NEW DIRECTIONS IN FAILURE TO THRIVE

Implications for
Research and Practice

NEW DIRECTIONS IN FAILURE TO THRIVE

Implications for Research and Practice

Edited by
Dennis Drotar

School of Medicine
Case Western Reserve University
Cleveland, Ohio

PLENUM PRESS • NEW YORK AND LONDON

Library of Congress Cataloging in Publication Data

NIMH Workshop on New Directions in Failure to Thrive (1984: Washington, D.C.)
   New directions in failure to thrive.

   "Based on the proceedings of the NIMH Workshop on New Directions in Failure to Thrive,
held October 9–10, 1984, in Washington, D.C."—T.p. verso.
   Sponsored by the Prevention Research Center, National Institute of Mental Health.
   Includes bibliographical references and index.
   1. Failure to thrive syndrome—Congresses. 2. Failure to thrive syndrome—Research—
Congresses. I. Drotar, Dennis. II. United States. National Institute of Mental Health. Prevention
Research Center. III. Title.
RJ135.N56 1984   618.92   85-28130
ISBN 0-306-42216-6

Based on the proceedings of the NIMH Workshop on New Directions in Failure to
Thrive, held October 9–10, 1984, in Washington, D.C.

© 1985 Plenum Press, New York
A Division of Plenum Publishing Corporation
233 Spring Street, New York, N.Y. 10013

Printed in the United States of America

This work is dedicated to the families of failure to thrive infants and those professionals who have made a commitment to them in their clinical work and research. It is hoped that the ideas, research, and approaches to intervention presented in this book will serve to enhance the lives of failure to thrive children by facilitating more effective research and clinical intervention.

PREFACE

Failure to thrive affects the lives of many infants and young children at critical times in their development and represents a significant public health problem in the United States. Moreover, this condition is invisible and can affect children for long periods of time before it is recognized. The long-term psychosocial sequelae of failure to thrive have only begun to be recognized but may be more severe than first realized. We do know that the costs to society in terms of acute pediatric hospitalization and long-term rehabilitation, foster care, and mental health treatment of young children who present with failure to thrive are considerable. Children who are diagnosed with failure to thrive represent a special challenge and opportunity for intervention, especially preventive intervention, because it is quite possible that many of the long-term consequences of this condition on psychological development can be lessened via early recognition and intervention.

However, the potential for preventive intervention in failure to thrive has been limited by the state of the art in scientific knowledge and practice. Despite the frequency with which failure to thrive is encountered in ambulatory and inpatient settings, there is little scientific information to guide practitioners. Research on the causes and consequences of failure to thrive has been very much limited by small sample sizes, lack of common definitions, and short follow-up periods. Uncertainties in the science of failure to thrive coincide with the considerable practical difficulties involved in diagnosis and intervention. Professionals from a variety of disciplines are called upon to make very difficult decisions concerning intervention, hospitalization and sometimes even foster care placement in the absence of suitable information to guide them. Because the families of failure to thrive infants are beset by many problems which limit their capacities to respond to treatment, professionals who work with failure to thrive infants and their families must design treatment approaches which can be accepted and utilized by family members.

The present volume presents a comprehensive description of research and practice in failure to thrive from the vantage point of an interdisciplinary group of professionals, each of whom have made a commitment to work with children affected by this condition and their families. This book is intended to stimulate research and practice in failure to thrive by presenting a detailed view of concepts, research methods, and questions to be solved. This work is based on the principle that the considerable challenges of research and practice concerning failure to thrive will not be solved by professional disciplines working in isolation. Rather, knowledge will be advanced by information sharing, interdisciplinary collaboration, and cross-center problem solving. It was in this spirit that the Prevention Research Center of the National Institute of Mental Health sponsored the conference: "Innovations in Research and Practice in Failure to Thrive: Implications for Prevention," held in Washington, D.C. in October, 1984 which stimulated the present volume. The hard work of the many individuals who participated in the development of this conference and the culmination of this volume is gratefully acknowledged.

Dennis Drotar

ACKNOWLEDGEMENTS

The work presented in this book represents the labors of a number of individuals who deserve special acknowledgement. Morton Silverman, formerly Director of the Prevention Research Center of the National Institute of Mental Health played a major role in the development of the conference which provided the impetus for the present volume. Vicki Levin, Program Specialist in Infancy at the Prevention Research Center, has been a tireless advocate for infants at risk and a facilitator of collaboration and information exchange among her grantees. Her support is gratefully acknowledged. The contributors to this volume put forth a singular effort in their writing. The final product is a testimonial to them.

A number of people provided special help to me in writing and editing. The past and present staff of the Infant Growth Project have been a source of insight and support throughout the course of this work. Juanita Warren and Claire Svet contributed significantly to this work in their typing of the seemingly endless chapter drafts. Finally, a very special acknowledgement is given to Mary Ball whose labors of typing and editing this entire volume were of the highest quality and very much appreciated.

CONTENTS

I. INTRODUCTION

These first three chapters provide an introduction concerning the topic of failure to thrive (FTT) and its relevance to preventive mental health. Silverman and Levin discuss the federal perspective concerning the prevention of psychological disorders of infancy. Tracing the history of the development of prevention perspectives and programs, Silverman and Levin describe the programs of the Center for Prevention Research of the National Institute of Mental Health. The Center for Prevention Research has maintained a consistent focus on infancy and early childhood amidst their funding of a diverse set of research projects concerning the prevention of mental illness and behavioral dysfunction as well as the promotion of mental health. Findings from such early intervention research projects will have exciting implications for the eventual clarification of complex interplay among biologic and environmental factors which contribute to mental disorders and to the nature, scope and cost effectiveness of interventions designed to avoid negative mental health outcomes.

Failure to thrive (FTT) is a condition which affects large numbers of children and contributes to the development of mental disorders in children. In order to clarify the relationship of FTT to mental health outcomes, one needs to understand the potential role of both biologic and psychologic risk factors in the development and sequelae of this condition. In her chapter, Frank describes the major categories of risk in FTT and the diagnostic and therapeutic implications. Frank's introduction to risk factors underscores the need for caution about diagnosing fixed neurologic or developmental disorders at a time when the child is acutely malnourished, the need for periodic reassessment of developmental and neurologic status, and the necessity for coordinated medical, nutritional, developmental, and psychosocial intervention.

Drotar presents a review of psychological risk factors and mental health outcomes pertaining to FTT, including the parent-child relationship, family risk factors, and the substantial costs of FTT which encompass the economic costs associated with diagnosis and treatment of this condition and the diminished human potential brought about by chronic intellectual, emotional, and physical problems. Salient gaps in knowledge concerning intervention and research are reviewed and contributions of the authors of this volume outlined in terms of the relevance to research and practice in prevention.

RESEARCH ON THE PREVENTION OF PSYCHOLOGICAL DISORDERS OF INFANCY:

A FEDERAL PERSPECTIVE***

Morton M. Silverman* ** and Victoria S. Levin*

Center for Prevention Research
Division of Prevention and Special Mental Health Programs
National Institute of Mental Health

OVERVIEW

Over the last decade, there has been an increasing concern within the Federal government, the Congress, and throughout the Nation regarding the heavy human toll and economic losses associated with alcohol, drug, and mental (ADM) disorders. There has developed a growing conviction that real success can be achieved in reducing the mortality, morbidity, and economic costs associated with the ADM disorders only if we systematically apply demonstrably effective and affordable prevention programs before the onset of these disorders. In response to these developments, the Alcohol, Drug Abuse, and Mental Health Administration (ADAMHA) has begun to address the numerous conceptual, methodologic, programmatic, and policy issues related to developing, implementing, evaluating and disseminating demonstrably viable strategies for reducing the incidence and prevalence of ADM disorders in the population (ADAMHA, 1984; ADAMHA, 1981).

Over the last decade, the National Institute of Mental Health (NIMH), one of the three Institutes comprising ADAMHA, has been conducting a multi-faceted program of prevention activities with two main foci: (a) to develop the field's capacity to address the many challenges of preventive intervention research, and (b) to encourage, support, and monitor ongoing prevention research activities. This chapter places these activities within a historical and conceptual framework. The scope and impact of the Nation's mental health problems are briefly described as a background to the need for effective preventive and promotive interventions, especially with high risk infants and children, such as those with environmentally based failure to thrive (FTT), who are the subject of this volume.

---

*The authors of this paper contributed in equal measure.
**Dr. Silverman is now Associate Administrator for Prevention, ADAMHA. He was formerly Chief, Center for Prevention Research,(NIMH). Ms. Levin is a Social Science Analyst who is the project officer for the NIMH high risk infancy research consortium.
***The opinions expressed in this manuscript do not necessarily reflect support or endorsement by the National Institute of Mental health or the Alcohol, Drug Abuse, and Mental Health Administration. This material is in the public domain.

THE SCOPE OF THE PROBLEM

Mental disorders and psychological dysfunctions have been estimated to affect between 15 and 20 percent of the Nation's population, or from between 35 to 46 million Americans (Regier, Goldberg & Taube, 1978; Albee, 1982a). Nearly 11 percent of all health care dollars in this country are spent on mental health. Studies have found that approximately 2 percent of the population can currently be diagnosed as schizophrenic, and that more than 16 percent suffer from a diagnosable affective disorder, primarily depression. New epidemiological findings make evident that significant increases can be expected in the prevalence of a wide variety of diseases and disorders of relevance to mental health which affect every age group from infants to the elderly. If one includes those classified as mentally deficient or retarded, or who experience mild to moderate depression, generalized anxiety, psychophysiological discomforts, insomnia, severe and persistent loneliness, and other indicators of emotional disorders, the numbers increase by several million (Weissman, 1978; Albee, 1982b). In recent years in the United States, there have been, annually, approximately one million divorces, shown by Bloom (1982, 1979) to be a significant source of stress for both parents and children, leading to any of the several different damaging emotional reactions. In addition, the stress of the loss of loved ones through death frequently results in severe emotional distress and/or reactive depression (Osterweis, Solomon & Green, 1984). Large numbers of other persons experience emotional crises related to stressful or traumatic life events. Involuntary unemployment, for example, has been shown by Brenner (1973) to produce any of several severe consequences including a rise in admissions to mental health clinics and mental health hospitals, an increased incidence of cirrhosis of the liver, alcoholism, fatal accidents, suicide, and an excess of deaths from all causes. In addition to these groups, various analyses indicate that there are 10 million persons with alcohol-related problems, a very large number of children and parents involved in child abuse, 5 million children with learning disabilities, 40 million physically handicapped Americans, and 6 million persons who are mentally retarded (Albee, 1982b). Exacerbating the situation is the fact that only about one-fourth of those suffering from a clinically significant disorder have ever been in treatment (Regier, et al., 1984). For those who suffer from some form of psychosis in general, or from schizophrenia in particular, untreated rates have been estimated at 40 and 20 percent, respectively.

DEVELOPMENTAL HISTORY

Since the mid-1970's, ADAMHA has been systematically examining all available public health models of disease prevention and health promotion for application to the reduction of the incidence and prevalence of ADM disorders. The Agency has done so in a gradual and considered fashion because of the need to weigh the similarities and dissimilarities between ADM disorders and the physical disorders which have been most responsive to prevention strategies, e.g., poliomyelitis, smallpox, and measles. Prevention efforts have been most successful in those cases in which a specific cause of a disease has been identified, its course understood, and interruption of one or both of these factors accomplished in cost-effective, efficient ways with minimal negative side-effects (Klein & Goldston, 1977). Not unlike many of the physical diseases, the ADM disorders are characterized by physiological, behavioral, and social aspects (Engel, 1977). The etiologies of the ADM disorders may, however, be somewhat more complex than those of many physical disorders and their developmental course from onset to manifest disorder may occur over longer spans of time. Nevertheless, a series of ADAMHA planning activities described in this overview have confirmed the general applicability of the traditional public health model of prevention to the ADM disorders (NIMH, 1983; ADAMHA, 1984).

An early important step in applying the public health model of prevention to the unique challenges associated with the ADM disorders occurred in the Fall of 1976 when ADAMHA sponsored a Tripartite Conference on Prevention (ADAMHA, 1977) with representatives from the United States, Canada, and the United Kingdom. Most were government officials responsible for the development of national health policies and the administration of programs targeted to alcoholism, drug abuse, smoking, mental health, and the psychosocial apsects of physical disorders. A number of conference proposals referred directly to prevention research activities, dissemination, and close collaboration between those involved in research and those involved in service delivery, including an emphasis on the social and environmental factors essential to developing effective prevention programming.

Two of the recommendations from the Prevention Task Panel of the Report to the President from the President's Commission on Mental Health (1978) were: "significant expansion of professional training and research opportunities in primary prevention" and "establish a Center for Primary Prevention at NIMH." In 1980, the National Institute of Mental Health created an Office of Prevention within the Office of the Director to coordinate all prevention activities within NIMH and to serve as a link with other Federal and State agencies concerned with prevention activities, and established the Center for Prevention Research within the Division of Prevention and Special Mental Health Programs in 1982. An additional recommendation was that "first priority in primary prevention be directed toward work with infants and young children (and their social environments)." The response to this recommendation will be addressed later in this chapter.

Beginning in 1977, the U.S. Public Health Service (PHS) undertook an intensive planning effort under the leadership of the Office of the Assistant Secretary for Health/Surgeon General. PHS prevention planning focused upon three major elements of health promotion and disease prevention -- lifestyle, environment, and personal preventive health services. Staffed by personnel from various PHS components, separate work groups were formed for each of these elements. Each group gathered and analyzed information about PHS prevention efforts, identified gaps in the available knowledge base, and recommended new prevention programs. The findings of these work groups formed the basis for the comprehensive report on health promotion and disease prevention, Healthy People, released in 1979, DHEW's Year of Prevention (DHEW, 1979). This Report emphasized that major improvements in the health status of the American people will occur through individual health-related behavioral changes and changes in the environment.

This landmark report expressed an emerging consensus among scientists and health professionals:

> There are three overwhelming reasons why a new strong
> emphasis on prevention -- at all levels of government
> and by all our citizens -- is essential... prevention
> saves lives... prevention improves the quality of
> life... (and prevention) can save dollars in the long
> run.

Two of the goals of this Report were the attainment of "Healthy Infants" and "Healthy Children." Specific subgoals included the reduction of the number of low birthweight infants and the enhancement of childhood growth and development.

Consistent with the PHS emphasis on disease prevention and health promotion, ADAMHA added prevention as its fourth priority, along with research, services, and training. In the Fall of 1979, nearly 300 participants attended an ADAMHA sponsored conference entitled "Conference on Prevention - Looking to the Eighties" (ADAMHA, 1979). The meeting provided an opportunity for State and local input as well as substantial representation from academia and research constituencies to assist the agency in developing its prevention policies. Among other topics, the Conference discussed: (1) "Health Promotion and Disease Prevention: Opportunities and Challenges," (2) "Commonalities in Prevention Programs for Children and Youth: Alcohol, Drug Abuse, and Mental Health," and (3) "Multicultural Approaches in ADM Prevention Programs for Children and Youth." Some of the recommendations included: the study of individuals/groups who are identified as at high risk for the development of ADM disorders, research on stressful environmental conditions, and assessment of the stages of development of children which would then determine criteria for, and types of, appropriate interventions.

Following the 1979 Conference, an ADAMHA workgroup in the Office of the Administrator's Division of Prevention continued meeting and, in early 1981, published ADAMHA's Prevention Policy and Program 1979-1982 (ADAMHA, 1981) which presented a discussion of prevention concepts, social change, evaluation, joint programming, and funding. As outlined in this document, the overall objectives of prevention efforts were to promote the strengths, resources, and competencies of individuals, families, and communities. The four main areas for future program directions were: knowledge development (research); development, testing, and dissemination of intervention models; increasing the prevention capacity of State and local mental health programs; and increasing the emphasis on prevention in mental health training programs.

In the Fall of 1980, following a major meeting in Atlanta of 167 invitees, DHHS published a companion document to the Surgeon General's Healthy People. The new report, Promoting Health/Preventing Disease: Objectives for the Nation, (DHHS, 1980) set out specific and measurable objectives for 15 priority areas that are key to improving the nation's health by 1990.

In the Spring of 1982, DHHS moved decisively to involve all PHS agencies in meeting the 1990 Objectives. This set in motion a large number of interrelated activities and responsibilities for all PHS Agencies. A total of 226 objectives grouped under 15 priority areas were identified and are to be achieved by the year 1990. They are described in full in Prevention '82 (PHS, 1982) and Promoting Health/Preventing Disease: Public Health Service Implementation Plans for Attaining the Objectives for the Nation (DHHS, 1983). Two of these Objectives include prevention priority areas addressing pregnancy and infant care as well as improved nutrition.

Since October 1981, and the advent of the Alcohol, Drug Abuse, and Mental Health Administration Block Grant to the States for service delivery, most of the resources for prevention program development, implementation, and capacity building have been transferred to the States. By law at least 20 percent of the block grant funds for alcohol and drug abuse services in each State must be used to support prevention and early intervention activities. The prevention activities carried out with block grant monies are described in detail in the DHHS Block Grant Report prepared in response to P.L. 97-35 and submitted to the Congress (ADAMHA, 1983).

RELATED ACTIVITIES

A number óf related National Academy of Sciences (NAS) activities and publications should be mentioned because of their influence on determining prevention policy during these critical years. In January 1978, the Institute of Medicine's (IOM) Division of Health Promotion and Disease Prevention published a staff paper monograph entitled "Perspectives on Health Promotion and Disease Prevention in the United States" (NAS, 1978). Clear emphases in this report were in the areas of behavioral factors in health and disease (including psychosocial stress), and mental disorders.

In June 1982, the Institute of Medicine's Division of Mental Health and Behavioral Medicine announced the publication of the final report of the Institute of Medicine's 2-1/2 year study, "Health and Behavior: A Research Agenda," which was funded jointly by ADAMHA and NIH. This document was published as a paperback entitled Health and Behavior (Hamburg, Elliott & Parron, 1982) and has become an important reference treatise within NIMH. Some of the topics included: "Stress, Coping, and Health," "Major Mental Disorders and Behavior," "Prevention Efforts in Early Life," "Prevention Efforts in Adolescence," and "Changes in Human Societies, Families, Social Supports and Health." A third IOM study, Research on Stress and Human Health (NAS, 1981), was supported in part by the NIMH Office of Prevention, and subsequently published as a monograph (Elliott & Eisdorfer, 1982). Again, recommendations were to increase research support in these critical areas.

With the gradual acquisition of (1) data concerning etiological factors, (2) epidemiological indicators of risk for mental disorders, (3) tested therapeutic modalities, and (4) reliable methods of outcome assessment, prevention research has become more scientifically feasible. Further, with the decision of the NIMH to focus its activities more on its research support programs in response to new initiatives and directions in the field of mental health research, the area of prevention research has become a highly visible one for rapid development.

INFANCY RESEARCH

At the Center for Prevention Research (CPR), a focus on infancy and early childhood has been a consistent theme in the funding of a diverse set of research activities related to the prevention of mental illness and behavioral dysfunction, as well as to the promotion of mental health. This focus was not a random choice, but one based on the timely confluence of the explosion of knowledge about the psychological complexity of infancy and the readiness of many prevention researchers to proceed from theory and conceptualization to clinical intervention trials with very young populations.

The earliest years of life have long been a focal point for theoretical scholarship, yet it has mainly been in the last two decades that basic knowledge of infancy has increased dramatically. Emotional and cognitive development within the first three years of a child's life are no longer seen simplistically but as an unfolding course in which sequential phases and tasks can be discerned. The accumulation of such normative data allows the progress of individual infants to be evaluated and developmental disturbances to be objectively detected and treated. The infant's own contribution of temperament and behavioral style is now fully acknowledged and evidenced in the transactional nature of the interchange between infant and caretakers. Video technology has validated clinical intuition, allowing us to document and decipher reciprocal interactions related to the growth of cognition, language, and social-emotional development. By its support of such pioneering researchers as Mary Ainsworth, T. Berry Brazelton, Stella Chess, Selma Fraiberg, Stanley Greenspan, Arnold Sameroff and others, NIMH has played a major role in advancing the field of infant mental health research, theory and practice.

Simultaneously, social scientists have been perfecting research tools, assessment techniques and statistical methods which permit objective measurement of behavioral change and increasing accuracy and precision in identification and classification of populations at high risk for mental illness or emotional dysfunction. Some predisposing risk factors may be categorized as static and unalterable, i.e., immigrant status, prior losses, or premature birth. Other risk factors are malleable, including social isolation, self-destructive lifestyle, or lack of age-appropriate parenting information, and can be modified by appropriate interventions. Better elaborated concepts of risk status and causation, more sophisticated research methods, and the scientific acceptance of basic and behavioral research on infancy have combined to create a readiness in the field to design and test interventions aimed at preventing dysfunctional emotional development in infants.

PSYCHOSOCIAL APPROACHES TO INTERVENTION

A basic, broadly generic psychosocial approach to preventive interventions with high risk infants and their families has been well represented among the variety of prevention efforts supported by the CPR. Some of the conceptual and methodological approaches characteristic of these comprehensive intervention strategies are described in the following section.

A consensus has emerged from research with a variety of normative and at-risk populations which identifies the quality of the bond between infant and caregiver as a pivotal factor leading to healthy social and emotional functioning in later phases of development, and to competence in other functional domains. Recent theory describes frequently observed patterns of attachment (Bowlby, 1969), conceptualizes the quality of the interaction, and provides a reliable and much used assessment procedure, the "strange situation" paradigm (Ainsworth, 1973). Empirical studies have also documented that positive or secure attachment is predictive of a variety of later adaptive patterns as the child reaches early school years (Waters & Sroufe, 1983). Thus, the thrust of preventive intervention methods have frequently focused on the nature of the dyadic interaction between infant and caregiver.

Another hallmark of these psychosocial interventions is the premise that the mother's emotional needs must be addressed before she can absorb didactic information about how to nurture or care for her baby. The intervenor recognizes the social and economic stressors impinging on the family and reaches out to explore solutions during regular home visits. By enhancing the mother's available coping strategies, the intervenor helps her to feel more in control of her life. When the mother feels she has a stable, caring, supportive relationship with a significant other, she will be better able to recognize and meet her baby's needs. Family systems theory provides a framework for psychosocial intervention by focusing on the cast of characters which affect the parent-infant nexus. The shifting balance of supports and pressures emanating from grandparents, siblings or men friends must be taken into account, as well as the frequently referenced role of social support as a mediator of stress.

Among conceptual underpinnings of these interventions is a recognition of the transactional nature of the interchange between infant and parents and between biologic and psychosocial risk factors (Sameroff & Chandler, 1975). This ongoing, dynamic process is reactive to the infant's contributions of temperament and behavioral style, as well as physical condition or developmental status. The spiralling effect of this mutual reactivity is one source of the perceived need to begin intervention early, prenatally if possible.

Taken together, these and other conceptual components represent a comprehensive approach to intervention, within which psychological, medical, social, and cultural functioning as well as physical development and cognitive outcomes are considered. Although specific intervention components will depend on the salient risk factors characteristic of the particular sample, a schematic representation of some basic components of a comprehensive intervention strategy is illustrated in Table 1:

Table 1

- <u>Provision of Emotional Support</u> to provide a model of a stable, nurturing relationship, addressing the mother's needs and fears

    <u>Aim</u>: increasing mother's emotional availability to her baby by meeting her own needs

- <u>Provision of Social Support</u> to reduce isolation; assist mother to improve her interpersonal skills and access her social networks

    <u>Aim</u>: lessening mother's level of stress through the mediating effects of increased social support

- <u>Provision of Information</u> about babies in general, their development and care; about this baby, his/her particular temperament and how to meet his/her needs; about community resources for mother, infant, and family

    <u>Aim</u>: increasing mother's sense of competence, satisfaction in caregiving, ability to cope; minimize intrusive and inappropriate behavior; promote sensitive, consistent handling of the child

The effectiveness of the intervention is typically assessed periodically, utilizing a combination of clinical and research evaluations. Table 2 illustrates a range of typically assessed outcomes:

Table 2

Child	Parent	Both
Physical Development motor, sensory, cognitive development language & hearing	Ability to enter into supportive, synchronous relationship with infant	Quality of interaction Mutuality of response
Attachment	Changes in social and community life skills	
Empathy	Level of support system	
Affect	Attitudes toward child rearing	
Mastery motivation	Marital harmony	
Social referencing	Quality of home environment	
Sociability with peers		

INFANCY PREVENTION PROJECTS

Among new grants supported by the Center during its first months of operation in 1982 were 5 projects which became the basis for a still-growing portfolio of extramural research on high risk infants and their families. The first projects to be funded had been proposed in response to a 1981 pioneering special NIMH grant announcement requesting proposals to conduct research concerning assessment and intervention for infants at high risk for impaired psychosocial developmental patterns and their families. These newly approved grants became part of the CPR portfolio because they exemplified basic components of state-of-the-art prevention research: focus on pre-symptomatic populations, randomly assigned control or matched comparison groups, replicable intervention trials, and interventions targeted specifically to the prevention of a potential emotional dysfunction which may later develop into more serious psychological disorders. Environmental failure to thrive is an example of such a condition, and Dennis Drotar's intervention study (Drotar et al., this volume) was one of the earliest research projects funded by CPR.

As of April, 1985, nine field-based studies are being funded by CPR (See Endnotes for further details). The current set of projects includes as foci:

- disorganized urban families which include a failure to thrive infant (Drotar)

- babies of young adolescent mothers (J. Osofsky)

- babies of women at risk on multiple medical, socioemotional, economic dimensions (Barnard)

- sick premature babies weighing less than 1500 grams born to low SES parents (Parmelee)

- preterm infants in Neonatal Intensive Care Unit (NICU) (Korner)

- babies born with a chronic physical handicap (Fleischman)

- insecurely attached 12 month old infants of recently immigrated Latino mothers (Lieberman)

- infants of low SES urban women who have high scores on a prenatal interview which predicts maladaptive parenting (O'Connor)

- first-time parents and their infants seen along a continuum of risk dimensions (H. Osofsky)

Interventions include both center-based, group, and individual home visitor designs, as well as an NICU intervention utilizing innovative waterbed flotation techniques to facilitate central nervous system integration of pre-term infants. Intervenors range from para-professional home visitors to specially trained public health nurses and nurse-midwives, as well as social workers and psychologists. In the above projects, intervention generally occurs for a 12 month period, with assessment of infant and family members continuing for an additional 18 to 24 months.

INTER-PROJECT COLLABORATION

To extend the significance of any single study's findings, the principal investigators of these projects have established an informal working consortium which is an innovative model for advancing programmatically linked research. Annual NIMH-supported research workshops have provided a forum for discussion of common research concerns and problem-solving techniques. An important product has been the creation of a common data base which emerged after an early collaboration blossomed into exchanges of instruments, pooling of data, and joint planning for future developmental assessment; three of the newly-funded researchers rearranged timing and choice of assessment instruments in order to collect commonly agreed upon data at 13, 20, 24, and 30 months on approximately 400 high-risk babies. This plan will provide a much needed data base concerning developmental transitions of key psychological parameters in at risk populations.

The infant researchers have also attempted to maximize the significance of their data by adopting each other's criteria for operationalizing similar pathological outcomes across studies. For example, Dennis Drotar's carefully refined set of criteria for psychosocial FTT in hospitalized infants, an intake measure in his study, was adopted as an outcome measure for those studies with populations (babies of adolescent mothers, psychiatrically disturbed inner-city parents, and sick prematures) at risk for FTT. The common use of such criteria insures that a more internally consistent statement can be made when data collection is complete as to what the various interventions did prevent.

Another direction for collaboration concerns the development of linkages among researchers. For example, a two day symposium with scientists from the MacArthur Foundation's Network on the Transition from Infancy to Early Childhood and the CPR infant researchers dealt with development of valid measurement instruments for the transition period from infancy to early childhood in the areas of attentional processes, cognitive development, language development and socioemotional development. Other work has included collaborative composition of a position paper referencing barriers and opportunities in the field of prevention research with high risk infant populations, as well as the benefits of multi-site cooperation (Consortium of NIMH Infancy Researchers, 1984).

IN-DEPTH ANALYSIS

A more detailed analysis of the three projects (Barnard, Osofsky & Parmelee) which are collaborating to collect a common set of data will illustrate how some of the intervention approaches are being applied to specific populations. These projects share a parallel structure. In each case, the research aims to measure the efficacy of adding a component to interventions that the community currently makes available to certain high risk groups. Practical advantages of this approach include the opportunity to make existing services truly preventive by modifying them after the efficacy of the innovative aspects of the research have been shown. In addition, the existence of a readily available comparison group bypasses an ethical dilemma for this type of clinical research in which withholding of service for the sake of a research design would be improper.

A more intensive, longer-lasting, and prescriptively designed home visitor intervention is central to research efforts for the following populations: babies born at less than 1500 grams with NICU histories and their low socio-economic status (SES) parents in Los Angeles (Parmelee, Beckwith, Cohen & Sigman, 1983); adolescent mothers and their babies in Topeka (Osofsky, 1985); and, in a nursing model, to multi-risk mothers and infants in Seattle (Barnard, 1983).

Infants born sick and neurobehaviorally immature are at high risk for forming maladaptive attachments. This may occur because of the baby's relative incompetence in eliciting and responding to the caretaking attempts of the parents, and because of the prolonged physical separation and lack of interaction during weeks or months in the NICU. Dr. Arthur H. Parmelee and his UCLA team begin their intervention with this population while the baby is in the NICU and continue through 13 months of corrected gestational age. Weekly or bi-weekly home visits are carried out by highly trained professionals, for example, a pediatric nurse practitioner with NICU experience. The focus of the intervention is on supporting and enhancing dyadic interaction, making it more pleasurable, satisfying, and contingent for mother and infant. The tone of intervention is non-didactic conjoint problem-solving, aimed at providing developmentally appropriate parenting information in the context of refining the mother's coping style and sharpening her observational skills. This approach is especially important for this population, because predictable difficulties in soothing and nurturing these frequently irritable babies may contribute to a mother's feelings of incompetence or being rejected by her infant. These feelings may be intensified by isolation and inexperience, particularly if the mother is still dealing with her shock and distress around an unexpectedly early birth and the loss of her dreamed-of "perfect" baby. If the intervention results in more satisfaction for the mother with herself and her baby, and if it reduces stress between mother and father, more secure attachment and a variety of improved future developmental outcomes for the baby should result.

Applying the psychosocial approach to preventive intervention for another high risk population, Dr. Joy Osofsky's project in Topeka focuses on preventing problems of development and adaptation in infants of adolescent mothers, 17 and under, as well as preventing psychopathology in the young mothers. Adolescent mothers and their babies can be thought of as two intertwined populations at risk, and many studies have indicated a high incidence of problematic outcomes for these young dyads. The mothers are faced with the necessity of nurturing an infant before their own developmental level approximates adulthood. In addition, the lack of educational and vocational opportunities, with related poor economic outlook and subsequent pregnancies sap their coping capabilities. Unrealistic expectations about motherhood may lead to inconsistent and inappropriate patterns of interaction with infants who are frequently born medically compromised after inadequate prenatal medical supervision.

In the Topeka study, 180 adolescent mothers and their infants are being followed in intervention, comparison and non-intervention control groups. Both intervention and comparison groups are participants in the Topeka-Shawnee County Health Department's Mother and Infant Project. This community program offers prenatal medical care, nutritional guidance, social service support and limited home visitation by nurses and social workers during the baby's first year. Paraprofessional home visitors, a 24 hour "warm line," and a drop in center constitute a more intensive and longer-term intervention for the target group. Each participant is introduced to her home visitor prenatally. Weekly visits in the early months of the child's life gradually decrease in frequency, but until the baby is 2 1/2, the intervenor remains available to help the young mother meet her baby's needs and to review her own situation.

In a third project, at the University of Washington at Seattle, Dr. Kathryn Barnard's research team is testing the efficacy of a nursing intervention model. Specially trained public health nurses utilize a clinical mental health protocol in home visits designed to foster the social compe-

tency of multi-risk women. Approximately 150 women, drawn from the prenatal clinics of a county health department, were recruited prior to the 20th
week of pregnancy and randomly assigned to one of two intervention models.
Criteria for selection included a high risk pregnancy, inadequate social
support and at least two of the following: previous psychiatric history,
drug or alcohol addiction, abuse or neglect of previous children, extreme
youth or poverty. Assessment of the impact of the two nursing models
occurs at regular intervals during pregnancy and the child's first three
years of life.

The mental health intervention is compared to a resource and information model designed to foster the pregnant woman's awareness of pregnancy
and motherhood and inform her about available resources. Both models,
delivered by public health nurses in home visits, begin during pregnancy
and continue through the first year of the infant's life. One of the
general hypotheses of the study is that women in the mental health nursing model will show greater improvement in their social and community
life skills and will subsequently demonstrate greater improvement in the
quality of interaction with the child and in providing a growth-fostering
environment for the child. It is further postulated that these positive
maternal traits will be translated into better developmental attainments
for the child.

Findings of this study are of great potential utility because the
public health nurse is widely thought of as the front line intervenor and
most appropriate, least stigmatizing home visitor both in the United States
and internationally. A system which is already in place could, with minor
modifications, deliver more effective intervention in high risk situations,
once the innovative model has been shown to be effective.

The collection of common data across these three projects will not
only permit the analysis of outcomes from a larger sample of comparable
subjects, but also the cross-sample analysis of specific subsets of high
risk participants. For example, premature babies which happen to be born
to the Topeka adolescent population or the Seattle multi-risk mothers can
be compared for characteristics and outcome of those of the Los Angeles
group where the intervention is specifically focused on prematurity. Similarly, the course of adolescent mothers in the Seattle and Los Angeles
projects can be compared with the Topeka group, etc. This strategy will
go a long way to enhance the generalizability of research findings.

FUTURE DIRECTIONS

It is hoped that prospective longitudinal follow-up of infant high
risk samples will establish long term effects of the interventions by
examining the potency of early positive outcomes as well as the subsequent
appearance of positive or negative latent effects as the infants become
young children and confront new developmental challenges. In combination,
the group of high risk infant research projects supported by CPR are also
expected to contribute significantly to our understanding of how genetic,
familial and environmental factors interact with prenatal and perinatal
vulnerabilities to produce mental disorders. These studies should also
make significant contributions to clarifying the nature, scope, and cost
effectiveness of interventions designed to avoid negative mental health
outcomes once these findings are available. Effective dissemination should
enable policymakers and service providers to utilize the fruits of the
researcher's labors on behalf of infants and their families who are most
at risk.

CONCLUSION

Since 1982, the NIMH has increased significantly its involvement in, and commitment to, the support of research and other prevention activities to strengthen the Nation's capacity to reduce the incidence and prevalence of mental disorders among all Americans in all age groups.

Researchers involved in developing and testing interventions to prevent disorders such as FTT and accompanying mental disorders appreciate the need to base those interventions on a sound scientific knowledge base and to approach their prevention goals in carefully planned incremental steps. To ensure continued growth in its capacity to increase the scientific and programmatic knowledge base necessary to identify and implement effective programs to prevent disorder and promote health, NIMH identifies and continuously reevaluates its specific research objectives. The task confronting NIMH is to determine the specific disorders for which the available knowledge base on etiology, prevalence, risk factors, etc., adequately allows for the design and testing of preventive intervention strategies, and those disorders for which intervention trials must be deferred until gaps in needed knowledge are filled.

The opinions expressed and data presented in this volume are evidence of a new beginning in the scientific biopsychosocial understanding and treatment of the vexing, life-threatening disorder of FTT. The NIMH Center for Prevention Research is pleased to have been involved in these initial steps toward the eventual prevention of psychosocial FTT and its long term consequences on the mental health of children. It represents a new beginning for all of us.

CPR SPONSORED INFANCY RESEARCH

Kathryn Barnard, R.N., Ph.D.
University of Washington
"Clinical Nursing Model for Infants and Their Families"

Dennis Drotar, Ph.D.
Case Western Reserve University
"Family Oriented Mental Health Intervention"

Alan Fleischman, M.D.
Albert Einstein College of Medicine
"Neonatal Project of the Preventive Intervention Research Center for Child Health"

Anneliese Korner, Ph.D.
Stanford University School of Medicine
"Assessment and Intervention with Premature Infants"

Alicia Lieberman, Ph.D.
University of California, San Francisco
"Preventive Intervention with Anxiously Attached Infants"

Susan O'Connor, M.D.
Vanderbilt University
"Prediction and Primary Prevention of Child Maltreatment"

Howard Osofsky, M.D.
University of Kansas Medical School
"Transition to Parenthood: Parent and Infant Risk Factor"

Joy Osofsky, Ph.D.
The Menninger Foundation
"Mental Health Program for High Risk Infants and Their Families"

Arthur H. Parmelee, M.D.
University of California, Los Angeles
"Early Intervention with Infants and Parents at Risk"

REFERENCES

Ainsworth, M.D.S. The development of mother infant attachment. In B.M.
    Caldwell & H.N. Riccuit (Eds.), Review of Child Development Research.
    Chicago: University of Chicago Press, 1973, 3, 79-97.
Albee, G.W. Preventing psychopathology and promoting human potential.
    American Psychologist, 1982a, 37(9), 1043-1050.
Albee, G.W. Testimony to Congress, 1982b.
Alcohol, Drug Abuse, and Mental Health Administration. Summary Proceed-
    ings: Tripartite Conference on Prevention. DHEW Publication No.
    (ADM) 77-484, 1977.
Alcohol, Drug Abuse, and Mental Health Administration. ADAMHA Conference
    on Prevention -- Looking to the Eighties. DHEW Proceedings (PHS)
    Sept. 12-14, 1979.
Alcohol, Drug Abuse, and Mental Health Administration. ADAMHA Prevention
    Policy and Programs 1979-1982. DHHS Publication No. ADM 81-1038, 1981.
Alcohol, Drug Abuse, and Mental Health Administration. Block Grant Report
    to Congress. Unpublished manuscript, 1983.
Alcohol, Drug Abuse, and Mental Health Administration. Prevention Activi-
    ties of the Alcohol, Drug Abuse and Mental Health Administration,
    Report to Congress. Unpublished manuscript, 1984.
Barnard, K., Eyres, S.J., Lobo, M. & Snyder, C. An ecological paradigm
    for assessment and intervention. In T.B. Brazelton & B. Lester (Eds.),
    New Approaches to Developmental Screening of Infants. New York:
    Elesvier, 1983.
Bloom, B.L. Focal issues in the prevention of mental disorders. In H.C.
    Schulberg & M. Killilea (Eds.), Principles and Practice of Community
    Mental Health. San Francisco: Jossey-Bass, 1982.
Bloom, B.L. Prevention of mental disorders: Recent advances in theory and
    practice. Community Mental Health Journal, 1979, 15(3), 179-191.
Bowlby, J. Attachment and Loss, Vol. I: Attachment. New York: Basic
    Press, 1969.
Brenner, M.H. Mental Illness and the Economy. Cambridge: Harvard Univer-
    sity Press, 1973.
Consortium of National Institute of Mental Health Infancy Researchers.
    Position Paper: The developmental process and early prevention;
    research needs and progress. Unpublished manuscript. Rockville, MD:
    National Institute of Mental Health, 1984.
Department of Health and Human Services. Promoting Health/Preventing
    Disease: Objectives for the Nation, 1980.
Department of Health and Human Services. Promoting Health/Preventing
    Disease: Public Health Service Implementation Plans for Attaining
    The Objectives for the Nation. Supplement to the Sept-Oct 1983 Issue
    Public Health Reports. PHS 83-50193A, 1983.
Department of Health, Education, and Welfare. Healthy People: The
    Surgeon General's Report on Health Promotion and Disease Prevention.
    Washington, D.C.: U.S. Government Printing Office, DHEW (PHS)
    Publication No. 79-55071, 1979.
Elliott, G.R. & Eisdorfer, C. Stress and Human Health: Analysis and
    Implications for Research. New York: Springer Publishing Co., 1982.
Engel, G.L. The need for a new medical model: A challenge for biomedicine.
    Science, 1977, 196, 129-136.

Hamburg, D., Elliott, G.R. & Parron, D.L. Health and Behavior: Frontiers of Research in the Biobehavioral Sciences. Washington, D.C.: National Academy Press, 1982.

Klein, D.C. & Goldston, S.E. (Eds.) Primary Prevention: An Idea Whose Time has Come. Proceedings on the Pilot Conference on Primary Prevention, April 2-4, 1976. Washington, D.C.: U.S. Government Printing Office, DHHS Publication No. ADM 77-447, 1977.

National Academy of Sciences, Institute of Medicine, Division of Health Promotion and Disease Prevention. Perspectives on Health Promotion and Disease Prevention. Washington, D.C., 1978.

National Academy of Sciences, Institute of Medicine, Division of Mental Health and Behavioral Medicine. Research on Stress and Human Health: Report of a Study. Washington, D.C.: National Academy Press, 1981.

National Institute of Mental Health. Center for Prevention Research Annual Report. Unpublished manuscript, 1983.

Osofsky, J. Perspectives on infant mental health. In M. Kessler & S. Goldston (Eds.), A Decade of Progress in Primary Prevention. Hanover: University Press of New England, 1985.

Osterweis, M., Solomon, F. & Green, M. (Eds.) Bereavement: Reactions, Consequences, and Care. Washington, D.C.: National Academy Press, 1984.

Parmelee, A.H., Beckwith, L., Cohen, S.E. & Sigman, M. Social influences on infants at medical risk for behavioral difficulties. In J.D. Call, E. Galenson & R.L. Tyson (Eds.), Frontiers of Infant Psychiatry. New York: Basic Books, 1983.

Public Health Service, Office of Disease Prevention and Health Promotion. Prevention '82. DHHS (PHS) Publication No. 82-50157, 1982.

Regier, D.A., Goldberg, I.D. & Taube, C.A. The de facto U.S. Mental Health Services System. Archives of General Psychiatry, 1978, 35(6), 685-693.

Regier, D.A., Myers, J.K., Kramer, M., Robins, L.N., Blazer, D.G., Hough, R.L., Eaton, W.W. & Locke, B.Z. The NIMH epidemiological catchment area program. Archives of General Psychiatry, 1984, 41(10), 934-941.

Report to the President from the President's Commission on Mental Health. Prevention Task Panel (Volume IV, pp. 1822-1863). Washington, D.C., 1978.

Sameroff, A. & Chandler, M. Reproductive risk and the continuum of caretaking causality. In F. Horowitz et al. (Eds.), Review of Child Development Research. Vol. 4. Chicago: University of Chicago Press, 1975.

Waters, A. & Sroufe, A.L. Social competence as a developmental construct. Developmental Review, 1983, 3, 79-97.

Weissman, M.M. & Klerman, G.L. Epidemiology of mental disorders: Emerging Trends in the United States. Archives of General Psychiatry, 1978, 35(6), 705-712.

BIOLOGIC RISKS IN "NONORGANIC" FAILURE TO THRIVE:

DIAGNOSTIC AND THERAPEUTIC IMPLICATIONS*

Deborah A. Frank

Department of Pediatrics, Boston University

Grow Team, Boston City Hospital

Failure to thrive is not a diagnosis but a symptom, the final common pathway of many possible physiologic insults. Traditionally, children with major organ system dysfunction sufficient to account for their growth failure are labelled "organic" FTT. When no such major organ system can be identified, children with growth failure are diagnosed as "nonorganic" FTT. However, the diagnosis of "nonorganic" FTT identifies children burdened by multiple biologic risks. These risks fall into three categories: 1) perinatal; 2) toxic-immunologic; and 3) neurodevelopmental. This chapter outlines the diagnostic and therapeutic implications of each of these three categories of biologic risk for the clinical care of the child with "nonorganic" FTT.

PERINATAL RISKS

For many children later diagnosed as "nonorganic" FTT, growth failure began in the womb. In clinical studies, ten to forty percent of children hospitalized for nonorganic FTT had birthweights below 2500 grams, compared to approximately 7% of the general population (Newberger et al., 1977; Shaheen, Alexander, Truskowsky & Barbero, 1968; Oates & Yu, 1971; MacMahon, Kover & Feldman, 1972).

Two research groups (Vietze et al., 1980; Pollitt & Leibel, 1980) have reported that, even within a population of newborns who were not below 2500 grams (the formal criterion of low birthweight), infants who later failed to thrive had significantly lower birthweights than infants who later grew normally.

While low birthweight clearly constitutes a biologic risk factor for failing to thrive, the factors mediating this relationship are not clearly elucidated. Published studies of nonorganic FTT do not distinguish low birthweight resulting from depressed rate of growth during gestation (in-

*Funding for this work provided in part by the Massachusetts Department of Public Health and federal grant numbers HD18401-02 and 1-R01-DA-03508-01.

The author would like to thánk Ms. Katherine M. Petrullo for her assistance in collecting data, editing the manuscript, and preparing the bibliography.

trauterine growth retardation) from that resulting from prematurity. This distinction is important clinically, since these two patterns of prenatal growth have prognostic implications for post-natal growth and development.

Prematurity

Prematurity may lead to an incorrect diagnosis of FTT, as a consequence of improper plotting of the infant's growth. Significant differences in growth percentiles will be obtained unless growth parameters are appropriately corrected for gestational age by subtracting the number of weeks the child was premature from post-natal age at the time of assessment. Such corrections should be done for head circumference until 18 months; for weight until 24 months; and for height until 40 months (Brandt, 1979).

Even when growth parameters are appropriately corrected for prematurity, it appears that infants born with very low birthweights (less than 1501 grams) and surviving without major handicaps may have impaired potential for post-natal growth. In these children, the distributions of height, weight, and head circumference up to the age of three are shifted downward so that mean weights fall between the third and twenty-fifth percentile of the NCHS grids: Mean heights, between the tenth and the thirtieth percentiles. As might be expected from this shift, the proportion of children from this very low birth weight population whose heights or weights are below the fifth percentile is three- to four-fold that expected for a normal birthweight population at this same post-conceptual age (Kimball et al., 1982; Pape et al., 1978).

In these very low birthweight infants, rate of growth rather than attained growth may be the most important clinical parameter. For this reason, children whose growth progressively deviates from a channel that is parallel to the NCHS curve, corrected for gestational age, should be carefully scrutinized for a post-natal and potentially correctable cause of growth failure.

Intrauterine Growth Retardation

Like prematures, infants whose rate of growth in prenatal life is depressed and who are born small for gestational age (conventionally defined as birthweight less than the tenth percentile for gestational age) are at increased risk for growth failure in early childhood. The degree of risk is not uniform for all intrauterine growth retarded infants, but depends on the nature of the prenatal insult and the early post-natal experience of the infant. To determine the growth prognosis of an intrauterine growth retarded infant, not only weight but also length and head circumference at birth must be determined. The pattern of relative deficit in these three parameters provides clues to the timing and nature of the prenatal insult and the potential for post-natal growth recovery. (See Peterson et al., this volume.)

The poorest growth prognosis is found in children who are symmetrically growth retarded at birth, with deficits in length, weight, and head circumference. These infants have usually sustained an insult during the first 24 weeks of gestation, often from intrauterine infection, chromosomal abnormality, or teratogen exposure (Gaston, 1982).

Common teratogens associated with symmetric prenatal growth retardation include cigarettes, anti-convulsants, opiates, and alcohol (Finnegan, 1984; Harrison, Branson & Vaucher, 1983). While the growth deficits associated with maternal cigarette smoking during pregnancy remain statistically significant into later childhood (Abel, 1980), they are not usually severe enough to account for a clinical diagnosis of FTT. In contrast, post-natal growth in children with symmetric prenatal growth failure from heavy prenatal alcohol, opiate, or anti-convulsant exposure can be so subnormal as to place the child below the fifth percentile, with deficits in head circumference more profound than those in somatic growth (Hanson, Jones & Smith, 1976; Hanson & Smith, 1975; Rosen & Johnson, 1983; Wilson, Desmond & Wait, 1981).

While prenatal exposure to opiates, alcohol, or anti-convulsants may be implicated in the child's growth failure, the clinician is also obligated to search for factors which contribute to on-going post-natal disruption of caretaking which may further compound the effects of prenatal deficits. For example, both opiates and alcohol (Hanson, Jones & Smith, 1976) may impair the maturation and coordination of the infant's early feeding skills. In addition, continued post-natal use of these addictive substances by the mother may decrease her caretaking competence.

As in the case of very low birthweight infants, the post-natal growth of symmetrically retarded infants should at least parallel the normal curve for height and weight. For this reason, progressive deviations from this pattern should not be dismissed as the inevitable consequence of the tera-togen exposure. Nutritional and environmental intervention may not enable these symmetrically intrauterine growth retarded children to achieve normal growth, but should protect them from the effects of post-natal problems which compound their initial deficits.

Asymmetric intrauterine growth retardation, where weight at birth is disproportionately more depressed than length or head circumference, car-ries a better prognosis for later growth. In these cases, the intrauterine growth retardation occurred later in the pregnancy, usually reflecting an insult such as maternal hypertension, maternal malnutrition, or placental infarction (Gaston, 1982). These asymmetrically growth retarded infants are often behaviorally difficult (Als, Tronick, Adamson & Brazelton, 1972), but with adequate post-natal nutrition are capable of significant catch-up growth in the first six to eight months of life, so that later growth trajectories may be within normal range (Scott, Moar & Ounsted, 1982; Villar et al., 1984). At the age of three, these youngsters score better on developmental assessments than symmetrically growth retarded infants but less well than infants of the same gestational age whose rate of intrauter-ine growth was normal (Villar et al., 1984). In these infants, early iden-tification of growth failure and intensive nutritional and environmental intervention are warranted, since the potential for catch-up growth to repair the intrauterine deficit is maximal in the first six months of life (Ounsted, Moar & Scott, 1982). The risk of developmental impairment for these infants can also be minimized by providing from birth an environment supportive of intellectual development (Zeskind & Ramey, 1978).

TOXIC AND IMMUNOLOGIC RISKS

Whatever their perinatal history, children with "nonorganic" FTT have usually suffered a serious post-natal organic insult: primary malnutri-tion. Children who fail to thrive have either not been offered, not taken, and/or not retained sufficient nutrients for normal growth. Nutrient deficiencies severe enough to impair growth jeopardize many other physio-logic functions as well. The medical concomitants of malnutrition include increased susceptibility to lead toxicity and immunosuppression with heightened vulnerability to infection. These conditions exacerbate and are exacerbated by malnutrition, depressing appetite and interfering with the absorption and utilization of nutrients once ingested. Any one of these conditions increase the probability that the child will become more mal-nourished, and thus susceptible to even more severe complications. To prevent cumulative deficits it is essential that these complications of malnutrition be identified and promptly treated.

Susceptibility to Lead Toxicity

Bithoney (1984) recently reported that children with FTT showed significantly higher blood lead levels than control children matched for age, race, and socioeconomic status. Although Bithoney is the first to report this phenomenon, it is not surprising. Increased susceptibility to lead poisoning can occur from micronutrient deficiency alone, at levels of nutritional deprivation too mild to produce obvious growth failure. As Mahaffey (1981) has outlined in detail, even brief fasting will triple the gastrointestinal absorption of lead. Dietary deficiencies of calcium, iron, and zinc, all prevalent in low-income children in general (Owen et al., 1974) and in FTT children in particular, not only enhance absorption of lead but also increase the tissue deposition and biochemical toxicity of lead once absorbed (Mahaffey, 1981). Lead intoxication, in turn, may further jeopardize the child's nutritional status by causing anorexia, abdominal pain, and vomiting (Graef, 1982). In addition, lead intoxication produces behavioral derangements such as irritability and hyperactivity (Graef, 1982) which may contribute to disordered parent-child interaction. The developmental sequelae of lead poisoning (i.e., fine motor dysfunction, language delay, and hyperactivity) may compound the deficits attendant on the nutritional and socio-environmental deprivation associated with FTT.

Any child with FTT living in geographic areas where lead poisoning is endemic (Mahaffey, Annest, Roberts & Murphy, 1982) should be screened for elevated blood lead at the time of presentation with FTT and should be treated as necessary.

Immunosuppression and Vulnerability to Infection

Malnutrition which is severe enough to produce growth failure may also cause impairments in immune function, particularly in cell-mediated immunity, complement levels, and production of secretory IgA (Suskind, 1981; McMurray et al., 1981). The severity of these deficits increases as the severity of malnutrition increases. In the developing world, Kielman and McCord (1978) showed that mortality from infection increases exponentially with each ten percent decrement in weight for age below eighty percent of the median weight for age. A child whose weight fell between seventy and eighty percent of standard for age, a not-uncommon level of malnutrition in FTT children in this country (Pollitt & Leibel, 1980; Mitchell, Gorrell & Greenberg, 1980), bore a four-fold risk of dying by age three compared to a child whose weight exceeded eighty percent of standard (Kielman & McCord, 1978).

In the United States, where more sophisticated medical care is available, it is rare for a child with FTT to die from infection. However, like their peers in the developing world, FTT children often show increased vulnerability to respiratory and gastrointestinal infections and decreased ability to recover from infections once acquired. Mitchell et al. (1980) found that children with FTT were significantly more likely than their better nourished peers to suffer from otitis in each of the first three years of life. Similarly, Sherrod et al. (1984) found that, compared to randomly selected controls, children with FTT showed significantly more infectious illnesses in the first year of life.

Clinicians treating children with FTT must be alert to the infection-malnutrition cycle (Scrimshaw, 1981). With each episode of illness, the child's appetite and intake decreases, while losses of nutrients are increased by the metabolic cost of response to infection, and perhaps exacerbated by diarrhea and vomiting (Scrimshaw, 1981). Unless the child's intake between illnesses is sufficient not only for normal growth but for restitution of the deficit acquired during the infection, the child will become more severely malnourished and more vulnerable to future severe and prolonged infections, which will further impair nutrition and growth.

The synergistic effects of infection and nutritional deprivation upon children's growth are so powerful that by the time the child is identified as FTT, it may be impossible to ascertain which process initiated the deterioration of the child. However, while the precipitant of the infection-malnutrition cycle may be unclear, the treatment is not. Parents of FTT children should be encouraged to seek medical care promptly at the first sign of infection. In addition, physicians should have a lower threshold for aggressive work-up and treatment of suspected infections in FTT children than in their better-nourished peers. Treatment should entail not only appropriate antibiotics when indicated, but also specific instruction about diets necessary for catch-up growth during and after the acute illness episode; diets outlined elsewhere in this volume. With restoration of normal weight for length and correction of micronutrient deficiencies, the vulnerability of children with FTT to toxic and infectious insults can be reduced to that of children of the same age who have never been malnourished.

NEURODEVELOPMENTAL RISK

Although appropriate nutritional and medical management can fully reverse the toxic and immunologic risks often associated with FTT, these therapies may not be able to restore completely the biologic damage inflicted on the developing nervous system by early nutritional deprivation. Children hospitalized with FTT show a range of neurodevelopmental deficits, including, in most series, low scores on standardized developmental assessments (Leonard, Rhymes & Solnit, 1966; Ramey et al., 1975; Field, 1984), abnormalities of posture and tone (Krieger & Sargent, 1967; Powell & Low, 1983), and depressed affect and social responsiveness (Rosenn, Loeb & Jura, 1980; Drotar, Malone & Negray, 1980). Most longitudinal studies show that after the acute episode of FTT, developmental deficits persist for months to years (Glaser et al., 1968; Elmer, 1969; Chase & Martin, 1970; Hufton & Oates, 1970) and are associated with academic delays and school failure (Glaser et al., 1968; Elmer, 1969; Hufton & Oates, 1970).

The mechanisms mediating the relationship between early FTT and persistent developmental impairment are complex, since nutritional deprivation is usually accompanied by other forms of socio-environmental deprivation (Casey, Bradley & Wortham, 1984) which can independently produce intellectual impairment. However, the effects of socio-environmental deprivation upon development appear to be magnified by the biologic derangements created by malnutrition. Research from the developing world demonstrates that, compared to children from similarly impoverished environments, children suffering acute or chronic malnutrition in early life show increased rates of intellectual deficit (Galler et al., 1983) and difficulties in modulation of attention and affect (Barrett, Radke-Yarrow & Klein, 1982).

What then are the biologic derangements which might in part explain the neurodevelopmental concomitants and sequelae of FTT? There is considerable evidence that malnutrition occurring in prenatal or early postnatal life can produce lasting damage to the structure and function of the developing nervous system - damage which may in part explain the long-term neurodevelopmental deficits identified in FTT children.

Brain structure is uniquely vulnerable to damage during the so-called "critical period" of maximal brain growth, when the brain has biosynthetic abilities that do not extend into later life (Dobbing & Sands, 1973). If adequate nutritional substrates are not available during this period, permanent deficits in brain size occur - deficits which are not reversible with later refeeding if the refeeding occurs after the critical period has passed (Dobbing & Sands, 1973). In humans, this critical period extends from the second prenatal trimester through the early post-natal years, with particularly rapid growth in the first year of life when the normal newborn brain increases 2.5 times in size, to two-thirds of its adult weight (Dodge, Prensky & Feigin, 1975). Children under age five dying from malnutrition show 15-50 percent reduction in brain weight compared to children dying of other causes (Rosso, Hormazabel & Winick, 1980; Winick, Rosso & Waterlow, 1970).

Survivors of severe early malnutrition show deficits in head circumference, which reflects brain size. Such deficits persist into adult life (Stoch & Smythe, 1982; Engsner & Vahlquist, 1975). In addition to overall reduction in brain size, severe malnutrition during the critical period of brain growth has been associated with identifiable structural deficits in the brains of human children, including decreased myelinization (Martinez, 1982; Rosso, Hormazabel & Waterlow, 1980) and decreased numbers of neurons and glial cells (Rosso et al., 1982; Winick et al., 1970; Chase et al., 1974) measured by DNA content.

While these data of necessity are derived from the autopsies of non-survivors, neurophysiologic correlates of malnutrition have also been demonstrated in living children. These include transient ventricular enlargement (Engsner & Vahlquist, 1975), persistent temporal-parietal hypoplasia (Stoch & Smythe, 1982), decreased velocity of peripheral nerve conduction (Kumar, Ghjar & Singh, 1977), and slowing of dominant EEG frequencies in sleep and waking (Dodge et al., 1975; Taori & Perena, 1974).

In addition to the structural and neurophysiologic derangements produced by early malnutrition, the behavioral effects of such derangements may impair the child's neurodevelopmental progress by impairing the child's ability to elicit and process stimuli from the inanimate and social environment. In both adults and children, malnutrition depresses discretionary activity, reduces motivation and arousal, and increases apathy and irritability (Beaton, 1983; Key et al., 1950; Lloyd-Still, 1976). These functional changes occur at levels of nutritional deprivation much milder than those required to cause gross structural alteration in the central nervous system, and may be obvious even before anthropometric deficits in body size have evolved (Beaton, 1083). Even iron deficiency alone, without obvious protein-calorie deficiency, can produce these behavioral alterations (Pollitt & Leibel, 1976). The physiologic mechanisms of these functional deficits are not clearly delineated, but may be related to alterations in neurotransmitter production and metabolism (Lytle, Whitacre & Nelson, 1984).

The neurodevelopmental deficits inflicted by malnutrition during the critical period of brain development are not all equally reversible with refeeding. EEG and peripheral nerve conduction abnormalities return to normal in months to years following nutritional resuscitation (Taori & Perena, 1974). While there are case reports of rapid catch-up growth of head circumference (and presumably of brain size) with intensive nutritional resuscitation (Dodge et al., 1975), research among clinical populations of malnourished children suggests that if the initial nutritional deprivation is severe or prolonged, some deficit in head circumference persists after somatic recovery (Stoch & Smythe, 1982; Engsner & Vahlquist, 1975). Depressed head circumference following malnutrition is associated with persistent developmental deficits (Engsner & Vahlquist, 1975).

Like structural deficits, functional abnormalities in behavior and development associated with early malnutrition may improve with refeeding (Grantham-McGregor, 1982), correction of micronutrient deficits (Oski et al., 1983), and improved handling by caretakers (Rosenn, et al., 1980), but not be restored to the level of function of children from the same background who were never malnourished (Grantham-McGregor, 1982; Barrett et al., 1982). If developmental intervention is provided in addition to nutritional and medical care, there is some evidence that the developmental quotient of formerly-malnourished children can be raised to that of better nourished peers of the same social class (Grantham-McGregor, 1982). Intervention to modify persistent deficits in attention and social-emotional functioning have never been formally assessed.

What are the diagnostic and therapeutic indications of these findings? Because the neurophysiologic derangements produced by malnutrition may be profound, clinicians should be cautious about diagnosing fixed neurologic or developmental disorders (such as cerebral palsy or mental retardation) at the time a child is acutely malnourished. Children should be periodically re-assessed neurologically and developmentally as their nutritional status recovers before any prognostic statements are made. Therapeutically, malnutrition during the period of critical brain growth should be identified early and treated vigorously to prevent possible central nervous system impairment. Although nutritional and medical therapy should be complemented by developmental stimulation and counseling to support caretakers in dealing with a delayed and behaviorally unrewarding child. Finally, planning for long-term remedial education may be necessary.

CONCLUSION

The term "nonorganic" FTT should not blind clinicians to the biologic risks which may adversely affect children's growth and development. Perinatal factors which may set constraints on a child's growth should be identified, to permit clinicians to make accurate diagnosis and realistic goals for treatment. The toxic and immunologic complications of malnutrition will jeopardize the child's recovery unless appropriate medical management is provided in addition to nutritional rehabilitation. The neurodevelopmental derangements produced by early malnutrition should be the subject of focused assessment and on-going treatment from the time that FTT is identified. These deficits may not be fully reversible but can probably be ameliorated. Moreover, with coordinated medical, nutritional, developmental, and psychosocial intervention, not only the child but the family may begin to thrive.

REFERENCES

Abel, E.L. Smoking during pregnancy: A review of effects on growth and development of offspring. Human Biology, 1980, 52(4), 593-625.
Als, H., Tronick, E., Adamson, L. & Brazelton, T.B. Behavior of full-term but underweight infant. Developmental Medicine and Child Neurology, 1976, 18, 590-602.
Beaton, G.H. Energy in human nutrition: perspectives and problems. Nutrition Reviews, 1983, 41, 325-340.
Barrett,D., Radke-Yarrow, M. & Klein, R.E. Chronic malnutrition and child behavior: Effects of early caloric supplementation on social and emotional funtioning at school age. Developmental Psychology, 1982, 18, 541-556.
Bithoney, W.G. Elevated lead levels in non-organic failure to thrive: A potential organic contributant. Presented at the 24th Annual Meeting of the Ambulatory Pediatric Association, San Francisco, April-May 1984.

Brandt, L. Growth dynamics of low birthweight infants with emphasis on the perinatal period. In F. Faulkner & J. Tanner (Eds.), Human Growth: Neurobiology and Nutrition. New York: Plenum Press, 1979.

Casey, P.H., Bradley, R. & Wortham, B. Social and non-social home environments of infants with non-organic failure to thrive. Pediatrics, 1984, 73, 348-353.

Chase, H.P., Canosa, C.A., Dabiere, C.S., Welch, N.N. & O'Brien, D. Postnatal undernutrition and human brain development. Journal of Mental Deficiency Research, 1974, 18, 355ff.

Dobbing, J. & Sands, J. The quantitative growth and development of human brain. Archives of Diseases of Childhood, 1973, 48, 757-767.

Dodge, P.R., Prensky, A.L. & Feigin, R.D. Nutrition and the Developing Nervous System. St. Louis: C.V. Mosby, 1975.

Drotar, D., Malone, C. & Negray, J. Intellectual assessment of young children with environmentally based failure to thrive. Child Abuse and Neglect, 1980, 4, 23-31.

Engsner, G. & Vahlquist, B. Brain growth in children with protein energy malnutrition. In M. Brazier (Ed.), Growth and Development of the Brain. New York, Raven Press, 1975.

Field, M. Follow-up developmental status of infants hospitalized for nonorganic failure to thrive. Journal of Pediatric Psychology, 1984, 9, 241-256.

Finnegan, L.P. Drugs and other substance abuse in pregnancy. In C. Stern (Ed.), Drug Use in Pregnancy. Boston: Science Press, 1984.

Galler, J., Ramsey, F., Solimano, G. & Lowell, W. The influence of early malnutrition on subsequent behavioral development. I. Degree of impairment in intellectual performance. Journal of the American Academy of Child Psychiatry, 1983, 22, 8-15.

Gaston, A.H. Small-for-gestational age (SGA) infants. In A.M. Rudolf, J. Hoffman & S. Axelrod (Eds.), Pediatrics, 17th Edition. Norwalk: Appelton, Century, Crofts, 1982.

Glaser, H., Heagarty, M., Bullard, D. & Pivchik, E. Physical and psychological development of children with early failure to thrive. Journal of Pediatrics, 1968, 73, 690-698.

Grantham-McGregor, S., Schofield, W. & Harris, L. Effect of psychosocial stimulation on mental development of severely malnourished children: An interim report. Pediatrics, 1983, 72, 239-243.

Graef, J.W. Clinical outpatient management of childhood lead poisoning. In J.J. Chisolm, Jr. & D.M. O'Hara (Eds.), Lead Absorption in Children: Management, Clinical and Environmental Aspects. Baltimore: Urban & Schwarzenberger, 1982.

Hanson, J.W., Jones, K.L. & Smith, D.W. Fetal alcohol syndrome. Journal of the American Medical Association, 1976, 235, 1458-1460.

Hanson, J.W. & Smith, D.W. The fetal hydantoin syndrome. Journal of Pediatrics, 1975, 87, 285-290.

Harrison, G.G., Branson, R.S., Baucher, Y.E. Association of maternal smoking with body composition of the newborn. The American Journal of Clinical Nutrition, 1983, 38, 757-762.

Hufton, L. & Oates, R. Non-organic failure to thrive: A long term follow-up. Pediatrics, 1977, 59, 73-79.

Key, S.A., Brozek, J., Henschel, A., Mickelsen, O. & Taylor, H. The Biology of Human Starvation, Volume II. Minneapolis: University of Minnesota Press, 1950.

Kielman, A. & McCord, C. Weight-for-age as an index of risk of death in children. The Lancet, 1978, 1, 1247-1250.

Kimball, K.J., Ariagno, R.L., Stevenson, D.K. & Sunshine, P. Growth to age three years among very low birth weight sequelae-free survivors of modern neonatal intensive care. Journal of Pediatrics, 1982, 100, 622-624.

Krieger, L. & Sargent, D. A postural sign in sensory deprivation syndrome in infants. Pediatrics, 1967, 70, 332-335.

Leibel, R.I., Greenfield, D.B. & Pollitt, E. Iron deficiency: Behavior and brain biochemistry. In M. Winick, Nutrition: Pre- and Postnatal Development. New York: Plenum Press, 1979.

Leonard, M.F., Rhymes, J.P. & Solnit, A.J. Failure to thrive in infants: A family problem. American Journal of Diseases of Children, 1966, 111, 600-612.

Lloyd-Still, J.D. Clinical studies on the effects of malnutrition during pregnancy on subsequent physical and intellectual development. In J.D. Lloyd-Still (Ed.), Malnutrition and Intellectual Development. Boston: Publishing Sciences Group, Inc., 1976.

Lytle, L.D., Whitacre, C.S. & Nelson, M.F. Mechanisms of nutrient action on brain function. In J. Galler (Ed.), Nutrition & Behavior. New York: Plenum Press, 1984.

MacMahon, B., Kover, M.G. & Feldman, J.J. Infant mortality rate: Socioeconomic factors. (U.S. Department of Health, Education and Welfare Publication # HSM 72-1045), National Center for Health Statistics, March, 1972.

Mahaffey, K.R., Annest, J.L., Roberts, J. & Murphy, R.S. National estimates of blood lead levels: United States, 1976-1980. Associated with selected demographic and socioeconomic factors. New England Journal of Medicine, 1982, 307, 573-579.

Martinez, M. Myelin lipids in the developing cerebrum, cerebellum, and brain stem of normal and undernourished children. Journal of Neurochemistry, 1982, 39, 1684-1692.

McMurray, D.N., Loomis, S.A., Casazza, L.J., Rey, H. & Miranda, R. Development of impaired cell-mediated immunity in mild and moderate malnutrition. American Journal of Clinical Nutrition, 1981, 34, 68-77.

Mitchell, W.G., Gorrell, R.W. & Greenberg, R.A. Failure to thrive: A study in a primary care setting: Epidemiology and follow-up. Pediatrics, 1980, 65, 971-977.

Newberger, E.H., Reed, R.P., Daniel, J.M., Hyde, J. & Kotelchuk, M. Pediatric social illness: Toward an etiologic classification. Pediatrics, 1977, 60, 175-185.

Oates, R.K. & Yu, J. Children with non-organic failure to thrive. A community problem. Medical Journal of Australia, 1971, 2, 194-203.

Ounsted, M., Moar, V. & Scott, A. Growth in the first four years: II. Diversity within groups of small-for-dates and large-for-dates babies. Early Human Development, 1982, 7, 29-39.

Owen, G.M., Kram, K.M., Garry, P.J., Lowe, J.E. & Lubin, A.H. A study of nutritional status of preschool children in the United States 1968-1970. Pediatrics, 1974, 53, 597-646.

Pape, K.E., Buncic, R.J., Ashby, S. & Fitzhardinge, P.M. The status at two years of low-birth weight infants born in 1974 with birth weights of less than 1,001 grams. Pediatrics, 1978, 92, 253-260.

Pollitt, E. & Leibel, R. Biological and social correlates of failure to thrive. In L. Greene & E.E. Johnson (Eds.), Social Biological Predictors of Nutritional Status, Physical Growth, and Neurological Development. New York: Academic Press, 1980.

Powell, G.F. & Low, J. Behavior in nonorganic failure to thrive. Journal of Developmental and Behavioral Pediatrics, 1983, 4, 26-33.

Ramey, C.T., Starr, R.H., Pallas, J., Whitten, C.F. & Reed, V. Nutrition, response contingent stimulation and the maternal deprivation syndrome: Results of an early intervention program. Merrill Palmer Quarterly, 1975, 21, 45-55.

Rosenn, D., Loeb, J.S. & Jura, M.B. Differentiation of organic from non-organic failure to thrive syndrome in infancy. Pediatrics, 1980, 66, 698-704.

Rosen, T.S. & Johnson, J.L. Children of methadone-maintained mothers: Follow-up to 18 months of age. Journal of Pediatrics, 1982, 101, 192-196.

Rosso,P., Homazabel, J. & Winnick, M. Changes in brain weight, cholesterol, phospholipid and DNA content in marasmic children. American Journal of Clinical Nutrition, 1970, 23, 1275-1279.

Scott, A., Moar, V. & Ounsted, M. Growth in the first four years: I. The relative effects of gender and weight for gestational age at birth. Early Human Development, 1982, 7, 17-28.

Scrimshaw, N.S. Significance of the interactions of nutrition and infection in children. In R.M. Suskind (Ed.), Textbook of Pediatric Nutrition. New York: Raven Press, 1981.

Shaheen, E., Alexander, E., Truskowsky, M. & Barbero, G.J. Failure to thrive - A retrospective profile. Clinical Pediatrics, 1968, 7, 225-261.

Sherrod, K.B., O'Connor, S., Vietze, P.M. & Altemeier, W.A. Child health and maltreatment. Child Development, 1984, 55, 1174-1183.

Suskind, R.M. Malnutrition and the immune response. In R.M. Suskind (Ed.), Textbook of Pediatric Nutrition. New York: Raven Press, 1981.

Taori, G. & Perena, S. Electroencephalograms and nerve conduction in survivors of kwashiorkor. British Journal of Nutrition, 1974, 31, 59-65.

Vietze, P., O'Connor, S., Sandler, H., Sherrod, K. & Altemeier, W. Newborn behavioral and interactional characteristics of nonorganic failure to thrive infants. In I. Martin, T. Field, S. Goldberg, D. Stern & A. Miller-Sostek (Eds.), High-risk Infants and Children: Adult and Peer Interactions. New York: Academic Press, 1980.

Villar, J., Smeriglio, V., Martorell, R., Brown, C.H. & Klein, R.E. Heterogenous growth and mental development in intrauterine growth-retarded infants during the first three years of life. Pediatrics, 1984, 74, 783-791.

Wilson, G.S., Desmond, M.M. & Wait, R.B. Follow-up of methadone-treated and untreated narcotic-dependent women and their infants: Health, developmental, and social implications. Journal of Pediatrics, 1981, 5, 716-722.

Winick, M., Rosso, P. & Waterlow, J. Cellular growth of cerebrum, cerebellum, and brainstem in normal and marasmic children. Experimental Neurology, 1970, 26, 393-ff.

Zeskind, P. & Ramey, C. Fetal malnutrition: An experimental study of its consequences on infant development in two caregiving environments. Child Development, 1978, 49, 1155-1162.

FAILURE TO THRIVE AND PREVENTIVE MENTAL HEALTH: KNOWLEDGE GAPS AND

RESEARCH NEEDS*

Dennis Drotar

Case Western Reserve University School of Medicine

Mental disorders and dysfunctional parent-child relationships which
have substantial economic and psychological costs to children, families and
society often begin in the earliest years of life (Rexford et al., 1976)
and present both short and long-term hazards to physical and psychological
well being (Lipsitt, 1979; Drotar, in press). In light of the increasing
numbers of American children who are vulnerable to severe disruptions in
early nurturing (Garbarino, 1977; Nagi, 1977), investigations of developmental processes which underly resilience to early parent-child relationship disturbances are of primary relevance to preventive mental health. To
the extent that the environmental and biological risks associated with
resilient versus dysfunctional psychosocial outcomes in infants at risk can
be documented, knowledge needed to develop preventive interventions to
ameliorate the effects of disruptive early experience on children will be
enhanced. Unfortunately, most childhood behavioral disorders associated
with maladaptive parent-infant relationships cannot be reliably detected
during critical periods of early development (Call, 1983). Hence, the
absence of objective markers which signal high probability of psychosocial
risk has been a considerable obstacle to research and intervention with
infants at risk.

Deceleration in rate of weight gain in the absence of primary organic
disease, the hallmark defining characteristic of FTT, is an objective
marker of early environmental dysfunction and psychological risk to the
child. Although FTT has long been recognized (Chapin, 1908, 1915; Spitz,
1945, 1946; Talbot et al., 1947; Patton & Gardner, 1962, 1963) as a sign of
deficient care, the implications of this condition for the study of risk
versus resilience in infants at risk have not been fully appreciated by
researchers. The unique advantages of environmentally-based FTT as a model
condition for studies related to prevention of mental disorders associated
with this condition include: 1) frequency; 2) objective early identification; 3) association with both acute and chronic mental, developmental, and
physical problems; 4) substantial costs to society related to diagnosis and
treatment of acute and chronic physical and mental disorders; and 5) potential modifiability of accompanying mental disorders and other sequelae
through early recognition and intervention.

---

*This work is funded by the National Institute of Mental Health Prevention
Research Center #30274.

FREQUENCY

Although systematic incidence and prevalence rates are not available, information from pediatric hospital admissions and ambulatory clinics throughout the U.S.A., consistently indicate that FTT affects large numbers of children and that the incidence may be increasing (Massachusetts Department of Public Health, 1983; Harvard School of Public Health, 1983). FTT accounts for between 1 and 5% of pediatric hospital admissions of infants (Berwick, 1980) and affects large numbers of children in ambulatory care. Frank, Allen & Brown's discussion of economic factors (this volume) also indicates that the numbers of affected children may be increasing.

POTENTIAL FOR EARLY IDENTIFICATION

FTT is unique among psychopathological conditions of infancy in that it can be objectively identified early in life through assessment of growth patterns and comprehensive physical and psychosocial diagnosis. (See Peterson et al., this volume.) A salient advantage of early recognition is that FTT children can be identified at critical phases in their development before they have developed severe and/or intractable emotional disorders. For this reason, FTT is a risk population in which the interrelationships among environmental risk, physical vulnerability, and mental health outcomes can be studied in accord with a transactional model (Cicchetti & Braunwald, 1984; Sameroff & Chandler, 1975; Seifer & Sameroff, 1982).

THE COSTS OF FAILURE TO THRIVE

Physical and psychological problems associated with FTT present major challenges for primary and secondary prevention. The costs associated with this condition are economic: those incurred by diagnosis and treatment; and human: lost potential owing to intellectual and emotional problems. The economic costs of pediatric hospitalization, especially considering relatively large numbers of FTT children hospitalized for this problem (Sills, 1978), are not trivial. Moreover, there is increasing recognition among pediatricians that it is difficult to interrupt, let alone reverse, the conditions that lead to chronic FTT and rehospitalization (Berkowitz, this volume). The costs associated with psychiatric hospitalization of children with histories of FTT may be more substantial than have thus far been documented. Preschool and school age children with histories of FTT are frequently admitted to psychiatric or psychosomatic units for treatment of severe feeding disorders and emotional difficulties (Rathbun, 1984). Other FTT-related costs are incurred by foster care (Hopwood & Becker, 1979), residential treatment for intractable behavior disorders (Money et al., 1983) and reduced academic achievement (Oates et al., 1985).

RISK IN FTT

It is important to differentiate among factors which contribute to a higher risk for the development of FTT versus those that increase the likelihood of associated nutritional, cognitive or emotional impairments among children already affected with FTT. The same factors that give rise to FTT may or may not be the same as those associated with the development of longer term impairments. Another important consideration in the study of risk is the need to clearly specify the domain of functioning that may be affected as a consequence of FTT. FTT can be associated with higher than average risk of impairment in a number of domains of functioning: physical health, physical growth, and nutritional status; cognitive development; and emotional development. Within each of these domains, a number of functions

can be affected and measured at different levels of specificity. It is
quite possible that the risk factors which contribute to acute or chronic
impairments in one domain, such as physical growth, may be very different
than those which are associated with acute or chronic impairments in another
domain, such as emotional development. Another useful distinction concerns
specification of the context (e.g. parent-child relationship, family context) in which FTT develops versus that in which it is maintained. It is
necessary to precisely specify the variable of interest in order to develop
theoretical frameworks that consider the interrelationships among different
variables.

The range of functions (nutritional status, health, cognition, and
mental health) that can be affected by FTT is one of the most compelling
features of this condition. Although a comprehensive review of the psychological sequelae associated with FTT is beyond the scope of this chapter,
interested readers might wish to consult review articles (Bithoney &
Rathbun, 1983; Drotar et al., 1979, 1980, in press; Breunlin et al., 1983;
Kotelchuck, 1980; Roberts & Maddux, 1982; Woolston, 1983).

Cognitive Deficits

Cognitive deficits associated with FTT range from moderate delays
(Leonard et al., 1966) to high rates of mental retardation (Ramey et al.,
1975). The cumulative results of studies indicate that a high frequency
(20 to 100%, median of 50%) of children initially diagnosed with FTT have
significant intellectual deficits as older children (Drotar et al., 1979,
1980). Although prospective studies are rare, most reports of preschool
and school aged children originally diagnosed with FTT in infancy show high
levels of chronic cognitive impairments compared to test norms (Bruenlin et
al., 1983; Chase & Martin, 1970; Drotar et al., 1980) and comparison groups
(Singer et al., 1983; Singer & Fagan, 1984). On the other hand, some
recent reports (Field, 1984) describe more optimistic cognitive developmental outcomes but delays in motor development.

Behavioral Disorders

The relationship of FTT to either DSM III diagnosis (American Psychiatric Association, 1980) or adaptational disturbances in preschool and
school-aged children is as yet unknown. However, some FTT infants can be
classified within DSM III categories such as Reactive Attachment Disorder
or Atypical Eating Disorder. In addition to emotional disorders diagnosed
in infancy, preliminary evidence indicates that FTT may be associated with
longer term effects on mental health (Bithoney & Rathbun, 1983). Clinical
researchers have reported rates of emotional disturbance from 25 to 80%
(median of 60%)(Drotar et al., 1979). Although controlled studies tend to
cite much less dramatic effects of FTT on psychological development than
clinical reports, a higher number of behavior problems (Pollitt & Eichler,
1976) and/or deficits in social responsiveness have been noted in infants
and preschoolers with FTT (Fitch et al., 1975). Moreover, the nature of
emotional problems associated with FTT varies with the child's age. The
social withdrawal initially demonstrated by many FTT infants has been
construed by observers as a classic sign of deprivation (Talbot et al.,
1947). In addition, a high incidence of depression has also been noted
among young children with histories of FTT who present to pediatric clinics
(Berkowitz & Barry, 1982). On the other hand, school age children with
histories of FTT may have high rates of conduct disorders. For example,
descriptive, uncontrolled studies report a high rate of behavioral disturbances (27-48%) among school aged children (Elmer et al., 1969; Glaser et
al., 1968; Hufton & Oates, 1977; Oates et al., 1985). Finally, preschool
and school-age children with a severe disturbance known as psychosocial
dwarfism, which can include an early history of FTT, demonstrate serious

behavioral problems including sleep disturbance, enuresis, encopresis, self-harming behavior, and conduct disorders (Williams & Money, 1980).

Feeding Disorders

Although the frequency of association of feeding disorders and FTT has not yet been established, feeding disturbances can be both a cause and consequence of FTT (Woolston, 1983) and have a substantial impact on family life. In view of the fact that feeding disorders often necessitate hospitalization, especially in association with FTT (Chatoor et al., this volume), the lack of research on this topic is unfortunate. Pollitt and Eichler (1976) reported that more FTT children had feeding difficulties as infants, ate skimpier and less regular meals, and had a poorer response to food. Feeding disturbances may originate in a diverse set of early experiences including parental insensitivity to the child's feeding cues (Chatoor & Egan, 1983) or family disorganization which increases distraction and sibling intrusion (Drotar & Malone, 1982) and precludes adaptive learning of self-feeding skills (see Linscheid & Rasnake, this volume).

Rumination

Rumination, defined as the voluntary regurgitation of previously swallowed food, is one of the most dramatic symptoms which can accompany FTT (Cameron, 1925; Flanagan, 1977; Lourie, 1955). In environmentally-based FTT, rumination is associated with severe parenting deficiencies (Richmond, Eddy & Green, 1955) and is sometimes accompanied by other behavioral symptoms, including increased alertness and self-stimulatory behaviors such as rocking. The factors which contribute to the development of rumination and its long-term impact are as yet unknown.

Attachment Disturbances

Although it is reasonable to assume that the processes which give rise to FTT also affect the child's attachment to his or her mother, empirical studies of attachment in FTT using objective criteria have been rare. Using a procedure similar to Ainsworth and Wittig (1969), Gordon and Jameson (1979) found that significantly more non-organic FTT children (50%) were insecurely attached to their mothers (either avoidant or resistant) than control children (15%). Drotar, Malone and Nowak (1985) found the following patterns of attachment in a sample of 12 month children who had been hospitalized and received psychosocial treatment: secure = 49%, avoidant = 33%, ambivalent = 12%, and unclassified = 6%. Taken together, these findings indicate a higher incidence of insecure attachment in FTT than the 35% found in middle class samples (Campos et al., 1983). At the same time, the variations in attachment patterns in individual children indicate that environmentally-based FTT is by no means synonymous with disturbed attachment. However, given the emerging data base which links patterns of early attachment and developmental competencies in socialization and problem solving (Matas, Arend & Sroufe, 1978; Pastor, 1981; Sroufe, 1979, 1983; Waters, Wippman & Sroufe, 1979), it is likely that some of the behavioral deficits found in preschool children with FTT (Pollitt & Eichler, 1976) may be mediated, at least in part, by an insecure attachment. On the other hand, a secure attachment may operate as a protective factor with respect to the development of serious psychological disturbances in FTT.

UNANSWERED QUESTIONS CONCERNING THE PSYCHOLOGICAL SEQUELAE OF FTT

Despite great variation in methodological sophistication in individual studies, cumulative findings indicate that FTT is a sign of psychological risk. However, scientific investigation of the precise interrelationship among FTT and psychological disturbance is very much in its beginning phases. A great many unanswered questions remain. For example, the incidence and prevalence of various psychological problems in FTT populations vs. comparison samples have not been established. In addition, the factors that contribute to the development of psychologic disturbance or those which operate as protective factors within the FTT population are not known. Such information is particularly important for planning for mental health services for the large numbers of affected children. Because FTT encompasses a range of caretaking problems and biologic vulnerabilities, each of which may have different long-term consequences, it would seem reasonable to concentrate services on those children in which prevention of serious mental disorders can be accomplished. For this reason, data concerning specific precursors and developmental processes which contribute to serious psychological disturbance in FTT has special relevance.

THE CONTEXT OF RISK

In view of the fact that the risks to FTT children cannot be considered apart from the relationships in which the child participates, the understanding of the contribution of child's relationship contexts to risk assumes special importance.

Parent-Child Relationship

The parent-child relationship is the most immediate context in which maladaptive patterns of feeding and social transaction are learned and hence is an important focus of intervention efforts. Although clinical observations have documented a variety of deficiencies and distortions in the relationships between maternal caregivers and FTT children (Greenberg, 1970; Fraiberg, 1980; Chatoor & Egan, 1982), empirical support for a causative link between relationship difficulties and FTT is more tenuous (see Finlon et al., this volume). Moreover, the marked variation in the nature of parent-child relationships associated with FTT: e.g., inconsistent over stimulation (Alfasi, 1982) and noncontingent behaviors (Ramey et al., 1972) have been noted as problematic and suggest that research needs to define a typology of individual differences in relationship disturbance (see Woolston; Chatoor et al.; Linscheid & Rasnake; this volume for more detailed discussions of these issues). One of the least understood aspects of FTT concerns the specific factors which affect the development of dysfunctional parent-child relationships.

Severe Parenting Dysfunction: Abuse and Neglect

The notion that FTT is part of a continuum of child maltreatment including child abuse and neglect has received empirical support (Altemeier et al., 1981; Kotelchuck, 1981; Newberger et al., 1977). In rare instances, FTT children suffer the extremes of environmental privation and abuse including starvation, and deliberate food restriction (Adelson, 1963; Koel, 1969; Krieger, 1974). Moreover, some abused children have below average physical growth, feeding and nutritional problems (Nakou et al., 1982; Newberger et al., 1977). On the other hand, in clinical practice the coincidence of FTT and abuse is infrequent but indicative of extraordinary risk to the child when it occurs (Bithoney & Rathbun, 1983).

Despite the fact that similar family stresses appear to be associated with FTT and child abuse, the two conditions may be characterized by different parent-child interactional patterns. For example, abuse is often associated with parent-child exchanges involving mutual coercion and parental aggression, which may be triggered by a specific stressful event

(Kadushin & Martin, 1981; Parke & Collmer, 1975; Patterson, 1979). On the other hand, FTT (especially early onset FTT) may represent a progressive disengagement between mother and infant which eventually can result in very low rates of parent-child interaction.

The complexity of FTT and the extraordinary problems involved in defining neglect (Aber & Zigler, 1981; Besharov, 1982; Cassidy, 1980) defies simplistic equation of these two problems and requires specification of behaviors (e.g., lack of appropriate supervision, failure to obtain medical care) assumed to be neglectful. Kotelchuck's (1980) data support the notion that FTT is not synonymous with neglect. Based on independent evaluations, 20% of families of FTT children were judged as neglectful and 24% of the children had characteristics of children known to be neglected. Although severely neglected children are subset of the FTT population, they present extraordinary clinical dilemmas to professionals (Berkowitz; Singer, this volume), require a great investment of services, and may be at very high risk for emotional disturbance. For this reason, scientific studies of the interrelationship of FTT and child maltreatment and the consequences for psychological development are very much needed (see Bradley & Casey; Sherrod et al., this volume for thoughtful discussions of research strategies that pertain to child maltreatment).

FAMILY RISK FACTORS

Despite the fact that clinicians have observed the association of severe family dysfunction with FTT for a number of years (Talbot et al., 1947; Patton & Gardner, 1962), the family context of FTT is perhaps the least well understood aspect of this condition. However, intrafamilial relationships, especially the quality of the marital relationship, may have a critical bearing on maternal nurturing capacities (Belsky, Robins & Gamble, 1984) and may be a primary factor in the origins and maintenance of FTT (Drotar & Malone, 1982). Moreover, family members are the child's major sources of nurturing and are the primary change agents in intervention. Hence, factors which either limit or enhance family response to intervention deserve greater scrutiny in future research.

Maternal Factors

Early clinical observations focused on the identification of deficits in the mothers of FTT infants (Roberts & Maddux, 1982) without precisely specifying the potential influence of these characteristics on child rearing and/or their interaction with the family environment. Maternal personality disturbances, which have been so striking in clinical observations (Elmer, 1966; Evans et al., 1972; Fischoff, Whitten & Pettit, 1969; Kerr, Bogues & Kerr, 1978; McCarthy & Booth, 1970) have not been as evident in controlled studies (Kotelchuck, 1979; Pollitt, Eichler & Chan, 1975; Newberger et al., 1977). Even if maternal personality, intellectual or psychiatric disorder can be shown to be associated with FTT, the precise manner in which the family support context affects the expression of maternal nurturing competence remains to be documented. For this reason, research designs should address the interrelationship of maternal personal resources and family environmental factors (Belsky et al., 1984) to the development of FTT and associated disorders.

Role of the Father

Although astute clinicians (Barbero, Morris & Redford, 1963; Elmer, 1966) have long regarded fathers as a salient influence in FTT, information concerning paternal contributions to the origins and consequences of FTT is largely anecdotal. However, Bruenlin et al.'s (1983) review documents a high incidence of paternal alcohol problems (45%) and unemployment (56%) and suggests that the role of fathers deserves much greater scrutiny than it has thus far received. Although the manner in which paternal functioning influences the expression of maternal caretaking competence has yet to be systematically described, fathers can have a powerful effect on maternal energy and self-esteem and hence on the quality of parent-child interrelationships. For this reason, one might expect that paternal contributions to family life, especially paternal absence and the quality of the father's relationship with family members, may have an important bearing on longer-term mental health outcomes in FTT children.

Family Stress and Structure

Family risk factors can be construed in terms of general factors such as stress, structure and organization (see Drotar et al.'s discussion of family systems influences in this volume). As yet, there is an emerging empirical basis to support the clinical observations that family functioning is a risk factor in the development of FTT (Bruenlin et al., 1983). A number of studies in the U.S.A. and other countries have suggested that family resources and organization are important in the development of nutritional privation in FTT (Kerr, Bogues & Kerr, 1978). Family factors that distinguish FTT from comparison samples of equivalent backgrounds include lower economic levels (Kanawati, Darwish & McLaren, 1974; Kanawati & McClaren, 1983), higher stress levels (Altemeier et al., 1981), lack of availability of extended family members for child rearing (Pollitt & Leibel, 1980) and social isolation (Bithoney, 1983; Newberger & Kotelchuck, 1983). Finally, the quality of the family environment may relate to the prognosis in FTT (Evans et al., 1972). For this reason, the identification of family factors which differentiate children with good vs. poor prognosis would be an important contribution.

CHALLENGES OF INTERVENTION

Although the acute nutritional deficits associated with FTT can be reversed in many situations, the longer-term consequences on development and mental health may be much more difficult to treat (Bithoney & Rathbun, 1983). Unfortunately, thus far, there is very little empirical data which systematically describes the outcomes of intervention, especially over the course of time.

Studies of Intervention Outcomes

Intervention in FTT can be considered along a continuum from primary prevention to early recognition and treatment. Psychosocial intervention in FTT can be considered along the following dimensions: (1) focus (e.g., the child or parents or family members); (2) target domain (e.g., physical growth, or cognitive development); (3) context (e.g., hospital, service agency, home); and (4) general goals (e.g., enhancement of child development, enhancement of parent-child relationship, improved family functioning, or problem solving). Theoretical frameworks which guide interventions (Fraiberg, 1980; Fraiberg et al., 1981) encompasse psychodynamic, family systems (Drotar & Malone, 1982) and behavioral (Linscheid, 1978). The range of intervention approaches reported in this volume are representative of the field. Unfortunately, the lack of empirical data concerning outcomes has as yet precluded the development of standards for diagnosis and treatment of the psychosocial problems that accompany FTT. The fact that so many outcome studies have had no control groups, short follow-up periods, and outcome measures restricted to physical growth and development (Drotar et al., 1979b) limits the conclusions that can be drawn from these studies. Social and emotional outcomes, which may be particularly important to the mental health of FTT children, have not been evaluated, except in a very general sense (Fraiberg et al., 1981). This is a general problem in early intervention research (see Halpern, 1984; Zigler & Trickett, 1982).

Descriptions of outcome in FTT show moderate (Fraiberg et al., 1981a, b; Leonard et al., 1966; Ramey et al., 1975) to little improvement (Fitch et al., 1975, 1976; Whitten et al., 1969) in psychological status. Although behavioral disturbances associated with FTT in young infants appear to be modifiable, at least in individual cases reported (Ferholt & Provence, 1976; Fraiberg, 1980), it is not yet known whether and to what extent longer term consequences on children's mental health can be ameliorated by early intervention. However, the growing number of studies which have documented chronic environmental deficiencies (Bradley, 1983), family problems (Bruenlin et al., 1983) and intellectual and academic impairments (Singer & Fagan, 1984; Oates et al., 1985) in FTT populations provide cause for concern about long-term psychological effects of FTT and additional impetus for systematic study of interventions.

In modern clinical practice, early pediatric recognition is the cornerstone of remediation. For this reason, specialized primary care clinics for the care of FTT children (Berkowitz, this volume; Casey et al., in press) represent an important resource for the diagnosis and treatment of FTT. The characteristics of such care, e.g. concentration of professional expertise, an organized approach to care, group support, and coordination of pediatric with community services may encourage earlier professional recognition of FTT, reduce the numbers of hospitalizations, and potentially affect psychological outcomes. It will be important to document the characteristics of populations served by such clinics, the initial physical and psychological deficits of children, and outcomes of these programs.

In some respects, the large numbers of children admitted to pediatric hospitals attest to the difficulties of prevention of FTT within current patterns of health-care delivery (see Brams & Coury, this volume for a detailed discussion of prevention). There are many reasons for the "failure" to prevent FTT: 1) the early warning signs of FTT are difficult to ascertain; 2) some of the parents of children who develop FTT are prone to miss their well-child visits which precludes early identification and treatment; 3) pediatric clinics are generally not equipped with the capacity to initiate outreach or other forms of early intervention to change the family context of FTT; 4) in some instances, FTT may not be recognized, undertreated or even mismanaged; 5) the factors which affect the development of FTT reflect the intersection of the family, parent-child and broader societal contexts, are poorly understood and difficult to manage.

In many settings, hospitalization is the major resource for the diagnosis and treatment of FTT. Pediatric hospitalization has both costs and benefits. Hositalization communicates the seriousness of the problem to parents who may be initially unwilling or unable to recognize it. In addition, hospitalization allows observation of behavior change and weight gain and a means to institute specialized interventions such as nutritional treatment, developmental stimulation, physical or occupational therapy, which can help improve the child's behavior and interrupt highly maladaptive patterns of parent-child interaction and/or feeding problems (see Altemeier et al.; Chatoor et al., this volume). On the other hand, the child's removal from the family context obscures the observation of family influences and can be disruptive to an already tenuous parent-child relationship. The hospital context is a highly charged evaluative situation which is stressful for parents and may contribute to increased parental defensiveness, especially if parental sensitivities are not recognized and addressed. Finally, hospitalization does not necessarily interrupt problems that have given rise to the child's FTT and may give a misleading picture

of progress. Given the complexities of hospitalization, more systematic
information is needed concerning which children are hospitalized, under
what conditions, and especially, the longer term outcomes of hospitalization.

In some instances, the FTT child's nutritional and developmental
problems may be so severe that they require extended rehabilitation over
and beyond what can be accomplished in an acute care hospital. In other
cases, the FTT child's family living situation may be so chaotic that the
child cannot be safely returned home at the point that the child is medically ready for discharge from the acute care hospital. In some communities,
pediatric rehabilitation hospitals provide a setting in which to continue
the psychosocial intervention with the FTT child and family needed to
stabilize and maintain nutritional and developmental gains (see Singer,
this volume). Another promising treatment option is a pediatric psychosomatic unit which has the potential advantages of a primary emphasis on
the understanding and management of family influences and individualized
structuring of nutritional and behavioral management.

Aftercare and Long-Term Follow-Up

There is general agreement that the benefits of hospitalization for
FTT are best realized if combined with aftercare interventions tailored to
the child's special needs. Such programs may include: developmental stimulation, advocacy and supportive help for the parents, family-centered
intervention, parent-centered education or psychotherapeutic intervention
for parents (Ayoub, Pfeiffer & Leichtman, 1983; Drotar & Malone, 1982a;
Fitch et al., 1975; Fraiberg, 1980). Intervention may concentrate on the
resolution of acute problems, preventionof long-term problems or both.
(See Drotar, Malone & Negray, 1979; for a comprehensive review of treatment
outcome studies.) In practice, the delivery of psychological interventions
depends on such variables as severity of FTT and associated problems, the
availability of services in individual communities, and the family resources
and acceptance. The fact that the families of FTT infants are often highly
stressed, disadvantaged and do not recognize the need for intervention
limits the usefulness of traditional mental health services and requires
specialized methods of outreach intervention based on coordination of
pediatric and community-based services (Ayoub et al., 1983; Drotar &
Malone, 1982; Maybanks & Bryce, 1979). In future research, it will be
important to document individual differences in the efficacy of intervention, and factors which differentiate between families who accept intervention vs. those who do not.

County Welfare Protective Services

In instances of abuse or neglect and whenever serious doubt is raised
about the family's capacities to care for the FTT child, referral to county
welfare protective services is in the child's interests. On the other
hand, large caseloads, a lack of support, and knowledge about FTT workers
can make it very difficult for county welfare protective service workers to
modify the extraordinary family problems sometimes associated with FTT.
More information is needed concerning the characteristics of FTT children
who are referred for county welfare protective services and the efficacy of
services. In principle, foster care provides a healthy and life saving
intervention for those FTT children who are in immediate danger or living
in families who are unable to provide basic care (Hopwood & Becker, 1979;
Money, Annecillo & Kelly, 1983). However, in practice foster care is by no
means a panacea and may introduce additional risks to an already vulnerable
child (Schor, 1982; Light, 1973; Wald, 1983) such as multiple placements
(Goldstein, Freud & Solnit, 1973).

UNANSWERED QUESTIONS CONCERNING FAILURE TO THRIVE

This review of available literature has indicated that substantial gaps exist in knowledge related to primary and secondary prevention in FTT. It is an ironic fact that so little is known about a condition that effects large numbers of children at critical times in their development in ways that can severely compromise their health, physical growth, and psychological development. Moreover, the lack of an empirical knowledge base, especially with respect to epidemiology and natural history of FTT handicaps the efforts of clinicians. Clinicians from a variety of professional disciplines who work with affected children and their families are charged with the responsibility to make decisions which may affect the lives of FTT children and their families in the presence of our uncertain knowledge base concerning diagnosis and prognosis. At the same time, clinical experiences with FTT children and their families can provide valuable insight into the nature of FTT and potentially effective interventions. In my view, advances in our knowledge of FTT will best come from an interplay between clinicians and researchers.

Obstacles to Research in FTT

Research is needed in almost every topic of FTT including epidemiology, etiology, prognosis, and intervention. When one considers the difficulty of conducting research in FTT, the reasons for the lack of research on this topic become more apparent. The very family problems that give rise to the condition also make the conduct of research extremely difficult. Families are highly stressed and may be reluctant to give consent for research. Once they have given their consent, they may be very difficult maintain contact with, especially over long periods of time (Fitch et al., 1975; Mitchell et al., 1980), which limits the generalizability of conclusions and the feasibility of prospective research designs. Although there is agreement that the ecological context of FTT deserves systematic scrutiny, many of the families of FTT live in neighborhoods where the realistic threat of danger precludes comprehensive observation and/or follow-up. Other practical problems relate to the fact that clinic or hospital settings, which are the front lines of pediatric care, are often not set up to conduct research. As a consequence, valuable opportunities for clinical research are lost (see Carey, Wortham & Nelson, in press, for a nice example of applied outcome research in a pediatric clinic setting). Research requires additional staff to conduct assessments and maintain contact with families. Such interdisciplinary teams are difficult to organize and maintain.

In addition to considerable practical problems of research, the complex, multidimensional nature of FTT raises unique methodological and conceptual problems (Bithoney & Rathbun, 1983; Bruenlin et al., 1983; Drotar, in press; Kotelchuck, 1980; Roberts & Maddux, 1982). The specific etiology of FTT is difficult to ascertain and must take into account multiple levels of influence. For example, environmental causes of diminished caloric intake, now well recognized to be the proximal cause of FTT (Rutter, 1982; Goldbloom, 1982; Woolston, 1983), may range from underfeeding based on ignorance of nutritional needs in the absence of other problems to chronic family disorganization (Evans et al., 1972; Altemeier et al., 1981). The fact that FTT has already developed and is in many instances chronic by the time the condition is first encountered makes it impossible to disentangle cause versus effect (see Woolston, this volume). The assessment of long-term risk in FTT also requires the capacity to understand and manage information related to outcomes in multiple domains; the child (physical health and growth, cognition and emotional development), the family relationship context (parent-child relationship, intrafamilial relations and resources). Finally, it is often impossible and not desirable for research teams to conduct research without providing services to families of affected children.

NEW DIRECTIONS FOR RESEARCH

The NIMH conference, "New Directions in Failure to Thrive Research: Implications for Prevention," that provided the impetus for the present volume was organized by present author and the Preventive Research Center of NIMH (Mort Silverman, Director and Vicki Levin, Program Specialist in Infancy) to address current research issues in FTT, present ongoing research representative of the current state of the art and to develop suggestions for future research in FTT with special relevance to prevention. The conference was organized with a number of principles in mind: First, there was recognition that advances in knowledge concerning FTT will require the talents of many professionals. The broad-ranging phenomena encompassed within the topic of FTT (physical health, growth, biologic and environmental risk factors, cognitive and emotional development, family functioning) tax the resources of single individuals and necessitates an appreciation of the contributions of many professional disciplines. The contributors to the present volume represent the disciplines of child development, child psychiatry, clinical child psychology, dietetics and nutrition, pediatrics, public health, nursing, and social work. In the interests of extending knowledge of FTT, this volume presents material in a way that transcends narrow professional boundaries. For this reason, a number of theoretical orientations are represented in the various chapters. The reader is left to choose the orientation that she or he finds most useful.

A second organizing theme involved our recognition that practicing clinicians and researchers at different centers throughout the country are already contributing important ideas and have the beginnings of a data base concerning the psychosocial and biologic aspects of FTT. However, their work has not yet been organized and presented in a unified way. The fact that research has thus far been conducted in individual institutions precludes the kind of sharing experiences, data, and ideas for future research that are most likely to advance knowledge of this heterogeneous condition.

Another organizing theme related to the need for more researchers and clinicians to know more about FTT and to eventually contribute information from their research and practice. Information about FTT is needed at a number of levels; clinical practice and service delivery, outcome and epidemiology. In the absence of an understanding of the major issues in FTT research, it is difficult for practicing professionals in various settings to contribute to existing knowledge.

The contributions to the conference and to the present volume were made by experienced practitioners and/or researchers who have made a commitment to the study of FTT. Although they do not by any means represent the entire scope of research or clinical practice in FTT, their work includes a broad spectrum of topics. It is hoped that this volume will stimulate others to begin sharing their work, and to begin new research projects. An additional hope is that this volume will serve to stimulate the cross-center collaboration needed to advance the state of the art in FTT research.

A final theme which guided the organization of the conference and the present volume was the notion that researchers and clinicians who work with the condition of FTT must carefully disentangle the complex issues in this condition and begin to carefully delineate the questions to be asked. Key issues that are considered in this volume include models of risk in FTT, a developmental perspective in FTT, individual differences in diagnosis, the family and societal context, intervention and prevention and methods of research.

STRUCTURE OF THE PRESENT VOLUME

The volume is organized around relevant themes in research and practice in FTT. One important theme is the conceptualization of risk in FTT.
Following Silverman & Levin's keynote introduction concerning prevention,
the present chapter provides an introduction to psychosocial risk in FTT.
Frank presents an overview of biologic risk factors and the implications
for practice which paves the way for subsequent discussions of risk.

Research and practice in FTT requires one to abandon simple models of
behavior and consider phenomena from a biopsychosocial perspective (Engel,
1977) in which biological, environmental and psychological factors interact.
One of the important ideas presented in this volume concerns the limitations
of the traditional organic vs. environmental dichotomy and the need to consider alternative models of FTT in research. A number of authors (Bithoney
& Dubowitz; Gordon & Vazquez; Casey, Collie & Blakemore) discuss this topic.
As research in FTT begins to take a more complex perspective, more sophisticated research questions which deal with various organic and environmental
subpopulations will undoubtedly emerge. The role of "organic" risk factors
as concomitant factors of environmental FTT, especially as they pertain to
the development of psychological outcomes, is a salient area for future
research (see Casey et al., this volume). As conceptual models begin to
clarify pathways by which risk factors influence outcome, one can look
forward to increasingly sophisticated research. Sherrod et al.'s threshold
model for risk in FTT is such a contribution.

Developmental Perspective

One of the most salient needs in future FTT research is for a developmental framework to guide studies of etiology and outcome. Research conducted within a developmental framework is likely to yield increasing
specificity concerning key processes that trigger and maintain FTT. In
addition, the understanding of precursors of mental disorders in FTT will
be enhanced by greater specificity of the developmental processes affected
by different kinds of compromised early experience. Lieberman & Birch and
Chatoor et al. present eloquent and intriguing ideas concerning a developmental framework of early parent-child relationships. Bradley & Casey
cogently discuss the need to apply developmental models of maltreatment to
the study of FTT and report an interesting illustration of the application
of this model from their research.

Individual Differences and Diagnosis

One of the biggest stumbling blocks to research in FTT has been the
implicit assumption of homogeneity in etiology, age of onset, or duration.
A number of authors (Woolston; Lieberman & Birch; Chatoor et al.,;
Linscheid & Rasknake) nicely articulate the complex nature of individual
differences in FTT and the implications for diagnosis, intervention, and
research.

The Family and Societal Context

Despite the fact that familial and societal contexts play a major role
in the origins and sequelae of FTT, research has not generally considered
these factors. Drotar et al. underscore the importance of the family
context to the development and treatment of FTT. Frank, Allen & Brown,
argue compellingly for the significance of economic factors as they impinge
on family life and contribute to the development of FTT. Gordon & Vasquez'
data links the presentation of FTT and economic factors in a metropolitan
area.

Intervention, Prevention, and Health Care Delivery

The salience of psychological and physical problems that accompany FTT necessitate greater attention to the development of innovative intervention strategies, especially preventive intervention. For this reason, treatment approaches need to become increasingly specific and to consider the developmental concomitants of FTT. Chatoor and her coworkers' and Lieberman & Birch's treatment approaches are tailored to the specific developmental concomitants of FTT. Linscheid & Rasknake's contribution concerns the use of behavioral methods in intervention with different subtypes of FTT. Drotar et al. describe the usefulness of a family centered treatment approach. These approaches are representative of the diverse theoretical orientations that will be needed to meet the considerable challenges of intervention in FTT.

There is a need for much better description of intervention strategies which occur in the context of health care delivery. A number of authors deal with this question, including Berkowitz, who describes an interesting interdiscplinary approach to pediatric health care delivery, and Altemeier et al. whose approach to hospital treatment is based on the results of their prospective research. Singer describes outcome in a pediatric rehabilitation hospital. Drotar et al., present an evaluation of a combined hospital and home-based approach to early intervention.

Studies of primary prevention of FTT are among the most needed yet difficult to accomplish. Coury & Brams (this volume) present a thought-provoking account of the difficult issues involved in prevention of FTT which should stimulate others to accept the challenges of prevention. Franket al. and Gordon & Vazquez consider the role of economic factors and public policy in prevention.

Research Methods

Research in FTT places considerable demands on researchers to become familiar with research methods in different fields that have potential applicability to FTT. The use of more comprehensive and sophisticated research methods will certainly enhance the quality of research in FTT. Contributions to the present volume pertain to methodological issues in the following areas: organic factors (Bithoney & Dubowitz), physical growth (Peterson, Herrera & Rathbun), behavioral observation (Finlon et al.), outcome studies (Drotar et al.) and prevention (Levin & Silverman; Brams & Coury).

We anticipate that the information offered in this volume will provide an introduction to the area of FTT. Each of the authors hope that their work will stimulate further interest and perhaps even a commitment to work in this area. One of the most primary needs is to attract the talents of a greater number of clinicians and researchers to work with FTT infants. We also hope that those who are already working with the FTT children and their families will find the information contained in this volume useful and informative. The information presented in this volume falls far short of answers to the problem of FTT. There is no shortage of cogent questions, however, which will lead to better answers and benefit the large numbers of children whose human potential is being affected by FTT and its associated disorders.

REFERENCES

Aber, J.L. & Zigler, E. In R. Rizley & D. Cicchetti (Eds.), Developmental Perspectives on Child Maltreatment. New Directions for Child Development: Vol 1. San Francisco, CA: Jossey-Bass, 1981.

Adelson, L. Homicide by starvation. The nutritional variant of the "battered child." Journal of the American Medical Association, 1963, 186, 458-460.

Ainsworth, M.D.S. & Wittig, B.A. Attachment and exploratory behavior of one year olds in a Strange Situation. In B.M. Foss (Ed.), Determinants of Infant Behavior: Vol. 4. London: Methuen, 1969.

Alfasi, G. A failure-to-thrive infant at play: Applications of microanalysis. Journal of Pediatric Psychology, 1982, 7, 111-123.

Altemeier, W.A., Vietze, P., Sherrod, K.B., Sandler, H.M., Falsey, S. & O'Connor, S. Prediction of child maltreatment during pregnancy. Journal of the American Academy of Child Psychiatry, 1979, 18, 205-219.

American Psychiatric Association Diagnostic and Statistic Manual of Psychiatric Disorders, 3rd Edition. Washington, D.C., 1980.

Ayoub, C., Pfeifer, D. & Leichtman, L. Treatment of infants with nonorganic failure to thrive. Child Abuse and Neglect, 1979, 3, 937-941.

Barbero, G., Morris, M. & Redford, M. Malidentification of mother-baby-father relationships expressed in infant failure to thrive. In, The Neglected Battered Child Syndrome: Role Reversal in Parents. New York: Child Welfare League of America, 1963.

Belle, D. Lives in Stress: Women and Depression. Beverly Hills, CA: Sage Press, 1982.

Belsky, J., Robins, E. & Gamble, W. The determinants of parental competence. Toward a contextual theory. In M. Lewis (Ed.), Beyond the Dyad. New York: Plenum Press, 1984.

Berkowitz, C.D. & Barry, H. Psychological assessment of children with failure to thrive. Annual Meeting of the Ambulatory Pediatric Association (Abstract). Washington, D.C., 1982. Berwick, D.M. Nonorganic failure to thrive. Pediatrics in Review, 1980, 1, 265-270.

Besharov, D.J. Toward better research on child abuse and neglect. Child Abuse and Neglect, 1981, 5, 383-390.

Bithoney, W.G. & Rathbun, J.M. Failure to thrive. In W.B. Levine, A.C. Carey, A.D. Crocker & R.J. Gross (Eds.), Developmental Behavioral Pediatrics. Philadelphia, PA: Saunders, 1983.

Bolton, F.G. When Bonding Fails: Clinical Assessment of High Risk Families. Beverly Hills, CA: Sage Press, 1983.

Bradley, R.H. Social and nonsocial environment of children who are nonorganic failure to thrive. Paper presented at the Biennial Meeting of the Society for Research in Child Development. Detroit, MI, April, 1983.

Bruenlin, D.C., Desai, V.J., Stone, M.E. & Swilley, J. Failure to thrive with no organic etiology: A critical review. International Journal of Eating Disorders, 1983, 2, 25-49.

Call, J.M. Toward a nosology of psychiatric disorders in infancy. In J.D. Call, E. Galenson & R.L. Tyson (Eds.), Frontiers of Infant Psychiatry. New York: Basic Books, 1983.

Cameron, H.C. Forms of vomiting in infancy. British Medical Journal, 1925, 1, 872-876.

Campos, J.J., Caplovitz, Barett K., Lamb, M.E., Goldsmith, H.H. & Stenberg, C. Socioemotional development. In P.H. Mussen (Ed.), Handbook of Child Psychology. New York: Wiley, 1983.

Cassidy, C.M. Benign neglect and toddler malnutrition. In C. Greene & F.E. Johnston (Eds.), Social and Biological Predictors of Nutritional Status, Physical Growth, and Neurological Development. New York: Academic Press, 1980.

Chapin, H.D. A plan of dealing with atrophic infants and children. Archives of Pediatrics, 1908, 25, 491-496.

Chapin, H.D. Are institutions for infants necessary? Journal of the American Medical Association, 1915, 64, 1-3.

Chase, H.P. & Martin, H.P. Undernutrition and child development. New England Journal of Medicine, 1970, 282, 993-999.

Chatoor, I. & Egan, J. Nonorganic failure to thrive and dwarfism due to food refusal: A separation disorder. Journal of the American Academy of Child Psychiatry, 1983, 22, 294-301.

Christiansen, N., Moro, J. & Herrera, M.G. Family-social characteristics related to physical growth of children. British Journal of Preventive Social Medicine, 1975, 29, 121-130.

Cicchetti, D. & Braunwald, K.G. An organizational approach to the study of emotional development in maltreated infants. Infant Mental Health Journal, 1984, 5, 172-183.

Drotar, D. Failure to thrive. In D.K. Routh (Ed.), Handbook of Pediatric Psychology. New York: Guilford, in press.

Drotar, D. & Malone, C.A. Family-oriented intervention in failure to thrive. In M. Klaus & M.O. Robertson (Eds.), Birth Interaction and Attachment, Johnson and Johnson Pediatric Round Table, Vol. 6. Skillman, NJ: Johnson & Johnson Co., 1982.

Drotar, D., Malone, C.A. & Negray, J. Psychosocial intervention with families of failure to thrive infants. Child Abuse and Neglect, 1979, 3, 927-935 (a).

Drotar, D., Malone, C.A. & Negray, J. Environmentally based failure to thrive and childrens intellectual development. Journal of Clinical Child Psychology, 1980, 9, 236-240.

Drotar, D., Malone, C.A. & Nowak, M. Early outcome in failure to thrive: correlates of security of attachment. Presentation to Society for Research in Child Development. Toronto, Canada, April, 1985.

Elmer, E. Failure to thrive: Role of the mother. Pediatrics, 1966, 25, 717-725.

Elmer, E., Gregg, G.S. & Ellison, P. Late results of the "failure to thrive" syndrome. Clinical Pediatrics, 1969, 8, 584-589.

Evans, S.L., Reinhart, J.B. & Succop, R.A. Failure to thrive: A study of 45 children and their families. Journal of the American Academy of Child Psychiatry, 1972, 11, 440-459.

Ferholt, J. & Provence, S. Diagnosis and treatment of an infant with psychophysiological vomiting. Psychoanalytic Study of the Child, 1976, 31, 439-459.

Field, M. Follow-up developmental status of infants hospitalized for nonorganic failure to thrive. Journal of Pediatric Psychology, 1984, 9, 241-256.

Fischoff, J., Whitten, C.F. & Pettit, M.G. A psychiatric study of mothers of infants with growth failure secondary to maternal deprivation. Journal of Pediatrics, 1971, 79, 209-215.

Fitch, M.J., Cadol, R.V., Goldson, E.J., Jackson, E.K., Swartz, D.F. & Wendel, T.P. Prospective Study in Child Abuse: The Child Study Program, Final Report of the Office of Child Development Project, Grant No. OCD-CR-371. Denver, CO: Denver Department of Health and Hospitals, 1975.

Flanagan, C.H. Rumination in infancy - past and present. Journal of the American Academy of Child Psychiatry, 1977, 16, 140-149.

Fraiberg, S. (Ed.) Clinical Studies in Infant Mental Health. New York: Basic Books, 1980.

Fraiberg, S., Lieberman, A.M., Pekarsky, J.H. & Pawl, J.H. Treatment and outcome in an infant psychiatry program, Part I and II. Journal of Preventive Psychiatry, 1981, 1, 89-111.

Freeman, H.E., Klein, R.E., Kagan, J. & Yarbrough, C. Relations between nutrition and cognition in rural Guatemala. American Journal of Public Health, 1977, 67, 233-239.

Garbarino, J. The human ecology of child maltreatment: A conceptual model for research. Journal of Marriage and the Family, 1977, 39, 721-735.

Garber, J. Classification of childhood psychopathology: A developmental perspective. Child Development, 1984, 55, 30-48.

Garmezy, N., Masten, A.S. & Tellegen, S. The study of stress and competence in children: A building block for developmental psychopathology. Child Development, 1984, 55, 97-111.

Glaser, H., Heagarty, M.C., Bullard, D.M. & Pivchik, E.C. Physical and psychological development of children with early failure to thrive. Journal of Pediatrics, 1968, 73, 690-698.

Goldbloom, R.B. Failure to thrive. Pediatric Clinics of North America, 1982, 29, 151-165.

Goldstein, S., Freud, A. & Solnit, A.J. Beyond the Best Interests of the Child. New York: Macmillan, 1973.

Gordon, A.H. & Jameson, J.C. Infant-mother attachment in parents with non-organic failure to thrive syndrome. Journal of the American Academy of Child Psychiatry, 1979, 18, 96-99.

Greenberg, N.H. Atypical behavior during infancy: Infant development in relation to the behavior and personality of the mother. In E.J. Anthony & C. Koupernik (Eds.), The Child in His Family, Vol. I. New York: Wiley & Sons, 1970.

Halpern, R. Lack of effects of home-based early intervention: Some possible explanations. American Journal of Orthopsychiatry, 1984, 54, 33-42.

Harvard School of Public Health. American Hunger Crisis: Poverty and Health in New England. Boston: Harvard University Press, 1983.

Hopwood, N. & Becker, D.J. Psychosocial dwarfism: Detection, evaluation and management. Child Abuse and Neglect, 1979, 3, 439-447.

Hufton, I.W. & Oates, R.K. Nonorganic failure to thrive: A long-term follow-up. Pediatrics, 1977, 59, 73-79.

Kadushin, A. & Martin, J.A. Child Abuse: An Interactional Event. New York: Columbia University Press, 1981.

Kanawati, A.A., Darwish, O. & McLaren, D.S. Failure to thrive in Lebanon, III: Family income, expenditure and possession. Acta Paediatrica Scandinavia, 1974, 63, 849-854.

Kanawati, A.A. & McLaren, D.S. Failure to thrive in Lebanon, II: An investigation of the causes. Acta Paediatrica Scandinavia, 1973, 62, 571-576.

Kerr, M.D., Bogues, J.L. & Kerr, D.S. Psychosocial functioning of mothers of malnourished children. Pediatrics, 1978, 62, 778-784.

Koel, B.S. Failure to thrive and fatal injury as a continuum. American Journal of Diseases of Children, 1969, 118, 565-567.

Kotelchuck, M. Nonorganic failure to thrive: The status of interactional and environmental theories. In B.W. Camp (Ed.), Advances in Behavioral Pediatrics: Vol. I. Greenwich, CN: Jai Press, 1980.

Krieger, J. Food restriction as a form of child abuse in ten cases of psychosocial dwarfism. Clinical Pediatrics, 1964, 13, 127-130.

Light, R.J. Abused and neglected children in America: A study of alternative policies. Harvard Educational Review, 1973, 43, 556-598.

Leonard, M.F., Rhymes, J.P. & Solnit, A.J. Failure to thrive in infants: a family problem. American Journal of Diseases of Children, 1966, 111, 600-612.

Lourie, R.S. Treatment of psychosomatic problems in infants. Clinical Proceedings of Children's Hospital, 1955, 2, 141-151.

Lipsitt, L.P. Critical conditions in infancy: a psychological perspective. American Psychologist, 1979, 34, 973-980.

MacCarthy, D. & Booth, E. Parental rejection and stunting of growth. Journal of Psychosomatic Research, 1979, 114, 259-265.

Massachusetts Department of Public Health Massachusetts Nutrition Survey, 1983.

Matas, L., Arend, D.A. Sroufe, L.A. Continuity in adaptation: Quality of attachment and later competence. Child Development, 1978, 49, 547-556.

Maybanks, S. & Bryce, M. Home-Based Service for Children and Families: Policy, Practice and Research. Chicago, IL: Thomas, 1979.

Mitchell, W.G., Gorell, R.W. & Goldberg, R.A. Failure to thrive: A study in primary care setting, epidemiology and follow-up. Pediatrics, 1980, 65, 971-977.

Money, J., Annecillo, C. & Kelley, J.F. Abuse-dwarfism syndrome: After rescue, statural and intelletual catch-up growth correlates. Journal of Clinical Child Psychology, 1983, 12, 279-283.

Nagi, S. Child Maltreatment in the United States. New York: Columbia University Press, 1977.

Nakou, S., Adam, H., Stathacopoulou, N. & Agathonos, H. Health status of abused and neglected children and siblings. Child Abuse and Neglect, 1982, 6, 279-284.

Newberger, E.H., Reed, R.P., Daniel, J.H., Hyde, J. & Kotelchuck, M. Pediatric social illness: Toward an etiologic classification. Pediatrics, 1977, 60, 178-185.

Oates, R.K., Peacock, A. & Forest, D. Long-term effects of non-organic failure to thrive. Pediatrics, 1985, 75, 36-40.

Parke, R.D. & Collmer, C.W. Child abuse: An interdisciplinary analysis. In M. Hetherington (Ed.), Review of Child Development Research: Vol. 5. Chicago, IL: University of Chicago Press, 1975.

Pastor, D. The quality of mother-infant attachment and its relationship to toddler's initial sociability with peers. Developmental Psychology, 1981, 17, 326-335.

Patterson, G.R. A performance theory for coercive family interaction. In R.B. Cairns (Ed.), The Analysis of Social Interactions, Methods, Issues, and Illustrations. Hillsdale, NJ: Erlbaum, 1979.

Patton, R.G. & Gardner, L.I. Influences of family environment on growth: The syndrome of maternal deprivation. Pediatrics, 1962, 30, 957-962.

Patton, R.G. & Gardner, L.I. Growth Failure in Maternal Deprivation. Springfield, IL: Thomas, 1963.

Pollitt, E. & Eichler, A. Behavioral disturbances among failure to thrive children. American Journal of Diseases of Children, 1976, 130, 24-29.

Pollitt, E., Eichler, A.W. & Chan, C.K. Psychosocial development and behavior of mothers of failure to thrive children. American Journal of Orthopsychiatry, 1975, 45, 525-537.

Pollitt, E. & Leibel, R. Biological and social correlates of failure to thrive. In L. Greene & F.E. Johnston, Social Biological Predictors of Nutritional Status, Physical Growth and Neurological Development. New York: Academic Press, 1980.

Ramey, C.T., Starr, R.H., Pallas, J., Whitten, C.F. & Reed, V. Nutrition, response contingent stimulation and the maternal deprivation syndrome: Results of an early intervention program. Merrill Palmer Quarterly, 1975, 21, 45-55.

Rathbun, J. Prospective outcome of children hospitalized for failure to thrive. Paper presented at NIMH Conference, New Directions in Failure to Thrive Research: Implications for Prevention. Washington, D.C., 1984.

Rexford, E., Sander, L. & Shapiro, T. Infant Psychiatry. New York: Basic Books, 1976.

Richmond, J.B., Eddy, E. & Green, M. Rumination: A psychosomatic syndrome of infancy. Pediatrics, 1958, 22, 49-55.

Roberts, M.C. & Maddux, J.E. A psychosocial conceptualization of nonorganic failure to thrive. Journal of Clinical Child Psychology, 1982, 11, 216-226.

Rutter, M. Prevention of children's psychosocial disorder: Myth and substance. Pediatrics, 1982, 70, 883-894.

Sameroff, A.J. & Chandler, M.J. Reproductive risk and the continuum of caretaking casualty. In F.D. Horowitz (Ed.), Review of Child Development Research: Vol. 4. Chicago, IL: University of Chicago Press, 1975.

Schor, E.L. The foster care system and the health status of foster children. Pediatrics, 1982, 69, 521-528.

Seifer, R. & Sameroff, A.J. A structural equation model analysis of competence in children at risk for mental disorder. Prevention in Human Services, 1982, 85-96.

Sills, R.H. Failure to thrive: The role of clinical and laboratory evaluation. <u>American Journal of Diseases of Children</u>, 1978, <u>132</u>, 967-969.

Singer, L., Drotar, D., Fagan, J.F., Devost, L. & Lake, R. Cognitive development of failure to thrive infants: Methodological issues and new approaches. In T. Field & A. Sostek (Eds.), <u>Infants Born at Risk: Physiological, Perceptual, and Cognitive Processes</u>. New York: Grune & Stratton, 1983.

Singer, L.T. & Fagan, J.F. The cognitive development of the failure to thrive infant. A three-year longitudinal study. <u>Journal of Pediatric Psychology</u>, 1984, <u>9</u>, 363-382.

Spitz, R.A. Hospitalism: An inquiry into the genesis of psychiatric conditions of early childhood. <u>Psychoanalytic Study of the Child</u>, 1945, <u>1</u>, 53-74.

Spitz, R.A. Hospitalism: A follow-up report. <u>Psychoanalytic Study of the Child</u>, 1946, <u>2</u>, 113-117.

Sroufe, L.A. Socioemotioinal development. In J. Osofsky (Ed.), <u>Handbook of Infant Development</u>. New York: John Wiley, 1979.

Sroufe, L.A. Infant-caregiver attachment and patterns of adaptation in preschool: The roots of maladaptation and competence. In M. Perlmutter (Ed.), <u>Development and Policy Concerning Children with Special Needs. Minnesota Symposium on Child Psychology: Vol. 16</u>. Hillsdale, NJ: Erlbaum, 1983.

Talbot, N.B., Sobel, E.H., Burke, B.S., Lindeman, E. & Kaufman, S.B. Dwarfism in healthy children: Its possible relation to emotional, nutritional and endocrine disturbances. <u>New England Journal of Medicine</u>, 1947, <u>236</u>, 783-793.

Wald, M.S. State intervention on behalf of endangered children. A proposed legal response. <u>Child Abuse and Neglect</u>, 1982, <u>6</u>, 345.

Waters, E., Wippman, J. & Sroufe, L.A. Attachment, positive affect and competence in the peer group: Two studies in construct validation. <u>Child Development</u>, 1979, <u>50</u>, 821-829.

Whitten, C.F., Pettit, M.G. & Fischoff, J. Evidence that growth failure from maternal deprivation is secondary to undereating. <u>Journal of the American Medical Association</u>, 1969, <u>209</u>, 1675-1682.

Williams, G.T. & Money, J. <u>Traumatic Abuse and Neglect of Children at Home</u>. Baltimore, MD: Johns Hopkins, 1980.

Woolston, J.L. Eating disorders in infancy and early childhood. <u>Journal of the American Academy of Child Psychiatry</u>, 1983, <u>22</u>, 114-121.

Zigler, E. & Trickett, P.K. I.Q., social competence and evaluation of early childhood intervention programs. <u>American Psychologist</u>, 1978, <u>33</u>, 789-798.

II. CONCEPTUAL MODELS: RESEARCH IMPLICATIONS

In this section, interactional models of organic and environmental influence in FTT and their implications for research are considered. It is an understatement to say that FTT defies easy description and conceptualization. The lack of agreement in definitions of FTT, which has been such a primary obstacle to progress in research and practice can be traced, at least in part, to the inherent complexities of defining FTT and conceptualizing its etiology.

Bithoney and Dubowitz recommend that FTT be considered in the broadest descriptive sense as growth deficiency defined by objective norms. From Bithoney and Dubowitz' vantage point, which is shared by many of the authors of this volume (See summary of conference discussion), the assessment of growth and nutritional status is the primary means of operationalizing FTT. Other associated characteristics, such as developmental delay, are best considered as separate dimensions (See Woolston, this volume).

Another salient problem identified by Bithoney and Dubowitz is the dichotomy between organic and nonorganic etiologic influences in FTT. Although this distinction has utility as a working assumption and is used by many authors in this book, Bithoney and Dubowitz challenge the dichotomy on the grounds that organic and non-organic processes are best understood not as discrete influences but as interrelated factors, and that the organic/non-organic dichotomy is based on a simplistic, linear causal model. Bithoney and Dubowitz recommend a broad etiological model which emphasizes the interrelationships between physical and psychosocial influences and review the organic influences on FTT and associated problems. Detailed consideration of these organic influences will help researchers clarify medical variables which might be expected to have a significant influence on the psychological status and outcome of FTT children.

Gordon and Vazquez trace the historical development of the concept of FTT and describe an expanded conceptual model which defines the circumstances under which FTT occurs, examples of clinical problems included in each category, and suggestions for future research based on this model. Gordon and Vazquez also underscore the limitations of the organic versus non-organic dichotomy in FTT and present a typology based on patterns of infant characteristics (e.g. physical health versus organic impairment) and environmental circumstances (normal versus adverse environment) which can be used to identify and define various subpopulations of FTT children. Researchers might wish to consider Gordon and Vazquez' typology in specifying research questions and subgroups of FTT infants as well as their recommendation that the implications of excluding infants from FTT populations be carefully considered.

In the introduction Casey, Collie & Blakemore describe an interactional model which considers environmental and organic influences in FTT. In this chapter, Casey and his colleagues focus on the potential impact of one class of organic risk factors: nutritional deficiency and one specific nutritional deficiency: the trace mineral zinc. The biologic and nutritional implications of zinc and clinical manifestations of zinc deficiency are reviewed. Casey, Collie & Blakemore cite information which suggests that zinc deficiency may play a significant role in a variety of physical and behavioral symptoms associated with FTT, including growth deficiency, diarrhea, impaired taste sensitivity and resultant loss of appetite, depressed mood and irritability. Casey and his colleagues develop the following hypothesis: that children who receive inadequate nutrition over time may become zinc deficient. This deficiency is more likely to occur in children living in deprived socioeconomic living conditions where diets are more likely to be inadequate in zinc-containing foods such as red meats and seafoods. Casey and his co-workers describe a research design which will allow the determination of the frequency of zinc deficiency in various diagnostic categories of FTT.

ORGANIC CONCOMITANTS OF NONORGANIC FAILURE TO THRIVE:

IMPLICATIONS FOR RESEARCH

William G. Bithoney and Howard Dubowitz

Comprehensive Child Health Program, The Children's Hospital
Boston, Massachusetts and the Harvard Medical School
Department of Pediatrics

The title of this chapter contains an apparent contradiction. If nonorganic failure to thrive (NOFT) has organic factors contributing to its etiology, then must "nonorganic" be a misnomer? This chapter will focus on these organic concomitants of NOFT. Before embarking on this description, examination of the traditional taxonomy of failure to thrive (FTT) is warranted.

It is evident from both the clinical and research literature that FTT has been defined in many different ways. There is a consensus about using growth parameters, but considerable variation in which specific measures are applied. Weight for age, height for age, and weight for height have all been used, alone or in combination. Specifically, weight or height below the third or fifth percentiles on sex-appropriate growth charts are most commonly used. There is also considerable controversy about which are the most valid measures and appropriate charts. Many researchers have used the Stuart charts, which are based on middle class white children in Boston (Stuart & Meredith, 1946). More recently, the growth curves of the National Center on Health Statistics (NCHS) have been suggested as the "gold standard," at least for the United States, and possibly for all countries (Hamill et al., 1977).

THE CONCEPT AND ASSESSMENT OF GROWTH DEFICIENCY

The term FTT means impaired growth, regardless of the reason. Reasonable determination of FTT requires precise knowledge of the norms for optimal or adequate growth that can be applied to individual children. Unfortunately, the knowledge base is not that well developed. The influence of genetic endowment on growth, particularly in the first few years, needs further clarification and consideration. For example, owing to different growth patterns, recent immigrants from Southeast Asia probably should not be plotted on NCHS charts. The expected growth patterns of children born prematurely or small for gestational age also need to be more completely delineated. These examples illustrate the need for the refinement of growth standards in order to make them meaningful for specific groups and individual children.

Undernutrition has been considered to be the primary basis of FTT. This raises another problem, in that arbitarily selected growth parameters might not reflect the presence of undernutrition. Some children are

"small" for other reasons (e.g. premature birth), and might be adequately nourished. In addition, a child whose weight for age is at the 25th
percentile, but with the genetic endowment to be at the 80th percentile, is
missed by the 5th percentile threshold. It seems that measures of growth
are rather indirect, and that direct evaluation of nutritional status would
be a preferred approach. A number of anthropometric and biochemical measures of undernutrition are being developed, but reliable standardized data
are not yet easily applicable, particularly for clinical purposes. (See
Peterson et al., this volume.)

Another criterion that has haphazardly been used for the diagnosis of
FTT is the presence of developmental delays. At times, delays are
considered, but in other reports they are not mentioned (Pollitt & Leibel,
1980; Barbero & Shaheen, 1967; Sills, 1978). Where delays are described,
specific details of what constitutes a developmental delay are not always
provided. In addition, different clinicians and researchers rarely apply
the same measures to assess developmental delays (Fitch et al., 1976;
Whitten & Fischoff, 1969). Although the developmental status of the child
who is growing inadequately is of importance, it should not be a necessary
criterion of FTT, since FTT is focused on growth and nutritional status.
The relationship between physical growth and the complex realm of child
development is frequently unclear and there appears to be insufficient
basis for linking them in a definition of FTT.

In light of the above criticisms, we suggest that FTT be considered
as, and renamed, growth deficiency. (This term will be used in the remainder of this chapter.) The term, growth deficiency, avoids the ambiguity of
"thrive" and the harmful connotations that "failure" might imply about a
family or parent. It is, in addition, suitably generic.

How might the concept of deficient growth best be operationalized?
Gomez has proposed a system to rate the degree of undernutrition (Gomez et
al., 1956). Using the Harvard growth charts, first, second and third
degree undernutrition would be 90%, 75%, and 60% of the reference weight
for age. Waterlow (1984) and Hansen (1984) offer valuable insights in
assessing the different anthropometric measures, and they show that no
single measure is able to capture all possible manifestations of deficient
growth. Further research is required to adequately refine a measure or
composite of measures that can satisfactorily describe deficient growth for
most clinical and research purposes.

What is needed is an instrument that can accurately and readily be
applied to an individual child. The threshold for concern and intervention
will necessarily vary depending on local growth patterns and available
resources. Waterlow (1984) has proposed to replace the terms "standard" or
"reference standard" growth charts with, reference growth chart. This
disclaims the notion of a single universal and optimal growth pattern for
all humans, and would be a meaningful improvement. At present, we need to
utilize the best appropriate reference charts and measures of growth that
we have, while remaining cognizant of their limitations.

If FTT is to be defined as growth deficiency, then undernutrition is
an important, but not the only etiological factor. The detection of growth
deficiency requires a method for ascertaining that the growth of an individual child is inadequate. Thus, direct measures of growth, such as
velocity of gain, are preferable for assessing the adequacy of growth.
Anthropometric measures of undernutrition are useful as an adjunct, but
do not provide diagnostic criteria.

THE ORGANIC VS. NON-ORGANIC DICHOTOMY

FTT has usually been dichotomized into two categories: organic and nonorganic. "Organic" refers to those instances where a specific physical disorder is identified as responsible for impeding growth. Virtually all serious pediatric illnesses, and also minor recurrent or chronic ones, can have this effect. "Nonorganic" pertains to cases without diagnosable organic disease. Generally, this designation has been made by a process of elimination i.e., the medical history, physical examination and laboratory investigations yield normal results, and preclude a medical diagnosis. The inference is then drawn that the psychosocial realm must be responsible; therefore, the term "nonorganic."

This perspective has two major limitations: first, organic and nonorganic processes are understood to be discrete, as not having any significant interrelationship. The implication is that either one set of factors or the other is the mechanism responsible for impeding growth. In this framework, physical factors are held apart from behavioral and psychosocial processes and the possibility of an interaction effect is minimized. The second and related problem is a causal model that is linear and, identifies the single agents held primarily responsible. This simplification minimizes the complexity of the pathways that lead to growth deficiency. The separate assessment of organic and psychosocial factors, analogous to the division of mind and body, and a reductionist approach are prominent characteristics of this traditional biomedical approach to FTT.

A recent study has challenged the organic - nonorganic dichotomy. Homer and Ludwig (1981) found that 23 percent of their FTT population could not neatly be fitted into either of these categories, and suggested the need for a third group of "mixed" etiology. The authors describe children with FTT whose organic disease was compounded by psychosocial difficulties, but other cases are characterized as "the totally organic and the purely psychosocial groups." The authors therefore adhere to the biomedical model and simply describe the concurrence of organic and psychosocial factors. They do not consider the feasibility, even in their "mixed" group, of a dynamic interaction with organic factors influencing the psychosocial realm and vice versa. The central questions concerning the current model, with its dichotomy of organic and nonorganic processes, are how accurate is the model, and how useful is it? Several scientists have argued against a focus on individual components of a process and have called for a more comprehensive, holistic approach (Bronfenbrenner, 1979; Engel, 1977, 1980; Illich, 1975). A premise of this approach is that nothing exists in isolation, and that one variable might influence another, and in turn be influenced by it (Sameroff & Chandler, 1975). This conceptual framework is derived from systems theory, which asserts that both the organized whole and the component parts are of importance.

We have good evidence that such interactions occur. For example, we know that infants born prematurely are neurologically less mature and that this can manifest in a difficult temperament (Bakeman & Brown, 1980). We also know that stressors on a parent diminish the ability to protect a child (Gaines et al., 1978). We know that infant feeding takes place in the larger context of the parent-infant relationship and interaction (Jackson, Wilkin & Auerbach, 1956). Moreover, it is clear that breast feeding practices are affected by cultural views, just as child rearing practices in general occur in the context of broader social mores (Robertson, 1961; Bronfenbrenner, 1979).

Clinical experience adds rich supportive evidence of the interaction between biological and behavioral factors: a sad, depressed mother struggling with her handicapped child, an anxious father hold his febrile infant

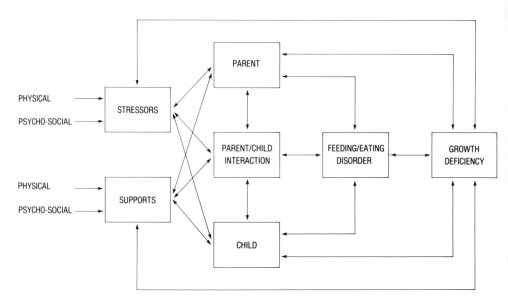

Figure 1

who will not be soothed, an anemic toddler who lacks a certain zest and energy, a competent parent who responds to her healthy child's needs in an appropriate, nurturing manner. Intuitively, we understand that we affect our environment and are also affected by it.

However, the etiological pathways of growth deficiency are not always clear. In different instances, individual factors exert varying influence. The patterns of interaction are dynamic and ongoing. An etiological model of growth deficiency is conceptualized in Figure 1, where the ideas of Engel (1977) are incorporated from his proposed biopsychosocial model.

ETIOLOGICAL PATHWAYS OF GROWTH DEFICIENCY

The case of John Rabb illustrates how this model can work. Alice Rabb completed high school and started working in a local store selling kitchen wares. When she was 19, she became pregnant after a brief affair and suffered from severe morning sickness for the first four months of the pregnancy. As a result, she was forced to quit her job, which in turn, led to her moving back home with her mother. Their relationship had long been a difficult one. Her father had died when she was 17 years old from alcohol-related liver disease. Alice's mother, Mrs. Rabb, wished to support her daughter during her pregnancy, but soon their differences led to frequent fighting. Alice felt badly about her situation and became quite depressed. When she started drinking heavily, her mother urged her to attend the local Alcoholics Anonymous meetings. After a few months delay, Alice began going to 3-4 meetings a week. Feeling better physically and emotionally, Alice applied to her former job, but was told that she would not be rehired. She resumed her drinking habit until the birth of her infant, John, who was born 3 weeks later, weighing 4 lbs and 6 ounces with a small head and other features of the fetal alcohol syndrome.

John's father felt ambivalent about having a child, and would drop in once or twice a week, occasionally offering some money. His relationship with Alice had ended just prior to John's delivery. Hospital staff filed a report to Social Services on the basis of Alice Rabb's alcoholism, and the service plan lead to her return to the AA meetings, albeit intermittently. Mrs. Rabb agreed to her daughter and grandson remaining with her, but she worked fulltime and was only occasionally willing to babysit.

Alice Rabb felt ambivalent about John. John had already resulted in her morning sickness, losing her job, returning to live with her mother, and the dissolution of her relationship with John's father. In addition, John was a difficult infant who would fret easily and demand much attention. At five months of age, he was still up half the night. Alice Rabb frequently became impatient with John and would respond by giving him a bottle of juice or milk, propped up, so that she could sleep or get on with her own activities.

Infants with the fetal alcohol syndrome frequently have developmental delays, and when John was 16 months and had still not said any words, Alice Rabb felt further discouraged about her son. As John grew older, he became increasingly active, and his mother was no longer able to take him to the AA meetings. Her AA attendance became even more sporadic, and she resumed drinking, although less heavily. Accordingly, the social worker increased her monitoring of the situation, which Alice considered intrusive and threatening. As a result, Alice frequently cancelled appointments with the social worker.

Alice prepared meals for John, but he was a very active toddler who preferred to play. Alice decided that rather than fight with him, he could eat as much or as little as he wished, and so she did little to encourage John to eat. John's weight, which had progressed just below the third percentile for age, steadily began to drop. Between the age of 2 and 3 years, John had several ear infections, and 3 bouts of gastroenteritis, which led to further decreases in his growth parameters.

Parenting was becoming increasingly difficult for Alice. An old high school friend became very concerned and asked Alice to join her at AA meetings. Mrs. Rabb agreed to babysit. Alice remained hostile towards her social worker, but was grateful when a day care placement was found for John, which allowed Alice to work part-time. John's behavior was still a significant problem, and Alice became very upset when she learned that John "might be mentally retarded." The AA group suggested that Alice seek counselling to help her "handle John." Four months later, Alice was feeling more competent with her child, and was able to attend to more of her own needs. Her relationship with John showed clear improvement. His eating increased, although he remained below the 3rd percentile of weight for age and at the 3rd percentile of weight for height.

This case clearly illustrates a biopsychosocial model which involves an interplay of organic and psychosocial factors, that beginning prenatally, are constantly interacting. Herein lie important diagnostic and therapeutic implications. Engel (1980) has demonstrated how this approach can greatly influence clinical management.

A good deal of clinical experience and research supports the biopsychosocial model. However, further research is needed to identify and clarify the interface between organic and psychosocial factors. These empirical data will provide for the critical test of the model. Minimally, there is the need for rethinking the current conceptual approach and classification system to growth deficiency. The biopsychosocial model also appears useful for enhancing our understanding and clinical management of growth deficiency.

Thus far, we have described our perspective on understanding the etiology of growth deficiency. It is in this context that we now shift the focus to a consideration of a number of "organic" factors that appear to have bearing on the development of growth deficiency. Some of these seem to play a causal role; others have been shown to be associated with deficient growth. Clarification of their contribution warrants further investigation, but these factors cannot be ignored in the assessment of growth.

ORGANIC FACTORS AND THE DEVELOPMENT OF GROWTH DEFICIENCY

Heredity

Clinicians are familiar with the assessment of a small infant whose parents reassuringly advise "but look at how small we are." There is little doubt that genetic endowment does, in part, determine growth, size, and shape, probably from the time of conception. The precise contribution and mode of transmission have been difficult to determine. Current thinking is that a child inherits a potential for growth and that the environment, particularly nutrition, determines to what extent that potential is realized. In those situations, when the environment is optimal for facilitating growth, it seems likely that heredity plays a major role in explaining the variation between children. In contrast, for children living in relatively adverse conditions, the environmental influence becomes increasingly important. To examine the discrete genetic contribution requires the careful parcelling out of potential environmental confounders. Therefore, a study that looked at birthweights of black and white infants in Baltimore crudely controlling for social class, needs to be interpreted cautiously (Penchaszadeh et al., 1972). The study showed an average birthweight of white infants of 3.27 kg compared to 2.97 kg for black infants. It remains possible that cultural and subcultural factors could still exert an influence, resulting in this difference. Only by controlling for all the known variables that have an impact on birthweight, such as nutritional and health status of mother during the pregnancy, parity, smoking history, use of drugs, medications, and complications of the pregnancy, might we be able to specify genetic influences more precisely. Even then, there might still be environmental factors of which we are simply unaware of.

Children born with phenylketonuria, an autosomal recessive disorder, and Down's syndrome, which is caused by an additional chromosome, provide clear illustrations of a genetic effect on birthweight. Infants with these conditions have been found to have birthweight reductions of 100 gm and 317 gm respectively (Saugstad, 1972; Chen, Chan & Falek, 1972). Robson (1978) has provided an excellent review of the literature examining the genetic influence on birthweight. Estimates of sib pair correlations vary between .41 and .62, and .50 is accepted as a reasonable estimate (Billewicz, 1972). She notes that the observed correlation of 0.50 supports the theory that birthweight is solely determined by fetal genotype. However, the common prenatal environment that sibs share also needs to be considered.

Penrose (1954) studied the correlation coefficients between twins and first cousins, and developed a method for discerning which factors explain what proportion of the variance in birthweight. Penrose (1954) suggested that maternal heredity explained 20% of the total variance, the general maternal environment 18%, the immediate maternal environment 6%, fetal genotype 16%, and unknown intrauterine environment the largest proportion. However, Robson (1978) has questioned some of the statistical assumptions used in this method. First cousins share one eighth of their genes, so that if birthweight were solely determined by fetal genotype, a correlation of 0.125 would be expected. However, the correlation that is observed is 0.014, which suggests a contribution by fetal genotype of about 11%. In comparison, correlations between maternal first cousins are approximately

0.135, a difference of 0.12 from other types of first cousins, that suggests the importance of maternal genotype (Robson, 1955). Considering that the genetic correlation between sisters is 0.5, this suggests a contribution by maternal genotypes of 24%.

Studies of twins have been marred by inadequate classification of monozygotic or dizygotic status, and lack of control for type of placentation. Monozygotic twins who share a placenta, i.e., monochorionic placentation, are frequently in quite disparate situations, where one fetus might be at risk for inadequate support. Corney and his colleagues (1972) found that the correlation of the birthweights in dichorionic monozygotic pairs exceeded that of dizygotic pairs by only about 0.04. Robson concludes that a contribution of 10% by the fetal genotype is a reasonable compromise, integrating the different methodological approaches. This and the 24% of the variance explained by maternal genotype remain relatively less important than maternal environment and unknown intrauterine factors.

Meredith (1970) has examined the birthweights of different populations around the world and demonstrated consistent racial differences. Other studies have shown a gap between black and white Americans in birthweight (Garns & Clark, 1976; Robson et al., 1975). It remains difficult, however, to distinguish the influence of subcultural factors, such as nutrition and other habits.

It has been postulated that the nutritional state of the mother during her childhood can later influence the birthweight of her offspring. The specific mechanism for this phenomenon has yet to be explained. To demonstrate such a relationship, it is critical to address potential confounding by such environmental factors as long-term low socioeconomic status and poor maternal nutrition during the pregnancy.

In a study of rats, Zamenhof and his colleagues (1971) have demonstrated that malnutrition prior to mating and during gestation may lead to fetal undernutrition in the offspring, and in turn, their offspring. Research with human subjects has been less conclusive. The British Perinatal Mortality Survey showed that shorter mothers had a higher incidence of low birthweight babies than did taller mothers (Butler & Alderman, 1969). Other studies have shown taller women to be more likely to produce larger babies (Ounsted & Ounsted, 1973; Thomson, Billewicz & Hytten, 1968). The questionable assumption has been made that taller mothers enjoyed superior nutrition during their childhoods, thus enabling them to achieve more of their growth potential.

Overall, the research indicates that the clinical assessment of an infant with low birthweight requires a thorough consideration of the genetic, as well as the environmental factors, that could play a determining role.

Eveleth (1979) has reviewed the research examining environmental and genetic factors influencing growth patterns in different populations. In those areas where nutritional standards are adequate, the major influence on height is genetic. During the last century, the offspring of each generation has tended to attain greater heights than their parents, and this is thought to reflect an improved environment, particularly with regard to nutrition. In populations that have been exposed to adequate nutrition over a period of time, this trend is likely to end as height begins to plateau. This is illustrated by Japanese children living in California. Gruelich (1957) found that the offspring of Japanese immigrants who were living in California in 1956 were larger than children of the same age raised in Japan. When the subsequent generation in California was measured in 1971, Japanese-American children were of similar size as the same age group of 15 years earlier (Gruelich, 1976).

Perhaps the most striking evidence of a genetic influence on growth and size are the differences between males and females seen on all the major reference growth charts. Race also appears to exert an effect. Many studies have shown Afro-Americans to be taller than Americans of European ancestry (Barr, Allen & Shinefield, 1972; Garn, Clark & Trowbridge, 1973). Asian children are similar to Europeans for the first 6 months, then fall steadily behind in height and weight (Terada & Hoshi, 1965). Smaller size at 1 and 4 years has been demonstrated for Asians living both in and outside Asia (Gruelich, 1957).

Adult stature has a near normal distribution, suggesting the likeli-hood of multiple determining factors. There is no indication of any gene dominance, since the correlations for father-son, mother-son, father-daugh-ter and mother-daughter pairs are all approximately 0.5 (Susanne, 1975). The highest correlations exist between the mean parental height and the child's height (Tanner, Goldstein & Whitehouse, 1970). Below age 2, the correlation coefficient is small and has little utility, but then steadily increases to 0.50 by age 9 years.

These data suggest that genetic endowment should be factored into the assessment of a child's growth. Sex of the child is universally considered. Race possibly requires separate growth charts, although this remains contro-versial and might not be practical for clinical purposes. Parental height is particularly important where the preceeding generation has experienced an environment conducive to optimal growth. However, if conditions were adverse, it is difficult to ascertain to what extent parental statures represent their actual genotypes.

Constitutional Short Stature

Constitutional short stature is defined as height that is less two standard deviations below the mean for age, retarded skeletal maturation, no family history of short stature (mid-parental height is well within normal range), and the absence of abnormalities according to a thorough medical history, physical examination and laboratory investigations (Horner, Thorsson & Hintz, 1978). At times, there is a family history of a similar growth pattern.

This phenomenon is largely seen during the first three years, with growth deceleration beginning at between three and six months of age and greatest during the first twenty-four months. It occurs in both sexes. While the ratio of skeletal age to chronological age has been found to be 0.63, the skeletal age to height age ratio was 0.98. This indicates that the height is appropriate for the skeletal age. By three years of age, a normal growth velocity is reached. It is thought that these children will ultimately attain normal adult stature as the correlation of the child's height to the mid-parental height increases with age (Rimoin & Horton, 1978; Tanner & Israelsohn, 1963; Smith, Truog & Rogers, 1976).

Gestational Factors

Infants suffering from intrauterine growth retardation due to poor maternal nutrition during pregnancy, congenital infection, or inadequate placental function are born small for gestational age (SGA). Their weight at birth is below the expected norms for gestational age. Fitzhardinge and Steven (1972), in a four year followup study of 96 infants, found that 35% of these infants were below the third percentile for both weight and height by age four. Infants with the poorest outcome in terms of growth had a lower socioeconomic status than the other study infants and were described

as having parents who did not stimulate them adequately. These children
are documented as suffering from an overall reduction in brain weight, cell
number, and neuronal myelinization (Chase & Martin, 1970). Such children,
given their difficult temperaments and problematic, trying behaviors are
overrepresented in childhood populations suffering from pediatric social
illnesses, such as child abuse and neglect as well as FTT (Brazelton, 1981).
These children are obviously different from their normally grown brethren
of normative weight/length at the time of birth. Head size is usually less
affected than weight and length (Crane & Kopta, 1979). Postnatal head
growth velocity is increased in these children, although not as much as in
normal prematures and head size continues to be less than the 10th
percentile in many of these children. Dodge, Prensky and Fegin (1975) have
confirmed past observations that SGA children have depressed neurologic and
psychological performance on standardized tests. Lipper and colleagues
(1981) has recently further refined these observations, however, noting
that only those SGA infants with depressed head circumferences have aberrant and delayed neurobehavioral functioning. Adequate maternal nutrition,
most especially during the period of hyperplastic placental growth (between
12 and 36 weeks - but especially between 32 and 36 weeks of gestation) is
imperative to prevent SGA birth. Most past studies of so-called "non-
organic" FTT have made no attempt to discern either the incidence of pre-,
peri-, and postnatal medical complications in their FTT probands or of
prevalence of SGA infants in their case samples. Given that 35% of these
infants have weight and height below the third percentile at age 4 years
because of an organic, prenatal insult, future studies of growth deficiency
should actively screen infants (see above) for the adequacy of their birthweight for length rather than including them as "non-organic" FTT cases.

Prematurity, per se, may also predispose to growth deficiency. The 10
to 40 percent incidence of low birthweight (LBW) infants who subsequently
fail to thrive is a significant overrepresentation from the 10% LBW rate
seen in the population at large (Elmer, 1960). The data concerning appropriate for gestational age (AGA) prematures are less clear cut.
Fitzhardinge & Steven (1972) found that at age 4 years, 11% of AGA prematures were less than the 10th percentile, implying a normal growth potential for AGA prematures. The high incidence of growth deficiency in LBW
infants may be due to a perinatal insult unrelated to low birthweight and
prematurity. A two-fold increase in the incidence of perinatal complications has been shown in children with deficient growth versus controls
(Riley et al., 1968). Such perinatal complications result in neural tissue
loss and are associated with subsequent effects on growth, cognition and
behavior. Past FTT research that did not examine or control for prematurity per se may now be seen as largely inadequate, given the high incidence of prematurity in the population at large.

Maternal Cigarette Smoking During Gestation. Over the past decade, a
number of authors have described the untoward effects on the fetus of
maternal cigarette smoking during pregnancy. For example, there is a
difference in the incidence of smallness for gestational age and low birthweight per se in the children of mothers who smoked during their pregnancy.
This effect seems to be linear with the children of mothers who smoke the
most suffering from a higher incidence of SGA and LBW.

Fetal Alcohol and Other Syndromes Associated with In Utero Toxin
Exposure. Several authors have noted a high incidence of alcoholism in the
families of undernourished FTT children (Elmer, 1960; Leonard, Rhymes &
Solnit, 1966; Pollitt & Thomson, 1977). It is now known that fetal alcohol
syndrome is caused by exposure in utero to alcohol and is seen most
frequently in the children of alcoholic mothers. More subtle effects are
seen in the infants of women who ingest significant amounts of alcohol, but
are not diagnosed as suffering from alcoholism (Oski & McMillen, 1980;

Graham, 1983; Behrman & Vaughan, 1983). Also, subtle fetal alcohol effects have been described in infants whose mothers drank moderate amounts of alcohol during pregnancy.

The physical disturbances of growth alone associated with heavy maternal alcohol ingestion include:

Abnormality	Percent of Patients
Prenatal growth disturbance	97
Postnatal growth disturbance	97
Microcephaly	93
Cognitive developmental delay	89
Fine motor dysfunction	80

Other abnormalities associated with the syndrome include craniofacial abnormalities: limb, vascular and cardiac abnormalities (Rosenberg & Weller, 1973). These children suffer severe impairments in growth that seems to persist throughout life. In neurobehavioral performance, they are much like SGA infants.

Other authors have described similar growth retardation and congenital anomalies associated with altered neurobehavioral performance in infants exposed in utero to hydantoin and trimethadione (Quinn & Rapoport, 1974).

All of the above syndromes are associated with in utero toxin exposure. Until these syndromes were recognized, children who demonstrated the associated findings -- decreased weight, height and head circumference along with developmental delay and irritability -- may have been diagnosed as suffering from "non-organic" FTT. These children along with premature and SGA infants may well confound the results of some past studies of undernutrition (FTT).

Minor Congenital Anomalies

Nelson's Textbook of Pediatrics (Behrman & Vaughan, 1983) lists multiple miscellaneous patterns of deformity that have been routinely associated with short stature and depressed weight. The list is long and such deformities as anteverted nostrils, microcephaly, and lateral displacement of the canthi all have been reported as identifiable syndromes associated with short stature and poor weight gain. Despite this, to date, no studies have been undertaken to catalog the incidence of these anomalous features in children who fail to thrive for "non-organic" reasons.

We have already listed the major features of fetal alcohol syndrome, and referred to fetal trimethadione, and hydantoin syndromes. It is reasonable to suspect that future research will elucidate other such syndromes associated with poor growth and altered behavioral patterns.

A number of authors have documented the often devastating effects of congenital anomalies on maternal-child bonding. Might anomalies of a more subtle nature lead to more subtle disturbances of bonding especially if associated with behavioral changes? Might these altered bonding patterns contribute toward deficient growth? No one at present knows the answer to these questions. A number of authors have demonstrated behavioral, attentional, temperamental and developmental deficits in children suffering from minor congenital anomalies that appear similar to those deficits described in malnourished children (Siva, 1976; Galler, Ramsey & Lowell, 1985; Barrett, 1983; Richardson et al., 1972; LaVeck, Hammond & LaVeck, 1980).

These children are overrepresented in series of children suffering from attention deficits and behavioral problems.

Undernutrition in Infancy and Toddler Years

All children who suffer from what has in the past been called NOFT have at least one organically based medical disease: malnutrition. (See Frank, this volume.) While this is self evident, and indeed tautological, in that FTT is defined as undernutrition demonstrated on standardized growth charts, the organic, temperamental, developmental, and interactional effects of malnutrition are all too infrequently considered by providers who treat children suffering from growth deficiency. In this section we will chronicle the multiple biomedical changes associated with moderate to severe nutritional inadequacy. These changes are biochemical, endocrinological, gastrointestinal, immunologic, neurologic, and behavioral.

I. Biochemical Alterations

Protein energy malnutrition induces many biochemical changes. These changes are mediated in a number of ways. Most obviously, decreased access on an intracellular level to the substrates of energy metabolism and the intermediates of metabolism, including adenosinetriphosphate (ATP), results in altered intracellular chemistry (McLean, 1966; Nichols et al., 1972; Viteri, 1981). Protein and amino acid chemistry is altered as the pool of available intracellular amino acids is depleted. This leads to an alteration of the baseline metabolic state from one of anabolism (growth, increase in cell size, number, muscle mass and adipose tissue) to one of catabolism (the autodigestion of adipose tissue and muscle proteins), in order to maintain the availability in the serum of an adequate pool of the substrates for energy metabolism. This attempt to conserve energy along with impaired muscle mass results in decreased activity and exploration of the physical environment by the child (Waterlow, 1975; Monckberg et al., 1964; Whitehead, 1968; Picou & Taylor-Roberts, 1969). Decreased and probably less satisfying interactions with caretakers may ensue. The child who is lethargic and interacts poorly is obviously at risk for delayed motor development. This, coupled with the central nervous system changes documented in undernutrition (see below), results in a child who might become progressively more developmentally delayed. The import of other biochemical changes such as depressed levels of urea cycle enzymes, decreased pyruvate kinase activity, decreased valine amino transferase, alanine hydroxylase, aldolase and other enzymes is less clear cut but possibly significant. The alterations in these and other enzymes demonstrates further abnormality of the biochemical baseline state in children suffering from undernutrition. It is important to note here, that elevations of serum transaminase enzymes (SGOT, SGPT) are routinely documented in undernourished children and these aberrancies have often led clinicians to do extensive medical workups pursuing the possibility of hepatic disease in these children (McLean, 1966). These enzymes are elevated in moderate to severe undernutrition per se, and in and of themselves, imply no organic pathology, only a catabolic nutritional state.

II. Endocrinological Alterations

Both hormonal levels and end organ activity are altered in childhood undernutrition. Decreased plasma insulin levels have been documented along with decreased amino acids in plasma. These changes are additive with increased cortisol levels and ACTH resulting in impaired incorporation of amino acids into muscle (the changes of catabolism) and increased amino acid release from muscles and organs (Goodlad & Munro, 1959). The above documented decrease in protein synthesis favors recycling of amino acids (catabolism) and decreased albumin synthesis resulting in the hypoalbuminemia and edema seen in the victims of severe protein energy undernutrition (Picou & Taylor-Roberts, 1969). Increased human growth hormone and adrenalin (possibly) along with glucagon further alter the metabolism of these children. The most severely malnourished children may become hypoglycemic and even hypothermic (Whitehead, 1968; Viteri, 1981). Reduced thyroid hormone levels and thyroid stimulating hormone levels may further contribute to the lethargy and slowed linear growth in children suffering from growth deficiency (Viteri, 1981).

III. Anemia, Micronutrient Deficiency

In our clinical experience, one-half of children suffering from growth deficiency are also anemic. While it is clear that most children who fail to thrive have many interactional and psychological problems, the anemia associated with undernutrition may have an important deleterious effect on social transactions (Howell, 1971) and thus may contribute to the etiology of growth deficiency.

Oski and Honig (1978) reported an improvement in the Bayley Mental Development Index of iron deficient infants within one week of treatment with intramuscular iron. The infants showed a statistically significant improvement in alertness, gross and fine-motor function. In this article, Oski concluded that there were behavioral and cognitive consequences of anemia and that they were, at least in part, rapidly reversible upon treatment with intramuscular iron. Howell (1978) reported decreased attentiveness and restricted perception in children with iron deficiency. Studies of both adults and children with iron deficiency show poor concentration, easy fatigability, malaise, and anorexia (Werkman, Shipman & Shelly, 1964). These deficits could be improved within five days, however, upon treatment with iron. Sulzer, Wesley & Leonig (1973), in a study of black, inner city children attending preschool, showed a significant depression of motoric output, recall of information, and decreased reaction time in children with hemoglobins less than 10.6. These impairments of functioning were worse in younger children. Housing, socioeconomic status, occupation of parents and other social parameters were well controlled in this study; the effect seemed related to iron deficiency alone. Webb and Oski (1973) found significant impairment of cognitive functioning in 72 iron deficient adolescent subjects. Further, Cantwell (1974) showed that anemia even without demonstrable deficiencies seems to be associated with an increase in the "soft" neurologic signs documented in attention deficit disorder (ADD).

While the effect of iron deficiency anemia on behavior is quite well documented, the mechanism by which iron depletion exerts its deleterious action is not well understood. It is unlikely that anemia per se causes these effects. Chodorkoff and Whitten (1963) found no relation between the degree of anemia and IQ scores in studies of patients with diagnosed sickle cell disease.

The behavioral changes associated with anemia and iron deficiency may be mediated by the effect of deficiency on the central nervous system (Cooper, Bloom & Roth, 1974; Sourkes, 1972). Monamine oxidase, an iron dependent enzyme, is important in the catabolism of all monamines, e.g. norepinephrine, dopamine, etc. This enzyme has been shown to have a decreased activity in iron deficiency which returns to normal upon treatment with iron within 6 days, well before the hemoglobin level approaches normal (Symes, Missala & Sourkes, 1971; Symes, Sourkes & Youdim, 1969). Children with iron deficiency have also been documented as having elevated excretion of urinary catecholamines (Voorhess et al., 1975). Catecholamine synthesis is also effected in the iron deficient state. Tyrosine hydroxylase, the rate limiting enzymatic step in norepinephrine synthesis, is an iron dependent enzyme, whose activity is decreased in the presence of inadequate iron stores. Since catechol "imbalance" is a well documented concomitant of depression in both adults and children, these findings of catecholamine abnormalities in children with anemia whose growth is deficient may be important. Further, the fact that some of the enzymes of the Krebs cycle (energy metabolism) are iron dependent results in increased caloric requirements in patients with iron deficiency and increased caloric requirements in patients with marked iron deficiency anemia (Dagg, Jackson & Curry, 1966; Jacobs, 1968; Picou, 1981). This implies that children with anemia and "FTT" may require more than normative calories before they gain weight. Certainly the depressed affect, delayed development and perceptual abnormalities seen in iron deficiency are identical to those ascribed to "FTT" per se. Most studies of growth deficiency, especially in the psychological literature, do not control for or even consider the severity of anemia or iron deficiency in these children. Thus, their interpretation of developmental findings may be partially confounded by the behavioral effects of iron deficiency. For this reason, further research in growth deficiency should categorize children based not only on their degree of undernutrition but also on their degree of iron deficiency. Subsets of the growth deficient population with developmental difficulties attributable at least in part to anemia need to be categorized. It is the authors experience that many children with growth deficiency and anemia have rapid improvement in their behavior, attention span and temperament fairly quickly after the institution of iron therapy even before significant weight gain or improved caretaker - child interaction occurs.

IV. Immunodeficiency

Undernutrition is also associated with an increased incidence of infection (Kulapongs et al., 1977). Impaired cell mediated immunity has also been documented. Lymphocyte function and numbers are adversely affected (Suskind, Olson & Olson, 1973; Alvarado & Luthringer, 1971; Keet & Thom, 1969). Impaired B- cell immunity has also been documented, although the absolute number of B- cells is not affected. While serum immunoglobulin levels are normal in mild undernutrition, the response to antigens and infections seems to be altered (Axelrod, 1971; Brown & Katz, 1966; Chandra, 1971; Hodges et al., 1962; Jose, Welch & Doherty, 1970; Wohl, Reinhold & Rose, 1949). This may be due to the absence of a number of specific nutrients necessary for the immune process to proceed (Kumate et al., 1971; Douglas & Schopfer, 1977). In addition to the above deleterious effects, the killing function of polymorphonuclear leukocytes is also impaired. In the polymorphs of undernourished children, cellular phagocytosis occurs normally along with vacuole formation. However, bacterial killing seems to be impaired in acutely infected, undernourished children although not in uninfected children (Douglas & Schopfer, 1977; Kumate, 1977). Finally, Suskind et al. (1976) have demonstrated impairment in the functional activity of serum complement in undernourished children.

These deficits in immune function may take their toll in mildly undernourished children, resulting in subclinical fluctuations in health status and recurrent mild infections. Obviously, children with severe growth deficiency who suffer severe infections due to pervasive immunodeficiency will have their growth severely impaired. However, even mild infections such as otitis media, which is now known to occur more frequently in undernourished United States children than comparison subjects, may result in functional impairments (Kaplan et al., 1973). Although the presenting symptoms of otitis media may be limited to irritability and poor appetite, such symptoms can exacerbate an already difficult feeding situation. Chronic otitis media has been associated with changes in psychologic adjustment, temperament, cognition and language impairment (Kaplan et al., 1973; Paradise, 1976; Lewis, 1976), similar to those symptoms typically associated with "nonorganic" FTT (Bithoney & Rathbun, 1983). The presence or absence

irritability		alteration		alteration in
pain	→	in child's	→	maternal-child
fever		temperament		interaction

<pre>
      ↑   ↓

otitis media   ←   immune   ←   undernutrition
                     compromise   (FTT)
</pre>

Figure 2

of chronic, recurrent infections may have an important effect on the clinical course of children with deficient growth by its impact on their capcity to learn and to interact positively with caretakers.

V. The Gastrointestinal Tract

Chronic malnutrition has a number of effects on gastrointestinal functioning. It can result in blunting of the intestinal villae of children experiencing severe undernutrition. Other alterations of the gut mucosa have been described (Schneider & Viteri, 1972). Decreased brush border heights and enzyme levels have been documented (Schneider & Viteri, 1972). Increased free bile acids (especially taurine conjugates) have been noted, thus altering the important ratio of free to conjugated bile acids. This can result in a deficiency of micellar forming capacity and subsequently in impaired fat absorption (Schneider & Viteri, 1974 a,b). Other authors have documented a relative decrement in intestinal absorptive capacity for glucose, d-xylose and vitamin B12 (Alvarado et al., 1973; Viteri et al., 1973). These intestinal changes are considered etiologic in the increased incidence of diarrhea seen in some undernourished children (Cook, 1974; Chadimi, Kumar & Abaci, 1973; Einstein, MacKay & Rosenberg, 1972; Rayfield et al., 1973; Torres-Pinedo et al., 1971). Overall, it is this tendency toward intestinal malabsorption in moderate to severe undernutrition that often complicates their rehabilitation. Also, many clinicians who observe relative malabsorption in their patients with FTT may believe the malabsorption to be etiologic in the malnutrition (i.e. an organic cause) when in fact it is secondary to the undernutrition itself.

VI. Central Nervous System Alterations

Structural Changes in the CNS. It has now been established that undernutrition especially during periods of rapid cellular growth results in irreversible changes in the central nervous system as well as significant damage to many other organ systems (Winick, 1976). Undernutrition occurring during the so called "critical periods" of brain growth duplication leads to decreased brain size, a marked decrease in brain weight and cell number (Cheek, 1968; Winick, 1976). Pathologically, these changes are associated with alterations in myelinization and in the type and number of nerve cell to nerve cell connections (Chase, 1980). These changes seem to result in neurobehavioral changes of importance to the growing child.

Functional Changes in the CNS. Engsner (1974) found delays in the motor nerve conduction rates of children suffering from malnutrition. Marasmic children displayed more marked delays in neuronal conduction rates than those with kwashiorkor. However, both groups demonstrated slowing compared to controls. Bartel (1980) examined the visual evoked responses of malnourished children versus comparison subjects . He displayed short, bright light flashes to both groups and he found that previously malnourished children had delayed neuronal responses on two of the six peaks normally seen in response to light. The changes were unilateral, occurring only in the right hemisphere and not in the left. While the significance of these alterations is not clear, the results may imply an alteration of visual perception in these children.

Bartel (1976, 1980) has also demonstrated alterations in the dominant electroencephalographic (EEG) frequencies recorded from malnourished children. Bartel described the EEGs of these children as demonstrating overall slowing and less alpha activity than normal children. Stoch and Smythe (1967) reported significant alterations in electrocortical stability between undernourished children and controls. Undernourished subjects' EEG patterns showed poor organization. A decrease in alpha activity was also seen. These authors saw their findings as consistent with organic brain damage. Baraitser and Evans (1969) have confirmed these findings in acute cases of kwashiorkor. Bartel (1976) concluded that while no definite diagnosis of brain damage can be made from the above recording patterns, they were suggestive of central nervous system maturational delay. Greisel (1983) found undernourished children to have altered galvanic skin responses and also slower responses to auditory stimuli. This author discusses the possibility that these findings suggest a generalized depression in physiological "arousal".

The final functional neurologic impairment we would like to discuss is the possible association of undernutrition with attention deficit disorder (ADD). Protein energy malnutrition has now been implicated as being associated with ADD in a number of studies (Barrett, Radke-Yarrow & Klein, 1982; Galler et al., 1983; Galler et al., 1982). These authors' findings are of great interest in that they suggest that the alterations in the central nervous system (CNS) described above may have significant impact on the future developmental capabilities of these children. Shaywitz, Cohen & Shaywitz (1978) have suggested that depletion of certain biogenic amines that act as neurotransmitters (norepinephrine and dopamine) is potentially etiologic in attention deficit disorder (ADD). Some authors using an animal model of ADD have been able to demonstrate a direct reduction of central levels of norepinephrine and dopamine (Shoemaker & Bloom, 1977). While the etiology of ADD remains controversial and is probably multifactorial and non-linear, these findings are suggestive of an association between growth deficiency and ADD.

Research and Clinical Implications

The above documented changes are the beginning of the elucidation of structural and physiologic bases for some of the neurobehavioral and psychological factors described in this text. However, their interplay with altered caretaker child interaction, fluctuating levels of medical illness, infection, temperamental aberration, anemia and underlying genetic endowment has yet to be explored. Future studies of growth deficiency must begin to utilize the more discrete classification systems used in the undernutrition literature from the third world. Documenting the degree of undernutrition in patients with FTT (first, second and third degree) is step one. We must also begin to quantify the medical variables we now know to be important in developmental functioning as we set out to do future research in undernutrition (FTT). It is not enough to say a child has "FTT." We must know his/her iron status, how many ear infections he or she has had and what percent of standardized weight for age the child is when we begin our research protocols so that the results will not be confounded by physiologic factors. Obviously, subgroups of children with third degree malnutrition will score less well on standardized developmental tests than first degree malnourished children. They should no longer be lumped together as "FTT" but rather classified according to severity.

The biopsychosocial model applied to growth deficiency could have important ramifications for clinical practice. Every child with this problem warrants a comprehensive assessment of possible contributory factors. This will allow for a thorough understanding of the child's deficient growth and so guide the optimal use of interventions.

REFERENCES

Alvarado, J. & Luthringer, D.G. Serum immunoglobulins in edematous protein-calorie malnourished children. Studies in Guatemalan children at INCAP. Clinical Pediatrics, 1971, 10, 174-179.

Alvarado, J., Vargas, W., Diaz, N. & Viteri, F.E. Vitamin B12 absorption in protein-calorie malnourished children and during recovery: influence of protein depletion and of diarrhea. American Journal of Clinical Nutrition, 1973, 26, 595-599.

Aref, G.H., Babr El-Din, M.K., Hassan, A.I. & Araby, I.I. Immunoglobulins in Kwashiorkor. Journal of Tropical Medicine and Hygiene, 1970, 73, 186-191.

Axelrod, A.E. Immune processes in vitamine deficiency states. American Journal of Clinical Nutrition, 1971, 24, 265-271.

Bakeman, R. & Brown, J.V. Early interaction: consequences for social and mental development at three years. Child Development, 1980, 51, 437-447.

Baraitser, M. & Evans, D.E. The effect of undernutritionon brain-rhythm development. South African Medical Journal, 1969, 43, 56-58.

Barbero, G.J. & Shaheen,E. Environmental failure to thrive: a clinical view. Journal of Pediatrics, 1967, 5, 639-664.

Barr, G.D., Allen, C.M. & Shinefield, H.R. Height and weight of 7500 children of three skin colors. American Journal of Diseases of Children, 1972, 124, 866-872.

Barrett, D. Malnutrition and child behavior: conceptualization and assessment of social-emotional functioning and a report of an empirical study. In Malnutrition and Behavior: Critical Assessment of Key Issues. Lausanne, Switzerland: The Nesle Foundation, 1983.

Barrett, D.,Radke-Yarrow, M. & Klein, R.E. Chronic malnutrition and child behavior: effects of early caloric supplementation on social and emotional functioning at school age. Developmental Psychology, 1982, 18, 541-556.

Bartel, P.R. Long-term electrocerebral sequelae of kwashiorkor, Special Report PERS 244. Johannesburg, South Africa: National Institute for Personnel Research, Council for Scientific and Industrial Research, 1976.

Bartel, P.R. Findings of EEG and psychomotor studies on malnourished children. In R.D. Griesel (Ed.), Malnutrition in Southern Africa. Pretoria, South Africa: University of Southern Africa, 1980.

Behrman, R.E. & Vaughan, V.C. Nelson Textbook of Pediatrics, 12th Edition. Philadelphia, PA: W.B. Saunders, 1983.

Billewicz, W.Z. A merit on birthweight correlation in full sense. Journal of Biosocial Science, 1972, 4, 455.

Bithoney, W.G. & Rathbun, J. Failure to thrive. In M. Levine, W. Carey, A. Crocker & R. Gross (Eds.), Developmental-Behavioral Pediatrics. Philadelphia, PA: W.B. Saunders, 1983.

Bollman, J.L., Flock, E.V., Grindlay, J.H., Mann, F.C. & Block, M.A. Alkaline phosphate and maylase of plasma after hepatectomy. American Journal of Physiology, 1952, 170, 467-470.

Brazelton, T.B. Nutrition during early infancy. In R.M. Suskind (Ed.), Textbook of Pediatric Nutrition. New York: Raven Press, 1981.

Bronfenbrenner, U. Contexts of child rearing: problems and contexts. American Psychologist, 1979, 34, 844-858.

Bronfenbrenner, U. The Ecology of Human Development: Experiments by Nature and Design. Cambridge, MA: Harvard University Press, 1979.

Brown, R.E. & Katz, M. Antigenic stimulation in undernourished children. East African Medical Journal, 1966, 42, 221-232.

Butler, N.R. & Alderman, E.D. Perinatal Problems. The Second Report of the 1958 British Perinatal Survey. Edinborough: E.S. Livingstone, 1969.

Butler, I.J., O'Flynn, M.E., Seifert, W.E. & Howell, R.R. Neurotransmitter defects and treatment of disorders of hyperphenylanemia. Journal of Pediatrics, 1981, 98, 729-733.

Cantwell, R.J. The long-term neurological sequelae of anemia in infancy. Pediatric Research, 1974, 8, 342.

Chandra, R.K. Immunocompetence in undernutrition. Journal of Pediatrics, 1972, 81, 1194-1200.

Chase, H.P. & Martin, H.P. Undernutrition and child development. New England Journal of Medicine, 1970, 282, 933-939.

Chase, H.P. Undernutrition and growth and development of the human brain. In J.D. Lloyd-Still (Ed.), Malnutrition and Intellectual Development. Lancaster, England: MTP Press, Ltd., St. Leonard's House, 1980.

Cheek, D.B. Human Growth. Lea and Febiger, 1968.

Chen, A.T., Chan, Y.K. & Falek, A. The effects of chromosome abnormalities on birth weight in man. II. Autosomal efectgs. Human Heredity, 1972, 22, 209-224.

Chodorkoff, J. & Whitten, C.F. Intellectual status of children with sickle cell anemia. Journal of Pediatrics, 1963, 68, 29-35.

Cook, G.C. Effect of systemic infections on glycylglycine absorption rate from the human jejunum in vivo. British Journal of Nutrition, 1974, 32, 163-167.

Cooper, J.R., Bloom, F.E. & Roth, R.H. The biochemical basis of neuropharmacology. Oxford, England: Oxford University Press, 1974.

Corney, G., Robson, E.B. & Strong, S.J. The effect of zygosity on the birth weight of twins. Annals of Human Genetics, 1972, 36, 45-59.

Crane, J.P. & Kopta, M.M. Prediction of intrauterine growth retardation via ultrasonically measured head/abdominal circumference ratios. Obstetrics and Gynecology, 1979, 54, 597-601.

Dagg, J.H., Jackson, J.M. & Curry, B. Cystochrome oxidase in latent iron defiency (sideropenia). British Journal of Haematology, 1966, 12, 331-333.

Dodge, P.R., Prensky, A.L. & Feigin, R.D. Nutrition and the Developing Nervous System. St. Louis: The C.V. Mosby Co., 1975.

Douglas, S.D. & Schopfer, K. White cell function in childhood malnutrition. In R.M. Suskind (Ed.), Malnutrition and the Immune Response. New York: Raven Press, 1977.

Einstein, L.P., Mackay, D.M. & Rosenberg, I.H. Pediatric xylose malabsorption in East Pakistan: correlation with age, growth, retardation, and weaning diarrhea. American Journal of Clinical Nutrition, 1972, 25, 1230-1233.

Elmer, E. Failure to thrive: role of the mother. Pediatrics, 1960, 25, 717-725.

Engel, G.L. The need for a new medical model: a challenge for biomedicine. Science, 1977, 196, 129-136.

Engel, G.L. The clinical application of the biopsychosocial model. The American Journal of Psychiatry, 1980, 137, 535-544.

Engsner, G. Brain growth and motor nerve conduction velocity in children with marasmus and kwashiorkor. In J. Cravioto, L. Hambraeus & B. Vahlqvist (Eds.), Early Nutrition and Mental Development. Sweden: Almquist, Wiksell & Uppsals, 1974.

Eveleth, P.B. Population differences in growth: environmental and genetic factors. In F. Falkner & J.M. Tanner, (Eds.), Human Growth. III. Neurobiology and Nutrition. New York: Plenum Press, 1979.

Fitch, N.J., Cadol, R.V., Goldson, E., Wendell, T., Swartz, D. & Jackson, E. Cognitive development of abused and failure to thrive children.

Journal of Pediatric Psychology, 1976, 1, 32-36.

Fitzhardinge, P.M. & Steven, E.M. The small-for-date infant: II. neurological and intellectual sequelae. Pediatrics, 1972, 50, 50-57.

Gaines, R., Sandgrund, A., Greene, A.H. & Power, E. Etiological factors in child maltreatment, a multivariate study of abusing, neglecting and normal mothers. Journal of Abnormal Psychology, 1978, 87, 531-540.

Galler, J., Ramsey, F., Solimano, G. & Lowell, W. The influence of early malnutrition on subsequent behavioral development. II. Classroom behavior. Journal of the American Academy of Child Psychiatry, 1982, 22, 16-22.

Galler, J., Ramsey, F., Solimano, G.V. & Lowell, W. The influence of early malnutrition on subsequent behavioral development. I. Degree of impairment in intellectual performance. Journal of the American Academy of Child Psychiatry, 1983, 22, 8-15.

Garn, S.M., Clark, D.C. & Trowbridge, F.L. Tendency toward greater stature in American black children. American Journal of Diseases of Children, 1973, 126, 164-166.

Garn, S.N. & Clark, D.C. Problems in the nutritional assessment of black individuals. American Journal of Physical Anthropology, 1976, 66, 262.

Ghadimi, H., Kumar, S. & Abaci, F. Endogenous amino acid loss and its significance in infantile diarrhea. Pediatric Research, 1973, 7, 161-168.

Gomez, F., Rimos-Galvan, R., Frenk, S., Cravioto, J.M., Chavev, R. & Vasquez, J. Mortality in third degree malnutrition. Journal of Tropical Pediatrics, 1956, 2, 77-83.

Goodlad, G.A.J. & Munro, H.N. Diet and the action of cortisone on protein metabolism. Biochemical Journal, 1959, 73, 343-345.

Graham, J.M. Congenital anomalies. In M. Levine, W. Carey, A. Crocker & R. Gross, (Eds.), Developmental-Behavioral Pediatrics. Philadelphia: W.B. Saunders, 1983.

Greulich, W.W. A comparison of the physical growth and development of American-born and native Japanese children. American Journal of Physical Anthropology, 1957, 15, 489-515.

Greulich, W.W. Some secular changes in the growth of American-born and native Japanese children. American Journal of Physical Anthropology, 1976, 45, 553.

Griesel, R.D. Psychophysiological sequelae of kwashiorkor. In Malnutrition and Behavior: Critical Assessment of Key Issues. Lausanne, Switzerland: The Nestle Foundation, 1983.

Hamill, P.V.V., Johnson, C.L., Reed, R.B. & Roche, A.F. NCHS Growth Curves for Children Birth-Eighteen Years. Publication #DHF 78-1650. Hyattsville, MD: National Center for Health Statistics, 1977.

Hansen, J.D.L. Comment and addendes. In J. Brozek & B. Schurch (Eds.), Malnutrition and Behavior: Critical Assessment of Key Issues. Switzerland: The Nestle Foundation, 1984.

Harris, J.W. & Kellermyer, R.W. The Red Cell. Cambridge, MA: Harvard University Press, 1970.

Hodges, R.E., Bean, W.B., Ohlson, M.A. & Bleiler, R.E. Factors affecting human antibody response. III. Immunologic responses of men deficient in pantothenic acid. American Journal of Clinical Nutrition, 1962, 11, 85-93.

Homer, C. & Ludwig, S. Categorization of etiology of failure to thrive. American Journal of Diseases of Children, 1981, 135, 848-851.

Horner, J.M., Thorsson, A.V. & Hintz, R.L. Growth deceleration patterns in children with constitutional short stature: an aid to diagnosis. Pediatrics, 1978, 62, 529-534.

Howell, D. Significance of iron deficiencies. Consequences of mild deficiency in children. Extent and meaning of iron defiency in the United States. Summary Proceedings of Workshop of the Food and Nutrition Boards. Washington, D.C.: National Academy of Sciences,

1971.

Illich, I. Medical Nemesis. Great Britain: Calder & Boyars, 1975.

Jackson, E.B., Wilkin, L.C. & Auerbach, H. Statistical report on incidence and duration of breastfeeding in relation to personal-social and hospital maternity factors. Pediatrics, 1956, 17, 700-715.

Jacobs, A. Leukocyte oxygen consumption in iron deficiency anemia. British Journal of Experimental Pathology, 1968, 46, 545-548.

Jose, D.G., Welch, J.S. & Doherty, R.L. Humoral and cellular immune responses to Streptococci, Influenza and other antigens in Australian Aboriginal school children. Australian Paediatric Journal, 1970, 6, 192-202.

Kaplan, G.J., Fleshman, J.K. & Bender, T.R. Long-term effects of otitis media: a ten year cohort study of Alaskan Eskimo children. Pediatrics, 1973, 52, 577-585.

Keet, M.P. & Thom, H. Serum immunoglobulins in kwashiorkor. Archives of Disease in Childhood, 1969, 44, 600-603.

Kulapongs, P., Suskind, R., Vithayasai, V. & Olson, R.E. In R.M. Suskind (Ed.), Malnutrition and the Immune Response. New York, Raven Press, 1977.

Kumate, J., Hernandez-Yasso, F. & Vasquez, V. Malnutrition and infection. Research Forum, 1971.

LaVeck, B., Hammond, M.A. & LaVeck, G.P. Minor congenital anomalies an behavior in different home environments. Journal of Pediatrics, 1980, 96, 940-943.

Leonard, M.F., Rhymes, J.P. & Solnit, A.J. Failure to thrive in infants. American Journal of Diseases of Children, 1966, 111, 600-612.

Lewis, N. Otitis media and linguistic incompetence. Archives of Otolaryngology, 1976, 102, 387-390.

Lipper, E., Lee, K., Gartner, L.M. & Grellong, B. Determinants of neuro-behavioral outcome in low birth weight infants. Pediatrics, 1981, 67, 502-505.

Logothetis, J., Lowenson, R.B. & Augostaki, O. Body growth in Cooley's anemia with a correlative study as to other aspects of the illness in 138 cases. Pediatrics, 1972, 50, 92-99.

McLean, A.E. Enzyme activity in the liver and serum of malnourished children in Jamaica. Clinical Science, 1966, 30, 129-137.

Meredith, H.V. Body weight at birth of viable human infants: A worldwide comparative treatise. Human Biology, 1970, 42, 217-264.

Mitchell, W.G., Gorrell, R.W. & Greenberg, R.A. Failure-to-thrive: a study in a primary care setting. Pediatrics, 1980, 65, 971-977.

Monckberg, F., Beas, F., Horwitz, I., Debancens, A. & Gonzalez, M. Oxygen consumption in infant malnutrition. Pediatrics, 1964, 33, 554-561.

Nichols, B.L., Alvarado, J., Hazelwood, C.F. & Viteri, F. Clinical significance of muscle potassium depletion in protein-calorie malnutrition. Journal of Pediatrics, 1972, 80, 319-330.

Oski, F.A. & Honig, A.S. The effects of therapy on the developmental scores of iron deficient infants. Journal of Pediatrics, 1978, 92, 21-25.

Oski, F.A. & McMillen, J. (Eds.) The Whole Pediatrician Catalogue. Philadelphia: W.B. Saunders, 1980.

Ounsted, M. & Ounsted, C. On Fetal Growth Rate. London: Heinemann Medical Books, 1973.

Paradise, J.L. Pediatrician's view of middle ear effusions. More questions than answers. Annals ofOtology, Rhinology and Laryngology, 1976, 85, 20-24.

Penchaszadeh, V.B., Hardy, J.B., Mellits, E.D., Cohen, B.H. & McKusick, V.A. Growth and development in an "inner city" population: an assessment of possible biological and environmental influences. John Hopkins Medical Journal, 1972, 131, 11-23.

Penrose, L.S. Some recent trends in human genetics. Caryologia, 1954, 6 (Suppl.), 521.

Picou, D. & Taylor-Roberts, T. The measurement of total protein synthesis

and catebolism and nitrogen turnover in infants in different
nutritional stages and receiving different amounts of dietary protein.
Clinical Science, 1969, 36, 283-296.

Picou, D.M. Evaluation and treatment of the malnourished child. In R.M.
Suskind (Ed.), Textbook of Pediatric Nutrition. New York: Raven
Press, 1981.

Pollitt, E. & Thomson, C. Protein caloric malnutrition and behavior: a
view from psychology. In R.F. Wurtman & J.J. Wurtman (Eds.),
Nutrition and Brain. New York: Raven Press, 1977.

Pollitt, E. & Leibel, R. Biological and social correlates of failure to
thrive. In L.S. Greene & F.E. Johnston (Eds.), Social and Biological
Predictions of Nutritional Status, Physical Growth and Neurological
Development. New York: Academic Press, 1980.

Quinn, P.O. & Rapoport, J.L. Minor physical anomalies and neurologic
status of hyperactive boys. Pediatrics, 1974, 53, 742-747.

Rayfield, E.J., Curnow, R.T., George, D.T. & Beisel, W.R. Impaired carbo-
hydrate metabolism during a mild viral illness. New England Journal
of Medicine, 1973, 289, 618-621.

Richardson, S.A., Birch, H., Brabie, E. & Yoder, K. The behavior of
children in school who were severely malnourished in the first two
years of life. Journal of Health and Social Behavior, 1972, 13, 276-
286.

Riley, R.L., Landwirth, J., Kaplan, S.A. & Collipp, P.J. Failure to thrive:
an analysis of 83 cases. California Medicine, 1968, 108, 32-38.

Rimoin, D.L. & Horton, W.A. Short stature. Part II. Journal of
Pediatrics, 1978, 92, 697-704.

Robertson, W.O. Breast feeding practices: some implications of regional
variations. American Journal of Public Health, 1961, 51, 1035-1042.

Robson, E.B. Birthweight in cousins. Annals of Human Genetics, 1955, 19,
262.

Robson, E.B. The genetics of birthweight. In F. Falkner & J.M. Tanner
(Eds.), Human Growth. I. Principles and Prenatal Growth. New York:
Plenum Press, 1978.

Robson, J.R., Larkin, F.A., Bursick, J.H. & Perri, K.P. Growth standards
for infants and children: a cross-sectional study. Pediatrics, 1975,
56, 1014-1020.

Rosenberg, J. & Weller, G.M. Minor physical anomalies and academic
performance in young school children. Developmental Medicine and
Child Neurology, 1973, 15, 131-135.

Sameroff, A.J. & Chandler, N.J. Reproductive risk and the constant
continuum of caretaking casualty. In F.D. Horowitz (Ed.), Review of
Child Development Research. Chicago: University of Chicago Press,
1975.

Saugstad, L.F. Birthweights in children with phenylketonuria and in their
siblings. Lancet, 1972, 1, 809-813.

Schneider, R.E. & Viteri, F.E. Morphological aspects of duodenojejunal
mucosa in protein-calorie malnourished children and during recovery.
American Journal of Clinical Nutrition, 1972, 25, 1092-1102.

Schneider, R.E. & Viteri, F.E. Liminal events of lipid absorption in
protein-calorie malnourished children: relationship with nutritional
recovery and diarrhea. I. Capacity of the duodenal content to achieve
micellar sclubilization of lipids. American Journal of Clinical
Nutrition, 1974, 27, 777-787.

Schneider, R.E. & Viteri, F.E. Luminal events of lipid absorption in
protein-calorie malnourished children: relationship with nutritional
recovery and diarrhea, II. Alterations in bile acid content of
duodenal aspirates. American Journal of Clinical Nutrition, 1974, 27,
788-796.

Shaywitz, S.E, Cohen, D.J. & Shaywitz, B.A. The biochemical basis of
minimal brain dysfunction. Journal of Pediatrics, 1978, 92, 179-187.

Shoemaker, W.J. & Bloom, F.E. Effects of undernutrition on brain morphology. In R.J. Wurtman & J.J. Wurtman (Eds.), Nutrition and the Brain. New York: Raven Press, 1977.

Sills, R.H. Failure to thrive, the role of clinical and laboratory evaluation. American Journal of Diseases of Children, 1978, 132, 967-969.

Siva, S.D.V. Minor physical anomalies and early developmental deviation: a biological subgroup of hyperactive children. In Mental Health in Children, Vol. III. New York: PJD Publications, 1976.

Smith, D.W., Truog, W. & Rogers, J.E. Shifting linear growth during infancy: illustration of genetic factors in growth from fetal life through infancy. Journal of Pediatrics, 1976, 225-230.

Sourkes, T.L. Psychopharmacology. In R.W. Albers, G.J. Siegel, R. Katzman & B.W. Agranoff (Eds.), Basic Neurochemistry. Boston: Little, Brown and Company, 1972.

Stoch, M.B. & Smythe, P.M. The effect of undernutrition during infancy on subsequent brain growth and intellectual development. South Africa Medical Journal, 1967, 41, 1027-1031.

Stuart, H.C. & Meredith, H.V. Youth body measurements in the school health program. American Journal of Public Health, 1946, 36, 1365-1386.

Sulzer, J.L., Wesley, H.H. & Leonig, F. Nutrition and behavior in head start children: results from the Tulane study. In D.J. Kalen (Ed.), Nutrition, Development and Social Behavior. DHEW Publication No. (NIH) 73-242. Washington, D.C.: Department of Health Education and Welfare, 1973.

Susanne, C. Genetic and environmental influences on morphological characteristics. Annals of Human Biology, 1975, 2, 279-287.

Suskind, R., Olson, L.C. & Olson, R.E. Protein calorie malnutrition and infection with hepatitis-associated antigen. Pediatrics, 1973, 51, 525-530.

Suskind, R., Edelman, R., Kulapongs, P., Sirishinha, S. & Pariyanonda, A. Complement activity in childen with protein-calorie malnutrition. American Journal of Clinical Nutrition, 1976, 29, 1089-1092.

Symes, A.L., Sourkes, T.L. & Youdim, M.B.H. Decreased monoamine oxidase activity in liver of iron-deficient rats. Canadian Journal of Biochemistry, 1969, 47, 999-1002.

Symes, A.L., Missala, K. & Sourkes, T.L. Iron- and riboflavin-dependent metabolism of a monoamine in the rat in vivo. Science, 1971, 174, 153-155.

Tanner, J.N. & Israelsohn, W.J. Parent-child correlations for body measurements of children between the ages of one month and seven years. Annals of Human Genetics, 1963, 245-259.

Tanner, J.N., Goldstein, H. & Whitehouse, R.H. Standards for childrens' height at ages 2-9 years allowing for height of parents. Archives of Disease in Childhood, 1970, 45, 755-762.

Terada, H. & Hoshi, H. Longitudinal study on the physical growth in Japanese. II. Growth in stature and body weight during the first three years of life. Acta Anatomica Nipponica, 1965, 40, 166-177.

Thomson, A.M., Billewicz, W.Z. & Hytten, F.E. The assessment of fetal growth. Journal of Obstetrics and Gynecology of the British Commonwealth, 1968, 75, 903-916.

Torres-Pinedo, R., Rivera, C. & Rodriquez, H. Intestinal absorptive defects associated with enteric infections in infants. Annals of the New York Academy of Sciences, 1971, 176, 284-298.

Viteri, F.E., Flores, J.M., Alvarado, J. & Behar, M. Intestinal malabsorption in malnourished children before and during recovery. Relation between severity of protein deficiency and the malabsorption process. American Journal of Digestive Diseases, 1973, 18, 201-211.

Viteri, F.E., Mata, L.J. & Behar, M. Metodos de evaluacion del estato nutritional proteinico-calorico en pre-escolares de condicions socio-economicas diferentes. Repercusion nutritional del sarampion en ninos eronicamente sub-alimentados. Archivos Latinoamericanos de Nutricion,

1973, 23, 13-31.

Viteri, F.E. Primary protein-energy malnutritioin: clinical, biochemical, and metabolic changes. In R.M. Suskind (Ed.), Textbook of Pediatric Nutrition. New York: Raven Press, 1981.

Voorhess, M.L., Stuart, M.J., Stockman, J.A. & Oski, F.A. Iron deficiency anemia and increased urinary norepinephrine excretion. Journal of Pediatrics, 1975, 86, 542-547.

Waterlow, J.C. In R.E. Olson (Ed.), Protein Calorie Malnutrition. New York: Academic Press, 1975.

Waterlow, J.C. Current issues in nutritional assessment by anthropometry. In J. Brosek & B. Schurch (Eds.), Malnutrition and Behavior: Critical Assessment of Key Issues. Switzerland: The Nestle Foundation, 1984.

Webb, T.E. & Oski, F.A. Iron deficiency anemia and scholastic achievement in yound adolescents. Journal of Pediatrics, 1973, 82, 827-830.

Werkman, S.L., Shifman, L. & Shelly, T. Psychosocial correlates of iron deficiency anemia in early childhood. Psychosomatic Medicine, 1964, 26, 125-134.

Whitehead, R.G. In R.A. McCance & E.M. Widdowson (Eds.), Calorie Deficiencies and Protein Deficiencies. London: J.A. Churchill, Ltd., 1968.

Whitten, C. & Fischoff, J. Evidence that growth failure from maternal deprivation is secondary to undereating. Journal of the American Medical Association, 1969, 209, 1675-1682.

Winick, M. Malnutrition and Brain Development. New York: Oxford University Press, 1976.

Wohl, M.G., Reinhold, J.G. & Rose, S.B. Antibody response in patients with hypoproteinemia, with special reference to effect of supplementation with protein or protein hydrolysate. Archives of Internal Medicine, 1949, 83, 402-415.

Zamenhof, S., van Marthens, E. & Grauel, L. DNA (cell number) in neonatal brain: second generation (F2) alteration by maternal (FO) dietary protein restriction. Science, 1971, 172, 850-851.

FAILURE TO THRIVE: AN EXPANDED CONCEPTUAL MODEL

Elizabeth F. Gordon and Delia M. Vazquez

Department of Pediatrics/Human Development, Michigan State
University and Hurley Medical Center; and Department of
Pediatrics, University of Iowa

HISTORICAL BACKGROUND

Growth failure or failure to thrive (FTT) in infancy has been a per-
plexing problem for more than a century. The first edition of the textbook,
The Diseases of Infancy and Childhood, by L.E. Holt (1899) addressed the
problem under the section "Malnutrition in Infants." During the first two
decades of the twentieth century, FTT was synonymous with infantile dystrophy, single dystrophy and marasmus (Holt & Howland, 1913).

The etiologies of FTT at that time, as now, were poorly understood.
However, it is instructive to consider the historical evolution of concepts
of FTT. The two major etiological factors that were implicated then, as
now, were food and surroundings. Specifically, faulty feeding, overcrowd-
ing, inadequate ventilation, lack of individual care and frequent infections
were considered to be causes of poor growth. This conclusion resulted from
observation of a high incidence of marasmus among young institutionalized
children (Holt & Howland, 1936).

Henry Dwight Chapin, a New York pediatrician, was a major early figure
in the quest for greater conceptual understanding of this baffling disorder.
His observations also concerned institutionalized children (Chapin, 1908).
He collected data from ten asylums in ten major cities and found that the
annual mortality was between 31.7 and 75 percent for infants under two
years old and 99 percent for those younger than one year of age (Chapin,
1915).

The Speedwell Society, founded in 1902, developed a program of care
for institutionalized children. These infants were boarded out to 24
trained families who were supported by visiting nurses and physicians.
Chapin reported to the American Pediatric Society, in 1908, that the use of
this system decreased mortality to 30 percent in those children less than
one year of age (Chapin, 1908).

Twelve years later, in 1920, Dr. Parrot, a pediatrician working in
French institutions, reported similar findings. He thought that these
infants were adversely affected by their immediate environment, and that
there was a great need for individual care and stimulation (Bakwin, 1949).

During this same period in history, other, more physiological explanations for growth failure were appearing in the literature. Three constitutional diatheses that predispose to malnutrition, were described by Shultz (cited by Abt, 1923). These were thymolymphatico - hyperplasia (allergies and infections), neuro-arthritic (neurotic, hypo-hypercalcemia), and inflammatory-exudative (inflamed sinuses). This represented an early effort to distinguish among disease states that could explain growth failure in young children. Finkelstein expanded this organic categorization by adding metabolic disturbance as a cause for growth failure (Abt, 1923).

Rene Spitz was one of the most influential historical figures to address the issue of growth retardation in infancy. Again, his findings were based on observations of institutionalized children. He coined the term "hospitalism" to describe the depressed orphans that he observed in foundling homes, and believed that the primary cause of their condition was the lack of emotional stimulation by a primary caretaker (Spitz, 1945). Another reasonable explanation is that the nutritional needs of those and other institutionalized children reviewed here, were not met. However, we were unable to determine from the literature whether nutritional factors were considered (see Pinneau, 1955 for a critique of Spitz' observations). Despite these ambiguities, Spitz' theory was widely accepted and stimulated much thinking, observation and clinical research, especially the influential monograph "Growth Failure in Maternal Deprivation" (Patton & Gardner, 1963).

Efforts to identify, categorize, simplify and manage FTT continued from the behavioral perspective. Emotional deprivation became an accepted term introduced indirectly in 1947 by Spitz. Bakwin (1949), described the characteristic features of the understimulated infant: "The outstanding features are listlessness, emaciation and pallor, relative immobility, quietness, unresponsiveness to stimulation, indifferent appetite, frequent stools, poor sleep, and appearance of unhappiness, proneness to febrile episodes and the absence of sucking habits."

While these early observations were all noted in institutions, reports of affected infants living in families were presented by Coleman and Provence (1957). The parental role in the infant's well-being became a critical focus. Bowlby (1951) introduced the new term, "maternal deprivation." Psychoanalytic and social learning theories gave importance to the negative consequences of separation or distortions of the mother-child relationship (Ainsworth, 1969). Attention was then shifted to the mother's role in FTT. Clinical studies were undertaken to describe the characteristics of the inadequate mother presumed to result in FTT (Elmer, 1960; Patton & Gardner, 1962; Fischhoff et al., 1971).

Historically, the importance of nutritional deprivation in FTT has been less emphasized than that of emotional deprivation. Talbot and coworkers (1947) clearly stated that there was a link between caloric malnutrition and emotional disturbances and that these two factors co-occurred to produce growth failure. Whitten and coworkers (1969) challenged the assumption that maternal deprivation was the primary cause of the disorder. They carried out one of the few prospective, quasi-experimental studies that has appeared in the FTT literature to date. These investigators, in keeping with the more current trend, excluded children with known organic disease (Goldbloom, 1982). The study groups were 1) low-level of mothering in the hospital plus adequate calories; 2) high level of mothering in the hospital plus adequate calories; 3) adequate calories in the home fed by the mother following hospitalization, and 4) adequate calories fed in the home by the mother prior to the parent's knowledge of the diagnosis. Their major finding was that when an adequate diet was available and accepted by the infant, weight gain did occur regardless of the level of mothering. Despite the methodological weaknesses (e.g. lack of random assignment to groups, absence of long-term follow up) of this study, these investigators addressed the important issue of the role of inadequate calories in the development of FTT. If increasing calories in the absence of increasing stimulation (mothering) results in weight gain, then an argument could be made that the primary cause of FTT is inadequate caloric intake, and not maternal deprivation. Appropriately designed studies would test this important hypothesis (Woolston, 1983).

Children with FTT were, until recently, placed in an organic category when the history, physical and diagnostic tests revealed an organic diagnosis (i.e. neurologic, cardiovascular, renal or endocrine disease), or in a nonorganic category upon the exclusion of physical findings. The trend in the conceptualization of FTT is currently moving away form the traditional organic-nonorganic dichotomy (Casey, 1983)(see Frank; Bithoney & Dubowitz, this volume). Homer and Ludwig (1981) suggested that a third category, "mixed," which includes a combination of organic and environmental components, would be necessary to accurately reflect the etiologic groups. This change represents an important advance in the development of a descriptive framework for FTT for at least two reasons. First, there has been a strong tendency to ignore the possibility of environmental factors in the growth failure once an organic disorder has been determined; and second, one would expect appropriate clinical intervention strategies to differ for each of the three categories.

This selective review of the history of FTT demonstrates that the final chapter on this common childhood disorder has not been written and that there is room to expand the framework of FTT.

EXPANDED MODEL

The development of conceptual or theoretical models is an essential step in scientific investigation. These models establish the basis for systematic research. We make this point for two reasons. First, it is of interest to note that the genesis of FTT remains a mystery even though the description of this disorder has appeared in the medical literature for nearly a century (Holt, 1899). Although numerous studies have been published, there is a paucity of controlled, systematic work. Perhaps, more effective use of testable conceptual models would result in more definitive research in this clinically important and theoretically interesting area. Second, the recent clarifications provided by Homer and Ludwig (1981) have made an immediate impact on the conceptualization of FTT (Bithoney & Rathbun, 1983; Casey, 1983; Chatoor et al., 1984).

The major purpose of the expanded model (Figure 1) is to present a comprehensive set of equations that define the circumstances under which FTT occurs. We also describe typical clinical situations that would be included in each category, and outline suggestions for future research.

Definitions for the terms FTT and adverse environment, as they are used in the model, are as follows: FTT is used to describe any child under two years of age who is not experiencing normal physical growth as defined by specified criteria. This description is in contrast to the current trend of automatically excluding cases where an organic etiology is determined (Goldbloom, 1982). Adverse environment refers to any factor or combination of factors present in the child's external environment that contribute, either wholly or in part, to the growth failure.

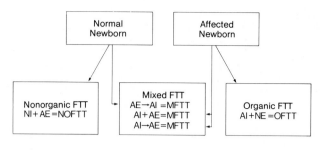

Figure 1

Reference to the newborn period is made explicit in this model to emphasize the importance of understanding the prenatal period of growth and development when confronted with FTT.

There are five components in three etiologic categories in this expanded FTT model. The major expansion occurs in the mixed category where three components are proposed as necessary to fully describe the mixed cases.

1) $\underline{NI + AE = NOFTT}$ (normal infant + adverse environment = nonorganic failure to thrive): Cases of FTT that would be included in this group would be those with no evidence of an organic disorder and positive findings for adverse environmental conditions. Diagnosis by exclusion of organic etiology alone would not be sufficient to include a case in this category. The same attention given to evaluation of the systems (i.e. endocrine, neurologic and cardiovascular) would be given to the evaluation of the environment of the child. The adverse components of that environment need to be as specifically defined as possible (i.e. stress from unemployment, lack of child care skills or attachment disorder). One important need is for objective assessment of the child's environment (See Bradley & Casey, this volume).

Clinical examples of this type of FTT include: 1) Situations where the caretakers did not know what and/or how to feed the child (i.e. feeding nondairy creamer and thinking it was milk, overdiluting formula, or feeding too infrequently), and 2) mothers who were depressed and not attending to the infants.

One of the major research tasks is to systematically study the specific ways in which adverse environmental conditions are associated with poor growth. Better understanding of the role of caloric intake (see Woolston, in press) is certainly needed. We point out that upon investigation most cases of NOFT may have as the primary cause, insufficient calories or specific nutrient deficiencies (i.e. zinc). If this would be empirically demonstrated, then the emphasis for intervention may be shifted toward developments of appropriate feeding plans for NOFT children.

Mixed FTT is the most complex etiologic category in the expanded model and occurs under three separate sets of circumstances. Each circumstance includes both environmental and organic factors.

2) $\underline{AE \rightarrow AI = MFTT}$ (an adverse environment precipitates an organically affected infant = mixed failure to thrive): Some children who are normal as newborns are born into adverse environments that, in time, precipitate organic symptoms/disorders. We suggest that these are specific problems that are known to be related to emotional stress and/or physical trauma.

Clinical examples for this group include the following: 1) Children with gastrointestinal disorders (i.e. chronic vomiting and diarrhea). The gastrointestinal systems in these children may represent the "point of least resistance" (Sibinga, 1983) making them vulnerable to these specific disorders when confronted with environmental stress. These disorders can be progressive (Nelson, Behrman & Vaughn, 1983). We do not include structural problems such as gastroesophageal reflux in this group. 2) The second clinical situation would be one where the child has experienced deliberate physical abuse. This would be, for example, a case where head trauma resulted in permanent neurologic damage.

3) AI + AE = MFTT (an organically affected infant + an adverse environment co-occur and = mixed failure to thrive). The disorders in these children could involve any system or combination of systems. Even though these problems co-occur rather than are caused by an adveerse environment, the severity of the organic disease may be exacerbated by the environmental conditions. Clinical situations where children with organic disorders are born into adverse environments could potentially include all disease states described in the pediatric literature (Nelson et al., 1983).

4) AI → AE = MFTT (an organically affected infant precipitates an adverse environment = mixed failure to thrive): These cases of FTT occur when the organic disorder of the child born into a normal environment, precipitates an adverse reaction that results in growth failure. The concept of the reciprocal relationshp between parent and child was introduced by Bell (1966) and applies in the situations described here. The child abuse literature makes reference to the part the physically disabled child plays in his or her maltreatment by eliciting negative parental reactions (Gordon & Gordon, 1979). This also applies to certain cases of FTT. Clinical examples include: 1) The child born with an apparent physical deformity that causes an adverse reaction from the caretaker and this interferes with the nurturing process; and 2) children with nonvisible impairment, where the parents' knowledge of the disorder interferes with the care.

5) AI + NE = OFTT (an organically affected infant + normal environment = organic failure to thrive): Children in this group would have a diagnosed organic disorder. These cases should be carefully evaluated to exclude adverse environmental factors that could be exacerbating the growth failure. The severity of the organic disorder should account for the degree of growth retardation. These clinical situations include all disease states of infancy where there is no evidence of adverse environmental factors that could be contributing to the growth failure.

We would like to propose that researchers interested in the effects of environment on growth, exercise caution prior to excluding any child with organic FTT from study. Some of these cases, upon more careful evaluation of the environment and/or child's condition, turn out to belong in the mixed etiology category.

Each of the models described in this chapter generate different populations and research questions. As the categories of FTT become more defined in accord with an expanded transactional model (Sameroff & Chandler, 1975), research questions will become more specific. For example, as the expectations for growth with organic conditions e.g. congenital heart disease become clarified, the salience of potential environmental influences as they effect feeding and growth can be documented more effectively. Similarly, with more objective assessment of the environment and with more refined typologies (Bradley & Casey, this volume) the impact of environmental factors on the course of organic and nonorganic FTT can be documented more clearly. The net effect of such research would be the development of increasingly specific intervention strategies.

REFERENCES

Abt, A.I. Abt's Pediatrics, (Vol II). Philadelphia: W.B. Saunders Co., 1923.

Ainsworth, M.S. Object relations, dependency and attachment: a theoretical review of the infant-mother relationship. Child Development, 1969, 40, 964-1025.

Bakwin, H. Psychologic aspects of pediatrics-emotional deprivation in infants. Journal of Pediatrics, 1949, 35, 512-521.

Bell, R.Q. A reinterpretation of the direction of effects in studies of socialization. Psychological Review, 1968, 75, 81-95.

Bowlby, J. Maternal Care and Maternal Health. Geneva: World Health Organization, 1951.

Casey, P.H. Failure to thrive: a reconceptualization. Developmental and Behavioral Pediatrics, 1983, 4(1), 63-66.

Chapin, H.D. A plan of dealing with atrophic infants and children. Archives of Pediatrics, 1908, 25, 491-496.

Chapin, H.D. Are institutions for infants necessary? Journal of the American Medical Association, 1915, 64, 1-3.

Coleman, R.W. & Provence, S. Environmental retardation in infants living in families. Pediatrics, 1957, 19, 285-292.

Elmer, E. Failure to thrive: role of the mother. Pediatrics, 1960, 25, 717-725.

Fischhoff, J., Whitten, C.F. & Pettit, M.G. A psychiatric study of mothers of infants with growth failure secondary to maternal deprivation. Journal of Pediatrics, 1971, 79 (2), 209-215.

Goldbloom, R.B. Failure to thrive. Pediatric Clinics of North America, 1982, 29 (1), 1951-1966.

Gordon, E.F. & Gordon, R.C. Child abuse: a review of selected aspects for the primary care physician. Southern Medical Journal, 1979, 72 (8), 985-992.

Holt, L.E. The Diseases of Infancy and Childhood, (1st Ed.). New York: Appleton and Co., 1899.

Holt, L.E. & Howland, J. The Diseases of Infancy and Childhood, (6th Ed.). New York: D. Appleton and Co., 1913.

Holt, L.E., Howland, J., Holt, L.E. Jr. & McIntosh, R. Holt's Diseases of Infancy and Childhood, (10th Ed.). New York: D. Appleton Century Co., 1936.

Homer, C. & Ludwig, S. Categorization of etiology of failure to thrive. American Journal of Diseases of Childhood, 1981, 135, 848-851.

Nelson, W.E., Behrman, R.E. & Vaughan, V.C. (Eds.) Nelson Textbook of Pediatrics (12th Ed.). Philadelphia: W.B. Saunders Co., 1983.

Patton, R.G. & Gardner, L.I. Influence of family environment on growth: the syndrome of maternal deprivation. Pediatrics, 1962, 30, 957-962.

Patton, R.G. & Gardner, L.I. Growth Failure in Maternal Deprivation. Springfield, IL: Thomas Press, 1963.

Pinneau, S.R. The infantile disorders of hospitalization and anaclitic depression. Psychological Bulletin, 1955, 52, 429-452.

Roberts, M.C. & Maddux, J.E. A psychosocial conceptualization of nonorganic failure to thrive. Journal of Clinical Child Psychology, 1982, 11 (3), 216-226.

Sameroff, A.J. & Chandler, M.J. Reproductive risk and the continuum of caretaking causality. In F.D. Horowitz (Ed.), Review of Child Development Research: Vol. 4. Chicago, IL: University of Chicago Press, 1975.

Sibinga, M.S. The gastrointestinal tract. In M.D. Levine, W.B. Carey, A. Crocker, & R.T. Gross (Eds.), Developmental-Behavioral Pediatrics. Philadelphia: W.B. Saunders Co., 1983.

Spitz, R. Hospitalism. In Psychoanalytic Study of the Child, (Vol. I).
    New York: International Universities Press, 1945, 53-74.
Talbot, N.B., Sobel, E.H., Burke, B.S., Lindemann, E. & Kaufman S.G.
    Dwarfism in healthy children: its possible relation to emotional,
    nutritional and endocrine disturbance. New England Journal of
    Medicine, 1947, 236, 783-793.
Whitten, C., Pettit, M. & Fischhoff, J. Evidence that growth failure from
    maternal deprivation is secondary to undereating. Journal of the
    American Medical Association, 1969, 209, 1675-1682.
Woolston, J.L. Eating disorders in infancy and early childhood. Journal
    of the American Academy of Child Psychiatry, 1983, 22, 114-121.

ZINC NUTRITION IN CHILDREN WHO FAIL TO THRIVE

Patrick H. Casey, William R. Collie, William M. Blakemore

Department of Pediatrics, University of Arkansas for Medical
Sciences; and National Center for Toxicological Research
Food and Drug Administration

An interactional causal model for failure to thrive (FTT), depicted in
Figure 1, undergirds our clinical and research thinking with children who
fail to thrive (Casey, 1983). Several aspects of these interactions have
been addressed at this conference. The focus for this chapter is one
corner of the model: undernutrition. Bithoney has stated that a common
organic problem in all children who fail to thrive is one of malnutrition
(Bithoney & Rathbun, 1983). We also believe that nutritional deficiencies
play a major role in the pathophysiology of these children. Medical and
nutritional scientists who evaluate children with malnutrition and FTT
typically examine nutrition in terms of calories consumed, and the diet's
adequacy of the major food types of protein, carbohydrates and fat. The
focus of this chapter will be on one specific nutritional deficiency: the
trace mineral, zinc. In order to describe why further clinical research
with zinc may be important to understand the course and treatment of chil-

HOME AND SOCIETAL ENVIRONMENT

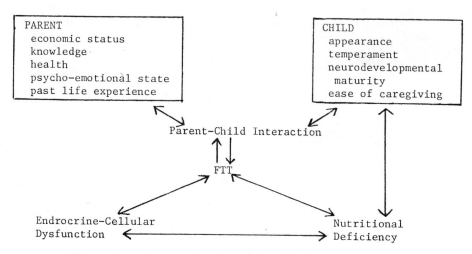

Figure 1.   Interactional model of failure to thrive.

dren with FTT, we will present the following: the biological role of zinc, the clinical problems which result from zinc deficiency, the epidemiology of zinc status in children in this country, and an introduction to what is known regarding the treatment of children with zinc deficiency. Finally, a controlled clinical trial of the incidence of zinc deficiency in children with FTT which is being performed currently in our clinic will be described.

We view this chapter as an opportunity to develop a hypothesis. In order to achieve this result for such a diverse range of professionals as those attending this conference, we will provide a basic introduction and a critical review of a selected group of commonly referenced clinical literature in the area. We do not intend this to be a definitive treatise on the biology of zinc, nor a complete review of the clinical literature. On the other hand, we hope the hypothesis will generate new thoughts in those who hear these ideas for the first time.

BIOLOGICAL ROLE OF ZINC

Zinc is an essential nutrient: it must be consumed in the diet as it is not synthesized by the human body. While zinc has a number of biological functions (Table 1), its predominant role is as an integral component of greater than 50 metalloenzymes (Solomons, 1981; Tasmon-Jones, 1980). A metalloenzyme is an enzyme that requires a fixed number of specific minerals for maximal catalytic activity. Through this function zinc plays a central role in multiple metabolic pathways and other essential physiological functions. Zinc is essential for normal cellular growth, differentiation, and division, as well as maintenance and regeneration of rapidly proliferating tissues such as skin, hair, and mucosa. One of the more critical roles of zinc is in the biochemical processes involved in the synthesis of Ribonucleic (RNA) and Deoxyribonucleic acid (DNA). Deficiency of zinc inhibits the formation of these essential nucleic acids. Zinc is important in immunity against certain pathogenic organisms. It has been reported that zinc is an essential component of a metallo-protein called Gustin which appears to have a significant function in the perception of taste (Hambridge, 1981). This latter function may be of particular clinical significance in children with FTT who often show little interest in eating.

ZINC IN NUTRITION

Foods with the greatest zinc content are seafoods, particularly oysters, and foods of animal origin, particularly red meat. Foods of plant

Table 1

Biologic Roles of Zinc

Cellular Growth (DNA, RNA)

Maintenance and Regeneration of
   Rapidly Proliferating Tissue
   (skin, hair, mucosa)

Sexual Maturation

Immunity

Taste and Appetite

Table 2

Zinc Content of Selected High-Zinc Foods

Food	Zinc Concentration mg per 100 g
Raw Atlantic oysters	75.0
Raw Pacific oysters	9.0
Cooked lean beef	6.2
Cooked lamb	4.9
Cooked chicken giblets	4.7
Turkey, dark meat	4.4
Steamed crabs	4.3
Cooked lean veal	4.2
Cooked lean pork	4.0
Cream of wheat cereal (dry)	3.6
Chopped chicken meat	3.4
Chopped turkey meat	3.4

After E.W. Murphy et al. Journal of the American Dietetic Association 66 (1975) p.345.

origin such as vegetables and fruits have extremely low zinc content. The zinc content of various classes of prepared baby foods are depicted in Table 2, as modified by Solomons (Solomons, 1982). Pre-cooked dry cereals have the highest zinc content, followed by strained meats and egg yolks. Again, strained fruits and vegetables have little zinc content. Studies in animals demonstrate that the efficiency of zinc absorption from human milk is superior to that of most cow's milk formulas used for infant feeding, and greater still than that of soy formulas (Johnson & Evans, 1978). As with iron, the molecular binding of zinc in human milk, as distinct from cow's milk, is thought to be the basis for this increased absorption by intestines (Solomons, 1982). Prepared infant milk formulas have been supplemented with zinc since the latter 1970's.

There are several factors and conditions which may contribute to zinc deficiency. A "simple" nutritional problem occurs when the element is deficient in a primarily adequate diet. Remembering the food types that contain zinc like seafoods and red meats, it may be anticipated that children who live in socioeconomically deprived environments in this country may develop zinc deficiency while receiving adequate protein and calories. A major dietary factor which is thought to inhibit absorption of zinc is the presence of high fibers and phytates in the diet (Reinhold, et al., 1973); the latter may inhibit zinc absorption in soy-based formulas (Lonnerdal, et al., 1984). There are suggestions in the literature that high dietary iron may also inhibit zinc absorption (Solomons & Jacobs, 1981). Zinc deficiency is more likely to occur in premature babies, children with more generalized and severe nutritional problems, and those who receive total intravenous alimentation. Several other medical diseases are known to have secondarily associated zinc deficiency, such as cystic fibrosis, chronic renal disease, and sickle cell anemia.

Zinc Deficiency: Clinical Manifestations

The range of clinical problems which result from clinical zinc deficiencies are presented in Table 3. That zinc deficiency exerts an independent effect which results in short stature and sexual immaturity in adolescence was first reported in the Middle East in the 1960's (Prasad, 1984). While this association in adolescence is now accepted, there is less convincing evidence that zinc deficiency in infants and pre-school children results in growth retardation. However, several controlled studies suggest that children in this country who live in deprived socioeconomic status

Table 3

Clinical Aspects of Zinc Deficiency

Growth Retardation

Skin - Alopecia
        Acral and Oral Lesions
        Acrodermatitis Enteropathica
        Wound Healing

Delayed Sexual Maturation

Anorexia, Hypoguesia

Depressed Mood, Irritability

Diarrhea

Increased Susceptibility to Infection

families are more likely to suffer from zinc deficiency and that zinc supplementation in this population increases caloric intake and rate of growth. These will be described in more detail below. To our knowledge, no studies have examined the incidence of zinc deficiency in infants and young children who suffer from FTT or other causes of growth retardation. In a major textbook of pediatric nutrition, Hambridge states that "one of the earliest and most prominent features of zinc deficiency in infants and children is impairment of growth velocity. Zinc deficiency has to be considered in the differential diagnosis of infants who fail to thrive" (Hambridge, 1981). The classic disease which results from zinc deficiency is acrodermatitis enteropathica, an inherited disorder of zinc metabolism which results in alopecia, unremitting diarrhea with associated vomiting, and extensive skin lesions about the diaper and oral areas (Neldner & Hambridge, 1975). Similar dermatologic problems have been demonstrated in children who received total nutrition intravenously in which inadequate amounts of zinc were supplied and in pre-mature infants who received inadequate zinc and nutrition (Solomons, 1982). That zinc deficiency results in impaired taste sensitivity (hypogeusia) and the loss of appetite is of particular importance to the topic of FTT. While these symptoms have not been clearly documented in human zinc deficiency syndromes, zinc restriction in livestock and other experimental animals has induced a dramatic reduction in spontaneous food intake (Chestess & Quarterman, 1970). Anorexia is a common feature of untreated acrodermatitis enteropathica and of experimental zinc depletion. In one study of middle class children in this country, zinc supplementation in ten children with zinc deficiency and short stature with associated anorexia and hyogeusia resulted in correction of taste deficits within one to three months (Hambridge et al., 1972). In a separate study, school aged children with reduced hair zinc content were more likely to demonstrate taste changes and abnormal growth (Buzina et al., 1980). Zinc deficiency is associated with depressed leukocyte chemotaxis and T cellular immunity. This deficiency is thought to increase the susceptibility to infections commonly seen in protein energy malnourished human beings (Gordon et al., 1981). Neuro-psychiatric symptoms such as depressed mood and increased irritability are listed as clinical effects of zinc deficiency. While these symptoms are commonly seen in zinc deficiency states and improve with zinc supplementation, research to date makes it impossible to isolate the zinc deficiency from multiple other clinical problems occuring at the same time. Still, it is of interest to consider this effect and its potential impact on FTT children.

Epidemiology of Zinc Deficiency

It is difficult from the clinical literature to determine normal zinc levels in various socioeconomic populations in this country or to determine the frequency of zinc deficiency in infants and pre-school children with growth problems. There are significant laboratory methodology problems in measuring plasma and hair zinc (Hambridge, 1981), the latter considered a more accurate reflection of chronic nutritional state. Norms are not clearly defined. Finally, the quality of clinical epidemiologic research across populations in this country is deficient. The group from Denver has produced the bulk of the clinical research in this area. In 1972, they found that hair zinc taken from 93 children between the ages of 3 months and 4 years fell below population norms in 45 percent of the cases (Hambridge et al., 1972). Subsequent articles compared hair and zinc plasma of children of lower socioeconomic status families to children of middle class families. Seventy-four of 350 children enrolled in a Head Start Program in Denver whose heights were below the tenth percentile on the Iowa grids were compared to a control group which consisted of normally grown children of similar age from middle class families. The average hair zinc (87 μgms/gm vs. 130.7 μgms/gm) and plasma zinc (74.6 grams per 100 milliliter vs. 84.2 micrograms per 100 milliliters) were significantly lower in the Head Start Group (Hambridge & Walvarens et al., 1976). The same group performed health and nutrition screening of children of Mexican-American migrant farm workers during a migrant health program. One hundred and two children age 2 through 69 months of 743 screened were found to have height, weight, or head circumference below third percentile for age. The hair and plasma zinc level of these children were compared to the same middle class children described in the earlier study above and were found to be significantly lower (Chase & Hambridge et al., 1980). While the differences between groups in these two reports were statistically significant, a bias is introduced in the selection of the subjects and controls. Comparing small children from poor families to normally grown middle class children exaggerates group differences, and this comparison obscures the ability to understand zinc's contribution to the growth problem relative to other socioenvironmental variables. This comparison also obscures an understanding of the incidence of zinc deficiency in normally growing poor children.

In summary, the published reports suggest that poor children are more likely to have lower hair and plasma zinc levels than normal-sized children from middle class families. However, the clinical literature lacks acceptable epidemiologic studies which assess the patterns of plasma and hair zinc levels of children across socioeconomic status in this country. Likewise, there is a similar deficiency of clinical studies which assess the incidence of zinc deficiency in infants and pre-school children from various economic levels who are growth deficient.

Intervention with Zinc Supplementation

Does zinc supplementation improve appetite, food intake, and growth? Three projects in which zinc supplementation was provided to children help to answer this question. In the first clinical trial, neonates were managed from birth until the age of six months, by random assignment, on one of two formulas, cow's milk formula or cow's milk formula supplemented with large doses of zinc (4 mgs. of elemental zinc per liter). The infants were term and normal sized, and the mothers were of comparable socioeconomic status. By six months of age, the mean growth increments of 14 supplemented male infants were 2.1 cm greater in length and 535 grams greater in weight than for 8 male controls. These differences between groups were statistically significant. Growth increments for female test and control infants did not differ (Walvarens & Hambridge, 1976). These results are subject to skepticism due to small number of subjects and the potential for selection bias resulting from loss of a significant number of children during the six months of the study. Forty-seven (47%) of the control infants and 20% of the subjects were lost during the six month follow-up. In another study, subjects were two to six year old Mexican-American children whose height for age percentiles were less than 10th on the National Center for Health Statistics Grids. Hair and plasma zinc levels were below expected norms for all children. The subjects were randomly assigned to receive zinc supplementation (10 mgs of zinc sulfate daily) for a year or a placebo for the same time period. An increase in the calculated intake of energy, protein and zinc occured during the study which the authors attribute to the zinc supplementation. As in the earlier study, this treatment effect was observed for the boys but not for the girls. Calculated daily energy intakes of the 10 test boys increased from the initial mean of 1,280 Kcalories to final mean of 1,880 Kcalories (Krebs, Hambridge & Walvarens, 1984). Finally, zinc supplementation was provided to 16 Jamaican children of 6 to 18 months of age who had already begun the recovery phase from malnutrition after caloric replacement. There was a statistically significant and clinically impressive increase in the plasma zinc levels and the rate of weight change, as well as a decrease in energy costs of tissue deposition in these children after zinc supplementation when compared to these levels before zinc was provided (Golden & Golden, 1981).

Despite methodologic weaknesses, these three intervention projects suggest that there may be a zinc deficiency syndrome which results in decreased caloric intake and linear growth, and that replacement of zinc may beneficially effect energy intake and linear growth at least in boys.

In this chapter, we have attempted to develop the background and to describe the potential clinical relevance of the specific nutrition problem of zinc deficiency in infants and pre-school children with FTT. Our hypothesis is as follows: children who receive inadequate nutrition over time may become zinc deficient. This is more likely to occur in children living in deprived socioeconomic living situations where diets are more likely to be inadequate in zinc containing food types such as red meats and seafoods. The children may then have increasing anorexia and loss of appetite resulting from zinc deficiency which compounds the primary growth problem. They may have concomitant psychoemotional symptoms such as depression and irritability which may compound the primary socioenvironmental problem which originally initiated the interactional abnormalities. Ultimately, the specific zinc nutritional deficiency may have an independent compounding negative effect on the child's growth and course.

We will now describe a clinical project which we have been performing in the Growth and Development Clinic at Arkansas Children's Hospital. Ours is a controlled epidemiological study designed to assess trace metal patterns, particularly zinc, in children with FTT, and to compare these to normally grown children of similar socioeconomic status. Although we will describe our methodology and our plans for statistical analysis, data analysis is not complete and thus results cannot be presented at this time. Specimens were collected at the time of initial evaluation from FTT children whose weight growth fell below the third percentile for age when corrected for gestational age, and/or whose weight crossed two standard deviation lines over time. During the eighteen month period of specimen collection, two thirds of these infants were evaluated in our outpatient clinic, and one third were evaluated in the inpatient service. Because our clinical setting has been described elsewhere (Casey, Bradley & Wortham, 1984; Casey, Bradley & Wortham, 1984), further details will not be presented here. Control children were selected from two sources. One third of the control group were children who are admitted electively to the hospital for surgical procedures such as inguinal hernias. Specimens were collected at the time of surgery after parental consent. A second group of control children were selected from the population of the Growth and Development Clinic who were assessed for developmental problems with no clinical evidence of growth or nutritional difficulties.

Specimens were collected to avoid contamination. Serum specimens were collected in specially prepared syringes. Hair specimens were cut from the nape of the neck as close to the scalp as possible. Specimens were analyzed by inductively coupled argon plasma emission spectrometry. A laboratory methodology using electrothermally atomized microsamples of liquids and solids for multiple element assay was specifically developed for this project by Dr. Blakemore, at the National Center for Toxicological Research. This sophisticated analysis is described in detail elsewhere (Blakemore, Casey & Collie, 1984).

All patients were categorized into clinical diagnoses of organic FTT, non-organic FTT, or interactional/mixed FTT. When organic disease was identified, the specific diagnosis was recorded. In addition, the following were recorded at the time of diagnosis: infant weight in grams, length in centimeters, the percent of average weight at the age of diagnosis, the percent of average length at the age of diagnosis (these latter two reflect the severity of FTT), the hemoglobin, red blood cell indices, and white blood cell count. The following socio-demographic date were also collected: the child's age, race, sex, maternal age, family income, and socioeconomic status. A total of 138 specimens were collected. Eighteen were diagnosed with organic FTT, 44 with nonorganic FTT, 39 with interactional FTT, and 37 were normally grown children without FTT. The average age for children in all groups was eighteen months. Our plans for statistical analysis are multiple: We intend to compare the hair and plasma zinc levels in FTT children with that of normally growing children. We will evaluate the percentage of all children with FTT who have abnormal levels of hair and/or plasma zinc. Similar assessments within the subtypes of FTT will be performed. We will perform a matched analysis by matching children with FTT with control children by socioeconomic status, age of the infant, sex, and race. We will evaluate the hair and plasma zinc of children with FTT, categorized by age and the severity of the FTT reflected by the percentage of average weight and percentage of average length at the time of diagnosis. Finally, we will evaluate the patterns of hair and plasma zinc in children with specific diagnostic categories.

IMPLICATIONS

Our brief review of the biologic roles of zinc, of zinc deficiency states, and the clinical literature regarding zinc supplementation allows one to suggest that zinc deficiency may contribute to the development and course of FTT. Unfortunately, the hypothesis we developed earlier remains conjecture to date. We believe the data are inadequate to draw concrete clinical implications and to make specific recommendations. The laboratory measurement of zinc presents a particular problem at several levels. First, many clinical laboratories do not possess the capability to measure trace metals. Second, extreme caution is required in collecting and preparing specimens, as specimens are subject to contamination, and the trace minerals are present in extremely minute quantities. Third, trace minerals act as acute phase reactants, and zinc levels may be depressed in the presence of acute illness. Thus low levels of serum zinc may inaccurately reflect chronic nutritional status. For this reason, researchers usually attempt to measure other samples such as hair. One should thus proceed cautiously in determining whether zinc deficiency is of such clinical significance in a particular child that the child should receive supplementation. On the other hand, this is an area ripe for research. A clearer understanding of hair vs. plasma zinc in clinical studies is required. Will the hair and

plasma zinc levels correlate well enough in clinical populations that hair
will not need to be measured in future clinical work? We expect that our
research will allow us to determine the frequency of zinc deficiency in
each diagnostic category of FTT. Additional research to determine the
frequency of zinc deficiency according to severity of FTT, the chronicity
of FTT, the age of onset of the FTT, the symptoms at the time of presentation, and the nutritional history will help determine clinical subtypes of
children with FTT who are more likely to have zinc deficiency. This epidemiologic information would allow design of a controlled clinical intervention of zinc supplementation in the group of children with FTT most
likely to have zinc deficiency. Such a controlled study would determine
whether supplementation would contribute to the management of children with
FTT.

In summary, clinicians and researchers who deal with children with FTT
need to be aware of the potential for this specific nutritional deficiency
to contribute to the heterogeneity of clinical types of FTT. Further work
in this area by clinicians and basic scientists is clearly required.

REFERENCES

Bithoney, W.G. & Rathbun, J.M. Failure to thrive. In W.B. Levine, W.C.
    Carey, A.D. Crocker & R.J. Gross (Eds.) Developmental Behavioral
    Pediatrics. Philadelphia: Saunders, 1983, 557-572.
Blakemore, W.M., Casey, P.H. & Collie, W.R. Simultaneous determination of
    10 elements in waste water, plasma, and bovine liver by inductively
    coupled plasma emission spectrometry with electrothermal atomization.
    Analytical Chemistry, 1984, 56, 1376-1379.
Buzina, R. et al. Zinc nutrition and taste acuity in school children with
    impaired growth. American Journal of Clinical Nutrition, 1980, 33,
    2262-2266.
Casey, P.H. Failure to thrive: A reconceptualization. Developmental and
    Behavioral Pediatrics, 1983, 4, 63-66.
Casey, P.H., Bradley, R. & Wortham, B. Social and non-social home environ-
    ments of infants with non-organic failure to thrive. Pediatrics,
    1984, 73, 348-353.
Casey, P.H., Bradley, R. & Wortham, B. Management of children with failure
    to thrive in a rural ambulatory setting: Epidemiology and growth
    outcomes. Clinical Pediatrics, 1984, 23, 325-330.
Chase, H.P., Hambridge, K.M. et al. Low vitamin A and zinc concentrations
    in Mexican-American migrant children with growth retardation.
    American Journal of Clinical Nutrition, 1980, 33, 2346-2349.
Chestess, J.K. & Quarterman, J. Effects of zinc deficiency on food intake
    and feeding pattern of rats. British Journal of Nutrition, 1970, 42,
    1061-1065.
Golden, M.H.N. & Golden, B.E. Effect of zinc supplementation on the dietary
    intake rate of weight gain, and energy cost of tissue deposition in
    children recovering from severe malnutrition. American Journal of
    Clinical Nutrition, 1981, 34, 900-908.
Gordon, E.F. et al. Zinc metabolism: Basic, clinical and behavioral as-
    pects. Journal of Pediatrics, 1981, 99, 341-349.
Hambridge, M. Trace element deficiencies in childhood. In R.M. Suskind
    (Ed.) Textbook of Pediatric Nutrition. New York: Raven Press, 1981,
    163-177.
Hambridge, K.M. et al. Low levels of zinc in hair, anorexia, poor growth,
    and hyoguesia in childhood. Pediatric Research, 1972, 6, 868-874.
Hambridge, K.M., Walvarens, P.A. et al. Zinc nutrition of preschool chil-
    dren in the Denver Head Start Program. American Journal of Clinical
    Nutrition, 1976, 29, 734-738.
Johnson, P.E. & Evans, G.W. Relative zinc availability in human breastmilk,

infant formulas, and cow's milk. American Journal of Clinical Nutrition, 1978, 31, 416-419.

Krebs, N.F., Hambridge, K.M., Walvarens, P.A. Increased food intake of young children receiving a zinc supplement. American Journal of Diseases of Children, 1984, 138, 270-273.

Lonnerdal, B. et al. The effect of individual components of soy formula and cow's milk formula on zinc bioavailability. American Journal of Clinical Nutrition, 1984, 40, 1064-1066.

Neldner, K.H. & Hambridge, K.M. Zinc therapy of acrodermatitis enteropathica. New England Journal of Medicine, 1975, 292, 879-883.

Prasad, A.S. Discovery and importance of zinc in human nutrition. Federation Proceedings, 1984, 43, 2829-2834.

Reinhold, J.G. et al. Effects of purified phytate and phytate-rich bread upon metabolism of zinc, calcium, phosphorous, and nitrogen in man. Lancet, 1973, 1, 283-288.

Solomons, N.W. Zinc and copper in human nutrition. In Nutrition in the 1980's: Constraints on Our Knowledge. New York: A.R. Liss, Inc., 1981, 97-127.

Solomons, N.W. Zinc bioavailability implications for pediatric nutrition. Pediatric Basics, 1982, 33, 4-11.

Solomons, N.W. & Jacobs, R.A. Studies on the bioavailability of zinc in humans. Effect of heme and nonheme iron on the absorption of zinc. American Journal of Clinical Nutrition, 1981, 34, 475-478.

Tasmon-Jones, C. Zinc deficiency states. Advances in Internal Medicine, 1980, 26, 97-115.

Walvarens, P.A. & Hambridge, K.M. Growth of infants fed a zinc supplemented formula. American Journal of Clinical Nutrition, 1976, 29, 1114-1121.

Walvarens, P.A., Krebs, N.F. & Hambridge, K.M. Linear growth of low-income preschool children receiving a zinc supplement. American Journal of Clinical Nutrition, 1983, 38, 195-201.

III. RESEARCH REPORTS

PART I: STUDIES OF RISK AND OUTCOME

Research concerning the psychosocial aspects of FTT is very much in its early phases. In the following section, the methods and data from a number of ongoing projects provide readers with information that should be useful to them in designing and evaluating future research concerning FTT.

Sherrod, O'Connor, Altemeier & Vietze examine various etiological models of maltreatment and pertaining to factors which differentiate child maltreatment from other populations. Children who had high rates of non-organic failure to thrive (NOFT) or abuse, and high rates of physical illness were compared with children who had a rate of illness similar to NOFT and abused children but who had no record of maltreatment. Compared on demographics, neonatal behavior, temperament, and maternal history, the groups differed in variables obtained from maternal history including nurturing, feelings about pregnancy, parenting skills, and family problems. The maltreatment groups also included infants with more difficult tempera-ments. Mothers who maltreated their children were reported more negative feelings about being pregnant, had more family problems when they were growing up and had a more punitive orientation toward parenting. On the other hand, the groups were comparable on main demographic factors, birth-weight and number of delivery complications and on neonatal behavior. The findings are consistent with a multidimensional, threshold model in which the number of various risk factors is more important in precipitating maltreatment than the precise subset of variables within an overall group. The findings suggest that researchers should begin to identify patterns of occurrence of risk variables in order to predict child maltreatment more effectively.

Bradley and Casey present a reanalysis of data from their ongoing investigation of factors in the home environments of NOFT infants that distinguish them from similar infants living in poor socioeconomic circum-stances. In presenting the rationale for their study, Bradley and Casey describe the necessity of relating research in FTT to developmentally focused research in child maltreatment, especially patterns of parent-child communication, attachment, and relationships.

Bradley and Casey's study involved a case control match for each of 23 NOFT infants to a child with normal weight for age according to age, race, sex, maternal education, family income and household crowdedness. Measures included home observation for measurement of the environment (Home) and a life events record (LER). A multiple discriminant analysis of Home and LER indicated significant separation between the two groups. (Correct identi-fication rate of 72%.) A detailed examination was made of the misclassifi-cations in order to develop hypotheses for future research. Factors asso-ciated with NOFT included having a primary caregiver who was extremely unre-sponsive and a caregiver who is extremely harsh. On the other hand, being from a small family seemed to afford some protection from FTT. Bradley and Casey suggest directions for future research, especially delineation of patterns of attachment and parental influences in order to establish a positive, empirically-based diagnosis based on the the child's environment.

In the next chapter, Drotar and his research team consider the evolution of methods and early outcome of a study of early preventive psychosocial intervention for infants with NOFT who were diagnosed following a hospitalization during their first year of life. The design of the intervention involved a restructuring of patterns of hospital-based care to provide greater continuity of care following hospitalization and intervention conducted in the home setting to address family and parent-child influences that were affecting the child. Drotar and his colleagues review the special logistics, problems, and methods involved in implementing this study. Preliminary findings indicate a general recovery in physical growth and maintenance of average cognitive development at 24 months for this sample but no differential effect of specific intervention plan. Early outcome within this population indicates that age of onset and family factors were protective factors related more to cognitive and language development and that children with fewer family stressors and shorter duration of FTT tend to be more securely attached. The implications of these findings for intervention research are discussed.

In the final chapter in this section, Singer describes the patterns of care and developmental outcomes of three groups of FTT children who received extended hospitalization at a pediatric rehabilitation hospital after an initial evaluation at an acute care hospital. These included a subset of children from the study described by Drotar and his colleagues, FTT children already in custody of county welfare and children with a mixed etiology which included neurologic impairments. The groups made similar progress in physical growth in their hospitalization and in physical growth and cognitive development on follow up. However, the children who had received outreach intervention were more likely to remain in custody of their parents and had much shorter hospital stays. The health problems presented by many children on follow-up reflected chronic environmental hazards. These findings underscore the need for additional empirical study of long-term developmental and physical outcomes of FTT children including those with a combination of neurologic difficulty and family problems, and children who are placed in foster care. For some children, provision for supportive outreach services to the families of FTT infants is a more cost effective intervention than extended hospitalization.

TOWARD A SEMISPECIFIC, MULTIDIMENSIONAL, THRESHOLD MODEL OF MALTREATMENT*

Kathryn B. Sherrod, Susan O'Connor, William A. Altemeier,
III, and Peter Vietze

Vanderbilt University, Nashville General Hospital, and
National Institute of Child Health and Human Development

Nonorganic failure to thrive (NOFT) is not well understood. Among the
few points that are accepted are the idea of the severity of the problem,
defined in terms of number of children affected (Altemeier, O'Connor,
Sherrod & Vietze, in press) and sequelae (Hufton & Oates, 1977; White et
al., 1980). One of the definitional aspects that is fairly generally
accepted is that NOFT that occurs in very young infants is different from
NOFT (often called psychosocial dwarfism) that occurs in toddlers or young
children (Green, Campbell & David, 1984; Money, Annecillo & Kelley, 1983).
Beyond that, NOFT appears to be a form of maltreatment, sometimes viewed as
related to abuse or as a precursor to abuse (Koel, 1979; Oates, 1982), but
more aptly viewed as a form of neglect, probably because it arises more
through acts of omission than commision. However, the manner in which NOFT
relates to other forms of maltreatment has not adequately been clarified or
addressed thoroughly. Books giving a general overview of maltreatment
invariably mention NOFT, although, unfortunately, few devote much space to
it (e.g., Giovannoni & Becerra, 1979; Oates, 1982; Pelton, 1981). There are
no books entirely focused on the psychological aspects of NOFT, although
there are medically oriented ones (e.g. Accardo, 1982; Patton & Gardner,
1963).

In the present chapter, we will briefly examine various etiological
models of maltreatment and will include some comparisons of NOFT in infancy,
abuse, and neglect as forms of maltreatment. In addition, complimentary
approaches to conducting research on maltreatment are discussed, using the
relationship of child illness to maltreatment as an example of research
approaches (a) that focus on what makes maltreaters or maltreated children

---

*This research was supported by the National Center on Child Abuse and
Neglect; the Children's Bureau Administration on Children, Youth, and
Families; Grants 90-C-419 and 90-CA-2138 from the Office of Human Develop-
ment Services of the Department of Health, Education, and Welfare; the
William T. Grant Foundation; Grant R01 MH31195-01 from the National Insti-
tute of Mental Health; Grant P01 HD15052 from the Research Program on
Retarded Intellectual Development of the National Institute of Child Health
and Human Development; and Bio-Medical Research Grant RG6000. We thank
Dottie Tucker for data collection and record checking, and Randy Parks and
Karen Weintraub for data analyses. Send reprint requests to Kathryn B.
Sherrod, Box 154, Peabody College for Teachers, Nashville, Tennessee 37203.

different from everyone else, or (b) that focus on what buffers or helps provide some compensatory mechanism for people who share characteristics with maltreaters or maltreated children, but who are not involved in maltreatment.

Researchers and practitioners who work in the area of child maltreatment have become accustomed to uncertainty regarding the causal factor(s) of child maltreatment. Some of this uncertainty derives from the competing theories regarding the etiology of maltreatment. Earlier theorists attributed a great deal of the cause of maltreatment to personality defects in the parents (e.g., Bennie & Sclare, 1969; Spinetta & Rigler, 1972; Steele & Pollack, 1968). A related factor, an inadequate childhood, has been posited by several authors (e.g., Benedek, 1959; Fraiberg, Adelson & Shapiro, 1975; Main & Goldwyn, 1984) who have described case studies that support their ideas. The difficulty with such single factor theories is that many experienced clinicians can cite examples of parents with personality disorders or who had unpleasant childhood experiences, but who do not maltreat their own children. Conversely, most clinicians can cite examples of parents without evident personality defects or who come from apparently more adequate backgrounds, but who do maltreat their children.

Similar discrepancies surround other theories on the cause of maltreatment. In the sociological model (see reviews by Belsky, 1978; Parke & Collmer, 1975), the stress and frustration of daily life are emphasized. Within this model, parents from the lower socioeconomic strata are assumed to experience heightened stress and hence are considered more at risk for maltreating their children than are those in higher socioeconomic strata. Although reported maltreatment, and apparently actual maltreatment, are more frequent in lower SES populations than in higher SES populations, the sociological model lacks precision because so many low SES families experience similar life events as do low income maltreating families, yet most manage to adequately nurture their children physically and emotionally.

Still another model is focused on the role of the child as elicitor of the maltreatment (Belsky, 1978). While this model is viewed as abhorrent and unacceptable by some, because it can be interpreted as a nonproductive instance of blaming the victim, it is incontrovertible that some children are more difficult to take care of than are others. There can be many reasons why children are difficult. Some are sickly, some irritable, and some unresponsive. Nonetheless, many more children are difficult than are maltreated; thus, being difficult is not sufficient for being maltreated. It may not even be necessary.

The difficulty of establishing etiological theories of child maltreatment may reflect more on the variety of causes of maltreatment than on the theorists' failure to posit etiologies. If it is the case that no one factor by itself is necessary or sufficient for causing maltreatment, this would precipitate a great deal of confusion for those trying to understand the phenomena of maltreatment. This is not to postulate that each of the factors and models delineated above lacks merit. That is not the case at all. The problem is that each of these factors and models lacks precision. While they are descriptive of some people who maltreat or of some children who are maltreated, they are also descriptive of many people who do not maltreat and many children who are not maltreated. The lack of efficacy of our present theories indicates that some shift in the theoretical explanation of maltreatment seems warranted. Because theory construction and methodology are inextricably interwoven, a shift in theory is most likely to follow a shift of methodological approach. Our previously utilized method of amassing data from which to derive theories has primarily been to look for factors found in maltreating parents or in maltreated children which distinguish them from others. A possible shift in approach might be to

focus on parents or children who have the same characteristics as parents
or children who are identified as having problems but who apparently are
avoiding the experience of maltreatment.

In some ways, focusing on the people who have characteristics associated with maltreatment, but who have shown no signs of maltreatment or
maltreating, is similar to the recent interest in invulnerable children
(e.g., Werner & Smith, 1982). Describing the people who are in precarious
or nonsupportive positions, but who nonetheless thrive, or at least manage,
may actually provide more useful hypotheses than focusing only on those who
fail to cope or thrive. For example, individuals who do not maltreat their
children, but who share some characteristics with people who do maltreat,
may have other characteristics that serve as compensatory mitigating factors. Similarly, children who are not maltreated, but who share some
characteristics with children who are maltreated, may have other qualities
that attenuate their risk status.

In terms of the implications for research, it is possible to combine
research methods. One approach would be for the same research team to
begin by searching their population for characteristics that are significantly associated with parents who maltreat or children who are maltreated,
and then to search the population again for individuals who share those
characteristics, but who do not appear to have the associated maltreatment.
One can then ascertain which other characteristics or set of characteristics differentiate between the families with maltreatment and those without. This combined approach is the one that will be emphasized in the
present paper.

Previously, our research team has focused on what differentiates
people who maltreat from those who do not. Initially, we showed that a
prenatally administered Maternal History Interview (devised primarily by
Altemeier) significantly predicted which children were at risk for abuse,
neglect, or nonorganic FTT (Altemeier et al., 1979). This earlier work has
been elaborated in three subsequent papers (Altemeier et al., 1982;
Altemeier et al., 1984a; 1984b). These studies showed that disturbed
childhood nurture, untruthfulness, poor rapport in an interview situation,
residency transience, unwanted pregnancy, and perhaps conditions that increased parent-child exposure were important predictors of maltreatment.
Additonally, we have shown that "rooming-in" tends to reduce the incidence
of deleterious outcomes in families at risk for maltreatment (O'Connor et
al., 1980; O'Connor & Vietze, 1982).

We also have focused on single factors that have been thought to be
associated with maltreatment. We have shown that children's health is
related to both FTT and to physical abuse, although not to neglect (Sherrod
et al., 1984). The relationship between health and maltreatment was that
the more often the children were ill during their first year of life, the
more likely they were to develop FTT or abuse. Having established that
health (or illness) and maltreatment are related, it seems reasonable to
approach that relationship from another perspective, that of trying to
ascertain what differences exist between families with ill children who
become maltreated and families with ill children who do not become maltreated. This will serve as an example of the general approach of seeking
parents and/or children who have characteristics associated with maltreatment, but who avoid maltreatment and comparing them with people who have
those characteristics and who do maltreat or are maltreated. For the
present study, data were available for mothers and their babies, but not
for other family members.

Because results from our studies have indicated that subjects in
different maltreatment groups are indeed different from one another and

warrant separate consideration, results are considered separately for children with NOFT, abuse, and neglect. Thus, even though this book is primarily focused on FTT, three types of maltreatment are considered in this chapter.

In order to explore the relationship between child illness and maltreatment, groups of children and/or their mothers were selected according to whether or not the children had experienced maltreatment and whether or not the children had high rates of illness. That is, children who were selected because they had NOFT or abuse also had higher rates of illnesses than did randomly selected control children (Sherrod, et al., 1984). (This was not the case for neglected children, who had equivalent rates of illnesses as the randomly selected control group.) For comparison purposes, a group of children who had a rate of illness similar to the NOFT and abused children, but who had no record of maltreatment was selected. These (a) maltreated; and (b) nonmaltreated, but often ill groups were then compared on other factors that have previously been related to maltreatment. The factors included demographic measures, Brazelton scores, Carey temperament scores, and Maternal History Interview scores.

METHOD

Subjects

The subjects in this study were 124 mothers and their children who were divided into several groups: Group 1 had 31 children with nonorganic failure to thrive (NOFT), Group 2 had 19 abused children, Group 3 had 14 neglected children, Group 4 had 24 randomly selected control children, and Group 5 had 38 control children who had an equivalent mean number of illnesses as the abused and NOFT children. Thus, Group 5 functioned as an illness control group. Group 2 was broken down into two subgroups for this study. The first subgroup contained 11 mother/child subject pairs, where the abused child in the family was the one born during the target pregnancy that brought the mother to the prenatal clinic and into this study. The second subgroup contained 6 mother/child subject pairs, where the abused child in the family was a sibling of the target child. The target child had no documented abuse within the first three years of life in those six cases.

Selection of Original Samples. The subjects and their mothers were drawn from families in a large prospective, longitudinal study (N = 1400) of the prenatal predictors of child maltreatment (Altemeier et al., 1979). The mothers were selected while they were patients at a prenatal clinic in a metropolitan hospital that serves a primarily lower-income population. From the original sample of 1400 women, two subsamples were created. Based on responses to a prenatal interview, 275 women were placed into one subsample considered at high risk for child abuse. (The prenatal interview was based on a review of child abuse literature and included such areas as interpersonal support systems among family and friends, and presence of abuse in the women's childhood.) The second subsample, 274 women, was randomly selected from the 1400 women (and had an overlap of 50 subjects with the high-risk sample). These two subsamples were followed fairly intensively for three years.

Selection of NOFT Sample. NOFT was determined by successive criteria. First, all babies whose weight gain ever fell below two-thirds of the Harvard 50 percentile growth curve were selected (Vaughn, McKay & Nelson, 1975); there were 61 such cases. Second, a determination of whether or not those children had FTT was made; children who appeared to be small of stature, but otherwise healthy were deleted at this point from the sample. Third, the 46 children who were left were divided into ten organic FTT cases and 36 NOFT cases. Reliability in the determination of whether a child had organic or nonorganic FTT was 87%. Of the 36 NOFT cases, clinic data were available on 31; they comprised the NOFT sample in this study. Twelve of the NOFT cases were admitted to the hospital. They gained weight in the absence of medical treatment, but with provision for demand feeding. This was considered diagnostic for NOFT. Other children were selected as NOFT cases after observation of an irregular growth curve, unusual weight, height, and head circumference correlations, and questionable feeding history given by the parents. Several of the organic cases were defined by (a) anatomic anomalies, such as congenital heart defects or pyloric stenosis, or (b) physiological problems, such as milk intolerance, or (c) illness, such as pneumonia or meningitis. Children who appeared to have components of both organic and nonorganic FTT were considered organic cases.

Selection of Abuse and Neglected Sample. The maltreated children in the present study were born to the women interviewed during their pregnancy and included all of those found to be maltreated from either subsample who had ever attended the hospital clinic. In addition, the previously mentioned six target children whose siblings were abused were included. No data were available to us about the siblings, other than that they were abused.

Abuse or neglect in the subject population was determined by checking the juvenile court records from the local county or by checking the state registry for abuse or neglect during the course of the study. State criteria for abuse include evidence of physical abuse (e.g. bruises, broken bones) or sexual abuse (e.g. ano-genital damage or disease). In the present study, all families in which sexual abuse occurred also had documented evidence of physical abuse. State criteria for neglect include evidence of medical neglect (e.g. failure to seek medical attention for a disease) and caretaking neglect (e.g. leaving small children unattended). All abuse or neglect cases for whom data were included in this study were substantiated by state-employed social workers.

Selection of Control Samples. Both the random control sample and the illness control sample were selected from the random subsample of 174 women. The 24 random control subjects in the present study were chosen by a computer program with a random number generator from those subjects in the random subsample who had no record of abuse, neglect, or NOFT. No other criteria were considered.

Thirty-eight other children from the random subsample were then picked by a computer sort program that selected children who had no record of maltreatment, according to number of acute illnesses they had experienced during the first three months of life for any variety of acute illness. An ANOVA was then run to compare the NOFT, abuse, and illness control subjects on number of illnesses within the first three months. There was no significant difference, nor even a trend toward significance. The illness control group was therefore considered to be group-matched for illness rate with the NOFT group and the abuse group. The three-month period was selected because, in earlier analyses, it was during the first three months of life that illness frequency best differentiated between two of the maltreated groups (NOFT plus abused) and the random control group (Sherrod et al., 1984). Illnesses did not seem to differentiate between the neglect group and the control group at any time, so no new control group was necessary for a study of the neglect group.

Table 1

Maternal Demographic and Infant Hospital Data

	NOFT N=31	Abuse Target N=11	Abuse Siblings N=6	Neglect N=14	Random Control N=24	Ill Control N=38
MOTHER*						
Race						
White	21	9	5	9	14	25
Black	10	2	1	5	10	10
Marital Status						
Married	18	8	4	8	16	17
Single/Divorced/Separated	13	3	2	6	8	21
Age (mean years)	20.5	22.1	24	20.1	22.2	20.1
Age Range	15-38	16-33	19-29	15-32	17-36	15-34
Education (mean years)	10.3	9.4	10.2	9.2	11.2	10.2
Education Range	7-12	4-12	8-13	7-12	8-14	6-13
Number of Siblings (mean)	.9	1.8	1.5	1.0	.9	.8
Sibling Range	0-4	0-6	1-5	0-3	0-4	0-7
BABY*						
Birthweight (grams)	3031	3118	3253	2983	3054	3207

94

	NOFT N=31	Abuse Target N=11	Abuse Siblings N=6	Neglect N=14	Random Control N=24	Ill Control N=38
Birthweight Range	1729-4345	2310-3827	2232-4011	1006-4260	907-4338	1708-4352
Gestational Age (mean wks)	38.8	39.6	38.3	38.4	38.8	39.6
Range	29-40	36-40	34-40	28-40	31-40	33-40
Apgar Score	7.1	7.5	7.0	7.5	7.0	7.6
Apgar Range	3-8	6-9	4-8	5-9	4-9	4-9
Delivery Complications						
None	22	8	4	10	12	27
Some	7	3	2	4	11	11
Nursery						
Complications						
None	18	7	4	7	12	23
Some	6	2	1	3	7	10
High Risk	5	2	1	2	4	5

* For some measures, missing data causes the actual number of subjects to be smaller than that listed at the top of the table.

Procedure

After the subjects were selected, data on the subjects' demographics were analyzed to be sure the groups were comparable. Some variables were analyzed using ANOVAs: mother's age, educational level, number of children, child's birthweight, gestational age, and Apgar score. There were no significant differences on these measures, except for years of education. Mother's educational level was significantly lower for the abuse targets and the neglect group in comparison with the random control group, but not in comparison with the illness control group. The abuse sibling group was not significantly different from either control group in educational level. Because education only discriminated abuse and neglect from the random control group, but not the illness control group, education did not seem to be a powerful discriminator among groups, nor a reasonable causal factor for maltreatment. Nonetheless, correlational analyses were run between educational level and the outcome measures and none of the results were significant. The other variables were analyzed using X^2: mother's race, marital status, number of delivery complications, and number of nursery complications. There were no significant differences on these measures. Data on these measures can be seen in Table 1.

Although the subjects included in this study were comparable on birth-weight and gestational age, in another study from this same project,. the children with NOFT were found to be lighter in weight and younger in gestational age than control children (Vietze et al., 1980). The characteristics of the NOFT children are similar in both studies despite deletion of four children from this study, who had no clinic visits from which to get health/illness data, but who were included in the Vietze et al. study. The difference between studies appears to be more due to the random control groups, each of which were separately selected by computer random number generating programs. In the present study, gestationally younger, smaller children happened to be included in the control group. This eliminated the differences between NOFT and control groups in the present study. It may well be that in reality, NOFT children as a group are smaller and gestationally younger than other children, but the difference is slight and thus is alternately revealed or hidden according to minor variations in subject selection.

In addition to the demographic and hospital data on these subjects, there were scores on the Maternal History Interview, the Carey Infant Temperament Scale (1970), and the Brazelton Neonatal Behavioral Assessment Scale (1973).

Maternal History Interview. All subjects first were given a questionnaire (Maternal History Interview) while they were waiting to be seen at the prenatal clinic. The questions included in the Maternal history Interview were derived in 1974 from reading the literature on maltreatment at that time. The scales were derived theoretically, not empirically. The questionnaire required about 30 minutes to administer. It included eight scales, measuring (a) mother's perception of her nurture as a child; (b) personality factors of self-image, isolation, and tolerance; (c) social support available from others; (d) positive and negative feelings about the pregnancy; (e) knowledge of parenting skills and disciplinary tactics; (f) alcohol, drug, and health problems in the family; (g) knowledge of developmental norms (KDN); and (h) a modified Holmes and Rahe Life Stress Inventory (1967).

The eight scales of the MHI were not generally highly intercorrelated. Eleven of the interscale correlations were r <.20 and only two of the intercorrelations were r >.40. The exact intercorrelations can be seen in Appendix 1.

The interviewers were trained to be reliable with each other in administering the questionnaire ($\underline{r}$ = .90 or greater between any pairs of four interviewers), and had regular reliability checks throughout the study to maintain that level. Interviewers were not clinically trained. They had educational levels ranging from completion of high school through a four-year college degree.

Carey Temperament Scale (1970). The Carey is a questionnaire which is administered to an adult (usually the mother) regarding the child's response to a variety of common foods, events, or social situations. From the mother's choice among the possible answers on each question, an overall score can be obtained indicating whether the particular child being considered is "easy " or "difficult" to take care of and relate to. It is also possible to obtain data on nine individual scales. For the present study only the overall score was used, where the higher the score, the more difficult the child is perceived to be.

The Carey was administered to the mothers in the present study when their babies were one and three months old. For babies on whom both one- and three-month Carey scores were collected, the mean of the scores was used. For babies on whom only one score was available, that score was used. The Carey was administered by research assistants who were not clinically trained. For the present study it was administered in the families' homes on the same day other data were being collected, but there is no indication at this time that location of administration alters the results and the Carey has even been used as a mailed questionnaire (Little, 1983). Thus, it is easily administered. It has been shown to predict problems other than maltreatment (Carey, 1972; see review on temperament by Campos et al., 1983). There is now a revised form of the Carey (Carey & McDevitt, 1978).

Brazelton Neonatal Behavioral Assessment Scale (1973). This examination was developed to assess interactive behaviors of normal infants. The main objective was to have a behavioral assessment, but some neurological items were included. There are 27 largely behavioral items scored on nine-point scales and 20 reflexes scored on a three-point scale. Scores on these items are combined into cluster scores. Brazelton has stressed that the examiner should work to achieve the newborn's best performance, rather than the average performance.

For this study, the Brazelton was administered to each child once, at a mean of 40 hours postnatally. This relatively early time was selected because so many of the mothers in this study leave the hospital after two days that waiting until the third day to test the infant (as is often recommended) was not feasible.

Individuals administering the Brazelton were either trained by Brazelton or one our testers who was trained by Brazelton. Reliability was established at $\underline{r} \geq .90$ and was checked between pairs of testers every four to six months. Testers were all master's-level psychologists.

RESULTS

ANOVAs were computed on the overall MHI score and on each of the scale scores. The overall MHI was significantly different across groups, with the maltreatment groups having the most negative MHI scores, $\underline{F}$ (5, 123) = 6.05, $\underline{p}$ <.001. The means of the MHI overall score and scale scores are in Table 2. Four of the eight scales of the MHI were also significant: nurture scale, $\underline{F}(5,123)$ = 44.71, $\underline{p}$ <.001; feelings about pregnancy, $\underline{F}(5,123)$ = 2.78, $\underline{p}$ <.025; parenting skills, $\underline{F}(5,123)$ = 6.69, $\underline{p}$ <.001; and family

Table 2

Means of Outcome Measures: Maternal History Interview, Carey, and Brazelton Scores

	NOFT N=31	Abuse Target N=11	Abuse Siblings N=6	Neglect N=14	Random Control N=24	Ill Control N=38
Overall Maternal History						
Interview	-18.0	-15.4	-31.3	-22.1	5.4	- 5.2
MHI Individual Scales						
Nurture	- 7.6	- 4.3	-14.8	-10.3	1.1	- 5.1
Personality	- 2.8	- 4.1	- 3.8	- 4.1	- .1	- .7
Support	- .8	.5	2.8	- 1.4	2.1	1.2
Feelings about pregnancy	- 1.7	- 1.5	- 5.7	- 2.1	1.7	1.0
Parenting skills	- 1.6	- 3.4[a,b]	- 5.8[a,b]	- 1.2[a]	1.6[b]	- .8[a]
Family problems	- 3.4	- 2.7	- 4.0[a]	- 2.9	- 1.0	- 2.3
Stress Inventory	9.4	8.4	11.0	5.4	4.6	7.2
Knowledge of Developmental Norms	7.2	7.9	8.3	8.3	6.2	6.1
Carey Temperament	3.0[a,b]	2.8[a,b]	3.0[a,b]	2.2[a,b]	1.9	1.8
Brazelton Scores						
Initial State	2.4	2.4	3.3	2.4	2.7	2.6
Predominant State 1	3.9	4.0	5.3	3.3	4.2	4.2
Social Cluster	2.3	2.1	2.3	2.0	2.3	2.2
Tone Cluster	2.0	1.7	1.7	2.0	1.8	1.7
State Cluster	2.2	2.0	2.7	2.2	2.2	2.0
Stress Cluster	1.8	1.5	1.3	1.8	1.9	1.6

[a]Post hoc tests established that this mean is significantly different from the random control group mean.
[b]Post hoc tests established that this mean is significantly different from the ill control group mean.

problems, $\underline{F}(5,123) = 2.70$, $\underline{p} <.025$. Post hoc tests (Fisher's LSD) were run comparing individual pairs of means. In most cases, no significant differences were observed due to exceedingly large variances within groups. In fact, several of the standard deviations were larger than the group means. The significant post hoc analyses that were observed are indicated in Table 2.

ANOVAs were also computed on the Carey easy/hard overall score and on the Brazelton Cluster scores. The Carey significantly discriminated among groups, with the maltreatment groups having higher scores (indicative of a more difficult temperament) than the control groups, $\underline{F}(5,123) = 5.7$, $\underline{p} <.001$. There were no significant differences on the Brazelton cluster scores.

Pearson product moment correlations were computed between the overall MHI score and the Carey, and between the eight MHI scale scores and the Carey. The overall MHI was significantly correlated with the Carey, $\underline{r}(83) = -.21$, $\underline{p} <.05$, such that the more negative the MHI score, the more difficult the mother rated her child on the Carey. Three of the eight subscales were similarly significant: nurture, $\underline{r}(83) = -.28$, $\underline{p} <.01$; parenting skills, $\underline{r}(83) = -.26$, $\underline{p} <.01$; and feelings about pregnancy, $\underline{r}(83) \leq -.20$, $\underline{p} <.05$.

DISCUSSION

As previously noted, we had shown in another report that infant illness is significantly associated with subsequent maltreatment (both for NOFT and abuse). Given that it is such a small step then to wonder if the illnesses might relate to the abuse in a causal fashion, it seemed imperative to identify a sample of infants who had an equivalent number of illnesses as the maltreated children did but who suffered no maltreatment. In the larger sample of children from which this present sample was drawn, we readily found 38 children who had a number of illnesses equivalent to that of the NOFT and abuse-target groups, but who were not maltreated. Having such a large illness-control group makes it clear that infant illness is not sufficient to cause or elicit maltreatment. However, the complications of having an ill child may potentiate an otherwise tense or unsettled family situation.

In contrast to other studies, the maltreatment and control subjects in this study were comparable on many of the main demographic factors which have been associated with maltreatment (e.g. see reviews by Belsky, 1978; Parke and Collmer, 1975). Hence, these demographic variables were unrelated to maltreatment for these subjects. Even the ranges of these demographics, which show the overlap of the measures across groups, indicate how unrelated these variables were to maltreatment in this study. Variables that were not significantly different between the illness control and the various maltreatment groups included race, marital status, mothers' age, mothers' education, number of children in the home, baby's gestational age, birthweight, Apgar score, number of delivery complications and number of nursery complications. These demographic measures, which have previously been found to discriminate among maltreated and nonmalteated groups, must neither be sufficient nor necessary in terms of causing maltreatment. They may, however, often be correlated with maltreatment, even though they were not correlated in the present sample.

The question remains, then, of why some children were maltreated and some not. Could the maltreated children have behaved differently than the illness-control children? Perhaps they were more disorganized or difficult to cope with and thus they elicited their own maltreatment. We have two measures of the infants' behavior to allow assessment of this question.

One, the Brazelton, is a fairly objective measure that was administered by trained master's level psychologists. The other, the Carey, is an interview tapping the mother's perception of her infant's behavior. The Carey is sometimes perceived as an objective measure because the questions on it are oriented toward the child's specific behaviors (e.g. eating and sleeping regularly) and are not oriented toward the mother's attitude toward the child. However, because the answers are collected from the mother rather than from observations, its status as an objective test remains questionable. An examination of the Brazelton scores shows that the Brazelton did not discriminate among groups of infants. In contrast, the Carey Temperament easy/hard score did discriminate among the babies. The lack of discrimination of the Brazelton might be related to the fact that it was given so soon after birth, when perhaps some children had not stabilized in behavior. It might also be related to the fact that the Brazelton was designed primarily to discriminate normal babies from abnormal babies, but not really to discriminate very preisely among normal babies (St. Clair, 1978). The Carey Temperament Scale was designed to discriminate among normal babies. It was administered later than the Brazelton was, at one or three months, by which time the babies had stabilized and the mothers had gotten to know them well enough to have formed definite opinions regarding their children's behavior and temperament.

Therefore, a simple and straightforward interpretation of these data would be that the maltreated children, while in the normal range (and thus not discriminably different from controls on the Brazelton) tended to be difficult children (and thus received higher Carey Scores than controls). This supports the contention that it is difficult children who are likely to be maltreated. However, in this study we were not limited to this interpretation because we also had the prenatally derived Maternal History Interview scores on the mothers. Both the overall score and four of the eight individual scale scores significantly discriminated among the groups. The mothers who maltreated were the ones who reported having the least adequate nurture when they were growing up, had the most negative feelings about being pregnant, had more family problems when they were growing up, and had the most punitive orientation toward parenting.

Given that the mothers of maltreated children had the least adequate nurture and reported the most punitive approach toward children, the possibility existed that they would evaluate their children less positively than other mothers. After all, whether or not a baby eats or sleeps with a regular pattern is a matter of opinion, not fact, because "regular" is a subjective term. If the mother's negative attitude about this pregnancy and her inadequate nurturance led her to be less satisfied with her infant, then her MHI scores should be correlated with the Carey scores. In the present study, the overall MHI as well as three of the individual scale scores were significantly correlated with the Carey in the expected direction. (A fourth scale, knowledge of developmental norms, showed a trend toward being correlated with the Carey, but it was not significant. Although we did not find that knowledge of developmental norms was a useful measure, others have [DeLissovoy, 1973; also see review by Elster, McAnarney & Lamb, 1983].)

The finding that prenatally collected MHI scores are significantly correlated with postnatally collected Carey scores could be interpreted in at least three ways. The first way is that the mothers' prenatal attitudes color their perception of their babies postnatally so the Carey is actually a projective measure. A second way is that the mothers' negative attitudes prenatally are reflective of a generally negative outlook and that this negative outlook is also reflected in complaints about the baby on the Carey. A third way is that the mothers' negative attitudes prenatally are associated with poor care of self and baby and that by one or three months after birth the babies are indeed difficult of temperament because they have received such poor pre- and post-natal care.

Although mothers' prenatal interview data were significantly correlated with babies' temperament scores, the amount of variance accounted for by those correlations is small. Thus, the relationship should not be over-interpreted as indicating that there were no real temperament differences among the groups of children. The babies who became maltreated may have been more difficult to care for from the time of birth as well as having mothers who may have been predisposed toward viewing them negatively.

In summary, health of the child appears to be related to maltreatment, but not directly causally related. The child's temperament may be related to maltreatment, or it may be only that mothers of maltreated children evaluate their children harshly. Mothers' rating of their children's temperament appears to be correlated with the mothers' prenatal feelings about the pregnancy and about their own nurture when they were growing up.

In conclusion, the data presented here are consistent with other reports emphasizing the influence of various factors on maltreatment. However, there is no support for the idea that any one of the variables examined here is necessary or sufficient for maltreatment to occur. What appears to be supported is a semispecific multidimensional model of maltreatment. The model is multidimensional in that various characteristics are all viewed as important to the model (e.g., emotional, familial, physical, demographic, and sociological characteristics). The model is semispecific in that, within this model, one might be able to specify a set of variables that contribute to maltreatment, but there is no precise subset of variables within this overall set that precipitates maltreatment. This is instead a threshold model, such that if a parent/child family unit (or the group of individuals who live together) has a threshold number of the overall set of variables, then maltreatment may occur. The greater the number of variables represented in the family unit, the more severe the maltreatment might be. But no one variable seems necessary or sufficient at this point; only in concert or in sets do they seem to precipitate maltreatment. Potentially, different sets of variables could predispose a family toward different forms of maltreatment. For example, neglect may be more associated with poverty than NOFT or abuse (e.g., Giovannoni & Becerra, 1981), NOFT may be more associated with physical problems or immaturity on the part of the child (e.g. Vietze et al., 1980), and abuse may be more associated with parental problems (e.g., Baker et al., 1976; Smith, Hansen & Noble, 1975).

What is needed now is to establish the overall set of variables and the threshold level. Among the variables related to NOFT and abuse (but less so to neglect) are child's health, child's temperament, mother's nurture, and feelings about her pregnancy and her child. Insufficient data exist to delineate a threshold level at this time.

As stated in the introduction to this chapter, the group comparisons presented here, which are focused on child-health measures, are viewed as an example of the approach of finding people who have characteristics associated with maltreatment, but no documented maltreatment. This has been a first step in the direction of seeking to determine if any variable is necessary or sufficient for maltreatment to occur. To pursue this idea, many other variables need to be examined. Our next step will be to search our data banks for mothers who had low Maternal History Interview scores (low scores are associated with maltreatment) but who did not maltreat their children so that we can begin to ascertain what other characteristics were different in those mothers, in their children, or in their situations and environments.

If this semispecific theory is correct, one by one we could control for each factor known to be associated with maltreatment and find individuals who had that characteristic, but who did not maltreat. If some factor were found for which no people could be located who (a) had that factor and (b) did not maltreat, then the semispecific theory would be violated and would be incorrect. If no such factors were found, then sets of factors could be examined to ascertain the impact of the various combinations. The specific sets of factors examined should be guided by a theoretical formulation of which factors would be expected to potentiate each other and which might act as buffering or mitigating factors for each other. Belsky, Robins and Gamble (1984) have presented some well-thought-out ideas to guide the search. They have isolated, in global terms, which of the factors they believe are more central to outcome than others. Their ideas have been derived partly from theoretical perspectives, and partly from the limited empirical data that exists. Their formulation of these factors is fairly general, being separated into three major categories, and will probably need to be broken down into finer partitions. Nonetheless, it is a useful formulation and warrants consideration.

The implications of these ideas and data affect prediction issues more than they affect treatment issues. That is, once maltreatment has occurred, there are certain treatment issues that inevitably arise. On the other hand, prediction of maltreatment, which is now woefully inaccurate, should be enhanced by procedures that draw on complex sets of variables such as family members' health status, parents' childhood nurture, and present support systems for encouraging healthy family development. However, it may be the pattern of occurrence of the variables, rather than the specific variables, that sets the stage for maltreatment.

REFERENCES

Accardo, P.J. (Ed.) Failure to Thrive in Infancy and Early Childhood. Baltimore: University Park Press, 1982.

Altemeier, W.A., O'Connor, S., Vietze, P.M., Sandler, H.M. & Sherrod, K.B. Antecedents of child abuse. Journal of Pediatrics, 1982, 100, 823-829.

Altemeier, W.A., O'Connor, S., Sherrod, K.B. & Vietze, P.M. Prospective study of antecedents for nonorganic failure to thrive. Journal of Pediatrics, 1984, 106, 360-365a.

Altemeier, W.A., O'Connor, S., Vietze, P.M., Sandler, H.M. & Sherrod, K.B. Prediction of child abuse: A prospective study of feasibility. Child Abuse and Neglect, 1984, 8, 393-400b.

Altemeier, W.A., Vietze, P.M., Sherrod, K.B., Sandler, H.M., Falsey, S. & O'Connor, S. Prediction of child maltreatment during pregnancy. Journal of the American Academy of Child Psychiatry, 1979, 18, 205-218.

Baker, E., Castle, R.L., Hyman, C., Jones, C., Jones, R., Kerr, A. & Mitchell, R. At Risk. London: Routledge and Kegan Paul, 1976.

Belsky, J. Three theoretical models of child abuse: A critical review. Child Abuse and Neglect, 1978, 2, 37-49.

Belsky, J., Robins, E. & Gamble, W. The determinants of parental competence: Toward a conceptual theory. In M. Lewis (Ed.), Beyond the Dyad. New York: Plenum, 1984.

Benedek, T. Parenthood as a developmental phase. Journal of the American Psychoanalytic Association, 1959, 7, 389-417.

Bennie, E. & Sclare, A. The battered child syndrome. American Journal of Psychiatry, 1969, 125, 975-979.

Brazelton, T.B. Neonatal Behavioral Assessment Scale. Philadelphia: Lippincott, 1973.

Campos, J.J., Barrett, K.C., Lamb, M.E., Goldsmith, H.H. & Stenberg, C.

Socioemotional development. In M.M. Haith & J.J. Campos (Eds.), Handbook of Child Psychology (4th Ed., Vol. II). New York: J. Wiley & Sons, 1983.

Carey, W.B. A simplified approach for measuring infant temperament. Journal of Pediatrics, 1970, 69, 676-682.

Carey, W.B. Clinical applications of the Infant Temperament Measure. Journal of Pediatrics, 1972, 81, 823-831.

Carey, W.B. & McDevitt, S.C. Revision of the infant temperament question- naire. Pediatrics, 1978, 61, 735-739.

DeLissovoy, V. Child care by adolescent parents. Children Today, 1973, 35, 22-25.

Elster, A.B., McAnarney, E.R. & Lamb, M.E. Parental behavior of adolescent mothers. Pediatrics, 1983, 71, 494-503.

Fraiberg, S., Adelson, E. & Shapiro, V. Ghost in the nursery. Journal of the American Academy of Child Psychiatry, 1975, 14, 387-421.

Giovannoni, J.M. & Becerra, R.M. Defining Child Abuse. New York: The Free Press, 1979.

Green, W.H., Campbell, M. & David R. Psychosocial dwarfism: A critical review of the evidence. Journal of the American Academy of Child Psychiatry, 1984, 23, 39-48.

Hufton, I.W. & Oates, R.K. Nonorganic failure to thrive: A long-term follow-up. Pediatrics, 1977, 59, 73-77.

Little, D.L. Parent acceptance of routine use of the Carey and McDevitt Infant Temperament Questionnaire. Pediatrics, 1983, 71, 104-106.

Main, M. & Goldwyn, R. Predicting rejection of her infant from mother's representation of her own experience: Implications for the abused- abusing intergenerational cycle. Child Abuse and Neglect, 1984, 8, 203-217.

Money, J., Annecillo, C. & Kelley, J.F. Abuse-dwarfism syndrome: After rescue, statural and intellectual catchup growth correlate. Journal of Clinical Child Psychology, 1983, 12, 279-283.

Oates, K. Child Abuse: A Community Concern. New York: Brunner Mazel, 1982.

O'Connor, S., Vietze, P.M., Sherrod, K.B., Sandler, H.M. & Altemeier, W.A. Reduced incidence of parenting inadequacy following rooming in. Pediatrics, 1980, 66, 176-182.

O'Connor, S. & Vietze, P.M. Rooming-in as a factor in reducing parenting inadequacy. In K. Oates (Ed.), Child Abuse: A Community Concern. New York: Brunner/Mazel, 1982.

Parke, R.D. & Collmer, C.W. Child Abuse: An interdiscipliinary analysis. Review of Child Development Research, 1975, 5, 509-590.

Patton, B.G. & Gardner, L. (Eds.) Growth Failure in Maternal Deprivation. New York: Charles C. Thomas, 1963.

Pelton, L.H. The Social Context of Child Abuse and Neglect. New York: Human Sciences Press, 1981.

St. Clair, K. Neonatal assessment procedures: A historical review. Child Development, 1978, 49, 280-292.

Sherrod, K.B., O'Connor, S., Vietze, P.M. & Altemeier, W.A. Child health and maltreatment. Child Development, 1984, 55, 1174-1183.

Smith, S.M., Hansen, R. & Noble, S. Parents of battered children: A controlled study. In A.W. Franklin (Ed.) Concerning Child Abuse. London: Churchill Livingstone, 1975.

Spinetta, J. & Rigler, D. The child-abusing parent: A psychological review. Psychological Bulletin, 1972, 77, 296-304.

Steele, B. & Pollack, C. A psychiatric study of parents who abuse infants and small children. In R. Helfer & C. Kempe (Eds.) The Battered Child. Chicago: University of Chicago Press, 1968.

Vaughan, V.C., McKay, R.J. & Nelson, W.E. Nelson's Textbook of Pediatrics. Philadelphia: Saunders, 1975.

Werner, E.E. & Smith, R.S. Vulnerable But Invincible: A Study of Resilient Children. New York: McGraw-Hill, 1982.

White, J.L., Malcolm, R., Roper, K., Westphal, M.C. & Smith, C. Psycho-social and developmental factors in failure to thrive: One- to three-year followup. Developmental and Behavioral Pediatrics, 1981, 2, 112-114.

Appendix

Intercorrelations Between Scales of the Maternal History Interview

	Feelings/ Pregnancy	Support Systems	Nurturing	Stress	Personality	Parent Skills	Mother Stress	KDN
Var. 1 Feelings/ Pregnancy	1.0000 (1400) P = .000							
Var. 2 Support Systems	.3891 (1400) P = .000	1.0000 (1400) P = .000						
Var. 3 Nurturing	.1393 (1400) P = .000	.2101 (1400) P = .000	1.0000 (1400) P = .000					
Var. 4 Stress	.3845 (1400) P = .000	.3101 (1400) P = .000	.3036 (1400) P = .000	1.0000 (1400) P = .000				
Var. 5 Personality	.3432 (1400) P = .000	.5186 (1400) P = .000	.3680 (1400) P = .000	.5251 (1400) P = .000	1.0000 (1400) P = .000			
Var. 6 Parent Skills	.2512 (1400) P = .000	.2042 (1400) P = .000	.2094 (1400) P = .000	.1897 (1400) P = .000	.2956 (1400) P = .000	1.0000 (1400) P = .000		

	Preg.	Support Systems	Nurturing	Stress	Personality	Parent Skills	Mother Stress	KDN
Var. 7 Mother Stress	- .0753	- .1769	- .2440	- .3058	- .2312	- .1210	1.0000	
	(1400) P = .002	(1400) P = .000	(1400) P = .000	(1400) P = .000	(1400) P = .000	(1400) P = .000		
Var. 8 KDN	.0015	.0050	.0022	.0015	.0151	- .0066	.2561	1.0000
	(1400) P = .478	(1400) P = .425	(1400) P = .467	(1400) P = .477	(1400) P = .286	(1400) P = .403	(1400) P = .000	(1400) P = .000

A TRANSACTIONAL MODEL OF FAILURE TO THRIVE: A LOOK AT MISCLASSIFIED CASES

Robert H. Bradley and Patrick M. Casey

Center for Child Development and Education; and the
Department of Pediatrics
University of Arkansas

INTRODUCTION

In a previous study, we attempted to identify factors in the home
environments of non-organic failure-to-thrive (NOFT) infants that distinguish them from similar infants living in poor socioeconomic circumstances
(Casey, Bradley and Wortham, 1983). A case controlled design was employed.
NOFT children were matched with normally growing control children on age,
sex, race, family income, family size, maternal education, and marital
status of mother. Findings from the study indicated that mothers of NOFT
infants were less accepting (more punitive) towards their infants, less
responsive to their infants, and less well organized in caregiving. On the
other hand, NOFT infants were not living in less stimulating environments
nor under generally more adverse or stressful circumstances.

This study, while an improvement over most previous studies of NOFT
due to its control of general SES circumstances and family structure,
still possessed some of the weaknesses of previous studies: It was not
longitudinal. It included only a limited array of family environment and
child development measures; and it had a sample size that was too small to
permit some multivariate statistical analyses. Given these limitations,
it was not possible to fully develop or test the transactional model of
NOFT which is addressed in this chapter.

It is probably a fair assessment of the medical literature to
say that NOFT has generally been diagnosed in a negative way or by exclusion (i.e., no apparent organic cause for the growth retardation is
found). Typically, organic diseases are sought by the traditional medical
approach of history, physical examination and laboratory evaluation. When
all medical diagnoses are excluded, then the child's problem is ascribed
to non-organic causes. It is probably an equally fair assessment of the
psychological literature on NOFT to say that this condition has been
conceptualized in a limited way. For example, there has been little
appreciation for individual differences in developmental patterns, acknowledgement of normal social-cognitive-emotional development in infants, few
attempts to ascertain differing parental responses to atypical child
characteristics, and insufficient attention to transactional models. It
is not that some of these ideas have not been broached in the litera
ture; but rarely have they been encountered altogether and almost never
have they been operationalized in research designs and statistical treat-

ments of data (Vietze, Falsey, O'Connor, Sandler, Sherrod & Altemeier, 1980). The basic state of affairs in collateral literatures on maltreatment such as abuse and neglect and malnutrition is roughly the same as with FTT. However, several recent advances in the maltreatment literature may point the way to a fuller understanding and future research on NOFT (Egeland & Sroufe, 1981; Rizley & Cicchetti, 1981; Belsky, 1980, 1984; Aber & Zigler, 1981; Vietze et al., 1980; Schneider-Rosen & Cicchetti, 1984; Riccuitti & Dorman, 1982).

The purpose of this paper is to offer a reanalysis and reinterpretation of data from our study within a transactional model, and to provide some suggestions regarding future research studies into diagnosis and treatment of NOFT. More specifically, an attempt is made to classify children as NOFT on the basis of their family environment, and to analyze misclassifications for clues toward a more complete organizational developmental model of this condition.

At present, transactional models offer a generic framework within which to view NOFT. A transactional model of NOFT conceptualizes synergistic interactions of factors at several levels with the central cause of NOFT viewed as a breakdown in parent-child interaction. In the maladapted parent-child interaction, the parent does not read and respond to the infant appropriately, and the infant has difficulty in eliciting attention and appropriate care from the parent. This bi-directional problem results in nutritional and nurturing deficiencies which cause NOFT. However, current transactional models are not sufficiently well delineated so that accurate diagnoses can be made using them.

Linking NOFT to Collateral Areas of Maltreatment

Aber and Zigler (1981) discuss difficulties in identifying maltreatment of children. They suggest that part of the difficulty arises in confusion of the concepts "emotional mistreatment" and "emotional damage." Mistreatment focuses on parental behavior while emotional damage focuses on developmental sequelae in the child. They go on to suggest that a second type of difficulty arises even after one has accepted "emotional damage" as the primary characteristic of maltreatment. Specifically, "...it is easier to specify in general theoretical fashion an overarching psychological construct (such as emotional damage)... than it is to operationalize the construct so that it can be used...(p. 17)." A review of the literature pertaining to NOFT indicates that both types of difficulties obtain with the definition and, hence, diagnosis of NOFT.

Cicchetti and Rizley (1981) approach the problem of defining and studying maltreatment a bit differently. They contend that "...the range of the phenomena covered by the term (maltreatment) is enormously varied (p. 35)." They argue that maltreatment varies in the way it manifests itself, etiology, and response to treatment. Again, there would appear to be parallels with NOFT. Although patterns of "maternal rejection" and "maternal deprivation" have frequently been referred to as causative of NOFT, clinical and empirical investigations have not shown consistent evidence that such patterns are present for most NOFT infants. Furthermore, although "response to hospitalization" is frequently used in the diagnosis of NOFT, the absence of weight gain in the hospital does not always indicate an organic problem, nor the presence of weight gain always preclude one. Perhaps most importantly, the transactional nature of NOFT is not exemplified in most attempts at medical diagnosis. This issue has been cogently presented with regard to the broad spectrum of maltreatment by Cicchetti and Braunwald (in press).

"...very few investigators have focused on theoretically meaningful, stage-salient tasks of socio-emotional
development of maltreated children during infancy and early
childhood. Abnormalities in the development of affective
communication between infants and caretakers have been
studied by Gaensbauer and his colleagues. Gaensbauer and
Sands (1979) identified six patterns of distorted affective
communications from infant to caretaker, including affective withdrawal, lack of pleasure, inconsistency/unpredic-
tability, shallowness, ambivalence/ambiguity, and negative
affective communications (e.g., distress, anger, sadness).
In a subsequent study , Gaensbauer, Mrazek, and Harmon
(1980) delineated four affective patterns that appeared to
be relatively consistent and that would represent the predominant communicative pattern of a mother-infant dyad.
These four groups were labelled as developmentally and
affectively retarded (characterized by lack of social responsiveness, emotional blunting and inattentiveness to the
environment), depressed (exhibiting inhibition, withdrawal,
aimless quality of play, and sad and depressed facial
expressions), ambivalent/affectively labile (showing sudden
shifts from engagement and pleasure to withdrawal and
anger), and angry (characteriazed by active, disorganized
play and low frustration tolerance, with frequent angry
outbursts). While the direction of causality of these
atypical communication patterns remains ambiguous, it is
apparent that deviant styles of affective displays, decreased responsivity and reciprocal interactions, aberra-
tions in the patterns of initiating, maintaining, or terminating interaction, and deviations in the capacity to
express emotional states, tend to characterize the dyad.
The work of Frodi and Lamb (1980) indicates that maltreating
parents have different psychological responses to the cries
of infants, thereby suggesting that these parents are less
effective than non-maltreating parents in responding to the
affective expressions of their infants. However, the
mutually reinforcing nature of the inadequacies in the
infant's communicative system, the differential impact of
emotional displays upon contingent, sensitive, responsiveness of the caregiver, may serve to perpetuate the deviant
patterns of interaction in this dyad and result in atypical
developmental outcomes in the emotional and behavioral
repertoire of the maltreating infant. (p. 5-6)"

Although the social and communicative competencies of NOFT infants
have not been well documented, the potential value of considering the
diagnosis and treatment of NOFT within the more general framework of
maltreatment may be seen in two recent studies. Sherrod, O'Connor, Vietze
and Altemeier (1984) reported a follow-up of 11 abused, 31 NOFT, 14 neglected, and 24 control families who were part of a prospective study in
Nashville. Earlier analyses had shown that 77% of those identified as
NOFT were judged "at risk" for maltreatment based on interviews with
mother during pregnancy. For all children, a record of problems was kept.
Outcomes for NOFT infants were similar -- albeit not quite as pronounced
-- to outcomes for abused children. Specifically, they had more illnesses,
a higher rate of family dysfunction, more hospitalizations, and a higher
rate of anatomical anomalies.

The Minnesota Mother-Child Project was also prospective in design
(Egeland & Sroufe, 1981). The design of the study was predicated on the
following generalizations from the maltreatment literature: 1) Maltreated

children often come from environments that are overcrowded and lacking in stimulation. 2) Parent-child relations among maltreated children are characterized by harsh treatment and a lack of praise and encouragement. 3) Patterns of cognitive development among abused children are quite varied. 4) Patterns of socio-emotional development among abused children are highly varied. 5) Most investigators have not attempted to define subgroups of abuse and maltreatment within the context of the broader caretaking environment. Some abused children are also physically and emotionally neglected; some are rejected, abandoned, or cared for in an inconsistent manner. 6) The relations between maltreatment and specific outcomes are not likely to be simple linear ones, but are cumulative and mediated by the child's developmental level.

For purposes of their longitudinal investigation, Egeland, Sroufe and their colleagues concentrated on 4 maltreatment groups: physically abusive, hostile/verbally abusive, psychologically unavailable, and neglectful. Although it was possible to separate the 4 groups according to patterns of parental behavior, there was considerable overlap between groups on parenting dimensions. Many families displayed 2 or more maltreating styles. Egeland and Sroufe (1981) felt that the most important outcome of the Minnesota Mother-Child Project was "...establishing the particular consequences of abuse and broadening the conception of maltreatment (p. 88-89)." They characterized the behavior of the groups as follows: (1) hostile and verbally abusive which included disruptions in attachment followed by frustration, anger and non-compliance; (2) psychologically unavailable defined as anxious/avoidant patterns of attachment, declining participation in feeding and play situations, continuous declines in cognitive and social functioning, low threshold and emotional unresponsiveness; (3) neglectful (without physical abuse) which included early anxious/resistent attachment followed by anxious/avoidant attachment, anger, frustration, whining, and low stress tolerance.

Although the Minnesota Project has begun to identify several maltreatment patterns (in terms of parenting behaviors and infant developmental sequelae), Cicchetti and Rizley's (1981) statement that maltreated children exhibit a wide variety of developmental disabilities seems an accurate summary of available research. Patterns of maltreatment result from a multiplicity of factors and there is clear evidence for individual patterns of effects. For example, Giovannoni and Becerra (1979) found FTT often coincided with gross neglect. Egeland and Sroufe (1981) found that children who were neglected or who were both neglected and abused tended to have anxious/avoidant attachments and low coping skills. They also found that children whose parents were extremely psychologically unavailable showed declining interest in feeding and playing. Thus, NOFT may result from several different transactional patterns or their combinations: gross neglect where insufficient food is given; active rejection where food is witheld; severe psychological unavailability where the child gradually loses appetite; temperamental factors which make the child hard to feed and which may become compounded if a parent is incompetent due to ignorance, stress, or emotional illness. A transactional model can take account of many such factors and assist in a more accurate diagnosis of NOFT. Of course, given the multiplicity of factors potentially involved and the timing of assessments, some misclassification is bound to occur.

METHOD

Sample

Forty-six children (23 NOFT, 23 non-FTT) and their families participated in the study. NOFT infants were obtained from the Arkansas

Children's Hospital Growth and Development Clinic. NOFT was defined using the following criteria: 1) age greater than 12 weeks; 2) weight below the third percentile corrected for gestational age and/or weight percentile declined over 2 standard deviations over time; 3) no evidence of organ system disease; and 4) residence within 30 miles of the hospital. All of the children were initially evaluated in the out-patient setting. Most had not been hospitalized, and none was hospitalized for more than a week. Their participation was requested at the time of the first clinic visit. No patient refused to participate.

The Growth and Development Clinic operates as a diagnostic and management unit for FTT children who are evaluated and given appropriate follow-up by a small team that consists of general developmental pediatrics, nursing, social work, and nutrition personnel.

An attempt was made to match each of the 23 NOFT infants to a child with normal weight for age according to age, race, sex, maternal education, family income, and household crowdedness. Precise matches were accomplished for 18 of the 23 NOFT infants; five infants matched in fewer than all six criteria. Eight non-FTT children were obtained from the Growth and Development Clinic, the remaining 15 were obtained using chart review from a community clinic.

Table 1 displays infant characteristics by group. Fifty-seven percent were male, and 25% were Caucasian in both groups. The mean age at time of diagnosis was 16 months. Family characteristics for NOFT and non-FTT groups are also displayed in Table 1. There were no significant differences in any of these variables. Mean maternal age and education were nearly identical in the two groups. Although the mean family income was slightly (though not statistically) lower in the NOFT group, the per capita income was somewhat higher for the non-FTT families.

Instrumentation

Home Inventory. An assistant naive to infant growth rate visited the homes of participating children within three weeks after the child was

Table 1

Infant and Family Characteristics for
Non-organic Failure to Thrive and Matched Controls

Infant Characteristics	FTT	Control
Mean % weight for age	73%	95%
Mean % length for age	94%	99%
% Male	57%	57%
% Caucasian	26%	26%
% Premature	13%	22%
Mean age at time of diagnosis (months)	16.4	16.9

Family Characteristics		
Mean maternal age (years)	24.7	24.8
Mean maternal education (years)	11.3	10.9
Mean income (dollars)	$5451	$6188
Per capita income (dollars)	$1273	$1170
Household crowdedness (# people)	4.5	5.4
% Married	35%	48%

identified. The Home Observation for Measurement of the Environment (HOME) Inventory was completed by this assistant in order to assess the quality of physical, cognitive, social, and emotional support available to the infant in the home environment (Caldwell & Bradley, 1984). Information needed to score the Home Inventory was obtained through a combination of observation and interview with the infant's primary caregiver. The HOME Inventory contains 45 items that are clustered in 6 subscales: 1) emotional and verbal responsivity of mother; 2) acceptance of child; 3) organization of the environment; 4) provision of appropriate play materials; 5) maternal involvement with child; and 6) variety in daily stimulation.

Life Events Record. The assistant also completed the Life Events Record for Preschool Children (LER) during the home visit (Coddington, 1972). This is an interview based inventory which attempts to quantitate the amount of psychological re-adjustments required by the child in order to cope with events occuring in the family over the previous year. The LER contains 30 items, each of which catalogs an event that necessitates some readjustment on the part of the child. Items are weighted in life change units according to the amount of adjustment required. The range is from 21 points (Has your money situation changed?) to 89 points (Has there been a death of a parent?).

RESULTS

Even though the number of children was small (N=46), a multiple discriminant analysis was performed using the 6 subscales from HOME and the LER in an effort to differentiate between NOFT and control infants. It was hoped that this statistical procedure might help identify key microenvironmental factors within the overall transactional model as characteristic in many cases of NOFT. This set of seven environmental variables was able to provide significant separation between the two groups (X^2 =14.23, $\underline{df}$=7, $\underline{p}$<.05). While the purpose of the study was not to "predict" NOFT, as might be done in a subsequent sample using the discriminant coefficients generated here, the number of correct classifications was examined. Thirty-three of the 46 infants were correctly placed into NOFT or control groups with an overall correct identification rate of 72%. Outcomes from the discriminant analysis can be seen in the four-fold Table 2.

In determining the placement of the 46 participants into groups, the factors given greatest weight were Maternal Responsivity, Acceptance of

Table 2

Classification of FTT and Controls
Using HOME Inventory and Life Events Record

Actual Condition	Classification Based on Environment	
	Failure to Thrive	Control
Failure to Thrive	16	7
Control	6	17

(N=46; X^2 = 14.23, p <.05 df = 1)

112

Child, and Organization of the Environment from the HOME Inventory. However, a discriminant analysis only provides the single best linear fit to the data, whereas a transactional model assumes that a simple linear combination of variables rarely provides a good fit to all the data. Indeed, a discriminant analysis done on a small group risks capitalizing on some chance difference between groups and, thus, erroneously categorizing certain individual cases. To help compensate for this limitation in the original study, an examination was made of the individuals who were not correctly placed using the discriminant function coefficients.

The first step taken in evaluating cases that were misclassified using the discriminant functions was to reclassify all cases using more stringent criteria. Since 2-group discriminant function analysis "places" cases into the more probable of two groups, individuals are assigned to whichever of the two groups has the higher probability -- even if the probability of membership in Group A is only 51% versus 49% for Group B. Given the fact that under such liberal case assignment even small measurement errors could result in erroneously assigning a person to NOFT or non-FTT groups, it was decided that more rigorous criteria for assignment might result in a clearer delineation of home environmental factors related to NOFT. Thus, the 46 infants were "reassigned" to one of three categories based on their discriminant function scores: (1) NOFT if the probability of being NOFT was 60% or greater; (2) Control if the probability of being non-FTT was 60% or greater; and (3) Uncertain if the probability for membership in NOFT and Control was less than 60%. Results of the reassignment are displayed in Table 3.

Of the 23 NOFT children, 15 were placed in the NOFT group with a probability of 60% or higher using their discriminant function scores. Similarly, 15 of 23 Controls were accurately placed using discriminant scores. The remaining 8 Controls, together with 4 NOFT infants, were placed in the Uncertain category. Four NOFT infants were "reassigned" to the Control category even when the more stringent 60% criterion was used.

All 4 of the NOFT children whose discriminant scores placed them in the Uncertain category had low scores on Variety of Stimulation, only 1 mother had completed high school, 3 of 4 had high life stress scores, 3 of 4 had at least 3 siblings, and half had no fathers living in the home. Two of the 4 reassigned to Uncertain status had low scores on Acceptance of Child, but were simply not low enough to be placed in the NOFT category with 60% probability.

Table 3

Classification of FTT and Controls
Using HOME Inventory and Life Events Record

Actual Condition	Classification Based On Environment		
	Failure to Thrive	Uncertain	Control
Failure to Thrive	15	4	4
Control	0	8	15

$$(N=46, \ X^2 = 22.69, \ p < .001 \quad df = 2)$$

Three of the 4 NOFT infants who were reassigned to the Control category on the basis of their discriminant scores presented an essentially coherent picture. They all had extremely low scores on both Variety of Stimulation ($\underline{M}$=1.00) and Maternal Involvement ($\underline{M}$=0.67). All 3 had unmarried mothers and several siblings ($\underline{M}$=3.3). While their scores on the home environment subscales most frequently characterized NOFTs (Maternal Responsivity, Acceptance of Child, Organization of the Environment) were not in the low range of scores that classified them as NOFT, They were not high and their scores on Acceptance of Child were marginal ($\underline{M}$=5.3). In essence, the mothers of these three NOFT infants did not appear so much hostile and grossly unresponsive as they were extremely unstimulating. Additionally, these 3 NOFT infants had few other sources of social or physical stimulation, except perhaps through siblings. Even the number of play materials available to them tended to be few ($\underline{M}$=4.3).

The remaining NOFT child who was reassigned to Control status on the basis of the more stringent criterion was almost certainly not growth retarded due to inadequate parenting. The mother, while young and unmarried, was experiencing only a moderate amount of stress, perhaps due to the birth of her second child. Scores on HOME subscale were uniformly high. Family income, while low, was slightly above mean for the total group and was roughly twice the per capita dollars available. Moreover, the child himself barely fell into the FTT range using our selection criteria since he was 77% or normal weight for age and 92% of normal height.

Of the 8 normally growing control children initially classified as NOFT (using the less stringent 50% criterion), none reached the more stringent 60% criterion for reassignment to NOFT. This was due to the fact that all had scores on Maternal Responsivity, Acceptance of Child, and Organization of the Environment that were marginal to slightly above. Neither did any of the non-FTT misclassifications have home environment profiles like the three true NOFTs reassigned to the Control category using the more stringent criterion. In only 3 of the 8 families did the mother show extremely low involvement with the child. In only 1 family was both Maternal Involvement and Variety of Stimulation low; but even there, the mother was better educated, there were more toys available, and fewer siblings in the family than for the 3 true NOFTs. Finally, 1 of the 8 controls initially classified as NOFT was only 81% of average weight for age, thus, barely missing the cut-off used for selecting FTTs.

DISCUSSION

Findings from this study would appear to offer support for a transactional model for NOFT briefly described in our earlier report (Casey, Bradley & Wortham, 1983) (i.e., synergistic interactions of factors at several levels with the central cause reflecting inadequacies in the social and physical aspects of the home environment). Furthermore, the findings appear to be generally in line with the organizational/developmental model for maltreatment detailed in Cicchetti and Rizley (1981). There appears to be no single set of factors or simple combination of factors that routinely results in NOFT. In the case of NOFT, the likelihood of significant growth retardation appears determined by extremes within two categories of factors which may be either temporary or enduring in nature. The result may be better understood as depicted in the following 4-fold table from Cicchetti and Rizley (1981).

As defined by Cicchetti and Rizley (1981), potentiating factors are those which increase the probability of maltreatment. Compensatory factors, by contrast, are those which decrease the probability of maltreatment.

Table 4

Risk Factors for Child Maltreatment

Temporal Dimension	Impact on Probability of Maltreatment	
	Potentiating Factors	Compensatory Factors
Enduring Factors	Vulnerability Factors: enduring factors or conditions which increase risk.	Protective Factors: enduring conditions or attributes which decrease risk.
Transient Factors	Challengers: transient but significant stresses.	Buffers: transient conditions which act as buffers against transient increases in stress or challenge.

From our data, potentiating factors for NOFT may include having a primary caregiver who is extremely unresponsive (8 of 10 infants who had Maternal Responsivity scores $\leq$ 6 were true NOFTs). Another potentiating factor seems to be a caregiver who is extremely harsh (all children whose Acceptance of Child scores were $\leq$ 4 were true NOFTs; 14 of 21 children whose Acceptance of Child scores were <6 were true NOFTs and 3 others had weights that were between 80% and 85% of average for age). A third potentiating factor may be gross understimulation (12 of 20 children who had Maternal Involvement scores $\leq$ 3 and Variety of Stimulation scores $\leq$ 3 were true NOFTs, 3 more had weights that were only 80% to 85% of normal for age). Only 3 of 23 NOFT infants did not manifest one or more of these three potentiating factors. However, the patterns also fit 5 infants with weights between 80 and 85 percent of average for age and 5 whose weight was clearly in the normal range. Consequently, the false positive rate using these factors to diagnose NOFT is either 33% or 17%, depending on how stringent the criteria are set.

It was clear that maternal education, number of children in the family, family income, and marital status of the primary caregiver were also potentiating factors. However, most families were from impoverished backgrounds so the extent to which these factors contributed to NOFT could not be clearly determined.

Given the generally impoverished circumstances of most participants, clues regarding "compensatory" factors were less easily distinguished. Among the 8 families where control children were initially classified as NOFT on the basis of their discriminant function scores, most came from small families (only 2 of 8 had as many as 6 members). Thus, being from a small family seems to afford some degree of protection from NOFT even when parenting is not optimal. Most of the misclassified control infants also came from homes that had not experienced a high level of disruption and stress over the past year. Unfortunately, no social support information was gathered for the families; thus, the potential value of social support as a compensatory factor could not be determined -- except perhaps in a rather indirect manner (3 of the 4 true NOFTs who were reassigned to the Control category using the 60% criterion not only had uninvolved mothers, but no regular involvement from other adults either -- the family was largely isolated from social involvement).

In sum, the discriminant function analysis along with the post hoc analysis of misclassifications suggests a number of potentiating factors in the home environments of NOFT infants, and a few compensatory factors as well. Nonetheless, there were 3 or 4 cases where none of the most typical patterns of environment fit the actual status of the infant. Thus, a transactional (or general systems) model that includes a number of factors from the micro-environment, yet retains some level of indeterminancy, appears to most adequately explain the current findings. The findings are reasonably consistent with those of Vietze and his colleagues (Vietze et al., 1980; Sherrod et al., 1984) given the considerable differences in timing of measurements for the two studies. An important addition to the model (and ultimately to the diagnosis of NOFT) may be some early measures of emotional and communciative functioning (Cicchetti & Braunwald, in press; Egeland & Sroufe, 1981; Gaensbauer, et al., 1980). At this point, it is important to offer a caveat concerning the results obtained in the study: the type of design and analysis used in the study do not -- strictly speaking -- permit one to conclude that any of the micro-environmental factors associated with NOFT actually "cause" or "potentiate" NOFT. Nonetheless, the findings provide useful hypotheses for a prospective, longitudinal study.

With regard to potential value of including some measures of early social, emotional, or communicative functioning in a model of NOFT, the results of the Minnesota Mother-Child Project are interesting to re-examine briefly (Egeland & Sroufe, 1981). Most particularly, infants who experienced maltreatment very often manifested non-optimal attachment patterns. In some cases, there were clear avoidance responses; in others there were less obvious "lack of effective approaches." Evidence of anger and low frustration tolerance was also observed in many maltreated infants. Infants who were seriously neglected often developed patterns of whining as they grew older and a decreased ability to cope. Those infants who had psychologically unavailable mothers showed devastating emotional consequences including decreased eating and playing, lack of emotional responsiveness, etc. These patterns of developmentally inadequate emotional/communicative functioning may both accompany growth retardation in many cases and also precipitate patterns of parental response that lead to continued problems with growth. Future investigations which include early measures of emotional development in a longitudinal design may help to clarify the complex organizational relationship between socio-emotional, cognitive and physical development as they relate to patterns of experience in the home environment.

Another potential useful addition to future studies of NOFT would be to place them in the transactional process model of parenting described by Belsky (1984). The Belsky model has several advantages from the standpoint of improved diagnosis of NOFT. Most importantly, it conceptualizes child development (including growth retardation) as a joint function of parental history, child characteristics, and the fmaily context of stresses and supports. It also delineates the dynamic interplay among personal and social factors as they relate to parenting. This model, with perhaps two additions (i.e., the physical environment and broader family dynamics) might usefully guide future research and diagnostic interpretations. These last two factors, while not assumed to be as salient as direct parenting from primary caregivers, nonetheless, are of potential significance. Three of the 4 misclassified NOFTs had very unstimulating environments (See also Dennis, 1973 and Skeels and Dye, 1939) -- nor was there any effective involvement from family members other than parents.

It is of interest to place these considerations of a transactional model in a clinical perspective. As described earlier, the typical diagnostic process in delineating organic from nonorganic FTT is focused

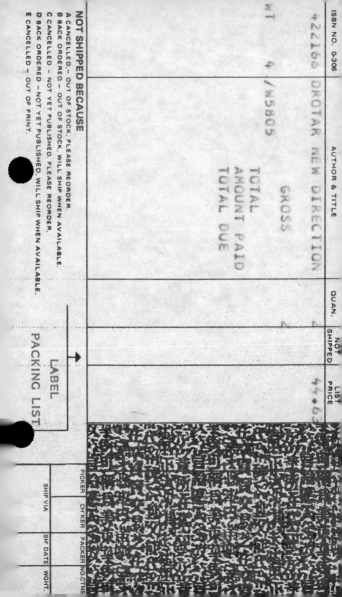

solely on the child. As a result, the diagnosis of NOFT is arrived in a negative way, by a process of eliminating various medical diseases. A more positive approach in diagnosis would account for the 3 categories of influence on parenting as described by Belsky (1984). We were able to accurately place most of our patients by using only a portion of the parenting process model. Further refinement of such a positive diagnostic model should occur as more research reports refine relevant subcategories of the transactional process.

Finally, it is important to recognize that the diagnosis of FTT is based on weight and height measurements. Some children with deviations from the expected growth pattern may not have an environmental problem at all and may be erroneously labeled as NOFT after the process of elimination described above. It should be noted that most clinical reports of FTT children have found no physical or environmental basis for below expected growth in 5% to 20% of the cases. A transient alteration in growth may be normal for this subgroup.

One potentially useful approach to future research on NOFT maybe to overlay the scheme of risk factors (potentiating vs. compensatory, enduring vs. transient) offered by Cicchetti and Rizley (1981) for child maltreatment on Belsky's (1984) process model of parenting (with the addition of the physical home environment and certain limited aspects of the broader family dynamics -- most particularly, interactions between the infant and other household members). For each of the categories in the expanded model of parenting, an attempt should be made to specify factors from the four cells in Cicchetti and Rizley's scheme (vulnerability factors, protective factors, challengers, buffers) that appear salient for NOFT -- with greatest emphasis on factors that are connected to or supportive of nutritional intake. The maltreatment literature in particular and the infancy literature in general suggest a broad array of child characteristics that should perhaps be considered for investigation. These include "state" factors (e.g. alertness), temperamental or style factors (e.g. mood, biological regularity), competence factors (e.g. social skills, communicative skills, emotional readiness), and motivational factors (e.g. person orientation, interest in the environment, refusal to cooperate). The use of the full model is probably not feasible within the limitations of most studies. However, the model may offer a fruitful means of structuring individual studies and in developing specific hypotheses to be tested.

Results from this study and other studies of maltreated children indicate that systematic observations of the child's home environment are likely to be productive in the diagnosis of NOFT. Structured interviews and clinic observations, while helpful, do not reveal the "texture" of actual interactions and events in the home environment. Bronfenbrenner (1979) decries the use of such procedures in child development research, arguing that the distortions involved in the procedures often obscure the actual flow and meaning of actions. As importantly, visitations to the home offer the opportunity of observing unintended events, objects or transactions that may be more significant than those addressed in clinical settings. A number of reliable, relatively easy-to-use instruments exist for the assessment of the home environment (Bradley & Caldwell, 1981; Bradley, in press). And, though home visits entail costs in terms of time and money, the cost may be easily justified by the usefulness of the information.

REFERENCES

Aber, J. & Zigler, E. Developmental considerations in the definition of child maltreatment. In R. Rizley & D. Cicchetti (eds.), Developmental Perspectives on Child Maltreatment. San Francisco: Jossey-Bass, 1981.

Belsky, J. Child maltreatment: An ecological integration. American Psychologist, 1980, 35, 320-335.

Belsky, J. The determinants of parenting: A process model. Child Development, 1984, 55, 83-96.

Bradley, R. Assessing the family environment of young children. In H. Fitzgerald, B. Lester & M. Yogman (Eds.), Theory and Research in Behavioral Pediatrics, Vol. 3. New York: Plenum (in press).

Bradley, R. & Caldwell, B. Pediatric usefulness of home assessment. In B. Camp (Ed.), Advances in Behavioral Pediatrics, Vol. 2. Greenwich, CT: JAI Press, 1981.

Bronfenbrenner, U. Ecological validity in research on human development. Paper presented at the Annual Meeting of the American Educational Research Association. Washington, D.C., 1976.

Caldwell, B. & Bradley, R. Home Observation for Measurement of the Environment. University of Arkansas at Little Rock, 1984.

Casey, P., Bradley, R. & Wortham, B. Social and non-social home environments of children with non-organic failure to thrive. Pediatrics, 1984, 73, 348-353.

Cicchetti, D. & Braunwald, K. An organizational approach to the study of maltreated infants. Journal of Infant Mental Health, 1984, 5, 172-183.

Coddington, R. The significance of life events on the etiologic factors in diseases of children - a study of a normal population. Journal of Psychosomatic Research, 1972, 16, 205-213.

Dennis, W. Children of the Creche. New York: Appleton-Century-Crofts, 1973.

Egeland, B. & Sroufe, A. Developmental sequelae of maltreatment in infancy. In R. Rizley & D. Cicchetti (Eds.), Developmental Perspectives on Child Maltreatment. San Francisco: Jossey-Bass, 1981.

Frodi, A. & Lamb, M. Child abuser's responses to infant smiles and cries. Child Development, 1980, 51, 238-241.

Gaensbauer, T., Mrazek, D. & Harmon, R. Affective behavior patterns in abused and/or neglected infants. In N. Freud (Ed.), The Understanding and Prevention of Child Abuse: Psychological Approaches. London: Concord Press, 1980.

Gaensbauer, T. & Sands, K. Distorted affective communication in abused/neglected infants and their potential impact on caretakers. American Journal of Child Psychiatry, 1979, 18, 236-250.

Giovannoni, J. & Becerra, R. Defining Child Abuse. New York: Free Press, 1979.

Ricciutti, H. Interaction of multiple risk factors contributing to high risk parenting. In V. Sassenrath (Ed.), Minimizing High Risk Parenting. New York: Johnson & Johnson Baby Products Co., 1983.

Rizley, R. & Cicchetti, D. Developmental Perspectives on Child Maltreatment. San Francisco: Jossey-Bass, 1981.

Schneider-Rosen, K. & Cicchetti, D. The relationship between affect and cognition in maltreated infants: Quality of attachment and development of visual self-recognition. Child Development, 1984, 55, 648-658.

Sherrod, K., O'Connor, S., Vietze, P. & Altemeier, W. Child health and maltreatment. Child Development, 1984, 55, 1174-1183.

Skeels, H. & Dye, H. A study of the effects of differential stimulation on mentally retarded children. American Journal of Mental Retardation, 1939, 44, 114-136.

Vietze, P., Falsey, S., O'Connor, S., Sandler, H., Sherrod, K. & Altemeier, W. Newborn behavioral and interactional characteristics of nonorganic failure-to-thrive infants. In T. Field (Ed.), High Risk Infants and Children: Adult and Peer Interactions. New York: Academic Press, 1980.

EARLY PREVENTIVE INTERVENTION IN FAILURE TO THRIVE: METHODS AND

PRELIMINARY OUTCOME*

Dennis Drotar, Charles A. Malone, Linda Devost, Corrine
Brickell, Carole Mantz-Clumpner, Judy Negray, Mariel Wallace,
Janice Woychik, Betsy Wyatt, Debby Eckerle, Marcy Bush, Mary
Ann Finlon, Debby El-Amin, Michael Nowak, Jackie Satola, John
Pallotta

Case Western Reserve University School of Medicine

The Infant Growth Project was designed to study the effects of preventive psychosocial intervention on the physical growth and psychological
development of infants diagnosed with environmentally-based FTT during a
pediatric hospitalization in their first year of life. This chapter describes the evolution of our project and preliminary findings concerning
children's psychological status and physical growth from study intake
through 24 months. In this report, emphasis is placed on the pragmatic
difficulties involved in conducting research with FTT children and the
implications for future research with this high-risk population.

EVOLUTION OF THE PROJECT

Obstacles to Comprehensive Hospital-Based Care

Clinical experiences over a number of years (Drotar, 1975; Drotar &
Malone, 1982 a, b) underscored the difficulties involved in providing
comprehensive psychosocial care for FTT children and their families in a
tertiary care hospital setting. In our hospital, children hospitalized for
envrionmentally-based FTT were often referred for psychological evaluation
following completion of physical diagnostic tests. However, pressures for
hospital discharge limited the nature and scope of psychological evaluation
and required us to make difficult decisions concerning disposition in the
absence of sufficient information about the child's family situation. The
pressures of clinical care also affected our capacity to engage in productive encounters with families, who were themselves under great psychological
constraint. For example, the parents of FTT infants were often unprepared
for the child's hospital admission. The sense of threat that parents experienced from the scrutiny of hospital staff and child's weight gain was often
considerable (Leonard, Rhymes & Solnit, 1966). In addition, beleaugered as
they were by the demands of other patients and their families, medical and

*The work described in the present research was funded by the Cleveland
Foundation and the National Institute of Mental Health Applied Research
#35220 and Preventive Research Center #30274.

nursing staff could not generally spend the time needed to inform highly-stressed family members about the child's physical and psychological status or to provide support needed by parents to cope with the considerable emotional demands of hospitalization. The fact that some families did not come into the hospital frequently also limited the extent of our involvement with them. As a consequence, it was not uncommon for communication between families of FTT infants and hospital staff to be seriously disrupted.

In addition to the difficulties of parent-staff communication associated with hospital-based care, the disjuncture between hospital and community based services posed considerable obstacles to productive intervention. Planning for adequate intervention following the hospitalization was often given short shrift. Moreover, even when appropriate follow-up services such as visiting nurse were available, it was often difficult to coordinate them with hospital-based services. In some instances, the severity of family problems outstripped available community services. As a consequence, it was not uncommon in our setting for FTT children to be discharged without after-care plans which addressed the problems that gave rise to the FTT (Drotar et al., 1981).

Structuring an Alternative Pattern of Care

We wondered whether the problems of delivering comprehensive psycho-social care to FTT children and their families might not contribute in some instances to chronic FTT, rehospitalization, and/or compromised long-term psychological outcomes. Further, we reasoned that it might be possible to prevent some of the chronic sequelae of FTT by restructuring care to provide greater continuity following hospitalization and to help family members ameliorate the problems which had given rise to the FTT. In our restructured model of care, hospitalization was construed as an initial phase of intervention which would provide: (1) diagnostic clarification of FTT, including the degree of nutritional deficit and the relative importance of various organic contributions; (2) treatment of acute physical symptoms and nutritional deficits; and (3) a setting in which to underscore the seriousness of the child's problem to family members and establish a relationship on which to base subsequent home-based intervention.

In designing this model of care, we recognized that the choice of hospitalization as a starting point for intervention and sample selection has a number of disadvantages and might not be applicable to many communities. From the standpoint of identifying children before the child's FTT becomes severe, the ambulatory setting is a more ideal setting for early intervention (Casey, Wortham & Nelson, in press; Berkowitz, this volume). However, in our community, specialized ambulatory services for the diagnosis and treatment of FTT did not exist. Hospitalization is a primary setting in which to identify FTT children who are at potential long-term psychologic risk (Drotar, Malone & Negray, 1979; Oates & Hufton, 1977; Oates, Peacock & Forest, 1985).

Selection of the home visit as a modality of intervention following hospitalization was predicated on clinical impressions that like other highly stressed families (Maybanks & Bryce, 1983), the families of FTT infants would not make use of traditional mental health services. The time and expense of outreach intervention was justified on the basis of the risk to the child. In addition, our pilot work indicated that outreach would be accepted by most families of FTT infants (Drotar & Malone, 1982a). At the time we began our project, Fraiberg and her coworkers (1980) had already established a precedent for productive use of the home visit in their pioneering infant mental health project.

Selection Criteria

Our major interest was in identifying a population of FTT infants in which the primary contributing factors were environmental rather than organic. The lack of valid independent behavioral criteria for envirionmental FTT (Kotelchuck, 1980) require that this diagnosis be made via careful medical judgement. Selection criteria for environmental FTT were based on recommendations of an interdisciplinary committee of experienced pediatric clinicians and researchers at our setting and are consistent with recommendations at the NIMH conference which stimulated the present volume. Study criteria and rationale were as follows:

1) Weight at or below the fifth percentile based on age expectations on National Center for Health Statistics (NCHS) norms (Hammill et al., 1979) and less weight than expected for length.

2) Deceleration in rate of weight gain from birth to study intake.

3) No identifiable organic cause for growth retardation or chronic illness from detailed medical history, physical exam, and laboratory analysis which always included complete blood count (CBC) and urinalysis. In addition, specialized tests (e.g., sweat chloride, thyroid, barium swallow) were given to delineate the etiology of other symptoms, e.g. vomiting, infections in accord with principles of pediatric management (Bithoney & Rathbun, 1983).

4) Weight gain (1-2 ounces per day) in the hospital over a period of at least 3 to 5 days. This criterion is recommended by Schmitt (1970) to demonstrate capacity to gain weight in another environment.

5) Birth weight of at least 1500 grams and weight appropriate for gestational age. "Small for dates" generally grow at slower than normal rates and have a higher risk for developmental problems were excluded (Lester et al., 1976). At the time of our study, little was known about the longer term growth patterns of very low birth weight infants. However, our pediatric consultants recommended inclusion of healthy, larger prematures based on clinical estimates and objective assessments (Dubowitz et al., 1970) to enhance the generalizability of findings. Physical growth of premature infants who eventually failed to thrive was assessed in reference to standards for gestational age (Lubchenco et al., 1966).

6) No identifiable physical disability, brain damage or neurological condition (based on physical examination) that might independently affect cognitive or motor development and hence performance on psychological or physical outcome measures.

7) Head circumference at or above the fifth percentile and above the level of weight percentile.

8) Absence of overt physical abuse by parents. Although FTT and child abuse are considered by some as part of a spectrum of maltreatment (Newberger et al., 1977), the developmental and family problems of children with FTT differ considerably from those of abused children, which to our way of thinking necessitated separation of these two groups (Fitch et al., 1975, 1976; Kotelchuck, 1980). Because we encountered relatively few instances of a combined presentation of FTT and child abuse, this criterion did

not exclude an unreasonable number of infants or decrease sample representativeness.

9) Between 1 and 9 months of age. Older infants and toddlers were excluded to: allow a more effective test of early intervention, provide for greater comparability of measures across a narrower age span, and reduce the heterogeneity of the population. This age restriction limits the generalizability of findings.

10) Infants must be living with and in legal custody of family members and not in foster care. Direct negotiation with parents concerning their child's participation in the study was considered necessary to conduct the study. In addition, FTT children who have already been placed in foster care may be a very different population than those who remain with their natural families. However, we did not preclude follow up of those children who were placed in foster care after being enrolled in the study.

12) Family must not live more than one hour's distance from the hospital. This criteria was based on logistical considerations.

It should be noted that the above criteria did not require that the FTT child have a developmental delay or specific behavioral deficits. We used open-ended criteria which did not specify the presence of psychological dysfunction because we did not wish to confound our criteria with potential psychological outcomes (see Bithoney & Dubowitz, this volume). Because the presence of a severe developmental delay is in itself a risk factor, FTT children selected on this basis may be a different population than those selected solely on the basis of physical growth deficits. In addition, developmental assessments of young infants hospitalized for FTT are often difficult to interpret. The severity of developmental problems can vary considerably with the child's nutritional state such that assessments made early in the hospitalization may not be strictly comparable with subsequent ones (Drotar, Malone & Negray, 1980). Although sequential developmental assessments are preferable, they are difficult to implement in practice, especially given the logistical constraints involved in sample recruitment at a number of hospitals. Finally, the predictive validity of infant assessment during the first year of life is limited (McCall et al., 1972), unless the child's developmental deficits are quite severe (Vanderveer & Schweid, 1974).

THE LOGISTICS OF EARLY INTERVENTION

Because we had reason to believe the young FTT infants would have less severe and/or irreversible psychological deficits than older children with chronic FTT, early recognition and intervention was a key ingredient of our research design. Whatever the attractiveness of the concept of early recognition, implementation proved to be more challenging than we expected for a number of reasons. Deceleration in rate of weight gain which eventually becomes severe enough to be labeled as FTT is often invisible in its early phases, unless it is accompanied by other symptoms and cannot be determined unless measurements are routinely plotted. In some clinic settings, infants with poor weight gain are not identified early because their weight is not consistently plotted. In addition, our requirement that the child's FTT be primarily attributable to environmental causes was difficult for practitioners. Some pediatricians equate environmental FTT with severe deprivation and do not consider FTT as non-organic unless the problem is dramatic.

A number of strategies were utilized to facilitate early recognition of FTT. Our research group established collaborations at hospitals in the

Cleveland area (a total of eight) in which FTT infants were admitted; and maintained a high level of visibility at the two major university-based pediatric hospitals (Rainbow Babies & Childrens Hospital and Cleveland Metropolitan General Hospital). Our project coordinator conducted a chart review at our base hospital to identify children who met the criteria. Our research group also visited pediatric practices and pediatricians, especially those who maintained practices in disadvantaged, high risk areas of the city. Although these procedures were helpful, the chart review, high visibility on the pediatric divisions, and the development of collaborations with staff, especially pediatric social service was most useful.

The integration of our research project with the clinical demands of patient care presented special problems. In making a referral to our project, many pediatricians were understandably more interested in our provision of immediate help to their children and families, than they were in the longer-term implications of our research. The fact that a number of FTT children referred to us did not fit the study criteria but were in need of service also required attention. Our provision of evaluation, treatment planning, and, in some instances, brief intervention to FTT children who did not fit our criteria necessitated a great deal of staff time but was in the interests of both families and practitioners.

Subject Recruitment and Attrition

Our project coordinator screened hundreds of referrals from pediatricians and social workers over a two year period to ensure that sampling criteria were met. Seven families out of 88 who met criteria did not wish to participate. The reasons for parental refusals are unknown. However, an analysis of available demographic and family characteristics of this group indicated no differences in physical status (physical growth, length or hospital stay) or demographic characteristics (e.g. family size, maternal age, income) from the sample who gave consent.

The initial sample who met criteria and signed informed consent was comprised of 80 children from 76 families (three sets of twins were included). From this original sample, a total of 11 (15%) have now been completely lost to follow-up. Most were lost in the initial phases of the study. Reasons for attrition were diverse and include four parents who signed initial consent but then decided that they no longer wished to participate. Children in this subgroup generally did sufficiently well in their weight gain following hospitalization that the parents no longer felt study follow up was necessary. In two of these cases, mothers initially signed consent, but then admitted that participation was not agreed upon by other family members. Four families moved out from the Cleveland area. Owing to distance and/or lack of information concerning their whereabouts, we have not been able to follow them. An additional two families are still in the immediate area but have proved to be impossible to track, even with assidious efforts to do so. Finally, one family counted as attrition began intervention, but we terminated the research contract after a few months because in the judgement of our treatment team and other professionals, the home environment was perilous to the child. Immediate action was taken by County Welfare Protective Services and all four children from this family were eventually placed in foster care.

This level of attrition is by no means inconsequential but is acceptable given the extraordinary difficulties involved in follow-up in the FTT population (Fitch et al., 1975) and the comprehensiveness of our protocol. One question concerns potential differences in the study versus attrition samples. To address this question, we compared the current sample with the attrition sample on demographic characteristics (birth order, family size, social class, age at admission, maternal age), physical status at birth (height, head circumference, weight, and weight for length), physical status at intake (height, weight for height, length of hospitalization), and psychological status at intake (Bayley, behavioral ratings). These analyses indicate that the two groups were not significantly different on the variables tested.

Working with Families in the Hospital Setting

As soon as it was determined that a child met the criteria, the intervenor who was assigned to the case (via random assignment) met the family at the hospital to explain the study to them. Despite the fact that parental right of informed consent was a primary focus of our initial contact with families, families experienced pressure from hospital staff to join the project as a consequence of the diagnosis of environmental FTT. In retrospect, such constraint may have prompted some families into prematurely accepting the study during the child's hospitalization only to subsequently refuse our involvement when the child returned home.

In the hospital setting, intervenors functioned as family advocates by providing information about the child's condition, interpreting findings and recommendations concerning physical diagnosis, and communicating to hospital staff about family adaptation and progress. Only in very few instances did parents recognize the importance of environmental factors in the child's growth deficit. Many parents tended to attribute the child's problem to organic factors (e.g. "my child is sick"), intrinsic character- istics ("he's just that way") or were very confused by their perception that the hospital staff had found "nothing." Some parents were angered and threatened by the hospitalization. Many parents, especially those whose children had been referred to county welfare protective services (15% of the sample) prior to the hospitalization, were most concerned about the fact that they might not get their baby back following hospitalization.

Our introduction to parents emphasized the reason for our involvement, e.g., the fact that family stress could affect the child in significant ways, the fact that we had worked with other families with this problem and the importance of the family working together with us to help the child. In our initial encounters with parents, we emphasized that we felt that the child's problem could be helped and that we felt we could also be helpful to the parents. Because hospital-based contact was the beginning of con- tact with families which would subsequently continue in the home setting, we were able to concentrate on building a relationship with the family during the hospitalization. To accomplish this, our project staff assumed a difficult role as advocate for family's needs and as consultant to the hospital staff. In some instances, our staff also collaborated with county welfare protective services in the intervention.

Home-Based Intervention

At point of hospitalization, families were randomly assigned to one of three intervention plans, each of which involved working with family mem- bers in their homes but differed with respect to frequency of contacts and focus of intervention. Intervention plans were based on clinical experience and available literature (Bromwich, 1976; Fraiberg, 1980). In one interven- tion plan, short-term advocacy, family members were seen for an average of six visits over a year as a control for frequency of intervention. In two others, parents or family members were seen for weekly home visits for an average duration of one year as follows: Family-centered intervention involved relevant members of the family group to enhance family coping and support and modify dysfunctional patterns of intervention to enhance child nurturing (see Drotar & Malone, 1982a; and Drotar et al., this volume for more details). Parent-centered intervention involved a supportive educational focus directed toward improving the other's (or major caretaker's) interactions, nutritional management, and parent-child relationship (Bromwich, 1976).

Differences in intervention plans were maintained by recruiting intervenors who with experience in either parent-centered or family-centered intervention, by supervision and structured care plans. Although family-centered intervention was expected to result in more permanent gains once treatment ended owing to greater involvement of the family network, no differences were predicted on initial outcomes (12-18 months) obtained while families still received intervention.

It should be noted that our initial study design was modified to include a comparison group matched on age, sex, race, economic level, prematurity, parental education, family size, and constellation. Recruitment of this sample has only recently been completed so that information about this sample is not included in the present chapter.

SAMPLE DEMOGRAPHIC CHARACTERISTICS

Child

Our research group identified FTT earlier (three months on the average) than ordinarily identified in practice (Drotar et al., 1981) or in most studies. The mean age at study intake was 4.9 months for 68 children (44 males and 24 females) from 65 families. The varied racial composition included 38 black, 27 white, and 3 Spanish. Children tended to be latter borns (M=2.6 birth order). Sixteen children were premature.

Family

Fifty-four families (82%) received Aid to Dependent Children. The other families were working class (3.7) based on Hollingshead & Redlich (1958). The average family income was $5,900. The average family size was five (M=2.4 adults, 2.6 children), average maternal age was 22.1, and maternal educational level, 10.9 school years. Demographics are comparable to other FTT samples which often, but not always (see Kotelchuck, 1980) show high rates of economic disadvantage (Bruenlin et al., 1983). Family structures based on household composition include married parents (42%), unmarried couples with a stable continuous relationship (23%), extended families (21%) and mother alone units (14%). However, the functional organization of these units was considerably more complex than reflected by these general patterns, in keeping with other observations of disadvantaged family life (Kellam, Ensminger & Turner, 1968; Stack, 1974, 1975).

Family Income and Structure

For families receiving welfare, income was determined from standard payments. Variations for the families on welfare corresponded to the number of eligible children and/or differences in social security payments. Family size and the ratio of adults to children living a household were corroborated with multiple observers. Family stresses were tabulated based on a checklist derived from Holmes and Rahe (1967).

CHILD OUTCOME ASSESSMENT

One of the unique features of our study was a comprehensive, prospective assessment of psychosocial functioning. The measures were chosen to tap competencies that could be affected either globally or selectively by dysfunctional parent-child relationships and that were relevant to subsequent mental health outcomes. Wherever possible, sequential assessment was used to assess the rate of the child's development over time, sample developmental competencies that emerge at different ages and hence predictive validity of outcome measures (McCall et al., 1972). Specific outcome measures were chosen for reliability of scoring, feasibility of administration and sensitivity to psychological deficits associated with FTT. Intake assessments were conducted in the hospital. Physically compromised children were not evaluated until they improved to the point where they could respond to the test items (Drotar et al., 1980). Outcome assessments were conducted in family homes by experienced examiners who were unaware of treatment or information about families.

The following domains and specific measures were sampled during the period of early outcome (intake to 24 months) reported in this chapter.

Physical Growth

Infants were weighed on equivalent scales (Health-O-Meter Pediatric Scale, Continental Model No. 322). Head circumference was assessed by the Inserta Tape, Ross Laboratories. All measurements were taken at study intake, 12 and 18 months. A number of derived measures were calculated from weight, length, and head circumference. Wasting was percentage of the child's weight typical for a given height, as specified by growth charts. Four general classifications were used (Waterlow, 1972) 0 = greater than 90% weight for height; 1 = 80-89%; 2 = 70-79%; 3 = less than 70%. Stunting refers to the percentage of expected length for age and was calculated by comparing the child's length with norms. In accord with the following classification schema (Waterlow, 1972): 0 = greater than 95% height for age; 1 = 90-95%; 2 = 85-89%; 3 = less than 85%.

Intellectual Development

Cognitive development was assessed with the Bayley Scale of Mental Development (Bayley, 1969) at study intake and at 12, 18, and 24 months.

Behavioral Ratings

Assessors filled out rating scales adapted from the Infant Behavior Record (Bayley, 1969) which assess the child's behavior during testing on a five point scale (a score of 5 was the most adaptive rating) in the following areas: Cooperativeness, Object Orientation, Social Orientation, and Goal Directedness. Inter-rater reliability ranged from 85 to 95%. Correlations between individual subscales and total composite ranged from .74 to .89. A composite score was utilized in this analysis.

Language Ability

Language ability was determined in children 18 months and older via a battery used by White et al. (1978) in a study of the competence of preschoolers from different socioeconomic backgrounds. Derived scoring categories, including vocabulary and comprehension of grammar were shown to have adequate inter-rater reliability (.90 to .99). Inter-rater reliability was above 90% in the present study.

Symbolic Play

Capacity to represent experience in the non-verbal medium of play was assessed by the Symbolic Play Test (Lowe, 1975), a structured procedure in which the child is given sets of play objects according to standardized format and observed in spontaneous play. Standardized on a sample of 240 children, this test has acceptable internal consistency (.92) and test-retest reliability (.81)(Lowe & Costello, 1976). Scoring categories based on objective, discrete behaviors assess the complexity of the child's play from very simple usage such as picking up a toy to relating objects to one another. Inter-rater reliability was above 90% in the present study.

Attachment

Attachment was assessed at 12 months of age via the Strange Situation, a laboratory procedure developed by Ainsworth and Wittig (1969) which consists of eight episodes presented in a standard order for all subjects in an 11 x 14 foot room. The order of episodes was so arranged that the infant experiences a series of increasingly (mildly) stressful situations. Episodes were videotaped and rated on the following dimensions (Ainsworth et al., 1978): (a) proximity seeking: The intensity and persistence of the baby's efforts to gain (or regain) physical contact (or more weakly, proximity) with an adult; (b) contact maintaining: The degree of activity and persistence in the baby's efforts to maintain physical contact with an adult once he has gained it; (c) proximity and interaction avoiding: The intensity, persistence, duration, and promptness of any active avoidance of proximity or interaction, even across a distance, especially in reunion episodes, and; (d) contact resisting: The intensity and frequency or duration of negative behavior evoked by a person who comes into contact or proximity with the baby, especially behavior accompanied by signs of anger.

These ratings are used to define three patterns of attachment as follows: secure, characterized by high proximity seeking with low avoidance and resistance, and insecure, including: (1) avoidant, characterized by low proximity seeking and high avoidance; and (2) resistant (ambivalent) which includes high proximity seeking and resistance. Videotapes were judged by two raters who were blind as to the subject's physical status and attachment classification. The inter-rater percentage of agreement for the behavioral dimensions was 86%.

Home Environment and Parent-Child Interaction

The present study also included the Home Environment Scale (Caldwell & Bradley, 1980) which was done at six month intervals and assessment of parent-child interaction using a computerized event recorder (Stephenson, Smith & Roberts, 1975; Stephenson, 1979). The child outcomes are described in this chapter. Preliminary findings for parent-child interactional variables are described in Finlon et al., this volume.

PRELIMINARY FINDINGS

Physical Health and Growth

As shown in Table 1, description of physical health and growth indicates the level of physical risk already experienced by this young sample. By age at intake (M=4.9 months), nutritional status was already significantly affected. Weight percentile dropped from M=32.8 at birth to less than the 5th %ile, length from M=37.9 to 19.0 %ile and head circumference from 33.3 to 24.9 %ile. Moreover, the impact of deceleration in rate of weight gain on nutritional status was demonstrated in significant changes in the percentage of weight for expected height from 97.1 at birth to 80.6 at intake. Most children (87%) showed at least a mild degree of wasting (acute nutritional impairment) and 7% were severely malnourished. Two children had severe rumination (Flanagan, 1967). Eighteen infants had prior pediatric hospitalizations, eight for FTT and/or related conditions and ten for acute infections or FTT related symptoms such as vomiting.

Table 1

Early Physical Growth and Psychological Outcome

	BIRTH M	S.D.	INTAKE M	S.D.	12 MONTHS M	S.D.	18 MONTHS M	S.D.	24 MONTHS M	S.D.
Ht (cm)	48.1 (38th %ile)	3.1	59.7 (20th %ile)	6.5	72.5 (25th %ile)	2.9	79.1 (27th %ile)	3.0	84.1 (23rd %ile)	2.9
Wt (kg)	2.81 (33rd %ile)	.5	4.6 (5th %ile)	1.3	8.6 (21st %ile)	1.1	10.1 (27th %ile)	1.2	11.06 (27th %ile)	1.5
HC (cm)	33.2 (33rd %ile)	1.8	39.9 (25th %ile)	3.2	45.7 (36th %ile)	1.5	47.2 (38th %ile)	1.3	48.1 (35th %ile)	1.5
Wt/Ht	96.4	12.5	80.5	8.9	94.5	9.5	95.3	8.7	95.1	10.3
Bayley MDI			99.3	16.3	109.6	15.1	102.4	13.6	93.0	14.8
Behavioral Ratings			11.2	2.6	13.8	2.5	12.1	3.0	12.4	2.7
Receptive Language Age (in months)			–	–	–	–	17.8	3.3	22.1	4.6
Symbolic Play			–	–	–	–	7.7	2.6	11.3	3.1

These findings indicate that FTT had become chronic for some children as early as the first year of life and underscore the necessity to consider physical and nutritional status in predictions of early psychological outcomes (Kotelchuck, 1980; Pollitt, 1969, 1973). Acute hospitalization for diagnosis and treatment averaged 15 days but was longer (average of 26 days) for 15 children whose problems required more extensive nutritional rehabilitation.

Initial Psychological Status

Owing to the difficult logistics of testing children in the hospital setting (Drotar et al., 1980), measures of psychological development during the hospitalization were limited to the Bayley Scale and ratings of behavior during testing. Initial assessments were done after the child was in the hospital for a period of at least a week to allow improvement in social responsiveness and a representative assessment to take place. Some children had to be seen a number of times to allow for a valid assessment. Sequential developmental assessment from point of hospitalization was impossible to implement because referrals came to us at varying times.

As shown in Table 1, cognitive development at intake was within normative expectations (M=99.4). Consistent with Field (1984), these findings indicate that young FTT infants have more intact intellectual abilities than those with chronic FTT.

EARLY OUTCOME

Our initial studies have described physical growth, nutrition, and early psychological outcome of FTT infants (see Table 1). Early outcome data for the entire sample indicated enhancement of physical growth, especially nutritional status as measured by weight for height percentile which changed from 80.6 at intake to 94.5 at 12 months. However, multivariate analyses of variance (adjusted for age at intake as a covariate) performed on physical growth and psychological competence variables (Bayley, Harvard Language, Symbolic Play), through 24 months indicated no effects of treatment group, sex, or race on any of the major variables. (It should be noted that treatment differences were not anticipated in analysis of early outcome but rather in longer term behavioral outcomes.) As a whole, the sample shows initial improvement in growth parameters, followed by stabilization. Average Bayley MDI shows a decrease from 12 months to 24 months but remains within normative limits. Average performance on Harvard Language and Symbolic Play Scale was consistent with norms at 18 months but somewhat below norms at 24 months.

The lowering of developmental competencies over time is consistent with other investigations of other high risk disadvantaged populations (Ramey et al., 1982) and affirms the selection of FTT as a risk population. Comparison of these outcomes compare favorably with prospective follow-up studies of FTT infants. For example, Casey, Wortham & Nelson (in press) reported that nearly half of their sample (48%) did not improve in rate of physical growth. Chase & Martin (1973) found a majority of preschool children still were below the fifth percentile in weight (53%), length (68%), and over a third in head circumference (37%). In this study, percentages of children below the fifth percentile included 22% for weight, 11% for length, and 12% for head circumference. At 24 months, average cognitive developmental levels of the present sample are higher (90 or above) than means of 84 and 78 reported at comparable ages in other samples (Fitch et al., 1975, 1976; Singer & Fagan, 1984).

Table 2

Prediction of Bayley MDI 18 Months

Variable	F Level	Signi-ficance Level	Multiple R	R^2	R^2 Change	Overall Signi-ficance
Income	2.41	.127	.09	.01	.01	.50
Family stress	.67	.416	.15	.02	.01	.55
Ratio AC	1.39	.243	.17	.03	.01	.69
Wasting	3.12	.084	.29	.09	.06	.37
Age of onset	9.83	.003	.50	.26	.17	.01
Chronicity	.02	.886	.50	.26	.00	.03

Overall F = 2.55
$\underline{p}$ = <.03

Predictions of Early Outcome

Initial multiple regression analysis at 12 and 18 months suggested that predictions of cognitive functioning on the Bayley Scale, followed an interactional model in which biologic variables such as acute nutritional status and family environmental variables contributed to variance in early outcome (Drotar et al., 1985).

The present analysis utilized hierarchical regression analysis which allows an ordered selection of variables and better statistical power than multiple regression analysis (Cohen & Cohen, 1978). In this analysis, three measures of family resources and claims were used: (1) income, (2) ratio of adults to children (AC), and (3) the number of stresses at intake. Three measures of biologic vulnerability were selected: (1) wasting at intake (wasting was chosen over stunting on the basis of its success in prior analysis), (2) the estimated age of onset (defined as the age the child reached the 5th percentile) and (3) chronicity defined as the discrepancy between the estimated age at which the child reached the 5th percentile and age at intake. The order of variable entry was income, stresses, ratio of adults to children, wasting, age at onset, duration.

As shown in Tables 2 and 3, the test model predicted the Bayley MDI at 18 and 24 months. In each of these predictions, the age the child reached the 5th percentile accounted for a significant amount of the variance. This analysis indicated that the older the child when reaching the fifth percentile, the better the level of cognitive development at 18 and 24 months.

On the other hand, a different pattern of predictions emerged for the receptive language measure. As shown in Table 4, family variables, especially the ratio of adults to children and the number of stresses at intake predicted Harvard language at 18 months. A higher ratio of adults to children and fewer stresses were associated with better outcomes. The predictive model was not significant for receptive language at 24 months.

Table 3

Prediction of Bayley MDI 24 Months

Variable	F Level	Signi-ficance Level	Multiple R	R^2	R^2 Change	Overall Signi-ficance
Income	.37	.541	.04	.00	.00	.73
Ratio AC	2.16	.148	.10	.01	.00	.76
Wasting	.07	.788	.10	.01	.00	.90
Age at onset	14.70	.0004	.49	.24	.23	.009
Stresses	.01	.912	.49	.24	.00	.02
Chronicity	.70	.406	.51	.26	.01	.03

Overall F = 2.58
   p = <.03

Attachment

Attachment classifications at 12 months of age were as follows: B
(secure 49%), A (avoidant 33%), C (resistant 12%), and 6% not classifiable.
These findings indicate that: FTT is not synonomous with attachment disturbance; however, the incidence of insecure attachment 45% is higher than
estimates of 25-30% in middle class samples (Campos et al., 1983), but
lower than estimates in various maltreatment populations (60-90%) (Campos
et al., 1983). The frequency of insecure attachment found in this study
are consistent with Gordon and Jameson (1980) who found a 50% incidence in
a FTT population. Finally, the most frequent pattern of insecure attachment, avoidance, is consistent with higher rates of avoidant vs. resistant
attachments associated with child maltreatment (Rizley & Cicchetti, 1981).

Preliminary analyses of factors which differentiate secure vs. insecure (avoidant and resistant) attachments indicate that physical (nutritional) and psychological status at intake did not discriminate attachment
classifications. However, children with insecure attachments had more
chronic FTT (M=2.5 months vs. 1 month) than the children who were securely
attached (F=9.20, df=1/61 p <.003). Family contextual factors also differentiated the two groups. Insecure attachment was associated with a greater
number of family stresses at intake (M=5.8 vs. 4.2) than secure attachment
(F=9.41, df=1/61, p <.008).

Other Outcomes

Our analysis of ongoing family adaptation over the period of early outcome family data is in process. However, it should be noted that during the
period of early outcome a number of families had chronic relationship stresses (45%), constellation changes (51%), and subsequent children (15%) which
may be expected to influence the child's outcomes. Other outcomes are important to note: Four children were rehospitalized for FTT. Another four
were hospitalized for accidents. Thus far, one child has been hospitalized
for a severe feeding disorder. Six families, less than 10%, have had continuing involvement of county welfare and protective services, which is
fewer than at study intake. On the other hand, owing to significant family
problems and/or maternal neglect, three children are now living with other

Table 4

Harvard Language 18 Months

Variable	F Level	Significance Level	Multiple R	R^2	R^2 Change	Overall Significance
Income	1.64	.211	.25	.06	.06	.07
Family stress	2.97	.095	.36	.13	.07	.03
Ratio AC	11.84	.001	.56	.32	.18	.0003
Wasting	.002	.959	.56	.32	.00	.001
Age of onset	.01	.096	.56	.32	.00	.001
Chronicity	.29	.591	.57	.32	.00	.002

Overall F = 4.33
  p = <.002

family members (aunt or grandmother) and two are in foster care. Such outcomes are difficult to evaluate owing to the lack of systematic information concerning the incidence of chronic neglect and foster care in FTT. However, at least for a subset of children, family participation in the study was associated with greater likelihood of the child remaining with his or her family versus foster care (see Singer, this volume).

DISCUSSION

Our preliminary findings have a number of implications for future research in FTT. Our models of clinical outreach intervention proved to be acceptable to families and within an acute-care pediatric hospital setting and urban community. Vigorous attention to early intervention resulted in early recognition of a sample of FTT infants which have thus far not demonstrated the severity of psychological deficits seen in more chronic populations. On the other hand, the follow-up period is relatively short. The failure to obtain differences as a function of specific treatment plan may have resulted from a number of factors. For example, the nonspecific effects of intervention (e.g., continuity of care from hospital to home, treatment contacts) may have outweighed specific effects. Because each intervention plan represented an improvement in care relative to current standards in the community, it is quite possible that the intervention resulted in enhanced outcomes in each group but no differential effects. Unfortunately, in the absence of baseline information concerning the natural history of the development of FTT infants, this is difficult to prove. It is also possible that the individual differences in age at onset, duration, and family response to intervention may have obscured group differences. Additional analyses will be directed toward the analysis of factors which discriminate children with positive vs. negative outcomes. Another possibility is that group differences may emerge upon analysis of subsequent outcomes, especially for variables reflecting socioemotional development. The developmental functions sampled in this early outcome assessment were heavily weighted toward cognitive development, which appears to be relatively resistant to the effects of early intervention, unless the intervention begins early, is continuous, and involves a substantial environmental change for the child (Ramey, Yeates & Short, 1984).

Prediction of Early Outcome: Cognitive Development

Analysis of factors which contributed to positive early outcomes within this FTT sample yielded interesting patterns, which differed depending on the criterion variable. Age of onset was a protective factor with respect to cognitive development. The older the child when the FTT presented, the better the outcome in cognitive development at both 18 and 24 months. This finding suggests that that very early onset vs. later onset FTT may have different developmental outcomes and underscores the need to differentiate between these groups. Children with later onset may have had a double advantage, including a shorter period of time in which their nutrition was compromised and earlier identification relative to the onset of FTT. It is unclear which is the more important factor. On the other hand, receptive language at 18 months was predicted by family factors. Fewer family stresses and a greater number of adult caretakers, relative to the children, were associated with better language outcomes, at 18 but not at 24 months. Families who had more adult caretakers and a fewer number of stresses may have presented their children with a more stimulating language environment than those who did not.

Attachment

Family ecological factors and chronicity of FTT discriminated security of attachment at age 12 months. Children from families which had greater stresses and a longer duration of FTT tended to have greater frequency of insecure attachments. These findings are consistent with studies of other populations which suggest that the family relationship context affects security of attachment (Egeland & Farber, 1984). Many of the families of FTT infants are burdened by a myriad of burdens (e.g., economic deprivation, large numbers of children) in a context of relatively few maternal resources for caregiving (Drotar & Malone, 1982a). Family stress, especially relationship stresses, may have burdened mothers of FTT with yet another set of competing claims in the context of relatively few supports and severely taxed their nurturing capacities and contributed to mutual avoidance. In the highly stressed, overburdened and depleted family situations that are often associated with FTT, an avoidant attachment can be construed as a mutual adaptation in which the child is expected to make do with fewer resources, defined as time and attention from his/her mother. The higher frequency of avoidant relative to resistant attachment patterns found in this sample is consistent with the link between psychological unavailability and avoidant attachment found among abused and neglected infants (Egeland & Sroufe, 1983).

Why should children with longer duration of FTT be more likely to have anxious attachments, especially avoidant attachments? In this sample, children with very early onset FTT (before two months of age) tended to have longer durations of this problem. It is possible that very early onset FTT is a distinct subtype, which may be associated with a greater level of family problems and problematic maternal-child attachment. Early onset coupled with a delay in identification of FTT, which is not uncommon in clinical practice, may also place the FTT child at greater risk for a compromised attachment.

The consequences of FTT associated with anxious attachment on children's psychological development remain to be explored. The present findings suggest that FTT is not necessarily synonymous with anxious attachment, especially in a sample of very early onset FTT who received intervention. One might expect different patterns of attachment for late onset FTT or for children from economically advantaged and less stressed families (Chatoor & Egan, 1983).

The present findings have a number of implications for future research. Taken together, these findings suggest that family status and individual differences in various parameters of FTT may relate to early psychological outcomes. Belsky's process model of parental competence provides an interesting conceptual model to guide studies of risk vs. protective factors in FTT (Belsky, 1984; Belsky, Robins & Gamble, 1984). In accord with this model, the combination of limited maternal personal resources, significant nutritional deficits in the child, and compromised family support may predict higher risk for chronic psychological difficulties among FTT children. In designing studies of psychological risk in FTT, it will be important to differentiate among acute versus chronic outcomes since these may be governed by different sets of risk factors. (Schneider-Rosen et al., in press). One interesting area for future research concerns the relationship of parental coping and decision making in families of FTT infants to subsequent. For example, how do overburdened family members choose to allocate financial and personal resources to their children? What are the costs/benefits of these decisions for children's development?

IMPLEMENTING OUTCOME RESEARCH IN FAILURE TO THRIVE

Our experiences raised a number of issues that may characterize FTT outcome research. We found that an interdisciplinary team can marshal different kinds of expertise which is very helpful working with this complex problem. In addition, a formation of a team is critical in providing the group support needed to work with the highly stressed families of FTT infants and to maintain them in a research project. Because such families are highly stressed and the energy of family members is often diverted into other issues, it seems important that the intervention actively impinge on family life, which takes a great deal of initiative from staff. The commitment of the research team to the families was a major factor in keeping attrition as low as possible. On the other hand, even with strenuous efforts, some families remained quite difficult to reach and required multiple visits on the part of our staff. Because many of the families move a great deal, it is important to keep a detailed record of their social networks. Other incentives for families were provided by to birthday cards, Christmas cards and baskets, reports of study progress, and payment for their time.

It should be noted that the implementation of an applied research such as this project raised a great many problems. For example, it was difficult for clinicians to operate under the constraints of a protocol involving random assignment, comprehensive record keeping, and in which they did not know detailed results of the outcome evaluations. Other issues which took a great deal of time and energy included maintainance of differences in intervention plans and separation of intervention from outcome evaluation. Perhaps the most troubling dilemmas was raised by our immersion in the chronic life stresses of the families of FTT children. Although we were comforted by the achievements that the child has made and our relationships with families, the more we became acquainted with some families, the more we came to appreciate the depth of the problems they experienced. Termination of intervention became a very difficult task. Following termination, we insured that the child's pediatric care was in place and that additional follow-up was maintained by communication. Some families remained in need of services from different agencies such as County Welfare Protective Service, Parents Anonymous, or Visiting Nurse. Although successful referrals could be made in some instances, the majority of families did not take advantage of such services. Other questions were raised by the applicability and feasibility of our intervention plans for hospital and community settings. Subsequent reports will deal with these issues.

LIMITATIONS OF THE PRESENT STUDY

The present study has a number of limitations that should be kept in mind in evaluating the findings. This sample was unique on a number of grounds: the families were highly stressed and disadvantaged, children were identified early in the first year of life, and all families received some kind of intervention. As a consequence, the findings may not be generalizable to other FTT populations, especially those comprised of older infants referred because of accompanying physical and/or behavioral problems.

The fact that all children received some kind of intervention makes it difficult to interpret some of our findings. Future studies might maximize the differences between intervention groups and reduce sample heterogeneity more completely than we did. In this regard, it would be very useful to design more specific interventions for subtypes of FTT (see Linscheid & Raskane, this volume). Another problem is raised by the problems involved in evaluating effects of repeated evaluations on outcome. The inherent problems of applied outcome research (Halpern, 1984) require investigators to somehow balance the rigors of method with the practical realities of implementation. As investigators begin to follow samples of FTT infants who have received various interventions, it will be possible to develop a better data base to determine factors which are associated with developmental and physical prognosis in various populations.

It is important to emphasize that the present findings reflect early outcomes on a limited number of measures. Our current plans are to follow our sample at least to preschool and, funding permitting, to early school age. Our test battery at age 3 includes a greater emphasis on socioemotional development than our early outcomes. For example, additional assessments include assessment of ego control and ego resilience (Block & Block, 1980), measures of child and family adaptation based on Q Sort (Block, 1978; Block & Block, 1984) and measures of adaptive problem solving (Goodman, 1979, 1981). Future analyses will be directed toward examination of the permanence of intervention effects, factors which predict chronic psychologic risk vs. resilience within the FTT sample, and the analyses of differences in longer-term risk between FTT and a matched comparison group.

REFERENCES

Ainsworth, M.D.S., Blehar, M.D., Waters, E. & Wall, S. Patterns of Attachment. Hillsdale, NJ: Erlbaum, 1978.

Ainsworth, M.D.S. & Wittig, B.A. Attachment and exploratory behavior of one year olds in a strange situation. In B.M. Foss (Ed.), Determinants of Infant Behavior: Vol. 4. London: Methuen, 1969.

Bayley, N. The Bayley Scales of Infant Development Manual. New York: Psychological Corporation, 1969.

Belsky, J., Robins, E. & Gamble, W. The determinants of parental competence. Toward a contextual theory. In M. Lewis (Ed.), Beyond the Dyad. New York: Plenum, 1984.

Bithoney, W.G. & Rathbun, J.M. Failure to thrive. In W.B. Levine, A.C. Carey, A.D. Crocker & R.J. Gross (Eds.), Developmental Behavioral Pediatrics. Philadelphia, PA: Saunders, 1983.

Block, J. The Q Sort Method in Personality Assessment and Psychiatric Research. Palo Alto, CA: Consulting Psychologists Press, 1978.

Block, J.H. & Block, J. The role of ego control and ego resiliency in the organization of behavior. In W.A. Collins (Ed.), Development of Cognition, Affect and Social Relations. The Minnesota Symposia on Child Psychology, Vol. 13. Hillsdale, NJ: Erlbaum, 1980.

Block, J.H. & Block, J. A longitudinal study of personality and cognitive

development. In S.A. Mednick, M. Harway & K.M. Finello (Eds.),
     Handbook of Longitudinal Research. New York: Praeger, 1984.
Bradley, R.H. Social and nonsocial environment of children who are nonor-
     ganic failure to thrive. Paper presented at the Biennial Meeting of
     the Society for Research in Child Development. Detroit, Michigan;
     April, 1983.
Bromwich R. Focus on maternal behavior in infant intervention. American
     Journal of Orthopsychiatry, 1976, 46, 439-446.
Bruenlin, D.C., Desai, V.J., Stone, M.E. & Swilley, J. Failure to thrive
     with no organic etiology: A critical review. International Journal of
     Eating Disorders, 1983, 2, 25-49.
Caldwell, B.M. & Bradley, R.H. Home Observation for the Measurement of the
     Environment. Little Rock, AK: Center for Child Development and Educa-
     tion, University of Arkansas, 1980.
Campos, J.J., Caplovitz-Barett, K., Lamb, M.E., Goldsmith, H.H & Stenberg,
     C. Socioemotional development. In P.H. Mussen (Ed.), Handbook of
     Child Psychology. New York: Wiley, 1983.
Casey, P.H., Wortham, B. & Nelson, J. Management of children with failure
     to thrive in a rural ambulatory setting. Pediatrics, in press.
Chase, H.P. & Martin, H.P. Undernutrition and child development. New
     England Journal of Medicine, 1970, 282, 993-999.
Chatoor, I. & Egan, J. Nonorganic failure to thrive and dwarfism due to
     food refusal: A separation disorder. Journal of the American Academy
     of Child Psychiatry, 1983, 22, 294-301.
Cohen, J. & Cohen, P. Applied Multiple Regression Correlation Analysis for
     the Behavioral Sciences. Hillsdale, NJ: L. Erlbaum, 1975.
Drotar, D. Mental health intervention in infancy: A case report on
     failure to thrive. Journal of Child Clinical Psychology, 1975, 4, 18-
     21.
Drotar, D. & Malone, C.A. Family-oriented intervention in failure to
     thrive. In M. Klaus & M.O. Robertson (Eds.), Birth Interaction and
     Attachment. Johnson and Johnson Pediatric Round Table, Vol. 6.
     Skillman, NJ: Johnson and Johnson, 1982 (a).
Drotar, D. & Malone, C.A. Psychological consultation on a pediatric infant
     division. Journal of Pediatric Psychology, 1982 (b), 7, 23-32.
Drotar, D., Malone, C.A. & Negray, J. Environmentally based failure
     to thrive and children's intellectual development. Journal of Clinical
     Child Psychology, 1980, 9, 236-240.
Drotar, D., Malone, C.A., Negray, J. & Dennstedt, M. Patterns of hospital
     based care for infants with nonorganic failure to thrive. Journal of
     Clinical Child Psychology, 1981, 10, 16-22.
Drotar, D., Nowak, M., Malone, C.A., Eckerle, D. & Negray, J. Early psych-
     ological outcome in failure to thrive: Predictions from an interac-
     tional model. Journal of Clinical Child Psychology, 1985, 14, 105-
     111.
Dubowitz, L.M., Dubowitz, V. & Goldberg, D. Clinical assessment of gesta-
     tional age in the newborn infant. Journal of Pediatrics, 1970, 77, 1-
     10.
Egeland, B. & Farber, E.A. Infant-mother attachment: Factors related to
     its development and changes over time. Child Development, 1984, 55,
     753-771.
Egeland, B. & Sroufe, L.A. Developmental sequelae of child maltreatment.
     In R. Rizley & D. Cicchetti (Eds.), Developmental Perspectives on
     Child Maltreatment. San Francisco, CA: Jossey-Bass, 1985.
Field, M. Follow-up developmental status of infants hospitalized for
     nonorganic failure to thrive. Journal of Pediatric Psychology, 1984,
     9, 241-256.
Finlon, M.A. & Drotar, D. Social competence and attachment behavior in
     failure to thrive infants. International Conference of Infant Studies.
     New York, April, 1983.
Fitch, M.J., Cadol, R.V., Goldson, E.J., Jackson, E.K., Swartz, D.F. &

Wendel, T.P. Prospective Study in Child Abuse: The Child Study Program, Final Report. Office of Child Development Project, Grant No. OCD-CR-371, Denver Department of Health and Hospitals, 1975.

Fitch, M.J., Cadol, R.V., Goldson, E., Wendel, T., Swartz, D. & Jackson, E. Cognitive development of abused and failure to thrive children. Pediatric Psychology, 1976, 1, 32-37.

Flanagan, C.H. Rumination in infancy - past and present. Journal of the American Academy of Child Psychiatry, 1977, 16, 140-149.

Fraiberg, S. (Ed.) Clinical Studies in Infant Mental Health. New York: Basic Books, 1980.

Frank, D.A. Malnutrition and child behavior: A view from the bedside. In J. Brozek & B. Schurk (Eds.), Critical Assessment of Key Issues in Malnutrition and Behavior. Bern, Switzerland: Huber, in press.

Garbarino, J. The human ecology of child maltreatment: A conceptual model for research. Journal of Marriage and the Family, 1977, 39, 721-735.

Goodman, J. The Lock Box: An instrument to evaluate mental organization in preschool children. Journal of Child Psychology and Psychiatry, 1979, 20, 313-324.

Goodman, J.F. The Goodman Lock Box Manual. Chicago, IL: Stoelting Co., 1981.

Gordon, A.H. & Jameson, J.C. Infant-mother attachment in parents with non-organic failure to thrive syndrome. Journal of the American Academy of Child Psychiatry, 1979, 18, 96-99.

Halpern, R. Lack of effects of home-based early interventions: Some possible explanations. American Journal of Orthopsychiatry, 1984, 54, 33-42.

Hammil, P.V.V., Drizd, T.A., Johnson, C.L., Reed, R.B., Roche, A.F. & Moore, W.M. Physical growth: National Center for Health Statistics Percentages. American Journal of Clinical Nutrition, 1979, 32, 607-629.

Holmes, T.H. & Rahbe, R.H. The social readjustment rating scale. Journal of Psychosomatic Research, 1967, 11, 213-218.

Kellam, S.G., Ensminger, M.E. & Turner, R.J. Family structure and the mental health of children. Archives of General Psychiatry, 1977, 34, 1012-1022.

Kotelchuck, M. Nonorganic failure to thrive: The status of interactional and environmental theories. In B.W. Camp (Ed.), Advances in Behavioral Pediatrics: Vol. 1. Greenwich, CN: Jai Press, 1980.

Leonard, M.F., Rhymes, J.P. & Solnit, A.J. Failure to thrive in infants: A family problem. American Journal of Diseases of Children, 1966, 111, 600-612.

Lester, B.M., Emory, E.K., Hoffman, S.L. & Eitzman, T. A multivariate study of the effects of high risk factors on performance on the Brazelton Neonatal Assessment Scale. Child Development, 1976, 47, 515-517.

Lowe, M. Trends in the development of representational play in infants from one to three years - an observational study. Journal of Child Psychology and Psychiatry, 1975, 16, 33-47.

Lowe, M. & Costello, A.M. Manual for the Symbolic Play Test. Windsor, Great Britain: NFER Publishing Co., 1976.

Lubchenco, L.O. Hansman, C. & Boyd, E. Intrauterine growth in length and head circumference as estimated from live births at gestational ages from 26 to 42 weeks. Pediatrics, 1966, 37, 403-407.

Maybanks, S. & Bryce, M. Home-based Service for Children and Families: Policy, Practice and Research. Chicago, IL: Thomas, 1979.

McCall, R.B., Hogarty, P.S. & Hurlburt, N. Transitions in infant sensorimotor development and the prediction of childhood I.Q. American Psychologist, 1972, 27, 728-748.

Moos, R. & Moos, B. A typology of family social environments. Family Process, 1976, 15, 357-371.

Newberger, E.R., Reed, R.P., Daniel, J.H., Hyde, J. & Kotelchuck, M. Pediatric social illness: Toward an etiologic classification. Pediatrics, 1977, 60, 175-185.

Oates, R.K. & Hufton, I.W. The spectrum of failure to thrive and child abuse. Child Abuse and Neglect, 1977, 1, 119-124.

Oates, R.K., Peacock, A. & Forest, D. Long-term effects of non-organic failure to thrive. Pediatrics, 1985, 75, 36-40.

Pollitt, E. Ecology, malnutrition and mental development. Psychosomatic Medicine, 1969, 31, 193-200.

Pollitt, E. The role of the behavior of the infant in Marasmus. American Journal of Clinical Nutrition, 1973, 26, 264-270.

Ramey, C.T., MacPhee, D. & Yeates, K.O. Preventing developmental retardation: A general systems model. In L.A. Bond & J.M. Joffe (Eds.), Facilitating Infant and Early Childhood Development. Hanover: University of New England Press, 1982.

Ramey, C.T., Yeates, K.G. & Short, E.J. The phosticity of intellectual development insights from preventive intervention. Child Development, 1984, 55, 1913-1925.

Rizley, R. & Cicchetti, D. Developmental Perspectives on Child Maltreatment. San Francisco, CA: Jossey-Bass, 1981.

Schneider-Rosen, K., Braunwald, K.G., Carlson, V., Cicchetti, D. Current perspective in attachment theory: Illustration from the study of maltreated infants. In I. Bretherton & E. Waters (Eds.), Growing Points in Attachment Theory and Research. Monographs of the Society for Research in Child Development, in press.

Schmitt, B. (Ed.) The Child Protection Team Handbook. New York: STM Press, 1978.

Singer, L.T. & Fagan, J.F. The cognitive development of the failure to thrive infant: A three year longitudinal study. Journal of Pediatric Psychology, 1984, 9, 363-382.

Stack, C.B. Strategies for Survival in a Black Community. New York: Harper & Row, 1974.

Stack, C.B. Who raises black children: Transactions of child givers and child receivers. In T.R. Williams (Ed.), Socialization and Communication in Primary Groups. The Hague: Mouton, 1975.

Stephenson, G.R. PLEXYN: A computer-compatible grammar for coding complex social interactions. In M.E. Lamn, S.J. Suomi & G.R. Stephenson (Eds.), Social Interaction Analysis. Madison, WI: University of Wisconsin Press, 1979.

Stephenson, G., Smith, D.P.B. & Roberts, T.W. The SSR system: An open format event recording system with computerized transcription. Behavior Research Methods and Instrumentation, 1975, 7, 497-515.

Vanderveer, B. & Schweid, E. Infant assessment: Stability of mental functioning in young retarded children. American Journal of Mental Deficiency, 1974, 79, 1-4.

Waterlow, J.C. Classification and definition of protein-calorie malnutrition. British Medical Journal, 1972, 3, 566-569.

Woolston, J.L. Eating disorders in infancy and early childhood. Journal of the American Academy of Child Psychiatry, 1983, 22, 114-121.

Zussman, J.V. Situational determinants of parental behavior: Effects of competing cognitive activity. Child Development, 1980, 51, 792-800.

EXTENDED HOSPITALIZATION OF FAILURE TO THRIVE INFANTS: PATTERNS OF CARE

AND DEVELOPMENTAL OUTCOME*

Lynn Singer

Rainbow Babies' and Children's Hospital and Case Western
Reserve University School of Medicine, Cleveland, Ohio

Introduction

Infants who fail to thrive without diagnosable physical disease remain
a frequent and frustrating treatment dilemma for pediatric and psychological practitioners, and have generated a large and expanding body of clinical research over the past decade. By far, much of the extant literature on psychosocial FTT has focused on the etiological factors associated
with the condition (Barbero & Shaheen, 1967; Bullard et al., 1967; Evans,
Reinhart & Succop, 1972; Fischoff, Whitten & Pettit, 1971; Leonard, Rhymes
& Solnit, 1966), the developmental sequelae for those children who experience growth failure in infancy (Drotar, Malone & Negray, 1979; Elmer,
Gregg & Ellison, 1969; Singer & Fagan, 1984), and innovative intervention
and treatment modes drawn from a variety of theoretical frameworks
(Fraiberg, 1981; Ramey et al., 1975; Drotar et al., 1979).

Investigators have repeatedly advocated the need for an interdiscplinary family-based approach to the treatment of FTT (Barbero & Shaheen,
1967; Drotar et al., 1979; Fraiberg, 1981; Leonard et al., 1966). However,
pediatric management through acute-care hospitalization continues to be the
primary mode of initial intervention (Hannaway, 1970; Shaheen et al., 1968;
Evans et al., 1972; Drotar et al., 1981). In addition, placement outside
the home, either through extended hospitalization, adoption or foster care,
remains a frequently recommended intervention option in many reports on
non-organic FTT (Evans et al., 1972; Silver & Finkelstein, 1967; Hopwood &
Becker, 1979; Berkowitz & Klaren, 1984).

The rationale for long-term hospitalization or foster care as a treatment for nonorganic FTT stemmed from early recognition that many instances
of growth failure in infancy occurred in conjunction with environmental
deprivation and improved with placement in a nurturing environment (Coleman
& Provence, 1957; Patton & Gardner, 1962). Although the nature and etio-

*The author wishes to acknowledge the following people for their help in
implementing this study: Gene Nowacek, Marilyn Malkin and staff and
families at Health Hill Hospital, Dennis Drotar, Joseph Fagan, the Cuyahoga
County Welfare Department, Sean Phipps, Barbara Lewis, Sandy Carrel, Jean
Montie, Pamela Schwartz, Sal Karanouh, and especially Barb Ekelman for data
analysis and Ann Marie Diemert for data collection.

logical path of the environmental disruption in the FTT "syndrome" have been debated, the notion that a change in environment could create positive effects on infant growth and psychologic status became almost definitional of the problem. Based on this conceptualization, placement outside the home, usually in foster care, remains an often recommended treatment for FTT (Powell, Brasel & Blizzard, 1961; Evans et al., 1972) and has played a significant role in shaping our concepts of this disorder.

Surprisingly, then, documentation of the course of and types of treatment in hospital intervention and foster care placement for FTT infants is severely limited. Only one study (Drotar et al., 1981) has described hospital based patterns of psychosocial care of nonorganic FTT infants in a naturalistic setting. Using an in-depth chart review, it was found that in-hospital treatment was highly oriented towards physical diagnosis, with poor utilization of psychosocial services and lack of follow-up after discharge. Most other reports of hospital treatment for nonorganic FTT infants have described short "shot-gun" hospitalizations in acute-care settings averaging about 1-4 weeks in which infants demonstrated relatively rapid weight gain (Hannaway, 1979; Evans et al., 1972; Elmer et al., 1969; Glaser et al., 1968; Field, 1984).

However, several reports have mentioned hospital treatment of longer duration. For example, Field (1984) noted that seven out of her sample of seventeen nonorganic FTT infants were admitted to a convalescent hospital for an average of six and a half weeks after physical work-up in an acute care setting. In Drotar et al.'s (1981) sample of such infants, twenty percent were discharged into a long-term rehabilitation hospital because of living situations characterized by severe neglect.

In an interesting series of studies, Graham & Adrianzen (1971, 1972), noted that a Jamaican cohort of severely malnourished infants and their siblings who were eventually adopted into healthier environments demonstrated "remarkable catch-up growth." These findings led to a planned intervention in which younger siblings of severely malnourished infants were admitted, at less than four months of age, to a convalescent unit of a hospital to ensure adequate diets (Baertle, Adrianizen & Graham, 1976). The infants thrived in the protected environment but showed declines in all growth parameters when returned to their natural homes.

Data regarding the use and effects of foster care placement in treatment of nonorganic FTT infants are even more sparse. Yet, up to 50% of some selected samples of FTT infants have been reportedly placed in foster care (Hopwood & Becker, 1979; Singer & Fagan, 1984), and foster care placement has at times been recommended as the "treatment of choice" for nonorganic FTT or deprivational dwarfism (Powell, Brasel & Blizzard, 1961; Patton & Gardner, 1976). In general, reports on the determinants and value of foster care placement in the treatment of FTT have been minimal, subjective, unsystematic and variable. For example, Evans et al. (1972) recommended immediate foster placement for children in families with gross psychopathology, physical abuse, or with an angry and hostile mother. Based on case information, one study of a very small sample of hospitalized nonorganic FTT infants found a number of factors associated with placement in foster care, namely: abuse of the child, a parental history of abuse or neglect, concerns about parental psychiatric status, parental lack of cooperation and a chaotic living situation (Haynes et al., 1983). However, Ranyon et al.'s (1982) empirically-based investigation of a large state-wide population of children seen for maltreatment found that additional factors not specifically related to intervention needs, such as geographic location and referral source, were associated with an increased risk of foster care placement. Investigators in this study found that over 83 percent of the variance in a multiple regression equation using foster care as the dependent variable was due to factors not in their data base. These findings led them to conclude that decision for foster care placement was "essentially a random process" across a large population.

Foster care remains a proliferating but controversial intervention for maltreated children, including FTT, the benefits and iatrogenic effects of which have not yet been adequately studied (Schor, 1982; Knitzer, 1981). The few studies which have described the outcome of nonorganic FTT infants who have been placed in temporary or permanent foster care have done so peripherally and without objective outcome measures. Silver & Finkelstein (1967) found nine children placed in foster care in their sample of FTT to be "significantly improved" in growth and "personality structure." In a study of older children with psychosocial dwarfism, Hopwood & Becker (1979) rated adopted FTT children as having the best adjustments, but noted a high incidence of multiple placements and behavior problems in their group of FTT children in foster care. The authors attributed the behavioral problems to continued contact with their natural families which they feel was disruptive to the children's adaptation. Casey (1984) also noted an improvement in some FTT children placed in foster care, but observed that others actually deteriorated with placement. In a study of nonorganic and organic FTT infants, Singer et al. (1984) found that home-reared infants fared better on standard cognitive measures at 20 months of age than did infants placed outside the home, irrespective of the medical or psychosocial basis of the growth failure. However, by 3 year follow-up, no differences between foster placed vs. non-placed infants were found.

Given the lack of data regarding the concomitants of placement outside the home in the treatment of FTT, the present study, then, sought to examine patient characteristics, hospital course, and long-term developmental outcome in a group of nonorganic FTT infants referred for extended hospitalization, and, in some cases, additional foster care, all following acute care hospitalization.

Subjects

Subjects included all infants 12 months of age or less admitted for evaluation and treatment of nonorganic FTT to a pediatric rehabilitation hospital in Cleveland, Ohio. All infants were recruited from Health Hill, a 50-bed specialty hospital for children which provides long-term care for infants with a variety of developmental problems. Since one purpose of the study was to investigate the range of infants receiving long-term hospital intervention for psychosocial growth failure, a broad definition of the condition was utilized. Thus, all infants referred to the hospital with an admission diagnosis of FTT, based on NCHS norms (Hamill et al., 1979), without documented organic etiology during a 2-year period were included for study. All infants in the present sample were referred after prior admission to an acute care hospital during which an initial diagnostic work-up had revealed no physical basis for the growth failure.

Demographic and medical characteristics for the total sample (N=35) are given in Table 1. Infants tended to come from impoverished homes (Mean Hollingshead index=4.7; S.D.=.6) with all but two families supported through public assistance. Most mothers had not graduated high school (Mean educational level=10.2 years, S.D.=1.9) and a significant number were either mentally retarded or with severe psychiatric disturbance (15%). Although information on fathers was not obtainable for all infants, at least twelve percent were noted to be imprisoned at the time of hospitalization. Approximately half the sample came from single-parent homes (54%). Sixty-three percent of the infants were black, 34% white and 3% were Hispanic. Males comprised 60% of the sample. At admission (mean age 5.9 months, S.D.=2.9), the majority of infants (66%) were in temporary or permanent custody of the County Welfare Department.

Table 1

Sample Characteristics of Infants Hospitalized Long-Term for Non-Organic Failure-to-Thrive

(N=35)

Variable	Mean	Standard Deviation	Range
Maternal Education (Years)	10.2	1.9	7-16
Socioeconomic Status (Hollingshead)	4.7	.6	3-5
Age at Hospital Admission (months)	5.9	2.9	1-12
Gestational Age at Birth (weeks)	38.2	3.7	24-40
Percentile of Weight for Age at Admission	6.6	9.5	1-50
Hospital Bayley Score (MDI)	85.1	17.5	50-129
Marital Status	37% married; 54% single; 9% other		
Race	34% white; 63% black; 3% Hispanic		
Sex	60% male; 40% female		
Abuse	83% no; 17% questionable		
CNS Problems	83% no; 17% yes		
County Welfare Custody	66% in custody		
Prematurity (less than 37 weeks gestation)	20% premature		

In terms of physical status, the mean percentile of weight for age for the group at admission was 6.6 (S.D.=9.5, Range=1-50). Variation in degree of growth failure at time of admission was due to the fact that all infants had been previously hospitalized in an acute-care hospital where, for most children, a degree of catch-up weight gain was established. For 83% of the sample, physical abuse had been ruled out; for 17% it was questionable but not evident. Mean gestational age at birth was 38.2 weeks (S.D.=3.7) with 20% of the sample premature. Seventeen percent of the group had some identifiable neurological abnormality, (i.e., mental retardation, unusual C-T scan, seizures) which was not thought to be a primary factor in the child's growth failure.

During hospitalization, all infants received specialized medical and nursing care, intensive physical and occupational therapies, and nutritional intervention. Each accessible family was assigned to a social worker for ongoing counselling and discharge planning. Outpatient rehabilitation therapies were available after discharge when needed. One-third of the sample, who were not in County Welfare Department custody, were simultaneously treated through the Infant Growth Project, a university-based research and intervention program which provided advocacy, family-centered intervention and consistent developmental follow-up for FTT infants prior to and after hospital admission. For these families, an Infant Growth Project worker remained involved with the family both during and after hospital treatment, providing additional supportive and therapeutic services. (See Drotar et al., this volume for more details.)

Subjects comprised three groups based on relevant medical and intervention factors in order to compare developmental outcome and patterns of care during and after hospitalization. Group 3 consisted of all children hospitalized while simultaneously referred to the Infant Growth Project, since these infants received specialized intervention services during and after the hospital admission. Admission criteria to the Infant Growth Project excluded all infants who were very low birth weight (less than 1500 grams) or small-for-gestational age at birth, who had severe neurological problems or physical disease, were mentally retarded or were in the custody of the County Welfare Department at the time of the child's initial hospitalization in the acute care hospital. Group 2 included all infants who matched Group 3 on the medical admission criteria of the Infant Growth Project but who had not participated in the project because they were already in county welfare custody and Group I consisted of those FTT infants who presented with additional neurologic problems. Admission characteristics of the three groups of infants are presented in Table 2. Means or percentages of occurrences of relevant sample characteristics were compared for the three groups through either one-way ANOVAS with post-hoc analyses for continuous variables or through single sample chi-square tests for categorical data. The analyses indicated that Group 1 differed from Groups 2 and 3 only on the variables relevant to group selection, i.e., Group 1 having lowered gestational age at birth ($F=6.2$, $df=2,32$, $p < .005$), and presenting more neurological problems ($F=12.2$, $df=2,32$, $p < .002$). Group 3, which received additional intervention through the Infant Growth Project, differed from the other two groups in frequency of County Welfare custody ($X =30.9$, $df=2$, $p < .001$). No infants in the Project were under county custody at time of admission while all infants in Groups 1 and 2 were in custody. Based on data from hospital records, there were no differences among the three groups on other factors which might reasonably affect outcome or care patterns, including years of maternal education, Hollingshead's (1957) index of socioeconomic status, age at hospital admission, birthweight, admission weight, hospital Bayley Mental Scale standard score, marital status, race, or occurrence of previous abuse.

Table 2

Means, Standard Deviations, Percentages and Tests of Significance
for Sample Characteristics of Sub-Groups of Failure-to-Thrive Infants

	Group 1 (N=13)		Group 2 (N=11)		Group 3 (N=11)		F or X^2
	X	S.D.	X	S.D.	X	S.D.	
Maternal Education (years)	10.7	2.6	10.1	1.5	9.7	1.5	.64
SES (Hollingshead)	4.5	.78	4.9	.32	4.8	.40	1.35
Age at Hospital Admission (mos.)	4.9	2.9	6.7	3.3	4.9	2.6	1.02
Gestational Age at Birth (wks.)	35.7	5.2	39.8	.60	39.5	1.0	6.20*
Birthweight (grams)	2593	1102	2903	703	2958	.65	.65
Admission Weight (percentile for age)	7.7	7.4	7.9	15.1	3.9	3.5	.61
Admission Bayley Score (MDI)	74.6	21.8	90.3	11.1	89.4	15.4	2.5
Marital Status (% married)	46%		46%		18%		6.3
Race (% minority)	54%		73%		64%		3.3
Abuse (% abused)	0%		0%		0%		
Presence of CNS Problems	46%		0%		0%		12.2**
County Welfare Custody	100%		100%		0%		30.9***

*   p <.005
**   p <.002
*** p <.001

Procedures

In order to examine hospital care patterns for the three groups of infants, information on physical status and discharge referrals were obtained from hospital records. Since infants were weighed daily in the hospital, the mean weight gain per week over the first two months of hospitalization was calculated as a measure of "catch-up" growth. A two-month time period was used as a means of controlling for the varying lengths of hospital stay among infants since growth would be expected to decelerate with longer lengths of stay. A two-month period was also useful for assuring the occurrence of accelerated growth with environmental change if growth could occur. Length of stay (weeks hospitalized) and the percentile for age of weight at discharge were also obtained. A variety of discharge recommendations were examined, including placement (parental, relative, foster or adoptive home or institution), educational, rehabilitation, psychological and health services.

At time of follow up, all legal caretakers of the infants were contacted by phone and requested to participate in the study. Procedures for intellectual assessment differed somewhat dependent on the status of the infants. All children in the Infant Growth Project (Group 3) were tested with the Stanford-Binet Intelligence Scale (Terman & Merrill, 1973) at three years of age as part of the ongoing intervention program. All other children were given the McCarthy Scales of Children's Development (McCarthy, 1972) by a trained graduate psychology student in their homes. For six children who were enrolled in the County Board of Mental Retardation or other specialized programs, results of recent assessments by licensed psychologists using standardized IQ tests were also used.   For each child, percentiles of weight and height for age were calculated using National Center for Health Statistics (NCHS) norms (Hamill et al., 1979). For some children, recent growth parameters taken at annual physical exams by their own pediatricians were used.

A standard interview form was used which documented information on caretaker socioeconomic status (Hollingshead, 1958), current living placement, number of placements subsequent to hospitalization, presence and type of health problems, current educational and therapy programs, services provided to families after hospitalization, and attrition.

Results

Hospital Course

Differences among the three groups of FTT infants in terms of hospital course and discharge planning are illustrated in Table 3. A series of one-way analyses of variance (ANOVA) with post-hoc comparisons were run to compare differences in treatment outcome for the three groups. Groups did not differ on either rate of catch-up weight gain during the initial phase of hospitalization or on the percentile of weight for age attained by time of discharge from the hospital. All groups had substantial growth in hospital, gaining, on the average, almost half a pound a week during the first two months of hospitalization. By discharge, the groups averaged a weight for age percentile of approximately 25 as opposed to a mean percentile of weight for age at admission of 6.6. The only reliable difference among groups in terms of hospital course related to length of admission (F=9.5, $\underline{df}$=2,32, p < .0006). Infants who received ongoing intervention services through the Infant Growth Project had the shortest length of stay (M=9.5 weeks, S.D.=7.1). Group 1 infants, who presented with known organic vulnerability had comparable lengths of stay (M=13.2 weeks, S.D.=10.2). Surprisingly, both groups had significantly lower lengths of stay than did Group 2 (M=31 weeks, S.D.=18) which matched Group 3 on all admission char-

Table 3

Hospital Course and Discharge Plans

	Group 1 (N=13)		Group 2 (N=11)		Groups 3 (N=11)		F or X^2
	Mean	S.D.	X	S.D.	X	S.D.	
Mean weight gain per week over first 2 mos. hospitalization (gms)	202	63	186	106	223	78	.53
Discharge weight (percentile for age)	26.2	23.1	34.4	35	16.8	22.4	1.1
Length of stay (wks. hospitalized)	13.2	10.2	31.0	18	9.5	7.1	9.5***
Discharge placement	62% parental home 31% relative home 7% foster home		18% parental home 46% relative home 27% foster home 9% institution		100% parental home		16.8**
Educational referral	70% none 30% Cty Bd Mental Retardation		100% none		100% none		7.6*
Therapy referral	77% none 23% OT/PT		64% none 36% OT/PT		36% none 64% OT/PT		NS
Visiting nurse	70% no 30% yes		82% no 18% yes		100% no		NS

*   p < .02
**   p < .01
*** p < .001

acteristics with the exceptions of County Welfare custody and Infant Growth Project intervention.

Groups also differed in terms of placement at discharge (X^2=16.8, df=2,32, p <.01) and post-hospital referrals. All infants from the Infant Growth Project (Group 3) returned to the care of their own parents after hospitalization. In contrast, only 18% of Group 2 infants returned to parental custody. Forty-six percent of infants in Group 2 were placed with relatives, and 36% were discharged into a foster home or institution. For those infants with mixed etiology, Group 3, 62% were placed with their parents, 31% were placed with relatives and 7% were admitted to a foster home.

Referrals for educational programs also differed by group (X^2= 7.6, p <.02), with, as expected, those infants with mixed etiology being referred more frequently for educational programs. Specifically, one third of Group 1 infants were referred for services to the County Board of Mental Retardation, in contrast to no referrals for that service from the other two groups. Groups did not differ on the basis of referral for therapy or visiting nurse services.

Follow Up Development

Table 4 describes the developmental outcome of the infants at long-term follow-up, which occurred for all children at approximately 3 years of age. There were no differences among the groups on any of the outcome measures of physical, intellectual or health status. All groups of children maintained the weight gains or their initial hospitalization with mean percentiles of weight for age at follow-up of 16.9 (S.D.=18.9), 40.2 (S.D.=36.3), and 42.3 (S.D.=31.6), respectively for Groups 1, 2, and 3. Percentiles of height for age followed a similar pattern with Groups 1, 2 and 3 achieving means of 24.4 (S.D.=18.5), 42 (S.D.=31.5) and 37 (S.D.=18.9), respectively. For all groups, intellectual status at follow-up was in the borderline range of functioning compared to age peers, with mean IQ scores achieved of 78.3 (S.D.=26.2) for Group 1, 84 (S.D.=11) for Group 2 and 79.2 (S.D.=9.4) for Group 3. Caretakers reported that 50 to 67% of the children continued to have health problems at follow-up, with groups not differentiated on this basis. Health problems cited at follow-up were pneumonia, otitis media, anemia, asthma, chronic eczema, elevated lead levels and accidental burns. One child, in Group 1 with mixed etiology, was later diagnosed as having autonomic dystonia which necessitated multiple subsequent hospitalizations. Her parents are suing the physician who placed her in custody of county welfare for nonorganic FTT. Another child, who had been born premature at very low birthweight, died an accidental death when she swallowed a bean in her home. A third child's mother was found murdered after a disappearance from the home.

Placement

Groups did differ reliably at follow-up on variables related to placement and socioeconomic status. All children in Group 3, which received ongoing intervention services from the Infant Growth Project, remained in parental custody at 3 years, in contrast to 70% of children from Group 1 and only 9% from Group 2 (X^2=20.9, p <.002). The number of placements in addition to hospitalization that a child had experienced also was different depending on group membership (F=7.5, df 2,26, p < .002). While Group 3 children experienced no placements beyond hospitalization as of the date of this follow up, Group 2 children averaged 1.2 (S.D.=.8) placements after discharge. Differences in caretaker socioeconomic status also emerged at follow-up (F=6.1, df 2,26, p <.006) with children in Group 2, the majority of whom had been placed in adoptive, foster, or relative homes, showing

147

Table 4

Developmental Outcome by Subgroup

Variable	Group 1 (N=9) X	S.D.	Group 2 (N=9) X	S.D.	Group 3 (N=11) X	S.D.	F or X^2
Age at follow-up testing (mos.)	42.	11.3	37.	12.7	34.	4.1	1.7
Number of placements	.5	1.0	1.2	.8	0	0	7.5***
Caretaker SES (Hollingshead)	4.3	.9	3.6	1.0	4.8	.4	6.1**
Current placement	70% parental home 20% relative home 10% foster home		9% parental home 36% relative home 28% foster home 27% adopted		100% parental home		20.9***
Presence of health problems	50%		67%		55%		.56
Current educational/therapy program	22% none 56% Men. Retardation Board 11% therapy 11% Head Start		63% none 25% Head Start		100% none		15.2*
IQ	78.3	26.2	84.	11.	79.2	9.4	.32
Age at follow-up in mos. (physical measures)	42.4	12.9	42.5	4.1	24.	4.1	2.4
Height (percentile for age)	24.4	18.5	42.	31.5	37.	18.9	1.3
Weight (percentile for age)	16.9	18.9	40.2	36.3	42.3	31.6	1.6
Attrition	1 lost/accidental death in parental home 2 lost/had refused services of MR home trainer		1 lost/moved out of state to relative home 1 adopted/parent refused follow-up		None lost to follow-up		

* p<.02
** p<.006
*** p<.002

higher socioeconomic status than those in Group 3, all of whom remained with their parents.

While no children seen by the Infant Growth Project were lost to follow-up, six children who had been in county welfare custody were not available for outcome study. Two of these children had moved out of state for placement in relative homes. The parents of one child who was adopted into a middle-class family refused to participate in the study. As noted previously, one child suffered an accidental death. Significantly, two other children who could not be traced had records of having refused the services of the County Board of Mental Retardation home trainer within several months after hospital discharge.

Discussion

The present study exmained medical and psychosocial characteristics, hospital course, and long-term developmental outcome in a group of infants admitted to a convalescent hospital for treatment of nonorganic FTT after initial diagnostic evaluation in an acute care hospital. Because a subset of infants simultaneously participated in a research intervention program (Drotar et al., this volume), a comparison of the effects of an intensive outpatient intervention on hospital course, discharge referrals and eventual outcome in this subsample could also be made. The findings, which should be considered in the context of the small sample size and limited nature of outcome studies, are nonetheless instructive

In this sample, FTT infants referred for long term hospitalization were an overwhelmingly impoverished group, with only one family of middle-class status based on Hollingshead's (1958) classification. Since the hospital from which patients were recruited is the only rehabilitation facility available in the state, the present sample probably accurately reflects characteristics of FTT infants who receive extended hospitalization in the geographic region served by this hospital. Although FTT occurs in all social classes, it is disproportionately reported in poor families (Glaser et al., 1968; Shaheen et al., 1968; Kotelchuck, 1977; Singer & Fagan, 1984). The percentage (97%) of patients from the lowest socioeconomic class in this sample is high, even in comparison to most other FTT samples, and suggests that infants from the most economically disadvantaged families may be more likely to be referred for long-term hospitalization and subsequently placed into county welfare custody (two-thirds of this sample).

Of some note is the substantial percentage of infants (35%) in this sample who presented with mixed etiology and who did not fit strictly into conventional criteria for nonorganic FTT Homer & Ludwig, 1981). These infants presented with poor weight gain in the context of other overt physical disorders, including mental retardation, extreme prematurity and seizures, which were not directly causative of their growth failure, but which may induce physicians to ignore the psychosocial environment of the infant as a factor contributing to poor growth (Elmer et al., 1969). In contrast, the "catch-up" weight gain achieved by this group during hospitalization would suggest that the occurrence of "interactional" FTT (Casey, 1983) may be high in selected populations, and emphasizes the need to consider the co-existence of psychosocial along with biological influences in the diagnosis and treatment of FTT.

In terms of degree of growth failure, admission developmental assessment, racial and sex characteristics, and rate of prematurity, the present sample compares favorably with most other groups of FTT infants described in the literature (Leonard et al., 1966; Fitch et al., 1976; Hufton & Oates, 1977).

Hospital Course and Discharge Plans

All three groups of FTT infants made similar "catch-up" weight gains in the initial phases of their long-term hospitalization, despite differences in the availability of outpatient services and the presence of other physical disorders among groups. For many of the infants, growth spurts achieved in extended care were a continuation of the reversal of malnutrition already begun in an acute-care setting. By discharge, weight for age for all groups of infants was also comparable.

On the other hand, differences among the groups in terms of length of hospitalization and patterns of discharge placement were striking, however. FTT infants concurrently treated through a home-based intervention, and those infants with associated physical problems, averaged two to three months of hospital stay compared to an average stay of eight months for FTT infants in county welfare custody who exhibited no other medical problems. In contrast, Field (1983) reported that a similar group of nonorganic FTT infants in her sample averaged one and a half months of stay in a rehabilitation hospital. Given the extreme length of time of infants' separation from caregivers involved, the long duration of institutionalization, and the staggering medical costs ($63,000 average per child in 1984 dollars) incurred, it seems important to evaluate the factors related to such lengthy hospitalizations. Since all groups were comparable on measures of socioeconomic status, education, unemployement and abuse, these factors do not account for the differences in duration of hospitalization. In the present sample, factors related to social factors, such as the family's capacities to nurture the child, seemd to outweigh medical factors in predicting length of hospital stay. A need for further medical treatment, and lack of family involvement have been cited in previous studies (Drotar et al., 1981; Field, 1984) as precipitants of a recommendation for extended hospitalization for FTT infants. Thus, infants in Groups 3 and 2 may have been initially referred for extended hospitalizations for differing reasons; Group 3 because of medical issues; Group 2 because of concerns about family functioning.

The present data then suggest that an outpatient family-based intervention program may mitigate against prolonged hospitalization for nonorganic FTT infants in extended hospital care. It is of some interest that those FTT infants who participated in an outpatient intervention program also had a significantly lower rate of referral for foster care and institutional placement. The fact that only 18% of the FTT infants in Group 2 returned to their parental home indicates that prolonged hospitalization, even with the extensive social service support provided by hospital staff and county welfare department, had little impact in ameliorating family dysfunction and preventing eventual separation of the infant from its family of origin.

Developmental Outcome

For all groups of FTT infants, later physical growth, intellectual development, and health status subsequent to hospitalization were comparable, independent of the placement of the child or the utilization of an outpatient intervention program. Three years after discharge from the hospital, all groups of infants sustained the weight gains achieved in hospital although no group approached the 50th percentile or higher in weight for age. Other long-term follow up studies of the physical status of FTT infants have documented similar weight stabilization after short-term hospitalization (Shaheen et al., 1968; Hufton & Oates, 1977; Elmer, Gregg & Ellison, 1969). All groups of infants continued to show intellectual delays consistent with previous long-term follow-up studies of such infants. While infants in the present study were of the lowest socioeconomic status, other reports have suggested that the cognitive deficits seen in FTT infants may not be solely a reflection of lowered socioeconomic class but may reflect different experiences, including number of placements (Singer & Fagan, 1984). Finally, a large percentage of FTT infants within this sample continued to present with significant health problems after the resolution of their growth deficits. Although later health status of FTT infants has thus far not been well documented, recent reports have also suggested that such infants may continue to demonstrate compromised health status (Sherrod et al., 1984). The health problems observed at follow-up in some of the present group of children reflected a complex and alarming level of chronic environmental hazards in multiple life contexts, including exposure to toxic substances (elevated lead levels), poor caretaking (accidental burns and death), extreme societal violence or nutritional deficit (anemia). Thus, while a poor growth pattern may have originally been the primary manifestation of the impact of family dysfunction on the young infant, the amelioration of the infant's growth disorder does not necessarily reflect a corollary resolution in severe family dysfunction, the effects of which may emerge at subsequent developmental stages.

Group differences at outcome were seen in the patterns of eventual placement of an infant, in caretaker socioeconomic status and in the number of placements outside his family of origin an infant had experienced. By 3 year follow up, differences among groups in terms of placement outside the home were even more pronounced than at hospital discharge. Only one child from the clearly nonorganic FTT group of infants remained in the parental home, while all infants in this subsample of a larger group of children who received home-based intervention after the hospitalization remained in parental custody. The present findings suggest that nonorganic FTT children placed in foster care are unlikely to return to their parents of origin, even though foster care is commonly construed as a temporary remedy during which social services are provided to assist the reunification of the family (Child Welfare League of America, 1959).

The fact that many of the foster care children in this sample experienced multiple placements beyond their lengthy hospitalization raises a number of questions, which can be addressed in future research. First, what are the long-term developmental sequelae of foster care and repeated placements on FTT children? While the present data demonstrate no difference in intellectual status in the early pre-school years between placed vs. home-reared FTT infants of similar socioeconomic status, outcome at school age is not known. In addition, social and emotional development, not assessed in the present study, might be particularly affected by the disruption of attachments and lack of emotional consistency associated with long-term hospitalization and foster care (Miller, Mackey & Magninn, 1981).

Which set of social, biological and environmental variables best account for dispositions involving extended hospitalization and/or foster care for nonorganic FTT children? The extremely low socioeconomic status of the present sample suggests that poverty is one important correlate of the FTT infant's removal from the family. However, the restriction in the range and quality of the retrospective data culled in the present study did not allow for critical information regarding family dynamics, social support, and psychological histories to be collected systematically, thus hampering the conclusiveness of the findings.

Finally, the serendipitous inclusion of a subgroup of FTT infants who received family-centered outreach program allows speculation about the role such a program might play in lessening hospital stays and decreasing the risk of a FTT infant's placement in county welfare custody and foster care. Of particular importance is the intriguing question of whether the group of infants who received the additional treatment program differed in some essential way from those children in county custody, or whether the treatment program played some protective role in preventing the need for county custody by providing an alternative disposition that provided help to the child while maintaining family integrity. In a climate of shrinking health care resources, the high cost of prolonged hospitalization and foster care needs to be evaluated in light of the potential benefit to the FTT infant, as well as in the context of the possible iatrogenic effects of the infant's long-term separation from caregivers, and the potential of multiple foster home placements (Knitzer, 1981). Such questions can only be answered through prospective studies with reasonably large sample sizes and comprehensive outcome measures which can better investigate factors related to either successful family resolution of an infant's growth problem and/or associated psychological difficulties versus further family deterioration and eventual removal of the infant from its parents.

REFERENCES

Baertl, J., Adrianzen, T. & Graham, G. Growth of previously well-nourished infants in poor homes. American Journal of Diseases of Childhood, 1976, 130, 33-36.

Barbero, G. & Shaheen, E. Environmental failure to thrive: A clinical view. Journal of Pediatrics, 1967, 71, 639-644.

Berkowitz, C. & Sklaren, B. Environmental failure to thrive: The need for intervention. Family Physician, 1984, 191-199.

Bullard, D., Glaser, H., Heagarty, M. & Pivchik, E. "Failure to thrive in the neglected child. American Journal of Psychiatry, 1967, 37, 680-690.

Casey, P., Worthham, B. & Nelson, J. Management of children with failure to thrive in a rural ambulatory setting: Epidemiology and growth outcomes. Clinical Pediatrics, in press.

Casey, P. Failure to thrive: A reconceptualization. Developmental and Behavioral Pediatrics, 1983, 4, 63-65.

Child Welfare League of America. Standards for Family Foster Care Services. New York, 1959.

Coleman, R.W. & Provence, S. Environmental retardation in infants living in families. Pediatrics, 1957, 19, 285-292.

Drotar, D., Malone, C.A. & Negray, J. Intellectual assessment of young children with environmentally-based failure to thrive. Child Abuse and Neglect, 1979, 3, 927-935.

Drotar, D., Malone, C. & Negray, J. Psychosocial intervention with the families of failure to thrive infants. Child Abuse and Neglect, 1980, 4, 23-31 (a).

Drotar, D., Malone, C. & Negray, J. Environmentally-based failure to thrive and children's intellectual development. Journal of Clinical Child Psychology, 1980, 9, 236-240 (b).

Drotar, D., Malone, C., Negray, J. & Dennstedt, M. Patterns of hospital-based care for infants with nonorganic failure to thrive. Journal of Clinical Child Psychology, 1981, 10, 63-66.

Elmer, E., Gregg, G. & Ellison, P. Late results of the failure to thrive syndrome. Clinical Pediatrics, 1969, 8, 584-589.

Evans, S.L., Reinhart, J. & Succop, R. Failure to thrive: A study of 45 children and their families. Journal of the American Academy of Child Psychiatry, 1972, 4, 453-476.

Field, M. Follow up developmental status of infants hospitalized for nonorganic failure to thrive. Journal of Pediatric Psychology, 1984, 9, 241-256.

Fischoff, J., Whitten, C. & Pettit, M. A psychiatric study of mothers of infants with growth problems secondary to maternal deprivation. Journal of Pediatrics, 1971, 79, 209-215.

Fitch, M.F., Cadol, R.V. & Goldson, E. Cognitive development of abused and failure to thrive children. Pediatric Psychology, 1976, 1, 32-37.

Fraiberg, S. (Ed.). Clinical Studies in Infant Mental Health. New York: Basic Books, 1980.

Gabinet, L. Shared parenting: A new paradigm for the treatment of child abuse. Child Abuse and Neglect, 1983, 7, 403-411.

Glaser, H., Heagarty, M., Bullard, D. & Pivchik, E. Physical and psychological development of children with early failure to thrive. Journal of Pediatrics, 1968, 13, 690-695.

Graham, G. & Adrianzen, T. Growth inheritance and environment. Pediatric Research, 1971, 5, 691-697.

Grahm, G. G. & Adrianzen, T.B. Late catchup growth after severe infantile malnutrition. Lancet, 1967, 1, 1-4.

Hamill, P., Drizd, T., Johnson, C., Reed, R., Roche, A. & Moore, W. Physical growth: National Center for Health Statistics Percentages. American Journal of Clinical Nutrition, 1979, 32, 607-629.

Hannaway, P. Failure to thrive: A study of 100 infants and children. Clinical Pediatrics, 1979, 9, 96-99.

Haynes, C., Cutler, C., Gray, J., O'Keefe, K. & Kempe, R. Nonorganic failure to thrive: Decisions for placement and videotaped evaluations. Child Abuse and Neglect, 1983, 7, 309-319.

Haynes, C., Cutler, C., Gray, J., O'Keefe, K. & Kempe, R. Implications of placement through analysis of videotaped interactions. Child Abuse and Neglect, 1983, 7, 321-328.

Hollingshead, A. & Redlich, F. Social Class and Mental Illness. New York: John Wiley & Sons, 1958.

Homer, C. & Ludwig, S. Categorization of etiology of failure to thrive. American Journal of Diseases of Childhood, 1981, 135, 848-851.

Hopwood, N. & Becker, D.J. Psychosocial dwarfism: Detection, evaluation and management. Child Abuse and Neglect, 1979, 3, 439-447.

Hufton, L. & Oates, F. Nonorganic failure to thrive: A long-term follow-up. Pediatrics, 1977, 59, 73-76.

Knitzer, J. Child welfare: The role of federal policies. Journal of Clinical Child Psychology, 1981, 10, 3-7.

Kotelchuck, M. Nonorganic failure to thrive: The status of interactional and environmental etiologic theories. In B. Camp (Ed.), Advances in Behavioral Pediatrics, Vol. 1, 1980, Greenwich, CN: Jai Press.

Leonard, M., Rhymes, J. & Solnit, A. Failure to thrive in infants: A family problem. American Journal of Diseases of Childhood, 1966, 111, 600-612.

McCarthy, D. Manual for the McCarthy Scales of Children's Development, Psychological Scales. New York: Psychological Corporation, 1972.

Miller, F., Mackey, W. & Maginn, V. The modern displaced person: The repetitive foster child. Journal of Clinical Child Psychology, 1981, 10, 21-26.

Money, J. & Annecillo, C. IQ change following change of domicile in the syndrome of reversible hyposomatotropinism (psychosocial dwarfism): Pilot investigation. Psychoneuroendocrinology, 1976, 1, 427-429.

Pardech, J. Multiple placement of children in foster care: An empirical analysis. Social Work, 1984, 29, 506-510.

Patton, R. & Gardner, G. Growth Failure in Maternal Deprivation. Springfield, IL: Charles C. Thomas, 1963.

Patton, R. & Gardner, G. Influence of family environment on growth: The syndrome of maternal deprivation. Pediatrics, 1962, 30, 957-962.

Powell, C.F., Brasel, J.A. & Blizzard, R.M. Emotional deprivation and growth retardation simulating idiopathic hypopituitarism. I. New England Journal of Medicine, 1967, 276, 1277-1278.

Ramey, C., Starr, R.,Pallas, J., Whitten, C. & Reed, V. Nutrition, response contingent stimulation and the maternal deprivation syndrome: Results of an early intervention program. Merrill Palmer Quarterly, 1975, 21, 45-55.

Ranyon, D., Gould, C., Trost, D. & Loda, F. Determinants of foster care placement for the maltreated child. Child Abuse and Neglect, 1982, 6, 343-350.

Schorr, E. The foster care system and health status of foster children. Pediatrics, 1982, 69, 521-527.

Shaheen, E., Alexander, E., Truskowsky, M. & Barbero, G. Failure to thrive - A retrospective profile. Clinical Pediatrics, 1968, 7, 225-261.

Sherrod, K.B., O'Connor, S., Vietze, P.M. & Altemeier, W.A. Child health and maltreatment. Child Development, 1984, 55, 1174-1183.

Silver, H. & Finkelstein, M. Deprivation dwarfism. Journal of Pediatrics, 1967, 70, 317-324.

Singer, L.T., Drotar, D., Fagan, J.R., Devost, L. & Lake, R. The cognitive development of failure to thrive infants: Methodological issues and new approaches. In T. Field & A. Sostek (Eds.), Infants born at risk: Physiological, Perceptual and Cognitive Processes. New York: Grune & Stratton, 1984.

Singer, L. & Fagan, J. Cognitive development in the failure to thrive infant: A three-year longitudinal study. Journal of Pediatric Psychology, 1984, 9, 363-383.

Terman, L.M. & Merrill, M.A. Stanford-Binet Intelligence Scale, Third Revision. Boston, MA: Houghton-Mifflin, 1972.

Turner, J. Reuniting children in foster care with their biological parents. Social Work, 1984, 29, 501-505.

III. RESEARCH REPORTS

PART II: METHODS

     Research concerning FTT necessitates special methods which incorporate
the perspective of scientists in a number of fields. In the following
section, authors methodological issues and examples of methods in two
different areas: (1) assessment and analysis of physical growth; and (2)
assessment of parent-child interaction.

     Peterson, Rathbun & Herrera describe the importance of the assessment
of growth status to diagnosis and treatment of FTT. Peterson and her
colleagues present a detailed description of method and technique in six
major areas: (1) anthropometric assessment techniques; (2) appropriate
reference growth standards; (3) auxological (growth) definitions of FTT and
malnutrition; (4) analysis and display of individual and group data; and
(5) correction of age bias inherent in auxological definitions of FTT and
malnutrition; and (6) use of growth velocity measures in clinical practice
and research. Peterson and her coworkers underscore the importance of using
methods and growth standards that can be generalized across settings. Specific suggestions for the measurement of weight, height, and head circumference and various systems for classification of growth and nutritional status
are described. The authors illustrate these approaches via the presentation
of growth data from a study of FTT children seen in a tertiary care setting.
The issues and problems in using various methods for analyzing growth data
that are described will be of special interest to researchers who are
designing studies of FTT, criteria for samples and describing growth data.

     Another area of methodology with special relevance to FTT concerns the
observation of parent-child interaction. Finlon, Drotar, Satola, Pallotta,
Wyatt & El-Amin describe a method of home observation of parent-child transaction which was developed in an ongoing prospective study of outcome in
non-organic FTT. Finlon and her colleagues summarize the literature concerning parent-child interaction in FTT, the special methodological problems
and outline the needs of future research. Using examples from their research, Finlon and her colleagues consider issues involved in choice of
observation methods, selection of behavioral codes, and family reactivity
to observation. The authors describe data reduction and analysis of data
collected via a computerized event recorder which allows detailed observation of interaction in real-time. Preliminary findings are presented which
illustrate the significant relationship of maternal interactional behavior
to early outcomes of FTT children in attachment (12 months), cognitive
development (24 months) and language (24 months). These findings suggest
that frequency of adaptive maternal interactions may predict psychological
resilience within a FTT population. The implications of these findings for
future research are described.

GROWTH DATA ANALYSIS IN FTT TREATMENT AND RESEARCH

Karen E. Peterson, Jennifer M. Rathbun,
and M. Guillermo Herrera

Harvard University School of Public Health
Harvard Institute for International Development and
Massachusetts General Hospital

Assessment of growth status in the FTT child is central to both diagnosis and treatment of this complex syndrome. In clinical practice and in
research, growth data analysis are used to assess the impact of organic and
nonorganic risk factors and to evaluate the effectiveness of treatment. In
the FTT child, growthis the indicator of overall progress. The short and
long term effectiveness of medical, nutritional, behavioral, and mental
health interventions is measured by the physical growth outcome. Likewise,
nutritional rehabilitation contributes to positive psychosocial outcomes,
such as improved developmental quotients and enhanced mother-child interactions.

The standard of FTT treatment has become the health care team emphasizing simultaneous consideration of multiple organic and nonorganic con-
tributants. The efforts of the pediatrician are generally more effective
when combined with the services of a nutritionist, primary nurse, social
worker or mental health professional, and a developmental specialist. Each
area of risk is investigated by the appropriate team member and a unified
treatment plan developed. In the context of multidisciplinary team management, the expertise of the nutritionist -- growth data analysis and nutritional rehabilitation -- is essential to the success of medical and psychosocial therapies. Similarly, effective nutritional therapy is enhanced by
the evaluation and treatment of underlying causes of feeding difficulties
and growth failure (see Berkowitz, this volume).

Nutritional management of FTT includes: 1) ongoing assessment of
nutritional status and rate of catchup growth, including regular collection
of anthropometric measurements; 2) provision of energy and protein in
amounts sufficient to meet requirements for catchup growth; and 3) individualized nutritional instruction with longterm follow-up at regular intervals. Assessment of dietary intake, modification of the diet to promote
catchup growth, and nutritional instruction are treated in detail elsewhere
(Murray & Glassman, 1982; Peterson et al., 1984; Rathbun & Peterson, 1985).
The present chapter will focus on the methodology used to assess the growth
status of the FTT child, and will consider the key role of growth data
analysis in the treatment and research of failure to thrive. The following
topics will be addressed: 1) anthropometric assessment techniques; 2)
reference growth standards; 3) auxological (growth) definitions of FTT and
malnutrition; 4) analysis and display of individual and group growth data;
5) correction of age bias inherent in auxological definitions of FTT and

malnutrition; and 6) use of growth velocity measures in clinical practice and research.

ANTHROPOMETRIC ASSESSMENT

Anthropometric measurements should be collected regularly according to a protocol which is simultaneously appropriate for clinical and research purposes. Personnel obtaining measures should be clearly designated and limited in number. Measurement error can be minimized by standardization of anthropometric measurements at periodic intervals, according to procedures detailed by the World Health Organization (WHO)(1983). Weight, height, and head circumference are obtained at presentation using techniques described in Table 1. During hospitalization, weight is monitored daily to assess effectiveness of therapy. Because daily weights will also reflect variations in hydration, net weight gain over a week's time should be emphasized. Other anthropometric data are collected at monthly intervals during lengthy hospitalizations and at all outpatient visits.

Routine use of upper arm measurements may not be indicated, unless mandated by specific clinical or research protocols. In malnourished children with edema, triceps skinfold and midarm muscle circumference provide a better index of nutritional status than weight for height, because the arm is relatively free of edema (Blackburn & Bistrian, 1977, Blackburn & Thornton, 1979). However, the measurement error for these indices is large because the range of distribution of normal values for arm measures is narrow and multiple measures of triceps skinfold are required to minimize variability in skinfold compressability. The techniques for obtaining the triceps skinfold thickness and mid-arm circumference are described in Table 2. Midarm muscle circumference is calculated from these two measures according to the formula:

Midarm Muscle Circumference (mm) = Midarm Circumference (mm)

$$- \pi \text{ (triceps skinfold (mm))}.$$

Triceps skinfold and midarm muscle circumference are converted to estimates of cross-sectional upper arm fat and protein areas and compared with reference standards (Frisancho, 1981). Measurements which are less than fifth percentile suggest depletion of body stores and indices between the fifth and fifteenth percentile indicate risk of depletion (Gray, 1980).

REFERENCE GROWTH STANDARDS

The growth charts of the National Center for Health Statistics (NCHS)(Hamill et al., 1976) should be used to plot all anthropometric data. The NCHS charts are based on semi-longitudinal data collected by the Fels Research Institute, Yellow Springs, Ohio, on white middle class children aged 0 to 36 months and on data from a large, nationally representative sample of U.S. children measured in the Health Examination Survey (HES) and the Health and Nutrition Examination Survey (HANES). Other growth charts in common use in industrialized countries are the Stuart-Meredith charts and the Tanner charts. The Stuart-Meredith or "Harvard" charts currently in use in many U.S. health facilities are based on a cross-sectional analysis of growth of children of Northern European descent living in Boston and Iowa in the 1930's and 1940's (Reed & Stuart, 1959; Stuart & Meredith, 1946). Tanner's standards are based on longitudinal anthropometric measurements of 80 children of each sex from birth to five years and a random, cross-sectional sample of London school children aged 5.5 to 15.5 years

Table 1

Technique for Measuring Weight, Height, and Head Circumference*

WEIGHT

1. A calibrated beam balance is needed to take the measurement.

2. Infants are weighed in the nude. Older children are weighed without shoes and wearing a minimum of clothing.

3. Weights are recorded to the nearest 10 grams for infants and 100 grams for older children.

4. On follow-up weighings the child is weighed on the same scale wearing the same amount and type of clothing.

RECUMBENT LENGTH (less than 24 months of age)

1. Measurement is taken using a wooden length board.

2. Infant is laid on the board, and the head is positioned against the fixed headboard; eyes vertical. The knees are extended and the feet are perpendicular to the lower legs.

3. The measurer moves the sliding foot piece to obtain a firm contact with the heels.

4. Measurement is recorded to the nearest 0.5 cm.

HEIGHT (24 months of age or older)

1. Measurement is taken using a measuring rod or scale fixed either to a wall or to the weighing scale itself.

2. The child should remove shoes and stand with feet parallel and torso and head erect.

3. Measurer gently lowers head piece to rest on top of head.

4. Measurement is recorded to the nearest 0.5 cm or ¼ inch.

HEAD CIRCUMFERENCE

1. Measurement is taken using a steel or fiberglass tape, not a cloth tape that may stretch.

2. The tape is placed around the head above the supraorbital ridges and the occiput, so as to obtain the greatest numerical value for the head circumference.

---

*Adapted from: Bithoney, W.B. & Rathbun, J.M. Failure to thrive. In Levine, M.D., Carey, W.B., Crocker, A.C. & Gross, R.T. (Eds.), Developmental Behavioral Pediatrics. Philadelphia: W.B. Saunders, 1983.

Table 2

Technique for Measuring Midarm Circumference and
Triceps Skinfold Thickness

MIDARM CIRCUMFERENCE

1. Child's right arm is bent at a right angle at the elbow.

2. Measurer anchors 0 point of steel measuring tape at the acromion
   process landmark using the left hand.

3. The tape is pulled out over lateral part of the arm to the top of
   the olecranon process, letting it hang free. Measurement is recorded to the nearest mm.

4. Measurer records the value of ½ the distance. Keeping the left
   hand anchor point firm, the measurer marks the midpoint with a
   horizontal line which extends toward the posterior surface of the
   arm over the triceps muscle, and toward the anterior side of the
   tape.

5. Measurer has the subject relax the arm at the side. The steel
   tape is extended around the arm at the level of the horizontal
   line. The tape is held in contact with the entire surface without deforming contours. The measure at the point the tape
   crosses the 0 point is recorded to the nearest mm.

TRICEPS SKINFOLD THICKNESS

1. Child's right arm is relaxed at the side. The measurer checks by
   gently shaking the subject's arm.

2. Using the left hand, the measurer places the thumb pointed downward on the medial side of the subject's arm. With the thumb and
   index finger placed 1 cm above the midpoint marking the mid-arm
   circumference, the measurer grasps the skinfold parallel to the
   long axis of the right arm over the triceps muscle. The skinfold
   is lifted from the underlying muscle surface and is shaken gently
   to be certain that muscle has not been included.

3. The caliper is applied at the level of the horizontal mark below
   the thumb and index finger of the left hand. The caliper jaws are
   held in place while the measurer counts three seconds. Reading
   is taken and recorded to the nearest millimeter.

4. The entire triceps measurement is repeated two more times. The
   triceps skinfold measurement value is recorded as the average of
   three measurements, which should agree to within 1.0 mm.

(Tanner, 1966; Tanner et al., 1970). These data were collected in the
1950's.

    Selection of the NCHS growth charts for screening and monitoring of
FTT in the United States is recommended for several reasons: 1) data have
been recently collected (1970's); 2) the NCHS sample was designed to be
nationally representative and includes healthy children of different racial
groups (Hamill, 1976); 3) the large, cross-sectional sample permits the
inclusion of a larger number of reference subjects so that outer centiles
can be determined more precisely (Tanner, 1978). The NCHS charts are also

Table 3

Gomez Criteria

Grade of Malnutrition	Percent Median Weight/Age
Normal	90–110
I Mild	75–89
II Moderate	60–74
III Severe	Less than 60

appropriate for assessing the growth of children who are refugees or immigrants to the United States. Based on a review of 55 reference standards,
the WHO Consultation on Growth Charts has recommended the use of the NCHS
charts for assessment of child growth worldwide (WHO, 1978). The alternative use of growth data from developing countries may not yield an accurate
assessment. For instance, their use as a reference to assess growth of
refugee children is inappropriate because these data usually include measures of acutely or chronically malnourished children, or children who show
evidence of intergenerational stunting.

DEFINITIONS OF FTT

Auxological (growth) definitions of FTT include: 1) weight less than
80 to 85 precent of the NCHS median (fiftieth percentile); 2) weight for
age less than the fifth percentile on the NCHS growth charts; and 3) a drop
in weight of two or more major percentile categories from a previously established growth channel (Bithoney & Rathbun, 1983). Percentile categories
are 95, 90, 75, 50, 25, 10, 5. Criteria of protein-energy malnutrition
(PEM) used in developing countries extend current definitions of FTT by: 1)
categorizing the relative severity of underweight; and 2) by examining the
relationship of weight to height to determine whether the child is acutely
or chronically malnourished, or both. These criteria have been commonly
used in the PEM literature for over two decades. Their utilization in
description of FTT samples permits a comparison with worldwide studies of
childhood malnutrition. The Gomez et al. (1956) criteria compare the
weights of individual children with normal values for a reference population by expressing weight as a percent of median weight for age (see Table
3). These criteria are comparable to the definition of FTT as a weight
less than 80 to 85 percent of median for age. In addition, the Gomez criteria are used to categorize the degree of underweight as mild, moderate,
or severe (Grades I, II, or III malnutrition). The Waterlow (1976) criteria
are used to ascertain the degree of wasting, or acute malnutrition by
examining the relationship of weight to height Height for age is compared
with reference standards to determine the severity of stunting, or chronic
malnutrition (see Table 4).

In clinical practice and research, auxological description of FTT
should be based on all three parameters: weight, height, and weight/height
ratio. Underweight for age alone is a coarse measure of malnutrition.
Definitions of FTT based solely on weight for age may include 3-5% of the
population who are genetically smaller but within normal limits of growth
and may exclude severely malnourished or chronically ill children suffering
from edema. Weight criteria alone will fail to differentiate children who
are acutely wasted and need immediate medical attention from those who are
chronically stunted but not wasted.

161

Table 4

Waterlow Criteria

Grade of Malnutrition	WASTING Percent Median Weight/Height	STUNTING Percent Median Height/Age
Normal	90–110	95 and greater
I Mild	80–89	90–94
II Moderate	70–79	85–89
III Severe	less than 70	less than 85

Growth data from a prospective growth study and retrospective psychosocial study of 86 children who presented to the FTT Team of Children's Hospital in Boston, Massachusetts, between October, 1979, and August, 1982, are used to illustrate the application of Gomez and Waterlow criteria to growth data analysis in the FTT population. Serial anthropometric measures of FTT patients were obtained using standardized techniques during hospitalization and at all outpatient visits. The mean age of subjects at presentation was 20.2 months, with a range of 1.5 months to 6 years, 11 months. Fifty-six percent were males; 44 percent females. Ethnic groups represented in the sample were: white (79%), black (14%), Hispanic (6%), and Oriental (1%). Using the Gomez and Waterlow malnutrition criteria to describe growth status of sample children, 95 percent were underweight for age (Grades I, II, III) at presentation (see Table 5). Ten children (12%) exhibited Grade III, or severe malnutrition (weight for age less than 60 percent of median, or fiftieth percentile). Sixty-eight percent of the group were acutely wasted, with low weight/height ratios relative to the reference median. Sixty-four percent of children were stunted (low height for age) and therefore considered to be chronically malnourished.

ANALYSIS OF INDIVIDUAL GROWTH DATA

Several patterns of growth may precede the presentation of FTT. In individual growth data analysis, careful note should be taken of events at the time when growth began to falter. History taking by members of the treatment team should be focused on that stage in the child's medical, developmental, and social history to pinpoint organic and nonorganic risks that may have been prominent (i.e. death in the family, active medical illness)(Rathbun & Peterson, 1985).

1) Wasting. The child whose weight/height ratio is below the fifth percentile on NCHS growth charts is classified as acutely malnourished, or wasted. Strictly speaking, such a child could still be growing normally since by definition five percent of the children in the reference population fall below this arbitrary cut-off point. However, the classification is useful because the likelihood of acute malnutrition is high in an individual whose weight for height falls below the fifth percentile of the reference population. In these children, weight for age is likely to be below the fifth percentile as well, but height may or may not fall below the normal range. If height is within the normal range, the weight for height deficit may be evidence of an acute nutritional deficit of relatively short duration. Patients in this category require immediate nutritional rehabilitation and treatment of associated organic and nonorganic risk factors to

Table 5

Grade of Malnutrition	Underweight (Weight/Age)		Wasting (Weight/Height)		Stunting (Height/Age)	
	N	Percent	N	Percent	N	Percent
Normal	4	5	21	24	26	30
I Mild	30	35	34	40	28	33
II Moderate	41	48	20	23	22	26
III Severe	10	12	5	6	4	5
Missing Data	1	1	6	7	6	7
TOTAL	86		86		86	

prevent more serious growth deficits. A drop in weight of two or more centiles followed by a decrease in height and ultimately in head circumference indicates that the child is passing from a state of acute to severe or chronic malnutrition. This stunting is an adaptive physiological phenomenon which preserves an adequate weight for height relationship in the face of prolonged nutritional deficits, at the expense of linear growth.

2) Stunting. Some children may present both underweight and short relative to reference standards (weight and height less than the fifth percentile) but have weight/height ratios within the normal range. These children may be genetically small or may have suffered nutritional deprivation earlier in life of sufficient duration to impair full catchup growth. In children without a history of prior nutritional insult, the possibility of constitutional growth deficit can be investigated by assessing midparental height (average height of both parents at any time between 25 and 45 years of age) using the Tanner-Whitehouse charts (Tanner et al., 1970). From ages two to nine, child height correlates well with the mean of parents' heights (average correlation coefficients are 0.53 for boys and 0.49 for girls)(Tanner, 1970). Any child whose height falls more than 2.5 standard deviations below that expected using the Tanner standards should be evaluated for FTT. Among certain groups, use of mid-parental height to assess constitutional growth deficit may be inappropriate. Correlation of child and parental height is based on the assumption that parents grew normally and have realized their genetic potential (Tanner et al., 1970). Children of parents who suffered FTT as children, immigrants from less developed countries, and families who have been chronically impoverished may show evidence of intergenerational stunting. The positive secular trend in height among groups in industrialized countries and studies of children in developing countries suggest that differences in growth among well nourished children of different ethnic groups are smaller than disparities noted between children of different social classes (Eveleth & Tanner, 1976; Habicht et al., 1974). With adequate nutrition and improvement of poor socioeconomic circumstances, children of families showing intergenerational growth deficits may exceed growth parameters predicted by assessment of mid-parental height alone.

3) Prematurity and Intrauterine Growth Delay. Premature and small for gestational age (SGA) infants comprise a heterogenous group of children who are small relative to reference standards at birth but exhibit different patterns of growth in infancy and early childhood. Potential for catchup

growth in high risk infants varies with degree of prematurity, severity of perinatal medical illness, and ponderal index classification, which reflects timing and duration of intrauterine growth retardation. Premature infants without serious medical problems and asymmetric SGA babies show catchup growth in the first 6 to 8 months of life (Davies, 1980; Fitzhardinge, 1972; 1975; 1976). Nutritional rehabilitation should be targeted to support maximal growth rates during this period. Symmetric SGA infants and more severely affected premature infants should not, however, be abandoned to a diagnosis of "small kid." These infants should be nutritionally supported so that their growth rates parallel reference curves and individual children are able to maximize potential for growth. In comparing growth of high risk infants to reference standards, age at measurement should be corrected for the number of weeks the child was premature (the difference between 40 weeks and gestational age). The difference between growth percentiles for corrected and uncorrected postnatal age is statistically significant from 18 months to three years, depending on the growth parameter (Brandt, 1976). Severity of growth deficit in premature infants will be overestimated if uncorrected ages are used to analyze anthropometric data. Age at measurement should be corrected for prematurity up to 18 months for head circumference, 24 months for weight, and 3.5 years for height (Brandt, 1976).

INTERPRETATION OF GROUP DATA

In the research setting, growth criteria (weight less than the fifth percentile or less than 80 to 85 percent of median) are used to define samples of FTT children. For purposes of study, children with anthropometric measures below these levels are considered to have FTT; those who do not meet criteria for growth failure are excluded from the sample. However, not all children who meet auxological criteria for FTT can be considered to have growth delay. In the clinical and research settings, affirmaive diagnosis of FTT rests not only on growth criteria but also on the identification of specific medical and psychosocial risk factors.

By definition, five percent of children in the reference population have growth measures below the fifth percentile and are growing normally. In group data, the number of children with anthropometric measures below the fifth percentile in excess of five percent of the sample reflects underweight in the study group. For example, in a survey in which ten percent of children exhibit weights less than the fifth percentile, ten percent are not malnourished, even though they meet criteria for FTT sample selection. Rather, the excess proportion of weights less than the fifth percentile (i.e., 5% excess) indicates the percentage of children in the sample who are underweight relative to reference standards. The World Health Organization has developed a format for displaying the excess proportion of malnourished children in a sample (WHO, 1985). The WHO format translates the growth chart into a bar graph which plots anthropometric measurements by deciles (Figure 1). In a reference population of healthy children, ten percent of anthropometric measurements can be expected to lie below the tenth percentile. Another ten percent of values will be plotted between the tenth and twentieth percentile, ten percent between the twentieth and thirtieth percentile, and so on. Percentages are plotted by

---

[The ponderal index is the ratio of weight (kg) to height (cm) (W/H3) and is used to describe the body shape of SGA infants at birth. Symmetric SGA infants are "proportional" or "non-wasted" and have a ponderal index greater than the tenth percentile on reference intrauterine growth curves (Lubchenco et al., 1963, 1966). Asymmetric SGA babies are "wasted" and have a ponderal index less than the tenth percentile.]

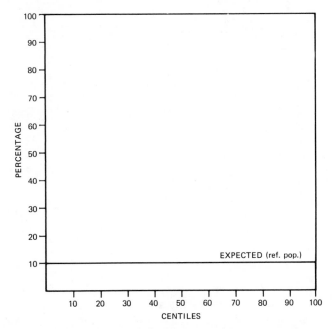

Figure 1. Percentage distribution by weight and height deciles

decile on the bar graph. The distribution of reference values forms a horizontal line under which ten percent of the reference group lies at each
decile.

When growth data on 86 FTT children in the Children's Hospital sample
are plotted by this method, the excess proportion of underweight, stunting,
and wasting relative to reference standards is evident (Figure 2A-C). A
subsample of 36 children were selected from the Children's Hospital sample
to illustrate group changes in anthropometric indices over a nine-month
treatment period. Children in the subsample had poorer initial growth
status relative to the study group as a whole. Many were chronically
malnourished, often presenting as inpatients and requiring longterm follow-
up. Improvement in the subsample with treatment is demonstrated in Figure
3A-C. The line solid line, indicating nine-month followup data is closer
to the horizontal line of the expected distribution in the reference population. Excess percentage of underweight children in the subsample decreased over a nine-month period. Reduction in the percentage of wasted
children (low weight/height ratio) is even more marked. The proportion of
children with stunted linear growth is relatively unchanged over the treatment period.

Median values for percentiles underscore group deficits, relative to
the NCHS reference population (Table 6).* Median rather than mean values
are chosen to summarize group statistics because percentiles on reference
growth charts reflect the distribution of reference values about the median,
or fiftieth percentile. This means that half of the values in the reference
population lie above the fiftieth percentile and half lie below. In the
Children's Hospital FTT sample, median values lie far below the median, or
fiftieth percentile of the NCHS reference population. For example, median
height percentile at presentation in the whole study group is 2.70, compared

---

*[Summary growth statistics were generated using computer programs provided
by the Centers for Disease Control (CDC) (Goldsby, 1972)]

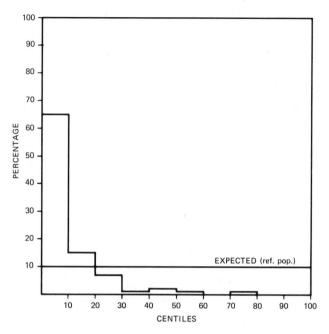

Figure 2A. Percentage distribution by height deciles at presentation.
FTT sample, Children's Hospital, 1979–1982

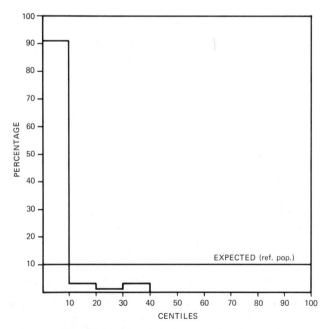

Figure 2B. Percentage distribution by weight deciles at presentation.
FTT sample, Children's Hospital, 1979–1982

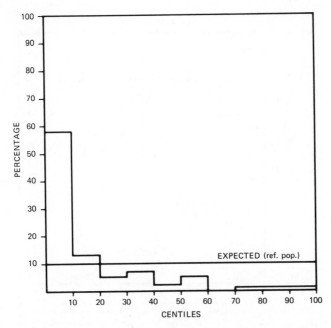

Figure 2C. Percentage distribution by weight/height deciles at presentation. FTT sample, Children's Hospital, 1979-1982

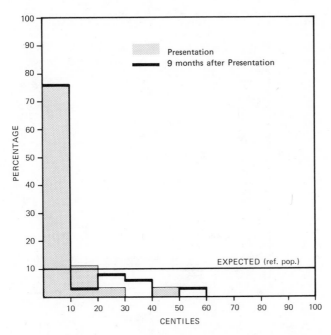

Figure 3A. Percentage Distribution by Height Deciles at Presentation and 9 Months after Presentation. FTT Sample, Children's Hospital, 1979-1982.

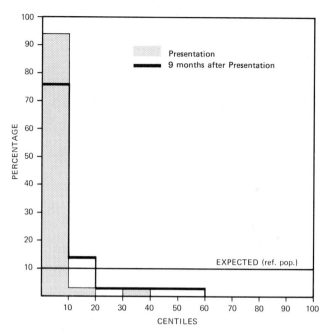

Figure 3B. Percentage Distribution by Weight Deciles at Presentation and 9 Months after Presentation. FTT Sample, Children's Hospital, 1979-1982.

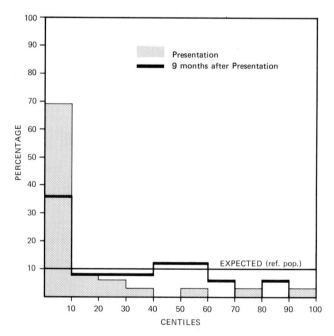

Figure 3C. Percentage Distribution by Weight/Height Deciles at Presentation and 9 Months after Presentation. FTT Sample, Children's Hospital, 1979-1982

Table 6

Median Percentiles at Presentation and Follow-up
FTT Sample, CHMC, 1979-1982

| | Median Percentile | | |
	Weight	Height	Weight/Height
Entire Sample (N = 86) Presentation	0.70	2.70	5.70
Subsample (N = 36) Presentation	0.20	0.85	3.55
Follow-up	3.55	1.75	23.50

with 50.0 in the reference population. Over the nine-month treatment
period, repair of deficits in weight for height is again evident. The
median weight/height percentile of the subsample (23.5) is within normal
range at followup.

USE OF Z SCORES IN GROWTH DATA ANALYSIS

An age bias inherent in the Gomez and Waterlow criteria of malnutrition and percent median definitions of FTT limits their utility as screening and research tools. These criteria express individual anthropometric
measurements as a percentage of fiftieth percentile values in the reference
population. At different ages, a given percentage of median does not,
however, correspond to the same proportion of standard deviation from the
median (see Figure 4). With increasing age, a static percent of median
corresponds to a progressively greater deviation from the median (see
Figure 4). For example, the line representing 75 percent of median weight
(Gomez criteria), the cutoff for Grade II underweight is close to the
fifth percentile at one month of age but far below the fifth percentile at
36 months. Percentage of median is thus an age-biased approximation of
standard deviation from the median. If anthropometric measures are translated into standard deviation units, or Z scores, the age bias is eliminated
(Heimendinger, 1981; Karlberg, 1980). The Z score shows how far an observation is from the NCHS reference median, expressed in standard deviation
units. The Z score for an anthropometric measurement is given by the
formula (WHO, 1983):

$$\text{Z score} = \frac{\text{Measurement value} - \text{Median for age value of reference population}}{\text{Standard deviation for age of reference population}}$$

Z scores can easily be derived by hand using tables of NCHS reference data
and standard deviations prepared by WHO (1983) or generated with computer
programs provided by the CDC (Goldsby, 1972). Deviation from the reference
mean for weight, height and weight/height ratio can be expressed as a continuous variable in Z units. For example, the Z scores of different aged
children can be pooled to assess the impact of an intervention. Relative
severity of underweight, wasting, and stunting can be categorized using
progressive decrements in Z scores (-2, -3, -4)(Gueri et al., 1980; WHO,

1983). When considering subjects individually, the data is interpreted as when using percentiles.

In normally distributed reference data, the median and mean will correspond so standard normal theory can be used to generate percentiles. Percentiles, like Z scores, express distribution of reference growth data about the median, or fiftieth percentile (Figure 5). Height and head circumference data are normally distributed in the reference population. In growth data analysis, weights are logrithmically transformed to achieve a more normal distribution of values (Heimendinger, 1981). The other classical criterion for selection of FTT samples, weight less than the fifth percentile, is not age-biased and corresponds to a Z score of -1.96. The fifth percentile criterion is thus a better screening tool than the definition of FTT as 80-85 percent of median. The fifth percentile cutoff is of

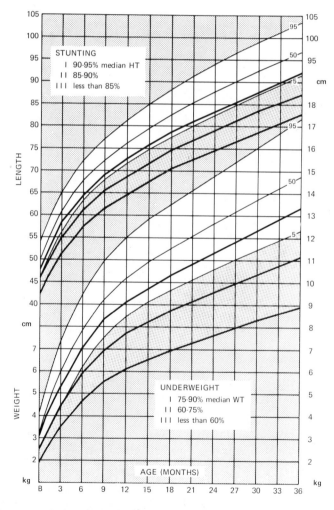

Figure 4. Gomez and Waterlow criteria of underweight and stunting relative to NCHS reference population

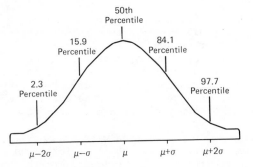

μ—Mean in unaerlying population from which sample
   is drawn
σ—Standard deviation

PERCENTILE	Z SCORE	MEAN $\pm$ STD. DEVIATION
50%	Z = 0	μ
15.9%	Z = -1	$\mu - \sigma$
84.1%	Z = +1	$\mu + \sigma$
2.3%	Z = -2	$\mu - 2\sigma$
97.7%	Z = +2	$\mu + 2\sigma$

The Z score shows how far the observation is from the
mean, expressed in standard deviation units:

$$Z = \frac{x - \mu}{\sigma}. \quad \text{Example: } Z = \frac{65-50}{10} = 1.5 .$$

(An observation of 65 is 1.5 standard deviation units
(σ = 10) from the mean of 50.)

Figure 5.   Percentile Points of the Normal Distribution.

particular use in the absence of longitudinal data confirming a history of
growth delay and in screening individual children at risk for FTT.

VELOCITY-BASED MEASURES OF GROWTH DELAY

Attained Growth vs. Velocity Measures

     An alternate definition of FTT is a decline in weight or height of two
or more centiles on distance charts. This description attempts to address
the question of normal and abnormal variation in growth velocity. In
infancy, some shifting of centiles is normal. Babies who are genetically
large may be born small if the mother (and hence the uterus) is small; the
converse is true for genetically small children born to large mothers
(Tanner, 1981). Correlations of height of Aberdeen children with final
adult height were low at birth (r=0.3), rose to 0.5 at six months, to 0.7
by one year and 0.78 by two years of age (Tanner et al., 1956). Smith et
al.'s (1976) study of 90 white middle class U.S. infants showed that the
majority of the 45 small infants (tenth percentile) in the sample shifted
upward to the fiftieth percentile in the first three to six months after
birth. Those who shifted downward from the ninetieth to fiftieth percentile did so between three and 18 months of age. Of note is the fact that
centiles used by Smith et al. (1976) were derived from the study sample

itself. Centile shifts in this more heterogenous reference group would be smaller in a larger, more diverse reference population Berkey et al. (1983) estimated the probability that NCHS reference children aged three months to six years would cross centile lines at a particular age, and found 1) a shift of two centiles toward the fiftieth percentile was more likely than a two-centile shift away (regression to the mean), 2) weight measurements shifted more than length measurements at these ages, 3) shift in centiles were uncommon after 1.5 to two years of age (Berkey et al., 1983).

Velocity charts used in conjunction with distance (attained growth) charts can help differentiate between those children who are small and those with concurrent growth failure. Velocity growth charts for children 0-18 years have been constructed from data on 818 participants in the Fels Longitudinal Study (Roche & Himes, 1980). Their use is appropriate in conjunction with the NCHS distance charts, which also drew from the Fels data base. Subnormal growth is indicated by a decrement in velocity greater than two standard deviations below the mean rate for age (velocity below the fifth percentile) over any three-month period during the first year of life and over six-month intervals during the second year of life (Fomon, 1974; Karlberg et al., 1980). Children who are not wasted but are proportionally stunted due to chronic or prior malnutrition will exhibit growth velocities between the fifth and fiftieth percentiles and normal weight/height ratios on distance standards. Such children may be differentiated from genetically small children by assessment of midparental height, dietary history, birth and medical history, social class and immigration status.

Velocity-Based Measures in Growth Data Analysis

Differences in attained growth, or degrees of malnutrition among groups of children, are frequently used as an outcome measure of treatment effect or differential distribution of risk factors. This method is appropriate for cross-sectional studies but results in a loss of statistical power in evaluating longitudinal growth data. Change in velocity is a more sensitive indicator of growth failure than attained weight. In 28 infants with a low rate of weight gain (decrease of at least 1SD unit in attained weight over a three month period) described by Kristiansson et al. (1980), 22 infants exhibited a subnormal rate of gain (decrease of at least 2 SD in attained weight over a three month period), whereas only 12 attained subnormal (less than -2SD) weight for age.

Altemeier et al. (1985) and Fomon (1974) have defined FTT as a deviation from median rate of weight gain, expressed in grams per day. Altemeier et al. (1985) employed a criterion for selection of an FTT sample of rate of weight gain over more than 10 days of less than 2/3 of the fiftieth percentile rate on the Harvard growth charts. This constitutes a decrease in rate of gain of approximately 1 SD over 10 days, corresponding to:

(2 weeks to regain birthweight)

less than 18 grams/day from 15-60 days of age
less than 12 g/d   61-270 days
less than 8 g/d   271-360 days
less than 5 g/d   361-540 days

Fomon (1974) describes FTT as rate of gain in weight or length less than   -2SD over at least 56 days in infants under 5 months of age and over an interval of at least 3 months in children aged 5 months or more. Attained weights at various ages for -2SD, 10th, 25th, 50th, 75th and 90th percentiles based on a longitudinal reference sample of Swedish urban children (Karlberg et al., 1968) are used to generate corresponding mean gains in length (mm) and weight (gm) per day between selected ages (birth, 8d, 14d,

Table 7

Z Scores as Measures of Change

	Presentation	9 Months
Age in Months	7.3	17.1
Weight in Kg.	4.8	10.0
Percentile	0.05	28.5
Z Score	-3.3	- 0.6
Z Difference		+ 2.7

28d, 42d, 56d, 84d, 112d, 3m, 6m, 9m, 12m, 18m, 24m, 36m).

Use of standard deviation units, or Z scores to represent gram values for weight used in the Altemeier et al. (1985) and Fomon (1974) velocity-based definitions of FTT eliminates the need for specifying different increments over different age intervals. Karlberg et al. (1980) has described measures of velocity using Z scores. The SD score/year is the rate of change in deviation over time, or the difference between the Z score of weight attained at two consecutive ages per unit time. Low rate of weight gain among infants is defined as a decrease in Z score in weight between 1 and 2 (-1SD to -2SD) over a period of three months. Subnormal growth is indicated by a reduction of 2 or more in Z score over three months. If greater precision is required in data analysis, the Z change measure can be further modified to correct for regression to the mean. For this purpose, weights are logarithmically transformed to achieve a more normal distribution of values. Measures are corrected for regression to mean using correlations between length, log weights, and log weight for length at various ages in the NCHS reference population (Birth; 3,6,9,12,18 and 24 months) (Heimendinger & Laird, 1983).

Tables 7 and 8 illustrate the use of Z scores as measures of change and treatment effect in an individual child and in the subsample of 36 children followed by the Children's Hospital group over a nine-month period. Changes in mean Z scores for weight and weight/height ratios are significant over a nine month period. Thus, underweight for age and deficits in weight for height, (acute malnutrition) can show marked improvement during a nine-month treatment period.

SUMMARY

In the FTT child, growth data are used to assess the impact of nonorganic and organic risks and to evaluate the effectiveness of treatment. Careful anthropometric technique and use of appropriate reference growth charts ensure the precision and validity of growth status as an outcome measure. Three types of growth indicators are used to describe the growth status of children:

1) Percent of Median Criteria. The FTT criterion of weight for age less than 80 to 85 percent of median and the Gomez and Waterlow malnutrition criteria express anthropometric measures as a percentage of the NCHS reference median, or fiftieth percentile. The Gomez (1956) criteria classify percent of median weight for age by severity of deficit: mild (Grade I), moderate (Grade II), and severe (Grade III) underweight. The Waterlow

173

Table 8

Treatment Effect at 9 Months

	Z_0	Z_9	Z_Δ	P
Height	-2.32	-2.21	0.11	NS
Weight	-2.84	-1.98	0.86	.001
Weight/Height	-1.73	-0.87	0.86	.001

criteria examine the relationship of weight to height to ascertain the degree of wasting, or acute malnutrition. Height for age is compared with reference standards to determine the severity of stunting, or chronic malnutrition.

2. Deviation from Median Criteria. Percentiles and Z scores express the distribution of reference data about the median. Z scores show how far anthropometric measures lie from the NCHS median, expressed in standard deviation units. Percentiles are equivalent to Z scores, since they indicate the percentage of anthropometric mesurements that lie a given number of standard deviation units from the reference median or fiftieth percentile (Figure 5). FTT samples are defined by attained weight more than 2 standard deviations (Z = -2) below the median or by weight less than the fifth percentile (Z=-1.96).

An age bias inherent in percent of median malnutrition criteria is eliminated in percentile and Z score measures. With increasing age, a given percentage of median corresponds to a progressively greater deviation from median (Figure 4). Percentiles and Z scores express attained measurements as an age specific deviation from median. In growth data analysis, Z scores of different aged children can be pooled without incurring an age bias.

3. Velocity-based Criteria. Decreased rate of growth is a more sensitive indicator of growth failure than attained growth. A decrease in growth velocity of two or more major percentile categories over three months is considered evidence of FTT. Change in growth velocity can also be expressed in standard deviation units (Z score). Low rate of weight gain is defined as a decrease in Z score between 1 and 2 (-1SD to -2SD) over a three month period. Subnormal growth is indicated by a Z score decrement of 2 or more (-2SD).

Growth criteria are used to define samples of FTT children and to diagnose individual cases of FTT. However, not all children who meet auxological criteria for FTt can be considered to have growth delay. In the reference population, five percent of children have growth measures below the fifth percentile and are growing normally. In group data, the number of children with anthropometric measures below the fifth percentile in excess of five percent of the sample reflects underweight in the study group. In individual children, the likelihood of malnutrition is indicated by anthropometric measures which meet FTT criteria. Affirmative diagnosis rests, however, not only on growth criteria but also on the identification of medical and psychosocial risk factors.

REFERENCES

Altemeier, W., O'Connor, S.M., Sherrod, K.B. & Vietze, P.M. Prospective study of antecedents for nonorganic failure to thrive. Journal of Pediatrics, 1985, 106, 360-365.

Berkey, C.S., Reed, R.B. & Valadian, I. Longitudinal growth standards for preschool children. Annals of Human Biology, 1983, 10, 57-67.

Bithoney, W. & Rathbun, J. Failure to thrive. In M.D. Levine, W.B. Carey, A.C. Crocker & R.T. Gross (Eds.), Developmental Behavioral Pediatrics. Philadelphia: W.B. Saunders Co., 1983.

Blackburn, G.L. & Bistrian, B.R. Nutritional support resources in hospital practice. In H.A. Schneider, C.E. Anderson & D.B. Coursin (Eds.), Nutritional Support of Medical Practice. Hagerstown, MD: Harper & Row, 1977.

Blackburn, G.L. & Thornton, P.A. Nutritional assessment of the hospitalized patient. Medical Clinics of North America, 1979, 63, 1103-1115.

Brandt, I. Growth dynamics of low-birth-weight infants with emphasis on the perinatal period. In F. Falkner & J.M. Tanner (Eds.), Human Growth, Vol. 2, Postnatal Growth. New York: Plenum Press, 1978.

Davies, D.P. Size at birth and growth in the first year of life of babies who are overweight and underweight at birth. Proceedings of the Nutrition Society, 1980, 39, 25-33.

Eveleth, P.B. & Tanner, J.M. Worldwide Variation in Human Growth. Cambridge: Cambridge University Press, 1976.

Fitzhardinge, P.M. & Steven, E.M. The small-for-date infant, I. Later growth patterns. Pediatrics, 1972, 49, 671-678.

Fitzhardinge, P.M. Early growth and development in low-birth-weight infants following treatment in an intensive care nursery. Pediatrics, 1975, 56, 162-167.

Fitzhardinge, P.M. Follow-up studies on the low-birth-weight infant. Clinics in Perinatology, 1976, 3, 503-510.

Fomon, S.J. Normal growth, failure to thrive and obesity. In Infant Nutrition. Philadelphia: W.B. Saunders Co., 1974.

Frisancho, A.R. New norms for upper limb fat and muscle areas for assessment of nutritional status. American Journal of Clinical Nutrition, 1981, 34, 2540-2545.

Goldsby, J.B. Pct19d anthropometry Fortran subroutines. Atlanta: Centers for Disease Control, Nutrition Division, Health Promotion and Education, 1972.

Gomez, F., Galvan, R., Frenk, S., Munoz, J.C., Chavez, R. & Vazquez, J. Mortality in second and third degree malnutrition. Journal of Tropical Pediatrics, 1956, 2, 77.

Gray, G.E. & Gray, L.K. Anthropometric measurements and their interpretations: Principles, practice and problems. Journal of the American Dietetic Association, 1980, 77, 534-539.

Gueri, M., Gurney, J.M. & Jutsum, P. The Gomez classification, time for a change? Bulletin of the World Health Organization, 1980, 58, 773-777.

Habicht, J.F., Martorell, R., Yarbrough, C., Maline, R.M. & Klein, R.E. Height and weight standards for preschool children: Are there really ethnic differences in growth potential? Lancet, 1974, 1, 611-614.

Hamill, P.V.V., Drizd, T.A., Johnson, C.L., Reed, R.B. & Roche, A.F. 1976 NCHS Growth Charts. Monthly Vital Statistics Report 25, No. 3 (Suppl.) DHEW Pub. No. (HRA) 76.

Heimendinger, J. & Laird, N. Growth changes: Measuring the effect of an intervention. Evaluation Review, 1983, 7, 80-95.

Heimendinger, J. The effect of the WIC program on the growth of children. Ph.D. Dissertation. Harvard School of Public Health, 1981.

Karlberg, P., Engstrom, I., Lechtenstein, H. & Svennberg, I. The development of children in a Swedish urban community. A Prospective longitudinal study. III. Physical growth during the first three years of life. Acta Paediatrica Scandinavia, 1968, 48 (Suppl. 187), 9-27.

Karlberg, P., Engstrom, I., Karlberg, J. & Kristiansson, B. Evaluation of growth during the first two years of life. In B. Kristiansson (Ed.), Low Rate of Weight Gain in Infancy and Early Childhood. Goteborg, Sweden: Department of Paediatrics, University of Goteborg, 1980.

Kristiansson, B., Karlberg, J. & Fallstrom, S.P. Infants with low rate of weight gain. I. A study of organic growth factors and growth patterns. In B. Kristiansson (Ed.), Low Rate of Weight Gain in Infancy and Early Childhood. Goteborg, Sweden: Department of Paediatrics, University of Goteborg, 1980.

Lubchenco, L.O., Hansman, C., Dressler, M. & Boyd, E. Intrauterine growth as estimated from liveborn birth-weight data at 24 to 42 weeks of gestation. Pediatrics, 1963, 32, 793-800.

Lubchenco, L., Hansman, C. & Boyd, E. Intrauterine growth in length and head circumference as estimated from live birth at gestational ages from 26 to 42 weeks. Pediatrics, 1966, 37, 403-408.

Murray, C. & Glassman, M. Nutrient requirements during growth and recovery from failure to thrive. In P.F. Accardo (Ed.), Failure to Thrive in Infancy and Early Childhood. Baltimore: University Park Press, 1981.

Peterson, K.E., Washington, J.S. & Rathbun, J.M. Team management of failure to thrive. Journal of the American Dietetic Association, 1984, 84, 810.

Rathbun, J. & Peterson, K. Nutrition in failure to thrive. In R. Grand, J. Sutphen & W. Dietz (Eds.), The Theory and Practice of Nutrition in Pediatrics. Boston: Butterworth Publishers, Inc., 1985.

Reed, R.B. & Stuart, H.C. Patterns of growth in height and weight from birth to eighteen years of age. Pediatrics, 1959, 24, 904-921.

Roche, A.F. & Himes, J.H. Incremental growth charts. American Journal of Clinical Nutrition, 1980, 33, 2041-2052.

Smith, D.W.,Truog, W., Rogers, J.E., Greitzer, L.F., McCann, J.J. & Harvey, M.A.S. Shifting linear growth during infancy: Illustration of genetic factors in growth from fetal life through infancy. Journal of Pediatrics, 1976, 89, 225-230.

Stuart, H.C. & Meredith, H.V. Use of body measurements in the school health program. American Journal of Public Health, 1946, 36, 1365-1373.

Tanner, J.M., Healy, M.F.R., Lockhart, R.D., MacKenzie, J.D. & Whitehouse, R.H. Aberdeen growth study: The prediction of adult body measurements taken each year from birth to 5 years. Archives of Disease in Childhood, 1956, 31, 372-381.

Tanner, J.M. & Whitehouse, R.H. Standards from birth to maturity for height, weight, height velocity, and weight velocity: British children, 1965. Archives of Disease in Childhood, 1966, 41, 454-471.

Tanner, J.M., Goldstein, H. & Whitehouse, R.H. Standards for children's height at ages 2-9 years allowing for height of parents. Archives of Disease in Childhood, 1970, 45, 755-762.

Tanner, J.M. Human growth standards: Construction and use. In L. Gedda (Ed.), Auxology: Human Growth in Health and Disorder. New York: Academic Press, 1978.

Tanner, J.M. Catchup growth in man. British Medical Bulletin, 1981, 37, 233-238.

Waterlow, J. Classification and definition of protein calorie malnutrition. In G. Beaton & J. Bengoa (Eds.), Nutrition in Preventative Medicine, W.H.O. Monograph Series No. 62. Geneva: World Health Organization, 1976.

World Health Organization. A growth chart for international use in maternal and child health care. Geneva: World Health Organization, 1978.

World Health Organization. Measuring change in nutritional status. Geneva: World Health Organization, 1983.

HOME OBSERVATION OF PARENT-CHILD TRANSACTION IN FAILURE TO THRIVE:

A METHOD AND PRELIMINARY FINDINGS*

Mary Ann Finlon, Dennis Drotar, Jackie Satola, John Pallotta,
Betsy Wyatt, and Debra El-Amin

Case Western Reserve University School of Medicine

Beginning with early clinical descriptions, FTT has long been characterized as having its origins in deviant maternal-child relationships
(Patton & Gardner, 1962). Although there is agreement among clinicians
that description of parent-child interaction has significant implications
for clinical intervention (see Chatoor et al.; Lieberman & Birch; Linscheid
& Raskane, this volume), the clinical import of this topic has not been
matched by systematic empirical studies. There are a number of reasons for
this. The logistics of observing FTT infants and their parents, especially
in their home setting are very difficult. In addition, formidable methodological issues are involved in the analysis and interpretation of observational data (Yarrow & Anderson, 1979). As a consequence, the parent-child
relationship in FTT remains largely uncharted by objective methods. In
order to explicate salient issues in the study of parent-child interaction
in FTT and stimulate future research on this topic, this chapter describes
a method for observation of parent-child interaction, preliminary data
which links observational variables to early psychological outcome in FTT,
and implications for future research.

STUDIES OF PARENT-CHILD INTERACTION IN FTT

Although FTT is thought by many clinicians to originate in deficient
or distorted parent-child relationships, in practice, parent-child interaction is not generally observed until after FTT has become apparent and is
often chronic. Unfortunately, such retrospective identification precludes
explicit inferences concerning the cause and effect relationship of parent-
child interaction to FTT for a number of reasons. After the child fails to
thrive, maternal perceptions of the child as physically sick may affect the
nature of parent-child interaction (Kotelchuck, 1980). In addition, some
FTT children are prone to recurrent infections or other health problems
which affect their behavior and social interaction. Finally, nutritional
status, which is often compromised in FTT and sometimes severely so, also
can affect social responsiveness and hence influence the character of
parent-child interaction (Pollitt, 1973; Pollitt & Thomson, 1977). For
this reason, the few available studies of the relationship of parent-child

---

*This research was funded by the National Institute of Mental Health
(Applied Research) #35220 and Prevention Research Center #30274.

interaction to weight gain prior to the development of FTT assume special importance. In a pioneering investigation, Pollitt, Gilmore & Vallarcel (1978) documented the relationship of parent-child interaction during the first feeding interaction and growth velocity during the first month of life. Variables predictive of weight gain included adaptive maternal behaviors such as frequency of feeding and caretaking, and infant behaviors such as visual alertness. Frequency of the child's refusal of the nipple correlated negatively with weight gain. This study provided empirical support for the clinical observation that the quality of the mother-child relationship can affect the child's rate of weight gain.

To the extent that FTT is associated with deviant parent-child rela- tionships, one would expect to see signs of early interactional difficulties prior to the development of FTT, especially in dyads at high risk to develop this problem. To our knowledge, Vietze et al. (1980) have conducted the only prospective exploration of parent-child interaction prior to the development of FTT. Vietze et al. (1980) noted that certain features of dyadic behavior observed during the neonatal period discriminated infants who subsequently developed FTT from physically healthy children who were also from high-risk environments. Given that the mother was responding in isolation, mothers of male children who subsequently failed to thrive were more likely to terminate their response than mothers of male children who did not develop FTT. In addition, there was a greater probability of mothers of healthy male infants to maintain their response when the infant was not responding than for the mothers of FTT infants. Finally, given that both mother and infant were responding, the mothers of male infants later diagnosed as FTT had a greater probability of dropping out of the interac- tion. The association of specific social interactional patterns with the subsequent development of FTT is unique in the literature and bears repli- cation, especially in view of the unexpected finding of sex differences and the failure to obtain more dramatic group differences. No differences were found between the groups on a variety of infant and/or maternal behaviors.

The need remains for researchers to describe the prospective course of interaction in dyads identified at risk in the neonatal period. For exam- ple, it would be important to know to what extent early signs of parent- child relationship difficulty (Gray et al., 1976) are expressed in subse- quent social transactions and/or eventually culminate in FTT.

Social-Interactional Concomitants

Although observations of parent-infant interaction after FTT has been diagnosed have limited ability to elucidate etiology, they can be very useful in defining transactional patterns associated with longer term psych- osocial functioning. In addition, controlled studies can help identify those elements of social transaction which differentiate FTT dyads from comparison groups. Although the group differences found in such studies are much less dramatic than what might be expected based on clinical obser- vation, deficiencies in social interactions between mothers and FTT chil- dren relative to comparison groups have been documented. For example, in a home observational study, Pollitt, Eichler & Chan (1976) noted that the mothers of FTT infants demonstrated fewer verbal and physical contacts and a less adaptive emotional climate, based on measures derived from the Home Inventory and the Childhood Level of Living Scale (Polansky, Borgman & Desaix, 1972) than mothers of physically healthy control children. These findings have been recently confirmed by Bradley (1983) who found differences on the HOME Scale in Maternal Responsivity, Maternal Acceptance, and Organization of Physical Environment between FTT infants and a sample matched on age, sex, and social class. A multiple discriminant analysis based on the HOME Scales and a life events measure yielded a 70% prediction rate of FTT vs. normally growing infants (see Bradley & Casey, this volume, for an interesting reanalysis of this data).

Dietrich, Starr & Weisfeld (1983) observed the feeding interactions of 53 mother-infant dyads from various diagnostic groups (nonaccidental trauma combined with FTT, nonaccidental trauma only, neglect only, and normal control). Infants and mothers in two groups: (a) nonaccidental trauma and FTT; and (b) nonaccidental trauma and iron deficiency anemia demonstrated the lowest interactional engagement as defined by a factor score based on maternal and child behaviors. Unfortunately, these findings are difficult to interpret because the infants with nonaccidental trauma and FTT also had significant developmental delays. Moreover, in view of the apparently low rate of coincidence of child abuse and FTT, these findings may not be generalizable to the majority of FTT infants.

Information based on studies of group differences would be greatly enhanced by studies of the prognostic implications of individual differences in interactional patterns within the FTT population. For example, one important direction for future investigation concerns the description and relevance of individual differences in parent-child interaction to psychological outcomes. Preliminary investigations, which have documented marked individual differences in social transaction between FTT infants and their mothers (Finlon & Drotar, 1983; Ryan, Whitt, Dalton & Lavigne, 1982), strongly suggest that there is no prototypic interactional pattern associated with FTT. For example, some parent-child dyads are characterized by conflict or intrusively high stimulation (Alfasi, 1982; Chatoor & Egan, 1983) rather than by the low frequency of interaction which has been characteristically identified with at least some types of FTT. For this reason, delineation of diagnostic subtypes (Chatoor et al. Lieberman & Birch; Linscheid & Raskane; Woolston, this volume) should lead to a more precise understanding of the interrelationship between early parent-child transaction and FTT. As yet, no theory has been developed to explain either the origins or nature of the specific deficit(s) in relationships between FTT infants and their mothers. However, Ramey and his coworkers hypothesized that one major interactional deficit in FTT involves response-contingent stimulation from mother to child (Ramey, Haeger & Klisz, 1972; Ramey et al., 1975). Moreover, clinicians who have worked extensively with mothers of FTT infants (Fraiberg, 1980; Shapiro, Fraiberg & Adelson, 1976) have postulated that maternal experiences of problematic nurturing as children (such as extreme parental inconsistency, abuse or neglect) may serve to disrupt their capacities to interpret their own children's signals and respond appropriately to their social bids. As yet, such highly intuitive clinical observations lack empirical documentation in larger samples.

THE PRESENT STUDY

Rationale

The overall design of the study is described by Drotar et al. (this volume) and will not be repeated here. Home observations were accorded a special place in our study design for a number of reasons. In view of the fact that the early parent-infant relationship might be expected to mediate psychological outcomes in FTT, observational variables were construed as key predictors of psychological outcome. As a process measure of interaction, home observations are a complement to other assessments of the family environment. Home observations provide a unique way of assessing the influence of potential competing activities on the child's nurturing. In addition, such variables as maternal or child reciprocal behavior, which can be best assessed via home observation, may be significant outcome variables in their own right. Finally, observational methods provide a unique vehicle to study individual differences in the developmental course

of social transactional patterns in FTT children which may underlie psychological resilience vs. deviance in various domains of psychological functioning.

The following sections describe: 1) the choice of method and its
development; 2) data reduction; and 3) predictive validation with cognitive
development and attachment.

Choice of Method

There is no one observational method that is the "best." Depending on
one's research goals, different observational methods have a variety of
costs versus benefits. We were most interested in preserving the content
and detail of specific interactions rather than in summary ratings of
interaction. Our interest in recording parent-child interaction in a
natural setting led us to consider methods that were appropriate for home
observation. Finally, we were interested in a method that allowed a flexi-
ble, multidimensional approach to data analysis. A specific method, the
SSR event-recording system (Stephenson, Smith & Roberts, 1975; Stephenson,
1979) was chosen for the following reasons: 1) the recorder is portable,
suitable for home observation, and thus provides an ecologically sound
method to sample a child's nurturing network; 2) computer compatibility:
data can be stored in a format for subsequent analysis programs; 3) the
system uses logically structured codes which ease the burden on the
observer; 4) the use of noninferential codes preserve the integrity of the
social transaction entered by an observer as a <u>subject</u> (e.g. mother) <u>action</u>
(e.g. feeds) <u>object</u> (e.g. infant) sequence. In this system, observations
of behavior are clearly distinguished from inferences about behavior, which
is not possible in clinical rating methods; 5) finally, the real-time data
base allows the use of data analytic techniques such as lag frequency
(Sackett, 1980) and dyadic states (Bakeman & Brown, 1977, 1980) which
sample the structure and organization of dyadic behavior.

On the other hand, significant disadvantages of this particular method
include the expense in training observers and data processing, the many
steps involved in data reduction and the difficulties of interfacing with
different computer systems. Finally, the method generates an extraordinary
amount of data which taxes the investigator's analytic capacities and requires one to develop specific conceptual frameworks to guide the analysis.

Behavior Codes and Observer Training

Behavior codes were developed from a series of pilot observations of
FTT and physically healthy infants which assessed a range of behaviors in a
variety of contexts (feeding, play, etc.) during the first two years of
life. The behaviors range from common behaviors, e.g. vocalizes, to rare
and more deviant behaviors such as echolalia. Observer training included
memorization of codes accompanied by practice demonstration with films,
live observation and an opportunity for practice with another observer who
is proficient with the SSR System. To enhance replicability of methods, we
have a videotaped illustration of each of the behavioral codes, including
different examples of the same behavior with different children and an
accompanying manual which includes detailed code description (Drotar et
al., 1981). The videotape and coder's manual can be made available to
investigators who wish to replicate this method. One safeguard against
bias concerns the fact that the observers were trained to observe specific
behaviors that do not require a great deal of inference and to strictly
attend to the flow of interaction. Observers were also unaware of treatment assignment and information about children and families.

Inter-Rater Reliability

To monitor inter-rater reliability to refine our coding system, a computer program was developed to allow detailed "matching" of protocols from two or more observers who are observing the same home visit and/or films. Inter-rater reliability studies were used to refine codes and summary variables. Given the wide ranges in inter-rater reliability on individual codes (from .30 to .85) and the large number of potential variables, only those variables showing reliability above .75 and nonsignificant observer effects based on generalizability analyses (Cronbach et al., 1972) are used. Inter-rater reliability was sampled throughout the study.

Specific Procedures for Home Observation

Baseline home observations were impossible since the child was not identified until pediatric hospitalization. The first observation was conducted in the home setting one month after hospital discharge and after the child's acutely malnourished state was improved relative to status at intake. Our procedure allowed us to sample family routine while imposing relatively few constraints on caregivers. Infants were observed in their homes at monthly intervals (duration of 45 minutes) over a ten month period to assess the evolving mother-child relationship in naturalistic contexts involving feeding, reciprocal social interchange, and play. This plan allowed the development of aggregate scores which are more reliable than single scores and the assessment of developmental change. Visits were scheduled at times when the infant was awake and interacting with its parent (major caretaker) and at a consistent time. At the start of observations, children ranged in age from 2 to 15 months (M=7 months).

Family Reactivity to Observation and Assessment

The question of family reactivity to observation is a difficult one to address. Studies using unobtrusive measures demonstrate that observer presence results in more socially acceptable behavior but does not produce significant changes in rates of deviancy (Patterson, 1982). Our experiences were consistent with these research findings. Once families were accustomed to observations, they demonstrated a range of behaviors, which sometimes included deviant behaviors such as inconsistent supervision of the child.

DATA ANALYSIS

The present findings were based on a subset of subjects (N=38) whose data collection and analysis has been completed, from a total possible sample of 66. Out of 68 infants who were initially enrolled in the project, one family refused home observations and another could not be observed with sufficient frequency to allow analysis.

Data Reduction

Data reduction was based on the logic of the SSR event recording system. The basic unit of observation is a subject-action-object sequence. Subject is defined as the actor (parent or child) who sends a communication or social signal, the action is the behavior that is observed, and the object is the social object of a communicative signal. Activity is defined as the total number of behaviors (including social and non-social) behaviors observed in a given family environment. A social signal or transaction is more specific and defined as a behavior emitted by a person or actor that is clearly directed toward or focused upon another person. In the SSR observational system, parent or child can direct social signals to a number of adults and/or children. In this way, we could assess the impact of such varibles as the number of persons in the home on child or parents' activity.

One first step in data reduction was the summary of behavior into general categories. Rates of social and nonsocial initiatives for each actor were subdivided into categories defined by whom the behavior was directed. For example, maternal behavior included mother to child initiatives, mother to other, mother to no-one (objectless), and self-directed behaviors (nonsocial initiatives). The child's general behavior categories are complementary to those defined for the mother and include social initiatives including child to mother, child to other and nonsocial initiatives defined as child to no-one and self-directed behaviors.

A second kind of summary category was derived to reflect specific content and function of behavior. Sample maternal behaviors are comparable to those used in other observational systems and include such behaviors as physical contact, child behaviors include feeds, vocalizations, etc.

Assessment of Dyadic State

The sampling of the structure and organization of dyadic activity is a useful complement to content-based methods based solely on frequencies. The concept of the communicative state (Bakeman & Brown, 1977, 1980) is an efficient way to assess dyadic process in ways that tap early social competence. A communicative state was defined by the presence of mother and/or the child's communicative behaviors within a given time interval (10 sec). Based on Bakeman and Brown (1977, 1980), four different dyadic states were defined: 1) Reciprocal: both child and mother send a social signal. 2) Mother Initiate: mother initiates signal to child, child does not signal. 3) Child Initiate: child initiates a signal. 4) Quiet or No Signalling: neither child nor mother initiates a social signal. In general, a competent or effective social dyad is one which is characterized by greater frequency of reciprocal states. In addition to state frequency, transitional probabilities (the frequency that one dyadic state follows another state or itself) were calculated. State transitions of particular interest were those in which maternal or child initiatives are followed by a reciprocal state. Finally, a standardized or z-score was also calculated to assess whether various state transitions occur above chance levels (Allison & Liker, 1982).

PSYCHOMETRIC STUDIES

Stability

Spearman rank correlations were done using a subsample of subjects who had at least 3 observations between the ages of 15 and 23 months to check the stability of the macro behavior categories and selected behavior categories. Most macro categories (e.g. mother to child initiatives, child social initiatives) had significant correlation between Time 1 and Time 2 (lag of 1 to 3 months) ranging from .45 to .79.

Factor Analysis

Maternal Behavior Categories. Principal component analysis with varimax rotation yielded three factors for the behavioral categories. The first factor (37.6%) consisted of: Physical Contact, Provide and Facilitate, Contact Breaking, Vocals and Parent-Infant Exchange. A second factor (23.4%) consisted of Negative Vocals, Negative Sanctions and Social exchange. A third factor (13.5%) consisted of Caretaking, Routine Physical Caretaking and Visual Attention.

Child Behavior Categories. For child behavior, Factor I (36.1%) consisted of Provide and Facilitate, Positive Affect, Object Oriented and

Social Exchange. A second factor (19.7%) included Vocals and Social Exchange. The third factor (13.2%) included Negative Child Behavior and Motor Behavior.

VALIDITY STUDIES

Predictions of Early Cognitive Developmental Outcome

A number of parent-child relationship dimensions may be relevant to outcome in FTT. For example, one might expect very depleted families of FTT infants to have low levels of social transaction which would constrain the child's opportunities for learning. In particular, the absence of maternal behavior focused on the child might be expected to relate to less competent outcomes. In addition, the consequences of child initiatives, especially whether they are effective in "claiming" additional interactions from caregivers may be a determinant of competence. For example, a FTT child who is significantly malnourished and/or who consistently withdraws from interaction will reduce the level of stimulation received from his caregivers (Pollitt, 1973). On the other hand, more resilient FTT infants may be more effective in claiming the effective attention of adult caregivers, even within the constraints of their family situations.

As an initial step, we were interested in studying the effectiveness of composite interactional behavior scores based on a summary of the 10 observations as predictors of future developmental outcome. In structuring this analysis, we assumed that the child's exposure to a rich maternal environment and practice of interactional skills are necessary to enhance development in a given domain. To test this, a stepwise multiple regression analysis used the following predictor variables: Child Vocalizations, Child to Mother Vocalizations, Mother to Child Vocalizations, Maternal Social Initiatives, Child Social Initiatives and the conditional probability for state transitions of Maternal and Child Initiate to the Reciprocal State to predict Mental Development Index (MDI) as measured by the Bayley (Bayley, 1969) and receptive language (White et al., 1978) at 24 months. As shown in Table 1, the results suggest that focal behavior or experience involving mother and child related to language is more likely to predict language outcome than general experience. The general initiatives categories for mother and child shared less than 3% of the variance in this predictive model compared to the Mother to Child and Child Vocalizations (Table 1).

Table 1

Prediction of Receptive Language at 24 Months

	Multiple R	R^2	R^2 Change	F	Sign
Child vocalizations	.422	.178	.178	6.48	.01
Mother to child vocalizations	.466	.217	.163	4.02	.03
Child social initiatives	.498	.248	.032	3.09	.04
Mother social initiatives	.519	.270	.021	2.49	.06

Table 2

Prediction of Bayley MDI at 24 Months

Variables	Multiple R	R^2	R^2 Change	F	Sign
Child to mother vocalizations	.384	.178	.148	5.19	.03
Mother social initiatives	.462	.214	.066	3.94	.03
Conditional probability of mother to reciprocal	.527	.278	.064	3.59	.03
Child social initiatives	.581	.338	.060	3.45	.02
Mother to child initiatives	.604	.365	.027	2.99	.03

As shown in Table 2, Child to Mother Vocalizations provided the best single predictor of Bayley MDI at age 24 months. However, maternal behavior, including Social Initiations and transition to the Reciprocal State, also had an influence (Table 2).

Correlates of Attachment

Attachment, defined as enduring affective tie between infant and caregiver (Sroufe & Waters, 1977; Ainsworth et al., 1978; Sroufe, 1979) is another outcome variable which may be relevant to psychological outcomes. As assessed from discrete behavioral reactions in a structured laboratory-based separation and reunion situation, the major dimensions of attachment behavior include: the child's proximity seeking to the mother or major caregiver and approach vs. avoidance following a brief separation. The most adaptive attachment pattern, secure (Ainsworth, 1978) is characterized by the child's explicit notice of the mother's departure, seeking of contact and comforting upon her return, maintenance of contact with her until comforted and then separation from the mother to return to independent play. In marked contrast, maladaptive or compromised attachment patterns are characterized by either marked resistance to physical contact, or avoidance of the caregiver.

Although the significance of attachment behavior for the development of competence has now been relatively well documented for normal populations (Main, 1981; Sroufe, 1979, 1983; Waters, Wippman & Sroufe, 1979), the specific patterns of early social transaction which underly adaptive vs. maladaptive attachment have not been well described, especially in risk populations such as FTT. However, one might expect that early parent-child transactions would provide the foundation for the development of adaptive attachment patterns. For example, dyads characterized by secure attachments might be expected to have a high level of social activity, a relatively high incidence of reciprocal dyadic states, and a high frequency of adaptive social bids which are effective in engaging caregivers in reciprocal interaction. On the other hand, maladaptive attachments, especially avoidant attachments, should be characterized by a low frequency of social initiatives, a diminished level of reciprocity as shown by fewer "Reciprocal" and more "No Signal" states and less effective child initiatives. Moreover, one might expect that these transactional patterns would be reinforced over time once the child established a given pattern of attachment.

Based on videotapes of behavior in the Ainsworth strange situation procedure subjects were classified into one of three categories: secure, resistant or avoidant (Ainsworth et al., 1979). The avoidant was the most frequent pattern of anxious attachment in this subsample and in the sample as a whole. Using a two-tailed t-test, only one significant difference was found between the securely attached (n=13) versus avoidant (n=16) group. The frequency of Self-Directed behaviors was higher in the Avoidant group (N=5.1, S.D.=3.2) than in the secure group (N=3.1, S.D.=1.4) (t=2.29, df=27, p= < .03). Although no differences were found for the other categories of social initiatives, most trends were in the direction one would hypothesize. For example, mothers in the securely attached group had a higher rate of Mother to Child Initiatives than the avoidant group. The rate of Child to Mother Initiatives was also higher in the secure group. Finally, mothers in the securely attached group directed fewer initiatives to others compared to those in the avoidant group. No differences were found between the groups on the rates of dyadic states and transitions.

Discriminant Function Analysis

The failure to obtain group differences based on single variables reflecting social initiatives and dyadic states suggested that our predictions may have been based on simplistic assumptions. In view of the fact that parent-child transactions are multidimensional processes (Bates et al., 1982), one might expect a cluster of variables to be more effective discriminators of attachment classifications than single measures. As a consequence, we chose to run two separate discriminant analyses for mother and child behaviors. Maternal behaviors included Social Initiatives, Mother to Child behavior, Mother to Other and Nonsocial Initiatives, and conditional probabilities of transitions from the Reciprocal State. Child behaviors included Social Initiatives, Child to Mother behavior, Self-Directed activity, Child to Other, and Nonsocial Initiatives and Child Efficacy. Child Efficacy was defined as the proportion of the infant initiative state and reciprocal states divided by the sum of the frequency of all states. This index was devised to provide a more precise assessment of the child's effectiveness in engaging his or her mother in interaction.

As shown in Table 3, the rate of child self-directed initiatives and efficacy combined to form a significant function. Securely attached infants had lower rates of Self-Directed behavior and higher rates of Efficacy than the children with avoidant attachments.

As shown in Table 4, maternal behavior also yielded a significant discriminant function. The rate of Mother to Other Initiatives and the likelihood that a Quiet (no interaction) state would follow a Reciprocal state were lower in the securely attached versus avoidant group.

IMPLICATIONS

Although based on a relatively small sample size, these preliminary findings have a number of potential implications. The fact that maternal to child and child vocalizations were predictive of subsequent language development at 24 months suggests that experience and practice in language-related transactions are associated with more competent language. The prediction of Bayley MDI at 24 months from rate of child vocalizations and maternal social initiative also makes intuitive sense and is consistent with the results of a number of other studies of high-risk, disadvantaged populations (Bee et al., 1981; Ramey, Farran & Campbell, 1979). These findings suggest that the frequency of adaptive maternal-child behavior may

Table 3

Discriminant Function Analysis: Child Behavior and Attachment

Step Number	Variable Entered	F Ratio	Cumulative Significance Level	Standardized Discriminant Function Coefficients in Final Steps
1	Child self-directed initiatives	4.44	.044	.972
2	Child Efficacy	5.74	.009	-.872

Table 4

Discriminant Function Analysis: Maternal Behavior and Attachment

Step Number	Variable Entered	F Ratio	Cumulative Significance Level	Standardized Discriminant Function Coefficients in Final Steps
1	Conditional probability of transition from reciprocal to quiet state	5.791	.023	.466
2	Mother to other social initiatives	3.558	.043	.855

serve as a protective factor with respect to longer-term cognitive impairment in the FTT population. It will be important to determine if these
findings are upheld for the entire sample and with long-term outcomes,
especially those pertaining to socioemotional development. Certain features of maternal-child transaction also discriminated attachment classifications at 12 months of age. For example, the finding of a higher frequency
of self-directed behavior in avoidant infants provides some validation of
the construct of avoidant attachment. In the laboratory situation, children classified as avoidant spend much of their time in self-directed
activity, which is coupled with active avoidance of the mother. The fact
that self-directed behavior was also characteristic of the behavior of
avoidant infants at home is support for cross-situational generalizability
of this attachment pattern. It should be noted that for a behavior to be
classified as self-directed, the child clearly had to direct communication
toward himself/ herself.

On the other hand, the fact that no other single variable differentiates securely attached vs. avoidant infants was contrary to prediction
and warrants discussion. It is possible that the small sample size, especially given the heterogeneity of the sample in terms of age, etc., limited
the detectability of group differences. The fact that trends were in the
predicted direction suggests that some of the predicted differences might
emerge with greater numbers.

Although the significant findings concerning the discriminant analyses
of attachment classification should be interpreted with caution given their
preliminary nature, the clusters of variables that emerged on this analysis
suggest that the pattern of children's initiatives in the home situation
are correlated with their pattern of attachment in a laboratory situation.
A high frequency of self-directed initiatives and a low rate of efficacy
were characteristic of children classified as avoidant versus securely
attached. The complementary pattern of low frequency of self-directed
initiatives and a high rate of efficacy was associated with a secure attachment. Maternal behavior also discriminated attachment classifications such
that an avoidant attachment was characterized by a higher probability of
the transition from the Reciprocal to Quiet state and by a higher frequency
of maternal initiatives to other people. Taken together, these findings
suggest that the child's behavior maintains the pattern of avoidant attachment. In addition, the frequency of competing activity (Zussman, 1978)
may contribute to the maintenance of an avoidant attachment, at least in
the present sample, in which FTT children tended to be latter born (mean
birth order of 2.6) and have multiple siblings. It is possible that mothers
of securely attached FTT children are more able to manage competing claims,
resist focusing behavior on other children, and hence focus their attention
on the FTT child more effectively than mothers of FTT children with avoidant
attachments. Reciprocal mother-child interactions may be of shorter duration in the avoidant group, as reflected by a greater occurrence of the
transition from the Reciprocal to the Quiet state. This finding suggests
that the allocation of social transactions in the FTT child's social network
(Lewis & Feiring, 1979) should be considered in evaluating psychological
outcome in FTT. The quality of the maternal-child interaction in FTT may
well depend on the manner in which the child's broader family context
supports or disrupts the maternal-child relations.

The obtained relationships between early maternal child behavior and
early psychological outcomes provide support for the notion that psychological outcome in FTT in a number of domains is at least partially related
to the frequency of parent-child interaction along specific dimensions.
Hence, these findings provide support for the potential efficacy of interventions designed to increase the frequency of parent-child interaction
either by working directly with the dyad or by working with the family

network to address factors which may be potentially disruptive to dyadic interaction. For this reason, it would be useful for studies of intervention in FTT to include observational measures as a component of outcome evaluation. To the extent that treatment results in positive changes in specific areas of parent-child interaction that can be linked to adaptive outcomes in the child, interventions may be designed with greater specificity and efficacy.

Certain limitations of the present findings should be mentioned. First, these data were gathered on a sample of FTT infants all of whom had relatively early onset, were hospitalized during their first year of life, and received some form of home-based intervention. As a consequence, the generalizability of these findings is limited to comparable populations. Second, the present analysis was based on summary scores which have the advantage of stability but may obscure developmental trends. Additional analyses are in progress to delineate the relevance of developmental trends in parent-child interaction to psychological outcome. In addition, the present analysis was based on variables which do not directly tap such constructs as maternal availability (Sorce & Emde, 1981) contingency (Watson, 1967, 1979), or maternal responsiveness (Coates & Lewis, 1985), which may be more predictive of children's competence than the current measures. Finally, the fact that the present measures were based on group data imposes certain limitations. Given the heterogeneity in parent-child transactions within the FTT population (Finlon & Drotar, 1983; Ryan et al., 1981), it is possible that detailed analyses of individual differences in interactional behavior (Thoman et al., 1981) may yield meaningful distinctions in this population. Although observations of early parent-child interaction yielded statistically significant relationships with outcome measures, such variables did not account for an especially large amount of the variance in outcomes. Perhaps, better predictions may be obtained by including measures of the family environment as predictors.

The present findings suggest a number of specific directions for future research. One productive area concerns investigation of the patterns of family ecology that are associated with positive vs. negative transactional outcomes. It would also be useful to document the relationship between diagnostically meaningful variables in FTT, e.g., age of onset, chronicity, and variables related to parent-child transaction and to determine whether observational variables contribute to prediction of outcomes over and beyond other child or family variables.

REFERENCES

Ainsworth, M.D.S. & Wittig, B.A. Attachment and exploratory behavior of one year olds in a strange situation. In B.M. Foss (Ed.), Determinants of Infant Behavior: Vol. 4. London: Methuen, 1969.

Allison, P.D. & Liker, J.K. Analyzing sequential categorical data in dyadic interaction: A comment on Gottman. Psychological Bulletin, 1982, 91, 383-403.

Alfasi, G. A failure-to-thrive infant at play: Applications of microanalysis. Journal of Pediatric Psychology, 1982, 7, 111-123.

Bakeman, R. & Brown, J.V. Behavioral dialogues: An approach to the assessment of mother-infant interaction. Child Development, 1977, 48, 195-203.

Bakeman, R. & Brown, J.V. Analyzing behavioral sequences: Differences between preterm and full-term infant-mother dyads during the first months of life. In D. Sawin (Ed.), Exceptional Infant: Vol. 4. Psychosocial Risks in Infant Environment Transactions. New York: Brunner-Mazel, 1980.

Bates, J.E., Olson, J.L., Pettit, G.S. & Bates, K. Dimensions of individ-

uality in the mother-infant relationship at six months of age. <u>Child</u>
<u>Development</u>, 1982, <u>53</u>, 446-461.

Bayley, N. <u>The Bayley Scales of Infant Development Manual</u>. New York:
Psychological Corporation, 1969.

Bee, H.C., Barnard, K.E., Eyres, S.J., Gray, C.L., Hammond, M.A., Spietz,
A.L., Snyder, C. & Clark, B. Prediction of IQ and language skill from
perinatal status, child performance, family characteristics, and
mother-infant interaction. <u>Child Development</u>, 1982, <u>53</u>, 1134-1156.

Bradley, R.H. Social and nonsocial environment of children who are nonorganic failure to thrive. Paper presented at Biennial Meeting of the
Society for Research in Child Development. Detroit, MI, April, 1983.

Chatoor, I. & Egan, J. Nonorganic failure to thrive and dwarfism due to
food refusal: A separation disorder. <u>Journal of the American Academy</u>
<u>of Child Psychiatry</u>, 1983, <u>22</u>, 294-301.

Coates, D.L. & Lewis, M. Early mother-infant interaction and infant cognitive status as predictors of school performance and cognitive behavior
in six year olds. <u>Child Development</u>, 1984, <u>55</u>, 1219-1230.

Cronbach, L.J., Gleser, G.C., Nanda, H. & Rajaratmon, N. <u>Theory of</u>
<u>Generalizability for Scores and Profiles</u>. New York: John Wiley &
Sons, Inc., 1972.

Dietrich, K.N., Starr, R.H. & Weisfeld, G.E. Infant maltreatment, caretaker-infant interaction and developmental consequences at different
levels of parenting failure. <u>Pediatrics</u>, 1983, <u>72</u>, 532-540.

Drotar, D., Negray, J., Metcalf, J., Blair, M. & Zwicker, K. <u>SSR Event</u>
<u>Recorder Coders' Manual</u>. Cleveland, OH: Case Western Reserve
University, 1981.

Finlon, M.A. & Drotar, D. Social competence and attachment behavior in
failure to thrive infants. International Conference of Infant Studies.
New York, April, 1983.

Gray, J. Cutler, C., Dean, J. & Kempe, C.H. Perinatal assessment of mother-
baby interaction. In R.E. Helfer & C.H. Kempe (Eds.), <u>Child Abuse and</u>
<u>Neglect: The Family and Community</u>. Cambridge, MA: Ballinger, 1976.

Kotelchuck, M. Nonorganic failure to thrive: The status of interactional
and environmental theories. In B.W. Camp (Ed.), <u>Advances in Behavioral</u>
<u>Pediatrics: Vol. 1</u>. Greenwich, CN: Jai Press, 1980.

Lewis, M. & Feiring, C. The childs social network: Social object, social
functions and their relationship. In M. Lewis & L.A. Rosenblum
(Eds.), <u>The Child and Its Family, Vol. 2</u>. New York: Plenum, 1979.

Main, M. Avoidance in the service of attachment: A working paper. In K.
Immelman, G.W. Barlow, L. Petrinovich & M. Main (Eds.), <u>Behavioral</u>
<u>Development</u>. New York: Cambridge University Press, 1981.

Patterson, G.R. <u>A Social Learning Approach. Coercive Family Process, Vol.</u>
<u>3</u>. Eugene, OR: Castalia Publishing Co., 1982.

Polansky, N., Borgman, R. & DeSaix, C. <u>Roots of Futility</u>. San Francisco,
CA: Jossey Bass, 1972.

Pollitt, E. The role of the behavior of the infant in Marasmus. <u>American</u>
<u>Journal of Clinical Nutrition</u>, 1973, <u>26</u>, 264-270.

Pollitt, E., Eichler, A.W. & Chan, C.K. Psychosocial development and behavior of mothers of failure to thrive children. <u>American Journal of</u>
<u>Orthopsychiatry</u>, 1975, <u>45</u>, 525-537.

Pollitt, E., Gilmore, M. & Vallarcel, N. Early mother-infant interaction
and somatic growth. <u>Early Human Development</u>, 1978, <u>1</u>, 325-336.

Pollitt, E. & Thomson, C. Protein-calorie malnutrition and behavior: A
view from psychology. In R.J. Wurtman & J.J. Wurtman (Eds.),
<u>Nutrition and the Brain, Vol. 2</u>. New York: Raven Press, 1977.

Ramey, C.T., Farran, D.C. & Campbell, F.A. Predicting IQ from mother-
infant interactions. <u>Child Development</u>, 1979, <u>50</u>, 804-814.

Ramey, C.T., Haeger, L. & Klisz, D. Synchronous reinforcement of vocal
responses in failure to thrive infants. <u>Child Development</u>, 1972, <u>43</u>,
1449-1455.

Ramey, C.T., Starr, R.H., Pallas, J., Whitten, C.F. & Reed, V. Nutrition, response contingent stimualation and the maternal deprivation syndrome: Results of an early intervention program. Merrill Palmer Quarterly, 1975, 21, 45-55.

Ryan, M.G., Whitt, J.K., Dalton, R.F. & Lavigne, J. Infant development, mother-child interaction and failure to thrive: A look at reciprocity. Annual Meeting of the American Association of Mental Deficiency. Boston, MA, June, 1982.

Sackett, G.P. Lag sequential analysis as a data reduction technique in social interaction research. In D. Sawin et al. (Eds.), Exceptional Infant, Vol. 4. New York: Brunner-Mazel, 1980.

Shapiro, V., Fraiberg, S. & Adelson, E. Infant-parent psychotherapy on behalf of a child in a critical nutritional state. Psychoanalytic Study of the Child, 1976, 31, 461-491.

Sorce, J.F. & Emde, R.N. Mother's presence is not enough: Effect of emotional availability on infant exploration. Developmental Psychology, 1981, 17, 737-745.

Sroufe, L.A. Socioemotional development. In J. Osofsky (Ed.), Handbook of Infant Development. New York: Wiley, 1979.

Sroufe, L.A. Infant-caregiver attachment and patterns of adaptation in preschool: The roots of maladaptation and competence. In M. Perlmutter (Ed.), Development and Policy Concerning Children with Special Needs. Minnesota Symposium on Child Psychology, Vol. 16. Hillsdale, NJ: Erlbaum, 1983.

Sroufe, L.A. & Waters, E. Attachment as an organizational construct. Child Development, 1977, 47, 1184-1199.

Stephenson, G., Smith, D.P.B. & Roberts, T.W. The SSR system: An open format event recording system with computerized transcription. Behavior Research Methods and Instrumentation, 1975, 7, 497-515.

Stephenson, G.R. PLEXYN: A computer-compatible grammar for coding complex social interactions. In M.E. Lamb, S.J. Suomi & G.R. Stephenson (Eds.), Social Interaction Analysis. Madison, WI: University of Wisconsin Press, 1979.

Thoman, E., Acebo, C., Dreyer, C.A., Becker, P.T. & Freese, M. Individuality in the interactive process. In E.B. Thoman (Ed.), Origins of the Infant's Responsiveness. Hillsdale, NJ: Erlbaum, 1979.

Vietze, P., Falsey, M., O'Connor, S., Sandler, H., Sherrod, K. & Altemeier, W.A. New born behavioral and interactional characteristics of nonorganic failure to thrive infants. In. T.M. Field, S. Goldberg, D. Stern & A.M. Sostek (Eds.), High Risk Infants and Children. New York: Academic Press, 1980.

Waters, E., Wippman, J. & Sroufe, L.A. Attachment, positive affect and competence in the peer group: Two studies in construct validation. Child Development, 1979, 50, 821-829.

White, B.L., Kohan, B.T., Attanucci, & Shapiro, B.B. Experience and Environment: Major Influences on the Development of the Young Child. Englewood Cliffs, NJ: Prentice Hall, 1978.

Yarrow, L.J. & Anderson, B. Procedures for studying parent-infant interaction: A critique. In E.B. Thoman (Ed.), Origins of the Infant's Social Responsiveness. Hillsdale, NJ: L. Erlbaum, 1979.

IV   NEW APPROACHES TO DIAGNOSIS AND INTERVENTION

   PART I: PEDIATRIC MANAGEMENT

      Pediatric diagnosis and management are the cornerstone of treatment
and prevention efforts. Pediatricians and nurse practitioners are among
the first to identify FTT and associated problems, to discuss these problems
with families and to initiate referral and intervention. Pediatric practitioners face a difficult burden in managing FTT in the context of unresolved
diagnostic issues and little available empirical information concerning
prognosis. In this section, two experienced pediatric practitioners present
approaches to the management of FTT in two different hospital settings.

      Berkowitz describes a multidisciplinary approach to the management of
FTT which was developed to insure adequate assessment and consistent follow-
up in an ambulatory setting. Over 300 patients from a variety of referral
sources have been evaluated in this clinic since 1980. In describing the
comprehensive approach of this clinic through case illustrations, Berkowitz
details the medical evaluation (history, physical exam, behavioral and
laboratory assessment), nutritional management (caloric deprivation, interactional and iatrogenic deprivation), psychological assessment and management, social service assessment, nursing assessment, and the role of observation of parent-child interaction. The clinic uses a team conference to
delineate diagnosis and a management plan. Although some patients have a
purely medical reason for their growth deficiency or isolated nutritional
problem, the majority of families require intervention on social, nutritional and/or medical basis. Special questions raised by coordination of
medical and community social services, foster care and ongoing follow-up
are discussed. Berkowitz and her coworkers also integrate clinical research
into the workings of the clinic.

      Altemeier, O'Connor, Sherrod, Yeager & Vietze describe an approach to
pediatric management of hospitalized FTT children that is based in part on
findings from an ongoing prospective study of antecedents which suggest that
NOFT is due to a disturbance in the mother-infant relationship characterized
by subtle maternal rejection. Altemeier and his colleagues discuss the
importance of breaking a potentially chronic cycle and maladaptive mother-
child relationship by enhancing maternal behavior, infant behavior or both.
In the authors' settings children receive their first well baby check
between two and four weeks of age to encourage early recognition of FTT.
Supportive intervention inludes specific feeding instructions, emphasis on
caloric intake, an optimistic attitude and close, active follow-up on the
part of the physician or nurse practitioner. Infants with severe NOFT, who
are hospitalized, are given intensive nutritional treatment, treatment of

medical problems, and intensive developmental stimulation. With coaching and support, responsibility for the child's feeding is gradually transferred from the nurses to the mother, who is informed concerning the child's weight gain, absence of organic illness, and the child's developmental gains. Suggestions for primary prevention of NOFT include provision of support to help a mother compensate for aberrant childhood nurture via such interventions as continuous support and friendship from a health care worker, the presence of a supportive family member during labor, early contact and/or rooming-in during the newborn period.

COMPREHENSIVE PEDIATRIC MANAGEMENT OF FAILURE TO THRIVE:

AN INTERDISCIPLINARY APPROACH

Carol Berkowitz

Department of Pediatrics
UCLA School of Medicine

The variety of medical, nutritional and psychosocial causes of FTT necessitate a comprehensive approach to the evaluation of this problem. The utilization of a multidisciplinary team allows each professional to contribute his or her area of expertise to the maximum. This model of care equates FTT with a puzzle, for which each team member obtains one piece. This chapter describes the evaluation process, management strategies, and results of a pediatric clinic established for the assessment of children with FTT.

BACKGROUND

The FTT Clinic was founded in June, 1980, by the author and a pediatric nurse practitioner. The impetus for the clinic came from a paper presented at the Ambulatory Pediatric Association meeting in Atlanta, Georgia in 1979, by Sahler et al. who noted that patients diagnosed as FTT had poor long term follow-up. When they re-evaluated 21 out of 30 children hospitalized for FTT two to four years after discharge, two-thirds were still below the 3rd percentile and half of the mothers were unaware of their child's diagnosis or treatment plan. Similar experiences have been reported by other investigators (White, Malcolm, Ruper, Westphal & Smith, 1981). Our experience suggested that similar outcomes existed at our institution. Prior to the development of the FTT Clinic, patients were evaluated in the emergency department or admitted to the hospital. Follow-up care was given sporadically, depending on the house officer who cared for the patient.

The FTT Clinic was developed to assure not only an adequate initial assessment but consistent long term follow-up. The Clinic is staffed by a team of individuals already employed by the institution. These individuals include a pediatrician, pediatric nurse practitioner (PNP), dietitian, clinical psychologist, clinical social worker, child abuse liaison specialist, occupational therapist and home nurse. No funds were required to start the Clinic, and all team members are salaried. In addition to providing a needed service to our patients, the Clinic is an integral part of the teaching program in pediatrics, psychology and nutrition. House officers and fellows all spend time in the FTT Clinic.

CLINIC SETTING

The FTT Clinic meets one morning a week from 8:30 a.m. to 1:00 p.m. in the Pediatric Clinic of Harbor-UCLA Medical Center. The Medical Center is located in Torrance, California, a middle class community which is part of greater Los Angeles, and serves a medically and economically indigent population. The hospital is also the southern campus of UCLA School of Medicine, and in addition to being a primary care facility for the area, is a tertiary care referral center. There are approximately 40,000 pediatric outpatient visits per year.

All patients register for the Clinic in a routine manner and undergo financial screening at which time financial responsibility for the Clinic charges are determined. Patients are weighed and measured by the pediatric nursing staff. The first person to evaluate the patient is the pediatrician or pediatric nurse practitioner who obtains a complete history and performs a comprehensive physical exam. Pediatric house staff discuss cases with the attending physician and determine which other team members need to evaluate the patient. This decision is based on the physician's assessment of nutritional status, social situation and developmental assessment. A complete evaluation takes from one to two hours depending on the number of patients being seen and the number of team members scheduled to do evaluations. An average of 15 to 20 patients are seen each week. Three or four of these are new patients and the remainder are seen for follow-up. Once all patients have been evaluated, the team convenes to review each patient, share findings and develop a management plan. Team conference lasts about one and a half hours. Team members present their findings and individual recommendations for disposition. Referrals are often made to the Visiting Nurse Association, and the visiting nurse presents findings from home visits. Decisions to refer families to outside agencies including Head Start, mental health, protective services or law enforcement are made by the team at the time of the conference. The team conference is discussed in more detail below.

Patient Characteristics

Over 300 patients have been evaluated in the FTT Clinic since 1980. Approximately 55% were male. Patients ranged in age from 18 days to 18 years, but three-fourths were under the age of 3 years and half were less than 1 year old. These findings are consistent with clinical observations. Fifty percent of children with FTT will manifest abnormal growth by 6 months (Hannaway, 1970). Some investigators restrict the term FTT to children under the age of 3 years, and utilize "psychosocial dwarfism" to characterize the older child with FTT (Gardner, 1972; Money, 1977; Silver & Finkelstein, 1967).

The ethnic background of the patients seen in the FTT Clinic was as follows: Latino 45%, black 25%, white 20%, and other including southeast Asian 10%. There was a slightly higher proportion of black infants seen in FTT Clinic than for the hospital in general.

Patient Referrals

Patients come from a wide variety of referral sources. Most patients (60%) are referred directly from our pediatric emergency room where they have been evaluated for an unrelated problem. Some patients (10%) are referred following hospitalization on the in-patient service. Occasionally a mother will request an appointment because of concern about her child's size. Other referrals come from private practitioners (5%), public health clinics (5%), the Department of Public and Social Services (DPSS)(15%), and law enforcement (5%). In recent years more children have been brought in by these latter two agencies.

Referrals from DPSS and law enforcement tend to involve children with multiple medical problems for whom the role of the environmental deprivation is difficult to ascertain. The resources of a multidisciplinary team in the evaluation of these children are particularly critical because the psychosocial aspects of the child's care are frequently overshadowed by the medical problems. In addition, children referred from private practitioners and public health clinics often have extensive medical and laboratory assessments, but little information has been obtained as to family functioning.

EVALUATION

Medical Evaluation

The medical evaluation, carried out by a physician or PNP focuses on obtaining a comprehensive history and performing a complete physical examination. The purpose of this evaluation is to assess the physical and emotional health of the child, and determine what if any organic factors are disrupting the patient's growth and emotional development. A detailed history rather than the laboratory will reveal the diagnosis in 95% of cases (Sills, 1978). In addition to having a primary effect on the child's growth, medical conditions may produce adverse effects on the mother-infant bonding and the family's financial and emotional resources. In addition, nutritional needs may be greater than normal in a child with an organic disorder. For this reason, the discovery of an organic etiology for FTT by the physicians does not obviate the need for assessment by other team members.

Birth History. The history of the pregnancy and birth provide important information concerning physical risk factors as they pertain to diagnosis. Maternal gravidity may be a clue to intrauterine growth retardation. For example, in one dramatic case we evaluated a 6 year old child who was the height of a 2 year old and was the eighteenth pregnancy for her then 37 year old mother. Multiple, closely spaced pregnancies deplete the uterus of its reserve as an organ of nutrition (Lin & Evans, 1984). In certain instances, a history of multiple spontaneous abortions may be a clue to a balanced chromosomal translocation in the mother (Nadler & Burton, 1980; Funderbunk, Guthrie & Meldrum, 1976). Abortions represent non-viable unbalanced translocation. For this reason, a history of multiple spontaneous abortions in the mother of an infant with FTT suggests the need for a genetics consult or a chromosomal karyotype.

Other salient risk factors involve maternal substance use during pregnancy. Although the effects of smoking on fetal size are well documented (Lin & Evans, 1984; Silverman, 1977), it is uncertain whether these effects are long term. Alcohol consumption during pregnancy has an adverse effect on fetal and post-natal growth (Jones, Smith & Vileland, 1973). The most common physical characteristics of the fetal alcohol syndrome include pre and post-natal growth retardation, psychomotor retardation, microcephaly, short palpebral fissures, long philtrum with a thin, smooth upper lip, skeletal anomalies including small distal phalanges, and occasional congenital heart disease (Smith, 1982). Our experience has suggested that asking a mother how much she drank, rather than if she drank during pregnancy is more likely to yield positive results. The toxic and teratogenic effects of many drugs have been well documented (Lin & Evans, 1984). Approximately 8% of children evaluated in our FTT Clinic have been exposed during gestation to alcohol or illicit drugs including marijuana, heroin, amphetamines and phenylcyclidine (PCP). Sixty-seven percent of these infants were small for gestational age, but the remainder (33%) showed growth deceleration after birth. It is important to note that although a history of maternal substance abuse was elicited in only 16% in the new-born period, further questioning during the clinic evaluation revealed a positive history in 89%.

The teratogenic effects of prenatal infection with organisms such as rubella, cytomegalovirus, toxoplasmosis are well-documented (Overall, 1981). Toxemia has a more limited effect on fetal growth because this maternal disorder is frequently limited to the final weeks of gestation. Birth weight may be reduced, but length and subsequent growth appear normal (Fischer, 1978).

In evaluating the significance of birth weight for subsequent growth, one must also decide if the infant was premature and appropriate for gestational age (AGA), or small for gestational age (SGA) and either premature or full-term. Multiple factors can lead to intrauterine growth retardation, and "catch-up growth" in such infants is unpredictable. Approximately 50% of AGA premature infants will achieve normal size usually by 3 years (Fischer, 1978). However, many premature infants develop multiple other problems such as intraventricular hemorrhage or bronchopulmonary dysplasia which interfere with their subsequent growth and development. In addition, premature infants have a higher than average (20-25%) incidence of being physically abused (Kennell, 1974). Although a number of factors operate to potentiate maternal-child relationship problems, the long hospitalization following a premature birth may interfere with maternal-infant attachment and heighten parental perception of the child as frail and vulnerable (Kennell, 1974).

SGA infants who are small in weight only have a better prognosis for catch-up growth than those with all three parameters at less than the 5th percentile. Potential ways to assess the adequacy of in utero growth include the ponderal index (P.I. = birth weight in gms/ crown to heel length in cm^3)(Miller & Hassanein, 1971) or the fetal/placental ratio. Ratios greater than 4.9 suggest placental insufficiency and in utero nutritional deprivation (Beargie, James & Greene, 1970).

Past History. Review of the past history should always include obtaining the child's previous growth measurements. Because growth velocity is so great during the first year of life, small but clinically significant decelerations may not be appreciated unless growth velocity curves are utilized. Weight velocity curves are very useful to illustrate the marked swings that occur in the growth of a child in different environments.

Although a complete review of systems should be obtained particular attention must be paid to a history of recurrent fevers or infections, diarrheal illnesses, enuresis or urinary tract symptoms (Cupoli, Hallock & Barness, 1980). Hannaway (1970) found that constipation was an infrequent complaint in children with FTT, being noted in only 7 of 100 children, 6 of whom had an organic reason for the FTT. We have also noted constipation to be infrequent in FTT, but to be equally prevalent in children with organic and non-organic FTT.

A complete developmental history should be obtained. The mother's assessment of her infant's temperament should be elicited, which may provide insight into the quality of mother-infant interactions. A useful question to ask is how the mother and child spend their day together.

Family Growth Patterns. In addition to the traditional questions about familial illnesses, we record the anthropometric measurements of the parents. We then utilize midparental height curves to determine the appropriateness of the child's height given the height of his parents. Approximately 15% of patients referred to our clinic have familial short stature. The mean height for mothers of children followed in our FTT Clinic was 61.5 in. and for fathers was 67.6 in. A random survey of heights of parents of children seen in other clinics was 63.65 inches (mothers) and 68.8 inches (fathers). Similarly, Beargie et al. (1970) noted that mothers of SGA infants averaged 2 inches shorter than mothers of AGA infants.

Physical Exam. Vital signs and body measurements including weight, length and head circumference should be recorded. Seventy percent of children with all three parameters less than the 5th percentile have an organic explanation for their FTT (Hannaway, 1970). If the head circumference is disproportionately low, fetal alcohol syndrome, congenital infection or central nervous system dysfunction may explain the FTT (Smith, 1982; Hannaway, 1970). On the other hand, disproportionately low weight is seen in non-organic FTT and malabsorption syndromes (Hannaway, 1970).

With respect to congenital malformations, the presence of 1 major anomaly or 3 minor anomalies suggest that a 2nd major anomaly may be found (Nadler, 1981). Cleft palate has been associated with both complete and partial growth hormone deficiency in 4% of all cleft patients and 32% of those with height less than the 3rd percentile (Rudman, Davis, Priest, et al., 1978). In addition, twelve percent of patients with cleft palate are below the 3rd percentile. However, it is interesting to note that none of the five patients with cleft palates referred to our FTT Clinic had growth hormone deficiency. A complete eye exam may reveal chorioretinitis or cataracts which are clues to congenital infection (Hiles, 1983).

The detection of a heart murmur may suggest a cardiac etiology of the FTT. Five out of 100 patients in Hannaway's (1970) study and 2 out of 185 in Sill's (1978) report had previously undiagnosed congenital heart disease. Eighteen percent of children with acyanotic heart disease are below the 3rd percentile and 40% of those with cyanotic heart disease are below the 3rd percentile. Ventricular septal defects (VSD) with pulmonary hypertension or congestive heart failure and complex atrial septal defects (ASD) are the acyanotic lesions associated with the greatest degree of growth retardation. Factors such as diminished tissue perfusion, anorexia and decreased caloric intake contribute to the slow growth associated with cardiac disease (Ehlers, 1978).

We have evaluated eight infants who had murmurs consistent with peripheral pulmonic stenosis. In each case, the murmur resolved with improvement in physical growth. Other patients have been referred to us from the Pediatric Cardiology service because the cardiologist felt that the growth retardation could not be attributed to the cardiac lesion. These children had pulmonic stenosis and simple VSDs.

Behavioral Assessment. A number of behaviors which characterize the FTT infant have been described including a watchful, wary, wide-eyed stare with overt gaze avoidance and poor eye contact (Rosenn, Loeb & Jura, 1980; Powell & Low, 1983; Berkowitz & Sklaren, 1984). Some infants are hypertonic, arch backwards when held and demonstrate scissoring of the lower extremities. Other infants may show little spontaneous movement, appear sad, listless and apathetic, and become irritable when handled. Such withdrawn infants spend a great deal time sleeping or in self-play and prefer objects to people. They are not cuddly to hold. It should be noted that a range of behaviors may be found in FTT and that accompanying behavioral characteristics vary greatly with age. For example, some children over the age of two years with FTT (often referred to as psycho-social dwarfism) manifest very deviant characteristics including bizarre and voracious appetite, marked hyperactivity and severe speech delay. In contrast to many children their age, they may often be very responsive to strangers and will willingly go with strangers or climb into their laps (Gardner, 1972; Money, 1977; Silver & Finkelstein, 1967).

Laboratory Assessment. In the past, the role of the laboratory in evaluating FTT was overemphasized. Sills' (1978) review of 185 patients hospitalized for FTT at Buffalo's Childrens' Hospital is instructive. Out of 2,607 laboratory tests averaging 14 tests/patient, only 1.4% of the laboratory studies were positive, and no study was positive without a specific indication from the clinical evaluation. The laboratory assessment can be viewed from three distinct indications. (1) Certain laboratory tests are obtained because they are part of routine well child care. These include hematocrits and urinalyses. (2) Tests may also be obtained because there is a history that suggests pathology in a specific area. For instance, evaluating a stool specimen for ova and parasites would be indicated in a child with chronic diarrhea. Older children with environmental FTT may manifest certain endocrinologic abnormalities which are helpful to document. These children have low norepinephrine and epinephrine levels, wich affect hypothalamic function. As a result, there is a relative lack of adrenocorticotrophic hormone manifested by an abnormally low baseline 17 hydroxycorticosteroids and inadequate response to metyrapone. There may also be an abnormally blunted response of growth hormone to stimulation with insulin, arginine, exercise or sleep (Powell, Brasel & Blizzard, 1967; Powell, Brasel, Raiti & Blizzard, 1967). Such endocrinologic abnormalities can reverse within one to two weeks of changing to a more nurturing environment (Silver & Finkelstein, 1967).

(3) Batteries of tests may be ordered in search of the etiology of the FTT. These include chemical profiles, thyroid panels, etc. However, this shot-gun approach to diagnosis is costly, counter-productive and relegates the diagnosis of non-organic FTT to one of exclusion.

The following illustrates the role of the history and physical exam in the diagnosis of non-organic FTT.

Case History. The patient, an 18 month old Latino male, was referred to our Clinic for severe growth and developmental retardation. He had been born to a 21 year old mother, who described this pregnancy as different from her others. She had a foul yellow vaginal discharge which failed to respond to penicillin for the final 3 months of the pregnancy. Fetal movements were diminished and labor was prolonged at 29 hours. The baby was not vigorous following the birth, and he required oxygen. In spite of being full term, he weighed only 1.5 kilograms (kg). He was kept in an incubator for 8 days, and was tube fed for 3 months. Developmental milestones were uniformly delayed, and he made no vocalizations except to cry. The family history was negative for any similar problem. Maternal height was 4'10". His past medical history included 5 previous episodes of pneumonia, 3 requiring hospitalization. He was described as being weak, with a poor appetite. Physically, he differed from his siblings because of his light hair. His exam showed growth parameters less than 5th percentile, unusual facies with narrow, almond shaped eyes, a thin upper lip with a long philtrum and a beaked nose. There were bilateral rales on ausculatation of the lungs. The scrotum was underdeveloped and the testes were not palpated. The neurological exam was remarkable for diffuse hypotonia and diminished muscle strength. The nutritional assessment revealed that the child was receiving less than half the calories and protein required for age. The patient demonstrated developmental delay based on a mental age of 5.8 months at 18 months of age using the Cattell

Infant Intelligence Scale. The findings of diminished fetal movements, hypogonadism, developmental delay, FTT, and characteristic facies were consistent with the diagnosis of Prader-Willi syndrome. Dietary counselling was instituted, and the child began to show an acceleration in weight with a steady increase in length. A repeat developmental assessment at 25-1/2 months using the Gessell Developmental Schedule showed him to be functioning at about 13 months.

Nutritional Assessment

All patients undergo a nutritional evaluation to determine if the patient's nutritional intake is adequate for growth and weight gain. The importance of adequate calories to the recovery of FTT cannot be emphasized strongly enough. In 1969 Whitten et al. reported that growth failure in maternal deprivation was reversible even in a "deprived" hospital setting if infants were given adequate calories. Rosenn et al. (1980) noted, however, that caloric intake in infants with non-organic FTT did not increase until behavioral abnormalities reversed. Only after infants began to interact socially in a more normal manner did their appetite improve and weight gain occur. Although these provocative findings need to be replicated, the role of caloric intake has been established as a primary factor in FTT.

Our experiences in nutritional assessment have also underscored the relevance of caloric intake to FTT. The nutritional assessment is carried out by a registered pediatric dietitian using a 24 hour diet recall, and a 3 day diet history recorded by the mother. Most parents are eager to provide us with this information in the hopes that some concrete recommendations will be made to improve their child's eating. When accomplished as part of a comprehensive care approach by experienced staff, the nutritional history is not an especially sensitive area for our patients. A nutritional assessment has been obtained in 80% of patients seen in our clinic. Sixty percent of these patients had some nutritional deficiency. Inadequate caloric intake was the most common deficit and was present in the overwhelming majority (85%) of patients who exhibited deficiencies in protein, vitamins and minerals. Although isolated deficiency in protein intake was noted in about 8% of patients, no infant had clinical kwashiorkor. Isolated vitamin, iron and calcium deficiencies were found in 1% of patients.

When assessing caloric adequacy, it is useful to calculate the intake for ideal body weight rather than actual body weight. In addition, children with certain medical disorders have increased caloric needs, sometimes approaching 200 calories/kg/day (Murray & Glassman, 1982). During our evaluations of children for caloric deprivation, we have recognized a number of distinctive patterns. Some children fail to grow despite a history of adequate calories. In children with a medical problem, such as congenital heart disease or cystic fibrosis, caloric requirements are greater than in normal children. Malabsorption syndromes or infections with parasites are a rare cause of an excess caloric need and intake (Lary & Bauer, 1978).

Patterns of Caloric Deprivation. First, the mother may be diluting the formula improperly. This may be done out of inexperience, her assessment that the milk is too rich or too thick, or more frequently because there is insufficient food for the other children. For example, infant formula obtained through the WIC program may be distributed throughout the family.

A second group of mothers are those who confabulate the diet history. These can be mothers who are depressed or overwhelmed with their own stresses, have no idea what their infant is taking, and make-up what they feel is an appropriate history. A similar group of mothers are those who are not actually caring for their children, though they may not acknowledge this. Sometimes they are part of an extended household, and no one individual has the primary responsibility for feeding the infant. The following case vignette illustrates the complexity of inadequate caloric intake as assessed in a home visit.

Case History. A 2 month old white infant was hospitalized because of poor weight gain. Weight at 2-1/2 months was 4.10 kg compared to a birth weight of 3.25 kg. Behavioral assessment showed minimal backarching, but good eye contact and an easy social smile. The mother was 29 years old, married, and had five other children, all under the age of 7 years. Initially, the mother reported an intake of 35 to 40 ounces of formula a day or 170 calories/kg/day. The baby, however, grew well in the hospital though had not grown well at home. Following discharge the mother kept a diet history which revealed that the infant was taking only 4 bottles a day for a total of 20-22 ounces or about 90 calories/kg/d. The visiting nurse also noted that the infant slept up to 6 hours, and did not demand feedings. The mother was so overworked with her other tasks that the infant's sleep was a welcome respite. The mother was instructed to awaken the infant to assure an adequate daily intake, and the baby has subsequently thrived.

Interactional Causes of Poor Intake. Inadequate caloric intake also occurs in infants with mothers not attuned to their own hunger cues. Some of these mothers are very petite and appear almost anorectic. They often report a seemingly adequate diet or suggest that their children are hungry or eating all the time. However, an adequate diet history will reveal long periods when the children are unfed. Hunger cues become suppressed in the children, who also stop demanding food. For example, two black siblings ages 1 year and 2-1/2 years, were referred to the FTT Clinic for an evaluation. In spite of a history that the children were good eaters and eating all the time, it was determined during a home visit that there were long intervals between meals. (The children had been fed at 8:00 p.m. the previous night, and still had not been fed by 1:00 p.m. the next day.) Both said they weren't hungry when asked, though ate when food was placed before them. The mother readily admitted skipping meals because she wasn't hungry or simply "forgot" to eat. The mother's poor motivation and lack of interest in food made this family particuarly difficult to deal with. The children's growth has been paralleling a normal curve, but has shown no acceleration in spite of dietary counseling.

Substance Abuse. A third category of children with nutritional deprivation are those who are the offspring of substance-abusing mothers. We have seen the most refractory cases of FTT in infants of PCP abusing mothers. In our Clinic population, 38% of infants of substance abusing mothers were noted to be very difficult feeders. They were irritable and hypertonic, and were felt to be neurologically impaired. Caloric intake was grossly inadequate. For example, a black infant was placed in a foster home after birth because of maternal PCP abuse. In spite of this, she showed very poor weight gain and had undergone extensive medical and neurologic evaluation, the conclusion of which was that the infant was hypertonic and developmentally delayed. At 13 months of age, she changed foster homes and was placed in the care of a foster mother who had cared for other FTT children. The new foster mother found her to be so irritable that it was exceedingly difficult to feed her. She was gavage fed for about 2 weeks, and then switched to oral feedings with excellent growth, including an increase in her head circumference from below the 5th to the 25th percentile. The foster mother felt that the irritability interfered with the child's ability to eat and the resultant hunger compounded the irritability. Tube feeding broke the cycle.

Iatrogenic Caloric Deprivation. A final example of caloric deprivation is that which is iatrogenically induced. Iatrogenic caloric deprivation occurs under a variety of circumstances. Sometimes an infant with acute gastroenteritis is kept on clear liquids or diluted formula for an extended period of time. Some infants with regurgitation are subjected to multiple formula changes. Such changes disrupt the normal feeding routine, and the mother is given the incorrect message that there is something wrong with her infant (Forsyth, McCarthy & Leventhal, 1982). The child with special dietary requirements may also develop iatrogenic malnutrition.

Case. A Latino male who had failure to thrive since age 10 months underwent hospitalization and comprehensive evaluation at age 19 months. At this time, it was determined that he was allergic to milk and soy protein. His mother was given extensive instructions about which foods to avoid. After one week on a milk and soy-free diet, his weight had fallen off even further. In avoiding all the prohibited foods, the mother was starving the child! With a change in the diet instructions (what to give rather than what to avoid) weight gain occurred.

Dietary Management. We have adopted a number of general strategies for enhancing the caloric intake of children who are picky eaters. For many children 6 "nutritious snacks" are more readily accepted than 3 well-balanced meals. Nutritious snacks include half a sandwich, pudding, granola bars. Supplemental formulas such as Ensure*, Ensure Plus*, and Sustacal* pudding are used in children over the age of 1 year. Milk shakes with Ensure*, plus ice cream, banana and chocolate syrup are encouraged, and may increase the caloric intake by over 500 calories a day. Polycose*, a glucose polymer, can be used to increase caloric intake in infants under the age of 1 year. One to two teaspoons are added to each bottle. Supplemental formulas may be given if the mother describes the child as a difficult or picky eater, or if she insists that he is taking a regular diet but not gaining weight. However, supplemental formulas are costly and should be tapered off as the nutritional status of the child improves. Overall, they are a useful adjunct in the management, and most patients experience an accelerated weight gain during the period of supplementation. Patients who fail to gain weight despite attempts at supplementation are often non-compliant which may be a sign that the mother is overwhelmed with her own stresses and not able to follow through with dietary recommendations.

Better nutrition improves the overall well-being of the infant. There is often an improvement in mother-infant interactions as the infant begins to gain weight. Developmental advancement has also been noted (Wachtel, 1982; Klein, Forbes & Nader, 1975; Chase, 1973).

Psychologic Assessment

The psychologist assists in the developmental assessment of children who are suspected of being developmentally delayed. Psychometric tests utilized in the Clinic include Cattell Infant Intelligence Test, Gesell Developmental Schedules, Bayley Scales of Infant Development Test, and Wechsler Intelligence Scale for Children-Revised. Sixty percent of patients seen in our Clinic have had psychometric assessments. Severe developmental delay was noted in 70% of those tested. Infants who are delayed are referred to treatment programs such as those provided by the Regional Centers of Los Angeles County. Children whose delay is secondary to a neurologic deficit such as cerebral palsy are referred to special schools developed by California Children's Services. In about half of these

---

*Registered Trademark

patients, serial testing has revealed marked developmental advancement which followed change in environment and/or enrollment in special stimulation programs.

The second function of the psychologist is to assess the emotional well-being of the child. This assessment is carried out using interview, drawings and/or play. The psychologist spends time with both the child and the caregivers. Although a brief interaction may occur at the time of the initial FTT visit, additional sessions are scheduled at a later date.

One common emotional problem which is associated with FTT is depression. Childhood depression may take one of 3 forms (Crytryn & McKnew, 1982; Child, Murphy & Rhyne, 1980). In acute depression, there has been a recent identifiable loss, such as the death of a parent, or a divorce. Symptoms such as sadness, anorexia, inability to sleep, constipation, or inability to concentrate are similar to those seen in adults. The child with chronic depression often has had multiple ongoing losses and may manifest similar symptoms. However, he may present with a masked depression or depressive equivalent which may take the form of hyperactivity, delinquency, truancy or fire-starting (Shapiro, 1975; Schowalter, 1981). For example, a 3-1/2 year old black male was brought to the FTT Clinic by his biological father with whom he had lived for several months following the death of his natural mother at age 27 years from a probable ampheta mine overdose. The past medical history was unknown to the father except for the fact the child was born after a 7 month gestation complicated by heavy amphetamine abuse. The patient was hospitalized for 2 weeks after birth for weight gain. Paternal height was 6'1", weight 220 pounds, and maternal height was 5'2". The physical exam was negative except for the abnormal growth parameters. The child was shy and withdrawn but cooperative. Nutritional assessment showed mildly decreased intake. Psychome tric evaluation revealed an IQ of 76 on the Stanford Binet Intelligence Scale. The child was markedly depressed. The father himself had suffered the loss of his own family, when his wife left him and moved to Utah taking his 2 healthy children along. The son and father were referred to child psychiatry but failed all appointments after the initial intake interview. The father, at the suggestion of the Clinic personnel enrolled the patient in a preschool. The child's appetite and affect improved. His weight changed only slightly though his height increased 5 cm in 6 months.

Childhood depression was noted in about one-fourth of the children seen in the FTT Clinic. In two-thirds, the depression was felt to be moderate to severe. The high incidence of depression in our patients probably parallels the high incidence of depression in the mothers. Children who are diagnosed as chronically depressed or who have behavioral disturbances (such as stealing, fire-starting, acting out) are referred for therapy. Depressed mothers and dysfunctional families may also be referred for psychologic counselling. Using an extended interview and the Beck Depression Inventory, we diagnosed maternal depression in 47% of mothers interviewed. Factors contributing to maternal depression are discussed below. A prior psychiatric history was noted in 18% of mothers and 11% were judged intellectually retarded (Berkowitz & Barry, 1982).

In cases in which significant emotional disturbance is diagnosed, the psychologist may provide on-going psychotherapy for the child and his family, or serve as a liaison between the family and outside agencies. We have found that recommendations for psychologic counselling are among the hardest to implement. Parental denial often interferes with the child's receiving the appropriate therapy. In our experience, psychotherapy recommendations are more often adhered to if they have been mandated by the court. Unfortunately, even when therapy is obtained, behavioral disturbances are often refractory, which reflects the chronicity of child and/or family problems.

Social Service Assessment

Approximately half the patients seen in the FTT Clinic undergo a comprehensive social assessment including an interview questionnaire developed by the clinical social worker. The purpose of the social assessment is to ascertain information about the family unit and its dynamics, including who the people are in the home, where the financial resources come from, whom the mother sees as providing emotional support, what past life and stresses for the mother have been, and what the mother's coping skills are.

Environmental factors are directly responsible for the FTT in 30% of patients seen in the Clinic, and an important contributing cause in another quarter of the patients. We have found the categorization of families of FTT children into three major groups described by Evans et al. (1972) to be very helpful. Group I consists of families where the mother has suffered an acute loss, such as the death of a close relative. Her unresolved grief reaction interferes with her ability to bond with and nurture her child. Supportive therapy and individual counselling are effective in assisting the mother, and the infant has a good prognosis for growth.

Group II consists of mothers who have had chronic losses. These mothers have often never developed adequate parenting skills. Thirty-seven percent of FTT Clinic mothers evaluated by observation of mother-infant interactions in the Clinic and in the home had poor nurturing skills (Berkowitz & Barry, 1982). These deficits can sometimes be traced to the mother's childhood. Selma Fraiberg and her colleagues (Fraiberg, Adelson & Shapiro, 1975) have described the impact of these childhood conflicts as "ghosts in the nursery," "as visitors from the unremembered past of the parents; the uninvited guests at the christening." (pp. 387). In addition to not having the benefit of a role model to learn parenting from, the parent who cannot remember significant childhood feelings of pain and anxiety will sometimes need to repeat such experiences with their own children (Fraiberg et al., 1975). For Fraiberg, the key to success in parenting when one has been a victim of inadequate parenting oneself is to be able to recall the feelings of childhood (Fraiberg et al., 1975). In addition to having the parents participate in parenting groups where the atmosphere is supportive and the focus is on teaching about nutrition, play, etc., parents need to be nurtured and listened to. Aggressive social service intervention, with frequent phone calls and home visits is needed.

Case History. The following case illustrates a Group II family. A 6 week old white female infant had been the 7 lb. product of a full-term pregnancy to a 22 year old mother. The prenatal course was complicated by a positive serological test for syphilis, treated with erythromycin for 2 months. The second child had died at 30 minutes of age. The history was pieced together over several visits. Feeding was with both the breast and bottle. There had been a trial of soy milk, but caloric intake was grossly inadequate. The physical exam was remarkable for a pale thin infant with mottled skin. Muscle tone was increased and the infant did not follow objects well, or respond to the bell. Psychological assessment, social service assessment and a home evaluation all confirmed that the mother was of limited intellect, had suffered many disappointments and losses in her own life, and that her 5 year old daughter had been removed because of alleged physical abuse. The mother was given specific feeding instructions to help her understand her infant's cues. Following supportive therapy which included visits by the home nurse, the infant began to grow.

Evans et al.'s (1972) third group has the worst prognosis. The child is viewed by the mother as bad, and the interactions between mother and infant are characteristically hostile. Despite the seriousness of the child's problems parental denial that anything is wrong is so strong that it interferes with implementation of any change. Foster placement is recommended early on for such families (Evans, et al. 1972).

In addition to doing a comprehensive diagnostic work-up, the social worker maintains close contact with the family, helping them obtain the necessary community and financial resources. Such resources include the WIC (Women and Infant Care) program, food banks, food stamps, Head Start or day-care programs for the patient or his siblings, homemaker services to assist with in home instruction, daytime respite care, and parenting classes or support groups. The social worker acts as the contact person if the case is referred to DPSS. She will inform DPSS of the progress of the child and his family. If the child is removed from the home, the social worker is the pivotal team member enforcing the image of a family advocate. Often the hospital or FTT team is viewed as a villain by the family for having made the referral that led to the removal of the child. Whereas the physician is defined as a child advocate, the social worker is seen as a parent advocate. He/she is contacted by the family who do not understand what is happening with respect to DPSS or the legal system and summarizes the data for use during court hearings. The social worker's role as an ombudsman is particularly important to assure continued medical care at the Clinic, especially after the child has been returned home. However, maintenance of medical care may be very difficult if the parents view the foster placement as punitive rather than necessary to insure a better outcome for the child.

Nursing Assessment

Home Visit. The home visit is utilized to provide further information about the living conditions of the child and assess the mother-infant interactions in a more natural setting than the pediatric clinic. Home visits have been carried out in about one-third of Clinic patients. These visits are conducted by either the pediatric nurse practitioner in the Clinic, or a member of the Visiting Nurses Association (VNA), who is also a member of the FTT team. The decision to conduct a home visit is made during the team conference. Home visits are carried out when the history suggests marginal living conditions (food supply in question, crowded quarters), a question exists as to who is caring for the infant, maternal depression is suspected, or maternal-infant interactions are judged to be abnormal.

Observation of Parent-Infant Interaction

Evaluation of mother-infant interactions is a critical component of the FTT work-up. We conducted a study in the Pediatric Clinic to determine if we could quantitate differences in interactions of mother-FTT infants and mother-thriving infants. These two groups were matched for age, sex, race, mother's marital status and socioeconomic background. Thriving infants were selected from patients attending the residents' group practice clinic and FTT infants were those seen for the first time in FTT Clinic. Mother-infant interactions were videotaped behind a one-way mirror. Twenty-one behavioral interactions were scored by two independent observers who reviewed the videotapes. Eleven mother-infant dyads were evaluated in each group. Statistically significant differences were noted in three broad areas: vocalizations, mutual behaviors, and contingency behaviors. There were fewer positive vocalizations, more negative vocalizations and more time spent ignoring their FTT infants by the study mothers compared to the controls. Mutual gazing, mutual interactions and contingency behaviors (baby does something and mother reacts) were also less in the study group (Senter, Berkowitz, Sklaren & Hasterok, 1983). Similar observations have been noted by others. For example, FTT infants showed more self-play and fewer vocalizations than control infants (Powell & Low, 1983).

To evaluate mother-infant interactions, our PNP utilizes the assessment scales developed at the University of Washington School of Nursing by Kathryn Barnard (1978). These scales consist of over 100 questions based on observations of the mother-infant interactions. These observations focus on the mother's ability to interpret her infant's cues. Special attention is given to the interactions which occur during a feeding, and the home visit is scheduled at a meal time.

Although the visiting nurse generally doesn't do as formal an assessment as our clinic nurse practitioner, she also makes a home visit during meal time and assesses the economic resources, mother-infant interactions, living conditions and food supply for the family. The visiting nurse uses time with the mother to make feeding or interactional suggestions.

Other institutions have utilized nurses, social workers or other health professionals to provide in-home counselling or support (Fraiberg, Adelson & Shapiro, 1975). These programs have been very successful in focusing on the needs of the mother, in order to help her focus her attention more effectively on the needs of her child.

Team Conference

Once all patients have been seen, the team convenes for about one and one half hours to discuss each case, develop management strategies and follow-up plans. Members of outside agencies such as law enforcement's Child Abuse Unit and DPSS may attend the Clinic and participate in the conference. The visiting nurse also attends the FTT team conference.

New cases are discussed first. The medical history, physical findings and laboratory studies are presented. The physician highlights the positive findings and makes a preliminary diagnosis based on the medical findings. Dietary findings and recommendations are then reviewed. The social worker then presents an assessment of the family needs to help formulate a comprehensive diagnosis. A typical assessment would be: "This is a child with familial short stature, who seems to have an adequate caloric intake, but whose mother seems overwhelmed with her six other children and the fact that her husband recently deserted the family."

The team delineates a management plan based on the information that has been gathered. Immediate admission to the hospital occurs infrequently (less than 5%), and is recommended if an infant appears acutely ill, severely malnourished (e.g. less than the 5th percentile weight for height) or removal from the home is needed but no foster home is available. Children over the age of 2 years with psychosocial dwarfism may be admitted to document abnormalities in their endocrine status. In contrast to other settings, we generally do not hospitalize infants with environmental FTT to document good in-hospital weight gain. The literature suggests that weight gain in such infants is variable and may require 2 to 3 weeks of hospitalization (Barbero & Shaheen, 1971; Berwick, 1980). Our experience has shown that 86% of infants with non-organic FTT hospitalized at our institution did gain weight. However, many of these infants also develop nosocomial infections, particularly gastroenteritis, which can lead to a prolonged hospital stay.

Approximately 10% of the children seen in the FTT Clinic are felt to be normal small children. These children are diagnosed as either familial short stature or constitutional delay. If there are no nutritional or social factors contributing to the child's growth retardation, the child is referred back to his primary care physician. If no primary care physician is available, our team will continue to follow the patient at intervals of 4 to 6 months to monitor growth.

A small number of patients are discovered to have a purely medical reason, such as congenital rubella syndrome, for the poor growth. Medical follow-up is given in the FTT Clinic or referral is made to a subspecialty clinic, such as Medical Genetics.

Approximately 10-15% of our patients have an isolated nutritional deficiency, sometimes based on limited family resources. With referral to WIC and food banks, and the temporary use of supplemental feedings, the outcome is very good. Follow-up visits with the team are important to assure that recommendations are being implemented, but the child can be referred back to the primary care facility once weight gain is achieved and progress continues.

The majority of families require intervention on a social, nutritional and/or medical basis. The decision to recommend a home visit by the VNA, WIC referral, placement of children in a Head Start program, or psychologic assessment is made during the conference. Overall, our team approach of aggressive supportive intervention appears successful in a majority of cases.

Another 20-30% of our patients come from families which are coping only marginally with life tasks. In such cases, family emotional and economic resources have usually been overwhelmed by the birth of the last infant. Such families are often open to help from outside agencies and follow through with WIC referrals, getting food stamps, state aid, and enrolling other youngsters in Head Start programs where they receive 2 meals a day. Prognosis is good for these infants and their families. We continue to follow these children initially on a weekly and then monthly basis.

More often (about 40-50%), families are not only overwhelmed by economic and emotional stresses but are unamenable to help. They deny that anything is wrong and fail to follow through on any of the team's recommendations. Some of these individuals do not allow the visiting nurse to come to their home and are very suspicious about the team's intentions. Occasionally, these families have been referred to DPSS before and are now understandably fearful that their children will be removed. Often their fears are realized because in our setting their failure to comply is an indication for a referral to DPSS and sometimes a recommendation for placement of the child in foster care.

Families in which a parent appears very angry or hostile are also referred to DPSS. Such families account for 10% or less of those seen in our Clinic. These parents often resist bringing the child in for an evaluation and deny that anything is wrong. They come into Clinic at the insistence of the court, DPSS or their private physician. They do not return for follow-up appointments, overwhelm the staff with their anger, and represent the most refractory FTT infants and families we deal with. Our experience suggests that some of these children do not only have to be placed in foster care, but may have to be relinquished for adoption to prevent physical abuse.

The decision to recommend removal of the child from the home is made after careful review of the medical, nutritional and social data. Some children have complicated medical needs which are not being met in their natural home. It is understandably difficult for members of the FTT team to be confronted by angry parents who can only view the removal of their child as a punitive act. Collegial support from other team members facilitates coping with the intensity of such anger.

We feel it is imperative that FTT children placed in foster care continue to be followed at the FTT Clinic. This assures continuity and consistency of medical care and allows the team to assess the effect that the natural environment made on the child's growth and development. Ongoing medical supervision is also important because not all foster homes are suitable for caring for FTT infants. Many of these children have complicated medical problems or are difficult to nurture for other reasons. For example, the infant suffering from environmental FTT is not a giving baby. Symptoms such as gaze avoidance, hypertonicity, and back arching make the infant uncuddly. A special foster mother is required to meet the child's needs. We have followed a number of infants who did poorly in one foster home, only to start growing and developing when their foster home was changed. In many instances, we also encourage the natural mother to come to Clinic with the foster mother.

The decision to return a FTT infant to the natural home is made by the court. However, this decision is based on the recommendation of agencies such as DPSS and the FTT Clinic team. We feel that infants should be gaining weight at a normal rate and all major medical problems appropriately taken care of before they are returned to their natural parents. In addition, parents should have demonstrated a willingness to get help for themselves by enrolling in parenting programs or individual therapy. If the children are spending time (e.g. weekends) with their natural parents, we question the foster mother as to the condition of the child when the weekend visit is over. Is the child appropriately dressed, well-fed, clean and well? Or is this a child who was making excellent progress until weekend visits were instituted? Are there any new stresses in the home that might interfere with the mother's ability to care for her infant? Has she had a new baby? Has the family had to move in with other relatives?

If the infant is returned to the natural parents, we feel that it is once again imperative that follow-up care be at the FTT Clinic. This permits careful monitoring of the infant's progress upon return to his natural environment. Once again, families may resist returning to the facility that recommended removal of their child. However, DPSS and the court can insist that care be rendered at our facility, and in some instances the supportive attitude of the team can facilitate the family's compliance with this recommendation.

Over the years we have developed strong liaisons with many community agencies dealing with FTT infants. These links were forged during training sessions given by members of our FTT team at local medical conferences, sessions of the Child Welfare League of America, American Humane Society and in-service sessions for the public health clinics of Los Angeles County. In addition, training sessions have been held for over 600 DPSS workers and foster parents. The FTT Clinic is recognized in the Los Angeles community as providing a unique, comprehensive and expert assessment of the child with FTT. We have found the team approach not only to be highly productive for patient care, but also to provide each team member with greater insight and understanding about the compelling disorder of FTT.

REFERENCES

Barbero, G.J. & Shaheen, E. Environmental failure to thrive: A clinical view. Journal of Pediatrics, 1967, 71, 639-644.

Barnard, K. NCAST Learning Resource Manual. Seattle: University of Washington, 1978.

Barnard, K. NCAST Nursing Child Assessment Feeding Scale. Seattle: University of Washington, 1978.

Barnard, K. NCAST Nursing Child Assessment Teaching Scale. Seattle: University of Washington, 1978.

Beargie, R.A., James, V.L. & Greene, J.W. Growth and development of small-for-date newborns. Pediatric Clinics of North America, 1970, 17, 159-167.

Berkowitz, C.D. & Barry, H. The psychological assessment of children with failure to thrive. In Program and Abstracts of the 22nd Annual Meeting of the Ambulatory Pediatric Association. Washington, D.C., 1982, 85.

Berkowitz, C.D. & Sklaren, B.C. Environmental failure to thrive: The need for intervention. American Family Physician, 1984, 29, 191-199.

Berwick, D.M. Non-organic failure to thrive. Pediatric Review, 1980, 1, 265-270.

Chase, H.P. The effects of intrauterine and postnatal undernutrition on normal brain development. Annals of New York Academy of Sciences, 1973, 205, 231-244.

Child, A.A., Murphy, C.M. & Rhyne, M.C. Depression in children: Reasons and risks. Pediatric Nursing, 1980, 9-13.

Cupoli, J.M., Hallock, J.A. & Barness, L.A. Failure to thrive. Current Problems in Pediatrics, 1980, 10, 1-43.

Crytryn, L. & McKnew, D. Proposed classification of childhood depression. American Journal of Psychiatry, 1972, 129, 149-154.

Ehlers, K.H. Growth failure in association with congenital heart disease. Pediatric Annals, 1978, 7, 35-37.

Evans, S.L., Reinhart, J.B. & Succop, R.A. Failure to thrive: A study of 45 children and their families. Journal of American Academy of Child Psychiatry, 1972, 11, 44-457.

Fischer, R. Growth patterns of low-birth-weight infants. Pediatric Annals, 1978, 7, 101-109.

Forsyth, B., McCarthy, P. & Leventhal, J. Feeding problems in early infancy and use of special formulas. In Program and Abstracts of the 22nd Annual Meeting of the Ambulatory Pediatric Association. Washington, D.C., 1982, 48.

Fraiberg, S., Adelson, E. & Shapiro, V. Ghosts in the nursery: A psychoanalytic approach to the problems of impaired infant-mother relationships. Journal of the American Academy of Child Psychiatry, 1975, 14, 387-421.

Funderbunk, S.J., Guthrie, D. & Meldrum, D. Suboptimal pregnancy outcome among women with prior abortions and premature births. American Journal of Obstetrics and Gynecology, 1976, 126, 55.

Gardner, L.I. Deprivation dwarfism. Scientific American, 1972, 227, 76-82.

Hannaway, P.J. Failure to thrive: A study of 100 infants and children. Clinical Pediatrics, 1970, 9, 86-91.

Hiles, D.A. Infantile cataracts. Pediatric Annals, 1983, 12, 556-573.

Jones, K.L., Smith, D.W. & Vileland, C. Patterns of malformation in offspring of chronic alcoholic mothers. Lancet, 1973, 1, 1267-1271.

Kennell, J. Evidence for a sensitive period in the human mother. In Klaus et al. (Eds.), Maternal Attachment and Mothering Disorders. Sausalito, CA: Johnson & Johnson, 1974.

Klein, P.S., Forbes, G.B. & Nader, P.R. Effects of starvation in infancy (pyloric stenosis) on subsequent learning abilities. Journal of Pediatrics, 1975, 87, 8-15.

Lary, V. & Bauer, C.H. Pathophysiology of failure to thrive in gastrointestinal disorders. Pediatric Annals, 1978, 7, 20-33.

Linn, C.C. & Evans, M.I. Intrauterine Growth Retardation: Pathophysiology and Clinical Management. New York: McGraw Hill Book Co., 1984.

Miller, H.C. & Hassanein, K. Diagnosis of impaired fetal growth in newborn infants. Pediatrics, 1971, 48, 511-522.

Money, J. The syndrome of abuse dwarfism (psychosocial dwarfism or reversible hyposomatotropism). American Journal of Diseases of Children, 1977, 131, 508-513.

Murray, C.A. & Glassman, M.S. Nutrient requirements during growth and recovery from failure to thrive. In P.J. Accardo (Ed.), Failure to Thrive in Infancy and Early Childhood. A Multidisciplinary Team Approach. Baltimore: University Park Press, 1982.

Nadler, H.L. Role of the general pediatrician in genetics. Pediatric Review, 1981, 3, 4-12.

Nadler, H.L. & Burton, B.K. Genetics. In E.J. Quilligas & N. Kretchmer (Eds.), Fetal and Maternal Medicine. New York: John Wiley & Sons, 1980.

Overall, J.C. Viral infections of the fetus and neonate. In R.D. Feigin, J.D. Cherry (Eds.), Textbook of Pediatric Infectious Diseases. Philadelphia: W.B. Saunders, Co., 1981.

Powell, G.F., Brasel, J.A. & Blizzard, R.M. Emotional deprivation and growth retardation simulating idiopathic hypopituitarism, I. Clinical evaluation of the syndrome. New England Journal of Medicine, 1967, 276, 1271-1278.

Powell, G.F., Brasel, J.A., Raiti, S. & Blizzard, R.M. Emotional deprivation and growth retardation simulating idiopathic hypopituitarism, II. Endocrinological evaluation of the syndrome. New England Journal of Medicine, 1967, 276, 1279-1283.

Powell, G.F. & Low, J. Behavior in nonorganic failure to thrive. Journal of Developmental and Behavioral Pediatrics, 1983, 4, 26-33.

Rosenn, D.W., Loeb, L.B. & Jura, M.B. Differentiation of organic from nonorganic failure to thrive syndrome in infancy. Pediatrics, 1980, 66, 698-704.

Rudman, D., Davis, T., Priest, J.H., Patterson, J.H., Kutner, M.H., Heymsfield, S.B. & Bethel, R.A. Prevalence of growth hormone deficiency in children with cleft lip or palate. Journal of Pediatrics, 1978, 93, 378-382.

Sahler, O.J., Simms, R., Rice, N. & Klijanowicz, A. A 2-4 year follow-up of children with failure to thrive. In Program and Abstracts of the 19th Annual Meeting of the Ambulatory Pediatric Association. Atlanta, GA, 1979, 29.

Schowalter, J.E. Depression in children and adolescents. Pediatric Review, 1981, 4, 51-55.

Senter, S.A., Berkowitz, C.D., Sklaren, B.C. & Hasterok, G. Mother infant interactions in non-organic failure to thrive. In Program and Abstracts of the 23rd Annual Meeting of the Ambulatory Pediatric Association. Washington, D.C., 1983, 66.

Shapiro, K. The masks of depression. Nursing Mirror, 1975, 140, 46-48.

Sills, R.H. Failure to thrive: The role of clinical and laboratory evaluation. American Journal of Diseases of Children, 1978, 132, 967-969.

Silver, H.K. & Finkelstein, M. Deprivation dwarfism. Journal of Pediatrics, 1967, 70, 317-324.

Silverman, D.T. Maternal smoking and birth weight. American Journal of Epidemiology, 1977, 105, 513-518.

Smith, D.W. Recognizable patterns of human malformation. Genetics, Embryologic and Clinical Aspects. Philadelphia: W.B. Saunders, 1982.

Wachtel, R.C. Malnutrition and the developing brain. In P.J. Accardo (Ed.), Failure to Thrive in Infancy and Early Childhood. A Multidisciplinary Team Approach. Baltimore: University Park Press, 1982.

White, J.K., Malcolm, R., Roper, K., Westphal, M.C. & Smith, C. Psychosocial and developmental factors in failure to thrive: One-to-three year follow-up. Journal of Developmental and Behavioral Pediatrics, 1981, 2, 112-114.

Whitten, C.F., Pettit, C.F., Fischhoff, J. Evidence that growth failure from maternal deprivation is secondary to undereating. Journal of the American Medical Association, 1969, 209, 1675-1682.

A STRATEGY FOR MANAGING NON-ORGANIC FAILURE TO THRIVE BASED ON A

PROSPECTIVE STUDY OF ANTECEDENTS

William A. Altemeier, III, Susan M. O'Connor, Kathyrn B.
Sherrod, Thomas D. Yeager, and Peter M. Vietze

Department of Pediatrics, Vanderbilt University Hospital
Nashville, Tennessee; Department of Psychology, Peabody
College/Vanderbilt University, Nashville, Tennessee; Mental
Retardation Research Centers, NICHHD, Bethesda, Maryland

Non-organic failure to thrive (NOFT) is a formidable problem at medical centers that provide care for low income families. The frequency is as high as six percent of all births in these institutions (Altemeier et al., 1985) and the sequelae are substantial for both victims and society. Although we lack an ideal study of outcome (for example, a long term prospective comparison of the full spectrum of NOFT with controls matched for family size, intelligence and socioeconomic level), the best information we have indicates that children with severe NOFT are at risk for delayed development and small stature when examined a decade or longer after the initial diagnosis (Oates et al., 1985).

The techniques used to treat this condition must be based upon an understanding of its etiology. The classical and most important category of growth failure without organic cause has been termed the "attachment" type because the mothers do not seem to be attached to these infants in the usual way. The evidence for this includes the fact that when these infants are fed in the hospital, rapid catch up growth is observed. Furthermore, retrospective studies of mothers who have children with NOFT indicate these women often have conditions that interfere with their ability to love and care for their infants. For example, these women were more likely to have substandard living conditions (Hufton & Oates, 1977), depression (Elmer, 1960; Evans et al., 1972), greater stress (Elmer, 1960) and isolation (Leonard et al., 1966) in their lives. The following is a report of characteristics of mothers with NOFT infants assessed prospectively by collecting data before the infant goes home from the nursery. The results provide further evidence that NOFT is due to a disturbance in the mother-infant relationship, that this disturbance is present before the infant

Supported by the National Center on Child Abuse and Neglect; Children's Bureau Administration on Children, Youth and Families; Office of Human Development Services/Department of Health, Education and Welfare Grant No. 90-C-419 and 90-CA-2138; William T. Grant Foundation; the National Institute of Mental Health, Grant No. R01 MH31195-01; (John F. Kennedy Center) Grant No. HD15052 Center for Research in Mental Retardation and Human Development and National Institute of Mental Health Grant No. MH 38373.

goes home from the nursery, and that maternal rejection of these infants seems to be subtle and not as overt as rejection in other forms of mal treatment such as child abuse. Our purpose was to use this prospective data to develop a strategy to prevent and treat NOFT.

METHODS

This study was performed at Nashville General Hospital (NGH) which provides outpatient, inpatient, and obstetrical care to low income families from Nashville. Details of methods have been published (Altemeier et al., 1985). Consent to be interviewed was requested from all mothers registering for prenatal clinic over a 15 month period, and 94% or 1400 agreed to participate. Trained research assistants administered a 40 minute interview concerning characteristics which retrospective studies found to be associated with child maltreatment. Immediately following interview, results were scored by an apriori method and the 20% who scored most negatively were estimated to be in a "high risk" category: the intent was to determine feasibility of predicting risk for NOFT during pregnancy. Because it was not possible to follow all 1400 infants, 274 mothers were randomly selected at interview and offered well and sick child care at the study hospital.

At the time of last data collection, the average age of infants born to these women was 12.8 months. However, progressively fewer children were available as the child's age increased because of variation in age at last data collection, the decreasing need for clinic visits with increasing age, and failure of subjects to return to the study hospital. Thus, at last data collection, 232 infants were at least 60 days old and all but 39 (a 17% "dropout" or missing data rate) had weights and clinical data available. Dropout rates were 33% of 175 infants between 2 and 9 months old, 63% of 188 potentially available between 9 and 12 months and 55% of 33 aged 12 to 18 months.

Failure to thrive (without considering organic versus nonorganic etiology) was defined as a daily weight gain, over at least 10 days, below 18 grams between 15 and 60 days of age, <12 grams between 61 and 270 days, <8 grams from 271 to 360 days, and <5 grams between 361 and 540 days. This translated to less than two thirds of the Harvard 50th percentile curve. Infants with FTT were divided into a dichotomy of organic versus nonorganic categories by pediatricians (authors SOC and WAA) who reviewed all clinical data while blind to all research information for the respective patients. Although some children had mixtures of organic and nonorganic sources for growth failure, no attempt was made to subdivide etiology further than these two categories. If the pediatrician felt a child's medical problem could have explained the growth failure, the patient was placed in the organic category. If not, the growth failure was considered nonorganic. Twenty one patients had growth failure at least once by these criteria, and six had a medical problem that could have explained this: two had pneumonia, two had gastroenteritis, and one each had cerebral palsy and persistent otitis media. The remaining 15 were categorized as NOFT.

The etiology of NOFT was explored by correlating interview and perinatal clinical data with NOFT using a pool of these 15 patients plus 86 children selected randomly from the remaining subjects. Perinatal clinical data were scored by the same two pediatricians, who reviewed maternal and neonatal medical records for the 101 subjects while blind to interview data and presence of absence of NOFT.

The study design was also blind in that physicians who diagnosed and managed medical conditions and growth failure were unaware of research data for their patients; and mothers were not aware of how they scored during the interview. The total subject population of 1400 mothers and their children were also involved in a parallel study of the antecedents of child neglect and child abuse at the time this NOFT research was underway.

RESULTS

The data will be presented in two formats. The next three sections present a brief overview of the results according to source. This will be followed by an organization of data temporally, as the characteristics would be expected to impact on the lives of a mother and her infant. The former sections report data; in the latter we speculate about how this data might fit into the development of this syndrome.

Incidence, Severity, and Age of Onset of NOFT

Fifteen of the 274 infants in this study were diagnosed as having NOFT. Thus, the overall incidence was 5.5% in our low income population. This compares with prior estimates of five to ten percent observed at our study hospital, and underscores the relatively high frequency of this syndrome. Actually, this must be accepted as a minimum incidence since some of the subjects were lost to follow-up and the average age of infants was only slightly over one year at the completion of the study.

We tried to set criteria that would capture a broad spectrum of degrees of NOFT, and the growth failure varied from mild to severe among our 15 infants. As summarized in Table 1, most children met our criteria for NOFT more than once. One child had growth failure below our minimum rates for at least ten days on four separate occasions, four met the criteria three times, four met the criteria twice, and the remaining six had NOFT recognized once. Five of these children had sufficiently severe growth failure to require hospitalization one or more times because of NOFT. At the time of first diagnosis, ten of the 15 were at or below the third percentile for weight while all but one of the remaining five were at or below the fifteenth percentile. A single infant dropped from the 90th to the 50th percentile the first time our criteria were met, and went on to have NOFT one additional time.

As illustrated in Table 1, the great majority of these infants first met the criteria for NOFT at a very young age: nine developed significant growth failure at approximately one month of age, and four more developed the syndrome near the third month. We attribute at least part of this high incidence in the first three months of life to the prospective approach of this study, although the fact that weights and clinical data were more complete for younger subjects may have also contributed to this tendency.

It was possible to predict high risk for NOFT to a moderate but significant degree: 49 of 274 mothers were classified as high risk on the basis of interview scores, and seven of the 15 children with NOFT were born to these mothers. Thus, the overall incidence of NOFT was 14% among the high risk and 3.5% among the remaining mothers (p <.05).

Antecedents of NOFT Identified by Prenatal Interview

The interview consisted of eight major sections: 13 questions explored a mother's perception of her nurture during childhood, nine dealt with her philosophy of parenting and parenting skills, eight with support from family and friends, eleven with self image and personality, six with alcohol, drug and health problems within the family, fourteen with her attitude about her current pregnancy, sixteen with her knowledge of child

Table 1

Weight Changes Used to Diagnose NOFT

Patient	Months of Age	At First Diagnosis Weight % tile	At First Diagnosis Weight Change Grams per day/# days	# Times Criteria for NOFT Met
1	1	< 3	−53/14	2
2	1	< 3	16/18	4
3	1	10	11/15	1
4	1	< 3	−20/11	1
5	1	3	9/15	2
6	1	50	−17/16	1
7	1	< 3	12/14	3
8	1	10	17/13	2
9	1	< 3	− 9/10	3
10	3	< 3	11/81	1
11	3	< 3	7/24	1
12	3	3	8/14	3
13	3	10	11/26	3
14	6	< 3	3/29	2
15	15	15	4/94	1

development, and finally, a Life Stress Inventory, modified from Holmes and Rahe (1967), identified the incidence of 21 maternal and 11 paternal stresses. The mother's perception of her nurture as a child ($r=-.328$, $p <.05$) and the Life Stress Inventory of both the mother ($r=.338$, $p<.01$) and father ($r=.270$, $p<.01$) were the only sections that correlated significantly with subsequent NOFT. Among the questions dealing with the perceptions of childhood nurture, those that were significant were: "do you feel you were loved as a child?" ($r=-.252$, $p <.05$); "was your childhood happy?" ($r=-.214$, $p <.05$); "would you like to be the same kind of mother that your mother was to you?" ($r=-.219$, $p <.05$); and "did you feel your parents were pleased with you?" ($r=-.195$, $p <.05$). The question "did anyone who took care of you ever beat you up?" did not correlate significantly with NOFT ($r=.177$, $p <.07$), but being beaten more than twice ($r=.197$, $p <.05$) and "did you see a physician for injuries?" ($r=.294$, $p <.01$) were significant.

The incidences of four maternal life stresses during the preceeding year were significantly higher among NOFT infants. These were: number of arguments with the father of the baby ($r=.236$, $p <.05$); separations from the father ($r=.410$, $p <.01$); "make up" with the father or his family ($r=.414$, $p <.01$); and death of a friend ($r=.254$, $p <.01$). Two paternal stresses were significant: leaving a job without being fired ($r=.219$, $p <.05$), and being arrested ($r=.363$, $p <.01$).

Table 2

Correlation of Perinatal Characteristics with NOFT

Pregnancy	Correlation
Duration prenatal care	-.066
Number prenatal visits	.047
Pregnancy complications	.231*
Weight gain	-.193*

Delivery	
Infant's sex	.035
Gestational age	-.195*
Dysmaturity	.013
Prematurity	.033
Birth weight	-.174
Birth length	-.228*
Twin birth	-.042
Caesarean section	-.112
Labor/delivery complications	.042
Apgar 1 minute	-.132
Apgar 5 minutes	-.065
Postpartum complications	-.080

Nursery Course	
Reduced feeding by mother	.233*
Weight loss in nursery	-.137
Breast fed	-.094
Nursery illnesses/complications	.035
Duration nursery stay	-.093
Neonate's discharge status	-.042
Residual medical problems	.235*

*$p < .05$ **$p < .01$

Antecedents of NOFT from Perinatal Clinical Data

Table 2 summarizes the relationship of pregnancy, delivery and nursery characteristics with NOFT. Mothers who would have infants with this condition gained less weight during their pregnancies, and had a greater number of pregnancy complications. Seven of the 86 or 8% of control mothers required hospitalization during their pregnancy compared to four (27%) of 15 in the NOFT group: two of the latter required hospitalization because of pregnancy associated hypertension, one because of dehydration from vomiting, and one because of premature labor. The only delivery complications related to subsequent NOFT were gestational age and body length at the time of birth. The average duration of gestation for NOFT infants was 38 weeks compared with 39 weeks for the controls, and no infant with NOFT had a gestation shorter than 36 weeks. Thus, differences between the groups were small but significant. The correlation of birth weight with NOFT approached but did not reach significance ($p < .07$). During the brief stay in the nursery, mothers in the NOFT group were more likely to have difficulty feeding these children: seven of the 15 notified nurses that they did not wish to feed, or had sufficient problems that the nurses elected to do most of the feeding. The nurses who fed these infants reported similar feeding problems for only one of these seven patients. Finally, at the time of discharge from the nursery, infants who would develop NOFT were more likely to have some unresolved question about their health: 5 of 15 were scheduled to return within the first few days for a bilirubin determination (3 patients), cytogenetics study for suspected Down's Syndrome which was negative (1 patient), and a heart murmur which disappeared (1 patient).

Speculation About the Sequence of Events Leading to NOFT

To gain insight into how this syndrome might develop, the following section presents characteristics from our prospective study organized sequentially as they appeared in the lives of mothers and their infants who developed NOFT.

The earliest differences between mothers in NOFT and control groups concerned perception of childhood nurture. Those who would have children with NOFT were more likely to: feel that they were not loved or accepted by their parents, consider their childhood less happy, and reject their mother as a model. These women also experienced more child abuse that was severe, but it was interesting that feeling unloved and unwanted seemed to be a stronger correlate of NOFT than outright abuse. This same pattern was observed in our studies of antecedents for child abuse (Altemeier et al., 1982). Many retrospective studies have found that abusive parents were often abused during their own childhood (Helfer, 1973; Park & Collmer, 1975; Solomon, 1973), and a few studies have also indicated that mothers of NOFT infants are likely to have experienced maltreatment during their own childhood (Kerr et al., 1978; Leonard et al., 1966; Pollitt et al., 1975). In any event, there is general agreement that aberrant nurture during childhood can interfere with the ability of an individual to experience strong and mature relationships with others, including one's own children. This suggests that NOFT may be due at least in part to a disturbed relationship between a mother and her infant.

At the time of interview, the significant correlates of subsequent NOFT were increased life stresses for both mother and father, and pregnancy complications ranging from medical problems serious enough to require hospitalization to inadequate maternal weight gain. Among the 21 maternal life stresses in the interview, four were significantly associated with NOFT, and three of these four expressed a tumultous relationship between the mother and the father of the infant she was carrying. Mothers in the NOFT group had significantly more arguments, separations, and reconciliations with this man. There are a variety of ways that a disturbed paternal relationship might be associated with subsequent NOFT. For example, the relationship might be an expression of a general inability on the part of the mother to form strong attachments related to the aberrant nurturing history mentioned above. Alternatively, a disruptive love relationship could, in itself, detract from the mother's ability to nurture and become attached to her infant. A third possibility is that both of these operate in conjunction. That is, the mother's inability to have mature relationships could result in a disruptive relationship with her mate which could further interfere with her ability to nurture her infant. It was also of interest that the two of 11 paternal life stresses that were significantly related to subsequent NOFT (increased incidence of changing jobs and being arrested) would also be expected to disrupt a relationship between parents. An association between increased life stress and NOFT has been observed by many workers (Elmer, 1960; Homer & Ludwig, 1981; Shaheen et al., 1968).

The increased incidence of pregnancy complications among mothers in the NOFT group might also disturb the mother's developing relationship with her unborn infant by distracting her (Cohen, 1966; Crnic et al., 1983) or perhaps causing her to resent the pregnancy. In similar fashion, the anxiety of unresolved medical concerns at nursery discharge could also

216

diminish a mother's emotional investment (Kennell & Rolnick, 1960), even though these health questions turned out to be of no direct consequence to the physical health of the neonate. The fact that the infants who would develop NOFT were slightly but significantly more premature and tended to be smaller than controls would also be expected to interfere with the mother-infant relationship. Premature infants have reduced ability to interact and therefore to reinforce nurturing behavior on the part of their mothers (Bakeman & Brown, 1980). The ability of an infant to interact with the mother appears to be an important aspect of their developing relationship and prematures would be at a disadvantage in this regard. Finally, Vietze et al. (1980) observed mother-infant interactions prospectively in a different group of subjects taken from this same study and found that mothers who would subsequently have infants with NOFT spent less time looking at their neonates at 48 hours after delivery compared to controls. Mothers of male but not female infants who would develop NOFT were also more likely to quickly terminate interaction at this time.

Since all of the above prospective observations correlated significantly with subsequent NOFT, and since all could, in some way, either reflect or contribute to a disturbed mother infant relationship, it seems likely that the latter may be the foundation for the pathogenesis of the early onset and disturbed maternal attachment type of NOFT. Actually, retrospective studies of NOFT have come to a similar conclusion based on different data (English, 1978). A comparison of predictors for child abuse and NOFT, as determined by our interview during pregnancy, may provide some further insight into the nature of this disturbed mother-infant relationship. The predictors for child abuse differed from those of NOFT in several ways (Altemeier et al., 1985; Altemeier et al., 1982). First, mothers of infants who would suffer child abuse had significantly more aggressive and violent tendencies compared to controls. The mothers in the child abuse group were also much more emphatic in expressing a negative attitude towards their pregnancy compared to the NOFT mothers (Altemeier et al., 1985). Finally, the interviewers were asked to subjectively estimate risk for child maltreatment based upon a mother's behavior during the interview. Their subjective comments and estimates were highly predictive for child abuse but did not correlate with NOFT, indicating the interviewers were able to recognize risk for child abuse but not for NOFT. This suggests the pathology behind the inability of a mother to provide adequate nurture for an infant is more passive, subtle and perhaps more subconscious than the personality problems that lead to child abuse.

The timing of the onset of NOFT may also have some relevance to unravelling its etiology. A prospective study should be more precise in identifying the earliest signs of problems in maternal feeding and inadequate weight gain. Nine of our 15 NOFT children first met the criteria for FTT at approximately one month of age while only two of the 15 had the initial onset after four months, suggesting the onset is quite early in life. It must be kept in mind that our study design emphasized younger infants since decreasing numbers of subjects were available at increasing ages, so it is possible that we missed some NOFT in older children. Even so, 13 or 5% of the 274 subjects in our study developed FTT before four months of age. It was also interesting that during the living-in period seven of the 15 mothers in the NOFT group either did not wish to feed their infants, or had sufficient difficulty with this, so that nurses elected to do most of the feeding. This rate was significantly higher than similar problems in control mothers. This provides further evidence of the early onset of attachment type NOFT and that the onset may often be a continuum that begins at birth.

Thus far we have only considered the role of the mother in the pathogenesis of NOFT without discussing whether the infant might also play a part in the development of this syndrome. As indicated above, some of our patients had illnesses that were not severe enough to cause their growth failure. It is difficult to know whether these organic problems might have had an adverse effect on the mother-infant relationship. Also, slight degrees of prematurity were associated with risk for NOFT. We speculated that this relationship could be due to a relative decrease in the premature's ability to reciprocate in mother-infant interactions. Thus, at least one infant factor may have been important. However, we were unable to find other differences in control and NOFT infants before they left the nursery. Brazelton scores near birth were not different, and nurses reported feeding problems in only one of the seven NOFT infants with maternal feeding difficulties.

The question of whether infants might themselves contribute to the development of this syndrome has been raised in the past, primarily because some patients with full blown NOFT are usually developmentally delayed and avoid or show disinterest in close social encounters (Rosenn et al., 1980). It is easy to see how it might be difficult to form an attachment with such an infant. As part of our overall study, mothers received the Carey assessment of perception of infant's temperament (Carey, 1970; 1972) administered at one and three months of age to NOFT and control women available for testing. Perception of difficult temperament correlated with subsequent NOFT at both ages (r=.296, p <.01 at one month; r=.351, p <.01 at three months). However, at these ages, most of the infants in the NOFT group had already met the criteria for FTT, and this perception of difficult infant temperament, as well as the above delayed development and asocial behavior seemed likely to be effects rather than primary causes of NOFT. Supporting this hypothesis is the relatively rapid improvement in social behavior and development that younger infants with NOFT often experience during a ten to twelve day hospitalization. In summary, except for prematurity, we were unable to find any infant characteristics that seem to be primary causes of NOFT. For this reason, we speculate the infant has relatively little to do with the onset of this condition. On the other hand, once NOFT develops, the developmental delay, antisocial behavior, and "difficult temperaments" of such infants may very well play a role in the continuation of the syndrome. That is to say, a vicious circle could develop by which disturbed maternal attachment may lead to inadequate feeding and nurture, which may lead to developmental and social delay, which may further disturb the mother-infant relationship.

CLINICAL MANAGEMENT OF NOFT

We speculate that the treatment of NOFT should be directed at breaking the cycle described above. If a disturbed mother-infant relationship is at the core of the syndrome, the strategy for treatment should be to improve this relationship by enhancing maternal behavior, infant behavior or both. The following is our treatment program developed on the basis of the above data and the programs of others. Our techniques of treatment are not very different form others described in the pediatric literature (Barbero & Shaheen, 1967; Leonard et al., 1966). It should also be pointed out that the study hospital is a city-owned indigent hosital with an abundance of NOFT patients but a shortage of resources so that a large multidiscplinary team approach is a realistic option for only the most serious cases.

Children born in the study hospital have their first well baby checks scheduled between age two and four weeks. The timing of this check is based upon the high incidence of NOFT in this population, the relatively early age of onset described above, and our experience that occasionally infants with severe NOFT will be in critical condition after age one month. At this and all subsequent well child visits, emphasis is placed upon accurate weighing and completion of growth charts to permit early recognition of FTT. Part of this emphasis is related to the impression (Powell & Blizzard, 1967) that the earlier this syndrome is recognized and treated, the easier it is to reverse NOFT and its sequelae. The infant seen in the clinics with severe NOFT is hospitalized at that visit because the compliance of NOFT mothers in keeping subsequent appointments is often poor, and the risk of a trial of outpatient management seems to be high.

If the growth failure is mild, the initial evaluation in the clinics will include a complete history and physical exam plus some laboratory screening tests such as a CBC, urinalysis and urine culture, tuberculosis skin test, and other laboratory procedures as suggested by clinical or laboratory findings. The mother is then given a supportive pep talk about feeding to make sure she understands appropriate feeding and to try to build her confidence. She is also given very specific feeding instructions such as "you should have all of this can of formula inside this baby by this time tomorrow." The mother is rescheduled for the clinic in seven to ten days, and the physician or nurse practitioner will often contact the mother by telephone the day after the clinic visit and sometimes subsequent to this to continue acting as a coach to promote a positive, optimistic attitude about the child and feeding. If the growth failure is reversed, follow-up is continued on an outpatient basis. If one to three weeks of outpatient efforts fail, the child is hospitalized.

Throughout the course of management, the mother is not directly accused of failing to feed her infant. This is done because such "accusation" is usually considered unacceptable by a mother and often produces anger and a subsequent lack of cooperation. Such maternal reactions are consistent with our speculation that NOFT probably reflects more of a subconscious rather than overt rejection of the infant. In the hospital, laboratory tests are kept to a minimum unless clinical or screening laboratory results suggest that more intensive evaluation would be fruitful (Homer & Ludwig, 1981). The primary strategy during the hospitalization is to interrupt the hypothetical cycle of disturbed mother-infant relationships leading to inadequate nurture, growth failure, developmental delay, and avoidant behavior, which in turn could produce increased disturbance in the mother-infant relationship. The mother is usually sent home "to rest" for the first few days while feeding is transferred to nurses. As soon as the infant enters a rapid stage of growth, we consider this supportive of a diagnosis of NOFT and temporarily suspend new laboratory investigation.

During the hospitalization, one important goal is to make the infant more acceptable to the mother, thereby enhancing the mother-child relationship. We try to make the child more appealing by achieving a one pound weight gain, treating any disfiguring conditions that may range from diaper dermatitis to plastic surgery for more serious defects. Otitis media and/or other minor medical problems are also treated at this point. In addition, hospital personnel nurture and play with the child as much as possible to advance social and developmental skills. It is often possible to change a socially avoidant two month old who has a monotone cry and does not roll over or smile into a playful, normal infant during an approximately ten to twelve day hospitalization. The latter is the duration usually required to accomplish most of the above changes for a younger infant. Again, our impression is that the older the infant is at the time of treatment, the longer it will take to produce weight gain and improve behavior. Although the new fiscal atmosphere under Diagnosis-Related Groupings (DRGs) makes it more difficult to keep a NOFT infant in the hospital for this duration, we feel that current knowledge about long term sequelae justify this approach. During the hospitalization, responsibility for the child's feeding is gradually transferred from the nurses (with coaching and support) back to the mother. The mother is also repeatedly (daily) told about each normal laboratory test, our inability to identify any organic problem, and the rapid weight gain the child is experiencing in the hospital. This is done in hope that she will herself realize the growth failure was due to inadequate feeding. We also point out the new skills acquired by the infant and encourage maternal interaction as the patient makes developmental advances while in the hospital. The goal is to have good weight gain while the mother is doing the majority of feeding and improve mother-infant play and interaction by the time of discharge.

Our impression is that this condition is one of the easiest psychosocial disorders to treat especially if early, aggressive diagnosis and intervention are utilized. The incidence of recurrence, however, is relatively high and these infants should be closely followed for at least the first year of life. As illustrated in Table 1, it is not uncommon to have multiple recurrences of NOFT that require repeated hospitalizations, even though there is adequate growth between episodes.

The primary prevention of NOFT should also probably be centered around improving the mother-infant relationship. Although difficult, the most ideal intervention may be directed towards modifying the effects of the aberrant nurture that mothers of NOFT infants experienced during their own childhood. Our prospective studies suggest that this may form the foundation for not only NOFT but other types of child maltreatment as well. Among the eight interview categories, this was the only one correlating significantly with all three types of maltreatment (NOFT, child neglect and child abuse). The scores of this category also correlated significantly with scores for all of the other interview categories except Knowledge of Child Development, indicating that negative childhood nurture was associated with negative pregnancy attitude, parenting skills, support, self-image, family substance abuse, health problems, and increased life stresses for both mother and father. An overall score of all childhood nurture questions was also correlated with each of the other interview questions. These correlations were significant at p <.05 in the expected direction for 56 of the 102 questions, again suggesting that aberrant nurture during childhood predisposes mothers to negative adjustments of a relatively broad scope during young adult life. Finally, a principle axis factor analysis was applied to the 42 interview questions which were significantly associated with either abuse, neglect, or NOFT using all 1400 subjects. The strongest factor was comprised of the majority of childhood nurture questions.

At first glance, it would appear very difficult to help a mother compensate for aberrant childhood nurture, but continuous support and friendship from a health care worker or volunteer might have some benefit, especially for mothers who are hungry for attention. Finally, interventions that are timed before or immediately after the pregnancy and directed to improve the mother-infant relationship might be preventive. For example, the presence of a supportive family member or other individual during labor, family counselling (especially if there are frequent arguments or separations between mother and father), early contact between mother and infant following birth, rooming-in during the obstetrical hospitalization, keeping nursery follow-up evaluations to a minimum and giving appropriate reassurance for unnecessary anxiety, all seem to be possible interventions to decrease the incidence of NOFT.

The above treatment and preventive regimens are speculative in that they have not been subjected to controlled trials, even though they are based upon prospective data. We recognize that other institutions may utilize much of the same strategies for management of this syndrome. A long-term, carefully controlled study of the sequelae of NOFT with and without various types of clinical management would be very helpful in determining the most effective care of these children.

REFERENCES

Altemeier, W., O'Connor, S., Sherrod, K. & Vietze, P. Prospective study of antecedents for nonorganic failure to thrive. Journal of Pediatrics, 1985, 106, 360-365.

Altemeier, W., O'Connor, S., Vietze, P., Sandler, H. & Sherrod, K. Antecedents of child abuse. Journal of Pediatrics, 1982, 100, 823-829.

Bakeman, R. & Brown, J. Analyzing behavioral sequences: Differences between preterm and full-term infant-mother dyads during the first months of life. In D. Sawin, R. Hawkins, L. Walker & J. Penticuff (Eds.), Exceptional Infant, Volume 4: Psychological Risks in Infant-Environment Transactions. New York: Brunner/Mazel, 1980.

Barbero, G. & Shaheen, E. Environmental failure to thrive: a clinical view. Journal of Pediatrics, 1967, 71, 639-641.

Carey, W.B. A simplified method for measuring infant temperament. Journal of Pediatrics, 1970, 77, 188-194.

Carey, W.B. Clinical applications of the Infant Temperament Measurement. Journal of Pediatrics, 1972, 81, 823-828.

Cohen R. Some maladaptive syndromes of pregnancy and the puerperium. Obstetrics and Gynecology, 1966, 27, 562-570.

Crnic, K., Greenberg, M., Ragozin, A., Robinson, N. & Basham, R. Effects of stress and social support on mothers and premature and full-term infants. Child Development, 1983, 54, 209-217.

Elmer, E. Failure to thrive. Role of the mother. Pediatrics, 1960, 25, 717-725.

English, P. Failure to thrive without organic reason. Pediatric Annals, 1978, 7, 774-781.

Evans, S., Reinhart, J. & Succop, R. Failure to thrive: A study of 45 children and their families. Journal of the American Academy of Child Psychiatry, 1972, 11, 440-457.

Helfer, R. The etiology of child abuse. Pediatrics, 1973, 51(Suppl 4), 777-779.

Holmes, T. & Rahe, R. The social readjustment rating scale. Journal of Psychosomatic Research, 1967, 11, 213-218.

Homer, C. & Ludwig, S. Categorization of etiology of failure to thrive. American Journal of Diseases of Childhood, 1981, 135, 848-851.

Hufton, I. & Oates, K. Nonorganic failure to thrive: A long-term follow-up. Pediatrics, 1977, 59, 73-77.

Kennell, J. & Rolnick, A. Discussing problems in newborn babies with their parents. Pediatrics, 1960, 26, 832-838.

Kerr, M., Bogues, J. & Kerr, D. Psychosocial functioning of mothers of malnourished children. Pediatrics, 1978, 62, 778-784.

Leonard, M., Rhymes, J. & Solnit, A. Failure to thrive in infants. A family problem. American Journal of Diseases of Childhood, 1966, 111, 600-612.

Oates, R., Peacock, A. & Forrest, D. Long-term effects of nonorganic failure to thrive. Pediatrics, 1985, 75, 36-40.

Parke, R. & Collmer, C. Child abuse: an interdisciplinary analysis. In E. Mavis Herington (Ed.), A Review of Child Development Research. Chicago, IL: The University of Chicago Press, 1975.

Pollitt, E., Eichler, A. & Chan, C. Psychosocial development and behavior of mothers of failure to thrive children. American Journal of Orthopsychiatry, 1975, 45, 525-537.

Powell, G.F. & Blizzard, R.M. Emotional deprivation and growth retardation simulating idiopathic hypopituitarism. New England Journal of Medicine, 1967, 276, 276-278.

Rosenn, D., Loeb, L. & Jura, M. Differentiation of organic from nonorganic failure to thrive syndrome in infancy. Pediatrics, 1980, 66, 698-704.

Shaheen, E., Alexander, D., Truskowsky, M. & Barbero, G. Failure to thrive: A retrospective profile. Clinical Pediatrics, 1968, 7, 255-261.

Solomon, T. History and demography of child abuse. Pediatrics, 1973,

51(Suppl 4), 773-776.

Vietze, P., Falsey, S., O'Connor, S., Sandler, H., Sherrod, K. & Altemeier, W. New born behavioral and interactional characteristics of nonorganic failure to thrive infants. In T. Field, S. Goldberg, D. Stern & A. Sostek (Eds.), High-Risk Infants and Children. New York: Academic Press, 1980.

IV   NEW APPROACHES TO DIAGNOSIS AND INTERVENTION

PART II: PSYCHOSOCIAL DIAGNOSIS AND INTERVENTION

Large numbers of children who are diagnosed with FTT have significant psychological and family problems which require intervention and research. In this section, new approaches to diagnostic classification and intervention in FTT are considered. These approaches represent a range of theoretical perspectives and should be of interest to practitioners in a number of disciplines.

Woolston begins this section with a discussion of diagnostic classification. For Woolston, a major impetus for greater diagnostic specificity in FTT is the need for research concerning subtypes of FTT, especially etiological subtypes. Woolston's proposed multiaxial diagnostic system, which has heuristic value for research, provides a clarification of diagnostic issues. Consistent with his pediatric colleagues in previous chapters, Woolston considers growth deficiency as the primary diagnostic feature of FTT. Additional diagnostic axes include physical illness, developmental delay, caretaker-infant interaction, feeding interaction, age of onset and cognitive/financial disability of caretakers. Clarification of diagnostic systems such as the one proposed by Woolston should allow increased specificity and refinement of therapeutic interventions.

Chatoor, Dickson, Schaefer & Egan describe a developmental classification of feeding disorders associated with FTT. The classification is illustrated with case examples derived from clinical experience in a tertiary care hospital setting. Based on a comprehensive assessment of child, mother, and mother-child interaction, Chatoor and her colleagues define four types of feeding disturbances: homostasis, attachment, separation and compounded disorders. Disorders of homostasis begin very early in life, involve problems in early regulation of state, and necessitate treatment directed toward the infant and mother-infant interaction. Disorders of attachment may begin somewhat later in life between two and six months of age, involve problematic parent-child interaction, and respond to a comprehensive program of nutritional rehabilitation, developmental stimulation, and emotional nurturance. Disorders of separation usually begin in the second half of the first year of life, have a peak incidence around nine months of age, and may be treated with a structured approach to reducing maladaptive feeding and parent guidance. Finally, compounded disorders are characterized by feeding problems which begin in one stage of development and compromise development in ensuing developmental stages. Chatoor and her colleagues illustrate how feeding problems can create, co-exist with or result from growth deficiency. Their proposed description of feeding disorders has helped Chatoor and her colleagues design and implement specific interventions and is now being tested in an ongoing research program.

Lieberman and Birch describe an interactional-developmental framework for understanding the psychological issues underlying the development of FTT at various ages. For Lieberman and Birch, FTT is rooted in a specific transactional impasse between the infant and the caregiver. The characteristics of this impasse vary with different developmental stages. Based on clinical experiences with FTT infants and their families, Lieberman and Birch describe specific developmental tasks during infancy and illustrate the way FTT represents a breakdown in developmental phases. These tasks include regulation of neuro-physiological process (first three months), focalization of attachment (3-7 months), initative and the balance of exploration and attachment (8-14 months) and emerging internalization (18-30 months). A number of well-detailed clinical vignettes provide graphic illustration of various transactional problems that are manifest as FTT in different developmental phases and the manner in which parents can be helped to nurture their infants more effectively. Lieberman and Birch's conceptual framework underscores the importance of assessment of the infant-caregiver dyad, the need for intervention based on specific features of developmental disturbances, and suggests directions for future research.

Linscheid and Rasnake illustrate the way in which behavioral principles can be utilized in the treatment of two subtypes of FTT: Type I which has an early onset, corresponds to the attachment disorder described by Chatoor and her colleagues and Type II, which is characterized by a later onset, and feeding disorder, corresponding to the separation disorders described by Chatoor. Linscheid and Rasnake underscore the importance of contingency experiences in the development of Type I FTT and describe a treatment approach which increases the infant's experience of contingency and the caregiver's learning of more effective interactional skills. For Linscheid and Rasnake, feeding problems associated with Type II non-organic FTT can be best understood by either a classical conditioning paradigm in which food is paired with maternal anxiety leading to food refusal or an operant conditioning model in which the child's refusal is reinforced by prolonged attention of the caregiver etc. Based on detailed observation of parent and child, highly specific and individualized treatment goals are developed which involve reinforcement and punishment contingencies and structuring these programs so that they can be implemented by parents. Linscheid and Raskane cite clinical examples which emphasize the importance of parental involvement and knowledge of effective feeding techniques.

In the final intervention approach described in this section, Drotar, Woychik, Mantz-Clumpner, Brickell, Negray, Wallace and Malone describe a family-centered conceptual framework as a guide for psychosocial diagnosis and intervention in FTT and for considering longer-term psychologic risk. A family-centered framework provides a means of understanding the manner in which intrafamilial relationships and resources affect parents, parent-child relationships and the FTT child. A conceptual schema of family resource allocation is presented which outlines various categories of family influence including: material resources (e.g. housing or food), parental personal resources (e.g. family support), family burdens and claims (e.g. relationship problems), and mediating factors (e.g parental development history) which can affect the FTT child's outcome. Case examples illustrate the importance of the family context in the development of FTT and implications for intervention. Drotar and his coworkers outline suggestions for family-centered assessment and intervention, the strengths and limitations of family-centered intervention, impact on intervenors and implications for future research.

In her summary of the intervention approaches this section, Rathbun points out that every clinician must define the problem and its etiology, set a goal of treatment, and develop a strategy for achieving treatment goals. Rathbun summarizes themes in the interventions described by the various authors and emphasizes the special importance of personal alliances and the building of trust. Rathbun suggests that we should consider whether the treatment goal chosen by professionals is the goal that the family of the FTT child would choose for themselves. Rathbun reminds of the dangers of undermining parental autonomy, the need to be cognizant of the limitations of treatment, and of the essential wisdom of prevention.

DIAGNOSTIC CLASSIFICATION: THE CURRENT CHALLENGE IN FAILURE TO THRIVE SYNDROME RESEARCH

Joseph Woolston

Yale Child Study Center

Diagnostic classification is the cornerstone for the development of valid research about virtually any phenomenon. Attempts to prevent, treat, or in any other way intervene, with an inherently heterogeneous problem without a valid classification system will be doomed to failure. One can imagine the dilemma in which medicine would be if "fevers" were still held to be a homogeneous disorder as was believed in the 18th century. Aspirin would be held to be a nearly universal treatment, while penicillin would probably be viewed as being about as effective as a placebo because of the many non-penicillin responsive courses of fever. One can imagine that such a classification might define such subcategories as high, acute fever; spiking fevers; and low, chronic fevers. Once again these subcategories would be highly misleading because of the etiological heterogeneity.

Research in failure to thrive syndrome must now address the task of attempting to define etiologically homogeneous subgroups so that research on prevention, treatment, epidemiology, and natural history can proceed more effectively. A striking development in recent research in FTT has been the dearth of robust findings which differentiate FTT infants and their families from other infants and their families matched for demographic factors (Kotelchuck & Newberger, 1983; Vietze et al., 1980). These results are in marked contrast to those of earlier, uncontrolled descriptive studies which described such severely dysfunctional and psychologically impaired caretakers that controls were thought to be unnecessary (Leonard, Rhymes & Solnit, 1966; Evans, Reinhart & Succop, 1972; Fischoff, Whitten & Pettit, 1971; Togut, Allen & Lelchuck, 1969). Recent studies have found that the only differences between FTT infants and normally developing infants and their respective families were that the infants were difficult to feed (Pollitt & Eichler, 1976), more sickly (Kotelchuck & Newberger, 1983), the families perceived themselves as more isolated (Kotelchuck & Newberger, 1983), and the mothers less verbal with their infants (Pollitt, Eichler & Chan, 1975). One explanation for the "washout" of the expected psychosocial features described in the earlier studies may be the heretofore unrecognized diagnostic heterogeneity in the FTT population. In addition, this washout of expected psychosocial characteristics strongly suggests that they are secondary, rather than primary factors in the development of FTT. A rather similar picture would be found in the study of tuberculosis. For example, if one looked at all of the people hospitalized for tuberculosis, one would find that most of them were poor, lived in substandard housing, had poor nutrition, education, and social support systems. Yet if one were to match this population of tuberculosis patients with a control group of similar demographic features, one would find all of the same features associated with poverty. FTT, like tuberculosis, may be influenced by psychosocial stress but not necessarily caused by it. A major task for future diagnostic research in FTT is to define the specific etiological "agent(s)" analogous to the tuberculin bacillus.

The disappointing results of carefully controlled studies highlight the multidimensional nature of FTT which has thus far confounded attempts at classification. FTT is a syndrome which is characterized by deficits in several spheres, including physical growth, cognitive development, and emotional development. There is considerable evidence that these deficits are related to insults in the analogous spheres of nutrition, intellectual stimulation, and emotional stimulation. To make matters even more complicated, there is a powerful feedback among individual elements of both the causes, as well as the effects, of FTT. Individual infants also display differing levels of impairments in each one of the spheres. It should also be noted that the clearest marker for FTT is growth failure which is frequently not noticed until many months after the syndrome has begun. Therefore, research concerning the interrelationships among various deficits and corresponding insults is, per force, retrospective.

With these cautionary notes in mind, it is important to review the features of a useful classification system. The most important (but usually most difficult to ascertain) element of a newly developing field is a definitive and comprehensive etiology. A major impetus for a more clearly defined diagnostic system in FTT is to enable more productive research into specific etiologies of subtypes of FTT. In the absence of a definitive comprehensive etiology of FTT, criteria may be established to define the disorder as a homogeneous population. For example the definition of the disorder should be operationally worded so that it produces a high degree of reliability and validity. Reliability is more easily achieved if simple and objective criteria are used to define the disorder. Validity is more difficult to establish. Two elements associated with validity of a diagnostic category are stability and predictability of symptomatology and epidemiology. Another aspect of validity is that independently derived measures of the disorder should determine the same population. One can compare independent measures in terms of sensitivity (number of false negatives), specificity (number of false positives), and predictive value (number of same diagnoses over a defined time period).

A MULTIAXIAL SYSTEM OF DIAGNOSIS

In a rush of diagnostic zeal, one is tempted to operationally define subcategories of FTT as concrete, stable entities to be tested for homogeneity in clinical features, response to specific treatments, and course of illness. Although such categorization is ultimately essential, it is currently premature because of the dearth of relevant data. Given the current state of the art, a much more appropriate strategy will be to define a multiaxial system of diagnosis in which each infant with FTT is rated in several different parameters. (See Table 1 for a listing of the different axes and their definition.) This profile of axial ratings would then be compared with a predicted "ideal" profile assumed to be typical of a proposed subtype. This strategy has the advantage of preserving much of the raw data so that different constellations of axial ratings can be examined later. In addition, each axis can be examined or defined by separate and independently derived measures so that convergent validity could be evaluated.

Table 1: Multiaxial Classification of Failure to Thrive

Axis I: Physical Illness

5. Illnesses which cause malnutrition (e.g., malabsorption syndrome)
4. Illnesses which contribute to malnutrition (e.g., mild heart disease)
3. Illnesses which are concurrent with malnutrition (e.g., cleft lip)
2. Illnesses which are caused by malnutrition (e.g., diarrhea of starvation, zinc deficiency)
1. No Illness

Axis II: Growth Failure

4. Severe (less than 70% of ideal body weight)
3. Moderate (between 70-79% of ideal body weight)
2. Mild (between 80-89% of ideal body weight)
1. None (90% or more ideal body weight)

Axis III: Developmental Delay

Motor: developmental quotient (Bayley)
Cognitive: developmental quotient (Bayley)

Axis IV: Caretaker-Infant Interaction

Greenspan-Lieberman Observations Scales, rated in spheres of:

Homeostasis
Attachment
Somato-psychological differentiation

Axis V: Observation of Feeding (Chatoor et al., 1984)

Mother

Physical interaction with infant
General interactive behavior with infant
Verbal behavior regarding feeding
Specific feeding behaviors
Response to infant's distress
Mother's general affect

Infant

Interactive behavior with mother
Specific eating behaviors
Infant's general affect

Axis VI: Age of Onset

Record as gestational-corrected age in weeks when infant met growth criteria for FTT

Axis VII: Cognitive/Financial Disability of Caretakers

Rate obvious cognitive, intellectual, educational or iatrogenic cause for
infant getting insufficient nourishment:

4. Severe
3. Moderate
2. Mild
1. None

The primary feature of children with FTT syndrome is a disturbance in
their physical growth. More specifically FTT syndrome is defined as a
marked deceleration of weight gain as determined by weight which is abnormally below the third percentile for gestation-corrected age or which
fails to proceed according to the expected growth pattern, demonstrating a
persistent deviation below the established growth curve (across two major
percentiles over time) (Casey, in press). There may be a concurrent
deceleration of linear growth and/or head circumference. In addition,
there may be a specific or generalized deceleration or regression in
developmental skills. According to this definition, the etiological agent
in FTT is inadequate (especially caloric) nourishment being supplied to
the infant's tissues.

ORGANIC VS. NON-ORGANIC FTT

It is at this juncture that the question of organic versus non-
organic FTT frequently arises. Although this diagnostic dichotomy has
been held sacred for several decades as the only "objective" means of
subcategorizing FTT, it is actually quite misleading. Many studies
(Berwick, Levy & Kleinerman, 1982; Casey, Wortham & Nelson, in press;
Holmes, 1979; Homer & Ludwig, 1981; Sills, 1978) which have examined FTT
on this diagnostic dichotomy have found 15-35% of the infants with a
"mixed" etiology. This is an unacceptably large percentage of infants who
fall between the two classifications. In addition, a rigid differentiation of organic versus non-organic causes does not make sense clinically
since many infants who fail to thrive have some organic features which
somehow contribute to, but certainly do not explain, the FTT. For example,
some infants with such congenital anomalies as cleft lip or moderately
severe cardiac disease may fail to thrive while others, with virtually the
same degree of organic impairment, grow normally. In addition, some infants
with these organic reasons for their FTT may begin to thrive if their
psychosocial environment is changed but their organic impairment is untreated.

Several studies (Bell & Woolston, in press; Krieger & Chen, 1969)
have shown that weight gain in moderately to severely malnourished infants
is directly proportional to their caloric intake regardless of the etiology
of their malnutrition. In these studies, caloric intake was assumed to be
equivalent to the calories available to tissue so that infants who did not
retain their food secondary to regurgitation or malabsorption were not
considered. Theoretically, one could imagine infants who had severely
inefficient metabolism secondary to an endocrinopathy but these infants
were not observed. In fact, there is predictable and linear relationship
between caloric intake and weight gain. Finally, it is clear that the
organic versus non-organic distinction is fundamentally misleading since
all FTT has an organic etiology: insufficient nourishment.

PHYSICAL ILLNESS AND NUTRITION

Rather than leaping to an organic versus non-organic diagnosis of the FTT, one must explore the cause for insufficient nourishment being delivered to the infant's tissues. If the infant has an intake which is adequate for growth in its state of nutrition and age, then the presumably physical cause for the inadequate absorption or utilization of nutrition must be evaluated. Such infants would get a high rating on a physical illness etiology axis for their FTT. On the other hand, if the infant has an insufficient nutritional intake, then the specific cause of this must also be evaluated. Certain physical disorders, such as infections, heart disease, and kidney disease, may interfere with feeding by making the infant too lethargic or weak to be able to eat. Other illnesses, especially central nervous system malformations, may interfere with the complex regulation of appetite, sucking, swallowing, and digestion. Disorders such as cleft lip may have little impact on primary aspects of feeding but may adversely affect the the caretaker-infant relationship and then secondarily disturb the feeding process. Finally, some physical conditions such as diarrhea are primarily the result of the malnutrition but then, in turn, feed back on the feeding disorder to exacerbate it.

Following this argument, there should be an axis which describes the presence of a physical illness and its presumed contribution to the malnutrition of the infant. (See Table 1) This axis might have a five-point rating scale to designate illnesses which cause the malnutrition, illnesses which contribute to the malnutrition, illnesses which are concurrent with the malnutrition, illnesses which are caused by the malnutrition, and no illness.

DEFINING THE IMPACT OF FTT

As has been indicated earlier, malnutrition, i.e., insufficient delivery of nourishment to the growing tissues, is proposed to be the etiological agent in the growth failure which characterizes FTT. Therefore a second diagnostic axis must be developed which measures the degree of impact of this malnutrition. The utility of such a rating of growth failure is evident for assessment, treatment, and prognosis. A variety of different studies (Berglund & Rabo, 1973; Eichenwald & Fry, 1969; Klein, Forbes & Nader, 1975; Richardson, 1976; Valman, 1974) have shown that this variable is crucial in all of the above areas. The primary rating scale that should be utilized is either the Waterlow classification (percentage of expected weight for length and sex) (Waterlow, 1972) or the McLaren Read Classification (percentage of expected weight for length, sex and age) (McLaren & Read, 1972). In addition, secondary scales should note percentage of expected length for age and head circumference for age. Other nonanthropometric measures (e.g., retinol binding protein and T3/rT3 ratio) could be added as independent means of assessing nutritional availability for tissue growth.

A hallmark of FTT which is second only to growth failure in its importance to the syndrome is developmental delay. This developmental delay can refelct either a deceleration of the acquisition of new developmental milestones or regression in certain areas. The developmental delays can occur in language, motor, cognitive, social and/or affective areas. Despite the frequency of developmental delay in FTT, there does not seem to be a characteristic pattern or profile which is characteristic for this syndrome. In addition, there has been considerable argument (Cupoli, Hallock & Barness, 1980; Goldbloom, 1982; Woolston, 1983) about the etiology of these delays, usually centering on emotional deprivation versus malnutrition. Rather clearly both kinds of chronic insults to the developing infant can and do cause developmental delay.

As in the case of growth failure, there must be an axis to rate quality and quantity of developmental delay. This requirement presents more measurement problems than rating growth failure. The Bayley Scales of Infant Development (Bayley, 1969) is an appropriate instrument for rating infant motoric and cognitive functioning. Affective functioning is crucial for our greater understanding of FTT but the most difficult to quantify. Emde (1980) has outlined the current state of the psychoanalytic theory of affective development but did not propose a quantitative schema for measuring this type of development. Gaensbauer (1982) presented an experimental paradigm which measured discrete emotional responses in infants 12-18 months of age. Although he found few changes in affective response with age, he reported striking differences between normal infants and high risk, low SES infants. For infants of this age group, his form of the "strange situation" might be a useful method to quantify affective response, if not affective development.

DIAGNOSTIC SUBTYPES

In addition to the point of view of specific degree of deficit in growth and development, FTT must be considered from the perspective of clinical presentation. For example factors such as age of onset and specific behavioral disturbances of the infant-caretaker dyad are crucial. Until very recently, FTT has been assumed to be a relatively homogeneous group of infants characterized by various developmental delays and insufficient or hostile bonding by the primary caretaker. These infants are proposed to have attachment disorders. Three other categories of infant FTT have now been proposed (Chatoor, Schaeffer, Dickson & Egan, 1984; Woolston, 1983) including (1) homeostatic disorders, (2) separation disorders, and (3) simple malnutrition. Infants with homeostatic disorders have a primary disturbance in the regulation of their feeding behavior with their primary caretaker. This disturbance encompasses very fussy infants who cannot be easily fed by any caretaker as well as caretakers who cannot adaptively feed their infants. Homeostatic disorders have their onset in the first two months of life. The second category, infants with separation disorders have a disturbance in their development of autonomy from their caretaker and somato-psychological differentiation. In a separation disorder, ingestion of food acquires a symbolic and affective significance quite distinct from the satiation of hunger. In this way the disturbance of the feeding is a secondary phenomenon. Finally, infants with simple malnutrition do not show any special disturbance in feeding, attachment, or separation/autonomy. Rather, for social, economic, or educational reasons, the infants are simply not being given enough to eat.

Although this diagnostic scheme has much to recommend it, one must keep in mind that the real world of FTT is more complicated than would seem from this categorization. For example, one can easily imagine a fussy, neurologically impaired infant born to a poor, depressed, mildly retarded mother. Such an infant could have a homeostatic disorder which, in turn, would predispose it to an attachment disorder. In addition, the mother might feed it excessively diluted formula as a result of insufficient funds. For this reason it is important to employ several more axes in addition to the physical illness, growth failure, and developmental delay axes. Another axis would examine the caretaker-infant interaction with scales which reflect homeostasis, attachment and somato-psychological differentiation. The Greenspan-Lieberman Observational Scales (GLOS) (Greenspan & Lieberman, 1980) would probably do very well in determining these areas of difficulty. A fifth axis would rate feeding interaction in areas relevant to homeostasis, attachment, and separation disorders. Chatoor et al. (1984) have described a feeding scale which measures these dimensions. A sixth axis would record the age (in weeks) of the infant at which he first met the growth criteria for FTT. A seventh axis would reflect the degree to which cognitive or financial disability of the primary caretaker directly caused the infant to be malnourished. This axis should be used to record only very gross and obvious features of the caretaker, such as a clear history of insufficient funds to provide food, a well-documented misunderstanding about infant formula dilution or pre-paration, or an iatrogenic mistake which led the infant to be fed the wrong amount or type of formula. The clearest proof that these factors are important is for the infant to begin growing rapidly as soon as the caretaker is provided with the proper food or nutritional information.

IMPLICATIONS

Many methodological problems remain before such a multiaxial diagnostic scheme of FTT can be implemented. Although the development of standardized, reliable, and valid rating scales for each of these axes is an enormous task, the potential benefits of such a system are many. It would permit the testing of the reliability, validity, and predictability of diagnostic subcategories. In addition, it would encourage refinement of therapeutic interventions aimed at specific etiological roots. It would make possible the exploration of other, independent systems of diagnosis, such as biological/endocrine parameters so that concurrent validity studies could be performed.

The description of several proposed subtypes of FTT has created an exciting potential for specific intervention strategies for each of the subtypes. However, this potential will be maximized by the development and utilization of multiaxial rating procedures which objectively assess features, such as presence of organic illness, severity of growth delay, quality of mother-infant interaction, and type of feeding disturbance. For example, a relatively homogeneous response to a specific intervention modality by one specific FTT subtype would provide additional evidence for the diagnostic validity of the subtype. However, if many of the various parameters proposed for a multiaxial rating score are not objectively recorded, a heterogeneous treatment response could be a result of varying syndrome severity, rather than problematic diagnostic validity. For example, if a specific type of intervention were used to treat infants with attachment disorders, one might find a very uneven treatment outcome in terms of catch-up growth, cognitive development, or even caretaker-infant interaction. In such an instance, one might then question either diagnostic validity or intervention efficacy, whereas varying treatment outcome might actually reflect differences in severity of the condition in an important parameter such as degree of growth delay. FTT is a complex, heterogeneous syndrome in which the causes and the effects occur in different dimensions and in which causes and effects feed back upon one another in a closed loop system. Recognition of this two-fold complexity is essential to enhance the generalization of further descriptive and treatment outcome research in FTT.

REFERENCES

Bayley, N. The Bayley Scales of Infant Development Manual. New York: Psychological Corporation, 1969.
Bell, L.S. & Woolston, J.L. Weight gain and caloric intake in failure to thrive. Journal of the American Academy of Child Psychiatry, in press.

Berglund, G. & Rabo, E. A long-term follow-up investigation of patients
    with hypertrophic pyloric stenosis--with special reference to the
    physical and mental development. Acta Paediatrica Scandanavia, 1973,
    62, 125-129.
Berwick, D.M., Levy, J.C. & Kleinerman, R. Failure to thrive: Diagnostic
    yield of hospitalization. Archives of Diseases in Children, 1982,
    57, 347-351.
Casey, P.H. A diagnostic approach for children who fail to thrive.
    Pediatrics, in press.
Casey, P.H., Wortham, B. & Nelson, J.Y. Management of children with
    failure to thrive in a rural ambulatory setting: Epidemiology and
    outcomes. Clinical Pediatrics, in press.
Chatoor, I., Schaeffer, S., Dickson, L. & Egan, J. Nonorganic failure to
    thrive: A developmental perspective. Pediatric Annals, 1984, 13,
    829-843.
Chatoor, I., Schaeffer, S., Dickson, L., Egan, J., Conners,   C.K. &
    Leong, N. Pediatric assessment of non-organic failure to thrive.
    Pediatric Annals, 1984, 13, 844-850.
Cupoli, J.M., Hallock, J.A. & Barness, L.A. Failure to thrive. Current
    Problems in Pediatrics, 1980, 10, 3-42.
Eichenwald, H.F. & Fry, P.C. Nutrition and learning. Science, 1969, 163,
    644-648.
Evans, S.L., Reinhart, J.B. & Succop, R.A. Failure to thrive: A study of
    45 children and their families. Journal of the American Academy of
    Child Psychiatry, 1972, 11, 440-459.
Emde, R.N. Toward a psychoanalytic theory of affect. In S.I. Greenspan &
    G.H. Pollock (Eds.), The Course of Life: Psychoanalytic Contributions
    Toward Understanding Personality Development, Vol. I. Bethesda, MD:
    NIMH, 1980.
Fischoff, J., Whitten, D. & Pettit, M. A psychiatric study of mothers of
    infants with growth failure secondary to maternal deprivation.
    Journal of Pediatrics, 1971, 79, 209-215.
Gaensbauer, T.J. Regulation of emotional expression in infants from two
    contrasting caretaker environments. Journal of the American Academy
    of Child Psychiatry, 1982, 21, 163-171.
Goldbloom, R.B. Failure to thrive. Pediatric Clinics of North America,
    1982, 29, 151-166.
Greenspan, S.I. & Lieberman, A.F. Infants, mothers and their interaction:
    A quantitative clinical approach to developmental assessment.   In
    S.I. Greenspan & G.H. Pollock (Eds.), The Course of Life: Psycho-
    analytic Contributions Toward Understanding Personality Development,
    Vol. I. Bethesda, MD: NIMH, 1980.
Holmes, G.L. Evaluation and prognosis in non-organic failure to thrive.
    Southern Medical Journal, 1979, 79, 693-698.
Homer, C. & Ludwig, S. Categorization of etiology of failure to thrive.
    American Journal of Diseases of Children, 1981, 135, 848.
Klein, P.S., Forbes, G.B. & Nader, P.N. The effects of starvation in
    infancy (pyloric stenosis) on subsequent learning abilities. Journal
    of Pediatrics, 1975, 87, 8-15.
Kotelchuck, M. & Newberger, E.H. Failure to thrive: A controlled study
    of familial characteristics. Journal of the American Academy of
    Child Psychiatry, 1983, 22, 322-328.
Krieger, I. & Chen, Y.C. Calorie requirements for weight gain in infants
    with growth failure due to maternal deprivation, undernutrition, and
    congenital heart disease. Pediatrics, 1969, 44, 647-654.
Leonard, M., Rhymes, J. & Solnit, A.J. Failure to thrive in infants.
    American Journal of Diseases of Children, 1966, 111, 600-612.
McLaren, D.S. & Read, W.W. Classification of nutritional status of early
    childhood. Lancet, 1972, 2, 142-151.
Pollitt, E. & Eichler, A. Behavioral disturbances among failure to thrive
    children. American Journal of Diseases in Children, 1976, 130, 24-

29.
Pollitt, E., Eichler, A.W. & Chan, C.K. Psychosocial development and behavior of mothers of failure to thrive children. American Journal of Orthopsychiatry, 1975, 45, 525-537.

Richardson, S.A. The relation of severe malnutrition in infancy to the intelligence of school children with differing life histories. Pediatric Research, 1976, 10, 57-61.

Sills, R.H. Failure to thrive: The role of clinical and laboratory evaluation. American Journal of Diseases in Children, 1978, 132, 967-969.

Togut, M., Allen, S. & Lelchuck, L. A psychological exploration of the nonorganic failure to thrive syndrome. Developmental Medicine and Child Neurology, 1969, 11, 601-607.

Valman, H.B. Intelligence after malnutrition caused by neonatal resection of illeum. Lancet, 1974, i, 425-427.

Vietze, P.M., Falsey, S., O'Connor, S., Sandler, H., Sherrod, K. & Altemeier, W.A. Newborn behavioral and interactional characteristics of nonorganic failure to thrive infants. In T.M. Field, S. Goldberg, D. Stern, et al. (Eds.), High Risk Infants and Children: Adult and Peer Interactions. New York: Academic Press, 1980.

Waterlow, J.C. Classification and definition of protein-calorie malnutrition. British Medical Journal, 1972, 566-569.

Woolston, J.L. Eating disorders in infancy and early childhood. Journal of the American Academy of Child Psychiatry, 1983, 22, 114-121.

A DEVELOPMENTAL CLASSIFICATION OF FEEDING DISORDERS ASSOCIATED WITH

FAILURE TO THRIVE: DIAGNOSIS AND TREATMENT

Irene Chatoor, Linda Dickson, Sharon Schaefer and James Egan

Departments of Psychiatry and Social Work
George Washington University School of Medicine and
Health Sciences, and the Children's Hospital National
Medical Center, Washington, D.C.

INTRODUCTION

In 1908 Chapin alerted pediatricians to the failure of growth and development associated with poverty and institutional care of infants and young children. Spitz (1945) gave new importance to Chapin's observations, demonstrating severe retardation in growth and development in children raised in institutions and in infants between six and twelve months of age whose mothers were abruptly withdrawn. Goldfarb's (1945) classic studies of the serious developmental disturbances of adolescents who had been raised in institutions added weight to the argument that relative maternal deprivation was a cause of FTT. Several studies have since explored general characteristics of the mother which might play a role in the development of non-organic FTT. Whereas Pollitt, Weisel, & Chan (1975) found that overt pathology was not more likely in FTT mothers than in mothers of normally thriving infants, most authors support the presence of psychosocial problems in FTT mothers (Fraiberg, 1975; Evans, 1972; Drotar, Malone & Negray, 1979).

Over the years, the literature has attempted to wrestle with what has been an awkward and, in many cases, not useful dichotomy, namely the differentiation of organic from non-organic FTT. Recently, Homer & Ludwig (1981) & Casey (1984) have suggested that a third category of FTT exists. These are patients who manifest a mixed picture, a combination of organic and non-organic factors, in the etiology of their growth disturbance. Thus a trend has begun which de-emphasizes the classical dichotomy between organic and functional FTT. Our clinical work has underscored the wide range of presentations of FTT.

A COMPREHENSIVE MULTIFACTORIAL APPROACH

In order to better understand our approach to FTT, a description of our setting will be helpful. Our particular setting is a large non-profit Children's Hospital located in a low-income neighborhood. The hospital provides primary, secondary, and tertiary care for children and adolescents from the metropolitan area of Washington, D.C. Because of this we see children from a wide spectrum of socio-economic and ethnic backgrounds.

The hospital, a 265 bed in and outpatient facility, is a training institution with a large department of Pediatrics and Adolescent Medicine including all pediatric subspecialities, a department of Surgery and a department of Child Psychiatry. Direct care of patients is usually performed by trainees under the supervision of attending staff. Within this context, the authors provide psychosocial consultations to patients hospitalized or referred by pediatrics or surgery. Our work with FTT patients has often been indirect through teaching and supervision of pediatric and psychiatric house staff, as well as through direct patient contact. Over the years, we have developed a close working relationship with the Department of Pediatrics. Patients with severe malnutrition are usually hospitalized by the primary physician and are under the care of the pediatric house staff. Organic and non-organic etiologies are optimally investigated simultaneously in the FTT workup.

We are limited by not having a psychosomatic unit or specially designated full time staff positions for working with the FTT population. However, we have created a program by involving the Chairman of Pediatrics, the nursing staff, an occupational therapist and nutritionist in a team which has provided interdisciplinary teaching and stimulation. The team meets on a weekly basis to discuss all hospitalized FTT patients. In addition, Dr. Chatoor conducts weekly teaching conferences for the pediatric house staff, addressing psychosocial problems in infants and toddlers with special emphasis on FTT. Through medical and community education, we have introduced our conceptual thinking about FTT to the pediatric community. This has resulted in referrals of patients with feeding problems from the entire metropolitan area to our outpatient clinic and for hospitalization. Patients who are referred to the psychiatric outpatient clinic have already undergone a medical evaluation of their feeding problem and growth failure by their pediatrician. However, patients who are hospitalized for FTT are referred to the FTT team soon after admission and a simultaneous diagnostic workup of organic and psychosocial factors resulting in growth failure is undertaken.

Our approach to diagnosis of FTT incorporates a number of perspectives Goldbloom (1982), in his recent review on FTT, emphasizes the need for a holistic approach to FTT. In establishing the etiology of the syndrome, he emphasizes the importance of gaining the medical and psychosocial history, the physical examination, and direct observations of parents and child rather than simply relying on laboratory "fishing expeditions." He refers to Sills' (1978) review of 185 children admitted to Children's Hospital in Buffalo, New York, with FTT, which showed that out of 2067 laboratory tests performed on these children only 36 (1.4%) were of positive diagnostic assistance.

To diagnose non-organic FTT via inclusionary and exclusionary criteria rather than solely on negative laboratory results, the clinician must have a full grasp of the various causes of organic and non-organic FTT. As Pasteur said, "In the fields of observation, chance favors only the mind that is prepared." Because mixed etiologies are common, the probability of making a proper diagnosis increases when the clinician is educated to look simultaneously for multiple contributing factors.

We have developed an approach to FTT which incorporates a multifactorial etiology of this syndrome. Through the medical and psychosocial history, the physical examination, and the videotaping of mother and child during feeding and play, we gain the following clinical information:

Infant --

1. Age of onset of the growth failure

2. Contributory organic conditions
3. Temperament
4. Cognitive, motor and speech development
5. Predominant feeling states (affect)
6. Interactive behavior with mother during feeding and play
7. Feeding history as given by mother and feeding behavior observed
8. Response to alternate caretaker

Mother --

1. Psychosocial stressors
2. Maternal pathology
3. Maternal affect
4. Interactive behavior with infant during feeding and play
5. Feeding behaviors

A DEVELOPMENTAL CLASSIFICATION OF FEEDING DISORDERS ASSOCIATED WITH FAILURE TO THRIVE

One feature which is frequently found in all varieties of FTT is the occurrence of feeding problems. The variety of feeding problems as well as the specificity of certain feeding difficulties at different ages has led us to search for a conceptual framework within which to understand eating and growth disorders in infancy and childhood. In our view, eating disorders in infants and toddlers can create, exacerbate, or be a sequela of FTT.

It was Anna Freud (1946) who first drew attention to the developmental aspects of feeding disorders and in so doing suggested that there was a developmental line from sucking to rational eating. Recently, Greenspan & Lourie (1981) have suggested a developmental classification of psychopathology in infancy and childhood that draws heavily upon observations of caregiver-child interactions. Building on the pioneering work of Freud (1946), Spitz (1945), Bowlby (1973), Mahler, Pine & Berman (1975) and Greenspan & Lourie (1981), Egan et al. (1980) suggested a developmental typology for failure to thrive in infancy and childhood. This approach has been further refined by Chatoor & Egan (1983) and by Chatoor et al. (1984).

Our observations of feeding disturbances leading to FTT or complicating an organic illness associated with failure to thrive incorporates Greenspan's stages of early infant development and Mahler's concept of separation and individuation. We classify three distinct stages of feeding development in which normal and pathological behaviors in both the infant and the mother can be identified: 1) Homeostasis, 2) Attachment, 3) Separation.

I. DISORDERS OF HOMEOSTASIS

From birth to two months the task of the infant is to achieve regulation of state. The infant must form basic cycles and rhythms of sleep and wakefulness, and of feeding and elimination. Stabilization of the autonomic and motor system enables the infant to interact more fully with the outside world. The caregiver attempts to provide an environment in which the infant can achieve a balance between internal state and involvement in the world. In the feeding situation we see a progression from reflex sucking to autonomously motivated oral feedings. Infants must develop from a state of nutritional equilibrium in utero to one in which they control the onset and termination of feedings by signals of hunger and satiation.

Feeding problems at this stage of development can stem from the infant's constitutional characteristics or medical difficulties. For example, infants with a labile autonomic nervous sytem show more difficulty in regulation of state and are frequently referred to as "colicky." The colicky infant seems particularly vulnerable to over-stimulation. It is important for the parents to discover the infant's sensory thresholds and to become aware of the relationship between stimuli such as loud noises or bright lights and the infant's irritability. Once they appreciate the connection between certain patterns of overstimulation and colic, the parents can then modify the environment to facilitate calmer feeding periods.

Another early feeding problem related to constitutional variations is a developmental delay in the coordination of the oral musculature or the integration of breathing and sucking. If the poor suck is recognized, the mother can learn specific techniques of positioning and oral support for the infant that will facilitate better feeding.

Infants with respiratory problems, especially premature infants with a prolonged course of hyaline membrane disease, may have particular difficulty in achieving homeostasis. Rapid respirations or intubation frequently prohibit oral feedings in the first weeks or months of life. Consequently, such infants do not make the usual transition from reflex sucking to autonomously motivated feedings. When they are introduced to oral feedings, they frequently don't know how to suck or swallow and seem to have no awareness of hunger or satiety.

Another group of infants with difficulties in homeostasis are those with congenital abnormalities of the gastrointestinal tract, such as esophageal atresia. Observing infants with esophageal atresia who had only gastrostomy feedings for the first months of life, Dowling (1977) noted that such children not only had severe difficulties learning to suck, chew and swallow but also marked delays in motor and speech development. The children lacked motivation and vitality and showed general dullness. Dowling's (1977) study demonstrates that the early feeding experience represents an organizer in the infant's overall development and that feeding disturbances interfering with the establishment of homeostasis result in severe problems in all areas of development.

The caretaker has an important role in facilitating the establishment of homeostasis. The mother must be able to provide a physical and emotional environment in which a baby can balance inner state and external stimuli. If the mother is unable to interpret the infant's cues, she might either under- or over-stimulate her infant. In some cases where the infant has constitutional or medical problems which interfere with the establishment of a regular feeding pattern, the infant's difficulties may be intensified by the mother's anxiety and her own disorganization. In other cases, the mother's inability to read the infant's cues, her noncontingent responses of too much or too little stimulation can disorganize even an otherwise healthy infant and lead to irregular feeding patterns in the infant.

Table 1 summarizes the diagnostic criteria for disorders of homeostasis.

Treatment of Disorders of Homeostasis

Early diagnosis of feeding difficulties provides the clinician with information needed to plan appropriate intervention. Intervention during the homeostatic period is critical because problems which develop at this early point of the infant's life impede physical growth and interfere with

Table 1

Diagnostic Criteria for Disorders of Homeostasis *

Feeding difficulties may stem from primary constitutional characteristics
or organic difficulties of the infant for which the mother is unable to
help the infant compensate because of her inexperience, her anxiety or the
infant's intractable homeostatic difficulties. Feeding problems may stem
primarily from the mother's inability to read the infant's cues of hunger
or satiety and her lack of ability to help the infant establish a regular
feeding pattern. In some cases there will be a combination of infant vulnerabilities and maternal factors adding to each other and resulting in
severe feeding problems.

INFANT	MOTHER

Age of Onset: Birth to two months;
beyond the first two months of life,
if the infant has organic problems
which delay the introduction of
oral feedings.

Common Contributory Organic Factors:
Respiratory distress prohibiting or
limiting oral feedings; anatomic
problems of the gastrointestinal
tract interfering with oral feedings (i.e. esophageal atresia,
duplication of the gastrointestinal tract, necrotizing en-
terocolitis); delayed maturation
of the coordination of the oral
musculature; delayed integration
of sucking and breathing.

Common Psychosocial Stressors: No
specific outside stressors; frequently stressed by the infant's organic
or temperamental difficulties and
their impact on her maternal self-
esteem.

Temperamental Vulnerabilities: Low
stimulus barrier resulting in excitability and irritability; passivity
associated with only short periods
of alert wakefulness.

Common Maternal Pathology: Adjustment disorder with anxious or depressed mood; narcissistic personality
disorder; post partum psychosis or
retardation.

Development; Primary delay in
gross motor area, less in fine
motor development; delay in speech
development.

Predominant Affect: Hypersensi-
tive and irritable or passive and
sleepy, dull affect.

Predominant Affect: Appears anxious,
easily distressed, or depressed and
overwhelmed.

Common Interactive Behaviors with
Mother: Cries, does not calm or
nestle when held; appears sleepy
in his responses; is difficult to
engage.

Common Interactive Behaviors with
Infant: Misses or overrides the infant's signals; responds with understimulation or over-stimulation and
projects negative attributes to the
infant's behavior.

Common Feeding Behaviors: Has poor
suck, tires easily and may fall
asleep after short feeding; gags
easily, spits up and vomits frequently; cries during feeding;

Common Feeding Behaviors: Misreads
the infant's cues of hunger or
satiety; feeds in erratic manner,
burps and changes the infant's posi-
(continued)

Table 1 (continued)

INFANT	MOTHER
Takes in adequate amounts of milk; has irregular and unpredictable feeding pattern.	tion frequently; handles the infant excessively; fails to establish a consistent feeding pattern.

Response to Alternate Caretaker:
Demonstrates similar interactive
and feeding behaviors with skilled
professional staff if the homeostatic difficulties stem primarily
from the infant's organic or temperamental characteristics, but
feeds better for an experienced
nurse if the difficulties stem primarily from maternal inability to
interpret the infant's cues.

*These characteristics were derived by clinical experience and are current-
ly tested by the authors in a research study.

motor and speech development as well as affective engagement.

Treatment can be directed toward the infant and toward the mother-
infant interaction. One infant intervention is the offering of the pacifie
during gavage feeding. Bernbaum, Pereira, Watkins, & Peckham (1983)
showed that regular offering of a pacifier during gavage feedings facilitated the infant's learning to suck and swallow. Later these infants
learned to feed more quickly and gained weight faster than did a control
group. Furthermore, although both groups of infants were taking in the
same amount of milk through gavage feedings, the infants who were stimulate
to suck a pacifier seemed to absorb their feedings more effectively.

A second intervention directed towards the infant is the use of sham
feedings during gastrostomy feeding in infants with esophageal atresia.
Dowling (1977), in a study of seven infants with esophageal atresia, notice
that those who had only gastrostomy feedings for the first months of life
had severe difficulties learning how to suck, chew and swallow and seemed
to have no awareness of hunger or satiety. He demonstrated that he could
prevent these feeding problems and developmental delays with a second group
of infants born with esophageal atresia when he introduced sham oral feedings. During gastrostomy feedings, the mothers were instructed to hold
their infants and to have them suck from a bottle with milk which was
collected from the esophageal fistula at the neck. Children who had been
fed this way quickly learned to signal their hunger and satiety. The
mothers could read these cues and feed the infants accordingly. Once the
esophagus was surgically corrected, the infants learned to feed orally with
out much difficulty.

For infants with homeostatic feeding difficulties resulting from delay
in the coordination of the oral musculature or in the integration of breath
ing and sucking, occupational therapy offers another intervention. The occupational therapist can teach the mother specific feeding and positioning
techniques to facilitate motor development and better feeding.

Mother-infant interactional problems which have been observed during
the assessment can be addressed by working with the mother. Videotaping of

the mother and infant during feeding and play is a standard part of the evaluation of FTT used at Children's Hospital National Medical Center. The therapist can replay the tape and watch it together with the mother, sharing observations with her and helping her to become a better self-observer. The therapist serves as an interpreter between mother and infant by reinforcing mutual cueing and helping the mother read her infant's signals more effectively. In the work with the mother, it is important that the therapist focus on positive and contingent maternal reactions to the infant rather than on maladaptive responses. Maternal self-esteem can be undermined easily if she experiences the therapist as unduly critical.

Another intervention to assist the mother can be the introduction of "a mother's helper." Depending on the financial resources of the family this can be achieved by hiring a nurse or housekeeper or sometimes a home-maker can be obtained through Child Protective Services in the community. Mother's helpers are particularly useful for infants who require extended periods of time for feeding. As demonstrated by Murray, Fink & Gaiter (1984), infants who present with abnormal sucking and breathing patterns tire quickly. They fall asleep after having taken in only small amounts of milk. They fail to thrive because their milk intake is inadquate. Their mothers may experience great anxiety and exhaustion. Effective intervention should consider the infant's difficulty in feeding as well as the mother's need for rest. A "mother's helper" can assist the mother and infant through this developmental crisis until the infant establishes a more mature sucking and breathing pattern. For example, some infants with severe feeding problems of this nature might need supplemental feeding through a nasogastric tube until they are able to suck and breathe without difficulty.

Case Vignette

Latisha, a three month old black infant who was the product of a full term pregnancy, was admitted to Children's Hospital because of FTT with concomitant vomiting and diarrhea. She had gained only 5 oz. and had intermittent vomiting and loose stools since birth.

On admission, Latisha was an irritable infant who was difficult to calm and to engage. She was noted to have poor muscle tone, poor head control and stiffening of the lower extremities when held. Otherwise her physical examination was unremarkable and her medical workup did not reveal any organic disease to explain her symptoms and FTT.

Latisha's mother was a single 22 year old woman of limited intellectual functioning. She had completed high school in a special program and had always lived with her mother who was employed fulltime. Consequently, mother had been in charge of her infant's care. The baby's father was not involved with mother or infant.

The mother gave a history of feeding difficulties soon after they returned home from the hospital after Latisha's birth. She reported that Latisha cried a lot, did not finish her bottle and spit up a lot.

A videotape and other observations of mother and infant showed an eager and affectionate mother who worked hard playing with and relating to her baby in spite of limited infant responsiveness. However, mother was observed to jiggle and dance the baby without awareness of the baby's increasing disorganization. The more she stimulated the baby with bounces and kisses, the more the baby appeared to become distressed. Her physical overstimulation of the baby was observed during feeding and play.

During feeding, the baby would tire out quickly, close her eyes and stop sucking, but the mother would jiggle and alert her again. The baby would drink a little more, become agitated and spit up. Unaware of the infant's distress, the mother would continue trying to get her to feed while the baby began crying and thrashing around in complete physical disorganization. Even then, mother responded with more bouncing of the baby to get her to calm down until the infant became exhausted and fell asleep in her arms. These observations illustrated mother's inability to read the infant's cues, which resulted in severe overstimulation and disorganization of the infant as evidenced in her dysregulation of muscle tone and movement and her dysregulation of her gastrointestinal functioning leading to vomiting and diarrhea.

During the hospitalization, mother was relieved of feeding the infant until Latisha had learned to regulate herself with the tender care of her nurses. Latisha became calmer, was able to feed longer and take in much more formula. As she began to gain weight, she seemed to feel better and began to engage her caretakers with smiles. At the same time, the social worker worked with mother using the videotape to help her understand her infant's reactions better. Mother was eager to learn and delighted with Latisha's progress although she struggled for a while with not being able to feed the baby herself. As Latisha became more robust and mother less anxious, they were united again during feedings, initially in the presence of Latisha's primary care nurse or mother's social worker. As mother became more competent in understanding her infant, Latisha stayed calm during feedings and mother and infant reinforced each other positively. After discharge mother and baby were visited by a nurse on a regular basis who reported ongoing progress in the baby.

II. DISORDERS OF ATTACHMENT

Having achieved some capacity for self-regulation, the adaptive infant is able to mobilize and engage caretakers in increasingly complex interactions. Consequently, between two and six months of age the infant is ready for the major psychological and affective task of the first year of life - the task of attachment.

Attachment develops within a reciprocal relationship. Either partner can facilitate or impede progress. Evidence of positive attachment behavior includes mutual eye contact and gazing, reciprocal vocalizations, and mutual physical closeness expressed through cuddling and molding.

Because most of the infant's interactions with the caretakers occur around feedings, regulation of food intake is closely linked to the infant's affective engagement with the caregiver. Certain feeding disturbances are characteristic of disorders of attachment. Infants with FTT as a consequence of impaired attachment frequently present with a history of vomiting, diarrhea, and poor weight gain. Observation of these mothers and babies during feeding reveals a general lack of pleasure in their interactions. The mothers appear listless, detached and apathetic. They hold their babies loosely on their laps without much physical intimacy. They rarely initiate verbal or visual contact, and seem unaware of the infant's signals. The infants also appear listless and apathetic. They often actively avoid eye contact with the mother. Some engage in rumination, which appears to be either a means of self stimulation or of relieving tension (Chatoor & Dickson, 1984). Some infants seem to be hypervigilant when scanning the environment, a process which has been described as radar gaze. When these babies are picked up they are unable to cuddle and mold to the caregiver's body. They usually show disturbance in body tone, being floppy or rigid. Many are developmentally delayed.

Much has been written about mothers whose infants suffer from disorders of attachment. They are frequently described as suffering from character pathology and affective illness (Fischoff, Whitten & Pettit, 1971; Pollitt et al., 1975). The mother's poor parenting, social isolation and economic hardship are also evident. Glaser, Heagerty, Bullard & Pivchik (1968) suggest that the highest risk exists when mother's needs take precedence over those of her infant. Fraiberg (1975) emphasized that the needs of parents reflect the "ghosts," the unmet needs, in their own growing years. Drotar et al. (1979) suggest that the manner in which a traumatic or deprived childhood experience can influence the mother/infant relationship is also affected by the current context of family life. Our clinical experience has particularly alerted us to the mother's feelings of isolation during pregnancy and birth, to current marital distress or unavailability of the father, and to recent death or other loss.

Certain individual infant characteristics can contribute to or exacerbate an attachment disorder. Infants who have problems with homeostasis, who are irritable and difficult to calm, and whose temperamental attributes are confusing or upsetting to the mother pose a threat to the attachment process. Infants with hypersensitivities to touch, sound, or to change of position are especially vulnerable to an attachment disorder because their avoidant behavior can easily be misinterpreted by the mother as rejection. On the other hand infants who are passive, sleep much and make few demands on the caregiver can easily be left alone by a depressed mother.

Table 2 summarizes the criteria for disorders of attachment.

Treatment of Disorders of Attachment

Frequently, a multiplicity of factors have interfered with the attachment process between mother and infant. These factors can be related to the infant, to the mother and to the social environment. Proper treatment entails directing therapeutic measures towards each of the component parts contributing to the dysfunction in the mother-infant relationship. Because of the complexity of the issues involved, a multidisciplinary team comprised of pediatricians, nurses, social workers, child psychiatrists, nutritionists, and occupational therapists is generally required for effective treatment. Best results are obtained when the same members have been working together over a period of time with a unified approach. In order to maintain a cohesiveness of purpose, these teams should meet on at least a weekly basis to review the patients currently under their charge. Because of the large number of personnel involved, the seriousness of the disorder and the frequency of severe malnutrition, hospitalization is frequently necessary for a thorough assessment and initiation of nutritional rehabilitation.

An initial hospitalization provides an opportunity for continued observations and for mobilizing the infant's capacities. For example, the improvement in the infant's feeding and affect can be used to activate the mother and to engage her in the treatment process. Hospitalization can be used to form an alliance between the mother and the mental health team which enhances the likelihood that treatment of the mother-infant dyad will continue after nutritional rehabilitation has been completed and the baby discharged from the hospital.

During the hospitalization, a number of specialized infant directed interventions can be carried out. These involve nutritional rehabilitation, developmental stimulation and emotional nurturance. In order to be successful with nutritional and developmental rehabilitation, it is essential that the infant be nurtured emotionally. This makes it very important to assign a primary care nurse and to keep the number of caretakers as low as possible

Table 2

Diagnostic Criteria for Disorders of Attachment*

Feeding difficulties stem from problems in mother-infant reciprocity, a lack of engagement between mother and infant. Since at this point of development much of the infant's interactions with the caretaker occur around feedings, regulation of food intake is closely linked to the infant's affective engagement with the caregiver. These infants are usually underfed and some engage in self-stimulatory activities such as rumination.

INFANT

MOTHER

Age of Onset: Two to six months.

Common Contributory Organic Factors: Prematurity or any illness requiring prolonged hospitalization and separation from mother; organic illnesses which result in homeostatic difficulties of the infant.

Common Psychosocial Stressors: Acute or chronic losses of close relatives or important attachment figures; move to new area with loss of support system; lack of financial resources; crowded living situation; several young children without adequate resources to care for them.

Temperamental Vulnerabilities: Passivity, and low responsiveness; low stimulus barrier resulting in excitability and irritability.

Development: Poor regulation of muscle tone, weak grasp, weak cry; general delay in fine motor and gross motor development; delay in speech development.

Predominant Affect: Appears sad, withdrawn or hypervigilant (radar gaze).

Predominant Affect: Appears detached, depressed or agitated, hostile.

Common Interactive Behaviors with Mother: Avoids eye contact; does not vocalize, does not smile, shows no anticipatory reaching out (in infant older than 5 months); stiffens or arches away when picked up; does not mold or cuddle when held.

Common Interactive Behaviors with Infant: Appears detached; fails to engage infant visually or vocally; holds infant loosely without physical closeness; does not respond to the infant's cues or needs; interacts with infant according to her own projected needs.

Common Feeding Behaviors: Drinks milk and eats without difficulty as reported by mother; might spit up or vomit frequently; might ruminate; looks away from mother during feeding.

Common Feeding Behaviors: Feeds mechanically or props bottle; holds infant loosely away from her body; does not seek visual engagement and does not talk to infant during feeding; is unaware of infant's nutritional needs.

Response to Alternate Caretaker: Initially will avoid interactions with professional but will usually feed well without difficulty. Gradually, will respond to sensitive caretaker with smiles, cooing and cuddling.

*These characteristics were derived by clinical experience and are currently tested by the authors in a research study.

in order to facilitate a special relationship between the infant and his caregivers. Once the infant becomes engaged with the primary care nurse, he will begin to smile and coo and his improved feeling state will also be reflected in better feeding and weight gain. In cases when malnutrition is very severe, we have found it helpful to supplement oral feedings during the day with continuous nasogastric feedings during the night. The additional caloric intake speeds up the infant's recovery, making him more available for social interactions and developmental stimulation.

Frequently these infants are developmentally delayed in a wide variety of areas and a thorough developmental assessment is necessary. This is generally the province of child psychiatrists and psychologists, but also frequently includes an occupational therapist. The occupational therapist often assesses the gross and fine motor development as well as certain aspects of perceptual and social functioning. The therapist may develop a plan for specific techniques of infant stimulation which are undertaken by the nursing and occupational therapy staff.

Following this multidisciplinary intervention, infants frequently gain weight and progress developmentally while in the hospital. But as Harris (1982) accurately emphasizes, "changes in growth and cognition are frequently rapid; changes in personality and behavior are much slower. Recovery from growth failure does not indicate that the parent child relationship is adequate, it is only a first step."

Because the mothers generally present with a variety of social, developmental, and psychological disturbances, their problems need to be addressed while work goes on with the infant's rehabilitation. Many of these mothers have experienced deprivation or losses during their own growing years. For this reason, nurturance of the mother is the first step in facilitating her potential to nurture the infant. As she develops a relationship with the therapist, the treatment of the mother involves strengthening her cognitive and emotional understanding of her infant, including the infant's emotional and nutritional needs, individual characteristics, and communication pattern. This method of mother-infant work was initially described by Fraiberg (1975) who emphasized the importance of addressing painful past experiences in the mother's background, the "ghosts" of the mother's childhood. The recognition of the baby as a potential transference object has been especially helpful in our work with these mothers. Not only the mother, but also the family in its relationship to the mother-infant pair need to be brought into the treatment of attachment disorders. Drotar et al. (1979) point to the influence of the family as a stress buffering or stress producing system. They emphasize a bidirectional-transactional model of development. "The infant affects and is affected by the marital, or parental partner relationship which in turn influences and is influenced by parenting." They suggest a family centered outreach program in the home. In some situations the pathology of the mother or the disruptions within the family are so severe that the infant needs to be placed in alternate full time care (Malone & Drotar, 1983). These are difficult decisions to make. A therapeutic trial with the mother should always be attempted before this intervention is suggested.

Case Vignette

Donald was admitted to the hospital for FTT and vomiting when he was 6 months old. Psychosocial and medical workup began simultaneously. The latter produced no evidence of organic disease. Donald was below the 5th% in weight, height was at the 10th %tile, head circumference was at the 25th %tile. He had been a full term infant with no known neonatal problems.

Donald was a sad looking baby who was extremely delayed. Still unable to hold his head up, he was delayed socially as well as motorically. He gazed with vigilance at staff members except during his feedings when he avoided eye contact. He was not a "good cuddler," had poor head control, and was hypertonic in the lower part of his body. It was extremely diffi- cult to elicit a smile from him, and he remained on his hospital bed for hours without a cry or whimper.

Donald's mother, Miss Q, was a single mother with a two year old and a three year old at home. She reported that Donald was an extremely good baby who slept a lot and was "happy all of the time." She was worried about his vomiting and blamed his failure to gain weight on that. When questioned as to whether he "preferred to be fed lying down or while being held," Miss Q revealed that he was fed from a propped bottle regularly because that made it "easy for him to fall asleep after feeding."

A videotape was made of the mother-infant dyad during feeing and during play. During feeding, Mrs. Q held Donald loosely, each looking away from the other for a place to rest their eyes. Mrs. Q spoke to herself a few times, never speaking directly to Donald during the feeding. She also held the bottle at half-mast feeding air as well as formula to Donald. The feeding was boring and empty for infant, mother, and videotape viewer. During the play situation, mother and infant were slightly more animated with each other, though clearly inexperienced at mutual play.

Donald was hospitalized for three weeks, but his mother spent only a few hours a day visiting. He gained weight rapidly during the hospitaliza- tion and became a much more responsive baby. He smiled more readily and became more comfortable with eye contact during his feedings.

Work with the mother was directed toward helping her better understand Donald's developmental needs and to understand that his "extremely good" behavior was not serving his needs well. His passivity in asking to be held or demanding enough formula needed to be understood by the mother as a problem which needed more active intervention from her. Mother was cooper- ative and showed some increased pleasure in interactions with her infant. However, because it remained clear, though, that the home and family situa- tion was overwhelming to Donald's mother and it was felt that the progress might end when mother and baby were back to their disorganized household, an alternate discharge plan was made. Donald was referred to a developmen- tal infant nursery, which he could attend five days per week, would be picked up and delivered by a van and be cared for, fed, and stimulated from 9:00 a.m. until 3:00 p.m. This option was employed because it was felt that Mrs. Q would not be able to come back to the hospital regularly enough for outpatient services and the community lacked the kind of infant outreac program which would be desireable.

Mother and infant were followed in the hospital pediatric clinic and Donald's progress while not optimal was acceptable. His weight lingered around the 20th %tile and he continued to progress developmentally. The mother-child relationship reflected a greater quality of attachment than when we first met this family, yet we knew that maternal behavior remained inconsistent. A child care worker at the infant center became a very special person for Donald.

III. DISORDERS OF SEPARATION AND INDIVIDUATION

Between six months and three years of age, the infant progresses through a developmental process characterized by Mahler (1975) as separa- tion and individuation. Both motoric and cognitive maturation occur during

this stage, enabling the infant to function with more emotional independence. As the infant is able to crawl away from the mother, he becomes
increasingly aware of his separateness and must deal with the developmental
issues of autonomy versus dependency. The cognitive capacity of the six
month old infant allows her to begin differentiating between "means and
end" and to understand basic schemes of causality. Part of this learning
process involves somatopsychological differentiation as defined by
Greenspan & Lieberman (1980). The normal infant begins to distinguish a
variety of somatopsychological feeling states including the differentiation
of hunger from such emotional feelings as affection, dependency, anger or
frustration. As during earlier developmental stages, both partners of the
dyad contribute to the successful resolution of the developmental task of
somatopsychological differentiation: the infant, by clearly signaling his
physiological or emotional needs, the caretaker, by reading her signals
correctly and by responding in a contingent way.

Egan, Chatoor & Rosen (1980) and Chatoor & Egan (1983) have observed an eating disorder which usually begins in the second half of the first
year of life and has a peak incidence around nine months of age. The
eating disorder is characterized by food refusal and represents a disturbance in somatopsychological differentiation as part of the infant's struggle for separation and individuation. The authors have labeled it a separation disorder. They postulate that feeling hungry and thus needing to eat
is compromised and clouded by needs to establish autonomy from the mother.
The separation disorder is characterized by certain patterns of behavior
both in infants and mothers. Characteristically, the infant grabs for the
spoon to participate in the feeding, but mother ignores this signal and
insists on feeding the infant herself, because she feels more effective in
getting the food into the infant's mouth herself. However, the infant
becomes angry because he is frustrated in his attempt at self-feeding and
refuses to open his mouth. The mother becomes anxious and tries harder to
get the food into the infant but is met by increasing refusal. The battle
of the spoons, so well characterized by Levy (1955), becomes a battle of
wills.

Numerous factors may precipitate a battle of wills. For example, the
infant might eat very slowly or reject mother's food because the taste or
texture is aversive. A mother can overpower the infant's food preferences
because caloric intake is a paramount variable in her mind. She begins to
coax the infant in every way imaginable to "to get him to eat." Soon the
infant learns that the less he or she eats the more attention he can elicit
from mother. His emotional needs come to dictate his eating behavior. As
time goes on, mother and infant become increasingly involved in these
maladaptive interactions around food.

Initially the child may only refuse to eat for the mother, but if the
condition persists, the oppositional food refusal will be generalized to
other caretakers. Not infrequently, the concern about the child's not
eating becomes an issue which pervades many aspects of family life. The
child's serious oppositional behavior frequently involves other areas of
his life, such as bedtime, toilet training or dressing.

Children with separation-individuation feeding disturbances do not
usually show delays in cognitive and speech development as do children
suffering from an attachment disorder. Gross motor development, however,
may be impaired because their food refusal may lead to chronic undernutrition and poor muscle development.

Mothers whose children experience separation disorders frequently come
from middle or upper-middle class families and have high expectations for
themselves in their role as mothers. These high expectations are frequently

coupled with a legitimate basis for anxiety about feeding during the infant's first year of life. For example, some infants may have had difficulty sucking in the first few months of life; others suffered from milk allergies or frequent infections which interfered with feeding and weight gain. In other cases seen by the authors, the infants had organic illnesses, e.g., congenital heart disease, which interfered with physical growth. The parents were told that the infant needed to gain up to a certain weight in order to undergo surgical correction of the heart condition. In still other cases where the infants had metabolic diseases such as diabetes, the parents might have been told by the physicians that it was critical that their child eat regularly.

In some cases, the child's developmental history did not provide an obvious reason for the mother's early preoccupation and concern with the child's eating. Instead, the etiology of the struggle appeared related to the mother's own history. These mothers frequently revealed that they have been in a battle over food with their own mothers during their growing years. Some were still having difficulty reading their own signals of hunger or satiety and continued to have eating disorders associated primarily with obesity.

The fathers of children with separation disorders presented a varied picture. In some cases they were intimately involved in the care of the infants, and were as much drawn into the infant's battle over food as were the mothers. In other cases, the fathers were physically or emotionally removed from the family and left the care of the infant almost completely in the hands of the mother. Some fathers were emotionally removed from the child as a result of marital conflict.

In most of these situations, the mothers felt lonely and isolated. The intense attachment to the infant substituted for the paucity of closeness to the spouse. However, during the second half of the first year of life, when the infant pushed for more autonomy the mothers were unable to negotiate issues of autonomy versus dependency, and the fathers were not available to lure the infant out of the symbiotic relationshp with the mother.

Table 3 describes the characteristics of disorders of separation.

Treatment of Disorders of Separation

The focus of treatment in a separation disorder is mealtime. The task is first to help mother and child negotiate issues of autonomy versus dependency in the feeding situation, followed by attention to other areas of the child's life. The intervention begins with the mother (or ideally with both parents) by explaining the developmental conflict of the child as outlined here: "The child has learned to assert his autonomy by refusing to eat. This has gotten mother anxious about the child's food intake and she has spent much time and effort in getting the child to eat. Although she has not been successful in increasing the child's food intake, her abundant attention around the child's feeding has encouraged his emotional appetite. The food refusal has worked for the child both ways: it has allowed him to assert his autonomy while his need for mother's attention has been met at the same time. He is in control and he loves it. His emotional hunger for mother's attention has outweighed his physiological hunger for food; he has failed to develop somatopsychological differentiation."

Following such an explanation of the child's developmental conflicts, the parents are instructed in behavioral techniques aimed at giving the child more autonomy during feedings and in setting firm limits on maladaptive behaviors at the same time. In order to enhance the child's develop-

Table 3

Diagnostic Criteria for Disorders of Separation *

Feeding problems stem from problems with infant's urge for autonomy. The parents give a history of food refusal and undereating in spite of all their efforts to increase their infant's food intake. The infant's conflict around autonomy versus dependency is carried out in the feeding situation and leads to a battle of wills over the infant's food intake.

INFANT

MOTHER

Age of Onset: Six months to 3 years; most commonly around 9 to 10 months of age.

Common Organic Contributory Factors: Homeostatic difficulties of the infant; any organic disease which results in poor weight gain or weight loss; organic illness which requires specific food intake, i.e., diabetes; organic illness in which weight gain is stressed for therapeutic interventions, i.e., surgery for congenital cardiac disease.

Common Psychosocial Stressors: Move to new area with social isolation of mother; frequent business travel by father leaving mother and infant alone at home; organic conditions or illnesses in the child which demand regularity or increased amounts of food intake.

Temperamental Vulnerabilities: Willfull, persistent, stubborn.

Development: Good to superior cognitive and speech development; if prolonged malnutrition, delay in gross motor development.

Common Maternal Pathology: Unresolved conflicts around separation and individuation; struggles around food with own mother during childhood; eating disorder, frequently associated with obesity; adjustment disorder with anxious or depressed mood because of child's physical illness.

Predominant Affect: Appears angry, defiant and irritable around feedings; curious and cheerful during play.

Predominant Affect: Appears anxious, insecure, worried, frustrated, discouraged or depressed.

Common Interactive Behaviors with Mother: Alternates between seeking closeness and asserting own will in defiant manner; engages mother in frequent battle of wills; shows limited range of responses to frustration and has difficulty in reconstituting.

Common Interactive Behaviors with Infant: Encourages infant's learning by visual and vocal stimulation; expresses pleasure in infant's new developmental accomplishments; may control interactions by overriding infant's drive for autonomy; fails to set appropriate limits.

Common Feeding Behaviors: Appears disinterested in food or losses interest in food quickly; refuses to to be fed by not opening mouth, turning away from food, or spitting food out; plays with food during meals and eats very little; engages in distracting game play instead of eating

Common Feeding Behaviors: Controls feeding by forcefeeding or playing distracting games without regard for infant's signals; does not facilitate or encourage self feeding; appears bothered by messiness and cleans infant excessively during feeding; is unable to read or trust infant's signals of hunger or satiety and feeds according to her projected needs.

---

*These characteristics were derived by clinical experience and are currently tested by the authors in a research study.

ment of somatopsychological differentiation, to help the child distinguish physiological hunger for food from emotional hunger for attention, the parents are made aware of one ground rule: to separate mealtimes from playtimes. They are instructed to feed the child at regular mealtimes and to schedule regular snacks if the interval between meals is too long. They are encouraged to offer the child a spoon, finger food, or whatever seems developmentally appropriate to facilitate self feeding. They are asked to assume a neutral stand about the child's food intake, not to praise if the child eats well and not to coax or force the child if he does not want to eat. In this way, the child's attention can be refocused on his inner state of hunger or fullness instead of being absorbed by the interactions with the parents. The parents are encouraged to set firm limits by terminating the meal if the child does not want to eat and to make up for the loss of attention during feedings by playing with the child before or after meals. Some parents who ask for written instructions are given the "Food Rules" (see Table 4).

Some parents can use this developmental guidance to alter their own and their child's behavior around feeding. Other parents have greater difficulty with change because of their own conflicts around parenthood or eating. Mothers whose infants develop feeding disturbances in the second half of the first year of life often have an elaborate defensive organization which may include use of reaction formation to protect themselves from aggressive, ambivalent feelings. In light of the generally neurotic level of character pathology involved, some of these mothers may benefit from exploratory psychodynamic psychotherapy as well as from straight-forward behavioral counseling.

Since many more of these children come from intact families, involving fathers in treatment is critical. The involvement of the father can diminish the mother's pathologic tie to the infant. For example, the father can encourage and support the mother as she attempts to disengage emotionally from the child. Father can be helped to become more assertive regarding their own needs which they may feel have been superceded by the mother's involvement with the child. In some cases, marital dysfunction is severe enough to interfere with successful treatment of the child's developmental problems, and couples therapy will be needed to address parental conflicts. Older toddlers and children can be helped directly through play therapy to address their conflicts around food and autonomy. With these multiple therapeutic interventions, one can begin to see significant improvement relatively quickly.

In some situations, hospitalization is indicated either for assessment or to provide a separation from parents so that the child can learn to establish more adaptive patterns of eating with an emotionally neutral caretaker. This approach requires limiting parent access to the child at feeding times. Frequently, one must impose strict rules prohibiting parental involvement during feeding. In such instances, the primary care nurse assumes total responsibility for the eating situation, preferably in the parent's absence. The mother's involvement is limited to non-nutritive issues. Following this intervention, the infant usually begins to eat more and gain weight.

Such progress often is received ambivalently by the mothers. They are relieved to see their child's weight gain and their anxiety about the child starving to death is reduced; nonetheless, they are hurt by the notion that someone else is better equipped at the moment to feed their child. Empathic work regarding these issues is essential in order to maintain a productive therapeutic alliance with the mother.

Table 4

Food Rules

1. Meals will be at regularly scheduled times; only planned snacks.

2. Nothing between meals will be offered, including bottles of milk or juice. The child may drink water if thirsty.

3. Solids will be offered first, fluids last.

4. Meals will last no longer than 30 minutes.

5. Child will be encouraged to self-feed as much as possible (finger feed, hold spoon, etc.).

6. A sheet under the high chair will "Catch the Mess". Wiping mouth and cleaning up only after the meal is over.

7. Child should learn to eat without approval or disapproval. Do not force food or comment on the child's intake. Mealtime should be in a neutral atmosphere.

8. Food should not be given as a present or reward.

9. No game playing at mealtimes. Don't use games to feed.

10. Food should be removed after 10-15 minutes if child seems to play with the food without eating.

11. Meal should be terminated if child throws food in anger.

Remember try to relax; with a neutral attitude he will eat when hungry.

After the child has established a healthy eating pattern, the mother and father are helped to resume feedings for their child. The children are frequently testy with their parents and try to resume the old patterns of interaction. The parents usually need much reinforcement to maintain a neutral stand about the child's food intake and to set firm limits on the child's provocative feeding behaviors. Once the child realizes that the old games don't work any more, he or she usually gives them up. Consequently, the parents feel strengthened in their ability of appropriate limit-setting and are better prepared to deal with other developmental issues of separation and individuation.

Case Vignette

Nora, a 25-month old white female was hospitalized for a medical evalution of her FTT and short stature. As the medical evaluation findings were negative, a psychiatric consultation was requested. The child's mother was a concerned woman who had no other children. Nora's father was away from home a great deal on business travel. The family lived with the mother's parents.

When Mrs. S. was asked to accompany the therapist to her office, Mrs. S. said she couldn't leave Nora, because Nora wouldn't let her. The mother related her sense of being trapped by Nora. She claimed that she had no life of her own and that she alternately wished and feared that Nora would die. Mrs. S.'s conflicting feelings made it difficult to leave Nora because "she might not eat and would starve to death."

The mother reported that Nora was the product of a planned, full term pregnancy. She was a "good baby" and had been the joy of her parents until she was about 10 months old. At that time, she began to walk and seemed to have "no interest in eating." Mother would play games with her to get her to eat, but the harder she tried, the less Nora seemed to eat. Nora would refuse to eat at mealtimes and waited for inconvenient moments to ask her mother to make her something to eat. Mother would then drop everything and prepare whatever Nora wanted, anxiously hoping that this time Nora would eat. Each time Nora refused. Other family members reported that Nora ate scraps surreptitiously, when she felt her mother was not watching.

Nora was a shy little girl who anxiously held on to her mother and became very distressed when separated from her. On the other hand, her play was creative and highly symbolic, and her language development was rather precocious. Early treatment interventions focused on helping the mother see how well she had done in areas of mothering other than feeding. We then dealt with the feeding difficulties and Nora's oppositional refusal to eat as an expression of her conflict around dependency and autonomy. The parents were encouraged to separate mealtimes from play times and to set firm limits to the length of the mealtimes. Once mother had convinced herself that Nora's food intake would be regulated by physiological feelings of hunger, she was able to follow through with the recommendations. On the first day, Nora refused two meals. Then she cried because her "tummy hurt." Her mother explained to her that she had hunger pains and that if she would eat, they would go away. Nora then proceeded to eat. This marked the turning point in her treatment. Mother and child did very well for a two-week period. When father returned from a business trip, Nora engaged him in the game play around food. After a short period of regression both parents were able to work together in helping Nora to separate her "emotional hunger" for her parents' attention from her physiological hunger for food.

After Nora established a regular feeding pattern, she began to have difficulty going to sleep. Mother would spend hours settling her at night. At that point in the treatment, Mrs. S. began to address her own conflicts around separation and individuation and her difficulties around limit setting.

IV. COMPOUNDED DEVELOPMENTAL DISORDERS

As we have studied infants and children with feeding disturbances, we have found cases where feeding problems which begin in one stage of development compromise development in ensuing stages. It has been our experience if the feeding problems and the interactional disturbances span more than one stage of development, treatment needs to address problems stemming from each stage of development, and is more complicated and time consuming.

Case Vignette of a Child with Homeostatic and Separation Difficulties

Leah, a little girl with pseudohypoparathyroidism, a rare metabolic disease, was referred at 19 months of age because of refusal to drink her special formula. Leah was the planned second child of a young middle-class couple. On her 3rd day of life Leah went into shock with a metabolic crisis and was hospitalized for the next two years. Her metabolic disease required very complicated dietary management and frequent intravenous infusions to maintain her electrolyte balance. In spite of her excellent care in the hospital, Leah experienced six near death episodes because of metabolic instability.

Leah spent most of her first year of life in the intensive and inter-
mediate care units of the hospital. Mother visited Leah almost daily
throughout the hospitalization in spite of the fact that she worked full
time and had another 4-1/2 year old daughter at home. She reported that
until age one, Leah did not seem to recognize her as mother, but seemed
quite attached to several nurses who cared for Leah on a regular basis.
Mother also recalled that Leah had not been given any oral feedings for the
first two months of life and that she had taken a long time to learn to
suck and swallow. Occupational therapists were called in to help with the
feedings. They instructed mother and nurses in special techniques; how to
position Leah and how to support her chin in order to facilitate a better
suck. When Leah was 10 months old, she seemed to have developed a good
suck and swallow, but never was very hungry because she was frequently kept
on continuous gastric infusions of her special formula.

In her second year of life, Leah stablized medically. She was moved
to the regular infant and toddler unit and began to make strides in every
area of development. At 16 months of age she began to walk. Her vocabulary
increased steadily. She was an engaging little girl, the pride of the
nursing and medical staff who had worked so hard to keep her alive. Along
with Leah's gains in motor and cognitive development came also a recognition
of her mother as a unique individual. Mother would usually come in the
evening to feed Leah her formula. But, around 15 months of age, Leah began
to cry when mother left and the feedings became increasingly difficult.
Mother found herself spending more time getting Leah to drink the formula,
and when Leah was finally referred at 19 months of age, she absolutely
refused to take any formula from her mother. The nurses who had initially
been more successful in feeding Leah also experienced Leah's increasing
refusal. Mother and nursing staff had fallen into a pattern of coaxing and
playing games and all experienced increasing frustration with their lack of
success.

Leah's history reveals that her metabolic disease and the associated
treatment had interfered with every stage of her feeding development.
First, Leah had missed out on learning to suck, swallow and regulate her
milk intake through feelings of hunger and satiety. In spite of assistance
from the occupational therapist, several months passed before Leah mastered
basic feeding skills. Leah's development of attachment was also complicated
because of the multiple caretakers a child in the hospital experiences.
However, special efforts to provide continuity of care by the nursing staff
and mother's regular visits in the evenings facilitated the development of
attachment to two nurses at 6 to 8 months and the emergence of a somewhat
delayed attachment to mother in the second year. About the same time, Leah
seemed to become aware of the special attachment to her mother. She learned
that by not drinking her formula she could delay mother's departure in the
evenings. Mother would try to coax her and play distracting games with her
to get Leah to drink her formula. Leah clearly enjoyed mother's attention.
However, the harder mother tried to get her to drink, the less Leah would
make an effort. Her mother's attention became much more important to her
than drinking her formula. The food refusal served both sides of Leah's
developmental conflict around separation and individuation. By not drinking, Leah asserted her autonomy towards her mother, and by getting her
mother to spend much time in playing distracting games to coax her to
drink, Leah's dependency needs were gratified.

Intervention needed to address Leah's interactional behavior around
feedings and her developmental conflict over separation and individuation.
Mother was advised to stop feedings temporarily and only to play with Leah
during visits in the evenings. The nurses were instructed in encouraging
self feeding but to stay neutral about Leah's food intake and to stop the
game playing. Whatever amount of formula Leah did not drink was substituted

through gastrostomy feedings after her meals. This removed the pressure from the nurses "to get formula into her" in order to avoid a metabolic crisis. After Leah had established a good feeding pattern while being fed by the nurses, mother was encouraged to resume feedings during her visits in the evenings. She was to feed first and play afterwards with Leah before she left. Firm time limits on her feedings were established to avoid a repeat of the pattern in the past. Mother needed much help in setting limits on Leah, especially when Leah was discharged home at 22 months of age. Mother's fear of a metabolic crisis resulting in Leah's death was very intense and made her vulnerable to "giving in" to Leah's manipulative game play around feedings. Not until Leah was three years old, did she master psychosomatic differentiation. She was able to drink her special formula independently and the gastrostomy was closed.

Case Vignette of a Child with Homeostatic Difficulties Leading to Attachment and Separation Problems

Susie, the full term product of a planned pregnancy, was born with a cleft palate and lip. She was referred at 5-1/2 years of age because her weight and height were below the 5th %tile, and mother reported chronic and constant battles with Susie around eating. Mrs. T feared for her daughter's health. She explained that Susie ate virtually nothing. Occasionally, Susie would indicate an interest in a particular food, and mother spared no effort to make that food as appetizing and interesting to Susie as possible and to prepare food for her at any hour of the day.

Discussion of Susie's functioning in other areas revealed a child who depended greatly on mother and a mother who interjected herself into many areas of her child's life. Mother dressed and groomed Susie. Mother accompanied Susie outside while Susie rode her bicycle. Mother went to Susie's gym class and participated in gym to "help Susie overcome her shyness at school." Susie was capable of tantrum behavior and tongue lashings which mother attempted to avoid at all cost. Mother described Susie as stubborn, willful, and "the boss" of the home. Not unexpectedly, Susie's father described himself as peripheral and relatively unimportant. He frequently felt exasperated towards Susie and mother and devoted much of his time to interests away from home. Mother expressed considerable resentment towards father who she felt had been unavailable to her and Susie during Susie's infancy and toddler years.

The history revealed that a severe cleft palate and lip, which was not corrected until Susie was 17 months, complicated the early feeding experience for both mother and infant. Mrs. T told of the desperation and humiliation she had felt when she had been forced to go to a veternarian's supply center to find a lamb's nipple for her infant Susie. Susie sucked poorly, gagged frequently, and when she spit up, milk came from her nose. Although Susie had been a wanted child, her mother's disappointment in her less than physically perfect infant was exacerbated by Susie's uneven temperament, her feeding difficulty, and Mr. T's apparent withdrawal from the child. Most of mother's rageful and aggressive impulses towards Susie during the early months appeared to have been repressed and managed by reaction formation defenses. Mother doted on Susie. She talked of having "swallowed" her disappointment. Mrs. T also described being afraid Susie would starve. She had some awareness of the numerous times when she herself had eaten, feeling it would help Susie. Her fantasy seemed to be that she could nourish Susie as she had done in the utero. At 17 months, Susie's defiance around eating caused mother to feel more angry as well as impotent and incompetent. Mother and Susie fell into a pattern of mother coaxing Susie to eat, alternating with angry outbursts and threats when nothing seemed to work.

The video taping of a meal revealed an anxious mother who appeared sensitive to any nuance of behavior or mood in Susie. The overall tone of the meal was that of a closed system. Mother and child appeared very involved with and dependent upon each other. Mother commented on each and every aspect of Susie's eating behavior, e.g. how the food tasted -- what food should be tried next, etc. Susie engaged Mrs. T during the meal time by looking at her mother as she was taking a bite and even reaching out to make physical contact with mother during the meal. However, Susie resisted all mother's direct attempts to encourage her to eat. She played with her food and sipped her soup broth but left the rest of the food untouched.

Treatment began by helping the parents understand how the early feeding difficulties stemming from Susie's cleft palate had interfered with every stage of her development. They were given some behavioral instructions on how to handle meal times and how to set limits on Susie's tyranical behavior. Susie was seen in individual play therapy to deal with her developmental conflicts around separation and dependency. Initially, the parents were seen together to support each other in limit setting and parenting issues. As treatment progressed, the parents focused on their ambivalent feelings towards Susie and the difficulties in their marital relationship which had been displaced to Susie. By the time treatment was terminated, Susie functioned with more autonomy. Her eating behavior, her oppositional behavior in the family and her social relationships had all become more age appropriate. Moreover, the parents marital relationship was improving and they were optimistic about the future.

Case Vignette of a Child with Attachment and Separation Difficulties

Jena, an 18 month old girl, was admitted to our hospital with gastroenteritis, scabies and FTT. Jena had been brought to the emergency room by her father who implied concern about his wife's ability to care for their child.

On admission Jena was below the 5th %tile for weight and height and developmentally delayed in speech, motor, and social development, functioning at about the 10-12 month level. She was indiscriminate in her appeals for physical closeness with adult strangers. She was without either an externally imposed or internally developed schedule for eating, sleeping, or other activities. We speculated that Jena had become used to snacking all day and never felt sufficient hunger or satiety to insure adequate calorie intake. Jena also shook her head "no" vehemently when mom pried her mouth open to force food in her.

Her parents did not visit for the first few days but did come in after some coaxing. Frightened, confused and emotionally labile, Jena's mother was difficult to communicate with initially. She projected her own feelings of anger on to the hospital staff and Jena. Mrs. Z's own history showed a 30 year old woman with limited intellectual functioning, poor social skills and very low self esteem. Her relationship with her own mother was characterized by frequent rejection and unavailability. Mrs. Z revealed that she had been unable to provide a structured routine or a consistant caring relationship for her child. She teased Jena or pushed her away and alternately felt angry and rejected by Jena for the child's approaches for affection to strangers. Mrs. Z was overwhelmed by her child's needs.

Mr. Z, a grocery store clerk, was also the product of a troubled abusive childhood. Although he professed great willingness to cooperate with the hospital staff, as he did at home, he left his wife to cope with her child (and us) while he spent much of his time in the local gay bars. The marital relationship was very troubled with frequent mutually abusive verbal behavior, anger, rejection, and tension. Nevertheless, both parents appeared invested in maintaining that relationship.

In this case, both issues of attachment and separation were prominent. From the beginning, the mother-infant attachment was fragile due to this mother's deprivation, which limited her capacity to nurture Jena and understand her needs. The concomitant separation difficulties arose as a result of the poor attachment, Jena's thwarted iniatives for individuation and limited opportunity for getting maternal assistance in developing autonomy. As Jena learned means-end differentiation, provoking mom became more important than satisfying her own hunger.

The treatment of this FTT child and her family consisted of the in-hospital treatment of mother and toddler, the development of an after-care plan, and long term out-patient follow-up. Hospitalization was aimed at enhancing the functioning of both mother and child. It was necessary to help Jena develop a regular eating and sleeping pattern. Autonomy in self-feeding was emphasized. As this goal was achieved, her weight began to increase. Scheduled activities were geared to foster growth and development of motor, speech, and social skills. Mrs. Z was gently nurtured and she became less frightened and more open about her fears and her feelings about herself and her child. She became quite dependent on the social worker and remarked that it was the first time she was ever treated like a "grown-up lady" instead of "retarded." Through this positive relationship she was helped to participate in her daughter's growth and development and then to feel responsible and effective in her own right for Jena's weight gain and improved development.

After a one month hospital stay, discharge was achieved with a complicated after-care plan. Mrs. Z and Jena continued to see the social worker-therapist once per week in the out-patient psychiatry department. Mother and child also attended the Speech Clinic and had close medical (weight) follow-up with the resident physician who treated Jena in the hospital. Day care outside the home was recommended but was not available. Mrs. Z also attended weekly a therapeutic infant center where mother and baby could be guided through new mutual developmental tasks. All of these plans were held together by a Protective Services worker who provided both weekly transportation to the hospital and a weekly visit by a parent-aide.

After two years of treatment and intervention, Jena's developmental progress was significant in all areas. Her weight was around the 10th percentile and her eating behavior was more appropriate. Mrs. Z maintained close contact with the extremely maternal and nurturing parent-aide and achieved increased self esteem and interpersonal maturity in her relationship with the clinical social worker at the hospital. Mrs. Z's growth in these two important relationships was associated with improvement in her interactions with Jena.

CONCLUSIONS

A comprehensive approach to the diagnosis and treatment of FTT necessitates an understanding of feeding disorders which can be associated with the FTT syndrome. The authors have proposed that as in other aspects of a child's development, eating behavior follows a sequential pattern. Therefore, feeding problems can best be understood within a developmental context. Three stages of development, each with characteristic eating behaviors and characteristic mother-infant interactive behaviors have been described: Homeostasis, Attachment, and Separation.

Problems of feeding and difficulties in mother-infant interaction frequently do not subside as one stage of development evolves into the next. Rather, problems wich begin during one stage of development can linger into the ensuing stage, thereby compromising the infant's growth and his emotional development. The chapter has described examples of this compounding effect and how it influences treatment. At each stage of development, feeding disturbances can be expression of difficulties emanating from the infant, from the mother, or from the infant/mother interaction.

The interface between feeding disorders and FTT is complicated. Feeding problems can create, co-exist with, or result from a growth problem. Thus, a multifactorial approach to the FTT syndrome is necessary. However, the authors postulate that the feeding situation may be viewed as an intersecting point where the many variables which result in FTT are expressed. For this reason, the feeding context provides the clinician with an opportunity to understand and interpret the organic, the emotional, and the social variables which are preventing growth.

The delineation of developmental subtypes has helped us to design our treatment interventions with more specificity. Thus far, our work has been primarily clinical. Presently, we are also examining and testing the validity of mother-child interactional patterns and individual characteristics in each of the three subtypes we have delineated. Further research needs to be directed toward evaluation of interventions designed to manage specific subtypes of FTT.

REFERENCES

Bernbaum, J.D., Pereira, G.R., Watkins, J.B. & Peckham, G.J. Nonnutritive sucking during gavage feeding enhances growth and maturation in premature infants. Pediatrics, 1983, 71, 41-45.

Bowlby, J. Attachment. New York: Basic Books, 1969.

Bowlby, J. Separation and Loss: Anxiety and Anger. New York: Basic Books, 1973.

Casey, P.H., Bradley, R. & Wortham, B. Social and nonsocial home environments and infants with nonorganic failure to thrive. Pediatrics, 1984, 73, 348-353.

Chapin, H.D. A plan of dealing with atrophic infants and children. Archives of Pediatrics, 1908, 25, 491-496.

Chatoor, I. & Dickson, L. Rumination: A maladaptive attempt at self-regulation in infants and children. Clinical Proceedings, 1984, 40, 106-116.

Chatoor, I. & Egan, J. Nonorganic failure to thrive and dwarfism due to food refusal: A separation disorder. Journal of the American Academy of Child Psychiatry, 1983, 22, 294-301.

Chatoor, I. Schaefer, S., Dickson, L. & Egan, J. Nonorganic failure to thrive: A developmental perspective. Pediatric Annals, 1984, 13, 829-843.

Dowling, S. Seven infants with esophageal atresia: A developmental study. The Psychoanalytic Study of the Child, 1977, 32, 215-256.

Drotar, D., Malone, C. and Negray, J. Psychosocial intervention with families of children who fail to thrive. Child Abuse and Neglect, 1979, 3, 927-935.

Egan, J. Chatoor, I. & Rosen, G. Failure to thrive: Pathogenesis and Classification. Clinical Proceedings of Childrens Hospital National Medical Center, 1980, 36, 173-180.

Evans, S.L., Reinhart, J.B. & Succop, R.A. Failure to thrive, a study of 45 children and their families. Journal of the American Academy of Child Psychiatry, 1972, 11, 440-457.

Fischoff, J. Whitten, C.F. & Pettit, M.G. A psychiatric study of mothers of infants with growth failure secondary to maternal deprivation.

Journal of Pediatrics, 1971, 79, 209-215.

Fraiberg, S., Anderson, E. & Shapiro, V. Ghosts in the nursery. Journal of the American Academy of Child Psychiatry, 1975, 14, 387-421.

Freud, A. The psychoanalytic study of infantile feeding disturbances. Psychoanaltic Study of the Child, 1946, 2, 119-132.

Glaser, H.H., Heagerty, M.C., Bullard, D.M. Jr. & Pivchik, E.C. Physical and psychological development of children with early failure to thrive. Journal of Pediatrics, 1968, 73, 690-698.

Goldbloom, R.B. Failure to thrive. Pediatric Clinics of North America, 1982, 29, 1.

Goldfarb, W. Psychological privation in infancy and subsequent adjustment. American Journal of Orthopsychiatry, 1945, 15, 247-255.

Greenspan, S.I. & Lieberman, A.F. Infants, mothers, and their interactions A quantitative clinical approach to developmental assessment. In S.I. Greenspan & G.H. Pollock (Eds.) The Course of Life, Volume I: Infancy and Early Childhood. Bethesda, MD: NIMH, 1980, 271-312.

Greenspan, S.I. & Lourie, R.S. Developmental structuralist approach to classification of adaptive and pathologic personality organizations: Infancy and early childhood. American Journal of Psychiatry, 1981, 138, 725-735.

Harris, J.C. Non-organic failure to thrive syndromes. In P.Y. Accardo (Ed.), Failure to Thrive in Infancy and Early Childhood. Baltimore: University Park Press, 1982, 240-241.

Homer, C. & Ludwig, S. Categorization of etiology of failure to thrive. American Journal of Diseases of Children, 1981, 135, 848-851.

Levy, D. Oppositional syndrome and oppositional behavior. In R.H. Hock & J. Zubin (Eds.) Psychopathology of Childhood. New York: Grune & Stratten, 1955.

Mahler, M.S., Pine, F. & Berman, A. The Psychological Birth of the Human Infant. New York: Basic Books, 1975.

Malone, C. & Drotar, D. A prospective study of failure to thrive: Outcome data for the children up to the age of two. Presented at the 30th Annual Meeting of the American Academy of Child Psychiatry. San Francisco, 1983.

Murray, S.L., Fink, R. & Gaiter, J. Nutritive sucking patterns in infants at risk for sudden infant death. Presented at the International Conference on Infant Studies. New York, NY, 1984.

Pollitt, E., Weisel, E.A. & Chan, C.K. Psychosocial developmental behavior of mothers of failure-to-thrive children. American Journal of Orthopsychiatry, 1975, 45, 525-537.

Sills, R.H. Failure to thrive, the role of clinical and laboratory evaluation. American Journal of Diseases of Children, 1978, 132, 967-969.

Spitz, R. Hospitalism, an inquiry into the psychiatric conditions of early childhood. The Psychoanalytic Study of the Child, 1945, 1, 53-74.

THE ETIOLOGY OF FAILURE TO THRIVE:

AN INTERACTIONAL DEVELOPMENTAL APPROACH*

Alicia F. Lieberman and Marian Birch

Infant Parent Program
University of California
San Francisco, California

The goal of this paper is to present an interactional developmental framework for understanding the psychological issues underlying non-organic FTT in the first two years of life. The central theses are that growth failure is rooted in a transactional impasse between the infant and the caregiver, that the specifics of this impasse vary at different developmental stages, and that the etiology of FTT may be best understood in the context of the developmental issues negotiated between infant and caregiver during each stage. In this framework, growth failure is interpreted as the most concrete (and hence most noticeable) manifestation of impaired infant functioning in a variety of areas, particularly in socioemotional development. This formulation has important implications for treatment. For example, if therapeutic attention is focused exclusively on nutritional issues at the expense of broader interaction between infant and caregiver, the distortions in socioemotional development may persist in the form of ongoing psychological vulnerabilities and maladaptive patterns of adjustment.

Current efforts to understand the genesis of FTT in infants have placed increasing emphasis on the interplay between multiple constitutional and environmental factors in the etiology of the condition. Drotar, Malone & Negray (1980) have developed a multifactorial model in which FTT represents the outcome of factors involving the infant, the caregiver, the family, and the broader socioeconomic environment impinging on various family members. Glasser & Lieberman (1984) outlined a classification based on the respective contributions of the infant and the caregiver to a dysfunctional interaction which results in the infant's FTT. Both of these approaches supercede the earlier view of FTT as the result of either medical illness (organic FTT) or of psychological deprivation, a term often used as a euphemism for maternal neglect. In prior investigations, the recognition of the role of socioemotional factors in the etiology of

---

*The authors wish to thank the following persons for their invaluable assistance in reviewing and commenting on the manuscript: Lester Eisenstadt, M.D.; Arthur Green, M.D.; Moses Grossman, M.D.: John Jemerin, M.D.; Elizabeth Mayer, Ph.D.; Jeree Pawl, Ph.D.; Stephen Seligman, D.M.H.; Calvin Settlage, M.D.; Robert Wallerstein, M.D.. Responsibility for the contents of this paper, however, rests solely with the authors.

FTT was crucially important in the understanding of the condition (Barbero & Shaheen, 1967; Leonard, Rhymes, & Solnit, 1966). However, recent evidence suggests that the concept of psychosocial deprivation overlooks the role of the infant and is insufficiently interactive to adequately describe, by itself, the dynamic process by which an infant fails to grow as expected (Ferholt & Provence, 1976).

Multifactorial and interactional approaches are promising because they emphasize that the understanding of FTT requires a more complex model than the long-accepted dichotomy between organic factors (originating in the infant) and emotional factors (originating in the mother). The challenge now facing investigators is to become increasingly more specific in identifying and describing each of the multiple contributing factors to the condition. While acknowledging the importance of a multifactorial perspective, we will focus specifically on the caregiver-infant interaction because we believe that, in the first two years of life, the effect of other high-risk factors such as poverty and family disorganization are funnelled to the infant primarily through their impact on the primary caregivers.

THE PROGRAMMATIC SETTING

The setting for our work is the Infant-Parent Program (IPP), an infant mental health program in the Department of Psychiatry of the University of California, San Francisco (UCSF). The program is located at San Francisco General Hospital, a teaching county hospital in the UCSF system. The Infant-Parent Program evolved from the pioneering work of Selma Fraiberg and her colleagues in developing methods for the assessment and treatment of high-risk and socioemotionally impaired infants and their families (Fraiberg, Adelson, & Shapiro, 1975; Fraiberg, 1978; Fraiberg, 1980). A basic feature of the Infant-Parent Program is the effort to integrate infant mental health services with pediatric care. The program has a close network of collaboration with the hospital's Department of Pediatrics. The program staff provide on-site consultation to the three major pediatric services: the newborn nursery, the well-baby clinic, and the pediatric ward. Approximately one-fourth of the referrals to the program come from these services. The remaining referrals come from pediatric providers at other local hospitals, from the San Francisco Department of Social Services and other child protective services, and from community agencies working with infants and their families (e.g., public health nurses, community mental health centers, day care centers, and parents' support groups).

Intervention always begins with an extended assessment consisting of five to seven weekly sessions. The assessment takes place primarily in the home, with an office visit scheduled for a videotaped developmental assessment of the infant and a free play sequence between infant and parents. One aspect of the assessment process involves the evaluation of the infant's affective, social, and cognitive functioning. The presence or absence of age-appropriate responses in each of these areas is observed, with much emphasis given to the quality of attachment behaviors, social responsiveness, the range and modulation of affect, and the adaptive coping mechanisms used by the baby. Unstructured home observations are supplemented by formal cognitive testing using either the Bayley Scales of Infant Development or the Stanford-Binet Intelligence Test, depending on the child's age.

A second aspect of the assessment involves appraising the parent's quality of caregiving, their emotional investment in the baby, areas of conflict in psychological and interpersonal relationships, and the implications of these factors for the infants' experience. This information is used to determine whether treatment is appropriate, and if so, what modality is likely to be most profitable for the family.

The treatment techniques themselves are multifaceted and arise from an understanding of each particular situtation. Frequently, the baby represents a powerful transference object for parents, and problems in the parents' relationship to the infant may be understood as both reenactments or vivid expressions of the parents' childhood experiences. These connections may be explored with the parents to a greater or lesser degree, but they inform the clinician's perceptions and guide the clinical choices made in the course of treatment. Information about development and about the emotional needs of infants is given to the parents in the context of their own spontaneous questions and concerns and of the specific difficulties that they experience in raising their child.

THE CLINICAL SAMPLE

Since the inception of the program in 1979, we have assessed and/or treated 53 cases referred by pediatric care providers with a diagnosis of non-organic FTT. Ten of the children were referred in the course of the hospitalization for this condition or immediately following discharge. The remaining children were referred as the measure of last resort before hospitalization. The majority of families referred belong to the lower socioeconomic level: approximately three-fourths of the heads of household worked as unskilled laborers, were unemployed, or received some kind of social assistance. The remaining families were middle or upper class.

DEVELOPMENTAL ISSUES IN FAILURE TO THRIVE: A CONCEPTUAL FRAMEWORK

Development is characterized by the emergence of progressively more complex levels of behavioral organization in the cognitive, affective and motor spheres. Developmental lines converge and interact in increasingly more intricate patterns at every new level of organization, leading to reorganizations in the links between behavioral systems and in the relationship between infant and the social and physical environment. In this sense, development has features of both continuity and discontinuity. It is continuous in the sense that difficulties at an earlier phase heighten the infant's vulnerability to stress at later stages, and conversely, secure and successful developmental negotiations in early development increase the infant's later resilience and resources for coping with new challenges adaptively (Escalona, 1968; Murphy, 1962; Sroufe, 1983). Yet, discontinuities occur with major organizational shifts which present qualitatively new and different challenges to the infant and the caregiver (Emde, Gaensbauer & Harmon, 1976; Spitz, 1965). Spitz characterized these shifts in embryological language, refering to them as "psychic organizers." Epigenetic views of development have been espoused by a number of theorists who have relied on child and infant observation and on experimental findings to outline shifts and reorganizations in development, and to describe developmental negotiations the infant must master in its transactions with the environment (Emde et al., 1976; Erikson, 1963; A. Freud, 1965; Greenspan, 1981; Piaget, 1952; Sander, 1962, 1976; Spitz, 1965; Sroufe, 1979).

In this context, FTT can be interpreted as a breakdown in the successful negotiation of developmental issues, an adaptational failure to attain mutually satisfactory regulation of the relationship between infant and caregiver. Such a failure signifies a concurrent disorder or distortion in the regulation of the infant's internal neurophysiological and psychological processes as well. The stage at which this breakdown occurs is a crucial factor in understanding the etiology of the disorder and devising appropriate intervention strategies. Succeeding developmental phases demand a reorganization and renegotiation of the infant-parent needs. Such transitions provide points of vulnerability for maladaptive or pathological resolutions. Indeed, one influential model of infant psychopathology (Greenspan, 1979; Greenspan & Lieberman, 1980; Greenspan & Porgess, 1984) relies on the concept of developmental transitions as a point of departure to describe adaptive and maladaptive patterns in the infant and in the environment and to show how these patterns may change at different stages. Our goal is to apply a similar outlook to the case of a specific disorder of infancy. Using our clinical data, we will describe how individual characteristics of infants and caregivers may interact in maladaptive ways around specific developmental tasks to increase the risk for the onset of FTT.

REGULATION OF NEURO-PHYSIOLOGICAL PROCESSES:
THE FIRST 3 MONTHS

The first developmental task facing the newborn infant concerns issues of neurophysiological organization, regulation, and homeostasis (Emde et al., 1976; Greenspan, 1981; Sander, 1962, 1975). This includes the regulation of state and sleeping-waking cycles, temperature regulation, and the stabilization of patterns of hunger, suckling and digestive processes. While maturation plays a significant role, it is not the only factor in these achievements: adaptive patterns of homeostasis have been shown to result from the interaction between the contributions of the infant and the characteristics of the caregiving environment (Burns, Sander, Stechler & Julia, 1972; Greenspan, 1981; Lewis & Rosenblum, 1974).

It is well established that there is much variability among infants along such dimensions as activity level, sensory threshholds, irritability, and arousability (Brazelton, 1973; Clemente, Purpura & Mayer, 1972). Infants have unique individual preferences and sensitivities in each sensory and motor modality, in the coordination between modalities, and in the patterns of integration between the sensory-motor responses and the neuroendocrine systems mediating arousal, attention, and distress. Thus, the individual infant has idiosyncratic, constitutional "biases" or characteristics which are of great importance in shaping adaptational responses to the environment (Brazelton, 1961, 1973; Escalona, 1968; Korner, 1974; Thomas, Chess, Birch, & Hertzig, 1963).

The challenge facing the caregiver of a very young infant is to perceive accurately and respond contingently to this configuration of characteristic biases (Papousek and Papousek, 1983) and in particular to those which make the infant vulnerable to disorganization or to those which make certain modes of stimulation and soothing particularly effective (Brazelton, Koslowski & Main, 1974; Escalona, 1968; Murphy, 1962). This task demands a true regression in the service of the ego in which the boundaries which normally separate one person's internal experience from another's become blurred. At the same time, the caregiver must retain the capacity to respond in an organized adult fashion to contingencies experienced in a non-verbal, empathetic way. This stage demands from the caregiver a remarkable blend of imagination and patient attentiveness to often subtle and confusing infant feedback. The baby has not yet differentiated hunger, cold, or fatigue from a global sense of distress and tension, and must rely on a caregiver not only to guess, provide for, and relieve the causes of the distress, but also to utilize the infant's frequently unclear signals to confirm and inspire caregiving behavior. The fact that this negotiation between infant signaling and maternal intervention is so often successful should not blind us to the remarkable nature of the achievement. Instances of failure to establish successful mother-infant negotiations and the developmental consequences of such failures have been extensively documented (Ainsworth, 1979; Brody, 1956; Stern, 1974).

In our clinical assessments of FTT infants and their families, we have found that in the first three months of life, the onset of the condition is often inextricably linked to such characteristics of the infant as muted signaling of need states, weak sucking, persistent irritability, unpredictable or unstable physiological states, and frequent gastrointestinal disturbances (regurgitation, vomiting, colic). This is so even when the pediatric workup has uncovered no medical cause of the condition. Cases where the infant shows these disturbances but there is no medical diagnosis of a specific illness necessarily raise the question of the outer semantic limits of the definition of organicity. In such instances, the absence of medical illness causally linked to the onset of FTT does not preclude the existence of organic factors such as those described which predispose the infant to the development of difficulties in feeding and may place the infant at high risk for FTT.

Of course, predisposing constitutional factors do not preclude the simultaneous presence of environmental risk factors. In our clinical population, we have seen families in which the parents have either an unusually high need for unambiguous infant signals or a low threshhold for discouragement when the baby fails to respond as expected. Such a parent may interpret the infant's lack of coordination or distractability when offered food as an angry refusal, indifference, or personal rejection. Such parental perceptions may lead to a self-perpetuating cycle in which the baby who does not immediately suckle or who is easily distractible and fatigued is not adequately fed because s/he is perceived as not interested in food or not hungry. Such a baby may have few if any satisfyingly completed feeding experiences, and the baby may then have ongoing difficulty in achieving a differentiated sense of hunger followed by relief as a result of feeding. In such a situation, the earliest rudiments of a reciprocal and gratifying engagement with the external world are not laid down. Such infants, in addition to nutritional deprivation, may suffer from deficits in the quality and quantity of interactive experiences needed to organize effective strategies for achieving a balance between neurophysiological equilibrium on the one hand and receptivity to environmental input on the other (Greenspan, 1981).

Clinical Vignettes

Vignette 1. Donna was referred at 3 months of age in the course of a hospitalization to clarify the causes of her failure to gain weight. Donna had gained weight in the hospital, and the medical staff felt concerned about the mother's brief though frequent hospital visits and about the relative absence of holding and physical contact, which the staff interpreted as maternal rejection of Donna.

In a number of ways, Donna fit the classic non-organic FTT syndrome. At home, she was repeatedly ill with GI disturbances and was unable to maintain or increase her weight, while during two hospitalizations she was able to gain weight adequately. Also, the nursing staff reported that Donna was a rewarding infant to work with, while her mother, Mrs. D., described her as an irritable and inconsolable baby who cried for hours and could not be soothed.

While no clear-cut organic cause for Donna's growth failure was ever found, a constellation of risk factors and the observations of the Infant-

Parent Program worker assigned to the case strongly suggest that Donna was an unusually difficult baby. Donna was born at 37 weeks and was small for gestational age. Her head circumference was disproportionately small. Since her birth, she had had several severe bouts of diarrhea, recurrent high fever, and a seizure of unexplained origin. Moreover, Donna was neurophysiologically immature and it required considerable persistent effort to console her when she was distressed. She was a weak sucker and easily distractible while feeding.

Home visits after Donna's discharge showed that Mrs. D was capable of responding appropriately to Donna, and could successfully feed her and interact with her if she had emotional support and no external distractions. But there were a number of circumstances which precluded this from happening with any regularity. Mrs. D. was a single parent who worked full time to support her two young children. When she came home, she felt torn between her duties towards Donna and towards her 18-month old son, and she often gave precedence to the insistent demands of the older child, which were both easier to understand and easier to respond to than Donna's. In addition, the strain of the repeated illness and, not least, the sense of blame Mrs. D. experienced from her contacts with the hospital staff, significantly contributed to this otherwise adequate mother's insecurity and uncertainty. These feelings fostered in turn a defensive stance of detachment toward her daughter and anger at the hospital staff for not finding an organic cause for Donna's illness. After sympathetic discussions of her predicament, and much support and help in identifying Donna's fleeting positive responses to her ministrations, Mrs. D. was able to do much better with her admittedly difficult infant, and the child's weight and medical condition stabilized. The improvements in the mother-child interaction and in the child's condition became even more marked after Mrs. D. married a nurturing man who provided financial support and who helped her with the two children.

Vignette 2. Bobby was referred to our program at 6 weeks of age after a 5-day hospitalization for FTT. The first child of a professional couple in their mid-thirties, he had lost weight since birth, although he appeared to be a healthy, competent and intact infant.

Bobby was an unusually quiet baby. He rarely cried, and his states were poorly defined and unpredictable. He appeared rather hypo-responsive to stimulation and gave little feedback to his mother about the effect of her ministrations. While his behavior was clearly within the normal range, it required some sensitivity and attentiveness to determine whether he was hungry or upset. His mother was very intelligent and seemed motivated to care for Bobby, but his weak signals found their match in her striking lack of access to her own inner needs and feelings, her failure to make a psychological claim on her baby, and her subsequent difficulty in empathizing with an infant who made weaker than normal bids for her sympathies. Quite true, Mrs. Y. often "forgot" to feed Bobby as well as herself and her husband, but Bobby was an infant who did not vigorously protest being forgotten.

Bobby was brought to nutritional adequacy with the combined support of the IPP therapist, the pediatrician, and the staff of the daycare center in which Bobby was enrolled. Therapeutic work with the mother involved both developmental guidance and efforts at understanding her pervasive ambivalent stance and her unawareness of her own feelings of hunger and satiety, need and satisfaction. Mrs. Y. became progressively more attuned to her feelings and more able to explore the psychological roots of her difficulties in feeling close to her son. Bobby, in turn, became an active toddler who took the initiative in drawing his mother's attention. However, signs of socioemotional impairment remained: at 18 months, Bobby had an extensive vocabulary, but no words for mother and bottle. Although his weight was adequate and his cognitive development above average, he showed some curtailment in the intensity of affective involvement with his parents and a delay in negotiating issues of autonomy, separation and control.

THE FOCALIZATION OF ATTACHMENT: 3-7 MONTHS

With the emergence of the social smile, which Spitz (1965) and Emde et al. (1976) consider as the indicator of the first "psychic organizer," a qualitatively new phase of development and behavioral organization begins. Mastery of the developmental tasks of the first phase (i.e. the achievement of fairly stable neurophysiological functioning) allow for an increased capacity for sustained attention to the environment, and the baby now begins to engage with both the animate and inanimate world in a far more focused and complex way. Behaviors which in the neonate were endogenously stimulated are now elicited by specific features of the environment. The purely reflexive behavior patterns of the neonate fade, probably by a process of active cortical inhibition, to be replaced by contingent responses to exogenous stimulation. The smile is the best researched example of this process (Emde et al., 1976; Sroufe and Waters, 1976; Wolff, 1963). This state is characterized by a new intensity in the expression of affective experiences (Sroufe, 1979). For the first time, the infant laughs in response to vigorous stimulation: pleasure has become an "excitatory phenomenon" (Escalona, 1968) which is linked to the infant's growing capacity to expect, anticipate, and engage in secondary circular reactions. These emerging capacities also bring the possibility of failed expectations and subsequent disappointments. As a result, frustration and rage now also appear.

Several factors converge to highlight social reciprocity during this period. The social smile, the onset of laughter, increased responsivity, and disappearance of early fussiness tend to heighten the caregiver's positive involvement (Emde et al., 1976; Stern, 1974). The infant begins to participate in social games (Sroufe and Wunsch, 1972), to explore the caregiver's face and body (Mahler, Pine & Bergman, 1975) and to initiate social interactions in a persistent, directed fashion (Escalona, 1968). The discrimination of the mother or primary caregiver as a preferred figure, particularly in situations of stress, becomes so reliable and clear-cut by the end of this period that the infant is considered to have become attached (Bowlby, 1969). The mother's sensitive responsiveness to the infant's social cues and need signals is considered a primary antecedent of the quality of attachment (Ainsworth, Blehar, Waters & Wall, 1978). This sensitivity, in turn, sets the stage for the infant's confident expectation that its social overtures will be responded to in kind. Mutually contingent interactions initiate the infant into the act of dialogue, of mutuality of response. Perhaps another way of describing this phenomenon is to say that at around 7 months, the infant develops a "theory of interfacable minds" (Bretherton and Bates, 1979) which allows the infant to have some self-apperception of an internal mental state, to attribute an internal mental state to a social partner, and, finally, to seek a reciprocal communication of these two mental states. Intentions can now be shared.

What is the developmental meaning of the feeding situation during this phase? Aside from its primary function of providing nutrition, feeding tends to be the most consistent and prolonged form of parent-infant interaction, and the degree to which it does or does not become a rich, mutually regulated exchange in which each partner has repeated experiences of being contingently responded to by the other may be a sensitive indicator of the overall quality of a parent-infant relationship. Greenspan and Lieberman (1980) have outlined two patterns of parental failure to respond to infants' signals which are relevant to the feeding situation as well as to other forms of interaction. They call these responses non-contingent and anti-contingent patterns. The non-contingent parent, for environmental or psychological reasons, is unable to provide consistent and reasonably predictable and appropriate responses to the infant's hunger signals or social initiatives. Food is offered in an apparently random fashion, feeding episodes may be frequently interrupted in response to external or internal pressures and distractions, and parental responses to infant initiatives may be absent, erratic, inconsistent, or bizarre. We have identified this non-contingent pattern in our clinical population in cases of severe parental thought disorder or depression, as well as in extremely chaotic and socioeconomically stressed families where there is no clearly defined person or persons principally responsible for feeding. In the second, anti-contingent pattern, the parent is consistent, even rigidly so, in her behavior and structuring of the feeding interaction, but her practices are informed by her own needs and by a conscious or unconscious need to control the infant's behavior. Thus, the infant who reaches for the bottle may have his hands restrained, the bottle may be arbitrarily removed as the infant is sucking, the infant who touches his food may have the food removed from his hands and forced into his mouth.

As for the infant's contribution, such innate but by this time environmentally modulated factors as activity level, distractability, irritability, and the degree to which the infant has the capacity to respond flexibly without becoming disorganized are important. How the infant responds to non-contingent or anti-contingent parental responses may make the difference between sustained weight gain and FTT: if parental behaviors regularly elicit rage or withdrawal in the infant, the result may be a breakdown in the feeding transactions in which the baby responds with disinterest in food or a battle to be fed on his own terms. Another significant factor is the baby's ability to "reward" the caregiver -- that is, to respond contingently to her overtures -- with smiles, with molding the body, with vocalizations and with other appealing behaviors. In one of our cases, 8 adults leading very chaotic lifestyles took care of two infants, the offspring of teenaged sisters. One, two months the older, was called "Bruiser" and was a healthy, robust infant who received and responded vigorously and positively to a great deal of admittedly rather casual and inconsistent but mostly benevolent attention. The younger infant, a quiet, rather unresponsive baby with chronic gastrointestinal problems, was diagnosed as FTT. It was clear that feeding him was seen by the adults as less rewarding than feeding his more responsive cousin.

Clinical Vignettes

Vignette #3. Jamal was referred to our program for non-organic FTT when he was 18 months old. However, the condition had been first identified by the pediatrician when Jamal was 6 months old and his weight had dropped from the 20th percentile at 4 months to below the third percentile at 6 months (Height and head circumference had stayed at the 25th percentile and 10th percentile respectively). In the intervening year between diagnosis and referral to our program, the pediatrician had conducted a comprehensive series of medical tests that had ruled out organic causes for the condition. The pediatrician then reluctantly considered the possibility that Jamal's FTT was due to psychological factors. In making the referral, he expressed his misgivings about this possible diagnosis by emphasizing how loving Jamal's parents were and how attached Jamal was to them.

Our initial home visits confirmed the pediatrician's impression that there were reliable affective bonds between Jamal and his parents. Jamal seemed like an active and competent toddler and his parents were quite proud of him, complaining only that he was unresponsive to limit setting and that he sometimes wore them out with his constant activity. However, other factors began to emerge as our visits continued. Jamal's mother was an extremely passive, almost inert woman, with a thought disorder that was at first masked by her apparent reserve. Her favorite activity was to watch TV, she seldom took the initiative in interacting with Jamal or setting limits, and she often did not notice behaviors that required prompt intervention, such as Jamal's climbing on a stool to reach a favorite toy. The father was more actively involved with Jamal and tended to set appropriate limits, but he was often out of the house and his arrivals and departures were rather sudden and unexplained. The home environment was an odd mixture of benignity and confusion. While Jamal appeared to be genuinely cherished by his parents, they themselves led highly unstructured, outwardly haphazard lifestyles in which the connections between intentions, actions, and results were strikingly obscure. Such a lack of organization was clearly reflected in the attitude towards eating. Nobody in the family ate regular meals, and there was no consistent pattern for Jamal's feedings: the mother was usually vague when asked whether Jamal had eaten, when and what he had eaten. Also, while Jamal occasionally took things from the refrigerator, he was sometimes praised proudly for his initiative, sometimes scolded for taking the wrong thing or making a mess, and sometimes ignored. On the few occasions when, at our urging, Jamal was actually fed, things tended to go wrong: the oatmeal was too hot and Jamal burned himself, bringing the meal to a sad end; or he was given a huge slab of ham that was not cut for him and that he hardly managed to nibble on; or the mother started to reminisce about her life and forgot to finish her cooking. Jamal continually had a bottle available to him which might contain milk or Koolaid or nothing, but he was never observed to use it for nutritional purposes.

Jamal's parents were not worried about his failure to gain weight, and responded to the pediatrician's and our concerns with benign puzzlement. They pointed out that Jamal had so much energy he could not possibly be weak from lack of eating, and were convinced that he would eventually catch up.

Our own view was that Jamal, an unusually active baby, had responded to his unstructured and unstructuring environment with precocious investment in motor activity to provide himself with more organized and manageable stimulation than his environment was able to offer him. Although he was well-coordinated, his constant activity had a compulsive, perseverative quality and a lack of goal-directedness that suggested a primitive form of self-stimulation. This inordinate investment in gross motor activity, which might have originated as a coping response to extreme absence of structure, seemed now to have become a partial determinant of Jamal's FTT because it interfered with his capacity to become aware of and respond to his hunger cues. In our view, Jamal's environment had not provided him at a crucial age with the reciprocal feeding exchanges necessary to help him develop adequate schemes of the relationship between hunger, feeding, and the social interaction mediating these experiences of need and satiation. Jamal's response to this environmental failure had been two-fold: a loss of interest in food and quick decline in weight, which stabilized below the third percentile, and a concomitant turn to motor activity as a source of self-contingency and self-stimulation in the face of his mother's failure to serve as a responsive partner in the establishment of reciprocal patterns of interaction.

Vignette #4. Claude was the second child of a single mother living in poverty and estranged from her family of origin since early adolescence. Mrs. S. and her two children lived in unstable and chaotic circumstances, sharing a small apartment with a large number of unrelated adults and their children. In spite of the difficult conditions, Mrs. S. was very committed to her children and, at 6 months, Claude clearly differentiated her as his primary caregiver. Mrs. S. brought Claude regularly for his pediatric appointments and established a close, nurturing relationship with a public health nurse who visited the home regularly and often. This situation was disrupted when Claude had to be hospitalized at 6 months for an intestinal obstruction. During the hospitalization, Claude's weight began to drop off, and by seven months it had declined from the 20th to the third percentile. Soon after his discharge, the friendly public health nurse was transferred to another service, and Mrs. S. refused admission to her successor. Extensive medical testing of Claude over the next two months failed to reveal organic causes for Claude's growth failure, and in his ninth month he was simultaneously referred to our program and hospitalized for the second time, now with a diagnosis of non-organic FTT.

From our observations and interviews with Claude and his mother on the ward and in our playroom, we came to feel that both mother and child had become acutely estranged from each other by the stresses of the first hospitalization and by the mother's bitter mourning for the almost simul- taneous loss of the public health nurse. The current circumstances had exacerbated latent conflicts about intimacy, mutuality and dependency which were rooted in the mother's early history of abandonment, neglect, and parental loss. Mother and child seemed overwhelmed by their own individual predicaments and emotionally unavailable to each other. Mrs. S., already stressed by her poverty and chaotic living conditions, now had to face her child's health difficulties and the implicit indictment of her mothering skills without the help of her cherished professional ally, the public health nurse. She responded with sullen anger and withdrawal, both from Claude and from our own efforts to understand her situation. Claude's age-appropriate capacity to initiate interactions and to respond positively were severely strained by the separation from his mother during his first hospitalization, by the stresses of surgery, and by his mother's psycholog- ical unavailability when he needed her the most to recover his develop- mental momentum.

During the months following Claude's second hospital discharge, we witnessed a mother-child interaction characterized by mutual aloofness and an intolerance on both sides for the expression of pleasure in the relation- ship or of dependency needs. Claude angrily rejected his mother's over- tures when she attempted sometimes to console him for some injury or to entice him to play. Mrs. S., on the other hand, tended to keep her dis- tance, and applauded Claude's displays of anger as expressions of "tough- ness" and "badness" which were valuable character traits in a hostile and unreliable world. The only mutuality of affect that we observed was in the form of sadomasochistic games which often ended in overt displays of mutual anger and subsequent disorganization, followed again by mutual aloofness. Thus, in this dyad, we saw not a failure to establish interac- tive rhythms and patterns around food or other dependency needs, but rather the establishment of a particularly rigid, dysfunctional and con- stricted interactive pattern.

INITIATIVE AND THE BALANCE OF EXPLORATION
AND ATTACHMENT: 8-14 MONTHS

When a child of 8-14 months declines to eat, we have a qualitatively different situation from that of the neonate who is not given and/or is unable to use available environmental support to coordinate focused sucking, or from the 3 to 7 month old who has failed to become an active partner in reciprocal and sustained rhythms of eating with his/her caregiver. In many of the referrals we receive where the onset of growth failure occurs in the latter part of the first year of life, onset coincides with weaning and the introduction of new foods. Many of these cases are rather quickly resolved as infant and environment adapt to the new development, labelled variously "separation-individuation" initiative (Mahler et al., 1975), "imitation and internalization" (Greenspan, 1981), "initiative and focalization" (Sander, 1962). The new phase is characterized by major maturational and developmental shifts in psychological organization. Its hallmarks are the beginning of independent locomotion, which brings with it the capacity for the concept of "if not here, then somewhere else" and the closely linked onset of fearful distress reactions to separations from primary caregivers. Ainsworth (1973) described the exquisite balance between exploration and attachment behaviors through the concept of the mother as a "secure base" which serves as the child's physical and emotional anchor for ever-widening forays. Active exploration of the environment becomes a permanent feature of infant behavior, and for the first time caregivers must monitor, facilitate and, inevitably interfere with infant initiatives. The adaptive caregiving environment (Greenspan, 1981) is able to make room for and encourage the infant's new initiatives in the area of feeding (as elsewhere) by permitting some self-feeding, respecting food preferences, and allowing some exploratory manipulation of food, while continuing to provide the structure and assistance which the infant still requires at mealtimes. In many ways, the so-called "independence" of the older infant makes far greater and more complex demands on the caregiver than did the relative helplessness and receptivity of the younger infant. It demands of the caregiver the capacity for continued libidinal availability (Mahler, 1975) in the face of the infant's developmentally prompted forays into increasingly independent and volitional functioning. The degree to which distal modes of communication (i.e. gaze, speech) are available to the dyad plays a crucial role in the psychological bridging of the increasing physical distance between caregiver and child.

A critical distinction between this phase and the one preceding it is the shift in the quality of the child's contribution. Whereas the younger infant makes some contingent adaptation to the caregiver's feeding practices, however pathological, the older infants are often actively refusing food via an ego-syntonic, choice-like mechanism made possible by the coalescence of a sense of self prompted by cognitive and, especially, motor advances. Chatoor and Egan (1983) described refusal to eat during this phase as an effort made by the infant to gain autonomy from the mother.

In our clinical population of infants with non-organic FTT beginning in the last quarter of the first year, we frequently find a striking environmental (parental) intolerance for infant initiative. These mothers tend to feel rejected by their infants' forays away from them and/or put upon by their infants' actively initiated demands.

Clinical Vignettes

Vignette #5. Candy, referred to us in her 11th month, was a friendly baby who, in our developmental assessment, showed an unusual capacity for sustained concentration on visual and fine motor exploration and relatively little active locomotion. She was quite compliant and responded somewhat precociously to maternal prohibitions. However, her mother, Mrs. M., complained angrily that in the past few months Candy had become "extremely active" and was "into everything." She felt intruded upon by the new need

269

to protect Candy from injuring herself, and to protect the family's more delicate possessions from Candy's "attacks." In fact, Candy had had several minor accidents in the month prior to the referral. Mrs. M. had attempted to resolve these difficulties by having Candy spend most of her time in a walker, which enabled the infant to move about the home but effectively prevented her from exploring her environment with her hands and mouth. Both when playing with Candy and when feeding her, Mrs. M. attempted to control her rather vigorously, to prevent bad habits (i.e. using her left hand or making a mess) and to instill good ones (i.e. waving bye-bye, being polite). Mrs. M. was clearly disturbed and angered by Candy's rather mild resistance to her efforts to control, and seemed actually relieved when Candy, who was often fed in the walker, wheeled away. No attempt was made to encourage and cajole her into continuing what appeared to be a frustrating interaction for both. In fact, Mrs. M. seemed rather quickly to become absorbed in activities of her own, and often responded with irritation and a sense of being intruded upon when Candy made active attempts to re-engage her or continue her feeding. As a result, Candy's food intake was less than adequate for her age.

Exploration with the infant-parent psychotherapist revealed a clear link between the mother's efforts to curtail Candy's sense of initiative and her buried resentment about the sacrifices and restrictions imposed on her by the role of wife and mother. In particular, the conflict between Mrs. M. and her much older husband, who staunchly objected to his wife's wishes to work, to learn to drive, and to have some interests independent from her husband and baby, found displaced expression in Mrs. M.'s intolerance of her infant's attempts to regulate her own activity.

Vignette #6. Habib, also referred in his 11th month, was a very active and determined little boy who resisted his mother's constant but ineffectual efforts to control him by writhing, kicking, spitting and enraged screams. One got the bizarre impression watching this dyad that the infant was the stronger of the two. While Mrs. H. clearly adored her baby, time and again she permitted him to defeat her. Habib's eating problem began during a severe gastrointestinal illness which lasted a month and during which Habib either vomited or had explosive diarrhea after every feeding. After recovery, Habib's appetite remained erratic and he often resisted being fed. Mrs. H., who was very young, illiterate and unsophisticated, clearly felt that it was cruel and sadistic to insist on feeding a resistant infant. In work with Mrs. H., it became clear that for her there were two possible modes of relating: communion or conflict. Negotiated settlements were not part of her repertoire. What she most enjoyed with Habib was holding him in her arms while he slept. She was frightened by the angry impulses his "naughty" behavior admittedly aroused in her, and seemed to compensate for this by seeing him as very powerful and precociously able to determine what he needed, both at mealtimes and in other situations. Further exploration revealed a buried conflict between Mrs. H. and her husband and his family, with whom she lived. It seems that in becoming pregnant with Habib, Mrs. H. had been more assertive than ever before, defying her husband's family's advice to have an abortion and wait until the family was more financially secure. In the face of their continuing criticism and hostility, Mrs. H. had retreated quietly into depression. We hypothesized that her buried rage and thwarted assertiveness had been projected and displaced onto her son, and that she derived a vicarious gratification from his ability to be in control.

EMERGING INTERNALIZATION: 18-30 MONTHS

In moving on to discuss the oldest infants in our clinical population, those with an onset of FTT between 18 months and 30 months, we enter what is clearly a transitional area between the primarily interactional conflicts of the earlier stages and the more truly intrapsychic conflicts of emotionally disturbed children and adults. While the histories of these older infants suggest that earlier feeding difficulties are instrumental in establishing a vulnerability to symptom formation in this area, we have found a group in whom avoidance of eating seems to meet the criteria for conflict-based symptom formation in that it has important symbolic significance and represents a compromise formation between conflicting tendencies in the infant.

This is an age at which, under normal circumstances, eating and other issues of body management begin to emerge from the context of the mother-infant relationship into the realm of autonomous function. If, as Winnicott said, "there is no such thing as a baby," there very definitely is such a thing as a toddler, as any healthy toddler seems at pains to make unmistakably clear. Behaviors, and in particular social negotiations, seem guided by what Brazelton (1983) called the "I am not you" principle. The infant becomes increasingly invested in self-managing, partly because new cognitive and motor achievements offer endlessly interesting possibilities in this regard and partly because his more sophisticated notions about self and other and the exponential increase in environmental prohibitions and expectations heighten the toddler's awareness of the potential conflict between his wishes and those of others and between opposing wishes inside himself (i.e. to possess something and to destroy it, to go and to come, etc.). This stage is characterized by the emergence of ambivalent conflicts which are complexly related to the development and structuring of internal self and object constancy. The toddler does not handle these conflicts smoothly, and is prone to acute behavioral disorganization and distress under their pressure. The caregiver is then called upon to function as an auxiliary ego to supplement the immature synthetic capacities of the toddler's ego. The caregiver is also called upon to be tolerant and supportive, and, by repeated efforts to negotiate, cajole, impose and concede, model for the infant less disruptive and disorganizing modes of conflict resolution. Parents whose own early history has left them with unresolved ambivalence and constricted and inflexible modes of conflict resolution find this modeling difficult to do, and often have grave difficulty helping the toddler in the management of aggression. In the two vignettes that follow, the eating inhibition seems in some degree to represent a symbolic expression of the infant's concerns regarding the consequences of aggression, as well as a response to maternal conflict in this area.

Clinical Vignettes

Vignette #7. Kirk was referred to us at 30 months for non-organic FTT, but his weight decline had begun when he was 20 months old and in the intervening 10 months he had failed to gain any weight at all. He was an emaciated child with a high activity level whose mother alternatively cradled him in her arms as if he was a baby, pushed him away from her, and warned him about the perils he was risking when he engaged in seemingly the most harmless of activities. Mrs. R.'s complaints about her son were endless, and the symptoms she described were indeed worrisome. He ran away from his mother in unfamiliar places, regularly ran away from home, was accident-prone, refused to be toilet trained, had frequent and prolonged temper tantrums and liked to destroy his toys. In Mrs. R.'s eyes, however, all these worries paled in comparison with Kirk's refusal to eat. The battles between mother and child at mealtimes ended either in Mrs. R. giving up and feeling like a helpless victim, or with her getting furious at Kirk and beating him up. During feedings, Mrs. R. expected Kirk to sit perfectly still in his highchair and to eat neatly from a daintily arranged dish. Kirk invariably climbed down from the highchair and wandered off, ignoring his mother's entreaties to return. Between mealtimes, Kirk exhibited an unusual behavior: he constantly helped himself from the shelves and the refrigerator to food items that he would taste, spit out, and throw away in places hidden from his mother's view.

Kirk's birth had created severe tension between Mrs. R. and her husband, who had several grown children from a previous marriage and wanted no more children. Mrs. R. had hidden her pregnancy from him, and managed to keep her weight at 96 pounds until her sixth month of pregnancy. She then revealed that she was pregnant and gained 50 pounds in three months. Mr. R., feeling shocked and betrayed, stopped talking to his wife until after Kirk was born. A successful businessman, he took on a grueling work schedule and spent most of the time away from home. Kirk's mother responded by bringing Kirk into the marital bed, while the father slept in his studio downstairs.

Kirk's mother returned to work soon after his birth and left him in the care of a warm and loving woman who he called "mommy." Kirk spent 10 hours a day in this woman's home.

Although described by his mother as a difficult and fussy infant, Kirk gained weight adequately until he was 20 months. At that time, Mrs. R. suffered a miscarriage and, beset by feelings of inadequacy and guilt, she quit her job, removed Kirk from the babysitter's care, and decided to devote all her energies to raising him. She found this a frustrating chore, and felt rejected and unloved by her son. Kirk's weight loss after the separation from his babysitter was particularly wounding to her.

We believe that, at 20 months, Kirk's increased resistance to eating represented an age-appropriate expression of distress and bewilderment over the loss of his babysitter. The symptom may have been determined both by depressive loss of appetite and by infantile theories about what makes things vanish (i.e. eating them) applied to the loss of his beloved caregiver. He may have closely associated eating with the comforting presence and pleasurable interaction with the sitter. His behavior of repeated tasting, spitting out, and throwing away food items, which is quite different from a flat refusal of or disinterest in food, suggests a disappointed expectation followed by anxiety, as if in a concrete way he expected that eating would invoke the comforting presence of his sitter, yet also associated food intake with her disappearance.

Kirk was not helped to resolve his feelings of grief through his parents' support because his father was physically and psychologically unavailable and because his mother interpreted his behavior as personal rejection. Feeding then became the arena in which the family conflicts that had been triggered by Kirk's conception and birth were most forcefully expressed. From what could have been a temporary response to object loss, food refusal became for Kirk an entrenched symbolic expression of his efforts at separateness from a mother who, in her own desperate loneliness, either attempted to engulf and seduce him, or who in exasperation abused him and pushed him away. The self-destructive character of Kirk's solution is apparent from the constellation of other symptoms that accompanied his FTT.

Vignette #8. Diana, referred to us at 24 months, started to show a weight decline at 20 months, coinciding with her mother's pregnancy. Diana's two older sisters were of school age, and Diana had been very close to her overprotective mother and unable to separate from her.

Mrs. H. was a recent immigrant who found herself socially isolated in an unfamiliar culture, missed her family of origin, and found herself often tearful and easily overwhelmed by the care of her children. Her new pregnancy had rekindled intense longings to return home, and she was often self-absorbed and affectively unavailable to Diana. Yet she remained a conscientious caregiver. She cooked the foods she had enjoyed in her own country, and she hovered, urged, and pressured Diana to eat while remaining oblivious to Diana's own cues. In fact, our observations showed clearly that Diana's intake was inversely proportionate to the amount of encouragement she received from her mother: she ate well if Mrs. H. was not attending to her.

Our formulation was that mealtimes became a setting for the distorted expression of conflict and aggression between mother and daughter. Mrs. H. was a passive woman who could not allow herself to express aggression and who could not tolerate it from her daughter; in fact, she conveyed the impression that she would be deeply wounded by even temporary withdrawal of her children's love. Her overprotectiveness and her excessive concern with Diana's food intake might be seen simultaneously as an identification with Diana and an expression of her wishes to be taken care of (for example, by eating again the food associated with her own childhood) and as a disguised expression of her hostility towards her daughter. For Diana, the direct expression of anger and autonomous strivings was likely to be a frightening experience given her mother's clear cues of vulnerability to perceived loss of love. Thus, Diana's refusal to eat might have the function of permitting some expression of aggression towards her mother while simultaneously effecting an inhibition of oral aggression. In other words, we speculate that Diana was experiencing a conflict between impulses to attack and separate from her mother and wishes to protect her and remain close to her. Refusing to eat was a symptom which represented a compromise formation between these two tendencies.

CONCLUSION AND IMPLICATIONS

The changing psychodynamic issues associated with the onset of eating disorders at different phases during infancy have been well recognized (Call, 1980, 1982; Chatoor & Egan, 1983). We have attempted to elaborate on this recognition by tracing a developmental line in severe disturbances of eating diagnosed as non-organic FTT. Such disturbances closely parallel and reflect the changing nature of the infant-parent relationship in the first two years of life. The onset of the condition is linked to an impasse or failure in the negotiation of adaptive solutions to the developmental challenges of a given phase. One might speculate that these disturbances serve a defensive purpose which might be akin to the pathological defenses in infancy described by Fraiberg (1982).

It is hardly necessary to belabor the clinical importance of distinguishing FTT cases that can be understood within this paradigm from cases where more simply (but perhaps more ominously) the failure to gain weight is due to actual withholding of food (e.g., Shapiro, Fraiberg & Adelson, 1976). In the cases described food withholding was not the primary reason for FTT. Instead, the condition was the result of a complex interaction in which both infant and caregiver were active contributors to an interaction dysynchrony.

Recognition of the mutuality of influences between infant and caregiver in the onset of FTT is important for nosological accuracy, for the conceptualization of approaches to treatment, and for future research. Each of these areas will be discussed below.

Nosological Accuracy

The more immediate implication of our findings is that assessment of
the infant-caregiver dyad is crucial in clarifying the etiology of FTT.
Dyadic interaction in itself presents important clues to the origins of the
disorder, and these clues differ with the unfolding developmental tasks
encountered by the dyad. In this sense, assessment of the dyadic interaction in infant psychopathology is akin to the assessment of clinical symptoms in child and adult psychotherapy. Winicott quipped that "there is no
such thing as a baby," meaning that a baby's individuality is inseparable
from the mother's caregiving. In assessing psychopathology in infancy,
attention to the transactional processes between infant and caregiver are
more promising for nosological accuracy than is diagnostic categorization
of the infant alone because the infant's condition has often not yet been
internalized as a stable individual pattern. Emphasis on the interactional
process may help to discard the clinically misleading dichotomy between
organic and non-organic FTT with maternal deprivation. In our clinical
experience, attention to the interactional manifestations that are concomitant with a child's failure to gain weight has frequently been useful in
ruling out psychopathology. In many cases the finding of basically adaptive interactional patterns has served to redirect the clinical inquiry to
familial genetic patterns or to as yet undetected medical problems.

Specificity of Treatment Approaches

Nosological accuracy should go hand in hand with specificity of
treatment, and the present framework has important therapeutic implications. Optimally, treatment approaches in infant mental health need to
weave together developmental guidance to the parents with a therapeutic
handling of the conflicts experienced by the parents towards the child.
Therapeutic techniques tend to work best when they are responsive to the
parents' spontaneous concerns and to observed areas of conflict in the
parent-child interaction, rather than when they follow a pre-determined
developmental curriculum (Fraiberg, 1980). The present framework provides
guidelines for the observation of developmentally relevant and affectively
charged areas of infant-parent interaction. These guidelines may alert
the therapist to the most salient areas for clinical enquiry at different
developmental stages.

Different emphasis in the intervention may be appropriate at different developmental stages. In cases where there are difficulties in the
regulation of neurophysiological processes, for example, much attention
may be given to helping the parents understand and accept the baby's
characteristics as an individual pattern and not as an expression of the
baby's rejection of them. The clinician may also support the parents in
experimenting with different feeding practices until they find methods
that seem comfortable for them and for their baby. In cases where there
is a failure to develop age-appropriate mutual responsiveness, the intervention may focus most profitably on helping the parents to notice and to
respond to the baby's signals in a variety of situations, both at mealtimes and elsewhere. When feeding has become a battleground over autonomy,
the clinician might do well to focus on this mutual struggle for control,
suggesting alternatives to defuse the negativism associated with mealtimes.
Finally, when the conflicts over food appear to have been internalized by
the infant, the mode of treatment may incorporate individual therapy
sessions with the child in addition to developmental guidance and infant-
parent psychotherapy.

Future Research

An important area for future research involves the usefulness of the present conceptualization for issues of prognosis. Are there different rates of recovery associated with onset of FTT at different developmental stages? What are the other factors that interact with the time of onset to predict the child's recovery?

Future research may also focus on the extent to which the infant's concurrent developmental functioning may be differentially affected by the time of onset of FTT. It is possible, for example, that in the first three months the child's failure to gain weight is the single major detectable symptom of malfunction, but that the quantity and severity of dysfunction in cognitive, affective and social development increase when the condition appears during later stages. This may give an indication of the relative function of FTT as a signal of infant distress at different developmental stages. While the major implication of our clinical findings is that FTT is an indicator of pervasive developmental disturbances, it would be helpful to have systematic documentation of the relationship between disorders of eating and growth on the one hand and developmentally specific dysfunctions in affective, social and cognitive functioning on the other.

REFERENCES

Ainsworth, M.D.A. The development of infant-mother attachment. In B. Caldwell & H. Ricciuti (Eds.), Review of Child Development Research (Vol. 3, pp. 1-94). Chicago: University of Chicago, 1973.

Ainsworth, M.D.A. Attachment as related to mother-infant interaction. In J.S. Rosenblatt, R.A. Hinde, C.Beer & M. Busnell (Eds.), Advances in the Study of Behavior (pp. 1-73). New York: Academic Press, 1979.

Ainsworth, M.D.A., Blehar, M., Waters, E. & Wall, S. Patterns of Attachment: A Psychological Study of the Strange Situation. Hillsdale, N.J.: Lawrence Erlbaum Associates, 1978.

Barbero, A.J. & Shaheen, E. Environmental failure to thrive: A clinical view. Journal of Pediatrics, 1967, 71, 639-644.

Bowlby, J. Attachment and Loss, Vol. I, Attachment. New York: Basic Books, 1969.

Brazelton, T. Psychophysiologic reactions in the neonate. Journal of Pediatrics, 1961, 58, 508-512.

Brazelton, T. Neonatal Behavioral Assessment (National Spastic Society Monographs, Clinics in Developmental Medicine No. 50). London: W. Heinemann & Sons (1973).

Brazelton, T. Infants can't wait. Opening address at National Training Conference, National Center for Clinical Infant Programs, Washington, D.C., November, 1983.

Brazelton, T., Koslowski, B. & Main, M. The origins of reciprocity: The early mother-infant interaction. In M. Lewis & L. Rosenblum (Eds.), The Effect of the Infant on its Caregiver (pp. 49-76). New York: Wiley, 1974.

Bretherton, I. & Bates, E. The emergence of intentional communication. New Directions, 1979, 4, 81-100.

Brody, Sylvia Patterns of Mothering: Maternal Influence During Infancy. New York: International Universities Press, 1956.

Burns, P., Sander, L., Stechler, A. & Julia, H. Distress in feeding: Short-term effects of caretaker environment on the first ten days. Journal of the American Academy of Child Psychiatry, 1972, 11, 427-439.

Call, J. Attachment disorders in infancy. In H. Kaplan, A.M. Freedman & B.J. Sadock (Eds.), A Comprehensive Textbook of Psychiatry, Vol. 3. New York: Williams & Williams, 1980.

Call, J. Towards a nostology of psychiatric disorders in infancy. In J.
    Call, E. Galenson & R.L. Tyson (Eds.), Frontiers of Infant Psychiatry
    (pp. 117-128). New York: Basic Books, 1982.
Chatoor, I. & Egan, J. Non-organic failure to thrive and dwarfism due to
    food refusal: A separation disorder. Journal of the American Academy
    of Child Psychiatry, 1983, 22, 294-301.
Clemente, C.D., Purpura, D.P. & Mayer, F.E. (Eds.) Sleep and the Maturing
    Nervous System. New York: Academic Press, 1972.
Drotar, D., Malone, C. & Negray, J. Environmentally based failure to
    thrive and children's intellectual development. Journal of Clinical
    Child Psychology, 1980, 236-240.
Emde, R.N., Gaensbauer, T. & Harmon, R.J. Emotional expression in infancy:
    A biobehavioral study. Psychological Issues, Monograph 10. New
    York: International Universities Press, 1976.
Erikson, E. Childhood and Society. New York: W.W. Norton, 1963.
Escalona, S.K. Roots of Individuality. Chicago: Aldine, 1968.
Ferholt, J. & Provence, S. An infant with psychophysiological vomiting.
    Psychoanalytic Study of the Child, 1976, 31, 439-459.
Fraiberg, S. Notes on Infant and Preschool Programs in Jerusalem.
    Unpublished manuscript, 1978.
Fraiberg, S. Clinical Studies in Infant Mental Health: The First Year of
    Life. New York: Basic Books, 1980.
Fraiberg, S. Pathological defenses in infancy. Psychoanalytic Quarterly
    1982, 51, 612-634.
Fraiberg, S., Adelson, E. & Shapiro, V. Ghosts in the nursery: A psycho-
    analytic approach to the problems of impaired mother-infant relation-
    ships. Journal of the American Academy of Child Psychiatry, 1976,
    14, 387-421.
Freud, A. Normality and Pathology in Childhood. New York: International
    Universities Press, 1965.
Glasser, M. & Lieberman, A.F. Failure to thrive: An interactional perspec-
    tive. In L. Zegans, L. Temoshok, C. Van Dyke (Eds.), Emotions in
    Health and Illness (pp. 199-207). San Diego: Grune & Stratton,
    1984.
Greenspan, S.I. Intelligence and Adaptation: An Integration of Psychoana-
    lytic and Piagetian Developmental Psychology. New York: International
    Universities Press, 1979.
Greenspan, S.I. Psychopathology and adaptation: Principles of clinical
    diagnosis and preventive intervention. Clinical Infant Reports, #1,
    National Center for Clinical Infant Programs. New York: International
    Universities Press, 1981.
Greenspan, S.I. & Lieberman, A.F. Infants, mothers and their interaction:
    A quantitative approach to developmental assessment. In S. Greenspan
    & G. Pollock (Eds.), The Course of Life, Vol. I: Infancy and Early
    Childhood (pp. 271-312). U.S. Department of Human Services, 1980.
Greenspan, S.I. & Porgess, S.W. Psychopathology in infancy and early
    childhood: Clinical perspectives on the organization of sensory and
    affective thematic experience. Child Development, 1984, 55, 49-70.
Korner, A. The effect of the infant's state, level of arousal, sex and
    ontogenetic stage on the caregiver. In M. Lewis & L. Rosenblum
    (Eds.), The Effect of the Infant on its Caregiver (pp. 105-121). New
    York: Wiley, 1974.
Leonard, M., Rhymes, J. & Solnit, A. Failure to thrive in infants.
    American Journal of Diseases of Children, 1966, 3, 600-612.
Lewis, M. & Rosenblum, L.A. The Effect of the Infant on its Caregiver.
    New York: Wiley, 1974.
Lieberman, A.F. Infant-parent psychotherapy during pregnancy. In S.
    Provence (Ed.), Infants and Parents: Clinical Case Reports (pp. 85-
    141). New York: International Universities Press, 1983.
Lieberman, A.F., Pekarsky, J.H. & Pawl, J.H. The integration of infant
    mental health and health care in a department of pediatrics: Toward

a comprehensive infant mental health program for a community. Symposium presented at the 10th International Association for Child and Adolescent Psychiatry and Allied Professions. Dublin, Ireland July, 1982.

Mahler, M., Pine, F. & Bergman, A. The Psychological Birth of the Human Infant: Symbiosis and Individuation. New York: Basic Books, 1975.

Murphy, L. The Widening World of Childhood: Paths Toward Mastery. New York: Basic Books, 1962.

Papousek, H. & Papousek, M. Interactional failures: Their origins and significance in infant psychiatry. In J. Call, E. Galenson & R. Tyson (Eds.), Frontiers of Infant Psychiatry (pp. 31-37). New York: Basic Books, 1983.

Pawl, J.H. & Pekarsky, J.H. Infant-parent psychotherapy: A family in crisis. In S. Provence (Ed.), Infants and Parents: Clinical Case Reports (pp. 39-84). New York: International Universities Press, 1983.

Pekarsky, J.H. Infant mental health consultation in a well-baby clinic. Zero to Three: Bulletin of the National Center for Clinical Infant Programs, 1-4, 1981.

Piaget, J. The Origins of Intelligence in Children. New York: International Universities Press, 1952.

Sander, L. Issues in early mother-child interaction. Journal of the American Academy of Child Psychiatry, 1962, 1, 141-166.

Sander, L. Infant and caretaking environment: Investigation and conceptualization of adaptive behavior in a system of increasing complexity. In E.J. Anthony (Ed.), Explorations in Child Psychiatry (pp. 129-166). New York: Plenum Press, 1975.

Shapiro, V., Fraiberg, S. & Adelson, E. Infant-parent psychotherapy on behalf of a child in a critical nutritional state. Psychoanalytic Study of the Child, 1976, 31, 461-491.

Spitz, Rene The First Year of Life. New York: International Universities Press, 1965.

Sroufe, L. Socioemotional development. In J. Osofsky (Ed.), Handbook of Infant Development (pp. 402-416). New York: Wiley, 1979.

Sroufe, L. Infant-caregiver attachment and patterns of adaptation in preschool: The roots of maladaptation and competence. In M. Perlmutter (Ed.), Minnesota Symposium on Child Psychology, 1983.

Sroufe, L. & Waters, E. The ontogenesis of smiling and laughter: A perspective on the organization of development in infancy. Psychological Review, 1976, 83, 173-189.

Sroufe, L. & Wunsch, J. The development of laughter in the first year of life. Child Development, 1972, 43, 1326-1344.

Stern, D. A microanalysis of mother-infant interaction: Behavior regulating social contact between a mother and her 3-1/2 month-old twins. Journal of the American Academy of Child Psychiatry, 1971, 10, 501-517.

Stern, D. Mother and infant at play: The dydic interaction involving facial, vocal, and gaze behaviors. In M. Lewis & L. Rosenblum (Eds.), The Effect of the Infant on its Caregiver (pp. 187-213). New York: Wiley, 1974.

Thomas, A., Chess, S., Birch, H. & Hertzig, M. Behavioral Individuality in Early Childhood. New York: New York University Press, 1963.

Wolff, P. Observations on the early development of smiling. In B. Foss (Ed.), Determinants of Infant Behavior. London: Methuen, 1963.

BEHAVIORAL APPROACHES TO THE TREATMENT OF FAILURE TO THRIVE

Thomas R. Linscheid and L. Kaye Rasnake

College of Medicine, The Ohio State University and Columbus

Children's Hospital

INTRODUCTION

The purpose of this chapter is three-fold: To differentiate two
distinct types of non-organic FTT; to show how behavioral principles are
utilized in the diagnosis and treatment of each type; and to propose an
interaction model as the appropriate paradigm for assessment and treatment
planning.

Surprisingly, it has only been in the last 10 to 15 years that the
infant has been viewed as contributing to the amount and type of interaction which it receives. In a series of studies, Richard Q. Bell (1968,
1971, 1974) developed a child-effect conceptual model in which infant
characteristics have major influences on parents' behavior. He summarized
his position by stating that "parent behavior is organized hierarchically
within repertoires in the areas of social response and control. Reasonable
bases exist for assuming that there are congenital contributors to child
behavior which (a) activate these repertoires, (b) affect the level of
response within hierarchies, and (c) differentially reinforce parent behavior which has been evoked" (Bell, 1968). Recent research has demonstrated
this reciprocity or bidirectionality of infant-parent interaction related
to variables such as infant temperament (Crockenberg & Smith, 1982), developmental status of the infant (Crawford, 1982; Green, Gustafson & West,
1980), sex of the infant (Block, 1976; Frisch, 1976) and abnormal infant
caregiver relationships (Crittendon, 1981; Frodi & Lamb, 1980).

Bell's (1968) assertion that infant or child behavior can differentially reinforce parents' behavior forms the core of the behavioral approach
to analysis and treatment of non-organic FTT. This will become apparent in
the following sections which describe not only the importance of contingency
-based interactions for normal development but how specific interactions in
the feeding situation itself can contribute to decreased food intake and
consequently FTT in infants and children.

The infant or child's ability to affect the behavior of the caregiver
was dramatically demonstrated in a single subject study reported by
Thompson, Palmer and Linscheid (1977). In their study, a 30 month old male
child whose diet was totally devoid of meats, fruits and vegetables was
treated using behavioral procedures to be described later. The mother was
observed feeding her child for three baseline sessions, the therapist then

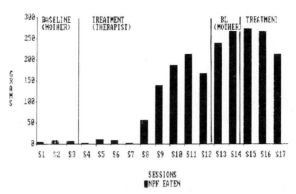

Figure 1. Behavioral feeding treatment

conducted nine feeding treatment sessions until the child had reached pre-
established treatment goals. Following treatment, the mother returned as
feeder for two return-to-baseline meals. The mother did not watch the
treatment sessions, was not told what techniques were being used or how her
child had done during treatment, and was not told what to do during the
return-to-baseline phase. Figure 1 demonstrates clearly that the child
learned to eat previously nonpreferred foods during the treatment phase and
continued to do so when mother returned to the feeding situation. A mother-
child interaction analysis revealed that mother's criticism of her child
dropped from 7 percent of her responses during baseline to 0 percent of her
responses during return-to-baseline. Positive statements (verbal positive
reinforcement) rose from 12 to 23 percent of her responses. The child
increased the percent of cooperative responses (e.g. eating, complying with
a request) from 18 to 53 percent and reduced noncooperative responses from
41 to 21 percent.

These data clearly demonstrate that the mother was capable of reducing
her criticisms and increasing her positive verbal comments to her child
based entirely on a change in her child's behavior. Observation of the
mother during baseline led most observers to conclude that she was overly
critical, was not capable of verbally reinforcing her child and was generally overinvolved with his behavior. Observation during return-to-baseline
revealed a mother who was appropriately and pleasantly interacting with her
child. The change in her behavior was entirely attributable to a change in
the child's eating behavior.

The Thompson et al. (1977) study demonstrates two very important
points. First, the feeder-child interaction is truly bidirectional in that
the child is capable of affecting the feeder's behavior significantly.
Second, the dramatic change in mother's behavior without specific instruction warns against ascribing the cause of the feeding problem to mother's
pretreatment behavior. Her ineffective pretreatment behaviors may well be
a result of her child's food refusal rather than the cause.

The two types of non-organic FTT which we will describe are primarily
differentiated on the basis of the child's age and the nature of the
caregiver-child interaction. While other authors have proposed two types
of non-organic FTT (Egan, Chatoor & Rosen, 1980; Harris, 1982), our formulation stresses the behavioral analysis of the caregiver-infant interaction
and the specific behaviors of each party which may contribute to the non-
organic FTT condition. We present Type I and Type II non-organic FTT as
working conceptualizations. Neither has been empirically established.

TYPE I NON-ORGANIC FAILURE TO THRIVE

The Type I non-organic FTT disorder is characterized primarily by the
early age of onset and by the dysfunctional nature of the caregiver-infant
relationship in multiple areas of interaction (not solely in the feeding
situation). This is the psychosocial disorder of infancy often diagnosed
as Reactive Attachment Disorder of Infancy (American Psychiatric Association, 1983). The DSM III diagnostic criteria include: (1) onset before 8
months of age; (2) lack of care that leads to the development of affectional
bonds; (3) lack of developmentally appropriate signs of social responsivity;
(4) weight loss or failure to gain not explained by physical disorders; and
(5) the presence of behavioral symptoms such as excessive sleep, a weak
cry, hypomotility, poor muscle tone. The diagnosis is confirmed if the
child begins to gain weight following institution of adequate caregiving.

Explanations for the presentation of the disorder focus on the concept
of attachment. In 1969, Bowlby enunciated an ethological-evolutionary
theory of attachment implying that an essential part of the ground plan of
the human species is the formation of an infant-caregiver attachment.
Attachment, in the simplest terms, is defined as an affectional tie that
one person forms to another specific individual. The child's attachment
behaviors function to predictably bring him/her and the mother-figure into
close proximity. This can occur through signals which attract the mother
or through the infant's own activity.

Behaviors that maintain closeness are not directed at a specific
individual during the first few weeks of life. However, with normal development, by six months of age, the child clearly identifies a primary caretaker and unique styles of interaction have evolved (Brazelton, 1975). The
interaction between the mother-infant pair is often described in terms of
the synchrony demonstrated. With normal attachment, evidence of reciprocity
exists so that the mother's attention level corresponds to the infant's
attention level. Other signs heralding the development of attachment are
the persistence of eye-to-eye contact between infant and caregiver, the
caregiver's sensitivity to the child's signals and ability to respond
immediately and appropriately, and the consistency in the mother's treatment of the child (Ainsworth, 1979).

The essential part of this ground plan is fulfilled except under
extraordinary circumstances when the infant experiences inadequate interaction with any one caregiver to support the formation of attachment
(Ainsworth, 1979). These circumstances frequently occur in overstressed,
multiproblemed families. The Type I non-organic FTT infant is likely to
present in a familial environment lacking financial, social and emotional
supports. This disorder may also appear in families experiencing recent
separation, such as loss of a loved one (Evans, Reinhart & Succop, 1972).
Although the infant's contribution to lack of attachment formation is
unclear, infant temperament has been consistently related to mother-infant
interactional styles (Crockenberg & Smith, 1982; Kronstadt, Oberlaid, Ferb
& Swartz, 1979; Thomas, Chess & Birch, 1968). Research findings indicate
that irritable infants, growing up in settings characterized by low support
for mothers, experience less responsive mothering and develop less secure
attachments. Whether a mother behaves responsively or unresponsively to
her infant, appears to be influenced by infant temperament, caregiver
attitudes and availability of social support systems (Crockenberg, 1981).

The research on maternal deprivation has not yet specified an acceptable minimum amount of interaction required for attachment formation.
Findings also do not permit identification of any one context of caregiver-
infant interaction as the most important for the formation of the attachment
bond. All caregiver-infant interactions provide the infant and the care-

giver with the opportunity to build up expectations of the other, whether the context is feeding, bathing, dressing, face-to-face interaction, or close bodily contact. These interactions can be viewed as opportunities for contingency experiences. Contingency experience generally refers to experiences which are controlled by or dependent upon the organism's behavior. The importance of contingency experience in facilitating infant development has been emphasized by numerous researchers (Ainsworth & Bell, 1974; Lewis & Goldberg, 1969; Ramey & Finkelstein, 1978; Watson & Ramey, 1972). Ainsworth and Bell (1974) maintain that the contingencies provided by maternal responsiveness allow the infant to learn that he/she can influence the environment. It is the infant's perception of a relationship between behavior and its consequences that is important. Ramey, Heiger and Klisz (1972) have suggested that FTT infants receive less response-contingent stimulation than normal infants. One study (Ramey, Starr, Pallas, Whitten & Reed, 1975) demonstrated that response-contingent stimulation can contribute to the remediation of developmental retardation in failure-to thrive infants. Given that the relationship between infant and caregiver is judged to be bidirectional, it can be assumed that the infant provides contingency experiences for the parent as well.

Goldberg (1977) offers an interesting view of contingency experiences in the caregiver-infant relationship which the authors believe is useful in understanding Type I non-organic FTT. Through a reconceptualization of White's (1959) theory of competence motivation, she proposes a model which "focuses upon conditions that contribute to feelings of efficacy generated in caretakers and infants by their interactions, namely the extent to which each member of the dyad provides the other contingency experiences." The infant experiences feelings of competency in the event of effective elicitation of attention and appropriate care from the environment. Feelings of effectiveness are generated in the caregiver through the ability to easily make decisions about interventions and when desireable outcomes follow the intervention decisions.

In the case of Type I non-organic FTT infants, one might interpret the dysfunctional nature of the relationship betwween caregiver and infant in terms of contingency experiences. The relationship has failed, and continues to fail to provide feelings of efficacy for either member of the dyad. The infant is unable to elicit appropriate care; the caregiver is unable to intervene effectively.

Perhaps, it should be noted that adequate nurturing encompasses a variety of behaviors; provision of the opportunity for contingency experiences is only one component. However, if we consider the presentation of Type I non-organic FTT to follow a sequence which includes behavioral mismanagement and underfeeding, the lack of contingency experiences may be the initial agent providing for the unfolding of the sequence. Little is known about how these factors interact. Certainly, the infant's lack of responsiveness, which may be a consequence of the undernutrition, perpetuates the problem.

Assessment

Assessment of Type I non-organic FTT primarily consists of two components. It is necessary to perform a direct observation of the caregiver-infant interaction. Particular attention is given to the effectiveness of the interaction and the presence or absence of contingency experiences. Is the infant demonstrating the ability to effectively indicate needs and have these needs met? Is the caregiver able to respond to the needs of the infant and feel a sense of accomplishment for appropriate intervention?

Additionally, assessment is made of the familial social environment.

What is the economic status of the family? What support systems are available to the caregiver and the family as a whole? Has the caregiver experienced a recent loss or separation?

Treatment

Interpreting Type I non-organic FTT in terms of contingency experiences results in a treatment approach aimed at developing a more functional caregiver-infant relationship. The incompetent dyad needs to be aided in establishing effective interactions. This can be accomplished through facilitating infant development and parenting skills.

More specifically, it is recommended that the infant be exposed to intensive stimulation in a variety of situations; bathing, diaper changing, feeding, playing. Since Type I non-organic FTT infants often have been sensorially deprived, it may be necessary to use a desensitization process, gently introducing physical contact and movement until the infant readily accepts this interaction (Evler, 1982). Stimulation should be provided for all senses; involving the infant in movement activities (i.e., rocking, bouncing, swaying), auditory activities (i.e., verbalizations, music), tactile activities (i.e., water, textures), olfactory stimulation, and exposure to a variety of tastes. It is important to systematically introduce activities/stimulation and to document in detail the infant's response. Nutritional treatment may be medically indicated and in and of itself can enhance the infant's responsiveness to stimulating interaction.

Within this framework, opportunities for contingency experiences should be maximized. The infant needs to learn that he/she can exhibit control over the environment. It is also necessary for the caregiver to be provided with contingency experiences to learn that they can control infant behaviors. Treatment must focus attention on the interactional system. If the relationship is to become a functional one for both members of the dyad, an effort to increase mutual contingency experiences must be made.

It is difficult to identify the amount of time required for caregivers to learn the necessary interaction skills. It is, however, known that infants can respond within approximately one week to appropriate stimulation, as evidenced by the usual course of hospitalization for Type I non-organic FTT infants. Once established, the process of contingency is self maintaining. Each member of the dyad is reinforced through generated feelings of efficacy.

Treatment typically begins in a hospital setting due to the need to medically stabilize the infant. This provides the opportunity to use a professional (i.e., nurse, developmental specialist) as a model for the caregiver in the initial phase of treatment. The professional can serve as the stimulator, helping to interpret the infant's behavior for the caregiver. It is important to point out behaviors exhibited by the infant which are purposeful and voluntary. This helps the caregiver develop the ability to read and predict infant behaviors. Emphasis should be placed on operationally defining infant behaviors, thus discouraging the caregiver from using general trait descriptors (e.g. stubbornness) as explanations of behavior. The need for immediacy of reinforcement delivery can be emphasized and demonstrated by the professional. The more immediate the reinforcement, the more effective the learning. This is particularly important with infants, due to the limited duration of their attention span. To enhance the intervention, synchronizing attention levels and establishing eye contact can be modeled for the caregiver. In addition, the ability of the infant to sense and react to the caregiver's emotional state (i.e., anxiety, fear, anger) and should be stressed. In staging the intervention, the professional should gradually transfer the responsibilities of infant care and stimulation to the caregiver, providing monitoring, coaching and support.

As noted earlier, the Type I non-organic FTT infant is frequently found within a family experiencing major financial and/or environmental stresses. Thus, engaging the caregiver in infant treatment and transferring responsibility from professional to caregiver may be very difficult tasks. Reality constraints, such as lack of transportation and care of additional children, often interfere with caregiver involvement. For this reason, it is vitally important that help from social services be provided for the family in order to establish support networks for reducing and alleviating these stresses. Additionally, the cognitive abilities of the caregiver may be a factor to be considered. Due to limitations in parents' cognitive levels, directions for caregiving may need to be stated explicitly, repeated, and modeled. If the caregiver demonstrates a limited ability to generalize, information about specific behaviors in each situation should be addressed and practiced with supervision. In such instances, simply presenting the general concept will be ineffective. In order to implement this approach the professional must work to establish a relationship with the cargiver to gain trust and confidence. This will lead to greater cooperation and acceptance of information and will provide the opportunity for the professional to help prevent the caregiver from resorting to "old habits" (i.e., patterns of interaction).

TYPE II NON-ORGANIC FAILURE TO THRIVE

Type II non-organic FTT is differentiated from Type I based on the factors of age and type of infant-caregiver interaction. Children with Type II non-organic FTT are usually at least eight months of age or older. Unlike their Type I counterparts, these children do not exhibit weight loss or failure to gain until some time after the first six months of life with the onset of the weight problem frequently occurring after 12 months of age. There is usually little or no evidence of gross neglect and the child's parent or parents may interact appropriately outside of the feeding situation. It is the feeding situation itself which becomes the focus of the struggle between parent and child. In addition to inadequate intake of calories, the child is likely to exhibit developmentally inappropriate feeding behaviors and food preferences (i.e., texture and variety). The Type II non-organic FTT child may show normal or slightly delayed development in areas other than feeding.

The authors view Type II non-organic FTT as occurring in situations in which the child is capable of explicit and very direct control over interaction situations. It makes sense then that this type of disorder begins to occur at a time of transition in the feeding process when control of feeding is being shifted from the caregiver to the child. One researcher (Egan et al., 1980) views Type II non-organic FTT as a separation disorder as opposed to Type I attachment disorder. In this conceptualization, the child is seen as engaging in a struggle with the parents for autonomy over the feeding process. Food refusal during meals may represent a more global struggle for independence and separation from the parent. The situation is aggravated when the parent has difficulty relinquishing control of the feeding situation which was appropriate with the younger child.

Type II non-organic FTT should not be confused with psychosocial dwarfism, a term which has been applied to children who do not grow at an expected rate. Psychosocial dwarfism describes a constellation of symptoms in children who present with bizarre eating, drinking and sleeping behavior; social distancing; impaired intellectual development and dysfunctional parent-child relationships (Money, 1977). Because children described as having psychosical dwarfism are frequently older, it is the authors' opinion that this term is not appropriate for the child three years of age and younger who demonstrate deceleration in weight gain in the absence of the extreme symptoms described above.

It is our opinion that the causes of weight loss and feeding disturbances in the infant and the child between eight months and three years of age are multidetermined and that it is misleading to attempt to label this problem with a name which implies either that there is an unresolved conflict between parent and child (separation disorder) or that the psychosocial environment of the child is entirely responsible for the observed condition. It is most productive and most parsimonious to view these problems as related to ineffective behavioral interactions between parent and child. The term ineffective is used guardedly and implies that the interaction is ineffective, from the parent's standpoint, because the child is not consuming an age-appropriate quantity or variety of foods. On the other hand, the interaction may be extremely effective in producing a number of reinforcing conditions from the child's point of view.

A short review of the development of normal feeding patterns is appropriate at this point. Until four to six months of life infants are maintained almost exclusively on a liquid diet. Foods such as infant cereals and pureed fruits and vegetables are usually introduced between four and six months of age. The infant begins to accept chopped or table foods at about eight months of age. Illingworth and Lister (1964) describe a critical or sensitive period for the introduction of solid foods. The authors believe this period ranges between seven and ten months of age and suggest that introduction of solids past this critical stage can result in a great deal of resistance. Indeed, there is clinical anecdotal evidence suggesting that children who are maintained past this critical period on artificial feedings or liquid only diets, usually due to medical reasons, have difficulty learning to accept and swallow solid food.

Normally by 12 months of age the infant is eating three meals a day and may have one or two light snacks inbetween meals. By 15 months of age the infant should be independently eating. This includes finger feeding which begins around the sixth to eighth month and self-feeding with a spoon or other utensil which is usually possible by 12 months (Christophersen & Hall, 1978).

Normal infants triple their weight in the first year of life. This rapid weight gain is associated with a rather consistent appetite from day to day and across feeding times. After 12 months of age the rapid weight gain experienced in the first year of life decreases dramatically. A child gains between 12 and 18 lbs during the first year of life. In contrast, gains of only approximately five pounds a year occur over the next three to four years (Schwartz, 1958; Smith, 1977). This decrease in the rate of weight gain is naturally accompanied by a decrease in appetite and extreme variability in appetite and food preferences. The child may eat large quantities at one meal and show absolutely no interest in food at the next. Likewise, the child may show a strong preference for a specific food for a short period and then completely reject it for no apparent reason.

Type II feeding problems generally have their origin between six months and 18 months of age. These problems are directly related to the introduction of solid food, the process of the child becoming an independent eater, and the decrease in appetite and food preference variability which naturally occurs after one year of age. Specifically, the most common problems are: prolonged subsistence on pureed foods, multiple food dislikes, mealtime behavior problems (tantrums, spitting, etc.), bizarre

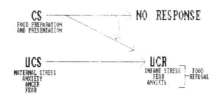

Figure 2. Classical conditioning model.

food habits and delays in self-feeding. While neurological impairment or developmental delays may contribute to these problems, they are primarily the result of behavioral interaction between the child and the caregiver.

It can be seen from the previous discussion that the type of problems described are those in which the child has voluntary control over his actions. For example, a child's refusal to accept any vegetable, despite accepting a wide variety of other food types, can only be attributed to a voluntary decision on the child's part. In performing a behavioral analysis of the disordered feeding situation two assumptions must be made. The first assumption is, except in extreme hunger, the motivation of a child for interaction with a caregiver can be stronger than the child's motivation for food itself. This is especially true once the child reaches an age in which appetite is variable. The second assumption is that stressful situations before or during meals can produce anxiety and specific fears in both the parent and the child. Additionally, these specific fears and anxieties can be elicited by elements of the feeding situation itself.

With these two assumptions in mind, Type II feeding problems can be analyzed and understood using both an operant and classical conditioning model. In the classical conditioning model (see Figure 2), caregiver anxiety is seen as the unconditioned stimulus which naturally elicits an anxiety response in the child. Food presentation is the conditioned stimulus which normally does not elicit anxiety. By pairing the conditioned stimulus (i.e., food presentation) with the unconditioned stimulus (i.e., maternal anxiety) food presentation itself will elicit anxiety in the infant. This anxiety then leads to food refusal.

Using an operant conditioning model, the feeding situation itself or food presentation per se can be seen as the antecendent event (see Figure 3). A number of consequences may serve to reinforce or increase the probability of food refusal behavior. The consequences of food refusal can be numerous but frequently include the withdrawal of the disliked food or food type, and replacement with a favorite food. Another consequence of food refusal may be the prolongation of attention from the feeder who increases attempts to get the child to accept the food. A third consequence may be that the child is removed from the feeding situation itself, which if the child is not hungry or is experiencing distress in the feeding situation, may be maintained through negative reinforcement.

Assessment

With these two learning models in mind, the first step in treating a Type II feeding problem is to assess the present feeding habits of both the feeder and the child. This is done by (1) collecting a thorough history of the child's feeding patterns, food preferences and a description of the typical mealtime, and (2) actually observing the child and feeder interacting during several meals.

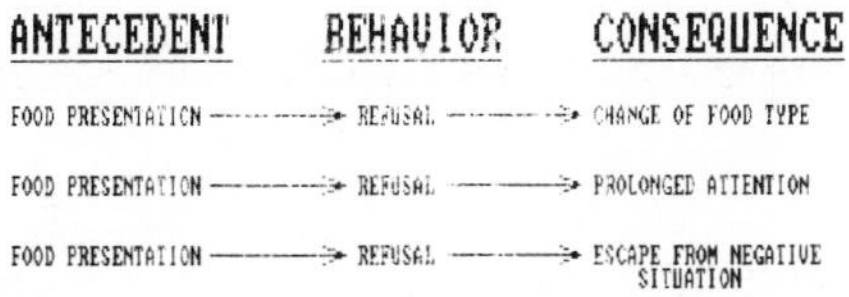

```
    ANTECEDENT    BEHAVIOR    CONSEQUENCE

FOOD PRESENTATION ------------->  REFUSAL --------------->  CHANGE OF FOOD TYPE

FOOD PRESENTATION ------------->  REFUSAL  --------------->  PROLONGED ATTENTION

FOOD PRESENTATION ------------->  REFUSAL  --------------->  ESCAPE FROM NEGATIVE
                                                            SITUATION
```

Figure 3. Operant conditioning model.

Questioning of parents or caregivers is very important in helping to determine how the problem developed and the specific nature of the problem at present. The parents should be asked objective questions which yield data based answers. Table 1 presents a sample questionnaire which can be used in collecting this background information. The questionnaire assesses present eating behaviors and interactions between feeder and caregiver.

In our experience, there are several strong indicators of a behaviorally-based feeding problem. The first of these is length of mealtime. Meals that last longer than 20 minutes are opportunities for parent-child interaction more than they are opportunities for food intake. Excessively long feeding sessions suggest that the parent is attempting many different techniques, spending a great deal of time coaxing, and possibly offering a great variety of foods. From the child's point of view, this represents a reinforcing, one-on-one interaction with a parent for an extended period of time. Any child behavior which serves to prolong the feeding session is reinforced by continued access to this rather intense interaction.

Another clue to the existence of a behaviorally-based feeding problem is the statement by parents or caregivers that the child has strong food preferences and that there has been a narrowing of the range of foods the child will accept. When parents indicate that there are a number of foods the child used to eat but no longer "likes," the assumption can be made that the parents are not continuing to present those foods based on their beliefs that the child will no longer eat them.

The location and timing of the feedings is an important factor to examine as well. Parents who do not present food at set mealtimes often develop a pattern of offering small quantities of food frequently throughout the day. This is often done in the form of foods which are portable in nature such as crackers, pieces of cheese, etc. When the child is given small quantities of food while wandering in his environment, it is difficult for parents to actually determine the exact quantity consumed on a day-to-day basis. The range of foods offered to the child is limited by the need for that food to be portable. Thus, the child who eats small amounts frequently throughout the day may not develop the cyclical appetite which leads to a sufficient amount of hunger to motivate expansion in the variety of foods eaten.

Parents who indicate a history of switching strategies during a meal itself or from meal to meal, often are unable to tolerate their child's distress for long enough periods to determine whether a procedure is effective. This is also suggestive of a feeding problem which is behaviorally based.

The next step in assessment is to actually observe the caregiver feeding the child in as normal a feeding situation as possible. Of interest is the interaction between the parent and child. Questions to be kept in mind are: What does the parent do if the child refuses food? What is the child's response to being placed in the feeding situation? What is the child's response to presentation of food? How long does the session last?

287

Table 1

Inventory of Behavioral Eating Skills

Child's Name _____   Informant _____

DOB __-__-_____   Weight _____

1. LIST FOODS CHILD CURRENTLY AND REGULARLY EATS:

2. LIST FOODS CHILD ATE AT ONE TIME BUT NO LONGER ACCEPTS:

3. LIST FOODS EATEN AS SNACKS:

4. WHO REGULARLY FEEDS THE CHILD?   (E.G. MOTHER, FATHER)

5.	WHEN SERVED	LENGTH OF MEAL	WHERE? (E.G., KITCHEN)	WHERE SEATED?
BREAKFAST				
LUNCH				
DINNER				

6. DURING THE MEAL DOES CHILD:

____	CRY	____	PUSH FOOD AWAY
____	SPIT FOOD OUT	____	VOMIT OR GAG
____	THROW FOOD	____	DROOL
____	TURN AWAY FROM SPOON	____	REFUSE TO OPEN MOUTH
____	FINGER FEED	____	USE A SPOON
____	USE A FORK	____	ATTEMPT TO LEAVE

---

7. TECHNIQUES USED DURING MEALS

____	COAXING	____	IGNORING
____	FORCED FEEDING	____	PUNISHMENT
____	THREATENING	____	MODELING
____	OFFERS OF REWARDS		

    (favorite foods or special privileges)

Is either parent or child distressed during the feeding session? The observer's goal is to assess the degree of stress and anxiety in the feeding situation and the degree to which the child's inappropriate feeding behaviors are maintained by reinforcement through parental attention, access to a preferred food, or withdrawal of the presentation of a nonpreferred food.

Treatment

    The first step in structuring a feeding treatment program is to delineate treatment goals. If the problem is a lack of variety, the goal may be to increase the number of preferred foods to include at least three or four from each of the major food group categories. If the problem is related to texture (e.g., pureed foods only), the feeding goal may be to train the child to accept foods with a more solid texture. In conjunction with this, if the feeding situation is characterized by crying or distress, a goal may be to eliminate crying behavior during the meal.

After delineating goals, a specific intervention is developed. While no two cases present alike, there is a basic structure based on behavioral principles which can be used to treat a number of feeding problems. This basic structure is predicated on the fact that the feeder has control of the two major reinforcers which operate in the feeding situation. First, the feeder has control over his/her attention and interaction with the child. Second, the feeder can and does control whether or not the child receives any food at all and therefore can manipulate the motivational variable, hunger. Essentially, the task is to structure the feeding situation so that the child receives these reinforcers when behaviors consistent with treatment goals are exhibited.

The literature contains numerous examples of single case studies utilizing these techniques (Bernal, 1972; O'Brien & Azrin, 1972; Palmer, Thompson & Linscheid, 1975; Riordan, Iwata, Wohl & Finney, 1980). Typically, these treatments include a description of a standardized feeding setting, the definition of feeding behaviors to both increase and decrease, specific reinforcement and punishment contingencies to be used, and a description of procedures for training parents or caregivers in the specific therapeutic techniques utilized. As stated earlier, while there are variations, what follows is a description of a typical feeding treatment as outlined along the above parameters.

Setting. Prior to initiation of treatment, a specific feeding setting is identified. Typically, the child is placed in an appropriate seating arrangment (i.e., high chair, feeding table). A therapist or parent sits beside the child or directly in front of the child in a distraction-free environment. The duration of treatment sessions is predetermined (e.g., 20 minutes) and sessions are scheduled three to five times per day. O'Brien and Azrin (1972) suggest the use of "mini-meals" of short duration occurring frequently throughout the day as a way to increase the number of training trials per day.

Requiring the child to eat at preset times and in a prescribed location increases the probability that time and location will come to be discriminative stimuli for the child and will signal appropriate eating behavior.

Baseline. Once the standardized feeding situation has been developed, prior to the initiation of the actual treatment, a number of baseline meals are offered to the child in that setting. During baseline meals, the child is given access to preferred foods and textures and to foods and textures which, by history, he or she is currently not accepting. No attempt is made to use specific contingencies to teach the child to eat at this point. The child is prompted to try foods and textures from both the preferred and nonpreferred groups during the feeding session. A record is kept of food acceptances and rejections and other target feeding behaviors such as crying, pushing food away, spitting food out, etc.

Treatment Procedures. Two basic behavioral techniques utilized in the feeding treatment situation are positive reinforcement and time-out from positive reinforcement. At the beginning of the feeding session the child is placed into the feeding apparatus (high chair), the therapist or parent sits beside or in front of the child. When the child is quiet, he/she is prompted to accept a bit of a nonpreferred food. Acceptance of a nonpreferred food is met with verbal praise, eye contact and a bite of a preferred food. Initially, the child may be reinforced for merely allowing the nonpreferred food to be held close to his/her mouth. Verbal praise, possibly coupled with a physical reinforcer such as patting the child on the head, and the presentation of a preferred food serve as reinforcers for acceptance of the nonpreferred food.

If the child refuses the nonpreferred food and engages in any avoidance behaviors such as pushing the food away, crying, etc., the parent or thera- pist physically turns away from the child and withdraws all attention for a preset time period (e.g. 15 seconds) or until the child is quiet, assuming the preset time period has expired. This systematic withdrawal of attention is a procedure known as time-out from positive reinforcement and in behav- ioral terms is a punishment procedure because it results in a decrease in the probability of the behavior which it follows. During the time-out period, the child should have no access to any positive reinforcement, that is he/she should not be able to receive a preferred food or to obtain any attention from the therapist or parent.

The meal is ended when the preset time period expires regardless of whether the child has eaten any of the foods or whether he/she seems willing to continue to eat. The reasons for ending the meal at the preset time period are two-fold. First, if the child is not cooperating and is not eating, continuation of the meal only provides an opportunity for the child to associate a distressing situation with the feeding setting. Second, even if the child is cooperating, termination of the meal after the preset time period will ensure that the child will be hungry at the next meal, thus increasing the probability of success. During the treatment phase no foods are offered to the child between meals. Water may be offered midway between meals to prevent dehydration.

Training Procedures. Parents or caregivers need to be involved in the treatment planning and the treatment itself. Anyone who will be feeding the child after treatment should be included in the planning and implemen- tation if at all possible. Participants may include grandparents, baby sitters, siblings, etc. and should include training in the behavioral principles involved and appropriate developmental expectations for the child, especially related to feeding (i.e., type and quantity of food and self feeding behavior). Our typical treatment plan involves having the therapist actually conduct the first several treatment sessions while parents or caregivers observe, either through a one-way mirror or from within the treatment room itself. The therapist serves as a model for the parents and answers questions following each session.

We find it very beneficial to have parents serve as observational data recorders. This process focuses their attention on objectively defined target behaviors and allows them to see the effects of consequences on behavior as treatment progresses. Observation also serves to increase parental enthusiasm and cooperation because they feel a part of the treat- ment process. When the parent becomes the feeder, the therapist acts as coach and provides verbal reinforcement for correct execution of treatment procedures and intervenes if the caregiver is inadvertently reinforcing inappropriate behavior or is failing to reinforce appropriate behaviors.

Treatment can be conducted on an outpatient or inpatient basis. Linscheid et al. (1978) suggest the following criteria for the selection of patients to be treated within the hospital:

(a) Is reduction of food intake, either the variety or the texture, interfering with intake of calories and nutrients needed for physical and mental growth? Has the child's weight or height dropped below the fifth percentile?
(b) Is mealtime behavior such that the relationship between caregiver and child is continually being jeopardized? Is this relationship

290

generalizing to other parent-child activities?

(c) Are the parents willing to participate in the process? With role
modeling and training can the parents be expected to follow
through on the behavioral techniques? Will experience in the
feeding area generalize to provide more positive, effective interaction in other areas?

Hospitalization provides the medical monitoring which is sometimes
necessary if the child's rate of weight gain has dropped significantly.
Hospitalization also makes it possible for contingencies to be consistent
from meal to meal. However, we have found that it is difficult to attain
consistency unless only one or two therapists are involved in the actual
treatment. In our experience, it has not been effective to have nurses
conduct the treatment because their other duties and changing shift schedules make consistency difficult to realize. Also, nurses most often do not
have the advanced training in behavioral techniques which is necessary to
conduct the intervention. We have been most successful when a small team
(i.e., one to three) of therapists, who have extensive training in behavioral principles, conduct and supervise the entire treatment. However,
this involves a substantial time commitment of usually three meals per day,
seven days per week, for one to six weeks.

Length of treatment may depend on factors such as type and duration of
the problem, child's health status, parental cooperation and treatment
history. From experience, texture related problems are more difficult to
treat than are taste preference problems.

If the child's rate of weight gain has not yet dropped to a level to
warrant close medical supervision and if parents are motivated to bring the
child to the treatment center three times per day during the course of
treatment, an outpatient program can be considered. However, outpatient
treatment requires highly motivated parents or caregivers who can monitor
their child closely at home and who can tolerate the child's distress,
which often occurs during the initial stage of treatment.

Follow-up sessions scheduled at regular intervals allow the therapist
to assess weight gain and to ensure that parents or caregivers are not
reverting to previous habits. In our experience, gains made during treatment are usually well maintained (Palmer et al., 1975; Thompson et al.,
1977). Two factors account for this. First, parents or caregivers know
the techniques can work if applied consistently and will return to these
procedures if the child regresses. Second, once the child begins to like
the taste of the new foods or textures, taste itself serves as a reinforcer.

SUMMARY

In this chapter we have described two types of non-organic FTT and have
described how behavioral principles can be used to analyze and treat these
problems. Type I and Type II non-organic FTT have their basis in faulty
contingent interactions between child and caregiver. In Type I, there
exists a generalized lack of contingency experiences between child and
caregiver. In Type II, the contingent interactions exist but do not lead
to the desired result. Also, failure of contingency interactions may be
specific to the feeding situation.

As a final note, behavioral interventions by their nature ascribe
problems to inadequate knowledge of effective techniques, not to maternal
emotional states. This seems a reasonable and parsimonious first step in
the remediation process. Certainly, we do not mean to imply that maternal

(parental) emotional status is not a significant factor in many eating problems. Three factors determine success in feeding: parental knowledge, food availability, and parental motivation to nurture. The behavioral approach addresses the first of these factors but recognizes the possible importance of the others as well.

Further research needs to be directed toward the documentation of successful feeding practices in children who are not showing growth problems. Such research will allow the documentation of differences in feeding practices between non-organic FTT children and normals. In addition, more extensive follow-up should be conducted with behavioral treatment to determine generalization and maintenance in other settings. Studies using group designs comparing treatment techniques need to be conducted. To date, most reports are case studies or single subject designs which provide important demonstrations of the principles of intervention but do not allow generalizability to various patient groups. The information presented here suggests that different types of FTT will respond best to programs of intervention which address the specific factors which are maintaining the maladaptive behavior patterns.

REFERENCES

Ainsworth, M. Infant-mother attachment. *American Psychologist*, 1979, 34, 932-937.

Ainsworth, M. & Bell, R. Mother-infant interaction and the development of competence. In K.G. Connolly & J.S. Bruner (Eds.), *The Growth of Competence*. New York: Academic Press, 1974.

American Psychiatric Association. *Diagnostic and Statistical Manual III*. Washington, D.C.: American Psychiatric Association, 1980.

Bell, R.Q. Contributions of human infants to caregiving and social interactions. In M. Lewis & L. Rosenblum (Eds.), *The Effect of the Infant on Its Caregiver*. New York: Wiley, 1974.

Bell, R.Q. Stimulus control of parent or caretaker behavior by offspring. *Developmental Psychology*, 1971, 4, 63-72.

Bell, R.Q. A reinterpretation of the direction of effects in studies of socialization. *Psychological Review*, 1968, 75, 81-95.

Bernal, M.E. Behavioral treatment of a child's eating problem. *Journal of Behavior Therapy and Experimental Psychiatry*, 1972, 3, 43-50.

Block, J. Issues, problems and pitfalls in assessing sex differences: A critical review of the psychology of sex differences. *Merrill-Palmer Quarterly*, 1976, 22, 283-308.

Bowlby, J. *Attachment and Loss: Vol. 1 Attachment*. New York: Basic Books, 1969.

Brazelton, T.B. Mother-infant reciprocity. In M.H. Klaus, T. Leger & M.A. Trause (Eds.), *Maternal Attachment and Mothering Disorders*. Johnson and Johnson, 1975.

Christophersen, E.R. & Hall, C.L. Eating patterns and associated problems encountered in normal children. *Issues in Comprehensive Pediatric Nursing*, 1978, 3, 1-16.

Crawford, A. Mother-infant interaction in premature and full-term infants. *Child Development*, 1982, 53, 957-962.

Crittendon, L. Abusing, neglecting, problematic and adequate dyads: Differentiating by patterns of interaction. *Merrill-Palmer Quarterly*, 1981, 27, 201-218.

Crockenberg, S. Infant irritability, mother responsiveness, and social support influences in the security of infant-mother attachment. *Child Development*, 1981, 52, 857-865.

Crockenberg, S. & Smith, P. Antecedents of mother-infant interaction and infant irritability in the first three months of life. *Infant Behavior and Development*, 1982, 5, 105-119.

Egan, G., Chatoor, I. & Rosen, G. Non-organic failure to thrive: Pathogenesis and classification. <u>Clinical Proceedings of Childrens Hospital National Medical Center</u>, 1980, <u>36</u>, 173-182.

Evans, S. L., Reinhart, J.B. & Succop, R.A. Failure to thrive: A study of 45 children and their families. <u>Journal of the American Academy of Child Psychiatry</u>, 1972, <u>11</u>, 440-457.

Evler, G. Nonmedical management of the failure-to-thrive child in a pediatric inpatient setting. In P.J. Accardo (Ed.), <u>Failure to Thrive in Infancy and Early Childhood</u>. Baltimore: University Park Press, 1982.

Frisch, H. The effect of designated and actual sex of infant on adult-infant play. (Doctoral dissertation, the University of Chicago, 1976). <u>Dissertation Abstracts International</u>, 1976, <u>37</u>, 874B.

Frodi, A.M. & Lamb, M.E. Child abusers' responses to infant smiles and cries. <u>Child Development</u>, 1980, <u>51</u>, 238-241.

Goldberg, S. Social competence in infancy: A model of parent-infant interaction. <u>Merrill-Palmer Quarterly</u>, 1977, <u>23</u>(3), 161-176.

Greer, J., Gustafson, G. & West, M. Effects of infant development on mother-infant interactions. <u>Child Development</u>, 1980, <u>51</u>, 199-207.

Harris, J.C. Nonorganic failure-to-thrive syndromes: Reactive attachment disorder of infancy and psychosocial dwarfism of childhood. In P.J. Accardo (Ed.), <u>Failure to Thrive in Infancy and Early Childhood</u>. Baltimore: University Park Press, 1982.

Illingworth, R.S. & Lister, J. The critical or sensitive period, with special reference to certain feeding problems in infants and children. <u>Journal of Pediatrics</u>, 1964, <u>65</u>, 839-848.

Kronstadt, D., Oberlaid, F., Ferb, T. & Swartz, J. Infant behavior and maternal adaptations in the first six months of life. <u>American Journal of Orthopsychiatry</u>, 1979, <u>49</u>, 454-468.

Lewis, M. & Goldberg, S. Perceptual-cognitive development in infancy: A generalized expectancy model as a function of the mother-infant interaction. <u>Merrill-Palmer Quarterly</u>, 1969, <u>15</u>, 81-100.

Linscheid, T.R., Oliver, J., Blyler, E. & Palmer, S. Brief hospitalization for the behavioral treatment of feeding problems in the developmentally disabled. <u>Journal of Pediatric Psychology</u>, 1978, <u>3</u>(2), 72-76.

Money, J. The syndrome of abuse dwarfism (psychosocial dwarfism or reversible hyposomatotropism). <u>American Journal of Disabled Children</u>, 1977, <u>131</u>, 508-513.

O'Brien, F. & Azrin, N.H. Developing proper mealtime behaviors of the institutionalized retarded. <u>Journal of Applied Behavioral Analysis</u>, 1972, <u>5</u>, 389-399.

Palmer, S., Thompson, R.J. & Linscheid, T.R. Applied behavior analysis in the treatment of childhood feeding problems. <u>Developmental Medicine and Child Neurology</u>, 1975, <u>17</u>, 333-339.

Ramey, C.T., Hieger, L. & Klisz, D. Synchronous reinforcement of focal responses in failure-to-thrive infants. <u>Child Development</u>, 1972, <u>43</u>, 1449-1455.

Ramey, C.T., Starr, R.H., Pallas, J., Whitten, C.F. & Reed, V. Nutrition, response-contingent stimulation, and the maternal-deprivation syndrome: Results of an early intervention program. <u>Merrill-Palmer Quarterly</u>, 1975, <u>21</u>(1), 45-53.

Riordan, M.M., Iwata, B.A., Wohl, M.K. & Finney, J.W. Behavioral treatment of food refusal and selectivity in developmentally disabled children. <u>Applied Research in Mental Retardation</u>, 1980, <u>1</u>, 95-112.

Schwartz, A.S. Eating problems. <u>Pediatric Clinics of North America</u>, 1958, <u>5</u>, 595-611.

Smith, D.W. <u>Growth and Its Disorders</u>. Philadelphia: W.B. Saunders, 1977.

Thomas, A., Chess, S. & Birch, H. <u>Temperament and Behavior Disorders in Children</u>. New York: New York University, 1968.

Thompson, R.J., Palmer, S. & Linscheid, T.R. Single-subject design and interaction analysis in the behavioral treatment of a child with a feeding problem. Child Psychiatry and Human Development, 1977, 8(1), 43-53.

Watson, J.S. & Ramey, C.T. Reactions to response-contingent stimulation in early infancy. Merrill-Palmer Quarterly, 1972, 18, 219-227.

White, R. Motivation reconsidered: The concept of competence. Psychological Review, 1959, 66, 297-333.

THE FAMILY CONTEXT OF FAILURE TO THRIVE*

Dennis Drotar, Janice Woychik, Carole Mantz-Clumpner, Corrine Brickell, Judy Negray, Mariel Wallace, and Charles A. Malone

Case Western Reserve University School of Medicine

In recent years, a family systems perspective has extended understanding of normal developmental processes (Belsky, 1984; Parke, 1979) and deviations ranging from child maltreatment to psychosomatic disorders (Garbarino, 1977; Minuchin, Rosman & Baker, 1978). Our clinical experiences with the families of FTT infants (Drotar & Malone, 1982) have underscored the unique advantages of a family-centered conceptual framework as a guide for intervention in FTT. In addition to its pragmatic value in facilitating treatment planning, a family systems perspective provides a valuable conceptual model to better understand the origins and course of FTT and concomitant risk. This chapter considers clinical assessment of family influences in FTT and the implications for intervention strategies and future research.

THE ROLE OF THE FAMILY IN FAILURE TO THRIVE

Although family environmental stress has long been identified as a potential causative factor in FTT (Patton & Gardner, 1962; Talbot et al., 1947), this relationship is by no means well established. Early studies have yielded interesting though uncontrolled clinical observations which highlighted the importance of the parental relationship in the development of FTT. For example, Leonard, Rhymes & Solnit (1966) presented a cogent portrait of the families of FTT infants as beset by multiple problems such as poverty, substandard housing, threats of eviction, unemployment, and relationship problems between the parents. Leonard et al. 1966 also linked FTT to insufficient family and maternal resources to cope with the burdens of raising many children in quick succession. Fathers of FTT infants were described as having great difficulty contributing to already depleted family resources and as taxing maternal nurturing capacities. Barbero, Morris & Redford (1962) highlighted the importance of the father's relationship with the child's mother in the pattern of family adaptation associated with FTT and the necessity to involve fathers in intervention. Elmer (1960) also identified problematic relationships between the parents as a salient family issue and described the importance of supportive intervention for

*This work is based on research funded by the National Institute of Mental Health, (Applied Research) #35220, the Prevention Research Center #30274 and the Cleveland Foundation.

the mothers of FTT infants to counterbalance the lack of paternal support.

Evans et al.'s (1972) comprehensive clinical description characterized
families of FTT children on the following dimensions: family living conditions, maternal affect (adjustment), maternal perception of the child as
ill or retarded, parent-child interaction, presence of severe loss, and
prognosis. The following family profiles were identified: (1) Good prognosis: good physical care, living conditions, depression and loss, and
severe object loss and strained mother-child interaction. (2) Guarded
prognosis: deprived living conditions, poor physical care of the child,
extreme maternal depression, perception of the child as ill or retarded,
chronic losses, closely spaced siblings with many problems. (3) Poor
prognosis: good living conditions, neglectful care, angry interaction with
child, child perceived as bad, mother hostile to staff. The Evans et al.
(1972) typology proposes an interesting but as yet untested model which
links family status and prognosis which certainly warrants further investigation.

The role of family factors in FTT has been recently reviewed by
Bruenlin et al. (1983). Family problems frequently cited included paternal
alcohol problems (45%), unemployment (56%), family size of more than four
children (55%), physical illness in family members other than the FTT child
(40%), alcohol use, marital difficulties, closely spaced (less than 18
months apart) children (69%), financial difficulties (68%). Bruenlin's
review highlights the association between family stress and FTT, the level
of family stresses and economic disadvantage varies considerably across
samples and is by no means universal (Kotelchuck, 1980; Kotelchuck &
Newberger, 1983). Moreover, it is not known to what extent the family
stresses identified with FTT are unique to this condition or are associated
with some other correlated risk factor, especially social class. Family
factors that differentiate families of FTT infants from comparison samples
in the U.S.A. and other countries include lower economic levels (Kanawati,
Darwish & McLaren, 1974; Kanawati & McLaren, 1973), higher stress
(Altemeier et al., 1981), lack of availability of extended family members
for child rearing (Pollitt & Leibel, 1980) and social isolation (Bithoney,
1983; Kotelchuck & Newberger, 1983). Using an unmatched comparison group
in a middle class sample of FTT children, Newberger et al., (1977) initially found no differences as a function of FTT in family composition, income,
housing density, extent of recent moves, job changes, stresses, maternal
health or access to child care help. In a more recent study, Kotelchuck &
Newberger (1983) indicated the major characteristic that differentiated the
two groups was the nature of family support systems. Mothers of infants
who fail to thrive much more often reported that their neighborhood was
unfriendly and that they were more isolated from family members.

OBSTACLES TO THE STUDY OF FAMILY INFLUENCES

The highly stressed and often times defensive families of FTT infants
do not easily lend themselves to participation in research or intervention.
In addition, the fact that observations are made in the health care context
rather than in the home situation severely limits the comprehensiveness of
family assessment. Clinicians who work in hospital settings often do not
have or seek access to family members such as the child's father or extended
family members who exert considerable influence on mother and child on a
day to day basis. As a consequence, a disproportionate amount of energy
may be directed to assessment of deficits in maternal functioning or mother-
child interaction (Fischoff, Whitten & Pettit, 1969) rather than the impact
of family environment on maternal nurturing. In addition, even when family
members are available, it is often very difficult for the clinician to understand the specific way in which family functioning has affected the

296

child's FTT or is likely to affect prognosis. The diagnostic situation is further complicated by the fact that many FTT children are from economically disadvantaged family environments characterized by high levels of stress and complex family structures (Drotar & Malone, 1982; Kellam, Ensminger & Turner, 1977; Stack, 1974; Stack, 1975). Such families require careful study over time to avoid misconstruing family adaptation to stressful life conditions such as economic privation as family psychopathology. Unfortunately, as is characteristic of research concerning the psychological status of culturally diverse groups, especially minorities (Howard & Scott, 1981), descriptions of family functioning in FTT have generally emphasized deficiencies rather than the functional interrelationship between family adaptation to conditions of life and nurturing patterns which would provide a more productive framework (Cassidy, 1980).

FAMILY INFLUENCES IN FTT

Concepts of Parental Competence

Our extensive observations of families of FTT infants in their home settings provided a wealth of material (see Drotar et al.'s discussion of early intervention in this volume for details on the design of this study). Our work suggested the need for a conceptual framework to encompass the diversity of factors which must be considered in FTT and which provided an alternative to deficit-centered clinical language.

The comprehensive family-centered contextual framework of parental competence recently described by Belsky has special relevance to consideration of the antecedents and concequences of FTT (Belsky, 1984; Belsky, Robins & Gamble, 1984). In this model, the major features of parental competence, parental involvement and sensitivity, are characterized by patience which enables the parent to hold their feelings in check, endurance, the ability to cope with the demands of parenting, and commitment, the continuation of investment of energy in a parental role. For Belsky, the level of parental competence depends on three interrelated influences: (1) parental personal resources; (2) child's characteristics; and (3) family support and functioning. Parental personal resources include developmental level, education, and emotional maturity. Belsky notes that the quality of the parents' prior nurturing and developmental experiences provides a template for successful nurturing experiences and sets the stage for the quality of parental nurturing (Fraiberg, 1980). A second set of factors involves individual child characteristics such as health, biologic risk factors, and temperament, which can influence the difficulty of child rearing. A final set of factors include stress vs. support of the parenting role which can include marital relationship, social networks and resources, and community and health supports. In this model, the quality of the marital relationship and informal support networks with friends, neighbors, relatives can buffer the effects of parenting dysfunction by providing key ingredients of emotional support, instrumental assistance, and social expectations which affirm the parental role. Social support can include emotional support, which communicates to the parent that she or he is esteemed or valued, and/or direct instrumental assistance such as the provision of goods, money and services which frees up parental physical energy. One of the most important features of Belsky's model is the role accorded to counterbalancing factors or buffers. Problems in one domain can be buffered by strengths in another domain. On the other hand, when parental competence is disrupted by problems in multiple domains, the child's nurturing is more likely to be affected.

Belsky's model calls our attention to the role of multiple risk factors in the development and maintenance of FTT. The families of FTT children appear to be affected in multiple domains, especially with respect to family support and parental nurturing history (Altemeier et al., 1980; Fraiberg, 1980). In addition, once the child develops FTT, the child's compromised health and/or nutrition may provide an additional stressor or burden on the parental system.

Table 1 lists certain factors in Belsky's model as applied to FTT. Family resources, claims, and mediating factors can affect the child's nurturing and eventually longer-term psychological outcome by affecting either availability (amount) or quality (type) of nutrition and/or attention given to the child. Nutrition and attention can be further subdivided into deficiencies of specific nutrients or types of stimulation (Wachs, 1971). Insufficient food can be a primary factor in the development of FTT as well as in enhancing risk for subsequent developmental and emotional deficits. In addition, inconsistent attention to the child, especially over a sustained period, is likely to be very disruptive. One advantage of this schema is that it differentiates among factors such as family organization and decision making, which may influence allocation of personal and/or material resources to the child, either directly or indirectly. For example, the quality of family functioning may affect child nurturing by affecting routines, especially those concerned with the timing and structure of mealtimes, and/or by exposing the child to noxious influences which disrupt the amount and quality of parental attention. The low energy levels found in some depleted families may be reflected in reduction of meal times and fewer opportunities for feeding. In addition, the noise and underorganized feeding which characterize certain families may limit the child's interest in food and hence food intake. Such familial factors may also influence the amount and quality of attention given the child, independent of the feeding situation and eventually affect the child's psychological status. One would anticipate that chronic depletions of nutrition and attention would be more deleterious than acute problems.

Economic Disadvantage

Economic disadvantage imposes special constraints on parental capacities to nurture children (Drotar & Malone, 1982). Family economic resources not only influence the amount of available food (see Frank, Allen & Brown, this volume) but also familial cultural practices. For example, those families of FTT infants who must operate on a level of subsistence and survival may have to endure periods of time in which there is not enough food for family members. Some cope with such depletions by reducing the allocation of resources to members. Watering down formula in order to save resources is an example of such a feeding practice which can have a direct bearing on nutrition. With fewer resources for food, possessions, or child care services families must also make especially cogent decisions about allocation of resources in order to avoid depletions which severely affect the child's nutrition. It is now recognized that economic disadvantage encourages special family and group adaptations which need to be understood in their own right. For example, Stack's anthropological studies of black inner city families in Chicago (1974) documented the importance of the supportive function of networks of kin and friends in trading and exchanging goods, resources, and the care of children as an adaptation to poverty. However, our clinical experiences with families of FTT infants have indicated that the well-functioning resource exchange units described so eloquently by Stack are by no means universal among economically disadvantaged, racially diverse families. In some families, significant relationship difficulties in the family network preclude adaptive resource allocation and priority setting with respect to infant care. In addition, families with multiple caretakers can share caretaking responsibility but must organize caretaking to avoid the kind of dispersion and/or discontinuity in caretaking that may be harmful to the child.

Table 1

Family Resource Allocation in Failure to Thrive

Material Resources	Personal Resources
Economic	Family structure, organization
Housing	and mutual support
Food	Intrafamilial relationships

Burdens/Claims

Relationship/conflict and strain
Economic depletion
Number of children
Child characteristics

Mediating Factors

Parental developmental level
Parental developmental history
Parental cultural practices
Parental educational level
Parental appraisal of child's needs

Parenting Outcomes

Availability: Amount and/or quality of nutrition and attention	Allocation of food and attention

Child Outcomes

Sociomotional development	Cognitive development
Physical growth and nutrition	

Family members may not always be aware of the specific impact of their adaptations to economic scarcity and/or relationship stress on their children. For example, one of our most interesting observations concerned parental attributions of the impact of nutritional privation on the child. Many of the parents of FTT infants did not appreciate (at least initially) how the infant was affected by the lowering of caloric intake. In some instances, this reflected insufficient knowledge of nutrition and development. However, such attributions sometimes coincided with beliefs about the resources that are needed by family members to survive in a culture of scarcity. For example, to the extent that "life is hard" and people in the family are expected to make do with less than optimal food and/or possessions, infants and young children may be expected to do the same, without regard for their unique developmental requirements for nutrition. Similar observations have been made to account for parental decision making concerning allocation of food to toddlers in other cultures in which resources are scarce (Cassidy, 1980). Other families were so preoccupied with their own relationship conflicts that the nurturing of infants could not be given the precedence needed to sustain the infant.

299

The Role of Family Conflict

Our experience suggests that the quality of intrafamilial relationshps
and support is perhaps the single most critical influence in the quality of
their exchange with one another. Families with the potential for adaptive
resource exchange do not necessarily utilize it. The families of FTT
infants sometimes cannot provide adequate support for one another and/or
make use of existing support systems owing to conflicts between the child's
mother and one or more parenting partner. (The parenting partner is defined
as a person in the mother's life who is potentially involved in the child's
nurturing and may include spouse, boyfriend, or grandmother.) Such family
conflicts may impinge directly on the child or indirectly via affecting
maternal nurturing (Parke, 1979; Pedersen, Anderson & Cain, 1980). Both
direct and indirect influences operate in the development of FTT. For
example, a severe family conflict may be directly stressful to a child by
disrupting the feeding situation and/or influence the child indirectly by
affecting the mother's emotional state and hence her capacity to effectively
nurture the child. Family dysfunction may also affect the child directly
by affecting the availability of money and food which may already be at
dangerously low levels owing to family economic circumstances (see Frank et
al., this volume). Families with severe relationship problems may have
particular difficulty taking advantage of available community resources
such as hunger centers or WIC benefits and responding to changes in the
availability or administration of nutritional and fiscal benefits. Disadvantaged families need to be quite resourceful to cope with bureaucratic
rules for the administration of benefits, such as showing up at specific
appointment times to continue benefits (see Pliven & Cloward, 1972; for a
cogent discussion of the nature and impact of bureaucratic regulation of
welfare families). It is quite possible that such patterns of bureaucratic
regulation may penalize poorly functioning families more than better functioning families, who are more able to create adaptive resource exchanges
in which money and child rearing are effectively shared.

In the course of our work, we observed a number of maladaptive patterns
of family life which were particularly disruptive to maternal nurturing
capacities. For example, in some families, exploitative exchanges, which
did not take the developmental capabilities of members into account, were
commonplace. For example, Fatima is a 16 year old mother who lives in a
Cleveland project in a separate apartment but nearby her mother and extended
family members. Fatima's birth of her first child, Nadine, was taken by
the family as a sign that she was "grown up" and hence, no longer in need
of protection at the same level as before. However, Fatima remained psycho
logically vulnerable. Her relationship with the baby's father was characterized by a significant commitment on her part but a more tenuous relationship on his part. Although he lived with her at the time of Nadine's birth,
he has another child and maintains two households. On her own, she could
not form a family unit and remained prey to other people or more distant
kin in the projects who come in and utilize hers and Fatima's food.

In other families, we confronted longstanding intergenerational patterns of scapegoating in which available resources were withheld from
family members as punishments or sanctions. For example, Teniesha was a
young mother of a FTT infant whose living circumstances: paint peeling off
the walls, a kitchen faucet that ran nonstop, a space heater in one room;
stood in stark contrast to her parents' beautifully furnished dining room
filled with diplomas signifying family achievement. Teniesha had failed to
live up to her family's expectations owing to her pregnancy. Her relationship with her parents required her to pay back many psychological debts.
She could never depend on anyone in her family to provide transportation.
Promises were made and often broken, and interfered with her keeping
appointments for her children's medical care. Moreover, Teniesha provided

her mother with some of her food stamps and paid extra rent but was not given economic support in return, a pattern which affected the availability of resources for the infant.

Conflicts between adult caretakers which interfered directly with allocation of time, attention or food to the infant were among the most powerful influences that we encountered. In accord with the complex organizational patterns often found in disadvantaged families (Kellam et al., 1972), family conflicts which affected infant nurturing often took on an unique character. For example, Samantha, a working class grandmother, was so angry at her daughter for bearing a child out of wedlock that she demanded agreement from local relatives that they refuse to babysit in an attempt to pressure her daughter into either relinquishing the baby or quitting her job.

In another family, Marie, the young mother with four children, maintained a relationship with Zeke, the father of two children, and Josh, the father of the baby. Both men visited regularly and tried to act as a father figure when visiting, wielding authority, and disciplining the children. Both were interested in Marie and would utilize their financial power as a sanction against her when they became jealous. A major financial crisis occurred when both men stopped their financial help at the same time. With no money for formula, the baby drank 2% milk.

FAMILY ASSESSMENT

What implications do these observations of family life have for assessment and intervention in FTT? The above vignettes illustrate the interdependence of family relationship problems, resource depletions, and maternal capacity to provide necessary attention and nutrients to the child. In planning interventions, we found it useful to consider the ways in which the intrafamilial social network was a source of competing claims rather than nurturance for the child. On the other hand, the number of available and potentially helpful adult caretakers relative to the numbers of young children was important to consider as a positive influence. If the family household has a number of available caregivers, the burden on the mother is substantially reduced, especially in disadvantaged families who cannot purchase child care.

The success of intervention will often depend upon the quality of family support. In highly stressed families, expecting mothers to make longlasting changes in their relationships with their FTT children without increased support from family members may be unrealistic, unless the mother has especially strong personal resources (Belsky et al., 1984). For this reason, intervention planning for FTT should take a number of factors into account: (1) the level of financial resources; (2) maternal relationships with other family members, especially the presence of conflict or emotional isolation; (3) family members' capacity to organize caretaking for the child; (4) family routines; (5) cultural practices concerning child rearing and feeding.

In this section, specific ways of gathering information concerning family functioning and FTT are considered. Information gathering concerning family functioning is best accomplished via a supportive approach in which one joins the caregivers in an exploration of how the family operates and effects the baby. The schema of family resource allocation described in Table 1 can be a useful means of organizing diagnostic information from different sources. One of the most useful practical tools to initiate information-gathering is the genogram (a detailed and expanded family tree) (Hartman, 1979). Since many people enjoy talking about their family to an interested listener, the tone of these interviews can often be relaxed and sometimes even spirited. In addition, the emphasis on family history inherent in the process of constructing a genogram communicates respect for the family's history, relationships and structure.

Convening the Family

In view of the fact that selective descriptions and other distortions easily can enter into history taking, direct observations are an especially useful means of evaluation. To gain further information and to lay the groundwork for engaging other family members, family functioning may be probed by inviting important family members into the hospital or clinic setting to visit and discuss the child's progress and their views of family life. "Important" family members can be identified partly by the genogram. The necessity of family involvement in the diagnostic process can be communicated to resistant members via statements like: "We often work with family members because we have found that the hospitalization is difficult for many families. We've also found that family stresses can affect the child's weight and development. For this reason, all family members are important in helping the child improve." Such introductory comments communicate the rationale for family involvement under the neutral and nonspecific label of stress, emphasize the impact of the child's problem and hospitalization on family members and highlight the importance of family members to intervention. In evaluating the family's response to an invitation for further discussion, one must be very careful about drawing premature conclusions about the nature of family committment to the child. For example, such reality factors as a lack of phone, transporation or babysitting resources may preclude family members from attending a meeting at the hospital or clinic and create a false impression of parental disinterest.

Direct Observation of Family Interaction

In addition to interviewing, it may be quite helpful to observe the family interaction with the child, especially during a feeding. Careful note should be taken about how the baby is being fed, how the adults interact with each other, and whether any other children are brought along. For example, a mother who is unsure of her ability to soothe a fussy baby may immediately hand the child to another family member. Bickering between spouses as the baby is being fed may signify a deeper level conflict between spouses that might be interfering with the quality of the child's care.

An example of how observation of family interaction can be used to develop an intervention plan is seen in the following case vignette: Joey was a two year old who presented with severe FTT and feeding problems. His maternal and paternal grandparents visited the hospital and were involved in his care. The grandparents also demonstrated a great deal of anxiety about his condition and concerns about his feeding behavior. At one point, these anxieties erupted in an active disagreement between Joey's mother and her grandmother about the proper way to feed Joey. Subsequent family interviews and home observations confirmed the fact that the grandparents maintained an active but ambivalent relationship with the parents. Joey's mother felt angered by their involvement but unable to set limits on their behavior. Subsequently, this intergenerational conflict became one focus of intervention conducted in the home setting.

The spontaneous visits of other family members, especially siblings, provide further opportunity for family-oriented assessment. For example, Kristen's (a young FTT infant) two older siblings, Justin, age 18 months and Rob, age 3 years, visited her in the hospital. Rob kept up a steady stream of conversation and was quite demanding. Subsequent discussion

302

revealed that Rob's behavior often interfered with Kristen's feeding at home by drawing his mother's attention away from feeding Kristen and resulting in tension filled mealtimes. Following the hospitalization, Kristen's mother was able to follow a recommendation to separate the mealtimes of the two children, which enhanced Kristen's caloric intake.

Home Observation

The complex nature of family functioning in FTT often requires more detailed observation than is possible in a hospital or clinic setting to discover what is actually hindering a child's weight gain and what can realistically be done to ameliorate the situation (Fraiberg, 1980). Home observation has a number of special advantages as a diagnostic procedure: Observing behavior in the home setting not only can put family members more at ease but provides data concerning the specific impact of family functioning on the child. For example, in the home a visitor might see the extent of visual deprivation of an infant by noting the high-sided white bassinette pushed in a dark corner where the baby lies. An intervenor might first meet the baby's father, who was too cautious to visit in the hospital but is actually interested and involved in the child's nurturing. Sometimes the immediate reasons for the child's FTT can be uncovered in a single home observation as in the following example: Nelson kept suffering from diarrhea. Stool cultures were negative. He'd stabilize on clear liquids, but as soon as he was back on his Isomil he became symptomatic. A home visit uncovered the problem: there was no working refrigerator in the house and the diluted liquid Isomil sat in bottles on the shelf, spoiling each day. The family did own a refrigerator, but since it wasn't working they used it as a cupboard. Two options were presented to the family: buy an ice chest and use it for the diluted liquid formula or arrange to get the formula dry and make it up bottle by bottle. They chose the former approach.

One of the most important advantages of home observation is a more accurate elucidation of household structure and the functional interconnections among family members than can ever be obtained in the hospital setting. In the course of our work, varied patterns of family structure were revealed which contrasted markedly with initial impressions based on information from hospital charts. In some instances, observation revealed that the family situation was much more depleted and conflictual than was first thought. Viewed in this context, maternal nurturing deficiencies became much more understandable. On the other hand, home visitation sometimes revealed unexpected strengths, especially additional family members who could be mobilized on the child's behalf.

The special advantages of home visitation have to be weighed against the disadvantages which include (among others) time, economic costs and stresses on the home visitor. Our experience suggests that when one considers the risk to children associated with FTT and the potential import of clinical decisions on the child's life, the benefits of home visitation outweigh the costs in most instances. However, if one is to undertake home visitation effectively, a great deal of emotional and supervisory support needs to be made available to those who conduct the visits (Fraiberg, 1980).

FAMILY CENTERED INTERVENTION

A family centered perspective can be helpful in identifying extremely disruptive family influences and in suggesting interventions that may be helpful to mother, child, and/or other family members. In addition, a family-centered approach can also suggest specific interventions to work with the family group and/or support the child's mother to make positive changes in the pattern of her relationships with other family members. Family-centered intervention can enhanced the child's nurturing by (1) helping family members increase the level of resources available to the child (money/food) through advocacy (Nagel, 1972; Nagi, 1980); (2) improving the overall organization and planning of family resources, especially those that pertain to the child; (3) reducing family conflicts and hence improving the quality of exchanges within the family; and (4) helping family members to protect the child from the influence of maladaptive family patterns.

Supportive and Educational Interventions

One of the most useful interventions in FTT is advocacy to help the family obtain resources and benefits to which they are entitled. In addition to direct concrete physical assistance, family centered advocacy can help encourage individual parents to cope more effectively with chronic relationship stresses. With many families, intervention can profitably proceed in stages on problems as they are acknowledged by the family. Educational and supportive intervention may be considered as a first level of intervention and as a probe concerning family members' capacity to utilize such information on their child's behalf. For example, history taking may show inadequate calories consumed by the child but the family may be unaware of the problem. In such a situation, the family might be receptive to nutritional education as well as counseling to modify the feeding patterns. (See Altemeier et al., this volume.)

Enhancing Intrafamilial Relationships

In cases in which family disruptions are pervasive, the child's FTT often cannot be addressed via a strictly educational approach. In such cases, intervention may help the child by improving the quality of the mother's social network, especially her relationships with parenting partners. In some instances, parents can be helped to ameliorate their difficulties with one another. In other instances, the mother may require support to extricate herself from troubled relationships. For example, at the start of intervention, Rasheeta, the mother of a young FTT infant was engaged in highly conflicted relationships with two men, father of her children which affected her relationship with her infant. Even with the extended family gone from her household, Rasheeta was sufficiently skillful to provide fairly well for the children's nutritional needs, as long as they were on WIC. However, because she was so isolated, getting to the WIC appointments by city bus was extremely difficult. She had only one stroller and negotiating city streets accompanied by her children was impossible. If her boyfriends, Ace or Bob didn't show for babysitting, Rasheeta had to miss WIC appointments. Having no phone, she could not immediately call to cancel the appointment. As a result, she was cut off WIC and began substituting homogenized milk for formula because it was cheaper. When intervention began, Rasheeta was most interested in Ace who was not divorced from his wife and did not follow through on responsibilities. Rasheeta's other boyfriend, Bob had proposed several times before. He had gotten a new job managing a restaurant and reported he stopped drinking. Rasheeta was tempted to accept his proposal, but accepted our advice to impose an engagement period to "test the waters" before she plunged herself into a commitment. Rasheeta was not pleased with what she eventually discovered about Bob; his position as "manager" was an exaggeration; he was only the cook, and he was still an active drinker. With support, Rasheeta eventually acknowledged that neither man was going to be able to meet her needs as a dependable co-parent.

With encouragement, Rasheeta began to seek the support of family members. She alerted her sister, Josie, that an apartment was available in her building. Josie moved in and they both began to cooperate on child-care arrangements. Both had children of kindergarten age and alternated taking the children to school or picking them up. Rasheeta had the luck to run into the daughter of one of her mother's friends, Beth, and they reactivated their friendship. This young woman came to function as a kind of alternate co-parent for the children. With Beth present during meal-times, both babies got the attention they needed as Rasheeta attended to one of the boys, while Beth helped with the other child. Both boys ate more and Rasheeta felt less exhausted and more successful following meal-times. As she developed her own sources of support, Rasheeta became more assertive with Bob and Ace and set limits on their involvement. For exam-ple, they could visit their children but they were not expected to babysit at critical times.

Aiding Resource Allocation

In families where conflictual relationships are affecting the child, intervention can help family members direct resources to the infant or to help the FTT family set limits on outright exploitation. For example, in families in which the resources were diverted away from the FTT child, our goal was to draw the attention of family members to the special needs of the FTT child and to encourage caregivers to restructure their dispersal of attention and food. This approach was useful in the case of Randy whose FTT appeared to relate to a disorganized familial approach to his feeding and inconsistent relationships with adult caregivers. Randy's complex assortment of caregivers included his mother, who lived alone with her four children, Randy, age 3 months and three siblings aged 18 months, 4 years and 6 years, and four adults: Randy's great grandmother who lived next door, his two uncles, and his aunt who visited regularly. Randy's mother was stressed by the burden of Randy's care and often required the other adults to spell her, especially when Randy had feeding problems or distress. However, the net effect of this pattern was to reduce her overall level of involvement with Randy and increase the inconsistency of his care which eventually culminated in decreased caloric intake and two hospitalizations for FTT. Following his second hospitalization, the family was encouraged to change their patterns of nurturing by increasing Randy's mother's in-volvement in his care, decreasing the numbers of caretakers, and enhancing the overall organization of his care. Randy's care was focused on two caregivers, his mother and great grandmother. His great grandmother was encouraged to utilize her energies in helping to feed Randy's sibling, who was quite demanding and claimed a great deal of his mother's attention. These interventions eventually resulted in improved nurturing and weight gain.

Separation and Individuation

One of the most common issues dealt with in family centered interven-tion concerned the relationship of the parents to their families of origin. In a number of cases, helping young families to cooperate with their ex-tended family networks while setting limits on the claims of family members presented formidable challenges as in the following example: Angela, a young mother with four children had just moved out of the apartment she had to escape her family that seemed to descend on her when she got the place. These "squatters" included her mother, her two adult brothers who didn't contribute money to the house, and a sister with her children. Everybody helped themselves to her food. There was never enough for the kids. Her mother could not set limits on this exploitation. Indeed, she was part of the problem. Angela found an apartment away from the neighborhood and moved in with the help of her children's father, swearing them to secrecy

about the location of her apartment and refusing to tell her family where
she was moving. Although this solved the immediate problem, it also left
her extremely isolated. To soften this effect, she alerted her one
"responsible" sister to a newly vacant apartment upstairs. Her sister
moved in and they were able to work out a mutually satisfactory relationship and child care.

Crisis Intervention

In families where the FTT child's hospitalization coincided with a
family crisis, adaptive resolution of this crisis became a primary goal of
intervention as in the following case example: Bobby was a 3-1/2 month old
white male admitted from the hospital emergency room for severe FTT, accompanied by vomiting and diarrhea. It came to light that Bobby's mother,
Debbie, was married to a man who stayed out late and often beat her when he
came home. In addition, they lived close to his mother who sided against
her and with her husband. She had long vowed she'd get a divorce if she
could get the money but needed support to make this break. While Bobby was
still in the hospital, our intervenor supported her decision and accompanied
her to a free legal clinic.

When Bobby was ready for discharge, Debbie announced her intention to
her husband of divorcing him. Once back home, Debbie's husband began to
harrass her by phone. Coincident with this stress, Bobby did not feed
easily and his weight gain stopped. He became anxious and was difficult to
soothe. In addition, her older son became quite demanding now that his
younger brother was home. Mealtimes were unscheduled, chaotic and tense.
Debbie was helped to see how reducing household tension and establishing
order were necessary to help Bobby. With support, Debbie was helped to
eventually limit her husband's harrassment, establish more dependable mealtimes, and a feeding schedule which included individual time to each child.
With these improvements, Bobby began to gain weight. Eventually, Debbie
moved closer to her kin, visited them weekly and maintained daily phone
contact.

THE LIMITS OF FAMILY-CENTERED INTERVENTION

Experienced clinicians will readily recognize that some of the families
of FTT infants remain resistant to change, even with intensive contacts.
When we encountered families whose pervasive structure and organizational
problems were recalcitrant to change, we considered intervention strategies
directed toward ameliorating the effects of family problems rather than
changing long-standing patterns of family relationships. Although some
families were not able to change their basic pattern of dysfunction, they
often could be helped to recognize the impact on the child and take steps
to limit the degree to which the infant was affected by family strife.
Unfortunately, some family environments remained potentially damaging to
the child. For example, in our experience one of the most recalcitrant
family problems involved chronically conflictual relationship between the
parents characterized by the father's abuse of the mother or substance
abuse, usually on the father's part. In such cases, the child's mother
could not easily separate from this relationship, nor could the family unit
be shifted from its dominance by the more impaired partner. For this
reason, continued surveillance by county welfare protective service to
monitor the family situation and, in some instances, foster care was necessary to ensure the child's well-being.

Impact on Intervenors

The special stresses engendered by working with the families of FTT infants in their home settings included the initiative that needed to be taken by the intervenor, the experience of personal vulnerability engendered by work in dangerous neighborhoods, and emotional reactions to families in great personal and economic distress. We often found ourselves immersed in personal pain and feelings of helplessness aroused by poverty and felt outraged that family members had to live this way. Steering a line between being the infant's advocate versus the family's advocate often resulted in divided loyalties which were hard for us to manage. Finally, the feelings of helplessness and frustration engendered by chronic, unchangeable family problems which defied intervention were especially troubling.

A number of strategies were effective in facilitating support to enable intervenors to work with the troubled families of FTT over an extended period of time: Informal groups were a key element in mutual support. These informal groups were facilitated by group meetings and weekly individual supervision. More specialized forms of support included self-defense lessons, which had both a pragmatic and psychological value. Finally, the recognition of the difficulties involved in reaching the families of FTT infants, caseloads were reduced and in most instances, averaged 10-15 for those doing weekly home visits.

IMPLICATIONS

The present findings have a number of implications for clinical intervention and research in FTT. Our experience has suggested that family-centered assessment can be a useful means of delineating the complex factors that influence the origins and maintenance of FTT. Because family assessment extends the range of assessment beyond the mother-child dyad, it can illuminate critical processes, especially the role of fathers and extended family members, as they influence the child directly and/or maternal nurturing. A number of investigators have begun to document a relationship between the quality of the parents' relationship and maternal-child interaction in samples of healthy children. For example, Pederson et al. (1979) have found that tension and conflict between husband and wife related to independent observations of the quality of maternal feeding competence; the more husbands criticized and blamed their wives, the more negative was the maternal interaction with five-month old infants.

Future research should be directed toward describing intrafamilial influences on FTT with greater precision. For example, the role of family support networks as they effect prognosis in FTT would be a fruitful area of investigation. Systematic description of family functioning via objective instruments is of key importance. Relevant variables include family structure, income, family size, spacing of children or household density (Pollitt & Leibel, 1980); social network and support (Cochran & Brassard, 1971; Weinraub, Brooks & Lewis, 1971); stress and functioning (Olson & McCubbin, 1983; Olson, Russell & Sprenkle, 1983). Family functioning may be rated by outside observers (Beavers & Voeller, 1983; Epstein, Bishop & Baldwin, 1982) or by family members (Moos & Moos, 1976). Finally, more detailed assessment of the family's interrelationship with neighborhood and support systems (Garbarino, 1977; Wahler, 1980) promises to extend our understanding of the origins and maintenance of FTT.

Clinical descriptions of family-centered intervention in FTT are very much needed, both as a means of sharing information about potentially effective techniques and a means of shaping more precise hypotheses about intervention effects. In addition to the heuristic value of studies of family functioning in generating hypotheses about the origins and consequences of FTT, assessment of the efficacy of family intervention, especially the fit between family intervention and subtypes of family functioning in FTT would be a useful future direction. As in family therapy (Gurman & Kniskern, 1981), family-centered intervention may be very useful for some families and contraindicated for others. For example, in some disorganized families, working with the family as a total system may be extremely difficult and even counterproductive. In such instances, it may be more effective to concentrate therapeutic resources on the mother to enable her to negotiate family problems more effectively. In either case, a comprehensive knowledge of the family system can be very helpful in ascertaining the nature of family problems. One of the goals of our future work will be to determine the factors which are associated with response to intervention, and with positive vs. negative longer-term outcomes in the child. Thus far, our findings have indicated that most families will accept intervention, that early outcomes in growth and cognitive development are age-adequate, and that the non-specific effects of intervention (e.g., contact, continuity of care) are important (see Drotar et al., this volume for a more detailed description of outcome).

Our preliminary findings have also suggested that family variables may be related to prognosis, especially in combination with measures of the child's physical status at intake. For example, better economic resources and personal resources for caretaking (as defined by the ratio of adults to children), were associated with positive early outcomes in cognition and language (Drotar et al., 1985). On the other hand, a greater number of family stresses at study intake were associated with risk factors such as insecure attachment, especially avoidant attachment at 12 months.

We believe that individual differences in chronic patterns of family functioning will emerge as a salient predictor of longer-term psychological outcome in FTT. Clinical observations suggested that families characterized by extreme instability (as defined by number of moves and relationship difficulties) were unable to provide basic needs for their children. Such families are often extremely difficult to work with because the family organizational difficulties are so extensive that the family is not able to engage in intervention. There is a great need for prognostic studies to identify families with children who have the poorest long-term outcomes. Although such families are difficult to follow, it may be possible to track health outcomes in the child such as readmission for FTT, infections, and illnesses and accidents.

Given the fact that the families of FTT infants share many of the same stressors, and economic disadvantages as other families, a question remains concerning the factors which differentiate the families of FTT infants from those who do not develop FTT. One hypothesis is that the families of FTT infants are more likely to demonstrate family functioning that is in some way dysfunctional and that these problems are chronic. Preliminary analysis of our comparison group data suggests that the families of FTT infants have a greater number of stressors and more pervasive problems than those with comparable economic levels and family structures whose children do not develop FTT.

Another interesting question for future research concerns the relationship of family functioning to individual differences in onset and presenting problems associated with FTT. For example, one might expect some correspondence between the developmental nature of relationship difficulties experienced by mother and child and patterns of intrafamilial relationships. The articulation of such relationships with respect to the families of FTT infants will have broad implications for the understanding of the family as a system (Minuchin, 1985).

REFERENCES

Altemeier, W.A., Vietze, P., Sherrod, K.B., Sandler, H.M., Falsey, S. & O'Connor, S. Prediction of child maltreatment during pregnancy. Journal of the American Academy of Child Psychiatry, 1979, 18, 205–219.

Ayoub, C. & Jacewitz, M.M. Families at risk of poor parenting: A model for service delivery, assessment, and intervention. Child Abuse and Neglect, 1982, 6, 351–358.

Barbero, G., Morris, M. & Redford, M. Malidentification of mother-baby-father relationships expressed in infant failure to thrive. In The Neglected Battered Child Syndrome: Role Reversal in Parents. New York: Child Welfare League of America, 1963.

Beavers, W.C. & Voeller, M.N. Family models: Comparing the Olson circumplex model with the Beavers system model. Family Process, 1983, 22, 85–98.

Belsky, J. The determinants of parenting: A process model. Child Development, 1984, 55, 83–96.

Belsky, J., Robins, E. & Gamble, W. In M. Lewis (Ed.), Beyond the Dyad, (pp. 251–279). New York: Plenum, 1984.

Bruenlin, D.C., Desai, V.J., Stone, M.E. & Swilley, J. Failure to thrive with no organic etiology: A critical review. International Journal of Eating Disorders, 1983, 2, 25–49.

Cassidy, C.M. Benign neglect and toddler malnutrition. In C. Greene & F.E. Johnson (Eds.), Social and Biological Predictors of Nutritional Status, Physical Growth and Neurological Development. New York: Academic Press, 1980.

Cochran, M.M. & Brassard, J.A. Child development and personal social networks. Child Development, 1979, 50, 601–615.

Drotar, D. & Malone, C.A. Family-oriented intervention in failure to thrive. In M. Klaus & M.O. Robertson (Eds.), Johnson and Johnson Pediatric Round Table, Vol. 6: Birth Interaction and Attachment. Skillman, NJ: Johnson and Johnson, 1982.

Drotar, D., Nowak, M., Malone, C.A., Eckerle, D. & Negray, J. Early psychological outcome in failure to thrive: Predictions from an interactional model. Journal of Clinical Child Psychology, 1985, 14, 105–111.

Elmer, E. Failure to thrive: Role of the mother. Pediatrics, 1960, 25, 717–725.

Epstein, N.B., Bishop, D.S. & Baldwin, L.M. McMaster model of family functioning: A view of the normal family. In F. Walsh (Ed.), Normal Family Processes. New York: Guilford, 1982.

Evans, S.L., Reinhart, J.B. & Succop, R.A. Failure to thrive: A study of 45 children and their families. Journal of the American Academy of Child Psychiatry, 1972, 11, 440–459.

Fischoff, J., Whitten, C.F. & Pettit, M.G. A psychiatric study of mothers of infants with growth failure secondary to maternal deprivation. Journal of Pediatrics, 1971, 79, 209–215.

Garbarino, J. The human ecology of child maltreatment: A conceptual model for research. Journal of Marriage and the Family, 1977, 39, 721–735.

Gurman, A.G. & Kniskern, D.P. (Eds.). Handbook of Family Therapy. New York: Brunner Mazel, 1981.

Hartman, A. Finding families: An ecological approach to family assessment in adoption. Beverly Hills, CA: Sage, 1979.

Howard, A. & Scott, R.A. The study of minority groups in complex societies. In R.H. Munroe, R.L. Monroe & B.B. Whiting (Eds.), Handbook of Cross Cultural Human Development. New York: Garland Press,   .

Kanawati, A.A., Darwish, O. & McLaren, D.S. Failure to thrive in Lebanon, III: Family income, expenditure and possession. Acta Paediatrica Scandinavia, 9174, 63, 849–854.

Kanawati, A.A. & McLaren, D.S. Failure to thrive in Lebanon, II: An inves-

tigation of the causes. Acta Paediatrica Scandinavia, 1973, 62, 571-
576.

Kellam, S.G., Ensminger, M.E. & Turner, R.J.   Family structure and the
mental health of children. Archives of General Psychiatry, 1977, 34,
1012-1022.

Kotelchuck, M.   Nonorganic failure to thrive: The status of interactional
and environmental theories.   In B.W. Camp (Ed.), Advances in Behavioral
Pediatrics: Vol. 1.   Greenwich, CN: Jai Press, 1980.

Kotelchuck, M. & Newberger, E.H.   Failure to thrive: A controlled study of
family characteristics.   Journal of the American Academy of Child
Psychiatry, 1983, 22, 322-328.

Leonard, M.F., Rhymes, J.P. & Solnit, A.M.   Failure to thrive in infants: A
family problem. American Journal of Diseases of Children, 1966, III,
600-612.

Maybanks, S. & Bryce, M.   Home-Based Service for Children and Families:
Policy, Practice and Research.   Chicago, IL: Thomas, 1979.

Minuchin, P.   Families and individual development: Provocations from the
field of family therapy.   Child Development, 1985, 56, 289-302.

Minuchin, S., Rosman, B. & Baker, L.   Psychosomatic Families.   Cambridge,
MA: Harvard University Press, 1978.

Moos, R. & Moos, B.   A typology of family social environments.   Family
Process, 1976, 15, 357-371.

Nagel, S.J.   Ombudsman among the poor.   In V.B. Ermer & J.H. Strange
(Eds.), Blacks and Bureaucracy.   New York: Thomas Crowell, 1972.

Nagi, S.Z.   A bureaucratic environment and gatekeeping decisions.   In S.
Salzinger, J. Antrobus & J. Glick (Eds.), The Ecosystem of the Sick
Child.   New York: Academic Press, 1980.

Olson, D.H. & McCubbin, H.I.   Families: What Makes Them Work?   Beverly
Hills, CA: Sage, 1983.

Olson, D.H., Russell, C.S. & Sprenkle, D.H.   Model of marital and family
systems.   Family Process, 1983, 22, 69-83.

Parke, R.D.   Perspectives on father-infant interaction.   In J.D. Osofsky
(Ed.), Handbook of Infant Development.   New York: Wiley, 1979.

Patton, R.G. & Gardner, L.I.   Influences of family environment on growth:
The syndrome of maternal deprivation.   Pediatrics, 1962, 30, 957-962.

Pedersen, F.A., Anderson, B.J. & Cain, R.L.   Parent-infant and husband-wife
interaction observed at age 5 months.   In F.A. Pederson (Ed.), Father-
Infant Relationship Observational Studies in the Family Setting.   New
York: Praeger, 1980.

Piven, F.F. & Cloward, R.A.   Regulating the Poor: The Functions of Social
Welfare.   New York: Vintage, 1971.

Pollitt, E. & Leibel, R.   Biological and social correlates of failure to
thrive.   In L. Greene & F.E. Johnston (Eds.), Social Biological
Predictors of Nutritional Status, Physical Growth and Neurological
Development.   New York: Academic Press, 1980.

Stack, C.B.   Strategies for Survival in a Black Community.   New York:
Harper and Row, 1974.

Stack, C.B.   Who raises black children: Transactions of child givers and
child receivers.   In T.R. Williams (Ed.), Socialization and Communication in Primary Groups.   The Hague: Mouton, 1975.

Talbot, N.B., Sobel, E.H., Burke, B.S., Lindeman, E. & Kaufman, S.B.   Dwarfism in healthy children: Its possible relation to emotional, nutritional and endocrine disturbances.   New England Journal of Medicine,
1947, 236, 783-793.

Wachs, T.D.   Proximal experience and early cognitive interrelated environment - the physical environment.   Merrill Palmer Quarterly, 1971, 17,
283-317.

Wahler, R.G.   The insular mother: Her problems in parent-child treatment.
Journal of Applied Behavior Analysis, 1980, 13, 207-219.

Weinraub, M., Brooks, J. & Lewis, M.   The social network: A reconsideration
of the concept of attachment.   Human Development, 1977, 20, 31-47.

ISSUES IN THE TREATMENT OF EMOTIONAL AND BEHAVIORAL DISTURBANCES IN FAILURE TO THRIVE

Jennifer M. Rathbun

Clinical Associate in Psychiatry, Massachusetts General
Hospital and Clinical Instructor in Psychiatry
Harvard Medical School

The therapeutic work described in these chapters hold great promise
for increased efficacy in interventions concerning emotional and behavioral
problems associated with FTT, a condition which certainly requires multiple
and specific problem-oriented interventions. Dr. Chatoor and her colleagues
and Lieberman and Birch demonstrate fine-tuned diagnostic and therapeutic
skills in the most difficult and often overwhelming arena of emotional
functioning in the mother-infant pair. Dr. Drotar and his colleagues' work
incorporates sensitivity to the value and strength of family ties surround-
ing the mother-infant pair, ties which offer vital therapeutic resources
for recovery. Drs. Linscheid and Rasnake's work is noteworthy for efforts
to directly address and correct behavioral burdens in the feeding situation,
offering a sense of immediate relief and control to families and a concrete
"shot in the arm" while other aspects of treatment are beginning.

All of us come to the arena of treatment in emotional and behavioral
disorders with our own professional training biases concerning what treatment means. Philosophically, however, we share a similar set of steps in
approaching the treatment questions:

Step I:	What is the problem?
Step II:	What is the etiology?
Step III:	What is the goal of treatment (i.e. the solution or resolution)?
Step IV:	How can the goal be reached in such a way as to return the (child) patient to a full range of his emotional capacities in developing, experiencing and partici- pating in the affective world?

Let me review with you how I have synthesized the various answers
presented in this volume into a broader view of treatment issues.

I. WHAT ARE THE PROBLEMS IN THE EMOTIONAL AND BEHAVIORAL DISTURBANCES ASSOCIATED WITH FTT

Dr. Chatoor tells us they are, in part: <u>feeding disturbances</u> as the
symptomatic manifestation of basic homeostatic, attachment or separation
difficulties in the feeding mother-infant pair. Dr. Lieberman tells they

are in part: <u>transactional impasses</u> between the infant and the caregiver at different developmental stages, manifested most concretely in growth failure but also in many other less obvious areas of impared socioemotional functioning in the infant. Dr. Drotar tells us they are, in part: <u>distressed interfamilial relationships</u> within the parent couple, the extended family or a dense sibling network that serves to influence and ultimately render at risk the adequacy of the infant's nutruting environment. Dr. Linscheid tells us they are, in part: <u>aberrant patterns of reinforcement</u> for feeding behaviors in the target child. These authors' work touches on each of four areas I had once constructed as critical problem areas in the psychosocial functioning of FTT families in our clinic (Bithoney & Rathbun, 1983).

I might offer along with Dr. Lieberman a fifth answer to "What is the problem?" in the emotional-behavioral treatment of FTT and that is:

> The initial and sometimes persistent resistance of many
> FTT families to letting their problem be known and
> understood by outsiders - in letting people get close.
> It is the problem of <u>personal alliances and the
> building of trust</u> as a foundation to emotional-
> behavioral treatment, a problem that insiduously weaves
> itself into every other treatment issue and can
> ultimately disarm a potential cure.

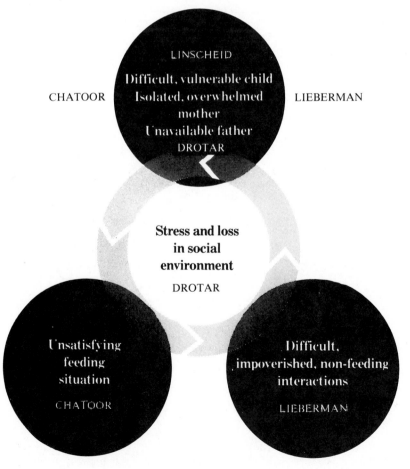

Figure 1

312

Going on to our review of treatment issues:

II. WHAT IS THE ETIOLOGY OF THE PROBLEM?

Dr. Chatoor offers failure of somatopsychological differentiation in the infant and ultimately in the caregiver, something Hilda Bruch has written about as well (Bruch, 1973). Dr. Lieberman tells us: failure in the mutual adaptation of the baby and mother to the challenges of a given stage of infant development. Dr. Drotar offers the absence of a family system's buffering capacities to stress and/or the loss of the extended family's special nurturing capacities to the mother-child pair.

III. WHAT IS THE GOAL OF TREATMENT?

The separate and unique goals of each presenter were clear:

Chatoor et al.: making mealtime a neutral arena;

Lieberman & Birch: disengaging external affect based in part on prior nurturing experiences from interactions with the infant;

Drotar et al.: freeing up the family network to mobilize for the child;

Linscheid & Rasnake: decreasing aberrant behaviors and increasing behaviors adaptive to successful eating.

Thus, each author has addressed within the spectrum of their own problem area, the goal of returning the FTT child and family to a fuller range of emotional capacity.

IV. HOW CAN THE GOAL BE REACHED IN SUCH A WAY AS TO RETURN THE CHILD PATIENT TO A FULLER RANGE OF HIS EMOTIONAL CAPACITIES IN DEVELOPING, EXPERIENCING AND PARTICIPATING IN THE AFFECTIVE WORLD?

In considering the goals of treatment, the following questions must also be asked: 1) Is our goal of emotional-behavioral treatment for the FTT child and family the same goal that the family would choose for themselves?; and 2) Does the treatment inflict no additional pain or harm into an already distressed system?

The unique pitfalls of treatment in FTT include those of becoming the too good and all intrusive parent who overcontrols and ultimately undermines parental autonomy, especially their attempts to learn the nurturance and healthy feeding of their child. Such a mistake can limit the chance for cure. The true gift of treatment is the caring transfer of our skills into the hands and hearts of your patients' families, returning the power and essence of parenting to its proper place. We ride a fine line in this work between benign neglect of our parents' needs and overintrusion and control of their domain. Both extremes can recreate in ourselves the parenting disorders we are attempting to treat: those that result in the relative neglect of our patients' and parents' emotional needs.

In some respects, these patients and families are vulnerable and easy to hurt. For this reason, professionals must take great care not to inflict iatrogenic harm in the course of treatment and to advocate for the safe passage of these families throughout the various systems they utilize. Through it all, the treating professional must stay cognizant of his or her own limits and needs. As Dr. Seuss so vividly reminds us when Horton the Elephant takes on more than he can manage nesting on the egg through blizzards of winter: it can be cold out there!

Let me close on a note of prevention:

I recently spent a lovely, restful week in Swansea, Wales at the International Conference on Anorexia Nervosa and Related Disorders and subsequently spent a day at Oxford with Dr. Christopher Fairbourne, a psychiatrist and permanent fellow at the University of Oxford. Dr. Fairbourne was fascinated by our high incidence of FTT in America. He offered, by contrast, his English experience of rare and primarily organic FTT in Britain. He went on to describe the system of care every new mother receives in England. Prenatal care in their medical system is free, available and widely used thanks to careful tracking of and outreach to all women found to be pregnant. Similarly, routine postnatal care includes home visits starting just after discharge by a mothercraft nurse to the homes of all new mothers. Careful attention, in these visits, is paid to the early establishment of healthy and mutually satisfying skills in feeding, developmental and behavioral management and nurturing the newborn. Often the father is present for these visits and is a part of the support given. Community mothercraft centers sit in the backdrop of these services as a further resource to young families.

Perhaps we can be inspired by this simple yet elegant preventive model. The intervention strategies we have heard today have a richness that might be incorporated into a public health preventive model. Dr. Beatrix Hamburg, Professor of Child Psychiatry at Mt. Sinai Hosital in New York, once commented that, in mother-infant pairs and young families, if you catch the problem early, it is only a tiny deviation to correct from the normal range of interaction. If you catch it late, the vacillations can be far, far off course.

REFERENCES

Bithoney, W. & Rathbun, J. Failure to thrive. In M. Levine, W. Carey, A.
    Crocker, & R. Gross, (Eds.), Developmental-Behavioral Pediatrics.
    Philadelphia: W. B. Saunders, 1983.
Bruch, H. Eating Disorders. New York: Basic Books, 1973.

V   PRIMARY PREVENTION

Primary prevention of FTT is one of the most important goals for future research and clinical practice. Given the large numbers of affected children and the considerable costs to society and individual families incurred by FTT, primary prevention of FTT and associated physical and psychosocial problems is of special importance. However, the issues involved in primary prevention of FTT and strategies of preventive intervention have not been a primary focus of research and practice. For example, investigators have generally not considered the influence of the broader societal context on the development of FTT, the potential of FTT as an indicator of childrens health as affected by family and societal conditions, and role of primary and/or secondary prevention in health care and community settings. The information presented in this section is designed to increase professional awareness of prevention issues in FTT and research and clinical practice that is related to prevention.

Brams and Coury consider research studies and concepts related to health promotion and primary prevention of FTT. Their review suggests that highly focused programs which are designed to enhance parental behavior may lower the incidence of FTT. Brams and Coury present a useful description of the components of primary prevention, the problems of definition in prevention, early identification, individual versus community prevention and suggestions for future research related to prevention. These authors consider the importance of educational efforts for pediatricians, possibilities for screening infants at risk for growth failure, the ethical and legal issues in screening and prospects for preventative services, such as parenting education, home visitors, nutritional support, and legislation concerning child abuse reporting laws.

Frank, Allen & Brown discuss the social policy implications of the primary prevention of FTT with special emphasis on the relevance of economic conditions to the development and maintenance of FTT. Frank and her colleagues describe the ways that poverty can affect the biologic and psychological status of children and note that amelioration of the family's level of material depletion is often a prerequisite to successful intervention. The evidence that poverty is linked to nutritional deprivation, the effects of reducing the availability of resources to economically disadvantaged individuals for obtaining food and the adverse effects on children's health and psychological status are described. Frank and her coworkers delineate implications case management, future research, and for programs which safeguard the health and nutrition of eocnomically impoverished families. Frank, Allen & Brown note that data and clinical examples which illustrate the impact of poverty on individual FTT children can be used to marshal political support to prevent cutbacks in programs such as food stamps or the Women, Infant and Children supplemental feeding program (WIC). These authors outline the need for future research concerning the effects of improved nutritional and concrete services on the prevention of FTT and concerning the link between economic privation and the development of FTT.

Gordon and Vazquez present data in support of Frank and her coworkers' contention that the incidence of FTT is related to economic factors such as high unemployment in a community. Gordon and Vazquez report findings from their descriptive retrospective study of the impact of an economic recession on children's physical health. More specifically, Gordon and Vazquez hypothesized that physical growth of young children is a sensitive marker of the economic conditions of a community. Their findings show a consistent increase in the total number of children with growth failure who were admitted to the Hurley Medical Center in Flint, Michigan during 1978-1982. The increased number of admissions for FTT and data concerning method of payment closely parallel the deepening recession and rising unemployment for that city. Gordon and Vazquez suggest that investigation of the relationship of economic conditions to the incidence and prevalence of physical growth and nutritional deficiency among children in various communities in the U.S.A. would be a fruitful area of future investigation which has special relevance to prevention.

PRIMARY PREVENTION OF FAILURE TO THRIVE

Jolie S. Brams and Daniel L. Coury

The Ohio State University and Columbus Children's Hospital

Over the past two decades the syndrome of FTT has received an increasing amount of attention from researchers. During this period, considerable effort has been made towards describing this problem and identifying and treating these children and families. However, relatively little research has focused on prevention of this disorder. In this chapter the authors will discuss the concept of prevention from both a "social epidemiological" and "health promotion" perspective; review the literature on prevention of FTT and related conditions such as child abuse and neglect; identify research and programmatic needs for prevention of this disorder; specify some methodological considerations; and discuss the goals, obstacles, and ethics which relate to the development of a primary prevention program.

The public health model of prevention was first developed during a time when great strides were being made in the field of infectious diseases. The relative simplicity and widespread acceptance of the medical-epidemiological model led to the outgrowth of social epidemiological models of psychological and sociological dysfunction. The medical epidemiological model follows a very logical cause and effect scheme and hence is well suited to illnesses with clearly defined etiologies, known complications, effective treatment strategies, and identifiable populations at risk. Armed with this knowledge of a disease process, a realistic plan can be devised for preventing the disease, altering or interrupting its course, and minimizing the sequelae. The types of interventions aimed at each of these stages of the disease process are known as primary, secondary and tertiary prevention efforts. Primary prevention is defined as the eradication of the disease process before it begins, either by elimination of the causal agent or immunization of the population at risk. One example of such an effort is the smallpox vaccination program. Secondary prevention is focused on interrupting the course of the disease and preventing future cases in others at risk. This is the point of impact of the great majority of child abuse programs, in which the child is first identified after the abuse has occurred and intervention efforts are aimed at preventing future abuse towards the patient as well as his or her siblings. Tertiary prevention efforts attempt to minimize the sequelae of the disease. In this framework psychotherapy for abused children would qualify as a tertiary prevention effort.

Many studies in the area of child abuse and FTT have been labeled as "primary prevention" efforts, but a purist might categorize these as attempts at health promotion. Such programs are less concerned with reducing the incidence of a pathological condition than they are with the promoting of physical and psychological health and thus indirectly decreasing the incidence of the "disease." In a joint statement by the National Mental Health Association and the National Institute of Mental Health it was clearly stated that primary prevention and promotion of mental health should not be used interchangeably.

For purposes of this chapter, research efforts which attempt to reduce the incidence of either FTT or child abuse will be noted and discussed, including both primary prevention and health promotion orientations. A review of child abuse prevention research is included for two primary reasons: One, the research literature on FTT alone is sparse, and several studies of child abuse prevention include FTT infants, although this syndrome is not primarily addressed in these reports. Two, the literature in child abuse presents many parallels to the problem of FTT (see Sherrod et al., this volume).

REVIEW OF THE LITERATURE

Health Promotion Programs

The facilitation of positive mental and physical health in children and families has been the concern of individual researchers as well as government programs. The primary aim of such health promotion efforts is to improve the quality of life by providing opportunities for optimal development, thereby decreasing the risk for the development of dysfunction. Thus, these programs are not necessarily concerned with prevention of a specific disorder, although disorders might be avoided through these health promotion activities.

In the late 1960's through early 1970's, a number of government efforts focused on bolstering the emotional and educational resources of children and families. For example, the Education for Parenthood program (Kruger, 1973; Marland, 1973; Rossoff, 1973) focused on facilitating parenting skills in high school students through didactic as well as participatory activities. Similar programs have been developed by Marion (1982) to expose students to basic information concerning child development as well as child development workers who modeled appropriate parenting skills. The aim of this program was to increase students' sensitivity to the needs of children, to individual differences, and to the realities of parenthood. This program also served to provide information as to where a parent could turn for assistance, and make students aware of the "value and methods of family planning" (Cohen, 1973). Unfortunately, while this and similar programs on local levels have assessed the participants' short-term responses to the program, there is no data concerning outcome in terms of actual parenting. As de Lissovoy (1978) notes, there is a paucity of data indicating that short-term measures of attitude change or limited behavioral change can produce long-term behavioral effects. In addition, he argues that adolescents may in fact be the wrong targets for parenting education: because of the natural egocentricity of that developmental period and the focus on identity issues, the adolescent may not be ready to become involved in the parenting process. De Lissovoy suggests that programs may be better suited to adolescent parents, although there is evidence that this target group is experiencing similar adolescent issues. In terms of prevention of FTT, it makes intuitive sense that an increased appreciation about children's physical and emotional needs would reduce the risk of infant growth failure, but this is not proven. In addition to programs aimed at adolescents, there have been a multitude of efforts directed at improving adults' parenting skills. These have ranged from well publicized efforts, such as parent-effectiveness-training (PET)(Gordon, 1971) to lesser known programs in local school or mental health systems, utilizing a variety of methods. These programs appear to serve an educational as well as a social purpose. For example, social isolation is reduced through participation and interaction (Alvy, 1975). However, again little data exists illustrating the effect of such programs on decreases in the rates of abuse or FTT.

While adolescent and adult parenting programs are widely used, other educational/supportive approaches to promoting optimal infant growth and development and preventing dysfunction have been suggested. Perhaps the most widely referenced suggestion is the "Health Visitor Concept" (Kempe, 1976). In this model, a health visitor, preferably a trained paraprofessional, would be assigned to every mother and her family from before the birth of the child through the preschool years. The primary goal of this program would be to assure that the basic health needs of every child are met. Health visitors would provide mothercrafting skills, as well as emotional support to families. Regarding FTT, nutritional information would be shared, and the infant routinely weighed, measured and have a record kept of physical growth. Although Kempe does not directly address this issue, such routine monitoring of infant growth might provide very early indication of growth deceleration and imminent FTT. Of course, such a program might also identify developing family difficulties that might lead to abuse. Thus, the "Health Visitors Concept" has a health promotion as well as primary prevention focus.

Health promotion activities may also take place in day care settings. This makes intuitive sense. As Barber-Madden (1983) states, "day care programs have the potential for providing growth experiences, supportive adult role models, and modeling parental skills in an atmosphere of understanding, respect and trust." However, for day care centers to be able to act in a health promotion role, Barber-Madden hypothesized that the staff needed to be educated to recognize problems in parenting and informed of the role of child care workers in prevention activities. Through a survey of 84 day care centers, it was found that day care programs in which staff had participated in brief training engaged in more preventative activities such as parent education and, although somewhat more in the category of primary prevention, high risk referrals. Although this study has a number of methodological flaws, including differences in sizes between "trained" and "untrained" groups and problems in subject self-selection, it is an interesting intitial attempt at examining the usefulness of day care centers as mechanisms of health promotion.

Deficits in parental knowledge may impact on the incidence of infant growth failure, and several studies of FTT as well as child abuse suggest that maternal and/or familial isolation may be causally related to the development of these problems (Garbarino & Crouter, 1978; Cochran & Brassard, 1979). Programs which strengthen social networks for parents may reduce the incidence of dysfunction by providing a mechanism for reducing life stress and lending emotional support to the parent(s). Such programs may also indirectly serve an educational purpose or act as a pipeline to avenues of assistance in the greater community. Powell (1980) discussed the effects of one community-based social support program on parenting. Preliminary results indicate a relationship between degree of involvement in the social support program and quality of maternal behaviors. Powell found that verbal and emotional responsivity were more likely with frequent contact with friends in the program and that similar variables also correlated significantly with the amount of child care assistance provided by group members.

However, other studies of the effectiveness of parent support groups, as described by Wandersman (1982), suggest that social support alone may not always result in the attitudinal and behavioral change necessary to prevent problems in parenting and child outcome. Although it seems "good sense" that improved social support should facilitate parental functioning, the evidence for this point is equivocal. Programs which have incorporated outcome measures have found a variety of outcomes, from no attitudinal or behavioral change to significant changes in maternal perceptions and beliefs, utilization of health care, and infant differences. More importantly, other studies have found that support groups may have less impact on parenting than do family and close friends (Colletta, 1981 Belle, 1981), and little evidence is available to support the idea that these groups greatly influence behavior (Harman & Brim, 1980). As they suggest, "parental behaviors are influenced by a wide range of factors including ability, unconscious factors, cultural values, network controls, family patterns, and ecological and physical constraints... increased supportive social contacts may increase the parent's satisfaction in a difficult transition but may have little impact on parenting behaviors which are enmeshed in the parent's social system." However, Wandersman suggests some mechanisms for facilitating the impact of parenting groups and her suggestions carry a special significance for families at high risk for FTT. She emphasizes matching program goals to the needs of the participants. Support does not necessarily produce behavior change, especially when such change is not valued or desired by the participants. However, at least one well designed study has suggested that behavior change is likely with a high risk group who perceives a need and participates in a structured program (Badger, 1981). In this study, infants of young adolescent mothers who regularly attended infant stimulation classes showed greater increases in mental development than did the infants of older, lower risk adolescents. In this regard, programs may also be more successful if they have a clearly defined behavioral focus. Programs which specify their emphasis, such as the group program created by Dickie and Gerber (1980), which focuses on parental responsiveness, or the program developed by Coysh (1981), which deals with family relationships, may be more successful in eliciting behavior change than programs with general goals. In terms of FTT, it might be effective to focus on specific parental behaviors which are expected to reduce the risk of growth failure in the infant.

Although the "purist" definition of health promotion would only include interventions aimed at benefiting "all" parents and children, rather than a selected "at risk" group, at least one health promotion effort has focused on families that self-selected as in need of assistance. Pillai et al. (1982) report preliminary data from families involved in an urban "walk-in center." Unfortunately, the data is descriptive in nature and many conclusions are based solely on clinical impressions. Although the results of this study are far from conclusive, the authors note that 38% of families demonstrated "overall improvement in child care and the parent-child relationship" and that there was a decrease in the area's number of reported cases of abuse.

Primary Prevention

Research which has been done on "true" primary prevention of nonorganic FTT is scant and has focused more on the following specific components of primary prevention programs: clearly defining the disease, methods of identifying those at risk, and development of effective treatment plans. There have been few comprehensive studies done of a complete primary prevention program.

Definition of FTT

The difficulty of clearly defining the target condition or "disease" in FTT has hindered prevention efforts. However, there is agreement on the physical parameters of the disease. Although various definitions are presented in the research and clinical literature, most professionals would likely agree that FTT is defined when an infant's weight is severely deficient in relationship to height and age. More specifically, the precise physical parameters used to define a child as failing to thrive fall into two categories. The first is the child who has a weight below the 5th percentile for age with a concomitant height at or above the 5th percentile for age; thus the child is underwieght for his height. The second category is not so much a precise placement as it is a downward trend in the child's growth pattern, more specifically defined as a drop across two major percentiles on a growth curve (Schmitt, 1978). Thus a child in this category might have had a birth weight and previous growth pattern along the 90th percentile but has now dropped to the 25th percentile. The single isolated finding of a child who is at the 25th percentile for weight does not draw undue attention, but the growth pattern which brought the child to that point is of concern. Utilization of either of these definitions allows for the identification of children who have encountered significant growth failure. (See Pederson et al., this volume for a detailed discussion of physical growth assessment.) Unfortunately it requires the growth failure to have progressed a great deal before being identified. Other proposed methods for identifying children who are failing to thrive, based on growth velocity or caloric intake for weight, are more difficult to utilize and are not as easily appreciated as the hard data seen on a growth chart. As a result, the first two definitions used here are those generally used in practice.

Although these physical descriptors provide an adequate definition of FTT for treatment purposes, they do not fit well with the medical epidemiological model of prevention because of the multiple possible organic and nonorganic causes for the child's growth failure (Casey et al., 1984; Chatoor et al., 1984; Woolston, 1983). (See Frank; Bithoney & Dubowitz, this volume). With so many varied causes under the classification of nonorganic FTT, it becomes necessary to devise a variety of methods to identify the cause in any one child. Similarly, the causal characteristics influence the treatment plan. Psychosocial assessment has been repeatedly recommended in the diagnostic evaluation of an infant with failure to thrive (Bithoney & Rathbun, 1983), but such global, lengthy, and nonvalidated techniques are not useful for screening large numbers of infants. Thus we see that nonorganic FTT conforms to the medical epidemiological model in having a definable end state but does not fit neatly into this model because of the many and sometimes interacting causes of growth failure.

Screening Efforts

Gray et al. (1977) utilized an interview, questionnaire, and observations during labor, delivery and the post partum period in an effort to predict mothers at high risk for abnormal parenting practices. Information obtained from the prenatal interview and the later administration of a 74-item questionnaire included parental attitudes toward discipline, expectations for the child, historical information, and data concerning the present living situation. Labor and delivery room observations focused on parental reactions to the birth, both verbal and nonverbal. Similar observations were made during the post partum period and social supports and stresses were also noted. Using the data generated from this perinatal evaluation, Gray and her colleagues divided a sample of mothers into "high" and "low" risk groups. Data from a two year follow up indicate that children in the high-risk group had encountered significantly different parenting practices. In addition, 10% of the high-risk group experienced serious abuse requiring hospitalization, while there was no incidence of severe abuse in the low risk group. In terms of the usefulness of the various predictive measures employed in this study, information generated from observations in the delivery room was most accurate in predicting potential for abnormal parenting practices; in contrast, prenatal interviews were the least useful in predicting outcome.

In a large, prospective study of 1400 pregnant women, Altemeier et al. (1979, 1984) and Sherrod et al. (1984) utilized a prenatal interview, chart review, Carey Infant Temperament Scale, and certain demographic factors in an attempt to identify those at risk for abuse and neglect. The authors found a number of fairly good predictors of maltreatment within the first three years of life. These included high risk status based on a prenatal interview, life stress, infant temperament, family dysfunction, child illness, maternal illness, low maternal eductional level, and mothers' impulsivity, as measured by her inability to wait in the clinic without leaving before being seen. Interestingly, in terms of a multifaceted model of causality of nonorganic FTT, this study demonstrates that a screening tool which addresses multiple theories of causality can be developed.

Lealman et al. (1983) attempted to use relatively simple measures in a prognostic study of child abuse, which included a nonorganic FTT subgroup. The authors devised a checklist of both "major" and "minor" risk factors, and considered an infant to be "at risk" if at least three factors were present at the time of birth. Major factors included a mother less than 20 years old, who had delayed prenatal care, or who was not married. Minor factors included step-children in the family, maternal psychiatric history, previous referral to a social worker, termination of pregnancy requested but refused (whether due to legal or medical reasons is unclear), complications of pregnancy or delivery, infant experiencing post-natal complications, or mother took own infant's discharge against advice. Of the 2802 cases screened, 511 cases (18%) were considered to be at risk and approximately two-thirds of the reported abuse occurred in that group during the 18 month study period. This study also suggested that families with previous contact with social agencies fared more poorly, especially in terms of the growth of their infants; 17.1% of infants in that group exhibited growth failure (defined as less than 85% of weight for height), as compared to 1.3% of the no-risk group. Although no statistical analyses were provided, it appears that high risk infants whose families had previous contact with a social agency were more likely to be on the "abuse register" during the study period. Although this study has many methodological weaknesses, it seems to indicate that simple demographic measures might be helpful in the prediction of child abuse and FTT.

Ayoub and Pfeifer (1977) described a list of "at risk" indicators for abuse, neglect and parenting problems. This tool was used in a hospital/ clinic setting to identify parents at risk, at which time special services were offered. Like other screening devices described previously, it focuses on biological, psychological, social and interactional criteria to alert the involved professional to the risk present. In later studies (Ayoub et al., 1983; Milner & Ayoub, 1980; Milner & Wimberley, 1979; 1980) they describe their Child Abuse Potential Inventory (CAP), as a companion instrument for further delineating the risk potential. Use of their "at risk" criteria results in selection of a population in which 58% score above the 95th percentile on the CAP. Although these studies indicate effectiveness in selecting parents in need of preventative services, they unfortunately do not describe the incidence of subsequent abuse or FTT among these treated families or a control group, making it difficult to assess the clinical usefulness of these tools.

Hunter et al. (1978) prospectively followed 255 premature and ill newborns, a group at high risk for abuse. At the end of a year, 10 of the 255 (3.9%) had been reported for abuse or neglect, including two cases of failure to provide adequate nutrition. Review of the information obtained at admission revealed significant differences between abusive and non-abusive parents on several psychosocial characteristics. Among these were social isolation, serious marital problems, closely spaced children, and a family history of child abuse and neglect. These criteria allowed the authors to identify 41 of the 255 patients as high risk, and all 10 reported cases of abuse were found among the high risk group.

While the previous studies have attempted to predict child abuse and failure to thrive with data primarily collected during the perinatal period, Rosenberg and his associates (1982) conducted a prospective study using data generated in an emergency room setting. Emergency room nurses, through the use of observations and a simple interview, assessed both the parent and child on a number of dimensions. Parental dimensions included 1) aggressive behavior, defined as demanding special service, 2) hostile behavior, defined by such behaviors as shouting or cursing, 3) critical or overdemanding behavior toward the child, 4) lack of bonding, defined by such behaviors as lack of eye contact with child or not providing physical support and 5) altered behavior, defined as being under the influence of alcohol, with altered gait or behavior. The child assessment included 1) whether the child was unkempt, defined as having a severe diaper rash, dirt under nails or on the soles of the feet, or having a body odor, 2) bald occiput, and 3) physical bruises, burns or bites. Patients were excluded if it was felt that they were victims of child abuse at the time of the initial examination or if a retrospective review of the records indicated they had been previously abused. Child abuse records of both the hospital and state were reviewed 12 months after the emergency room visit, with a total of 456 subjects. Several factors were predictive of later child abuse. Altered parental behavior was the only isolated parenting pattern which proved to be significant. Children who were unkempt or who had abnormal bruises, burns, or human bites were also at greater risk for later abuse. When these factors were found in various combinations, their predictive usefulness increased. Although this relatively simple emergency room screening technique did not successfully identify all children who were later abused, this study suggests that some time and cost effective measures might serve as fairly good predictors of abnormal child outcome.

The preceeding review clearly indicates that although several interesting attempts have been made at predicting child abuse, and to a much less extent, FTT, highly effective screening measures have yet to be developed. While certain measures and factors might correctly label children as future victims of abuse or FTT, a large number of "false positives" are also identified. Thus, most of these reported measures have high "sensitivity" (the ability to correctly identify potential victims) but they also have low specificity (the ability to correctly identify those children who will not be victims). The ethical and logistical implications for this "high sensitivity/low specificity" problem will be addressed in a later section.

Prevention Directed Specifically at Child Abuse and FTT

Few primary preventative efforts have been attempted with FTT, although there have been considerably more efforts aimed at reducing the incidence of child abuse. Some of these efforts are conceptually quite close to the "health promotion" efforts previously cited. Such programs attempt to foster particular attitude and behavior changes, usually in parents, which theoretically should lead to reduction in the incidence of the disorder in the study group. Other programs hope to reduce the incidence of child abuse, neglect, and FTT through community-wide activities, which usually have components of education, referral, interagency and interdisciplinary cooperation, and counseling for "high-risk" families. Still others are more "sociologically-based," focusing on broad changes in the attitudinal, institutional, and financial structures of society. All of these approaches certainly have merit, but all are plagued by problems inherent in prevention research in general. Most importantly, it is extremely difficult to determine ultimate outcome in most prevention efforts in this area. This difficulty appears to primarily stem from the low base rate of the disorder; statistical significance cannot be demonstrated unless large numbers of subjects are included. While many studies can document changes in knowledge, behavior, attitude, or societal factors, documenting significant changes in incidence rate is not an easily attained goal. For the purpose of this chapter, only programs directed at attitudinal/behavioral change within a circumscribed population will be reviewed. For the interested reader, details of community-based prevention efforts in child abuse can be obtained from the National Committee for the Prevention of Child Abuse.

A recent review of prevention literature (Helfer, 1982) suggested that only two studies met standards for adequate research on prevention. Both of these studies focus on the facilitation of adequate caregiving through the provision of supportive services and experiences which promote caregiver/infant bonding.

Siegel et al. (1980) studied the effects of early and extended postpartum contact, as well as paraprofessional home visits, on maternal attachment, reported child abuse and neglect, and health care utilization in a sample of low-income mothers. Pregnant women who received health care at a public prenatal clinic were recruited and assigned to one of four study groups; 1) early and extended hospital contact with their newborn and home visits by a paraprofessional infant care worker; 2) early and extended contact only; 3) home visits only; and 4) routine hospital and follow up care. Dependent variables included home observations of mother/infant interaction in areas such as feeding, dressing, and play. Factor analysis of a 92 item "Attachment Inventory" yielded a number of factors at various infant ages; maternal acceptance, stimulation, and consoling. Maternal background variables were obtained from interviews conducted during the third trimester of pregnancy. Variables included race, marital status, parity, education, age, and a global intelligence score. Interestingly, although the interventions provided accounted for a small proportion of the variance in terms of the outcome measures, the background variables explained substantially more variance in maternal behavior.

The results of the Siegel study are in contrast with those found by O'Connor et al. (1980). These authors found that extended mother/infant contact during the neonatal period correlated with fewer subsequent cases of parenting inadequacy, as measured by physical or sexual abuse, FTT, relinquishment of caretaking responsibilities, abandonment, medical or physical neglect, or admission related to a mother/infant problem. It is important to note that more than 90% of the women who did not experience extended contact with their infants did not demonstrate problems in parenting. Thus, while this contact may facilitate bonding in some mothers, lack of this exprience is not universally detrimental. The authors suggest that extended contact may be especially beneficial to mothers predisposed to parenting problems.

One additional study focused on preventative interventions with families. Larson (1980) found that home visitors make a positive impact on the functioning of the mother and infant, but only when the home visitor makes contact prior to the birth of the infant. Using a working class population Larson found a reduction in the rate of accidents, higher scores on assessments of home environment and maternal behavior, a lower prevalence of interactional and feeding disorders, and a greater father participation in groups where the health visitor made a prenatal visit compared to groups who received a visit six weeks post partum or controls. Although no evidence is presented to indicate that these increases in positive functioning reduced the incidence of child abuse or FTT, the findings regarding feeding disorders and interactional problems are suggestive of reduced risk in these areas.

CURRENT STATUS OF PRIMARY PREVENTION IN FTT

The Problem of Definition

As suggested previously in this chapter, there are three general steps in creating an effective primary prevention program. The first step is defining the problem to be prevented. Some useful measures have been developed to standardize the labeling of FTT infants; in particular, the relationship between height, weight and age is considered. In addition, standardized medical evaluations have been developed so that the differentiation of organic and nonorganic etiologies is more definitive. Thus, the state of the art allows us to define, with a reasonable degree of accuracy, the physical and medical parameters of failure to thrive. Less clear are the behavioral and developmental factors which might be present in children failing to thrive. Difficulties in feeding, social withdrawal, irritability, and other biobehavioral irregularities have been noted but not in all infants suffering from growth failure. It is likely that subgroups of FTT infants present with varying degrees of other abnormalities in thse areas; however, in the absence of objective definition these factors cannot yet be used in determining FTT outcome.

Identification of Those at Risk

The second component of a successful primary prevention program for FTT is to develop methods of identifying those at risk, before the problem occurs. The end result of identifying individuals who are at risk can be accomplished on a "case by case" basis, or can occur as the result of a mass screening effort.

Individual vs. Community Prevention

Emory Cowen (1982), an eminent scholar in the area of prevention research has formulated what is perhaps the "ideal" definition of primary prevention research. One of his stipulations is that "true" primary prevention must be "mass-oriented," although the programs themselves might incorporate individual contacts. This requirement for a "community" approach is pragmatic, especially in light of his stress on data to demonstrate positive program effects. This is ideally what good FTT prevention programs should accomplish; reduction in the incidence of this disorder which can be documented in a scientifically valid manner. However, we must seriously ask ourselves if this is a reasonable goal for the present. We need to examine the potential benefits of better preventative health and nutritional care for a given individual infant. There is some question among practitioners involved in clinical activities with FTT and other high risk infants as to whether there has been sufficient dissemination of information about FTT to the general health care community (the authors are presently conducting a survey of knowledge of this disorder among health care professionals). Frequently by the time a child finally presents for evaluation to a hospital based child abuse and neglect team, the child's growth deceleration has been occurring for a prolonged period of time. Often the team evaluating the child are surprised that the referring physician has waited so long before initiating a more extensive evaluation. Some of these cases are understandable, such as when a pediatrician has a single visit or two with which to judge the child's growth velocity. As previously described, those children with a relative FTT (that is, a drop across two major percentiles) are not immediately recognized by one or two points on the growth curve. Also, these children in whom growth deceleration has been long standing may appear to be following a normal curve along or below the 5th percentile. Without prior information regarding the child's growth during the early months of life, such a pattern may be interpreted as normal for that child. In addition, family members are often quick to point out that other siblings or adult family members were small at that age also but have "turned out okay." The family's explanation and comments, along with the absence of obvious organic or social pathology, often leads the physician to believe that there is indeed no cause for concern.

The problem of "overlooking" infant growth failure can be illustrated by the case of an eleven month old infant, Tony, who was admitted to our teaching hospital after his mother brought him to the outpatient clinic for treatment of a "cold." Tony was pale, thin, but quite active and engaging. When his weight and height were plotted on a growth chart, it was found that his height was at the 50th percentile, but his weight was far below the 5th percentile. Tony's mother presented as pleasant but not exceptionally bright or well versed in child rearing, despite the fact that Tony was her third child. She stated that Tony was a "sickly baby" and that she often took him to her doctor "down home" for health care. This was verified by Tony's records from his community physician, as was his consistent decrease in growth over the past 6 months. Why had his growth failure not been treated previously? Conversations with his previous physician revealed that while the growth failure was noted, the physician found it difficult to believe that it was a serious problem as "all of the siblings were small," and "Tony's mother was so nice and reliable." He had failed to discover that Tony's father refused "welfare" and that none of the children were enrolled in WIC or given free school lunches. It took many months, and the consistent understanding of the clinic nurse and protective services case worker, to convince the family of the importance of adequate infant nutrition. Most importantly, it took a physician who was particularly concerned with infant growth failure to ask the "right" questions to define the etiology of the problem.

There are other reasons responsible for the failure to primary care physicians to become involved at an early point in the child's growth deceleration. As noted, too often the physician is willing to go along with the family's explanation that the child will "start growing when he's ready." At other times, however, failure to appropriately intervene may be due to failing to routinely chart the child's growth. It is unfortunate that some physicians feel a growth chart is necessary only if growth appears to be abnormal. Consistent record keeping of infant growth along with examination of the growth curve on each visit can uncover inadequate growth long before the child has to experience the complications of malnutrition. Still other problems in the early management of children who are failing to thrive appear to be due to misunderstandings regarding the etiology of this syndrome. Traditional medical teaching has emphasized the organic causes, and often the medical evaluation is a "wild goose chase" for a rare disease process in spite of the fact that the child manifests no symptoms of the diseases being sought. Knowledge and understanding of nonorganic factors is often limited to erroneous assumptions that mothers must demonstrate severe psychopathology or that the child should also show signs of abuse. Such approaches tend to result in inappropriate and often incomplete evaluations of the child's illness.

Perhaps an initial step in primary prevention is to educate health care professionals so that they will be better able to recognize imminent growth failure and implement appropriate interventions. Such a program may not be able to statistically demonstrate a reduction in growth failure for a large population, but improvement in nutritional status might be documented for a circumscribed population, such as in a clinic in which training in FTT was given to staff. In general, efforts need to be made to encourage training programs in nursing, medicine, social work and other allied health professions to devote more time to the diagnosis and management of infant growth problems, at least in proportion to its incidence and seriousness as compared to other clinical problems which are being taught. It is the authors' experience that teachers and faculty in such programs welcome input and training materials. We are presently developing a multidisciplinary training package which focuses on both didactic material and clinical experiences, through the use of videotapes. Similar programs could be developed that could be used in other settings.

Mass Screening for Infants at Risk for Growth Failure

Several of the studies described in the literature review focus on screening large populations of infants to determine who might be at risk for later growth failure or other psychosocial disability. While many of these have had rather promising results, i.e. they were reasonably good predictors of later difficulties, implementation of such efforts on a widespread basis poses numerous difficulties.

As noted by Starr (1979), as promising as these results may be, use of these measures will result in a "disproportionately large number of false positive cases because of a low base rate (of the disorder)." For example, he considers a screening measure which has a sensitivity of 85% (sensitivity refers to the ability to identify correctly infants who will later fail to thrive) and a specificity of 82.5% (specificity refers to the ability to identify correctly infants who will grow appropriately). We screen 100,000 infants at birth and assume an incidence of failure to thrive of 1%. As described by Starr, we would find that 850 potential FTT infants would be correctly identified, 150 potential FTT infants would be missed, and 17,325 infants would be "false positives." What about the usefulness of such a measure? As Starr notes, "whether such a predictive measure would be useful would be a question of policy and values." Starr gives his opinion that given present policy and resources, prediction would be futile. However, it is possible that some of these barriers might be overcome.

One obstacle to mass screening involves the logistics of implementing such a program. It makes sense to screen factors which have the best predictive validity, and to conduct this screening in settings which best lend themselves to the necessary organizational processes and in which such needed information can be generated. Previously reviewed studies have suggested that screening might best be conducted in a variety of health care settings, with different types of predictive information generated in each setting. Given this premise, what are some possibly effective settings for collection of needed information?

One setting has been previously suggested by several authors including Gray (1977): the obstetrical wards of hospitals. The study by Gray has strongly suggested that pertinent predictive data includes observations of mother/infant transaction during the perinatal period as well as observations during delivery. This is also a good time to gather other psychosocial and family information, which has been shown to have some predictive value. Hospitals routinely collect some of the needed information and it may be possible that their routine data collection during the perinatal period could be expanded so as to include observations similar to those noted in the Gray study.

Other health care settings also hold potential for utilization in predictive screening programs and in fact are already gathering pertinent information. The federal Women, Infants and Children nutritional program

(WIC) screens infants and expectant mothers for nutritional risk and monitors infant growth on a regular basis. Data from this program concerning
nutritional and health status and certain psychosocial factors might be
used in a predictive manner, either alone or in conjunction with information generated from other sources. Expansion of their data gathering to
include assessment of psychological factors could be a tremendous aid in
collecting much needed predictive information. Like the WIC program, the
federal Early and Periodic Screening, Diagnosis and Treatment Program
(EPSDT) assesses and monitors the health of children (especially those at
some level of psychosocial risk) on a regular basis. Mandated screening
procedures in this program include a health and developmental history,
unclothed physical examination including physical growth assessment, immun-
izations, assessment of nutritional status, vision and aural testing,
various laboratory procedures, and dental examinations. In terms of the
age of onset of FTT, six of the recommended twelve exmainations should take
place between the ages of 0 and 24 months. Thus, in terms of both type of
information generated and in terms of age at screening, the EPSDT program
might be an ideal source from which to gather useful screening information.
As noted in the literature review, the possibility of using the EPSDT
program to screen for child abuse has been suggested (Reis & Herzberger,
1980).

Lastly, in terms of appropriate settings for collection of predictive
data, pediatric clinics as well as emergency rooms may be an additional
source of useful information. As found by Rosenberg et al. (1982), information generated in an emergency room setting may be a good predictor of
later abuse. In a similar vein, the prospective studies by Altemeier et
al. (1979, 1984) suggest that data gathered in a pediatric clinic setting
is useful in prediction of maltreatment. Both of these studies utilized
information that was either routinely collected, or added some additional
observational or "paper and pencil" measures.

So far we have suggested mechanisms by which predictive information
could be gathered without excessive financial cost to society. However the
ethical and legal costs have not yet been addressed. Many questions could
be raised concerning the right of some higher organization to gather the
data needed to predict infant growth failure. Other questions certainly
include whether the cost to society in terms of money as well as "invasion
of privacy" is worth the end result. Given the high number of false
positives likely in even the best screening program, especially when compared to the number of correctly identified potential failures to thrive,
it is likely that many will balk at the efficiency of such a program.
Thus, even though actual monetary costs may not be exorbitant, the rather
low specificity of available screening measures may be problematic. All of
these questions are valid; as child advocates we must be open to questions
and criticisms of even what we hold to be near and dear, in this case the
eradication of infant growth failure and its potentially serious sequelae.
However, such questions can not be meaningfully dealt with until all parties
have a greater understanding of this disorder, including the lay public as
well as our colleagues in the health professions. In addition, and perhaps
equally important, it is very likely that mass screening procedures will
never become accepted on a wide scale (although certain circumscribed
programs may be implemented) until more effective predictive measures are
developed for FTT per se.

Duquette (1982) in a discussion of these legal and ethical arguments
and considerations notes that up to now, the courts have "run the risk of
occasional coercion and perhaps unwarranted invasions of family privacy and
personal integrity in exchange for swift identification and response to
child abuse and neglect and related family problems" (p. 196). Infringe-
ment of parental or family rights has generally been balanced against the

possible risk to the child. For example, in most states a hospital may
detain a child who is the suspected victim of abuse without parental permis-
sion until legal intervention can be secured. Here, the degree of certain-
ty that the child is at risk is apparently relatively high, as determined
by the judgement of medical and other experienced helping professionals.
Parental rights are sacrificed to some degree in light of the child's risk
for immediate physical harm. However, with implementation of mass screening
for potential abuse or FTT several additional questions are raised.
Duquette notes that if screening measures have "reasonable specificity and
sensitivity," parents labeled as high risk may be reported as suspected
abusive parents. Federal guidelines as well as many state guidelines
usually mandate that reports should be filed on cases which demonstrate
"harm or threatened harm" to the child. Thus, screening for parental
problems implies, in most cases, possible legal action against the parents
and mandatory services. While many other screening processes are mandatory
and may result in a loss of liberty or other rights as defined by the
Constitution, they differ in many respects from a "FTT" screening program,
as it would exist today. First, many of the problems that are presently
addressed through screening programs are clearly definable. Preschool
screening for tuberculosis is a mandatory requirement for school entry, but
the screening technique used has a high sensitivity and specificity. In
addition, there is a definite medical response to a "positive" screening
result. Lastly, the danger to the child, as well as those in contact with
the child is quite clear. This is quite unlike the situation with FTT
screening. In this case, available measures are not highly specific or
sensitive. As noted by Duquette, this relative lack of specificity and
sensitivity results in the creation of four groups of parents, three of
which may be at risk for some degree of legal or ethical insult. Only
parents correctly identified as not at risk are generally risk-free. Those
in the "false negative" group (incorrectly identified as not at risk) may
not be offered needed services. Parents in the "false positive" group
(incorrectly labeled as at risk) suffer the effect of false labeling and
possible legal consequences. Parents correctly labeled as at risk also
experience the adverse effects of labeling and may also be coerced into
accepting services and/or additional invasion of rights or privacy. Unfortunately, at present there is no well defined, tested, curative response
available for the family who appears to be at risk.

What legal changes can be implemented to encourage the use of screening measures and yet protect the best interests of both child and parents?
Duquette argues that informed consent prior to screening may be a necessary
due process safeguard. He states that "the concept of informed consent
requires that a patient be provided sufficient information about the risks
attendant upon a particular course of therapy and that the patient, being
aware of the risks, consents to the procedure." Thus, the law strives to
protect personal integrity by allowing the patient to control what is to
happen. Informed consent may be a mechanism to safeguard personal liberties in a predictive screening program. Parents should be informed, in a
noncoercive environment, about the possible ramifications of screening.
This may create some problems, especially in states where the results of
the screening might mandate a report to a child protection agency. It is
even more difficult if state court decisions suggest that such screening
results may be legally used against the parent at some later time. Duquette
notes that such risks must be shared with parents, but a more reasonable
solution to the problem of informed consent is to reform the child abuse
reporting laws so as to reduce the risk to parents. Obviously, the number
of parents willing to undergo voluntary screening will be affected by the
possible consequences of that screening. It appears to make more sense to
screen large numbers of willing parents who are free of the threat of
coercive action and offer them voluntary services, than to screen smaller
numbers of parents for whom the likelihood of abnormal parenting might be

less, given their willingness to cooperate in the face of possible legal and social action.

Technology and the Prediction of FTT

Available computer technology could prove to be valuable in the prediction and very early assessment of FTT, and such technology is presently available in many health care settings in which these infants and families are presently being served.

First, computers are obviously well-suited to information storage and compilation. Our preceeding literature review suggests that information from a number of sources (e.g. perinatal observations, routine demographic data, emergency room visits) all contribute to the accurate prediction of problematic child outcome. Putting aside for the moment the legal and confidentialty issues involved in collecting such data, the technology exists at present to collect this and other data on large numbers of individuals and organize and store this information in a readily accessible form. Most health care settings use computers regularly to bill patients, schedule appointments, and store medical data. Within hospitals, it is very often the case that data collected from outpatient clinics is interfaced with data collected from the emergency room. Between health care settings, such data management might be more difficult, but not impossible, especially if this type of prediction is labeled as a priority and staff time is allocated for this purpose. The type of data collected is not so much a new process; rather, it is the process of evaluating this data in a more routine fashion which is being advocated here.

One example of such a coordinated data management system is the Columbus Partnership for Adolescent Health (CPAH) at Columbus Children's Hospital. The purpose of this project is to coordinate interventions in the areas of health care, schooling, and other psychosocial areas for a group of at risk adolescents. A coordinated data management system might allow for early identification of at risk families in a cost-effective manner. However, it is apparent that such a system could not be implemented without seriously addressing the many ethical and legal issues previously discussed.

Computers may also be used to assist health care professionals in recognizing growth failure in an individual infant before it becomes extreme. If clinic computer facilities could be used to plot infant growth and "red flag" infants who were significantly deviating from their previous growth velocities, early intervention might be more likely.

Very Early Intervention Programs

Once the problem of FTT is defined, and screening measures implemented, the last step is to develop programs which prevent serious growth failure. The literature review suggests several possible areas for intervention.

Parenting Education

While no research literature appears to exist which focuses on a direct relationship between parenting knowledge and skills and infant growth failure, the rather extensive literature on parent training suggests that such intervention may have a positive impact under certain conditions. As suggested by Wandersman (1982), programs which result in behavior change rather than just attitudinal change have a specified behavioral goal and a group of motivated parents who are at high risk. The FTT literature suggests a number of possible etiologies for growth failure, including poor parental feeding techniques, lack of knowledge of nutrition, and interactional problems, especially in terms of response-contingent stimulation (e.g. Ramey et al., 1972; 1978). It follows that parent education programs should focus on skills in these areas, such as nutrition education, practice in feeding, and infant stimulation. In addition, the failure to thrive as well a child abuse literature consistently suggests that social isolation may be a contributory factor in these psychosocial problems. Structuring parent education so as to provide social outlets and support should also prove to be beneficial.

There are a number of settings in which such education could occur, as noted by Gray (1982). She suggests that education should be provided prenatally, perinatally, and in later follow up. Preparation for childbirth classes would focus on parenting education as well as providing a mechanism for networking. Ongoing educational programs could be offered to obstetricians and other medical professionals to facilitate their acquisition of recent and relevant findings in the area of child development and related areas. She notes that these professionals would be taught "the earliest warning signals of impaired potential for healthy parent-child relationships" with the implied understanding that this knowledge would be conveyed to the patients. Lastly, Gray notes the importance of follow up. This has proven to be related to positive outcome in several previously reviewed studies, in which home visits by paraprofessionals were conducted.

The Home Visitor Concept

The use of a "home visitor" (a supportive and informative volunteer or paraprofessional) to facilitate parenting and child development has received considerable attention (Kempe, 1976). To date, several intervention studies have implemented variations on this concept with encouraging results overall. In terms of prevention of infant growth failure, it appears that such a program would be valuable. The health visitor could provide education as well as demonstration of proper feeding techniques, could weigh and measure the infant at regular intervals, and could ensure that financially needy parents were receiving WIC and other nutritional support. Although it is doubtful that such a program would be implemented on a widespread basis in the near future, similar interventions for at-risk infants might be feasible.

Changes in the "Child Abuse" Reporting Laws

At present, many states do not consider FTT to be a condition that requires involvement by child protection agencies, although this is rapidly changing. The inclusion of FTT as a reportable condition is very important in terms of secondary and tertiary prevention. However, by the time an infant has suffered enough nutritional insult so that he or she is reported to the appropriate agency and intervention is begun, that child is already in a compromised physical state. Early reporting of growth failure may not seem feasible at present but perhaps should be a goal of those who wish to prevent serious infant growth failure. In many instances, supportive services, such as transportation to health care services, use of a "homemaker," and parenting classes are only available to those who are involved with a child protection agency. Thus, these services rarely serve a primary prevention function. If these services could be made available at the initial signs of growth failure, more serious problems in growth and development might be prevented.

One method of providing these services at an early stage might be through the concentration of medical and psychological diagnostic services for failure to thrive infants and children in a specific pediatric setting within a community. Referral to such a clinic could follow two paths -- referral from the county child protection agency which has an identified case of failure to thrive, and referral from hospitals and community health care providers who would refer "at-risk" patients. Those referred by child protection agencies would receive treatment in the form of secondary prevention. In contrast, those patients referred before the occurrence of severe FTT would receive more preventative interventions. The end result of such a program would be to have as many of the community's non-thriving infants and children as possible followed through this center, just as one hopes that all patients with heart disease are followed by the heart specialists in the community. Through identification and referral of these patients to the center of expertise, evaluation, treatment, and prevention can all be conducted by appropriately trained personnel in a consistent manner. Both expertise and consistent care are important in managing these complex cases, but such a center could exist in a variety of settings. The diagnostic resources for such a center are relatively few, and consists primarily of appropriately trained staff rather than complicated and expensive equipment. Although a tertiary care center is most likely to provide the personnel and such expertise, development of such a center outside of the hospital setting might be advantageous. Problems such as transportation and location might be overcome with an out-of-hospital placement.

If early referrals could be made to a specialized center for the evaluation, treatment, and prevention of FTT, perhaps more serious growth failure could be prevented. This does not seem to be an unrealistic goal, given the state of the art and the potential resources available in most communities.

Provision of Nutritional Support

Studies of nutritional status of children enrolled in the WIC program (Edozian et al., 1979; Pearson & Windom, 1984; Miller et al., 1985), and studies of the relationship of federal support for childhood nutrition programs and child outcome (see Frank et al., this volume) illustrate the positive impact of such programs on the growth and development of infants and children. The evidence that these programs are successful are unequivocal and a major primary prevention effort should be the encouragement of the development of these programs by interested professionals. Equally important, educational and support programs need to be created to facilitate the use of such programs by eligible families. Programs might include education during the prenatal and perinatal period as to the benefits of participation in terms of infant health or provision of money or bus tickets for transportion to required WIC checkups.

IMPLICATIONS FOR PRACTICE AND FUTURE RESEARCH

The future for the primary prevention of FTT is very much dependent on an increase in our knowledge of the causes, risk factors, and effective treatments available for this disorder. At a basic level it is imperative that medical personnel have adequate knowledge of normal and abnormal growth patterns. Once this knowledge is disseminated more completely, their attitudes must be adjusted towards one of advocating more aggressively for the child and seeking to identify those children in the early stages of growth deceleration. Without this orientation toward prevention, adequate knowledge is useless. Development of this knowledge and attitudes can be addressed through continuing medical education, journal articles, and workshops or seminars.

With more knowledgeable and appropriately oriented health care professionals seeking out children at risk for FTT, the need for more community services and improved communication between these services and health care providers becomes much more important. This is the vital step for an adequate treatment or intervention portion of a prevention program. Establishment of centralized medical and psychological services for FTT infants could meet the needs of both educating community caregivers and creating a forum for the exchange of information between the health facility, community agencies and health professionals.

There is still a need to better describe what the disorder is and the factors associated with its development. Just as there have been studies analyzing the incidence of various organic diseases in the causation of FTT, more detailed evaluations of the nonorganic causes are in order. Such topics as the relative frequency and types of parental psychiatric disorders, overt neglect, feeding disorders, inadequate access to nutrition, and social factors must all be evaluated. In this way screening tools can be developed which will identify more children through close approximations of the major causes of nonorganic FTT. Additional longitudinal studies need to be performed to assess the predictive value of those risk factors which have already been identified with the complete form of FTT. This would primarily involve the type of prospective research programs such as those conducted by Altemeier, Sherrod and their associates.

Treatment programs such as the health visitor concept need to be carried out on larger populatioins with more specific focus on the prevention of infant growth failure. These programs would utilize the information obtained from prospective studies to focus their preventative efforts. Additionally, there is still some need for medical studies in the area of unidentified causes of organic failure to thrive. Recent studies commenting on the incidence of elevated lead and presumed zinc deficiency have shown that there still may be organic causes for what appears to be a nonorganic illness (See Bithoney & Dubowitz; Casey et al.; this volume). Lastly, research as well as prevention of infant growth failure must take into account the mechanisms by which perhaps "minor" organic factors may play a role in the development of primarily nonorganic FTT. The effects of chronic, albeit mild pediatric illness, such as otitis media or upper respiratory infection, must also be considered.

Infant growth failure has long been a source of confusion and frustration to health professionals as well as researchers working with this population. Prevention of a disorder whose etiology is still unclear, but certainly complex, poses further challenges. However, in spite of many obstacles, ensuring adequate growth and development for all children is a goal which is both attainable and worth pursuing.

REFERENCES

Altemeier, W.A., O'Connor, S., Vietze,P., Sandler, H. & Sherrod, K. Prediction of child abuse: A prospective study of feasibility. Child Abuse & Neglect, 1984, 8, 393-400.
Altemeier, W.A., Vietze, P., Sherrod, K., Sandler, H., Falsey, S. & O'Connor, S. Prediction of child maltreatment during pregnancy. Journal of the American Academy of Child Psychiatry, 1979, 18, 205-218.
Alvy, K.T. Preventing child abuse. American Psychologist, 1975, 30, 921-928.
Ayoub, C., Jacewitz, M.M., Gold, R.G. & Milner, J.S. Assessment of a program's effectiveness in selecting individuals "at risk" for problems in parenting. Journal of Clinical Psychology, 1983, 39, 334-339.
Ayoub, C. & Pfeifer, D.R. An approach to primary prevention: The "at risk" program. Children Today, 1977, 6(3), 14-17.
Badger, E. Effects of parent education program on teenage mothers and their offspring. In K.G. Scott, T. Fields & E. Robertson (Eds.)

Teenage Parents and Their Offspring. New York: Grune & Stratton, 1981.

Barber-Madden, R. Training day-care program personnel in handling child abuse cases: Intervention and prevention outcomes. *Child Abuse & Neglect*, 1983, 7, 25-32.

Belle, D. The social network as a source of both stress and support to low-income mothers. In *Stress and Coping in Families with Young Children*. Symposium conducted at the meeting of the Society for Research and Child Development. Boston, MA, April 1981.

Bithoney, W.G. & Rathbun, J.M. Failure to thrive. In M.D. Levine, W.B. Carey, A.C. Crocker & R.T. Gross (Eds.), *Developmental-Behavioral Pediatrics* (pp. 557-572). Philadelphia: W.B. Saunders, 1983.

Casey, P.H., Bradley, R. & Worthham, B. Social and nonsocial home environment of infants with nonorganic failure to thrive. *Pediatrics*, 1984, 73, 348-353.

Chatoor, I., Schaefer, S., Dickson, L. & Egan, J. Non-organic failure to thrive: A developmental perspective. *Pediatric Annals*, 1984, 13, 829-843.

Cochran, M. & Brassard, J. Child development and personal social networks. *Child Development*, 1979, 50, 601-616.

Cohen, D.J. Meeting adolescents' needs. *Children Today*, 1973, 2(2), 28-29.

Colletta, N.D. The influence of support systems on the maternal behavior of young mothers. Paper presented at the meeting of the Society for Research in Child Development. Boston, MA, April 1981.

Cowen, E. Primary prevention research: Barriers, needs and opportunities. *Journal of Primary Prevention*, 1982, 2, 131-137.

Coysh, W. The impact of a group-focused preventive intervention. Paper presented at the Annual Meeting of the American Psychological Association. Los Angeles, CA, August 1981.

De Lissovoy, V. Parent education: White elephant in the classroom? *Youth and Society*, 1978, 9, 315-338.

Dickie, J.R. & Gerber, S.C. Training in social competence: The effect on mothers, fathers and infants. *Child Development*, 1980, 51, 1248-1251.

Duquette, D.N. Protecting individual liberties in the context of screening for child abuse. In R.H. Starr (Ed.), *Child Abuse Prediction: Policy Implications*. Cambridge, MA: Ballinger, 1982.

Edozian, J.C., Switzer, B.R. & Bryan, R.B. Medical evaluation of the Special Supplemental Food Program for Women, Infants and Children. *American Journal of Clinical Nutrition*, 1979, 32, 677-692.

Frank, D.A. Malnutrition and child behavior: A view from the bedside. In J. Brozck & B. Schweich (Eds.), *Critical Assessment of Key Issues in Research on Malnutrition and Behavior*. Switzerland: Hans Huber Bern, (in press).

Garbarino, J. & Crouter, A. Defining the community context for parent-child relations: The correlates of child maltreatment. *Child Development*, 1978, 49, 604-616.

Gordon, T. *Parent Effectiveness Training*. New York: Wyden, 1971.

Gray, E.G. Perinatal support programs: A strategy for the primary prevention of child abuse. *Journal of Primary Prevention*, 1982, 2, 138-152.

Gray, J.D., Cutler, C.A., Dean, J.G. & Kempe, C.H. Prediction and prevention of child abuse and neglect. *Child Abuse & Neglect*, 1977, 1, 45-58.

Harman, D. & Brim, O.G., Jr. *Learning to be Parents - Principles, Programs and Methods*. Beverly Hills, CA: Sage Publications, 1980.

Helfer, R.E. A review of the literature on the prevention of child abuse and neglect. *Child Abuse and Neglect*, 1982, 6, 251-261.

Hunter, R.S., Kilstrom, N., Kraybill, E.N. & Loda, F. Antecedents of child abuse and neglect in premature infants: A prospective study in a newborn intensive care unit. *Pediatrics*, 1978, 61, 629-635.

Kempe, C.H. Approaches to preventing child abuse: The health visitors concept. American Journal of Diseases of Children, 1976, 130, 941-947.

Kruger, W.S. Education for parenthood and the schools. Children Today, 1973, 2(2), 4-7.

Larson, C.P. Efficacy of prenatal and postpartum home visits on child health and development. Pediatrics, 1980, 66, 191-197.

Lealman, G.T., Haigh, D., Phillips, J.M., Stone, J. & Ord-Smith, C. Prediction and prevention of child abuse - An empty hope? The Lancet, 1983, 1, 1423-1424.

Linscheid, T.R. Eating problems in children. In C.E. Walker & M.C. Roberts (Eds.), Handbook of Clinical Child Psychology. New York: John C. Wiley, 1983.

Marion, M. Primary prevention of child abuse: The role of the family life educator. Family Relations, 1982, 31, 575-582.

Marland, S.P. Education for parenthood. Children Today, 1973, 2(2), 3.

Miller, V., Swaney, S. & Deinard, A. Impact of the WIC program on the iron status of infants. Pediatrics, 1985, 75, 100-105.

Milner, J.S. & Ayoub, C. Evaluation of "at risk" parents using the child abuse potential inventory. Journal of Clinical Psychology, 1980, 36, 945-948.

Milner, J.S. & Wimberley, R.C. Prediction and explanation of child abuse. Journal of Clinical Psychology, 1980, 36, 875-884.

Milner, J.S. & Wimberley, R.C. An inventory for identification of child abusers. Journal of Clinical Psychology, 1979, 35, 95-100.

O'Connor, S., Vietze, P.M., Sherrod, K.B., Sandler, H.M. & Altemeier, W.A. Reduced incidence of parenting inadequacy following rooming-in. Pediatrics, 1980, 66, 176-182.

Pearson, H.A. & Windom, R.D. Eradication of iron deficiency anemia in an inner city childhood population: An endangered triumph or prophylaxis. Pediatric Research, 1984, 18, 246A.

Pillai, V., Collins, A. & Morgan, R. Family walk-in center - Eaton Socon: Evaluation of a project on preventive intervention based in the community. Child Abuse and Neglect, 1982, 6, 71-79.

Powell, D.R. Personal social networks as a focus for primary prevention of child maltreatment. Infant Mental Health Journal, 1980, 1, 232-239.

Ramey, C.T., Bryant, D.M., Sparling, J.J. & Wasik, B.H. A biosocial systems perspective on environmental interventions for low birth weight infants. Clinical Obstetrics and Gynecology, 1984, 27, 672-692.

Ramey, C.T. & Finkelstein, N.W. Contingent stimulation and infant competence. Journal of Pediatric Psychology, 1978, 3, 89-96.

Ramey, C.T., Hieger, L. & Klisz, D. Synchronous reinforcement of vocal responses in failure-to-thrive infants. Child Development, 1972, 43, 1449-1455.

Reis, J. & Herzberger, S. Problem and program linkage: The early and periodic screening, diagnosis and treatment program as a means of preventing and detecting child abuse. Infant Mental Health Journal, 1980, 1, 262-269.

Rosenberg, N.M., Meyers, S. & Schakleton, N. Prediction of child abuse in an ambulatory setting. Pediatrics, 1982, 70, 879-882.

Rosoff, S.R. Education for parenthood: An overview. Children Today, 1973, 2(2), (inside front cover).

Schmitt, B.D. The Child Protection Team Handbook. New York: Garland, 1978.

Sherrod, K.B., Altemeier, W.A., O'Connor, S. & Vietze, P.M. Early prediction of child maltreatment. Early Child Development and Care, 1984, 13, 335-350.

Siegel, E., Bauman, K.E., Schaefer, E.S., Saunders, M.M. & Ingram, D.D. Hospital and home support during infancy: Impact on maternal attachment, child abuse and neglect, and health care utilization. Pediatrics, 1980, 66, 183-190.

Starr, R.H. Jr. Child Abuse. American Psychologist, 1979, 34, 872-878.

Wandersman, L.P. An analysis of the effectiveness of parent-infant support groups. Journal of Primary Prevention, 1982, 3, 99-115.

Woolston, J.L. Eating disorders in infancy and childhood. Journal of the American Academy of Child Psychiatry, 1983, 22, 114-121.

PRIMARY PREVENTION OF FAILURE TO THRIVE:

SOCIAL POLICY IMPLICATIONS

Deborah A. Frank, Deborah Allen, and J. Larry Brown

Grow Team, Boston City Hospital, Department of Pediatrics
Boston University School of Medicine; Community Health
Improvement Program, Harvard University School of Public
Health; Physician Task Force on Hunger in America, Harvard
University School of Public Health

INTRODUCTION

Although FTT occurs in children of all social classes, researchers
have consistently noted that clinical populations of children with FTT are
drawn disproportionately from low income families (Evans, Reinhart &
Succop, 1972; Glaser, Heagarty, Bullard & Pivchik, 1968; Mitchell, Gorrell
& Greenberg, 1980; Pollitt, 1975; Shaheen, Alexander, Truskowsky & Barbero,
1968). The mechanisms which link poverty to growth failure in childhood
are varied and complex; biology, psychopathology, and prevailing socioeconomic conditions interact to produce FTT. The biologic sequelae of poverty
begin prenatally. Low income mothers are at increased risk of bearing low
birthweight infants (MacMahon, Kover & Feldman, 1972), infants who constitute 10-40% of reported clinical series of children later hospitalized with
FTT (Mitchell et al. 1980; Shaheen et al. 1968; Oates & Yu, 1971), but only
7% of all newborns. Children reared in poverty bear an increased burden of
post-natally acquired illnesses, any one of which may interfere with growth
(Holmes, Hassanein, Miller, 1983). Finally, the Preschool Nutrition Survey
(Owen et al., 1974), the Ten State Nutrition Survey (Garn & Clark, 1975),
and the Health and Nutrition Examination Surveys (U.S. Department of Health
Education and Welfare, 1975) all link poverty to the primary biologic risk
for FTT - diets of inadequate quality and quantity (Goldbloom, 1982).

Poverty does not act upon children by biologic mechanisms alone. The
economically depleted family is emotionally depleted as well. Parents
preoccupied with the basic prerequisites of physical survival have dimin-

---

*Funding for this work provided in part by the Massachusetts Department of
Public Health, Federal Grant numbers HD18401-02 and 1-R01-DA-03508-01, and
the New World and Field Foundations. The authors would like to express
their gratitude to Drs. Dennis Drotar and Michael Reinhart for their
thoughtful review of the manuscript and helpful suggestions, many of which
have been incorporated into the text. The authors would also like to
thank Ms. Katherine M. Petrullo for her invaluable assistance in collecting data, editing the manuscript, and preparing the bibliography.

ished emotional resources to invest in their relationship with their child. As Maslow (1968) recognized long ago:

> Safety is a more prepotent, or stronger, more pressing, more vital need than love, for instance, and the need for food is usually stronger than either.

Conversely, children stressed by cold, hunger, or illness may be too apathetic or irritable to provide a positive affective response to their parents. As Sameroff and Chandler (1978) have made clear, the biologic and psychologic concomitants of poverty each exacerbate the other to produce suboptimal physical and psychosocial development. Traditionally the families of children who fail to thrive have been portrayed as lacking affective resources for nurturing their children, a lack ascribed primarily to emotional deprivation in the parents' own childhood (Fraiberg, 1980). However, the contribution of ongoing material deprivation to the child's growth failure has been largely ignored. There is a temptation pathologize and scapegoat parents, while ignoring financial and social circumstances beyond the family's control, circumstances which would make it difficult for any adult, no matter how emotionally resilient, to address a child's physical and emotional needs. Family function and economic conditions do not operate independently but interact to affect the child's growth and development. At one extreme, parental psychopathology may be so severe that children lack adequate physical and emotional care in a setting of material affluence. At the other extreme, material conditions may be so catastrophic, as, for example, during a famine, that no parent, however competent, could provide a child with adequate food. In many clinical situations, the problem does not fit so neatly into either extreme category. Rather, disadvantaged families struggle to maintain delicately balanced survival strategies, strategies which are readily disrupted by emotional stress and family conflicts which in more privileged settings would cause psychic pain but not acute nutritional deprivation of the child.

Although health providers and mental health professionals have long been aware of the association between poverty and FTT, poverty itself has not been a focus of medical study or intervention. Our therapeutic and investigative efforts tend to be directed at the biologic or psychologic concomitants of poverty, which our professional training prepares us to perceive and address. However, we would argue that effective primary prevention requires us to investigate not only the concomitants of poverty, but also the economic conditions and social policies which produce poverty. In clinical experience, we find that ameliorating the family's material depletion is often the prerequisite to successful biologic and psychotherapeutic intervention. Families must be enabled to meet their children's basic physical needs for food, shelter, and health care, before they can focus on improving the intangible aspects of family function. This model, derived from clinical experience with individual families of FTT children, can logically be applied to the population of children at risk. This does not mean that we believe that FTT would no longer occur if all families could be assured of the minimal economic resources necessary to meet the concrete needs of their children. Such material resources are a necessary but not always a sufficient condition to assure optimal growth and psychosocial development. However, this chapter will focus on the conditions and programs which either endow or deprive families of such resources, leaving others to elaborate on ways of enhancing the emotional resources families can offer their children once a basic foundation of material safety is established. As a basis for devising strategies for the primary prevention of FTT, this chapter will examine the nature of childhood poverty in the United States in the 1980's. The following questions will be addressed:

1) How does the government define poverty?

2) Who is poor and why are they poor?

3) What is the evidence that poverty is linked to nutritional deprivation of families and children?

4) What is the evidence that such nutritional deprivation is adversely affecting children's growth and health?

5) What are the implications of these findings for diagnosis, treatment, and prevention of failure to thrive?

6) What are the implications of these findings for further research?

7) How can clinicians and researchers contribute to the implementation of strategies to protect the health and nutrition of families in poverty?

HOW DOES THE GOVERNMENT DEFINE POVERTY?

The term poverty, as used by government agencies, has a very specific meaning. This definition exerts a great deal of power over the lives of poor people. It determines the way they are counted by the census, and thus the extent to which their circumstances are perceived as a significant social problem. The official definition of poverty also serves as a baseline from which eligibility criteria and benefit levels for various government assistance programs are determined. It is useful, therefore, to understand this definition as a starting point for understanding the social context in which poor children "fail to thrive."

The federal government first constructed poverty guidelines for different sized families in 1964, at the start of the War on Poverty. Two studies provided the numbers from which the income levels said to define poverty were initially derived. The first, conducted by the United States Department of Agriculture (USDA) in 1955, looked at the way income is expended by American families and determined that the average family at that time spent 1/3 of after-tax income on food. This 1/3 figure became a norm for government thinking about appropriate food outlay. The second study, also conducted by USDA, looked at food costs and determined the minimum amount necessary for a family of a given size to meet minimal nutritional needs. This expenditure level is called the Thrifty Food Plan (TFP). To develop poverty guidelines the government combined these two studies: "poverty" was defined at three times the cost of the TFP. This 1964 formulation still constitutes the basis for poverty guidelines; the numbers are adjusted annually for inflation but are derived the same way.

Our experience suggests that the assumptions underlying this formulation, that the TFP constitutes an adequate diet and that three times the cost of an adequate diet is sufficient income to cover all living expenses, are both invalid. First, the TFP does not now and never did constitute a sufficient level of expenditure for good nutrition over long periods. The USDA technicians who devised the plan recommended it only for "temporary or emergency use when funds are low" (USDA Agricultural Research Service, 1969). Moreover, the TFP is set according to average food prices nationally. Those living in areas where food costs exceed the national average are unable to afford even this inadequate diet. Predictably, the USDA's 1977-

1978 Nationwide Food Consumption Survey found that 88% of families whose budget for food was actually limited to the level set by the TFP were unable to meet the Recommended Daily Allowances for essential nutrients (Peterkin, Kerr & Hama, 1982).

Second, the proportion of family income which, on average, is spent on food has changed significantly since 1955. While all prices have risen since then, disproportionately high inflation of energy, housing and health care costs have reduced the proportion of income spent on food. Other items take up larger shares of the family income than in the past. Three times a minimum food budget, even an adequate food budget, no longer represents an income sufficient to assure a minimally decent standard of living.

The poverty level thus defines a family's income as at least three times the amount required to purchase an inadequate diet -- not a very reassuring statistic. Families with low incomes below the poverty level are by definition at high risk of nutritional deprivation, as are many "near poor" families whose incomes barely exceed the formal poverty threshold.

WHO IS POOR AND WHY ARE THEY POOR?

In August 1984, the Census Bureau reported that the number of Americans living in poverty had risen from 24.5 million in 1979 to 35.3 million in 1983 (Bureau of the Census, February, 1984; August, 1984). This increase did not simply reflect population growth -- the rate of poverty climbed from 11.7% of the population in 1979 to 15.2% in 1983 (Bureau of the Census, February, August, 1984), the highest it has been since the beginning of the War on Poverty. The rate of childhood poverty has risen even more rapidly than the overall rate. This is particularly true of children under six, the group at highest risk for FTT. As figure 1 shows, there was a 31% increase in child poverty from 1979-82; the increase for children under six was 51% (Bureau of the Census, August 1984). In 1983 one out of every four American children under the age of six lived in poverty. The rate of poverty is higher still among minority children. Almost 50% of black children under six and over 40% of Hispanic children are poor (Children's Defense Fund, 1984).

There has been debate about the validity of these figures since they were released. Currently, the census classifies families as above or below poverty based on cash income alone. The figures cited above reflect this definition. Critics of this approach, many of them in government, point out that the poor receive significant benefits that are not in the form of cash -- Medicaid. They propose that the value of such benefits be incorporated into the measure of income which determines poverty status. It has been suggested that this change would eliminate the apparent increase in the poverty rate reported above. The underlying implication is that poverty is not a growing social problem but a statistical artifact.

Whatever the merits of such a change in the way that poverty is classified, it would not, in fact, reverse the upward trend in American poverty. Interpreting such non-cash benefits as income would lower the absolute number of people termed poor. However, the increase in the rate of poverty is actually greater when these benefits are incorporated into the measure of income. Using the current census definition, poverty rose 28% from 1979 to 1982. When in-kind benefits are counted the increase is between 37% and 47%, depending on how the benefits are valued. Poverty is on the rise, however it is measured (University of Wisconsin Institute for Research on Poverty, 1984).

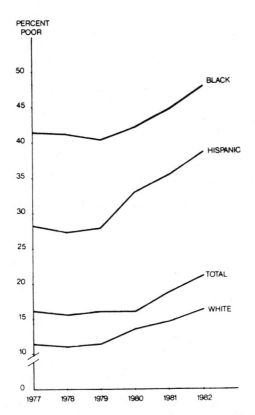

Figure 1.   Poverty rate among children, 1977-1982
(Children's Defense Fund Budget, 1984)

        Strategies for prevention of FTT associated with poverty require an
understanding of the forces producing this soaring rate of poverty, especially among children. Economists attribute the increase to two forces:
(1) economic recession with concomitant unemployment; and (2) reduction in
public programs which have, in the past, cushioned the impact of hard
times on poor families. Although unemployment has declined from its peak
of 10.8% (reached at the height of the recession in December, 1982) as of
March 1983, there were still 7 million children with at least one parent
out of work (Children's Defense Fund, 1984). The impact of unemployment
upon family resources is especially severe now because the majority of the
unemployed are not presently covered by unemployment insurance. This is a
very new phenomenon in American life. During the recession of 1975, for
example, 78% of jobless Americans were covered by unemployment insurance.
In the summer of 1984 only 30% received benefits (U.S. Department of
Labor, 1984). Many of the individuals involved have been unemployed for
long periods. Their families have significantly depleted any resources
they may have amassed during better times.

        Nationally, unemployment in winter 1984 stood at around 7%. That
figure obscures, however, extremely high unemployment among particular
population groups. Black unemployment was approximately 16%, down from its
1982 peak but not down as much as the overall figure. Even sharper is the
discrepancy in long-term unemployement (unemployment beyond six months).
While the rate of long-term unemployment for whites has increased 1.5% from
1980 to 1984, the rate for blacks has grown 72%. Over 30% of the long-term
unemployed in the U.S. are black (Center on Budget and Policy Priorities,
October 1984; Data from Bureau of Labor Statistics, 1984).

Two-parent families deprived of earned income and uncovered by unemployment insurance are in particularly severe straits. Although the states have a federal option to provide AFDC to two-parent families where the principal wage earner is unemployed, 26 states, more than half, do not do so. Recent Maternal and Child Health legislation reinstituted Medicaid coverage for pregnant women and children under five in these families, but the basic AFDC grant is not available.

Since 1981, 725,000 families with 1.4 million children have lost AFDC. About a half million of these families have been working poor (Congressional Research Service, 1984). Cuts in program funding and new limits on program eligibility which came just as recession hit have forced many families below the poverty level and placed their children at risk of nutritional deprivation. The poorest families have borne a disproportionate share of these cutbacks. For example, "means tested" programs, those targeted to the poor, have proven far more politically vulnerable than programs such as Medicare, which are available across the income spectrum.

Families who continue to receive AFDC have experienced a 36% reduction in real spending power from 1970 to 1983 as grant levels lagged far behind inflation. The net effect is as follows: for the typical AFDC family, combined AFDC, food stamps, and low income energy assistance, the cash benefits available to poor families, have declined nearly 1/5 from 88% of the official poverty level in 1970 to 71% in 1981. This downward trend is still going on (Sneeding, 1984).

Constriction of eligibility criteria has not necessarily resulted in redirection of benefits from the less needy to the most needy. On the contrary, resources have been transferred from the most needy to the most affluent. The net result of tax cuts plus benefit reductions has been a 7.6% decline in real disposable income for the poorest quintile families, whose average income in 1982 dollars including food stamps has declined from $6,913 in 1980 to $6,391 in 1984 (Moon & Sawhill, 1984). At the same time, the average income of the most affluent quintile has increased from $37,618 to $40,888.

WHAT IS THE EVIDENCE THAT POVERTY IS LINKED
TO NUTRITIONAL DEPRIVATION?

Unfortunately, there is no national system for providing timely information about the nutritional status of children (or any other group). Data from the NHANES collected in 1976-1980 is only now becoming available in the most preliminary form (U.S. Department of Health and Human Services, 1982, 1983). There is no comparable population-based data publicly available to assess the impact of economic and social policy changes since 1980 on the nutritional status of the poor.

Despite this lack of definitive information on nutritional status, there is some evidence (albeit rather patchwork in nature) that hunger and malnutrition are serious problems for poor families and their children. We can look at the following kinds of information: 1) information about the resources available to poor people for obtaining food; 2) surveys conducted since 1980 documenting that poor people report periodically lacking food for themselves and their children; 3) statistics kept by private providers suggesting that while the need for such aid is increasing, the resources to meet the need are inadequate; 4) perinatal vital statistics and anthropometric surveys of children presenting to emergency rooms and primary health care settings. We will examine each of these briefly.

Resources Available to Poor People for Obtaining Food

The Food Stamp Program provides a critical nutritional resource for poor families, since food stamps can be used like cash for food purchase. Everyone on the program has had benefits reduced through a variety of regulatory changes. For example, in 1981, the USDA decided to base food stamp allotments on 99% rather than the full amount of the TFP, a reduction not reversed until the FY '85 congressional budget (Children's Defense Fund, 1984). Other reductions in the program remain in effect. One restriction particularly devastating for the population at risk for FTT is a change in the way program regulations determining eligibility for food stamps define a household. Any child or sibling living with a parent, even if economically independent, is assumed to be part of one household for assignment of benefits. An adolescent or indeed any single mother forced to move in with her parents will find their resources counted as her income. Food stamps for many young mothers have been reduced or withdrawn entirely as a result (Bowden & Palmer, 1984).

Given such cuts, the allotment available to a family getting the average food stamp benefit is 47 cents per person, per meal (Amidei, 1984). Many families get less. Consistently, families who depend on this benefit for any significant portion of their food budget run out of food between the second and third week of each month (Citizen's Commission on Hunger in New England, 1983).

In addition to reductions reflecting clear-cut regulatory or legislative changes, food stamp recipients have been affected by a variety of administrative procedures put in place by states in response to threat of federal sanction if the food stamp error rate is too high. These changes generally involve requirement of exhaustive documentation and verification of information clients must provide on food stamp applications. Many advocacy groups report that low-income individuals, particularly those who are unable to speak or read English or who are inexperienced at negotiating the system (often the very people who are in greatest need), may be intimidated and choose not to even apply. Others are removed from program rolls because of procedural errors even when eligibility and need are absolutely apparent (Casey, 1983). It is important to note that states are sanctioned only for errors of liberality; there is no penalty for exclusion of eligible recipients.

These restrictive policies, introduced in the uncontroversial guise of administrative reform, have prevented access to food stamps for many potential eligibles (Brodkin, 1983). Overall, the federal spending for the food stamp program has been cut 14%; seven billion dollars have been lost to food stamp recipients since 1981 (Children's Defense Fund, 1984). This point has been subject to debate as some in government argue that the number of food stamp participants has remained stable in the early 1980's. As figure 2 shows, however, stable enrollment must be compared to the increase in the number of families and children living in poverty (Children's Defense Fund, 1984). Of 35 million Americans below poverty, plus another 10 million with incomes below 130% of poverty who are also technically eligible for food stamps, only 22 million currently receive food stamps. Historically, the USDA predicts a one-million person participation increase and a $500 million increase in program costs for every percentage hike in unemployment. Increased population below poverty has been linked to program expansion as well (Bowden & Palmer, 1984). Thus, the current participation level reflects a major program cut.

The Child Nutrition Programs, school lunch and breakfast, child care and summer feeding, have been cut back even more sharply than food stamps:

28% between 1981 and 1985 (Children's Defense Fund, 1984). About 2,000 schools which include one million poor children have lost school lunch. The breakfast program was never fully implemented – at its height only about 12% of eligible low-income children were enrolled (Amidei, 1984). Since 1981, 650 schools have dropped the program, cutting out 250,000 poor youngsters (Children's Defense Fund, 1984). One-half million children have lost access to summer feeding since a regulatory change made only public schools (most of which close in summertime) or municipal buildings acceptable sponsors. Child care feeding, available at both family and center-based day care facilities for low-income children, now subsidizes only two meals and one snack per child regardless of the length of the program day.

Of all the programs supporting the nutrition of children and families, only WIC, the Women, Infants and Children Supplemental Feeding Program, has been able to achieve modest growth in this period of increased need. Cuts in WIC have been proposed every year by the Administration but each proposal has been rejected by Congress. Even with slightly increased funding, the WIC program serves only three million women and children. The USDA estimates 8.3 to 10 million, almost three times as many, are potentially eligible (Amidei, 1984).

Surveys Documenting Lack of Food

As public resources available for feeding children decline and the number of families and children in need increases, it is not surprising that poor parents report that they and their children periodically go hungry. In April, 1984, the General Accounting Office (GAO) reported that of 493,000 single-parent families terminated from AFDC since 1981, over

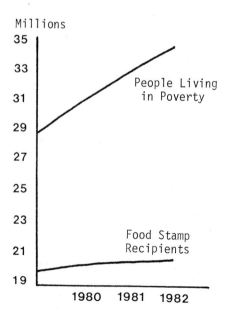

Figure 2.   Food stamp recipients vs. people living in povery, exclusive of Puerto Rico. Source, General Accounting office, USDA.

half had run out of food at least once since termination (General Accounting Office, 1984). A Gallup Poll conducted in 300 sites across the United States from January 27-30, 1984, found that 20% of the 1562 adults questioned stated that there had been times in the past year when they did not have enough money to buy food for their families (Los Angeles _Times_, 1984). Smaller studies by local organizations tell the same story; poor people report consistently that food stamps, AFDC, unemployment benefits - the basic resources available to them - are not enough to meet minimal nutritional needs (University of Wisconsin, Institute for Research on Poverty, 1984; Citizens' Commission on Hunger in New England, 1984).

Demand for Emergency Food

Faced with inadequate food and hungry children, families turn increasingly to private sector food programs - soup kitchens, which provide on-site meals, and food pantries, which provide a several-day allotment of food to be prepared at home.

The network of such organizations has grown with astonishing rapidity over the last three years. Two examples drawn from larger programs which keep relatively precise records illustrate this growth. The Second Harvest network includes 74 food banks across the United States. Starting with 2.5 million pounds in 1979, Second Harvest projects distribution of 60 million pounds by the end of 1984 (Ramsey, 1984). All of this food goes to programs which serve almost exclusively low-income recipients. In fact, some food banks will not even feed food stamp recipients - reserving their resources for those with no means of acquiring food at all (Citizen's Commission on Hunger in New England, 1984).

Salvation Army programs that distributed food over the same period report similar findings. The number of families receiving emergency assistance has increased from 1.6 million in 1980 to 3.7 million in 1983. Meals served to individuals have gone from 7 million to 10 million between 1980 and 1983 (Salvation Army, 1984).

It has been charged that such figures may indicate something other than greater need such as a change in program availability or in client attitude. The Salvation Army, like other programs to whom this question is posed, reports no change whatsoever in the way their services are publicized or portrayed. The change, they say, comes from the circumstances faced by the poor. Program initiators report universally that they started up services in response to obvious need on the part of parishioners, neighborhood residents or social service agency clients, depending on the nature of the sponsoring organization (Citizens' Commission on Hunger in New England, 1984). In addition, providers see a change in clientele - the indigent male alcoholic, typical of program users in the past - has been replaced by the young mother or family with children as the predominant client in many programs. Of 298 major emergency food providers from 36 states and the District of Columbia surveyed in 1984, 60% reported that families with children comprise the majority of their cases (Food Research and Action Center, 1984). No obvious cultural change would explain the dramatic increase in participation in such a short period of time. On the contrary, providers report that clients are generally embarrassed to be taking advantage of such programs (Citizens' Commission on Hunger in New England, 1984).

Two further points should be made in discussing emergency sources of food for the poor. First, the diets available through these emergency feeding programs, while sustaining in times of extreme need, are by no means nutritionally sound. Food Banks may find themselves flooded with foods that are nutritionally questionable if they are what happens to be locally available, while fresh fruits and vegetables and good sources of protein are hard to come by. Infant formula and other foods appropriate for infants and young children are much sought after but not consistently available (Citizens' Commission on Hunger in New England, 1984).

Furthermore, the amount of food available through the emergency provider network, while not negligible, does not begin to replace the food resources lost to poor families through federal budget cuts. Food providers report that they are unable to meet the ongoing chronic needs they observe. Most have placed limits on the number of times an individual or family can turn to them in a given period regardless of the legitimacy of need. One study placed the emergency food available in 1982 in Massachusetts, a state with a relatively extensive system of providers, at approximately 2% of the federal food removed from that state in that one year (Citizens' Commission on Hunger in New England, 1984).

Evidence of Adverse Effects on Children's Health and Growth

As the numbers of children in poverty increase and the allocation of resources for their nutrition and medical care decreases, one would expect clinical and epidemiological evidence of adverse effects on poor children's health and growth. Two bodies of such evidence exist: 1) perinatal vital statistics, and 2) anthropometric surveys of children presenting to emergency rooms and primary health care settings.

Although multiple health factors and access to health services influence pregnancy outcome and infant health, the nutrition of the mother is a critical determinant of infant birthweight and thus of infant survival (Worthington-Roberts, Vermeersch & Williams, 1981). The post-natal nutrition of the infant may also influence survival, since, as outlined below, undernutrition increases susceptibility to overwhelming infection. The infant mortality rate (IMR), a measure of the mortality rate of infants under a year of age, reflects both pre- and post-natal conditions. Increases in IMR and rates of low birthweight (LBW) in some parts of the country in recent years and the persistent gap in IMR and LBW between rich and poor, white and non-white, gives grounds for concern about the nutritional resources available to poor pregnant women and to their children.

For example, a survey conducted by the Children's Defense Fund revealed that the IMR increased in eleven states in 1982. For non-white children, 13 states reported increases in the IMR over the same period (Children's Defense Fund, 1984b). While 1983 data are just becoming available, current vital statistics reveal that the national death rate for black children under one rose between 1982 and 1983 (National Center for Health Statistics, 1984). This is the first such increase for black or white children in over ten years.

The most revealing infant mortality data is that drawn from small geographic areas, for which more precise economic and social characterization is possible. Figure 3 shows the dramatic differential that emerges when the IMR of Boston's poorest census tracts are compared to the level of previous years (Boston Department of Health and Hospitals, 1984). Similarly, in Pittsburgh, which has the highest black infant mortality rate of any city, the 1982 rate was 29.7 per 1000, up from 22.8 per 1000 in 1981. White infant mortality in that city was lower than the national average: 10 per 1000 in 1982 (Lewis, 1984).

In New York City, district by district figures are available not only for infant mortality but also for low birth weight, which is both the leading cause of infant mortality, and in babies who survive, a risk factor for FTT. The range in infant mortality among the city's 30 health dis-

tricts is striking: from 5.8 per 1000 in the Sunset Park section of
Brooklyn and 7.5 per 1000 on Manhattan's East Side - rates among the
lowest in the world - to 27.6 per 1000 in Central Harlem and 25.3 in
Brownsville, two predominantly black, very disadvantaged communities.   In
1982, the percentage of low birthweight babies born rose in eleven of the
city's 30 health districts.   Again, the highest figure reported was for
Central Harlem and the lowest for the nearby but very affluent East Side
(Public Interest Health Consortium, 1984).

There is unfortunately no comparable population-based data on the
post-natal growth of children under current economic and social conditions.
However, available data is remarkably consistent - a substantial proportion
of low-income children seen by medical providers show anthropometric
evidence of acute or chronic undernutrition.   Weight for age, the only
measure available in some clinical settings, is a composite indicator of
acute and/or chronic undernutrition.   Acute under-nutrition is defined as
depressed weight for height; chronic, as depressed height for age
(Waterlow, 1972).

Three clinical audits have been conducted in pediatric emergency
rooms serving indigent urban populations: in Toledo, Ohio; Boston,
Massachusetts; and Chicago, Illinois.   In Toledo, 23% of 100 children
under 12 were found to have weights for height below fifth percentile; 14%
showed heights below the fifth percentile.   A survey of 208 children under
5 using the emergency room at Boston City Hospital during one week in
February 1983, revealed that 15% were below the 5th percentile in weight
for age and/or weight for height.   None were significantly dehydrated
(Spivak, 1983).   At Cook County Hospital in Chicago, 30.5% of 325 children
under the age of two were found to be below the 10th percentile for height
and/or weight.   The same hospital reported a 24% increase in admissions
for failure to thrive, diarrhea and dehydration in the summer of 1983
compared to the summer of 1981 (Lattimer, 1983).

While both acute and chronic malnutrition are common in emergency
room settings, chronic malnutrition is also surprisingly prevalent in low-

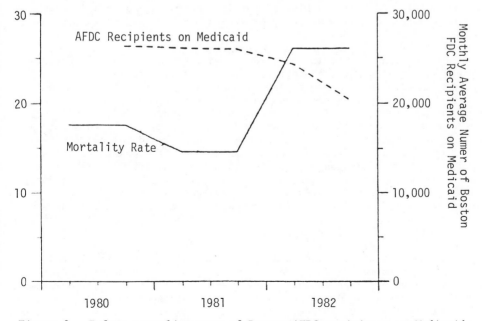

Figure 3.   Infant mortality rate of Boston AFDC recipients on Medicaid

income children receiving pediatric primary care. For example, the 1983 Massachusetts Nutrition Survey (MNS) which assessed 1337 low-income children presenting to primary care clinics between the ages of six months and six years, found that 10.5% of the children with family incomes below poverty, and 8.8% of children whose family incomes were 100 to 200% of poverty had heights below the fifth percentile. Eighteen percent of the sample had one or more indicators of inadequate nutrition defined as depressed height for age, depressed weight for height, or anemia (Massachusetts Nutrition Survey, 1983). Recent data from the Center for Disease Control, based on data from 32 states on children from birth to four years enrolled in WIC or Early Periodic Screening Diagnosis and Treatment sites, found a consistent increase in the prevalence of height for age below the fifth percentile as age increased until by age four the prevalence was as high as 16% in Hispanic and native American children (Trowbridge, 1984).

The proportion of children with sub-optimal growth identified by these surveys is not an artifact of the multiethinic nature of the low income populations studied. In infancy and early childhood, dietary quality and quantity and intercurrent illness are more powerful predictors of height and weight than is ethnic membership (Habicht, 1974; Graitcer, 1981). Hispanic children from Central and South America, raised in upper class homes capable of offering adequate nutrition, show in early childhood a distribution of growth patterns approximating U.S. norms (Habicht, 1974). Similar data is not available for native Americans, but there is no scientific reason to assume that these children should differ so greatly from other populations as to be incapable of showing improved growth with improved nutrition.

The evidence that a substantial proportion of low income children have inadequate diets has disturbing implications for the current physical health and long term cognitive and emotional development of these children. Children with nutritional growth deficits show impairments of immune function manifested by increased vulnerability to respiratory and gastrointestinal infection and decreased ability to recover from infections once acquired (Suskind, 1981). The malnourished child also shows increased susceptibility to toxic morbidity from lead poisoning, a hazard endemic in the central cities where many poor children live (Mahaffey, Annest, Roberts & Murphy, 1982).

In addition to exerting detrimental effects on the child's physical health and growth, chronic undernutrition in early life may jeopardize the child's intellectual capacity, school performance and social-emotional functioning in the preschool and school age years. Cross-sectional studies, in populations at nutritional risk because of poverty, have found that, compared to children of similar socioeconomic status, children whose heights are depressed show delay in neurointegrative development (Cravioto & Delicardie, 1979), decreased scores on standardized cognitive tests, particularly those of language abilities (Ashem & Jones, 1978; Freeman et al., 1977; Lasky et al., 1981; Lacey & Parkin, 1974; Edwards & Grossman, 1980), and poor school achievement (Lacey & Parkin, 1974; Edwards & Grossman, 1980). Observed differences may reflect both nutritional and non-nutritional aspects of the child's pre-and post-natal environment which effect both growth and cognitive functioning.

In addition to depressed cognitive functioning, chronically undernourished youngsters manifest an increased incidence of impaired memory and attention, and deficits in social responsiveness and modulation of affect, characteristics which may impede later school achievement and economic productivity (Barrett, Radke-Yarrow & Klein, 1982). Thus, the chronic nutritional deprivation faced by many low income children jeopardizes not only their growth but their mental and physical health and long term developmental potential.

Neither emergency room nor primary care surveys can be generalized unequivocally to the total population of poor children. Primary care surveys probably underestimate the severity of nutritional deficits in the general population since they reflect only the children currently receiving preventive health services and not those going unserved. Conversely, malnourished children may be overrepresented in emergency room studies since, as outlined above, such children are more likely than their better-nourished peers to acquire infectious diseases. Nevertheless, the available data suggests that children ultimately referred for FTT represent the extreme end of a continuum of nutritional deprivation and its medical and developmental correlates, deprivation afflicting a significant proportion of the increasingly large population of poor children.

WHAT ARE THE IMPLICATIONS OF THESE FINDINGS FOR
DIAGNOSIS, PREVENTION AND TREATMENT OF FAILURE TO THRIVE?

A first step towards addressing FTT in its social context is the collection of information about the circumstances of our patients and their families. We must begin to obtain not only careful medical and psychiatric histories but also meticulous economic histories. This will not be a simple matter. It is humiliating for parents to have to confess that they are unable to feed their children. Interviewing the parent(s) in the home may moderate the stressfulness of the experience. Further, it allows the provider to make firsthand observations of the family's material resources and their allocation.

Whether conducted at home or in a clinical setting, the interview should consist of questions phrased in a neutral fashion that conveys neither the assumption that the respondent is living in squalor nor that disclosure of poor living conditions would reflect negatively on the parent. The interviewer should explore both the material conditions currently prevailing at home (adequacy of heat and hot water, operation of utilities, availability of refrigerator and stove, number of persons and rooms, etc.) and the nature and adequacy of financial resources available to the family. Special attention should focus on current and past participation in child nutrition programs including food stamps, WIC, day care and school feeding programs. Use of emergency food distribution programs in churches and other agencies should also be explored.

It is particularly enlightening to elicit the monthly schedule for benefits and/or wages and then inquire specifically how the family eats immediately before and immediately after these resources become available. We have found families in which parents eat almost nothing and children are sustained on minimal and unbalanced diets without milk or other fresh food in the week before food stamps or the paycheck arrives.

In addition to assessing current economic status, one should ascertain whether there has been any loss or gain in the months preceding the onset of FTT in the family's resources as a result of changes in work or benefit status or of catastrophe such as theft or fire. Documentation of changes in family resources may provide critical diagnostic information. As figure 4 shows, sometimes a child's growth pattern exactly reflects the family's resources for food purchase.

Once inadequate material conditions have been implicated in the child's failure to thrive, clinicians are obligated to intervene. A team approach involving a social worker or client advocate is usually necessary

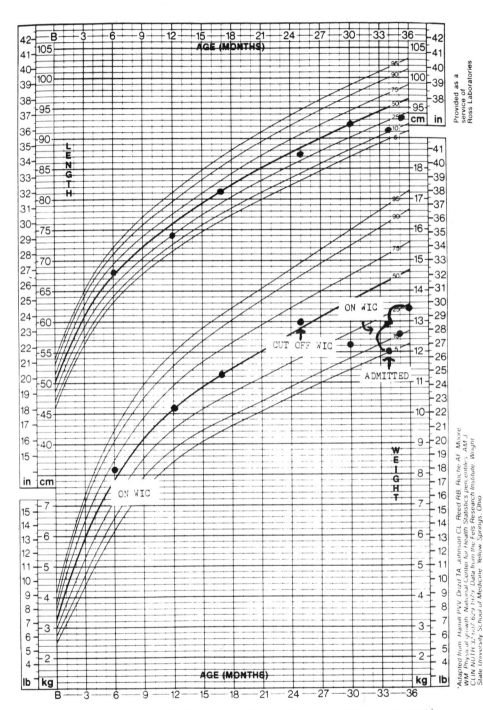

Figure 4. Boys 0-36 months physical growth NCHS percentiles

since few physicians or psychotherapists have the expertise necessary to help patients negotiate with obstructive bureaucracies to obtain needed public benefits or private relief. However, a personal letter or telephone call from a health professional may sometimes facilitate the process of mobilizing needed services. In addition to advocating with public programs to help families receive food and medical care, clinicians must also be aware of local emergency food sources. As for other psychiatric and medical conditions, periodic follow-up with families regarding the continuing availability of food and medical care is essential.

A caveat is necessary here. Clinicians should be aware that data from the Third World suggests that once malnutrition has occurred, food and medical care alone are necessary but not sufficient to reverse behavioral and developmental sequelae. Physical growth improves with refeeding and treatment of intercurrent illness but developmental deficits often persist (Galler, Ramsey, Salimano & Lowell, 1983, a, b; Hoorweg & Stanfield, 1976; McLaren et al., 1973). Focused and sustained center or home-based developmental intervention beginning before age two, in addition to nutritional supplementation and medical care, has been shown in several Third World studies to have an ameliorating effect on cognitive impairments following early malnutrition (Grantham-McGregor, Schofield & Harris, 1983; McKay et al., 1978; Herrera et al., 1980). However, interventions to reverse the social-emotional and attentional deficits associated with early malnutrition have never been formally assessed. One would expect that treatment of FTT children in this country demands attention to developmental and emotional as well as nutritional and medical needs.

While nutritional supplementation and medical care alone cannot reverse the deficits that occur once a child has become malnourished and fails to thrive, they may be essential and often sufficient for primary prevention of FTT associated with poverty. Existing data supports the contention that provision of nutrition and health care to poor families during children's prenatal and early post-natal life can, without any formal psychosocial intervention, reduce the risk of growth failure and developmental impairment in low income children.

There have been two studies using sibling controls to minimize the confounding effects of family characteristics and genetic differences on the growth and cognitive outcomes assessed. One conducted in South Africa involved 14 families in which younger siblings of children hospitalized with kwashiokhor received nutritional supplementation from two to 30 months of age (Evans, Bowie, Hansen, Moodie & van der Spuy, 1980). The other study took place in rural Louisiana where Hicks and colleagues studied 21 sibling pairs where the youngest child received WIC supplementation beginning prenatally and continuing into the early preschool years, while siblings were not supplemented until after the first birthday (Hicks, Langham & Takenaka, 1982). Both studies showed that during supplementation, supplemented children showed better growth in both height and weight than their unsupplemented siblings. Although supplementation was discontinued prior to school entry in both studies, positive developmental effects persisted. In both studies, children who had received early nutritional supplementation, when tested during primary school, showed scores on standardized intelligence tests 10 points or more above that of their older unsupplemented siblings, with particularly strong positive effects on verbal skills. The WIC study also found that children who had received WIC from prenatal life achieved higher grades in first grade and manifested a significantly lower number of behavior problems than their siblings. This finding is consistent with the work of Barrett and colleagues (Barrett, Radke-Yarrow & Klein, 1982), who demonstrated in a study of 138 children in Guatemala that children who had received high levels of nutritional supplementation beginning prenatally and continuing until age four, manifested improved attention, memory, social responsiveness, and modulation of affect at school age when compared to less well-supplemented peers.

WHAT ARE THE IMPLICATIONS OF THESE FINDINGS FOR FURTHER RESEARCH?

The issues outlined above suggest areas of potential research to clarify further the relationship between social-economic conditions, child health in general, and the clinically-recognized FTT syndrome in particular. As discussed elsewhere in this volume, research would be facilitated by uniform criteria for diagnosis of FTT and a national system for ongoing reporting of the number of children diagnosed with this condition. Potential areas for future investigation include:

1) What factors determine which of the large number of nutritionally deprived children in poverty are diagnosed as FTT, and referred to medical and psychosocial services? What characteristics of the child, the family, or the referring professional influence the labelling of some malnourished children, but not others, as FTT?

2) What is the sensitivity of diagnosed FTT as a sentinel condition for assessing the health and well-being of the child population as a whole?

3) Are periods of high job loss followed by increased numbers of children diagnosed as FTT? Conversely, do the number of children with FTT decline when there is economic expansion?

4) Are reductions or increases in funding of public nutrition and income maintenance programs reflected in the number of clinically recognized cases of FTT?

5) Could the incidence of FTT in high risk populations in this country be reduced by provision of universal nutritional supplementation and medical care?

6) Can treatment of low income children who have already failed to thrive be best accomplished by the provision of concrete services (nutrition, medical care, job training, day care) alone; psychotherapeutic services (mother-child therapy, family counseling) alone, or a combination of both modalities? Does the same relationship between the efficacy of material resources alone as prevention for childhood malnutrition but not as treatment that has been identified in the Third World also pertain in this country?

HOW CAN CLINICIANS AND RESEARCHERS CONTRIBUTE TO THE IMPLEMENTATION OF STRATEGIES TO PROTECT THE HEALTH AND NUTRITION OF FAMILIES IN POVERTY?

Since the etiology of FTT is multifactorial, no single intervention will be entirely successful as primary intervention. However, the weight of the evidence suggests that assuring access to adequate nutrition and health care for all children, regardless of their family's income, would be the most productive strategy for minimizing the population at risk. A commitment to primary prevention requires professionals to go beyond advocacy for individual patients to advocacy for families and children in poverty as a group. Clinicians who systematically collect information on patients' material circumstances can marshal both statistical data and case examples to inform politicians who fund programs and the public who elect them of the impact of their decisions on real children from real American families. Despite their professed disdain for anecdotes, particularly when those anecdotes illustrate unpopular political realities, politicians and voters are sometimes more responsive to stories of identified lives than to statistical summaries. Both kinds of information are critical for truly informed decision-making. Clinicians and researchers should be able and willing to provide both.

To reduce the risk of FTT for American children, no new programs or additional bureaucracies are needed. Expansion of the existing nutrition (WIC, food stamps, child nutrition), health (Medicaid), and income maintenance programs (AFDC, unemployment) could rapidly end the epidemic of nutritional risk. However, this is by no means the perception which shapes current federal policy. As described above, these programs, except WIC, all experienced drastic cuts in the early 1980s even as need was increasing, yet only half of the proposed cuts were actually enacted by FY '85. In 1985, the new Congress will be under Administration pressure to reduce the federal deficit by further cuts in domestic programs. WIC, Child Nutrition, and Food Stamps will be particularly vulnerable since they will be up for re-authorization in the 1985 Congress. The voice of the medical community has in the past protected WIC from cutbacks planned by the Administration. The challenge now is to maintain this advocacy to prevent destructive cuts and permit indicated increases not only in WIC but in the other crucial feeding programs.

Substantial funding increases and regulatory changes would be necessary to permit effective primary prevention of FTT. Detailed recommendations are beyond the scope of this paper, but the broad outlines of policies meriting support include: 1) Expanding WIC to reach 100% of eligible women and children; 2) Increasing the asset and income limits for food stamp eligibility; 3) Increasing food stamp benefits 30% to prevent families from running out of food during the last third of every month; 4) Permitting young mothers and their children to be considered as a separate household from their parents in determining food stamp eligibility; 5) Reinstituting outreach to assist needy families in obtaining food stamps and other benefits; 6) Raising the eligibility levels for reduced-price school meals; 7) Expanding AFDC grants to bring families up to the poverty level; 8) Extending Medicaid to cover children of unemployed parents up to the age of 18; 9) Passing legislation to end administrative harassment of Americans applying for federal programs such as Social Security Disability and food stamps.

These of course are only short-term solutions to the longer-term problem of ending poverty in America through providing jobs and child care for all who are able to work. However, children cannot wait for more distant economic transformations. The existing programs, if funded to meet the true level of need in families with children at risk, would protect children's health and growth in the present and thus their potential for a brighter future.

The United States is not a poor nation without the means to feed its children or tend their health. Other less wealthy industrialized nations protect the nutrition and health of all their children. At a time of budget cutting frenzy, it is well to remember that a country which spends $18 billion each year to prevent farms from growing food could nourish all its children if it chose to do so. As the AMA (Council on Food and Nutrition, 1970) has pointed out:

The existence of hunger in a society that can afford to
abolish it is morally and economically indefensible...
The cost of a massive attack upon hunger and malnutrition will be great in money; the cost of doing nothing
will be immeasurable...

REFERENCES

Amidei, N. Hunger in the Eighties: A Primer. Washington, D.C.:Food and
    Research Action Center, 1984.
Ashem, B. & Jones, M. Deleterious effects of chronic undernutrition on
    cognitive abilities. Journal of Child Psychology and Psychiatry,
    1978, 19, 23-31.
Barrett, D., Radke-Yarrow, M. & Klein, R.E. Chronic malnutrition and
    child behavior: Effects of early caloric supplementation on social
    and emotional functioning at school age. Developmental Psychology,
    1982, 18, 541-556.
Bowden, D.L. & Palmer, J.L. Social policy: Challenging the welfare
    state. In The Reagan Record. Cambridge, MA: Ballinger, 1984.
Brodkin, E.Z. The Error of Their Ways: Reforming Welfare Administration
    Through Quality Control (unpublished doctoral thesis). Massachusetts
    Institute of Technology, 1983.
Casey, T. The In-human Resources Administration's Churning Campaign.
    New York: Community Action Legal Services, 1983.
Center on Budget and Policy Priorities. Falling Behind: A Report on How
    Blacks have Fared under the Reagan Policies. Washington, D.C.,
    1984.
Children's Defense Fund. American Children in Poverty. Washington,
    D.C., 1984
Children's Defense Fund. A Children's Defense Budget: An Analysis of the
    President's FY 85 Budget and Children. Washington, D.C., 1984.
Citizens' Commission on Hunger in New England. American Hunger Crisis:
    Poverty and Health in New England. Boston: Harvard University School of
    Public Health, 1984.
Congressional Research Service. Background Material on Poverty.
    Washington, D.C.: United State House of Representatives Committee on
    Ways and Means: Subcommittee on Public Assistance and Unemployment
    Compensation, 1984.
Council on Food and Nutrition. Malnutrition and hunger in the United
    States. Journal of the American Medical Association, 1970, 213, 272-
    275.
Cravioto, J. & Delicardie E. Nutrition, mental development, and
    learning. In F. Falkner & J Tanner (Eds.) Human Growth: Neurobiology
    and Nutrition. New York: Plenum Press, 1979.
Edwards, L.N. & Grossman, M. The relationship between children's health
    and intellectual development. In Health: What is it worth? Measure
    of Health Benefits. Pergamon Policy Studies. New York: Pergamon
    Press, 1980.
Evans, D., Hanson, J., Moodie, A. & Van Der Spuy, H. Intellectual
    development and nutrition. Journal of Pediatrics, 1980, 97, 358-363.
Evans, S., Reinhart, J.B. & Succop, R.A. Failure to thrive: A study of
    45 children and their families. Journal of the American Academy of
    Child Psychiatry, 1972, 2, 440-459.
Federal Register. 4-19-84, 49,77,15590.
Food Research and Action Center. Bitter Harvest: A Status Report on the
    Need for Emergency Food Assistance in America. Washington, D.C.,
    1984.
Fraiberg, S. Clinical Studies in Infant Mental Health: The First Year
    of Life. New York: Basic Books, 1980.
Freeman, H.E., Klein, R.E., Kagan, J. & Yarbrough, C. Relations be-

tween nutrition and cognition in rural Guatemala. American Journal of Public Health, 1977, 67, 233-239.

Galler, J., Ramsey, F., Solimano, G. & Lowell, W. The influence of early malnutrition on subsequent behavioral development. I. Degree of impairment in intellectual performance. Journal of the American Academy of Child Psychiatry, 1983, 22, 8-15.

Galler, J., Ramsey, F., Solimano, G. & Lowell, W. The influence of early malnutrition on subsequent behavioral development. II. Classroom behavior. Journal of the American Academy of Child Psychiatry, 1983b, 22, 16-22.

Garn, S.M. & Clark, D.C. Nutrition, growth, development, and maturation: Findings of the Ten State Nutrition Survey 1968-1970. Pediatrics, 1975, 56, 306-319.

General Accounting Office. An Evaluation of the 1981 AFDC Changes: Initial Analyses. Washington, D.C., 1984.

Glaser, H., Heagarty, M., Bullard, D. & Pivchik, E. Physical and psychological development of children with early failure to thrive. Pediatrics, 1968, 73, 790-798.

Goldbloom, R.B. Failure to thrive. Pediatric Clinics of North America, 1982, 29, 151-165.

Graitcer, P.L. & Gentry, E.M. Measuring children: One reference for all. The Lancet, 1981, 2, 297-299.

Grantham-McGregor, S., Schofield, W. & Harris, L. Effect of psychosocial stimulation on mental development of severely malnourished children: An interim report. Pediatrics, 1983, 72, 239-243.

Habicht, J.-P., Yarbrough, C., Martorell, R., Malina, R. & Klein, R. Height and weight standards for preschool children: How relevant are ethnic differences to growth potential? The Lancet, 1974, 1, 611-614.

Herrera, M., Mora, J., Christiansen, N., Ortiz, N., Clement, J., Vuori, L., Waber, D., De Paredes, B. & Wagner, M. Effects of nutritional supplementation and early education: Physical and cognitive development. In R. Turner & F. Reese (Eds.), Life-Span Developmental Psychology. New York: Academic Press, 1980.

Hicks, L.E., Langham, R.A. & Takenaka, J. Cognitive and health measures following early nutritional supplementation: A sibling study. American Journal of Public Health, 1982, 72, 1110-1118.

Holmes, G.E., Hassanein, K.M. & Miller, H.C. Factors associated with infections among breast-fed babies and babies fed proprietary milks. Pediatrics, 1983, 72, 300-306.

Hoorweg, J. & Stanfield, J. The effects of protein energy malnutrition in early childhood on intellectual and motor abilities in later childhood and adolescence. Developmental Medicine and Child Neurology, 1976, 18, 330-350.

Institute for Research on Poverty. Poverty in the United States: Where do we stand now? In Focus. Madison,WI: University of Wisconsin, 1984.

Johnson, N. Testimony before Citizens' Commission on Hunger in New England, October 31, 1983 by Director of Boston Food Bank, 1983.

Lacey, K.A. & Parkin, J.M. The normal short child: Community study of children in Newcastle-upon-Tyne. Archives of Diseases of Childhood, 1974, 49, 417-424.

Lasky, R.E., Klein, R.E., Yarbrough, C., Engle, P.L., Lechtig, A. & Martorell, R., The relationship between physical growth and infant development in rural Guatemala. Child Development, 1981, 52, 219-226.

Lattimer, A. Testimony Before House Agricultural Committee, Subcommittee on Nutrition, October 20, 1983.

Los Angeles Times. Gallup Poll: Poor Families. January, 1984.

MacMahon, B., Kover, M.G. & Feldman, J.J. Infant Mortality Rate: Socioeconomic Factors. U.S. Department of Health, Education and

Welfare, Publication No. HSM 72-1045. Washington, D.C.: National Center for Health Statistics, March, 1972.

Mahaffey, K.R., Annest, J.L., Roberts, J. & Murphy, R.S. National estimates of blood lead levels: United States, 1976-1980 Associated with selected demographic and socioeconomic factors. New England Journal of Medicine, 1982, 307, 573-579.

Maslow, A. Toward a Psychology of Being. Princeton, NJ: Van Nostrand, 1968.

Massachusetts Department of Public Health. Preliminary Findings. Boston, MA: Boston Department of Health and Hospitals, 1984.

Massachusetts Department of Public Health, Division of Family Health Services. 1983 Massachusetts Nutrition Survey. Boston, MA, 1983.

McKay, H., Sinisterra, L., McKay, L., Gomez, H. & Lloreda, P. Improving cognitive ability in chronically deprived children. Science, 1978, 200, 270-277.

McLaren, D.S., Yatkin, U.S., Kanawati, A., Saggagh, S. & Kadi, Z. The subsequent mental and physical development of rehabilitated marasmic infants. Journal of Mental Deficiency Research, 1973, 17, 273-281.

Mitchell, W.G., Gorrell, R.W. & Greenberg, R.A. Failure to thrive: A study in a primary care setting: Epidemiology and follow-up. Pediatrics, 1980, 65, 971-977.

Moon, M. & Sawhill, I.V. Family incomes: Gainers and losers. In The Reagan Record. Cambridge, MA: Ballinger, 1984.

National Center for Health Statistics. Monthly Vital Statistics Report. October 5, 1983,31,13; September 21, 1984, 32, 13.

Oates, R.K. & Yu, J. Children with non-organic failure to thrive. A community problem. Medical Journal of Australia, 1971, 2, 194-203.

Oatis, P., Bobo, R. & Herman, D. Nutritional status of hospitalized children (Effect of socioeconomic status). Pediatric Research, 1982, 4, 583.

Owen, G.M., Kram, K.M., Garry, P.F., Lowe, J.E. & Lubin, A.H. A study of nutritional status of preschool children in the U.S. 1968-1970. Pediatrics, 1974, 53, 597-646.

Peterkin, B., Kerr, R.L. & Hama, M.Y. Nutritional adequacy of diets of low income households. Journal of Nutrition and Education, 1982, 14 (3), 102.

Pollitt, E. Failure to thrive: Socioeconomic, dietary intake, and mother-child interaction data. Federation Proceedings, 1975 34, 1593-1597.

Public Interest Health Consortiums for New York City. Prenatal health care in New York City. City Health Report, 1984, 1.

Ramsey, J. Personal Communication, Director, Second Harvest National Food Bank Network, September 1984.

Salvation Army, Regional Statisticians: Eastern, Central, Southern, Western Territories. Personal Communications, September 1984.

Sameroff, A. & Chandler, M.J. Reproductive risk and the continuum of caretaking casualty. In P.D. Horwitz (Ed.), Review of Child Development Research. Chicago, IL: University of Chicago Press, 1978.

Shaheen, E., Alexander, E., Truskowsky, M. & Barbero, G.J. Failure to thrive - A retrospective profile. Clinical Pediatrics, 1968, 7, 225-261.

Smeeding, T. Is the safety net still intact? In D.L. Bowden (Ed.), The Social Contract Revisited: Aims and Outcomes of President Reagan's Social Welfare Policy. Washington, D.C.: The Urban Institute Press, 1984.

Spivak, H. Unpublished Data, 1983.

Suskind, R.M. Malnutrition and the immune response. In R.M. Suskind (Ed.), Textbook of Pediatric Nutrition. New York: Raven Press, 1981.

Trowbridge, F.L. Prevalence of growth stunting and obesity: Pediatric nutrition surveillance system. Mortality and Morbidity Weekly Report, 1984, 32 (55), 23-26SS.

U.S. Department of Agricultural Research Service, Consumer and Food
     Economics Research Division. Family Food Plans Revised, 1964.
     Washington, D.C., 1969.
U.S. Department of Commerce, Bureau of the Census. Estimates of Poverty
     Including the Value of Noncash Benefits: 1979-1982. Washington,
     D.C., 1984.
U.S. Department of Commerce, Bureau of the Census. Estimates of Poverty
     Including the value of Noncash Benefits: 1983. Washington, D.C.,
     1984.
U.S. Department of Health, Education, and Welfare. Preliminary Findings
     of the First Health and Nutrition Examination Survey, United States,
     1971-1972: Dietary and Biochemical Findings. HRA 74-1219-1,
     Washington, D.C., 1975.
U.S. Department of Health and Human Services. Dietary Intake Source
     Data: United States (1976-1980). Vital Health Statistics. 2, 231,
     PHS 83-1681, Washington, D.C., 1983.
U.S. Department of Health and Human Services. Hematological and Nutri-
     tional Biochemistry Reference Data for Persons 6 Months - 74 Years
     of Age: United States 1976-1980. 2, 32, PHS 83-1682, Washington,
     D.C., 1982.
U.S. Department of Labor. The Employment Situation, July, 1984.
     Washington, D.C., 1984.
Waterlow, J.C. Classification and definition of protein-calorie malnu-
     trition. British Medical Journal, 1972, 3, 566-569.
Worthington-Roberts, B., Vermeersch, J. & Williams, S.R. Nutrition in
     Pregnancy and Lactation. St. Louis, MO: C.V. Mosby, 1981.

FAILURE TO THRIVE AND THE ECONOMICALLY DEPRESSED COMMUNITY

Elizabeth F. Gordon and Delia M. Vazquez

Department of Pediatrics, Michigan State University and

University of Iowa

Failure to thrive (FTT) that has occurred outside of institutions, has typically been viewed as a disorder involving the growth retarded infant and the mother (Elmer, 1960; Patton & Gardner, 1962; Ainsworth, 1969; Fischhoff et al., 1971). Recently Roberts and Maddux (1982) have proposed that additional causative factors within the family system need to be identified and used as a guide to the complex management of this common pediatric disorder. Specifically, they suggest that situational, infant and paternal variables should also be considered as important in understanding the causes of FTT. We further propose that growth failure in young children may result, indirectly, from factors that are present in the larger community system. The study reported here was initiated to address this issue.

The world-wide economic recession began over a decade ago (Thompson, 1981). The degree to which countries and their regions have experienced its impact has depended, to a great extent, on the sources of economic stability within each area. One source of economic stability that has been severely affected by the recession has been the automobile industry. Michigan, the capital of the American automobile industry, had the note-worthy distinction in 1980 of having the highest rate of unemployment in the United States. Twelve percent of that state's workers were idle (Editor, 1981). Flint, Michigan, "the Buick City," second only to Detroit in car production, reported 23.1% or 54,700 individuals unemployed at that time (Angell, 1980; Editor, 1983).

The health of a community is one of the most important issues related to long-term unemployment. Mortality is known to increase during economic fluctuations, and infant mortality is regarded as one of the most sensitive indicators of the general economic level (Brenner, 1973a; Brenner, 1973b; Colledge, 1982). Higher suicide rates (Brenner, 1973a; Colledge, 1982; Durkheim, 1952) and a greater number of deaths from heart disease (Colledge, 1982; Morris & Titmuss, 1941) have been reported. Morbidity is also a good indicator of economic conditions. Significant rises in blood pressure (Brenner, 1973a; Kasl & Cobb, 1970), psychological problems, alcoholism and drug abuse (Angell, 1980; Brenner, 1973a) have been found following unemployment.

The most complete studies concerning economic cycles and health were carried out by M.H. Brenner, a sociologist and economist at Johns Hopkins

University. Brenner, considered a pioneer in the study of the effects of the economy on the health of a community, hypothesized that pathological reactions follow increased unemployment and that these reactions will be dispersed over time so that there will probably be a time lag between the stress of being unemployed and the onset of illness (Colledge, 1982). Morbidity, including hypertension, heart disease, and mental illness, would, therefore, be quicker indicators of economic crisis than mortality.

While Brenner was objectively identifying predictors and indicators of association between economic fluctuations and illness, Hill (1978) was developing a theory of psychological transition following unemployment. He described three stages of the unemployed: disbelief, pessimism, and unemployment. In the first stage, there is optimism that the present situation is temporary. Then pessimism ensues and reality becomes unavoidable. The overall feeling of "holiday" is over and money and benefits are running short. The individual is characterized by loss of self-esteem and takes on the unemployed identity. The last phase, "unemployment," occurs when the idea of having no occupational identity is accepted. Time structure is lost as well as activity, sense of purpose, and confidence.

While the review to this point has focused primarily on the worker, it is important to point out that most workers live within a family unit and the effects of unemployment on the health and well-being of all family members must therefore be considered. Studies of the impact of unemployment on family life have identified several significant effects and suggested the following stages: 1) living standards are lowered; 2) families lose interest in events that are not directly related to meeting basic needs; 3) time loses its meaning; and 4) the family becomes resigned and may experience despair. This process, when it occurs in a large number of families, can result in deterioration of community health (Colledge, 1982).

There is a paucity of research on the effects of adverse economic conditions on the health of the children living in unemployed families. The only area of systematic study on the relationship of adverse economic conditions and morbidity in children has been in child abuse. A number of articles have reported increases in child abuse during periods of economic stress (Garbarino & Sherman, 1980; Steinberg et al., 1981). Light's (1973) extensive review of child abuse and neglect in America concluded that "... the variable that shows up most frequently as somehow related to child abuse is the father's unemployment" and that this occurs more often when the unemployment is recent.

Our brief review of the literature on economic conditions and health supports the premise that high unemployment is related to increases in morbidity and mortality and that both the worker and other family members are affected. Michigan, for reasons previously stated, would be expected to have an increase in community health problems.

The major purpose of this study was to initiate a preliminary investigation into the possible effects of the recession on the health of the children in Flint, Michigan. Specifically, we hypothesized that the physical growth of young children would be a sensitive marker of the economic conditions of a community and that (FTT) would be increased in cities such as Flint.

METHOD

This retrospective, descriptive study was conducted at Hurley Medical Center, a 600 bed, Michigan State University affiliated hospital located

360

in Flint, Michigan. The medical center has the major pediatric facility
for this midwestern community.

SUBJECTS

Subjects were all children two years old or younger who were admitted
during a five year period (1978-1982) with a diagnosis of FTT defined as a
disorder that occurs in the child two years old or younger who has body
weight below the fifth percentile or who has a drop of two or more percentile ranks on the National Center for Health Statistics (NCHS) growth
charts. All weights are corrected for gestational age. The total number
of cases was 204. In patient data were collected for each admission and
included: 1) age, sex and race; 2) social history; 3) discharge diagnosis;
and 4) employment status of the family and method of payment of the hospital
bill. The method of payment was determined for all children two years old
or younger who were admitted during the study period with a diagnosis of
meningitis. This infectious disease has no apparent relationship to FTT or
socioeconomic status, and could thus be used as a partial control. Employment data for Flint, Michigan were obtained for the years 1978-1982 from
the Michigan Employment Security Commission. Simple chi square (X) analyses were completed for selected categorical data.

The age, sex, race, and mean length of the hospital stay data were
analyzed. A significant majority of the patients were one year of age or
younger for each of the five years studied. There were significantly more
males than females in the nonorganic FTT group in 1978 and in the organic
FTT group in 1979 and 1981. There were significantly more White than Black
patients with a diagnosis of of nonorganic FTT in each of the five years.
The only other significant finding for race was a higher number of Blacks
with organic FTT in 1978. There were no significant differences for length
of hospital stay between the organic FTT and nonorganic FTT groups for any
of the five years.

All major organic disease categories were represented in this study.
There was a significantly greater percentage of cases of gastrointestinal
disorders compared to the other specified diagnoses for each of the five
years studied.

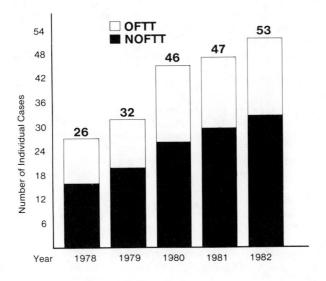

Figure 1

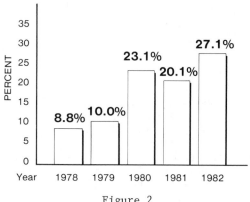

Figure 2

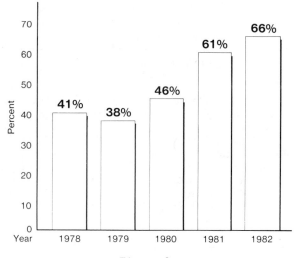

Figure 3

The numbers of children admitted with FTT are shown in Figure 1. There was a consistent increase in the cases between 1978 and 1982. Increasing rates of unemployment for Flint, Michigan and for the families of the patients studied, are shown in Figures 2 and 3 respectively. Comparison of Figures 1, 2, and 3 demonstrates similar trends of an increasing number of cases of FTT and rising unemployment in both the city of Flint and the families of the children with FTT.

As shown in Figure 4 the following changes in the method of payment were demonstrated: 1) Insurance as a method of payment rose in 1979 and 1980 and then significantly declined in 1981 and 1982; 2) Use of medicaid held steady until 1981 and 1982 and then increased; 3) Use of private funds for payments steadily declined over the five years. The recent HMO insurance plan is in evidence for 1981 and 1982 as a method of payment.

The method of payment data for the cases of meningitis during the five years of the study are shown in Figure 5. Insurance was the most frequently used method for the payment of hospital bills for each year.

The major purpose of this study was to begin to address the issue of the possible effects of an adverse economy on the physical growth of young children. Specifically, our findings demonstrate that there has been a

children. Specifically, our findings demonstrate that there has been a
consistent increase in the total number of chldren with growth failure who
were admitted to Hurley Medical Center in Flint, Michigan during 1978-1982.
These increases closely parallel the deepening recession and rising unemployment for that city.

Method of payment related to economic crises has been studied and
found to show a distinct pattern of hospital payment during recessions.
Immediately after employment lay off, there is a period of time where
health care benefits are present. Insurance is used to take care of those
health problems that arise or that had been postponed. When health care
benefits are terminated, emergency room care is sought using cash as method
of payment. Medicaid is the final solution for the unemployed who have

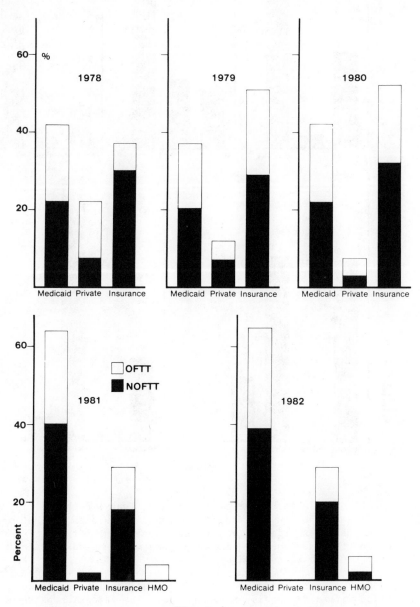

Figure 4

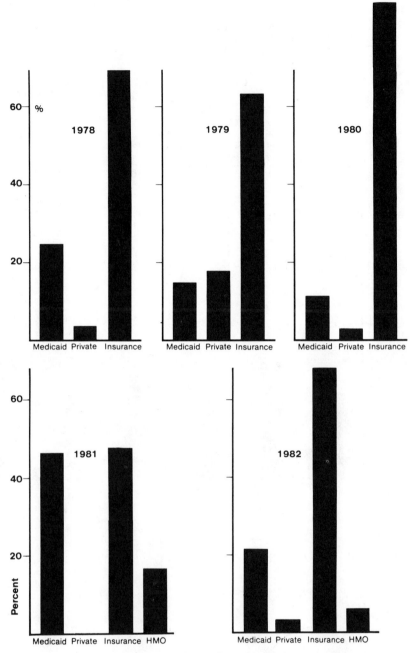

Figure 5

exhausted all other alternative payment plans (Tway & Bachafer, 1980; Fox, 1983). A similar pattern of payment was found in this investigation. Insurance payments experienced an increase during the first two years of the study and then declined. Medicaid became widely used while cash utilization became extinguished by 1982.

Method of payment was also analyzed for all children seen during the study period with a diagnosis of meningitis. The recession pattern of payment was not evident and use of private insurance continued to be the predominant method of payment during the 1978-1982 period.

While it is not proposed that all or even most of the infants with growth failure were admitted to Hurley Medical Center, the authors suggest that perhaps the increase found here reflected an increase in the community at large. The retrospective nature of this investigation, however, poses serious limitations on the interpretation of these data.

IMPLICATIONS

This study was intended to generate an interest in the possible effects of adverse economic conditions on the physical growth of young children. We recommend that future work in this area be done prospectively using the aggregate longitudinal approach suggested by Steinberg and coworkers. They used this method to test the economic stress/child abuse hypothesis. Specifically, economically meaningful geographic units would be identified and monitored over time. These Standard Metropolitan Statistical Areas are defined as cities with a minimum population of 50,000 persons and their socially and economically dependent suburbs (Steinberg et al., 1981). Once the appropriate geographic areas of study are identified, unemployment figures are then obtained.

The next and most difficult issue related to the development of an appropriate research strategy, is the determination of the number of young children with growth failure. Unlike child abuse, there are no mandatory reporting laws for FTT. The reader is reminded that even with the presence of child abuse legislation, the actual number of cases is estimated to be twice that of the number reported (Gordon & Gordon, 1979).

While it may be unrealistic to expect to identify all children with FTT, investigators can identify all sources in the geographic study area where growth data would be available. These would include all hospitals that see pediatric patients. Pediatric clinics as well as the inpatient services should be monitored. An additional study related to the one reported here was conducted in the pediatric outpatient clinics in this setting. We found that 18 percent (169 cases) of children seen in 1983 had growth failure as previously defined. This demonstrates that the outpatient settings are also appropriate monitoring sites for FTT. The authors point out that the primary reason for the visits was typically an acute pediatric problem rather than FTT. Physical growth, therefore, must be carefully and deliberately evaluated for each child, regardless of the presenting complaint. Other sources of growth data would include physician offices and public health departments.

The possible mechanisms that relate adverse economic conditions to growth failure need to be considered as part of future investigations. Frank et al. (this volume) points out that the "economically depleted family is emotionally depleted as well." For this reason, analysis of biological, psychological and sociological factors are necessary to determine how unemployment is related to FTT.

If results of systematic studies support the hypothesis that adverse economic conditions in the community result in FTT, we will be one step closer to initiation and maintenance of effective preventive interventions.

REFERENCES

Ainsworth, M.S. Object relations, dependency and attachment: a theoretical review of the infant-mother relationship. *Child Development,*

1969, 40, 964-1025.

Angell, D. Michigan hospitals assess recession's impact in confusing, contradicting variety of ways. Michigan Medicine, 1980, 465-468.

Brenner, M.H. Mental Illness and the Economy. Cambridge, MA: Harvard University Press, 1973a.

Brenner, M.H. Foetal, infant and maternal mortality during periods of economic instability. International Journal of Health Service, 1973b, 3 (2).

Colledge, M. Economic cycles and health: Toward a sociological understanding of the impact of the recession on health and illness. Social Sciences & Medicine, 1982, 16, 1919-1927.

Durkheim, E. Suicide: A Study in Sociology. New York: Free Press, 1952.

Editor. Recession backfires on Michigan doctors. Medical World News, 1981, 39-41.

Editor. Economic report of the governor: Employment. Michigan Employment Security Commission, 1983, 123-124.

Elmer, E. Failure to thrive: Role of the mother. Pediatrics, 1960, 25, 717-725.

Fischhoff, J., Whitten, C.F. & Pettit, M.G. A psychiatric study of mothers of infants with growth failure secondary to maternal deprivation. Journal of Pediatrics, 1971, 79 (2), 209-215.

Fox, J.E. Recession seen taking hold on health benefits. U.S. Medicine, 1983, 19 (5), 1-11.

Frank, D.A. & Allen, D. Primary prevention of failure to thrive: Social policy implications. In D. Drotar (Ed.) New Directions in Failure to Thrive: Research and Clinical Practice. New York: Plenum Publishing Corp., 1985.

Garbarino, J. & Sherman, D. High risk neighborhoods and high risk families: The human ecology of child maltreatment. Child Development, 1980, 51, 188-198.

Gordon, E.F. & Gordon, R.C. Child abuse: A review of selected aspects for the primary care physician. Southern Medical Journal, 1979, 72 (8), 985-992.

Hill, J.M. The psychological impact of unemployment. New Society, 1978, 19, January, 1978.

Kasl, S. & Cobb, S. Blood pressure change in men undergoing job loss: A preliminary report. Psychosomatic Medicine, 1970, 32.

Light, R. Abused and neglected children in America: A study of alternative policies. Harvard Educational Review, 1973, 43 (4), 556-598.

Patton, R.G. & Gardner, L.I. Influence of family environment on growth: The syndrome of maternal deprivation. Pediatrics, 1962, 30, 957-962.

Roberts, M.C. & Maddux, J.E. A psychosocial conceptualization of nonorganic failure to thrive. Journal of Clinical Child Psychology, 1982, 11 (3), 216-226.

Steinberg, L.D., Catalano, R. & Dooley, D. Economic antecedents of child abuse and neglect. Child Development, 1981, 52, 975-985.

Thompson, H.L. Containing health care costs - world recession is changing the fact of medicine. The Medical Journal of Australia, 1981, 2 (9), 447-448.

Tway, J. & Bachafer, H. Recession in hospitals. Voluntary Effort Quarterly, 1980, 2 (1), 2.

VI   CONFERENCE SUMMARY

The complex, biopsychosocial nature of FTT necessitates the involvement of many professional disciplines in clinical practice and research.
One of the special advantages of an interdisciplinary approach is the
sharing of perspectives and approaches that simply cannot emerge from the
efforts of any single professional discipline. The NIMH conference that
was the impetus for this book provided a unique forum for experienced
researchers and practitioners to share opinions concerning the problems and
prospects of research and practice in FTT. This final section is a summary
of the major themes that emerged when the conference participants had a
chance to talk together in an open forum concerning research on FTT. The
reader will recognize that the problems and issues that emerged in this
discussion are reflected in individual chapters in this book. One issue
concerned the need to address the considerable heterogeneity in the FTT
population and to develop more explicit definitions of subcategories and
risk populations. Conference participants also discussed another major
question in FTT research, that of description and definition of growth
deficiency. In view of the fact that an operationally defined, generalizable definition of FTT is a critical first step toward scientific progress,
the conference participants' recommendations for descriptive definition are
an important first step. The final general topic considered was one with
special relevance to the mandate of the Prevention Research Center of
NIMH: the effects of FTT on mental health. The environmental conditions
and biologic risk factors that give rise to and maintain growth deficiency
can have very significant effects on children's physical and mental health.
The tasks of charting those areas of human potential and competence that
are most affected by FTT and associated risk factors and implementing
effective research pose formidable challenges. The chapter authors and
conference participants suggest ways of meeting these challenges that provide information for others to build upon in future research and practice.

SUMMARY OF DISCUSSION AT NIMH CONFERENCE: "NEW DIRECTIONS IN FAILURE TO

THRIVE RESEARCH: IMPLICATIONS FOR PREVENTION,"   OCTOBER, 1984

Dennis Drotar

Case Western Reserve University School of Medicine

The participants in the NIMH conference which stimulated this book had
an opportunity to discuss the state of the art in research in FTT.   The
following summary of this discussion recapitulates themes that recur in
this volume, offers the reader the feel for a working discussion which
occurred among these researchers and practitioners, underscores areas in
need of future research, and outlines special methodological problems.

DIAGNOSTIC SUBTYPES OF FTT

Although there was widespread agreement that diagnostic subtyping is
an important topic in FTT, various opinions were expressed concerning the
directions such research might take.   For example, Brams noted that there
is an important need to understand the differences in FTT populations as a
function of demographic characteristics and patterns of diagnosis and treatment in different centers.   Bithoney reminded the group of the ascertain-
ment bias in FTT as a function of whether the child presents in a primary
vs. a tertiary care hospital setting.   One of the implications of this bias
is that sampling characteristics encountered in individual settings will
have an important bearing on obtained psychological and physical growth
outcomes in FTT populations.   As a consequence, investigators should carefully delineate the features of their particular setting, referral and care
delivery patterns, and the nature of the child's accompanying physical,
developmental, and emotional problems at study intake.

Woolston pointed out that as yet we do not yet know whether the
proposed diagnostic subtypes of FTT exist and/or how frequently they are
encountered in practice.   For this reason, empirical validation of diagnostic subtypes is needed via standard criteria.   The identification of subtypes requires an understanding of dimensions that are potentially relevant
to subtyping.   Chatoor et al., Lieberman and Birch, Linscheid and Rasknake,
and Woolston (this volume) all make potentially important distinctions
concerning diagnostic factors that are in need of empirical validation.
Peterson noted that other variables potentially relevant to outcome in FTT
include social class, family functioning, and biologic/nutritional status.
There was agreement in the group that it would be very useful for investigators to separate FTT children with vastly different psychosocial and
environmental etiologies.   This point has been cogently made by a number of
authors in this volume including Linscheid & Rasknake.   Rathbun felt that

the difference between early onset FTT, especially if accompanied by environmental deprivation, and later onset FTT is worth pursuing in future research. Linscheid underscored the necessity to differentiate between families of FTT infants who have sufficient economic resources but for some reason cannot use them effectively vs. those who do not have sufficient economic resources. Toward this end, objective descriptions of the FTT child's home environment (see Bradley & Casey, this volume) are very much needed.

While the benefits of subtyping, especially in terms of increased precision were clearly apparent to the group, a number of cautions were also raised. For example, Levin questioned whether the purpose of subtyping was to develop more and more categories (an exciting but eventually futile task) or to use the framework of diagnostic subtypes to identify populations of special research interest, such as those at very high risk to develop emotional disorders. Given the heterogenity of the FTT population and the potential numbers of subtypes, especially relative to sample size, it is important for investigators to keep the purpose of their subtyping expedition clearly in mind. Lieberman reminded the group that individual differences in a given FTT population may reflect the characteristics of children who are referred by practitioners for treatment in a given setting. The impact of referral bias is particularly powerful in samples gathered in settings who are known to specialize in the psychological treatment of certain kinds of problems which accompany FTT. This built-in "match" between the population referred and the treatment plan characteristic of a given setting limits the generalizability of conclusions that can be made about FTT from any one sample. For example in her setting, San Francisco General Hospital, Lieberman sometimes sees early onset FTT in middle class families and separation disorders in lower class families, a clustering of characteristics which differs somewhat from that described by Chatoor and her colleagues at Childrens Hospital in Washington, D.C. (Chatoor & Egan, 1983) and illustrates the differences in settings. Owing to such problems of generalizability, Brams felt that the field needs a better documentation of FTT populations on such parameters as age of onset, family characteristics and severity. With sufficient numbers of children, it would be possible to use empirical methods such as cluster analysis (Lorr, 1983) to empirically group descriptive characteristics along different dimensions. Rathbun reminded the group that although she respects complexity a great deal, that there is a need to simplify and limit the number of dimensions that are assessed and most especially to begin with an objective, straightforward description and definition of FTT.

DEFINITION OF FTT

Not having achieved complete closure on the issue of subtypes but nonetheless undaunted, the group turned to the knotty question of the definition of FTT. There was agreement that one of the major stumbling blocks in the research of FTT was the lack of comparable definitions of this condition. The fact that investigators have used so many different definitions of FTT makes it difficult to ensure comparability of populations and to evaluate research findings. Variation in obtained outcomes in FTT may be related to sampling characteristics, which is a knotty problem in all kinds of risk research (Kopp & Krakow, 1982). Bithoney noted that the question of the definition of FTT is further complicated by the difference between diagnostic clarifications needed in clinical practice versus those required by research definitions. In clinical practice, one is concerned with distinctions that have implications for treatment. On the other hand, in research, one is concerned with accurate description of a sample, especially to establish objective inclusionary and exclusionary criteria.

The group agreed that a descriptive definition of FTT on the basis of anthropometric criteria is a cornerstone of further research which must precede etiological classification. However, establishing criteria for FTT on an anthropometric basis is much more difficult than it would appear. For example, one issue in such definitions concerns the normative standards which are used in making a determination. This group of researchers agreed that the National Center for Health Statistics (NCHS) norms (Hamill et al., 1979) are the most representative currently available and should be used by clinicians and investigators.

The next question that concerned us was: How does one identify and discriminate children who are failing to thrive vs. those who are not? Two broad methods of classification have been used: (1) an absolute criterion which includes children whose growth is less than the 5th percentile based on norms and (2) a velocity-based definition in which children are identified via significant deceleration in rate of weight gain compared to norms (see Peterson et al., this volume for more details). Two main issues in the application of a velocity-based definition, which appear to be more sensitive than a static definition for the identification of environmentally-based FTT, are the time period and criteria of deceleration that are used. A number of alternatives were discussed: For example, Fomon (1974) described conservative criteria such as the failure to grow at a normal rate for 56 days under five months or 90 days or more over a five month period. Altemeier et al. (1981) in the Nashville Prospective Study have developed detailed velocity based criteria which were discussed. These criteria are based on a rate of weight gain over a period of time that is less than 2/3 of 50th percentile on norms. A more complete description of criteria is also found in Altemeier et al. and Sherrod et al. in this volume. Altemeier noted that once children had been identified via this criteria as failing to grow in accord with normative expectations, a second step involved determination of etiology. Each case was reviewed separately. If it could be determined by a group of pediatricians that the weight gain could be explained by organic factors it was not counted as a case of environmental FTT. Altemeier also noted that a velocity based measure also identified most children who were failing to thrive based on absolute criteria (less than the 5th percentile).

There was a great deal of support for the use of velocity based criteria such as that proposed by Altemeier. At the same time, Reinhart pointed out that in practice, it is often difficult to obtain a sufficient number of points to apply a detailed velocity based measure and that 10 days may be too short a period for determination of growth failure. Drotar et al. (this volume) used both absolute criterion (less than the 5th percentile) and a velocity based definition (children had to fall below their weight percentiles at birth). In view of the fact that the target population was environmental FTT, children with patterns of chronically delayed growth were excluded from Drotar's sample as were children who were small for gestational age (SGA). Frank pointed out that it was important to correct for prematurity in evaluating children's physical growth and to carefully consider the growth norms for premature samples, such as those of Brandt (1979).

The next issue that was discussed concerned the question of the medical work-up for FTT. Berkowitz felt that the clinician's perspective is very important to consider in research. Diagnostic tests used in the assessment of FTT include among others, complete blood count, urinalysis, and stool analysis. (See Bithoney & Rathbun, 1983.) It is important to recognize that pediatricians differ with respect to specific tests that are ordered reflecting individual differences in training, approaches to FTT and clinical populations. Berkowitz underscored the critical importance of history taking including prenatal, birth, and perinatal history (these issues are also covered in Frank; Berkowitz; Bithoney & Dubowitz in this volume). Greenspan raised the significance of early feeding history, infant temperament, and sensitivities to foods in building a comprehensive picture of the child's early history.

The discussion concerning the diagnosis of FTT underscored a number of issues: (1) it is important that psychosocial research be carried out in the context of an interdiscplinary team in order to clarify criteria and establish protocols; (2) variations in clinical presentation and clinical criteria of FTT from setting to setting place a difficult burden on the shoulders of investigators who must carefully consider how clinical proce-dures in individual hospitals fit with the state-of-the-art consensus for a FTT work-up by researchers and clinicians in other settings. This is particularly important in making distinctions between FTT that is primarily organic versus environmental and in defining populations with mixed environ-mental vs. organic diagnostic etiologies; (3) research criteria will vary considerably according to one's aims. For example, depending on the pur-poses of the investigation, one might want to use highly specialized cri-teria which identify only a subset of FTT children or general criteria which identify a broader population. General criteria are useful for most research purposes. However, exclusionary criteria should be chosen with special care because of the potential impact on outcomes. When using general criteria, it is also very useful to describe factors relating to the child's health history, health and nutritional status at presentation, and developmental status in detail, since these factors might have a bearing on outcomes. As research questions become increasingly refined, objective criteria for specific subgroups of FTT children will need to be developed. For example, if one is interested in those FTT children with micronutrient deficiency or anemia, then one would have to carefully specify that criteria to identify those subgroups. The subset of FTT children who present with a developmental delay can be defined on the basis of objective cognitive assessment. On the other hand, if one is interested in studying a general sample of FTT, developmental delay is not be an optimal inclusionary cri-teria (see Bithoney & Dubowitz, this volume).

The general consensus of the group concerning the definition of FTT was unanimous and worth highlighting: As an initial step, FTT should be identified on the basis of anthropometric measures.

RISK AND EMOTIONAL DEVELOPMENT

Having addressed the question of criteria of growth deficit and achieved a rare consensus, our discussion forged ahead to consider the question of the relationship of FTT to the development of behavior disorders in children. One of the special but as yet not well researched features of FTT is its status as a risk category for the development of emotional disorders (Drotar, this volume deals with this topic). The group recognized that in some respects the acute and long-term psychological consequences of FTT are even less well understood than the antecedents of this condition. Levin noted that research areas of topical interest to NIMH include, the potential role of maternal bereavement as a stressor in FTT, the link be-tween maternal depression and FTT and the relationship of FTT to childhood depression. The group discussion suggested a number of interesting ques-tions for future research concerning the relationship of FTT to emotional disorders of children which extend beyond the narrow confines of the DSM III definition of FTT (American Psychiatric Association, 1980). Brams suggested that disturbances in regulation of behavior including attention deficits and self-control may be an important longer term consequence of infant FTT. Another area of risk may involve modulation of affect and depression (Gaensbauer & Mrazek, 1981). Various lines of research were

cited as being especially relevant to the study of the psychological
sequelae of FTT. Galler et al.'s (1983) work concerning the relationship
of early malnutrition to affective behavior was cited by Frank as an example of a fruitful approach. Language development was mentioned as another
area of potential vulnerability in FTT children, especially because many
FTT children have evidence of language as well as other cognitive deficits
which might be expected to affect their behavior and competence. Sherrod
pointed out that there may be a relationship between the language deficits
that some FTT children manifest and disturbances in social development.
For example, children with compromised language development may be more
prone to use strategies of social interaction that involve action which may
be difficult for their peers to handle. The question of the relationship
of early FTT to subsequent social development, social interaction and
competence, was cited as another understudied area. Gottman et al.'s
(1975) and Garvey's (1976) research involving detailed description of
social interchanges were cited as examples of basic child developmental
research which have relevance for FTT outcome. In addition, Barrett's
research on malnourished children (Barrett, in press; Barrett et al., 1982)
was felt to illustrate a creative approach to the assessment of social
development. Other dimensions of emotional development in preschool and
school aged children that are relevant to FTT outcome include Block &
Block's (1980) measures of the personality dimensions of ego control and
ego resiliency. Levin pointed out that the need for empirical determination of those subgroups of FTT children who are most vulnerable to psychological deficits in later life is especially great.

Another topic for future research deemed as important was treatment
and intervention. It was felt that retrospective evaluations of intervention were not adequate and needed to be supplemented with prospective
assessment of treatment outcome. The group recognized that many children
are not currently being referred for intervention in many communities and
that patterns of pediatric care vary widely from community to community.
Brams noted the importance of educating community physicians concerning the
mental health implications of FTT, including the need for early identification as a means of prevention of psychological disturbance (see Altemeier
et al.; Brams & Coury, this volume for discussions of early intervention).

As the group considered questions relating to intervention, there
was recognition of the need for greater information sharing concerning
treatment approaches among professionals who work with FTT infants.
Lieberman pointed out that agreement on those dimensions thought to be
especially relevant to clinical intervention and research will be important
to establish a common language among researchers and practitioners. The
conference participants agreed that cross-center collaboration will eventually be a necessary strategy to enhance the generalizability of research
in FTT. As a first step, it was felt to be useful to share methods of
assessment and procedures of record keeping that are currently being used
in various clinic settings and research studies. Sharing of assessment
protocols would provide a way to determine similarities and differences in
data gathering across settings and eventually establish greater comparability of diagnostic procedures and FTT populations. The present group of
authors and conference participants represented are anxious to expand the
ranks of professionals who are currently working with FTT children and
their families. Interested readers should feel free to contact individuals
for additional details about their work. Those interested in general
questions concerning FTT can contact the editor of this volume who will
either find the answers to questions and/or direct inquiries to the appropriate person.

CONFERENCE PARTICIPANTS

In addition to the chapter authors who are listed at the beginning of this book, participants who made valuable contributions to the conference include Joseph Fagan, Ph.D. (Department of Psychology, Case Western Reserve University) who has conducted follow-up studies of FTT using his own laboratory derived measure of infant recognition memory; Stan Greenspan of Maternal and Child Health, Washington, D.C. who is well known for his studies of infant psychopathology; J. Kenneth Whitt, Ph.D. (Departments of Pediatrics and Psychiatry, North Carolina University, School of Medicine, Chapel Hill, North Carolina) who has conducted observational studies of FTT and has a particular interest in diagnostic classification; Michael Reinhart, M.D. (Department of Pediatrics, University of California at Davis Sacramento, California) who is very interested in clinical management of FTT and improving the quality of research in this area; and Bonnie Sklaren, R.N. (Gulfport, Florida, formerly of the UCLA School of Medicine) whose interests include comprehensive nursing care of FTT.

REFERENCES

Altemeier, W.A., Vietze, P., Sherrod, K.B., Sandler, H.M., Falsey, S. & O'Connor, S. Prediction of child maltreatment during pregnancy. Journal of the American Academy of Child Psychiatry, 1979, 18, 205-219.

American Psychiatric Association. Diagnostic and Statistic Manual of Psychiatric Disorders, 3rd Edition. Washington, D.C., 1980.

Barrett, D. Malnutrition and child behavior: Conceptualization and assessment of social-emotional functioning and a report of an empirical study. In J. Brozek & B. Schurch (Eds.), Critical Assessment of Key Issues in Research on Malnutrition and Behavior. Bern, Switzerland: Huber, in press.

Barrett, D.E., Radke-Yarrow, M. & Klein, P.C. Chronic malnutrition and child behavior: Effects of early caloric supplementation on social and emotional functioning at school age. Developmental Psychology, 1982, 18, 541-566.

Bithoney, W.G. & Rathbun, J.M. Failure to thrive. In W.B. Levin, A.C. Carey, A.D. Crocker & R.J. Gross (Eds.), Developmental Behavioral Pediatrics. Philadelphia: Saunders, 1983.

Block, J.H. & Block, J. The role of ego control and ego resiliency in the organization of behavior. In W.A. Collins (Ed.), Development of Cognition, Affect and Social Relations. Minnesota Symposia of Child Psychology, Vol. 13. Hillsdale, NJ: Erlbaum, 1980.

Brandt, I. Growth dynamics of low birth weight infants with emphasis on the perinatal period. In F. Falkner & J.M. Tanner (Eds.), Human Growth, Vol. 2, Post Natal Growth. New York: Plenum, 1978.

Chatoor, I. & Egan, J. Nonorganic failure to thrive and dwarfism due to food refusal: A separation disorder. Journal of the American Academy of Child Psychiatry, 1983, 22, 294-301.

Fomon, S.J. Infant Nutrition. Philadelphia: Saunders, 1974.

Gaensbauer, T.J. & Mrazek, D. Differences in the patterning of affective expression in infants. Journal of the American Academy of Child Psychiatry, 1981, 20, 673-691.

Galler, J., Ramsey, F., Solimano, G., Lowell, W. The influence of early malnutrition on subsequent behavioral development, II: Classroom behavior. Journal of the American Academy of Child Psychiatry, 1983, 22, 16-22.

Garvey, C. Some properties of social play. In J.S. Brunner, A. Jolly & K. Sylvia (Eds.), Play: Its Role in Development and Evolution. New York: Basic Books, 1976.

Gottman, J., Gonso, J. & Rasmussen, B. Social competence, social interaction, and friendship in children. Child Development, 1975, 46, 709-718.

Hamill, P.V.V., Drizd, T.A., Johnson, C.L., Reed, R.B., Roche, A.F. & Moore, W.M. Physical growth: National Center for Health Statistics Percentages. American Journal of Clinical Nutrition, 1979, 32, 607-629.

Kopp, C.B. & Krakow, J.B. The issue of sample characteristics: Biologically at risk or developmentally delayed infants. Journal of Pediatric Psychology, 1982, 7, 361-375.

Lorr, M. Cluster Analysis for Social Scientists. San Francisco: Jossey Bass, 1983.

Woolston, J.C. Eating disorders in infancy and early childhood. Journal of the American Academy of Child Psychiatry, 1983, 22, 114-121.

CONTRIBUTORS

DEBORAH ALLEN, Harvard University School of Public Health, 677 Huntington Avenue, Boston, Massachusetts 02115

WILLIAM A. ALTEMEIER, III, Department of Pediatrics, Vanderbilt University Hospital, Nashville, Tennessee 37210

CAROL BERKOWITZ, Department of Pediatrics, University of California at Los Angeles, School of Medicine, 100 West Carson Street, Torrance, California 90509

MARIAN BIRCH, Infant-Parent Program, University of California, 1001 Protero Avenue, San Francisco, California 94110

WILLIAM G. BITHONEY, Comprehensive Child Health Program, The Children's Hospital, Boston, Massachusetts and the Harvard Medical School, Department of Pediatrics, 300 Longwood Avenue, Boston, Massachusetts 02115

WILLIAM M. BLAKEMORE, National Center for Toxicological Research, Food and Drug Administration, Washington, D.C.

ROBERT H. BRADLEY, Center for Child Development and Education, University of Arkansas at Little Rock, 33rd and University, Little Rock, Arkansas 72204

JOLIE S. BRAMS, College of Medicine, The Ohio State University and Columbus Children's Hospital, 700 Children's Drive, Columbus, Ohio 43205

CORRINE BRICKELL, Private Practice, Telluride, Colorado 81435

J. LARRY BROWN, Harvard University, School of Public Health, 677 Huntington, Boston, Massachusetts 02115

MARCY BUSH, Department of Psychology, Case Western Reserve University, Cleveland, Ohio 44106

PATRICK H. CASEY, Department of Pediatrics, University of Arkansas for Medical Sciences, 804 Wolfe Street, Little Rock, Arkansas 72202

IRENE CHATOOR, Department of Psychiatry, George Washington School of Medicine and Health Sciences and the Children's Hospital, National Medical Center, 111 Michigan Avenue North West, Washington, D.C. 20010

WILLIAM R. COLLIE, Department of Pediatrics, University of Arkansas for Medical Sciences, 804 Wolfe Street, Little Rock, Arkansas 72202

DANIEL L. COURY, College of Medicine, The Ohio State University and Columbus Children's Hospital, 700 Children's Drive, Columbus, Ohio 48303

LINDA DEVOST, Department of Social Service, Rainbow Babies' and Children's Hospital, Cleveland, Ohio 44106

LINDA DICKSON, Department of Social Work, George Washington University, School of Medicine and Health Sciences and the Children's Hospital, National Medical Center, 111 Michigan Avenue North West, Washington, D.C. 20010

DENNIS DROTAR, Rainbow Babies' and Children's Hospital and Departments of Pediatrics and Psychiatry, Case Western Reserve University School of Medicine, 2101 Adelbert Road, Cleveland, Ohio 44106

HOWARD DUBOWITZ, Comprehensive Child Health Program, Children's Hospital, Boston, Massachusetts, and the Harvard Medical School, Department of Pediatrics, 300 Longwood Avenue, Boston, Massachusetts 02115

DEBBY ECKERLE, Department of Psychiatry, Case Western Reserve University School of Medicine, Cleveland, Ohio 44106

JAMES EGAN, Department of Psychiatry, George Washington University, School of Medicine and Health Sciences, and the Children's Hospital, National Medical Center, 111 Michigan Avenue North West, Washington, D.C. 20010

DEBBY EL-AMIN, Department of Psychiatry, Case Western Reserve University School of Medicine, Cleveland, Ohio 44106

MARY ANN FINLON, Jennings Computer Center, Crawford Hall, Case Western Reserve University, Cleveland, Ohio 44106

DEBORAH A. FRANK, Department of Pediatrics, Boston University, Grow Team, Boston City Hospital, 818 Harrison Avenue, Boston, Massachusetts 02118

ELIZABETH F. GORDON, Department of Pediatrics, Michigan State University, One Hurley Plaza, Box 7, Flint, Michigan 48303

M. GUILLERMO HERRERA, Harvard University School of Public Health and Harvard Institute for International Development, Cambridge, Massachusetts 02138

VICTORIA S. LEVIN, Center for Prevention Research, Division of Prevention and Special Mental Health Programs, National Institute of Mental Health, 5600 Fisher's Lane, Rockville, Maryland 20857

ALICIA F. LIEBERMAN, Infant-Parent Program, University of California, 1001 Protero Avenue, San Francisco, California 94110

THOMAS R. LINSCHEID, College of Medicine, The Ohio State University and Columbus Children's Hospital, 700 Children's Drive, Columbus, Ohio 43205

CHARLES A. MALONE, Department of Psychiatry, Case Western Reserve University School of Medicine, 2040 Abington Road, Cleveland, Ohio 44106

CAROL MANTZ-CLUMPNER, Kaiser Permanente, Willoughby, Ohio 44094

JUDY NEGRAY, Rainbow Babies' and Children's Hospital, 2101 Adelbert Road, Cleveland, Ohio 44106

MICHAEL NOWAK, Department of Psychiatry, Case Western Reserve University School of Medicine, Cleveland, Ohio 44106

SUSAN M. O'CONNOR, Department of Pediatrics, Vanderbilt University Hospital, Nashville, Tennessee 37210

KAREN E. PETERSON, Harvard University, School of Public Health, 665 Huntington Avenue, Boston, Massachusetts 02115

L. KAYE RASNAKE, College of Medicine, The Ohio State University and Columbus Children's Hospital, 700 Children's Drive, Columbus, Ohio 43205

JENNIFER M. RATHBUN, Massachusetts General Hospital and Harvard Medical School, 300 Longwood Avenue, Boston, Massachusetts 02115

JACKIE SATOLA, Department of Psychiatry, Case Western Reserve University School of Medicine, Cleveland, Ohio 44106

SHARON SCHAEFER, Department of Social Work, George Washington University, School of Medicine and Health Sciences and the Children's Hospital, National Medical Center, 111 Michigan Avenue North West, Washington, D.C. 20010

KATHRYN B. SHERROD, Department of Psychology, Peabody College, Vanderbilt University and John F. Kennedy Center for Research in Mental Retardation and Human Development, Box 40, Nashville, Tennessee 37203

MORTON M. SILVERMAN, Alcohol, Drug Abuse and Mental Health Administration, 5600 Fisher's Lane, Rockville, Maryland 20857

LYNN SINGER, Rainbow Babies' and Children's Hosital, Department of Pediatrics, Case Western Reserve University School of Medicine, 2101 Adelbert Road, Cleveland, Ohio 44106

DELIA M. VAZQUEZ, Department of Pediatrics, University of Iowa, Iowa City, Iowa 52240

PETER M. VIETZE, National Institute of Child Health and Human Development, 7910 Woodmont Avenue, Bethesda, Maryland 20205

MARIEL WALLACE, Planned Parenthood, East Cleveland, Ohio 44112

JOSEPH WOOLSTON, Yale Child Study Center, 230 South Frontage Road, New Haven, Connecticut 06510

JANICE WOYCHIK, E.A.P. Systems, 100 Tower Office Park, Woburn, Massachusetts 01801

BETSY WYATT, Department of Psychology, Kent State University, Kent, Ohio 44242

THOMAS D. YEAGER, Department of Pediatrics, Vanderbilt University Hospital, Nashville, Tennessee 37203